TRACTS,

HISTORICAL AND STATISTICAL,

ON

INDIA

TRACTS,

HISTORICAL AND STATISTICAL,

ON

INDIA

WITH

JOURNALS OF SEVERAL TOURS THROUGH VARIOUS PARTS OF THE PENINSULA

BENJAMIN HEYNE, M. D. F.L.S.

GYAN

Published by

GYAN

Gyan Publishing House
5, Ansari Road
Daryaganj, New Delhi-110002
Phone: 011-47034999, 9811692060
E-mail: books@gyanbooks.com

Distribution Network
gyanbooks.com
India, USA, Canada, UK, Australia, France

ISBN: 978-81-212-9122-4 (PB)
First Published, 1814

2nd Impression 2023

Printed at: Gyan Press, Delhi.

TRACTS, HISTORICAL AND STASTISTICAL, ON INDIA
AUTHOR: BENJAMIN HEYNE

To face Title

Neele sc Strand.

The Rock of Trichinopoly 330 feet high; The Bramins carrying Water to the Temple, and a View of the Barracks.

TRACTS,

HISTORICAL AND STATISTICAL,

ON

INDIA;

WITH

JOURNALS OF SEVERAL TOURS THROUGH VARIOUS PARTS OF THE PENINSULA:

ALSO,

AN ACCOUNT OF

S U M A T R A,

IN A SERIES OF LETTERS.

BY BENJAMIN HEYNE, M. D. F. L. S.

MEMBER OF THE ASIATIC SOCIETY OF CALCUTTA, AND THE LEARNED SOCIETIES OF BOMBAY, BERLIN, &C. AND SURGEON AND NATURALIST ON THE ESTABLISHMENT OF FORT ST. GEORGE.

ILLUSTRATED BY MAPS AND OTHER PLATES.

LONDON:

PRINTED FOR ROBERT BALDWIN, PATERNOSTER-ROW;
AND
BLACK, PARRY, AND CO. BOOKSELLERS TO THE HON. EAST INDIA COMPANY, LEADENHALL-STREET.

1814.

TO

THE HONOURABLE

THE COURT OF DIRECTORS

OF

THE EAST INDIA COMPANY,

These Tracts,

WHICH ARE THE RESULT OF OBSERVATIONS AND RESEARCHES

MADE WHILE FULFILLING THE OFFICIAL DUTIES OF HIS SITUATION,

ARE,

WITH ALL DUE DEFERENCE AND RESPECT,

INSCRIBED

BY THEIR FAITHFUL AND OBEDIENT SERVANT,

BENJAMIN HEYNE.

PREFACE.

THE greater number of the Tracts which constitute this volume, were written during the earlier part of a residence of about twenty years in India: some of them have been published, but without my knowledge, and without receiving the necessary correction; others, which had been laid before the Government of Fort St. George and forwarded to the Honourable the Court of Directors, were deposited in their library; the rest, as some journals, letters, and translations, had been communicated to private friends only: none were thought by me of sufficient importance to lay before the world. To ascertain, however, whether they contained any information worth preserving, I submitted them to several of my friends, and ultimately to Dr. Thomas Thomson, for whose advice in selection, and assistance in revising the MS. for the press, I am very deeply indebted. To Dr. Wilkins I feel very grateful for his support in recommending to the Honourable Court of Directors to permit those papers to be published which had come officially before them.

Owing to circumstances, which it is immaterial to state, I have not been able to arrange the Tracts either according to the succession in which they were written, or to the connexion of their subjects. In all, I have given my opinion very honestly, which, when it differs from the established notions, or the ideas of celebrated writers on the same subject, I trust will not be imputed to idle or impertinent presumption.

Throughout the work, except in particular instances, I have used the manner of spelling Indian words as adopted in the Asiatick Researches, for which the general rules are—that all vowels are sounded like those in the Italian language; that they are pronounced short, or are lengthened by a line - over them, as ā, ē, ī, ō, ū; that the consonants are sounded as in English; the letter y in the middle of words as an English i, in the beginning as usual in English, and at the termination of a word as an English e. Words which are in general use, and have been adopted in the English language, I have spelled according to the common usage, as, Hindoo, Cooly, Palankeen; likewise most names of places of note; as otherwise it would have become necessary to write them as they are pronounced by the natives, which would in most instances have rendered them perfectly unintelligible to every body in Europe: as, thus it would have been, Chamerlacotta for Samulcotta, Striringapatam for Seringapatam, Tiruchināpaly for Trichinopoly, Rajamahendram for Rajamundry. In the maps I have throughout used the common way of specifying the names of places and districts.

I could have wished to be more particular in mineralogical and geological descriptions, but found myself so often at a loss for want of specimens to refer to, that I have seldom attempted it, and in general omitted all such as I conceived would not be found perfectly correct. I must lament here the loss of large collections, which I was obliged, during the latter years of my residence in India, to leave behind me at different places, from want of means to carry them with me in the country, or of sending them to a place of safety. The diamond in the rock, or matrix, if it may be so called, I found at Banaganpilly; the Right Honourable the Countess of Powis did me the honour to receive it among her valuable collection of Indian minerals, and now to permit me to represent it by a plate.

The botanical names that occur in these Tracts will be found correct, as they have been taken mostly from Dr. Roxburgh's manuscripts, or on the authority of my most respected friend the Rev. Dr. Rottler: most of the plants I have seen and examined myself.

It was thought advisable to publish the Meteorological Tables in the Appendix; as few of the kind yet exist which have been taken even with so much accuracy as these possess. The completest copy of it, which contains, besides other periods, one of a year and a half of my stay at Cuddapa, has been either mislaid at the packing of my things in India, or is among some parcels which have not yet come to hand.

My observations on mere scientific subjects I have neither found leisure nor means, during my stay in England, to elaborate in such a manner, as to venture on laying them before the public; but as I have yet several years to reside in India, I shall, if God grant me life and health, and my Honourable Masters continue their patronage, have an opportunity of increasing them, and afterwards of rendering them more deserving of notice. I have in the mean time not been sparing in communicating my specimens to such as will be able to make them useful; and this, on the whole, was and is the primary object. It matters but little whether it be known by whom a thing is collected, provided it only be used for the good of the community. Many of my friends seem to be of the same opinion!

During my former residence in India I have met with some obstacles in my pursuit, particularly in latter times; but in general I gratefully acknowledge having experienced the greatest encouragement. The Government of Fort St. George, and its Governors, the Right Hon. the Earl of Buckinghamshire, Earl of Powis, and Lord W. Bentinck, have most graciously patronised my pursuits: many gentlemen in the Civil and Medical Service, as Mr. W. Petrie, Mr. T. Cockburn, Dr. W. Roxburgh, Dr. J. Anderson, and others, have generously supported; and individuals, among whom I name the late Mr. Andrew Ross with sentiments of the liveliest gratitude, have most kindly encouraged me. Delicacy forbids me to say more of those who are yet alive. May God still preserve them long in health and happiness.

London, June 20, 1814.

CONTENTS.

TRACT I.

TRACT II.

TRACT III.

TRACT IV.

TRACT V.

TRACT VI.

TRACT VII.

TRACT VIII.

TRACT IX.

TRACT X.

TRACT XI.

TRACT XII.

TRACT XIII.

TRACT XIV.

List of the Plates referred to in this Work.

Plate II. to face page 74.

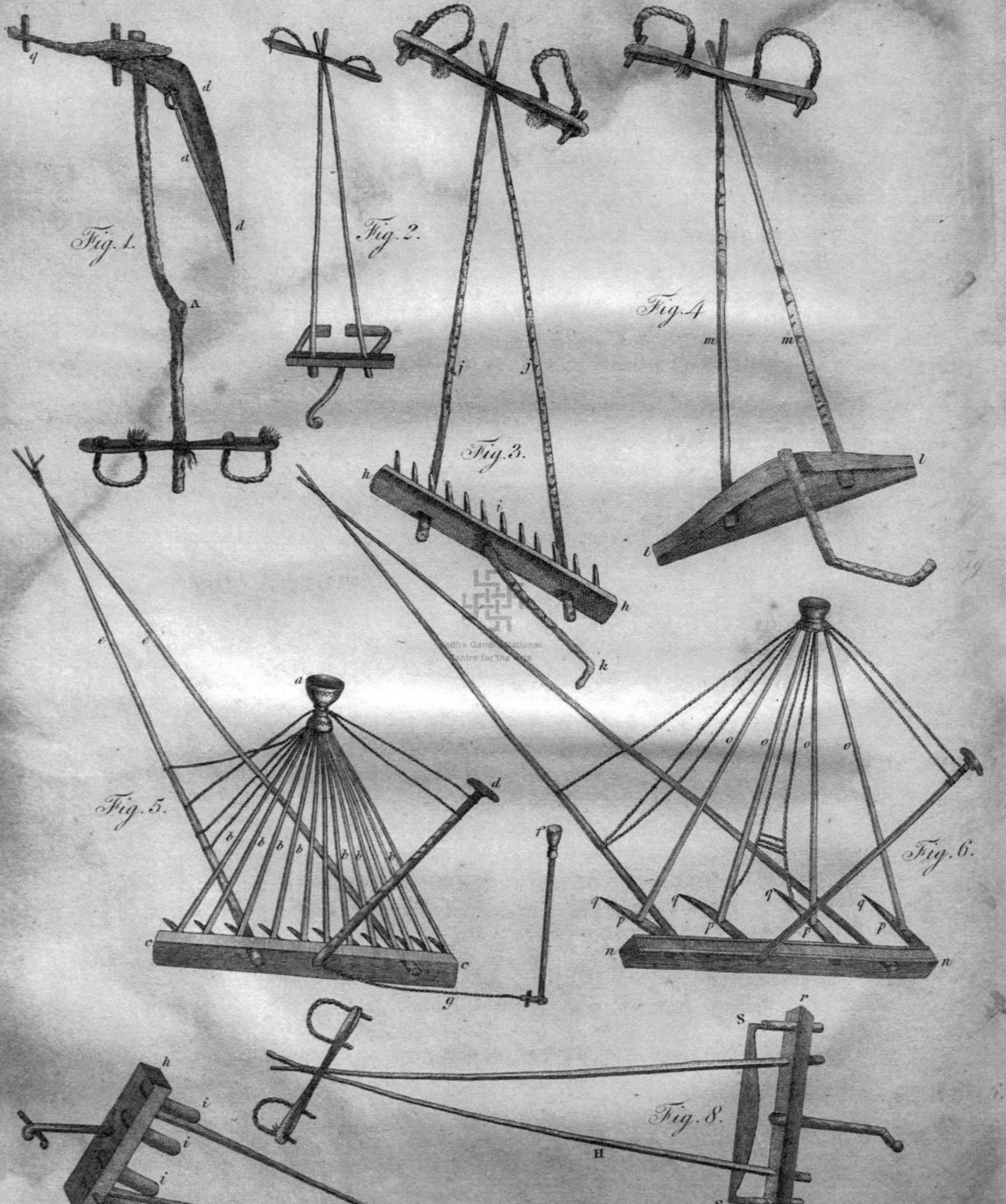

Engraved for Dr. Heynes Tracts on India. Published by Black Parry & Co. and R. Baldwin 18th May 1814.

A Diamond in the Rock from the Mines at Banaganpilly.

Engraved for Dr. Heyne's Tracts on India, Published by Black, Parry & Co. and R. Baldwin, 18th May 1814.

Plate IV. page 190.

Method of drawing Water from deep Wells.

Iron Furnace.

Engraved for Dr. Heynes Tracts on India Published by Black Parry & Co. and R. Baldwin 18th May 1814.

Plate V. Page 191.

Neele & Strand.

Virra Malli, a romantic Rock in Tondiman's Woods 40. Miles south of Trichinopoly.

Engraved for Dr. Heyne's Tracts on India. Published by Black Parry & Co. and R. Baldwin 18th May 1814.

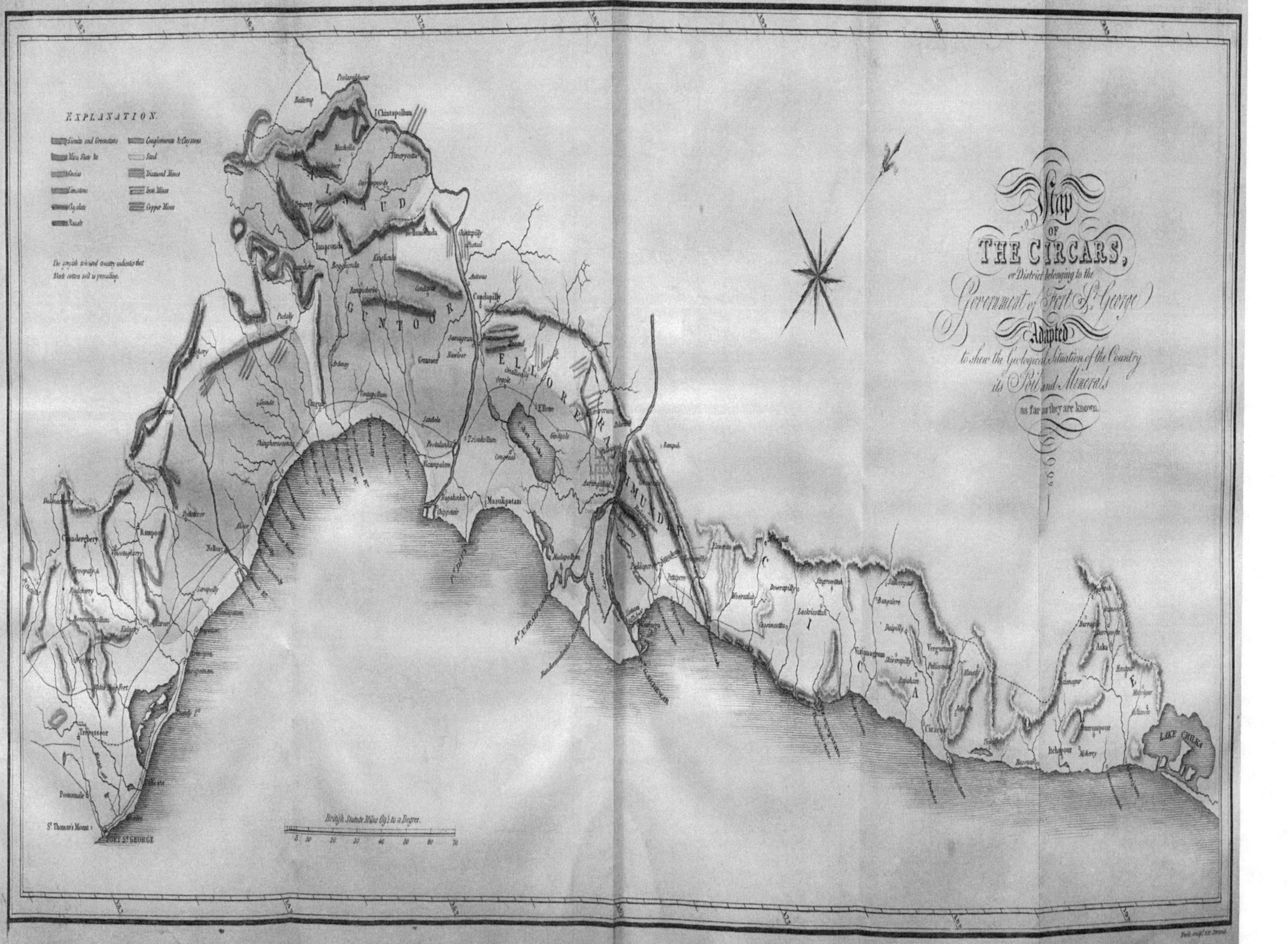
Map
OF
THE CIRCARS,
or District belonging to the
Government of Fort St. George
Adapted
to shew the Geological Situation of the Country
its Soil and Minerals
as far as they are known.
EXPLANATION.
Mica Slate &c
Gneiss
Limestone
Clay slate
Basalt
Conglomerate & Claystone
Sand
Diamond Mines
Iron Mines
Copper Mines
The greyish coloured country indicates that
Black cotton soil is prevailing.
GUNTOOR
ELLORE
Masulipatam
Nellore
Chintapollum
LAKE CHILKA
St. Thomas's Mount
FORT ST. GEORGE
British Statute Miles 69½ to a Degree.

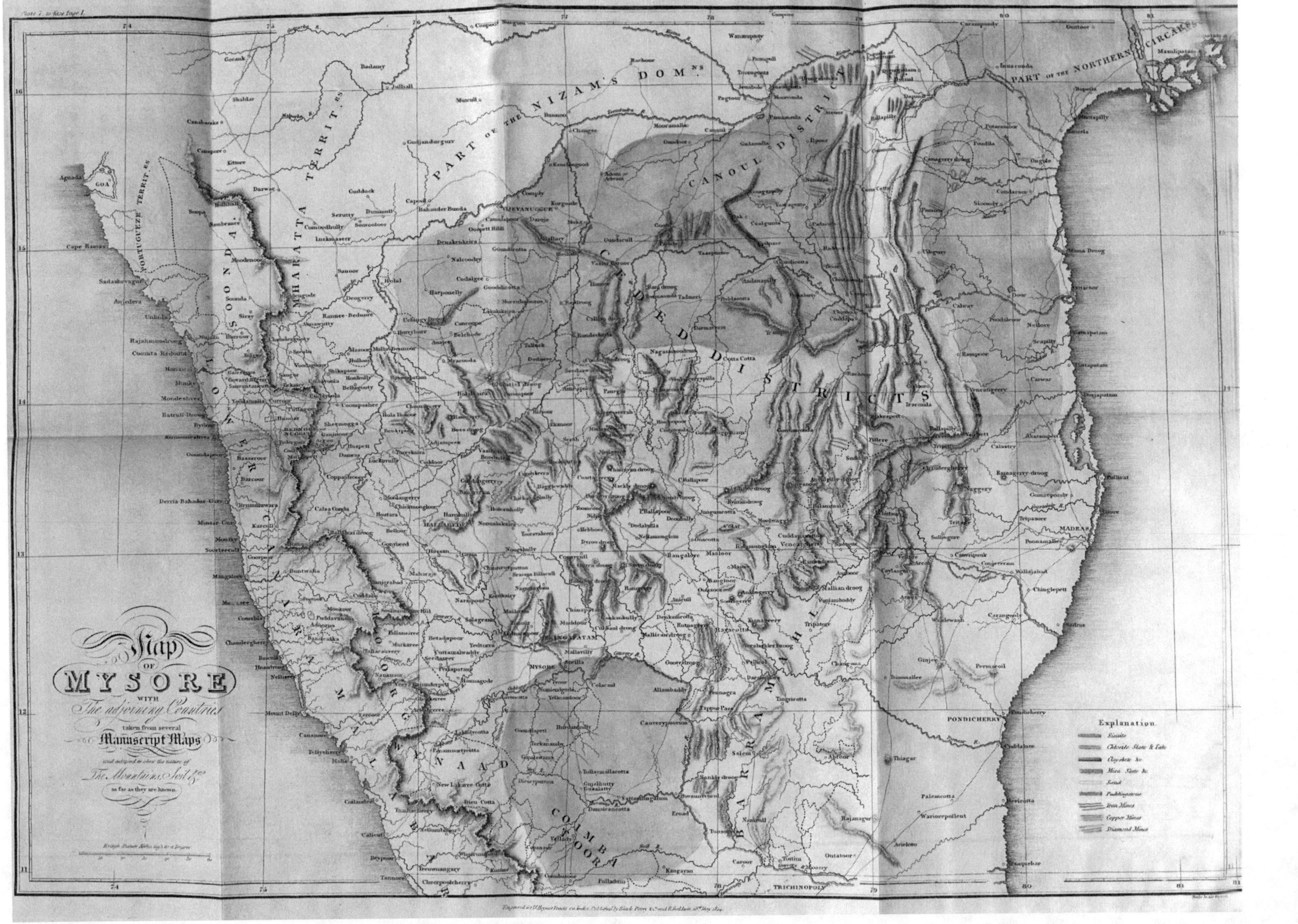
Map of MYSORE
with The adjoining Countries
taken from several
Manuscript Maps
and adapted to shew the nature of
The Mountains, Soil &c.
as far as they are known.
PART OF THE NIZAM'S DOM.NS
PART OF THE NORTHERN CIRCARS
MHARATTA TERRIT.ES
PORTUGUEZE TERRIT.ES
SOONDA
CANOUL DISTRICT
CEDED DISTRICTS
LOWER CANARA
COORG
WYNAAD
MALABAR
BARAMAHL
COIMBATOOR
MYSORE
MADRAS
PONDICHERRY
TRICHINOPOLY
GOA
Explanation.
Sienite
Chlorite Slate & Talc
Clayslate &c.
Mica Slate &c.
Sand
Puddingstone
Iron Mines
Copper Mines
Diamond Mines

TRACTS,

HISTORICAL AND STATISTICAL

ON

INDIA.

TRACT I.

STATISTICAL FRAGMENTS ON THE CARNATIC.

WHAT is at present called the Carnatic consists of a tract of land extending along the peninsula of Hindostan, lately the territory of the Nabob of Arcot, from north latitude 15° to about 10°. Its present capital is Madras, well known as the seat of a British governor, and remarkable for the celebrated struggle between the British and French nations, which was terminated by the peace of 1763, and which laid the foundation of the British dominions in India. A residence of nearly twenty years in that country or its neighbourhood having afforded me abundance of opportunity of making myself acquainted with it, I might easily describe it at great length. But as this has been already repeatedly done by others, I shall satisfy myself, in this Essay, with a few statistical remarks, which may not perhaps be without their utility.

I. SOIL.

The soil of that part of the Carnatic which lies nearest the sea is a mixture of loam and sea sand, sparingly intermixed with the remains of marine animals, and bears evident marks of having been formerly covered by the sea. It is affirmed in the Pooranas, and has been handed down by tradition, that great part of the Coromandel coast was suddenly elevated out of the sea; but the appearance of the low land renders it evident that this tradition cannot be correct. The land must have been formed gradually, and must have elevated itself above the sea precisely in the same way as the *marsches* on the coast of Sleswigh, Holstein, &c. The inland regions of this part of India contain mountains of sienite, with a very small proportion of felspar. The fragments of these mountains, washed by the torrents into the sea, constitute the sand of this coast; and the small proportion of felspar in these rocks probably occasions the badness of the soil; at least it accounts for the want of the proper admixture of clay, and for the superabundance of iron.

I consider the whole soil of this part of the Carnatic to be composed of the debris of the decomposed sienitic mountains. According to local circumstances it is either a loam mixed with sand and gravel, and strongly impregnated with iron, or in low and wet places a stiff red loam mixed with vegetable earth and fine sand, or in eminences gravel and sand. And it is often so much impregnated with common salt, that it presents a saline efflorescence in dry weather.

Near Madras it is a heavy, sterile, salt loam, mixed with silicious sand; and along the sea-coast, and for some miles inwards, we meet at certain depths with marine productions, such as cockle and oyster shells, indicating, as before observed, that this part of the country consists of land recovered from the sea.

By some the soil near Madras has been thought vitriolic or aluminous at a certain depth, in consequence of the efflorescence that forms on it when it is exposed to the air. But the taste of this saline substance announces it to be common salt.

An exact determination how far inland this saline soil extends is an important subject of inquiry; because the success of plantations of trees that strike deep roots into the ground depends upon it. For trees will not thrive in the saline soil, as has been often experienced in the neighbourhood of Madras. From the appearances of the country I conceive, that the saline soil does not extend farther than the mount called Little St Thomas, and that on the west side of this spot gardening and planting may be prosecuted with success.

Between Mount St. Thomas and Vellore the soil is sandy, and nearly as poor as in the neighbourhood of Madras; but it is not poisoned by the saline impregnation. In the valleys, which are watered by tanks and rivers, it is more fertile than on the barren downs, which form a range of low hills parallel to the coast. I may mention, as examples, the Conjeveram valley, and the villages Damerla, Samindenghy, and others which are watered by branches of the Polar. About Conjeveram the soil is more clayey, owing to the decomposition of the felspar which abounds in the granite of that region: it is scarcely necessary to observe, that the high ground, such as those in the neighbourhood of Arcot, are always poorer than the contiguous valleys, because the finest particles of the soil are gradually washed away by the rains, and deposited in the valleys.

Here and there in the inland parts of the country, we find large spots of salt ground, containing either common salt, or a mixture of that salt and soda, which, from the use to which it is applied in India, is known by the name of *washermen's earth.* The fertile soil called *black cotton ground,* I have observed only in one place, namely, Kuckalom, where cotton was sown together with jonnaloo, or the holcus sorghum of botanists.

In the valleys along the Ghauts, and between the ranges of hills between Vellore and Peddanaikdoorgum, the soil is chiefly loamy, mixed with sand, and with a considerable proportion of vegetable mould which gives it the dark shade of brown by which it is distinguished. Near the hills it is often stony, but not so much so as I have observed it in other parts of the country, where the rock, constituting the neighbouring mountains, is not so liable to decomposition as the sienite of the Carnatic.

The vegetable admixture and loaminess are to be ascribed to the great quantity of water with which it is inundated for a very great part of the year. Rice, or *paddy*, as it is called in India, is the principal produce, and on that account the inhabitants are at great pains to inundate their fields from the neighbouring rivers and tanks which abound in the country.

II. WATER.

The water all over the peninsula of Indostan is upon the whole pretty good. In rivers it is best after rain; tanks, though muddy, being composed of rain water, are usually sweet. The water in wells is often a little brackish, owing to a mixture of some common salt or muriate of lime; for these are the only saline bodies that I have found by analysis in the waters at Madras and other places. Mineral waters, as far as I know, do not occur on the coast: indeed I have heard of only one hot spring in the peninsula; it is situated in the middle of the Godavery, near Badrachellum, about one hundred miles west from Rajahmundry. Springs issuing from the surface of the ground are almost as scarce as mineral waters; they occur only on the tops of high mountains, as on all hill forts: the water which they yield is usually excellent.

If we dig almost any where, veins of water may be found proceeding from the high land and the Ghauts, which run all along the peninsula. The depth at which these veins occur is various: I have observed, that in some valleys near the mountains they are more superficial. In the Polnaud, for example, near Samulcotah, they occur at the depth of four or five feet below the surface; along the Carnatic Ghauts they are deeper, owing, I think, to the elevation of the respective countries between them and the sea; for the valleys in the Circars are nearly on a level with the sea shore. The intervening country is considerably elevated, while the lower parts of the Carnatic valleys are a good deal higher than the coast. It is in consequence of the intermediate high ground between the valley and the coast in the Masulipatam circar, that the Godavery cannot be applied to any use in watering the countries through which it flows, while the rivers in the Carnatic are of immense use in this respect.

I can speak with confidence of the Godavery, as the bed of that river has been levelled by Mr. Topping as far as its entrance into the low country, and has been found not above a foot higher than at the place where it disembogues itself into the sea; and as I have lived for many years either upon its banks or on the very high ground that intervenes between the valley of the Ghauts and the coast.

The goodness of water depends, in a great measure, on the nature of the strata through which it runs. If these strata be impregnated with common salt, or any other similar substance, we may expect to find the water brackish: a calcareous or gypseous soil will produce hard water, because a portion of the calcareous salts will be dissolved by the liquid. In clayey soil the water will be muddy, but generally soft and good, unless the clay happen to contain a mixture of iron or martial pyrites: in primitive tracts of country the water is always transparent and good.

III. AGRICULTURE.

The general division of lands on the coast is into high and low land. On the former all kinds of small grain are cultivated: on the latter chiefly rice, or paddy, as it is called, which requires to be inundated till it is almost ripe. The Tamuls call the latter grounds *nanjic*, and the former *punjie*. The Telingas distinguish them by the names of *pallum* and *merka*.

For both, the cultivators use the same measure, settled, as it is said, by Raychie the Dewan of the former nabob of the Carnatic.

The fundamental measure is the *kola*, which is a measuring stick twenty-four feet in length: a square kola is called a *kunta*, and one hundred of these a *cawny*, equal to two thousand four hundred square feet of English land measure, or somewhat more than the eighteenth of an English acre.

On nanjie, paddy, as has been observed, constitutes the principal crop. When the soil happens to be very fertile and level, this grain is sown by the hand, but in most cases it is transplanted from beds on which it had been reared till it was nine inches or a foot long. For two cawny it is said one *kalum*, equal to ninety-six pounds of seed, is required, the produce of which differs according to the season in which it has been planted.

The farmers raise four different crops in the year, and two of these are raised on the same ground. The first is called *kauroo punta*, and is sown from the middle of the month of May to the middle of June, and is cut in September. In good seasons it produces fifty kalums, or an increase of fifty-fold. The second crop is distinguished by the same name *(kauroo punta)* but is planted in June and July, and is expected to give a forty-fold return. The third crop, called *sambha*, is planted in July, August, and September, and is ripe in January and February: like the second crop it is expected to yield a forty-fold return. The fourth crop, called *navara punta*, is sown between the middle of November and the middle of January, and ripens in April and May. It is the least productive of all, yielding between twenty and thirty-fold.

The sheep and goat keepers, provided they be fed themselves by the farmer during the interval, will drive their flocks for a few weeks on the fields, after the removal of the first paddy crop: in such cases the farmers are enabled to sow jonnuloo raghie *, or pessaloo †, bobberloo‡ or kanduloo §, and expect a ten or twelve-fold return.

For the cultivation of one kalum (or forty-eight pucca seer) of paddy, the farmers consider one pair of bullocks to be sufficient. Their ploughs are made of the *waggisa* or *mimosa latisiliqua* of Linnæus, a hard and brittle wood which does not readily absorb the moisture to which it is exposed in ploughing the nanjie. The ploughshare is a thin piece of iron of about eight inches long, and an inch thick, which in a soil abounding with moisture is sufficiently strong to pierce the ground and admit the wooden plough. The share projects little more than an inch, and is obtusely pointed.

The mode of renting the ground to the farmers depends on the way in which it can be watered. If by pacotas (navarie), and consequently attended with much labour, it is let to them at a stipulated sum amounting to ten or twelve rupees || per cawny. This, supposing it to produce from twenty to thirty kalums, leaves them (where rice sells moderately dear) ten or twelve rupees for their share of the profit, after one-tenth of the whole produce, calculated according to the bazar or shop price, has been deducted. This portion is called *malavarâm*, and, in the northern Circars, *malvatty*.

Lands that can be watered by channels from rivers or tanks are let out for shares, of which the Circar gets five and a half, and the farmer four and a half, out of which he is obliged to pay the malavarâm, or the one-tenth, at the bazar price. Two sets of appraisers, one appointed by the Circar¶, the other by the farmer, estimate the amount of the crop, and report their opinion to the renter and the people assembled, and the medium of their appraisement is taken as the real quantity for which the Ryot is answerable till what belongs to the Circar is threshed out and delivered to its servants. Cultivators, who are not inhabitants of the village, receive exactly one half of the produce, and out of this pay the malavarâm.

The *punjie* or high ground, which cannot be watered, produces small and dry grains, the following are the principal of these—aruga *(puspalum frumentaceum)*, raghie *(eleusine corocana)*, of which there are three varieties, sajja *(holcus saccharatum)*, jonna *(holcus sorghum)*, chauma *(panicum miliaceum)*, and corra *(panicum italicum*, or millet). The three first of these are sown in the beginning of the rains in June, are ripe in September, and

* Eleusine corocana. † Phaseolus mungo. ‡ Dolichos catjang.
§ Cytisus cajam. || An Arcot rupee is 2s. 4d. ¶ Government.

yield on an average a twenty-fold produce; the next are sown in August and are ripe in November.

As the first four of these grains, especially the jonna, require strong ground which is ploughed with difficulty, four pair of bullocks are considered as requisite for the cultivation of one kalum of seed. But it ought to be observed that this quantity requires much more ground than a kalum of paddy. A kalum of chauma requires only two pair of bullocks.

The plough for cultivating high ground is made of maddie (*ficus*), a tough kind of wood which is strengthened by a much larger ploughshare than that for the low grounds, in order to overcome the superior hardness of the soil.

A little of the following kinds of grain is sown in October, and is ripe in January—minuma (*phaseolus minimus*), pessara (*phaseolus mungo*), wulawa (*glycine tomentosa*), kanda (*cytisus cajan*), bobbara (*dolichos catjang*), alsanda (*dolichos sinensis*).

The punjie is let out at a stipulated rent which is regulated by the kind of grain sown on it, or rather by the quality of the ground which renders it capable of producing certain kinds of grain. A cawny of the soil on which leguminous grains are sown is rented at from one and a half to three rupees. It is the worst kind of soil, being sandy and barren, and very little tillage is bestowed upon it. The soil on which what are called small grains are sown, as jonna, aruga, raghie, &c. rents at from three to six rupees the cawny, besides the malavarâm, or one-tenth of the whole produce at the bazar price.

Natchini or raghie is the kind of small grain most cultivated, as it finds a ready market every where among the lower classes of people who chiefly subsist upon it. But in the Pollams * the fields which can be watered by the rivers or tanks are chiefly attended to. Sugar is cultivated only in small quantities, probably because the soil in general is not rich enough for the cultivation of the sugar cane. But indigo I have found near Amboor in a tolerably flourishing state; and if the demand were greater this plant might be cultivated to much advantage. I am of opinion that indigo manufactured from dried leaves †, as is practised in the Carnatic, forms a more durable dye than when it is prepared in a different manner. I draw this conclusion from a trial which I made upon a large scale. I brought at a considerable expense a dyer from Porto Novo with a quantity of his indigo. As long as it lasted I made blue cloth of as fine and as durable a colour as can be ob-

* The valleys between the Ghauts.

† The dyers in Europe are much prejudiced against this as well as that made by boiling.

tained in that part of India. But as soon as we employed indigo manufactured by boiling, which is apparently the best mode of preparing it, the cloth, though at first beautiful to look at, lost its colour rapidly, and was in every respect similar to cloth dyed in the northern Circars.

The cotton chiefly cultivated on the coast is the common *dwarf cotton*, (*gossypium herbaceum*). It grows best on what is called the black cotton soil; but it may be raised upon any soil whatever, provided it be not mere sand. I have seen it growing on the hills, as on Kailasghur *, very luxuriantly between the stones. Perhaps it may have originally been in a wild state upon that hill, but at present the cotton is collected there. Nor have I any doubt that with a little attention on the part of the servants of Government the other hills along the coast might be made to produce this most valuable article. At present most of the cotton used in the Company's dominions is imported from the inland countries. A perpetual or a long exemption from all the Circar claims would probably be the best encouragement that could be given to the ryots for their attention to the culture of grounds, which have been hitherto allowed to remain in a state of nature. It is true that there is a good deal of uncultivated ground in the low country; but the soil in all such places is exceedingly bad: that of the hills though in general very stony is much better. Hence they are every way entitled to the preference when cultivation is to be attempted.

After proceeding several miles inland few cocoa-nut trees are to be seen, except those in the villages of the Jaghire, which are planted in rows before the houses of the inhabitants, and appear to thrive remarkably well. The high value of the ground is probably the reason why this useful tree is so little attended to in the Carnatic. Fields planted even with fruit trees do not yield so much profit as paddy fields. But as this apology does not apply to the streets of the villages, they might be stocked with cocoa-nut trees to great advantage.

IV. WEATHER AND CLIMATE.

As I have not had an opportunity of observing the different seasons of the year in the Carnatic, I have derived my knowledge of this subject chiefly from the writings of the natives themselves. The passages which I employ I must, however, confess I did not extract from the works myself; they were

* A hill fort near Vellore.

given me by a Bramin, to whom I am likewise indebted for the explanation of them.

The Hindoo year is divided into six seasons, the names of which are descriptive of their principal properties.

The first season is the *wasanta rutuwoo.* It begins with the Hindoo year in the middle of March, and lasts till the middle of May. The pleasures and occupations of Gods and men during this season are described with all the poetical luxuriance of the Indian bards. It is the season of the Gods, as it is emphatically called. The weather is serene and clear; the farmer's occupations are mostly over, and he has time to celebrate the yearly marriages of his Gods and friends. Many of their favourite trees are then in blossom, as the mango, from the young beautiful leaves of which Mammudoo * makes his shafts; and the inhalation of its vivifying pollen (called Mammudoo's sparks) is believed to raise similar passions in men and flowers. The southerly breezes that blow during the night are the Zephyrs of the western regions, to which the voluptuousness of the vernal season is particularly ascribed.

The second season is the *greeshma rutuwoo,* the hottest part of the year. As Krishna is represented of the darkest bluish black hue (cloud colour), a tinge of the skin that can be only produced by long exposure to a sun-burnt climate, I thought it not unlikely, as I had been told by many Bramins, that the name of this season was derived from that black deity. The difference between the initial G and K I did not consider as a sufficient objection, because I found them in many other cases used indifferently. But in the books which I have already noticed *Greeshma* is derived from the Shanscrit word *Greeshmaha, sweat;* so that *greeshma rutuwoo* is to be translated the *sweating season.*

All countries within the north tropic must be hottest at this season, because the sun is nearly vertical. But it is the blowing of what are called the *land winds* during this season along the coast of Coromandel that renders this country so disagreeably hot at this period. Like all great changes in nature, they do not come all of a sudden or surprise us unprepared. The most remarkable of the forerunners are the *whirlwinds* which, at the end of March and beginning of April, show themselves between eleven and twelve at noon, increasing daily both in strength and number, and moving from west to east in varying directions all over the country. They carry dust and light things along with them, and are called by the natives *peshashes,* or devils. After

* The Indian Cupid.

the whirlwinds have continued for some weeks they are succeeded by heavy clouds which appear at the same time of the day, and becoming gradually larger they at last burst forth in heavy showers of rain, accompanied by violent peals of thunder and lightning. These violent rains come mostly from south-west, while the land winds usually blow from due west. They begin in the west, for they are earlier felt inland near the ranges of hills than on the coast; they are always preceded by a long calm, and carry before them a cloud of dust. The atmosphere while they blow is always hazy and apparently thicker than in common, and the sun when rising appears as if involved in mist or dust.

They set in about ten or eleven o'clock in the forenoon, and increase in violence and heat till they are stopped by an easterly wind called the sea breeze, which begins to waft delight and health along the coast about two in the afternoon or sometimes earlier. The sea breeze is preceded by a short lull or calm. If the sea breeze fail, as sometimes happens, the land wind continues blowing, but gradually decreases in strength, and finally dies away in the beginning of the night, having slowly veered round to the south-west. About morning a little motion of the air is perceptible; but it is very weak, until at the usual time the wind sets in stronger and hotter than on the preceding day.

The land winds are said to be dry, and on that account productive of an uneasy sensation all over the body, with a dryness of the skin as if the perspiration had been suddenly stopped. This sensation is peculiarly felt in the eyes, which we are frequently obliged to shut while walking in this wind, because they become quite stiff.

These winds are frequently so hot that they destroy men and animals if exposed to them for a short time. It is not very uncommon to see large kites and crows, while on the wing, drop down at once as if they had no life in them. Nor is it an unfrequent occurrence for a place, containing from five to ten thousand inhabitants, to lose four or five in a day in consequence of exposing themselves to this wind for too long a time. This happens chiefly at the setting in of the wind, when people are caught unprepared. Pains of the bones and general lassitude are universally felt, and paralytic or hemiplectic affections are by no means uncommon.

Along the coast, and for a few miles inland, the inhabitants are relieved by the sea breeze; but at the distance of ten or twenty miles from the sea its good effects are not so much experienced; for it arrives late in the afternoon, and is already heated by the tract of country over which it has passed. Nothing can be more distressing than the failure of the sea breeze for several successive days, when the land wind blows all night and heats every thing so much as to become distressing to the touch. This was the case in the year 1799 in the northern Circars for almost a fortnight. The thermometer at mid-night stood at 108°, and at eight o'clock at 112°. Neither wood nor glass is capable of bearing this heat for any length of time; the latter, as shades, globe lanthorns, &c. crack and fly in pieces; the former warps and shrinks. The nails fall out of the doors and tables. I have never myself seen the thermometer higher than 115° in the coolest part of the house. Some persons affirm that in such cases they have seen it as high as 130°.

Nightly illuminations of the Ghauts or of the hills in their neighbourhood are seen at this season, after it has continued for some time without rain. These appear always about the middle of the mountain, seldom or never reaching the top. They frequently present very interesting and beautiful scenes. As far as my observations go they are confined to those hills which are covered with bamboo bushes. The natives account for these spontaneous combustions by the friction of the bamboos against each other, an explanation which appears to me satisfactory. In Europe I know these spontaneous combustions have been much discredited, because they could not be explained by means of favourite theories invented within the walls of a college, or perhaps a less respectable place.

The natives use no other means of securing themselves against the effects of the land winds, than shutting up their houses and bathing in the morning and evening. Europeans cool their apartments by means of wetted tats, made of straw or grass, and sometimes of the roots of the *wattie waeroo* *, which when wetted exhales a pleasant but faint smell. It will appear incredible to those who have never witnessed it, when I say that the water evaporates so fast that several people are constantly employed throwing it upon the tats, the dimensions of which are eight feet by four. Without this labour the requisite degree of coolness could not be obtained. I have known several gentlemen who, during the continuance of the land wind, have kept people constantly employed in pouring water over them both night and day, and apparently without suffering any inconvenience in point of health.

It is natural to ask the question here, how comes the land wind to be so

* Andropogon Muricatulum.

much heated? The usual answer is, by passing over the surface of a considerable tract of heated country. But this, though it may, to a certain extent, be true, does not appear to me sufficient to account for the very high temperature which this wind has acquired. If this peninsula, like Zaara, in Africa, or the northern parts of Arabia, were a tract of desert dry sand, over which the land-wind swept, we should not be surprised to find the temperature of that wind as high as 115° or 130°. But this, though a hilly, is a cultivated country. I am disposed to believe that the valleys winding through the Ghauts are the places where the temperature of the atmosphere is so much elevated. The hills that form the boundaries of these valleys will reflect the rays of the sun towards the centre, and this must be attended with a prodigious increase of temperature. The atmosphere, remaining stagnant for some time in these valleys, must be very much heated; and when it is at length forced outwards by the pressure of the air on the higher grounds, it constitutes the land-winds, which blow with such disagreeable regularity during summer in Coromandel. This accounts too for a circumstance which has often been observed, that the land-winds are hotter near the mouth of these valleys than any where else.

If I were disposed to speculate farther on this subject, I would conjecture that the vast quantity of vapour condensed during this season, in these parts, into clouds and rain, must set at liberty a considerable quantity of heat, which probably contributes to raise the temperature of the land-winds.

The land-winds in India are not considered as prejudicial to the health, probably because a few only suffer during their continuance. But if we consider the effects which such heat must have upon the human body, and if we consult the registers of mortality for many successive years, we shall find that soon after the termination of these winds in the month of June, bilious fevers finish the career of many persons, particularly of the old and debilitated. It is a common and a true saying, that an old valetudinarian will not long survive the land-winds.

In the latter part of this season, the water of the Cavery comes into the Carnatic, and gives fresh life and animation to the cultivator. During this dry season in the Carnatic, the violent monsoon rains fall on the Malabar coast. The sages among the natives say that this river comes from the neighbourhood of a Mount called Sampia, which lies in the Sanda country. About this time, and a little before it, violent storms of thunder and hail sometimes blow from the west, which gives to this season the title of the little monsoon.

The third season is the *warasha rutuwoo, or rainy season.* But though this name may be accurately applied on the Malabar coast, and in the higher provinces of India, this is not the season when the heaviest rains fall in the Carnatic. The air is sometimes cooled by showers, and the sky is cloudy; but the true rainy season is

The fourth season, called *siradra rutuwoo*, or the *drying season.* In it the heavy rains fall in the Carnatic, fill the tanks, and often inundate the country. The rains and the wind are said to come chiefly from the east and north-east, and are at least a fortnight or a month later than in the Circars. It is an established opinion in Hindostan, that the rains are in proportion to the heat of the Greeshma season; and this opinion is supported by my observations. The weather and the wind which prevail in this season are said to make people drowsy and sleepy.

It may be worth while to notice here several of the meteorological opinions of the Indians, as affording some means of judging of the state of their knowledge.

In the *Megha Sandusha Grandum*, it is said of thunder—When the smoke, lightning, water, and wind combine together, and rise towards the regions in which the probhunda wind * reigns, a friction is produced between these substances, which occasions the discharge of bolts with the accompanying thunder.

According to the *Chumpoo Ramayana*, the following predictions may be formed from the colour of the lightning. If the lightning be of an impure green colour, it precedes strong wind; if red, the weather will be afterwards hot; if yellow, strong thunder and rain will follow; and if white, or black, it presages a season without rain, and consequently dearth.

The first of the works from which these quotations are taken, treats of nothing but clouds; the second is one of the many Ramayana, or Epic Poems, celebrating the feats of Rama.

In the Almanacs of the Hindoos, regular notice is taken of the quantity of rain that will fall in the different seasons, computing it by conchums †. For example, in the Cholam country will be three, in the Guntoor six conchums of rain, &c. I thought this, at first, a prophecy without meaning, but learnt afterwards that many persons are in the habit of keeping an account of the rain as it falls. Their rain gauge is merely a common cutcherry pot, which

* A wind that blows at some height above the surface of the earth.

† A measure of eight pounds.

is placed before the house, and emptied as often as the rain has filled it. Among the remarkable news of the weather, the sages of the village are in the habit of inquiring how many pots it has rained.

The fifth season is the *hementa*, or *cool season*, from the middle of December to the middle of February. The countries along the Ghauts, and in the valleys, are, in the wasanta season, hotter than in the open country; but in this season they are much colder. The dews are much heavier than in the plains, and they increase in proportion to their vicinity to the mountains. The greatest cold is felt immediately after the deposition of the dew, an hour after sun-rise, probably proceeding from the evaporation of the dew, which, after the sun gets higher, is not so much felt.

The last season is the *sisa rutuwoo*. In it the wind blows from the south-east, and is called the *along shore wind*. It is strong, and, on account of the sand which it carries with it, very unpleasant; and it is usually reckoned unhealthy. The weather is serene, moderately cool, and indeed what the *wasanta rutuwoo* is represented to be by the Indian poets. Hence I should conclude that the division and description of the seasons have been made in the northern provinces of Bengal, where the names are much more expressive or descriptive of nature in those seasons.

The following translation is supposed to be pronounced by a Bramin to a Rajah, as a kind of blessing, and literally translated can scarcely be understood. Indeed the Indian poets are so unreasonable as seemingly to wish not to be understood without their comments.

"May you enjoy in Hemanta the congenial warmth of your wife; in Sisa, the gentle heat of the sun; the pleasures of a shady garden in Wasanta, and of cool bathing in Greeshma; a comfortable high room in Warasha, and a copious draught of fresh milk in Siradra. And may your enemies disappear, as the day in Hemanta, like the lotus flower in Sisa, like sexual bashfulness in Wasanta; may they be as short-lived as the nights in Greeshma, and vanish like dust in Warasha, and moisture in Siradra."

V. ROADS.

The roads in this part of the Carnatic are, generally speaking, pretty good, and indeed excellent, when compared with those in the northern Circars. This observation, however, applies only to the best season of the year for travelling. In order to judge of them in the rainy season, we must consult the general face of the country. In all cases, the goodness of the roads is invariably as the state of cultivation. Where rice, sugar, or jonnaloo are cultivated in any abundance, we may be assured that the roads, in the wet season, will be both narrow and bad, while high and sandy tracts of ground, which cannot be watered, and therefore produce only dry grains, will have good roads even at that season. Hence I conclude that the roads between the Mount and Conjeveram are tolerably good in every season, and perhaps in some places, where the deep sand is distressing in the dry, they will be best in the rainy season; and bad between Vellore and the Ghauts in the latter.

The avenues of trees, and the numerous choultries, render the roads in this country very pleasant and commodious for travellers of all descriptions. The avenues, however, are by no means regular, either with respect to the distance and number of trees, or their breadth, or even their continuity. Sometimes vacancies of many miles occur, as between Raychie, Choultry, and Conjeveram. The trees are usually planted sufficiently close, with underwood between them; and the greater number are banyans *. Tamarinds and mangos *(mangifera indica)* supply their place near villages, where frequent *topes* † of the same kind of trees occur. The Madras avenue tree, and the portia *(hybiscus populneus)*, are not often seen. The latter has not been so much attended to as it merits, from its quick growth and fine shade, probably on account of the kind of catterpillar that feeds upon it, which, when it falls on the skin, occasions blisters and ulcerations. The Madras avenue tree ‡ is deservedly neglected, as it affords no shade in the hotest seasons of the year, when it is most wanted.

Among the smaller trees, I frequently observed the galeduppa pungam, the kanuga of the Gentoos; the seeds of which yield a medicinal oil. It grows, in many places, to a large handsome tree.

The Choultries are much more numerous than are requisite for the number of travellers. They are all terraced, and built of quarry stones, or brick and chunam §. The smaller ones are single square rooms, open towards the street, where the roof is supported by large square pillars. In the walls are excavations for lamps, which are lighted in the night. But they have no windows. The larger ones, as Veerapermal Suttrum, four coss west of Stree Permatore, and Raychie Choultry, near Conjeveram, are fine extensive buildings. The former has an open court in the middle, surrounded by a spacious covered

* Several species of *ficus*, by sending their roots in different directions down along the trunk, and from the branches into the road, spoil it for wheel carriages.

† Copses. ‡ Odina. § Mortar.

veranda, which, in the houses of the natives, is always the most frequented part of the habitation. Doors enter from it into the more secret recesses.

Notwithstanding the characteristic cleanliness of the natives of India, these choultries, with the exception of a very few, where attendants are kept to clean and sweep them, are disgustingly dirty. Rather than stay in one of them, I would, even in the hottest season, prefer the shade of a tree. The smoke produced by their culinary operations is one of the most disagreeable things. It heats the place and blackens the walls, and we seldom find a choultry free from it, because the Fakeers, and many other people, are too lazy to dress their food at a distance from the choultry. In the rainy season, these choultries are comfortable to all ranks and descriptions of travellers, and, by a little attention of the police, might be rendered very pleasant temporary abodes. The turn of the richer classes of natives for building such places of accommodation for travellers might be improved, by encouraging them to extend their charity to countries more in want of it than the vicinity of the capital. Some honorary privilege, for example, might be held out to them, which they value much more than money.

Every choultry has a pond or tank near it, partly to serve for the daily ablutions of the Hindoos, and partly to allay their thirst, which the natives in general are much less capable of bearing than the Europeans. I have been astonished during my excursions, to find them complain of want of water, in cases where I underwent at least as much fatigue as themselves, without feeling any inclination to drink: they were equally astonished when I refused a draught of turbid water, which they happened to find in a little nasty pool, to partake of which they never fail to invite the whole party, by crying out emphatically, "good water." In consequence of this propensity, it becomes a very charitable action, during the hot land-wind season, to erect temporary buildings near the road side, where water, whey, or butter-milk is served out to travellers by a Bramin or Soodra. This custom prevails much in the northern Circars, where indeed I myself established a place of the kind.

The preceding remarks apply almost correctly to the road from Conjeveram to Wallajahbad and Vellore, excepting that in those places where rice is cultivated in any quantity; as about Conjeveram itself, at Damerla, and Samindinghy, the road is necessarily bad and deep in the wet season. We must except also the bed of the river Polar, between Arcot and Vellore, which is very broad, and a deep distressing sand in the dry season.

The road from Vellore, in the valley of Ambore, to Santghus, was very pleasant and good in the season that we passed, but probably bad in the rainy season, from the torrents of rain from the neighbouring mountains that must inundate the country. The best, though the steepest, road in the country is the Peddanaikdoorgum pass, which, with great labour, has been cut through rocks by the pioneers, a set of people, by the wise regulations of government, as useful in times of peace as they are in those of war.

Whether the want of large wheel carriages rendered the establishment of public roads unnecessary in the opinion of the former rulers of India, or whether the want of roads prevented the use of wheel carriages, I cannot determine. But this circumstance shows the little progress they had made in civilization, even when compared with the other Asiatic nations. The Japannese, for example, look upon the preservation of roads as one of the principal charges incumbent on their government: indeed in all well-formed governments the importance of roads, both in time of peace and war, will not suffer them to be neglected, especially as the establishment of convenient ones is one of the greatest encouragements that can be held out for increasing manufactures and inland trade: it is true that we can convey goods from the Mysore, and other parts of India, to the coast, on the backs of bullocks; but it is no less true, that four bullocks in a four-wheeled carriage will draw more than sixteen or twenty can carry on their backs. In mercantile transactions, nine maund, or two hundred and sixteen pounds, are allowed for the load of a good bullock, but they seldom carry more than two hundred pounds, and often less.

To give a plan where and how roads should be constructed does not come within my province; but a few hints, derived from observation, will not be thought, I hope, too presumptuous.

The best materials for roads would be the disintegrated sienite, common all over the country near the hills, or the bed which is found by digging several feet under ground, all along from Conjeveram and farther east, which is a decomposed granite. These materials, especially the sienite, would harden much, I conceive, if some lime-stone or marl were mixed with it, substances which, in small quantities, may be found every where: it would then be nearly similar to the Nellore clay, which hardens when exposed to the air.

The loam or sand taken from the surface of the country would not, for obvious reasons, afford a lasting good road.

In countries where rice is cultivated, sluices might be made, or rather arched channels, at the bottom of the road, at proper distances for the communication of the water: if this is not attended to, the ryots will, in spite of all prohibitions, contrive to cut channels across the road, either to get rid of their superabundance of water, or to get a share of water belonging to their neighbours, which they conceive themselves to have a right to. It should by no means be allowed to employ the road as a dam to collect water as in a tank, as this might materially hurt it; and a sudden rain might even break the road, as often happens to the strongest tank embankments.

Besides avenues of trees on the sides of the road, palmeyra or date trees might be planted in close rows on the ascent of its sides; as, not to mention the use of the trees in future times, they would soon remarkably strengthen the roads.

Malefactors of all kinds, and especially palankeen boys and servants convicted of malpractices towards their masters, or run-aways, I would recommend as the fittest persons to keep the roads in repair. People of this description are never wanting.

It would contribute much to the beauty of the road, if the species of tree constituting the avenues were changed every mile, or at fixed distances. Such a regular succession would point out to the traveller the number of miles he had gone.

I conceive the following to be the best trees for avenues.

1. Hibiscus populneus: but this tree should not be too abundant, as it feeds a very troublesome caterpillar.

2. Artocarpus integrifolia, or jack fruit. This is a fine shady tree of quick growth, and producing a nourishing fruit: I have seen it planted by the road side in some parts of the Mysore, chiefly about Ooscottah, by the order of Tippoo.

3. Tamarind. This tree, though of slow growth, affords a fine shelter in the hottest season of the year, not to mention the usefulness of its pulp and leaves; but this tree ought to be sparingly planted, because it is believed by the natives to diffuse noxious vapours during the night. No other vegetable will grow under it.

4. Bassia longifolia. It grows luxuriantly in the worst soil: from its seeds an oil is expressed.

5. Mimusops elengi. A fine tree with good fruit.

6. Mango. This is a shady useful tree, that thrives in any soil, and is not slow in growth.

7. Melia azedarachta. This is also a very useful and handsome tree, the leaves, bark, and fruit of which possess medical virtues. It is of quick growth.

8. Tectonia grandis, the teak tree. It grows best in hilly countries. The seeds are often a year in the ground before they come up, but afterwards its growth is not slow. Probably it may not be advisable to plant this tree in the low countries.

9. Mimosa latisiliqua, the tirisina of the Gentoos. It grows soon to be a large fine tree, the flowers of which are remarkable for their grateful odours; the wood is durable and hard, and answers better than any other for sugar mills and ploughs.

10. Bastard cedar (bubroma). It is of quick growth, and is of sufficient size for an avenue tree.

VI. REMARKABLE PLACES.

The most remarkable places on our road to the Ghauts were Conjeveram, Wallajanagar, Vellore, and Sautghur. I shall notice what has come to my knowledge respecting these places, that I do not consider as too trite or too well known to deserve a place here.

Conjeveram, renowned in the ancient history of the country, and known to Europeans by the military transactions of the Carnatic wars, is still a very large and populous place. It lies in a kind of valley, which has a cheerful appearance. The village is five or six miles long; the streets are mostly broad, and planted on both sides with cocoa nut and bastard cedar trees: many gardens and topes are conspicuous in it, under the shade of which the weavers have their looms. Round the whole village is a bound hedge, chiefly of the agave americana, which, together with the gates, is capable, during war, of keeping off any irregular body of horse: such troops, during the late wars of Hyder and Tippoo, proved exceedingly destructive to the Carnatic. The small river Wegavatty, which runs along the western skirts of the village, contributes much to the fertility of the valley: its bed is very sandy, and water is found every where by digging a few feet through the sand. Hencc the saying that the water of this river is in some seasons above, in others under, its bed.

Many tanks of a large size have been constructed in this valley, chiefly at its west end, because the country on that side is sloping, and consequently favourable for collecting water: there are tanks likewise in the village near the numerous pagodas. We encamped near a very remarkable one, for which it is said the gods collected water from no less than three millions of rivers: it lies on the west side of the great pagoda. Every Bramin who visits the place for the first time must perform his ablutions in this tank, and spend some money in charity, or rather in furnishing food to a number of Bramins of the place in honour of the manes of his forefathers.

There are three religious divisions in this place, namely, Siwa conjie, Wishnoo conjie, and Jina conjie. The largest pagoda is dedicated to Sewa, where he is worshipped under the usual form of a lingum, or the creative attribute of Deity. As the Hindoos acknowlege five elements, water, earth, fire, air, and ether, so also they worship five different lingums, called *Pancha lingāloo.* The lingum here is made of earth, and consequently represents that element. The other four are made of stone, distinguished by their colours according to the element which they are to represent. It *appeared* (for this is the theological expression) under a mango tree, the tree sacred to Mammudoo, or the God of Love, who makes his shafts from the young leaves of it.

In Wishnoo conjie, the deity called Wishnoo is worshipped, but it is here by no means so celebrated as the former, there being but few of this sect in the Carnatic. Jina conjie is scarcely worth mentioning; there are a few houses on the west side of the river where they have a temple, containing a a representation of Bhouda.

According to the stalapurānam * this must have been a famous place in ancient times, as places at the distance of five yojanums on each cardinal point of the compass are represented as its gates or keys. To the east is Mahavellyporam, to the west Wirinjiporam, to the north Narrainawannam, and to the south Tindiwanam. A yojanum is equal to four coss, or eight miles, so that each of these places should be forty miles from Conjeveram, and this is very nearly the case. As we find pagodas of some note at all these

* The best if not the only geographical account of ancient Hindostan: it deserves to be translated.

places, we have reason to think that by *gate* is meant places of worship, to be visited before pilgrims are allowed to prostrate themselves before the principal deity. The pious Hindoos are obliged in all small pagodas to worship Puliăr or Wikneswandu,* and Bayrudu, inferior deities represended, the first by a god with an elephant's head, and the second by a dog, before they can have access to the principal deities of the place.

The real age of this large pagoda is lost in obscurity; but the Hindoos affirm that it was built by Weswakarmadu, the chief architect of the Dewatas. He lived in the golden age, and the gates were constructed by him of gold, which, in that happy æra, constituted the common material. The Annagunda Krishnarailu, it is said, built the very extensive porticos erected on no fewer than a thousand pillars; and I think it probable that, under the reign of that prince, the pagoda acquired much of its celebrity. It is now a noble building, and well worth seeing; but as the Bramins would not allow me to view the interior, I disdained to take any notice of the exterior. The arrogance and contumely with which the Bramins in the Carnatic are allowed to treat Europeans, is almost proverbial; and as it proceeds entirely from the motives which the Madras Dubashes are inculcating and spreading, it is becoming more and more intolerable. Something is due to inveterate prejudices, but to countenance them, and to suffer them to be encouraged, is acting with too much liberality.

The only people at Conjeveram that have the means of building or repairing pagodas, are the weavers, a great number of whom reside here. They are always the most dissolute, but at the same time the most useful set of men. They earn their money by great industry, and spend it like fools, in every kind of play. Owing to their sedentary life, they resemble their brethren in other countries in their sickly and meagre appearance. They are not jealous of one another. The manufactures of this place are red handkerchiefs, turbans, and dressing cloths for men and women. Punjums, and other useful cloth, might no doubt be manufactured here as well as in other parts of the Carnatic. Saltpetre might be made also, as the earth contains it in many streets in great abundance. Indeed I saw them collecting it, but whether to procure saltpetre from it, or to manure their gardens, I do not know; for it constitutes an excellent manure for sugar canes, chillies (capsicum annuum), and for natchemy fields. I saw little appearance of saltpetre in other parts of

* Ganesa.

the Jaghire, or in the Arcot country, except at Wirinjiporam, where it is manufactured for sale. A banyan pays yearly fifty rupees rent to the Nabob, and sells his product, which amounts to about twenty candies, at eighty rupees per candy, to the country people. This amounts to 464¼ pagodas. Now, if we deduct 160 pagodas for the expense of the manufacture and for the rent, there will remain a handsome profit of 250 pagodas.

Wallajanagur is a little town containing about 300 houses, twenty-five miles distant from Conjeveram, and three from Arcot. It is better known by the trade which it carries on all over the country than by its situation, or external attractions. It was built about forty years ago, by Raychie, the Nabob's Dewan, who encouraged tradesmen from all quarters to settle in it, by promising them an exemption for five years from all duties, assessments, and customs, which are usually levied with great severity upon the houses, shops, persons, &c. of banyans, and other traders. The consequence was a considerable concourse of people, who have, by their industry and frugality, rendered its trade extensive and flourishing. Every article that India furnishes can be procured here, and even money transactions are carried on to a great amount.

The situation of this place has been judiciously chosen, though probably owing to an accident, which pointed it out as a lucky spot. As its position is nearly central, it is well calculated to unite the trade of the Marattas, the Nizam, and the Mysore countries, who send down annually a great host of lombardies, with their productions. They take, in return, salt, and some European articles, such as red cloth, knives, looking-glasses, &c. These the merchants keep ready while the lombardies go to the coast for salt.

The want of rivers, and of wheel carriages, is not so much felt in India as they would be in other countries, because a set of people called Lombardies, or Brinjaries, dedicate the whole of their time to the transportation of goods from one province to another. They make their appearance at certain seasons with droves of many thousand head of cattle; and as long as the roads continue in their present state, these people must remain the sole carriers of Indian merchandize.

No other encouragement but a short exemption from assessments and customs was necessary to render Wallajanagur a flourishing place; the same method would succeed in procuring similar establishments all along the coast. They would be of the utmost consequence to the English territory in that country, and to the revenue of the Company. Those places would be best fitted for the purpose where nature herself has opened a communication between the upper and lower countries: for example, near all the great rivers or passes where we find the lombardies enter the low country. Rajanagram, near Rajamundry, is I believe well situated, and would require but little encouragement to render it flourishing. Another place of the kind in the Muglatore, one between Ellore and Masulipatam, and several on both banks of the Kistnah, and near Ongole, would give a favourable turn to trade in the Circars.

Vellore, or as the natives call it, Ray Ellore, or Stone Ellore (to distinguish it from Ellore in the Circars, called Upper Ellore, or Salt Ellore) is well known in this country, as it has been constantly one of the principal stations of the Company's forces. Tradition says it was built about five hundred years ago by a Polygar called Bomma Naidoo, who, having discovered a concealed treasure, was anxious to secure his independence. His family continued masters of the place during about one hundred years, when they were obliged to resign themselves to the mercy of Kirstmarailoo of Annagunda, who appeared with a large force before the place. About fifty years ago it came into the possession of the Nabob of Arcot, who still possesses* the revenue of the country, of which Vellore is the capital.

The hill fort is now almost entirely neglected, but the lower is said to be very strong. In the broad and deep ditch are many alligators, turtle, and large fish: the alligators are not molested, and seemingly do not attempt to attack the human species. The Pettah is very large and populous; the inhabitants are chiefly Malabars† and Moormen, many of whom belong to the sons of Tippoo Sultan, to whom Vellore has been assigned as their future place of residence.‡ The palaces built for them are on a very large scale, and accommodated to their own notions of comfort and elegance.

The country round Vellore is very well cultivated, and diversified with many chains of hills: it is indeed one of the larger valleys formed by those ranges of hills called the Mysore Table-land, which I conceive to be nearly on a level with the summits of the highest among these mountains.

Sautghur is the last place in our way through the Carnatic of any consequence, and it is more remarkable for what it has been than what it is at present. By the Hindoos it is called Sewana Kandala Dūrgum. It con-

* At the time this was written.

† Properly Tamuls.

‡ Since the mutiny at Vellore in 1807, they have been removed to Bengal.

sists of seven fortified hills (as its Moorish name expresses); but as the names of these are Telinga, it is evident that it was originally a Hindoo establishment. Its founder, according to tradition, was a Soodra of the name of Pīrmalnaidoo, who fortified these hills about five hundred years ago, at a time when this part of the country was in the hands of a great number of independent Polygars. There is abundance of fine water on the hill called Gunga Sagragadda in a bason of the rock, which is said to be unfathomable: this bason is about half-way up the hill, and has no appearance whatever of having been the crater of a volcano. The hill is composed of sienite, and is in all respects similar to the other mountains of the Carnatic: the soil produced by the decomposition of this rock is favourable to vegetation. Hence these hills are covered with a variety of trees and shrubs: the trees however are small, because the soil is not deep, and the roots soon penetrating to the rock, the plants are stinted in their growth.

From the top of these hills there is a very extensive prospect of a highly cultivated country; in the valley immediately below, a branch of the sandy bed of the Palaroo was seen winding along. When we saw it it was destitute of water, and this I understand is the case during the greatest part of the year: hence the natives call it Goddaeroo, or the empty sterile river. The valleys towards the Gauts are very narrow, and indeed nothing but empty chasms. There is a very fine view of them from this place, especially of the Peddanaikdurgum pass, in which we saw with the naked eye travellers ascending.

This place is very unhealthy in the rainy season; on this account the Nabobs of Arcot formerly kept their state prisoners here, when policy or some other motive prevented then from putting them to a violent death. In the warm season this valley, which is contiguous to that of Ambore, is remarkably hot.

Hurryhur, 7th October, 1800.

TRACT II.

STATISTICAL FRAGMENTS ON THE MYSORE.

THE information collected in this Tract was acquired while I acted as assistant to Col. Mackenzie, superintendant of the Mysore survey. In the year 1800 I was appointed to this situation, and received a set of instructions; according to which I have digested all the particulars that have come to my knowledge. Indeed this Tract may be considered as simply an abridgement of a report laid before the Government of Fort St. George.

I. STATE OF THE THERMOMETER.

The greatest variation of the thermometer, in the course of one day during sixteen months, was 28°: this happened in the month of April 1800. The greatest difference in one month was 36°, and in the course of sixteen months 51°. For the thermometer stood at 56° in the palace of Bengalore, on the 26th December, 1800; and in my tent on the 8th of May, 1800, it was as high as 107°: but I must observe, that the thermometer had been carried in a box on a man's head during the greatest part of the day, on our march from Bengalore to Madāvaram, and that it stood at 107° immediately on being put up in my tent: so that it was perhaps rather the direct heat of the sun, than of the atmosphere, that produced this elevation. The greatest heat in the houses during the month of April is 87° or 88°.

In the palace of Bengalore the thermometer, during the year 1800, never rose higher than 82°, and in the coldest season of the same year, it fell in a tent to 52°. In the palace at the same time it was 56°.

II. STATE OF THE BAROMETER.

The weather and temperature have very little effect on the barometer in India. The greatest variation in the course of a day during sixteen months amounted to 0·3 inch: the regular daily variation is about 0·05 inch.

To try what influence solar heat might have on the column of quicksilver, I exposed a barometer, with a thermometer attached to it, to the sun for about an hour; another corresponding barometer and thermometer I kept in my tent. The difference between the thermometers was about 30°, and that of the barometers about 0·05 inch. The real change in bulk ought to have been nearly twice as great, as we learn from the experiments of General Roy and Sir George Shuckburgh Evelyn: but my barometer was not sufficiently delicate for measuring minute alterations in length. I made no attempt to ascertain the amount of the diurnal rise and fall of the barometer between the tropics, as first pointed out by Bouguer, and lately determined with considerable accuracy by Messrs. Langsdorf and Horner: such observations would have required better barometers than I was provided with, nor is it likely that observations, made in an inland district, should have been attended with such regular results as those made at sea by the Russian philosophers above mentioned.

III. PREVAILING WINDS.

The prevailing winds in the eastern and northern parts of the Mysore, according to the accounts of the natives and my own observations, are the following. About the beginning of June and in July, the wind blows steadily from the west and the south-west, and ought to bring abundance of rain. This was the case particularly in the years 1800, 1801, and 1805, in the southern districts of the Mysore; while the northern with the same wind had no rain.

In August and September the wind varies from the south-west to the north-west, bringing rain from both quarters. In the latter end of September and in October the wind veers round to the east and north-east, and from that quarter the heaviest rains are expected. About Hurryhurr rain is invariably expected in this season, after the wind has blown for three days successively from the north or north-east.

In November and December the northerly winds prevail, and to them are ascribed the coldness of this season, as well as the frequent fevers and other disorders.

In January and February the wind blows chiefly from the south, and is said to be healthy and pleasant. On the coast the *along-shore* winds (blowing from the same quarter) prevail during this season; they are esteemed very unpleasant, strong, and unhealthy: they do not extend in the bay to any great distance from the shore.

The different effects of winds upon the human body seem to be connected with their degree of moisture and dryness. The along-shore winds seem to stop the perspiration, while the land winds promote it. Hence probably the difference of their salubrity at least in some degree.

In April and May the winds are changeable, commonly blowing in the forenoon from the west, and in the afternoon from the east. These east winds bring violent storms, showers of rain and hail, accompanied by loud peals of thunder and vivid flashes of lightning.

The weather before rain becomes invariably sultry and calm, then the wind blows hot and dry from the rainy quarter, and effects the sensations in the same way, though not in the same degree, as the land wind on the coast.

IV. RAIN.

As the Mysore participates of two monsoons, namely, the Malabar monsoon from June to September, and the Coromandel monsoon from September to December, more rain falls in it than in any other part of India. The rain of the former monsoon is attended with distant murmuring thunder, and frequent lightning, and seldom falls very heavy; while that of the latter pours down with great violence, fills the largest tanks in a few hours, and often lasts for many days with little intermission. The thunder is louder and the flashes of lightning more vivid.

The rains in April and May are of the accidental kind, heavy short showers from the east quarter. The drops are large and fall at a distance from each other.

V. ATMOSPHÈRE.

The atmosphere is, generally speaking, serene and clear from January to May; during the first part of this season, however, the mornings are foggy, and about the end of it, in May, particularly the afternoons, are cloudy. The clouds begin to show themselves at noon along the eastern Ghauts, and draw from all eastern points, in different directions, to the western hemisphere.

From the month of June to September the clouds come from the westward, and often obscure the sky for whole weeks: they have the appearance of detached broken bodies, and the rain from them is drizzly and persevering.

From the latter end of August to October, heavy clouds in the east before and after sun-set, of a crimson and fiery colour, prognosticate immediate rain. They often assume the appearance of a fiery meteor. Hence I am disposed to suspect, that the meteor seen on the 13th December, 1801, at Madras, and visible also in the Mysore, was nothing but a cloud of this kind.

The clouds in all seasons appeared to me to draw with the wind.

VI. FOGS.

In some parts of the country heavy fogs, or rather mists, precede rain: thus about Chittledroog, from August to October, the hills are obscured till about ten in the forenoon. In general, fogs prevail all over the country in the months of December and January, after the rains are over, and have been abundant: they begin after midnight, and render the atmosphere chilly till seven in the morning, or a little later, when they are dispersed by the heat of the sun. No rain ever falls in these months. Hence these fogs are highly useful to the growth of plants, as they clear them from dust, and open their pores, and supply them with nourishment, which they could not obtain from the earth in this season. Without these irrigations very little salt petre could be made, as the earth which contains it can be recognised only after is has attracted this moisture.

I had an opportunity of becoming well acquainted with the changes in the atmosphere, and the circumstances attending the rising of heavy fogs, when I had the superintendance of the saltpetre works in the northern Circars, and was obliged to ride early in the morning on horseback to distant villages. Before three o'clock the weather was usually serene and calm, but about that time a gust of warm wind set in, and almost immediately afterwards I was involved in clouds of mist, so thick, that frequently I could not see my horse keeper a few yards before or behind me: I found it often so cold that I dismounted and walked until day light.

In this season, and by means of the heavy fogs, is the vinegar of Sennagalu obtained, which is so much prized by the Moormen and rich Hindoos.

It is made by spreading pieces of muslin cloth on the flowering sennaga (*cicer arietinum*, Bengal *gram*) after sun-set, and removing them before the sun gets through the clouds of mist. The moisture, with which they are quite wet, is wrung from them, and preserved for use. This acid juice, according to the analysis of Vauquelin, contains oxalic, malic, and a little acetic acid.

VII. DEWS.

Dews are heaviest in December and January, before the fogs set in. They become perceptible about eight or nine o'clock in the evening, at a time when the atmosphere is perfectly serene and clear. On the Coromandel coast, we are not so much afraid of exposing ourselves to them as they seem to be in other parts of the world. Many Europeans, and almost all the natives, sleep during the night in the open air, without the least injury to their health.

VIII. HAIL.

Hail falls only in the hottest season, in April and May. It is usually in pieces of the weight of half an ounce, but sometimes of very considerable magnitude*. It is accompanied by heavy thunder, and storms or gusts of wind from the eastward. Showers of hail are more frequent above the Ghauts than below them. The natives call the hail *rainstones*, and ascribe to it great invigorating virtues.

IX. THUNDER.

The loudest peals of thunder take place in the month of May. The coruscations are then very vivid and frequent, and followed almost immediately by the thunder clap. This is the only season in which buildings, trees, and animals are struck by lightning. The natives of India, however, do

* Masses of immense size are said to have fallen from the clouds at different periods: in the latter part of Tippoo Sultan's reign it is on record, and well authenticated, that a piece fell near Seringapatam of the size of an elephant, which by the Sultan's officers was reported to produce "the effect of fire on the skin of those who touched it:"—a comparison naturally made by persons ignorant of the sensation of extreme frigidity. It is stated that two days elapsed before it was entirely dissolved, during which time it exhaled such a stench as to prevent people from approaching it: fear probably occasioned the latter report. That this account is in the public records of Tippoo's reign, I have from a gentleman of the greatest respectability of character, and high in the civil service of the Honourable Company.

not betray any fear. Like the vulgar in Europe, they believe that the damage is done by thunderbolts, or stones that are discharged from the clouds.

The clouds in this season are hurried along by violent storms, often accompanied by whirlwinds, from all parts of the eastern Ghauts; and when they meet each other, a dreadful scene of thunder and lightning, and whirlwinds, immediately presents itself; but it does not continue long; for the clouds are again dispersed in quick motions to the westward, and leave the atmosphere serene and delightful.

During the rainy season (seven months in the year), thunder is almost daily heard; but at a great distance. Flashes of lightning are seen very often. The peals are rather louder during the rains of the Coromandel monsoon.

X. EARTHQUAKES.

These commotions of the earth are never violent, and by no means frequent in this country, occurring only about once in five years. I felt one at Toomkoor, on the 23d of October 1800. It is remarkable that, at the same time, a violent hurricane raged along the coast from Ongole to Masulipatam. The shock was felt at Bengalore, and in most other parts of the Mysore; and it was stronger in the south than in the province where I was. It seemed to come from the north; proceeding southward, along the inland range of hills, and to be guided farther by those of which Sīvaganga and Sewendroog are the most conspicuous.

During the violent hurricane of Ongole, just mentioned, large masses of fire were seen to fall upon those hills so well known for their influence on the needle; and rain fell at both places, during the time, in the greatest abundance. These hills are composed chiefly of a kind of magnetic ironstone.

XI. GENERAL APPEARANCE OF THE COUNTRY.

The peninsula of Hindostan is called, with great propriety, a promontory of Asia, as it consists of chains of mountains stretching from that immense continent into the Eastern Ocean, to within a few degrees of the equinoctial line. The eastern side of the peninsula, called Coromandel and Orixa, has, at most places, a gradual ascent from the sea shore to the interior; but the western, or Malabar coast, is all along, I understand, mountainous, rising abruptly from the sea into high ridges of hills.

The inland country is longitudinally intersected, at unequal distances, by single or aggregated chains of hills, running north and south, or in a direction nearly parallel to the two coasts. These mountains belong all to the primitive class of rocks, and consist, as far as I have examined them, of sienite, mixed here and there with granite. In some places they are capped with beds of newer rocks, and floetz mountains are observed here and there crossing the country, and joining, as it were, the primitive chains to each other. It must not be supposed that the mountains keep these directions with mathematical accuracy; on the contrary, deviations are by no means uncommon. We sometimes find small chains of primitive mountains running east and west, and sometimes floetz mountains running north and south. But, upon the whole, the directions of the mountains are as I have stated them.

The principal ranges of the peninsula present themselves best to our view when we cross the country from east to west. They lie at uncertain and unequal distances from each other, and, accordingly, sometimes form wide and sometimes narrow valleys. Of the latter kind are the valleys between the eastern Ghauts, called Pollams; and of the former, different parts of the Mysore.

The usual height of the hills, reckoning from the base to the summit, scarcely exceeds 800 or 1000 feet. But as the country is continually rising, the height of the inland mountains, above the level of the sea, frequently amounts to 4000 feet.

The eastern Ghauts form the frontier of the Mysore country, by which it is separated from the Carnatic. They constitute the exterior of the east ranges of hills, which run along the whole length of the peninsula from Cape Commorin, stretching up to the continent of Asia. In many parts, the ascent over them into the Mysore is very high and difficult, while in others it is more sloping and protracted. These places are called passes; and there is a considerable number of them. The pass at Peddanaigdūrgum has, reckoning from the bottom of it to the first resting place, or choultry, in a distance of between six and seven miles, about 600 feet of elevation. That between Kistnagherry and Ryacotah, is nearly as high, but it is much longer, not less than fourteen miles, and consequently not so steep.

The Mysore country, above the Ghauts, is often called the Table Land, a denomination very little descriptive of its appearance; as it is by no means plain or flat, but in some parts mountainous, and every where undulating.

The part which presents itself first for our consideration, is that situated between the eastern Ghauts, and the first parallel chain of mountains to the west of them. These two chains, in the northern part of the country, are about eighty or ninety miles distant from each other; but they gradually approach as we proceed south; and near Ryacotah they seem to run into each other. The northern extremity is marked by interrupted chains of hills, which run from the Ghauts towards the western range. Nundydroog is the highest hill of that chain, and the hill fort of Nidjoil one of the most western. The distance between this east and west chain and Ryacotah, is about eighty miles.

The countries adjoining to this part are, the Carnatic, or rather the Pollams, to the east; the ceded districts, to the north; the inland country of Mysore, to the west; and part of the Borramahl, to the south. Formerly the whole of this district belonged to the Mysore; but at present, the eastern and southern parts are annexed to the Company's dominions; the remainder belongs to the Mysore Rajah.

This tract of country seems to constitute the highest part of the whole peninsula of Hindostan. It rises gradually from the Ghauts towards Bengalore. At the end of the Peddanaigdurgum pass, the barometer stood at twenty-eight inches, nearly at the same height as it did on the top of Sautghur, one of the highest hills below the pass. At Baetamungalum it stood at 27·5 inches: and at Bengalore, at 27·2 inches. These determinations give us the respective heights of these places above the level of the sea, as follows:

	Feet.
Peddanaigdurgum,	1907
Baetamungalum,	2435
Bengalore,	2807

According to the same mode of calculation, the top of Siwagunga, the highest mountain in this part of the Mysore, is about 4600 feet above the level of Madras.

The high tracts of ground, which give this district an undulating appearance, generally run from north to south, or following the direction of the great mountain ranges. The soil on these high grounds is red and gravelly, and very often rocks of sienite, or granite, appear upon its surface. These masses of stone have usually so little cohesion, that they may be easily broken by means of iron crows; and they admit even wooden tent pins to be driven into them. The lower parts of these high grounds are intersected by nullahs, or deep ravines torn up by the torrents of water that are precipitated from the heights in the rainy season.

The tops of these ridges are usually very barren, producing nothing but a small jungle, chiefly composed of *dodonæa viscosa, convolvulus cuneatus, erythroxylon areolatum*, and a thorny new species of *barleria*, very similar to the *barleria prionitis.*

The soil in the valleys is quite different; for, during the rains, the finer particles of the decomposed rocks are deposited in them, and form a good and loamy mixture. The lowest part of the valley is cultivated with rice, or sugar. The latter requires the best soil; while, for the former, a copious supply of water is necessary. This is easily obtained in the wet season, from the rivulets, or nullahs, and in the dry, from tanks (or reservoirs of water), for the construction of which this country is remarkably favourable. Plantations of cocoa nuts, jack, and other trees, are likewise found here, particularly near the villages, which are built on the first ascent from the valley, where the soil is of a middling quality, namely, a mixture of loam, sand, and oxide of iron, with a portion of vegetable and animal matter. Raghie, and some other small and dry grains, are also cultivated here. Higher up, towards the top of the ridge, a silicious sand prevails in the soil, which produces nothing but horsegram, a grain, on that account, very cheap in this part of the Mysore. Below the superficial soil, there is commonly a bed of gravel, which immediately covers a sienitic or granitic rock, very often in a state of disintegration, considerably advanced.

As the proportion of the constituents in these rocks is far from uniform, a corresponding diversity is observable in the soil produced by its disintegration. We find capacious veins, consisting of nothing but quartzy gravel of different sizes. In other places, where felspar has prevailed, we find a fine white pipe-clay in great abundance; and where hornblende has been the prevailing constituent, we find abundance of yellow ochre. Both the pipe-clay and ochre are used by the natives for different purposes.

The district on the north of this is similar, both in its aspect and boundaries, being surrounded on all sides by ranges of hills. But it is lower than the district which has just been described. The descent from Bengalore, as we proceed northwards, is perceptible, though by no means rapid. At Sîrah, on the high ground near the large Mussulman mausoleum, the barometer stood at 27·85, which makes it, in a distance of eighty-four miles, about 584 feet lower than Bengalore, or about 2223 feet above the level of the sea. The loftiest mountains in this part of the country are in the eastern range; but I do not suppose that any of them is 4000 feet above the level of the sea. Those of the Chittledroog are much lower; and the highest from the bottom to the top, not quite 900 feet. Some smaller hills and ridges cross the country in different directions. They are usually composed of stratified rocks, low and flat on the top, and clad with fine long grass. Whereas the primitive rocks are covered with trees and different kinds of underwood.

The soil of this part of the country is similar to that already described till we come to Sîrah, where the stratified hills make their appearance. It then becomes alternately black and red, sometimes gravelly and stony. Through its surface appear perpendicular layers of slate, which are often intersected with quartz or marl. The slate is iron-shot, and always decomposing and red.

The culture is the same as in the last described district, except in the country where the stratified hills occur. On the black soil jonnaloo and cotton are the principal crops; while on the red soil raghie flourishes best. The underwood on the uncultivated land, which is véry extensive, consists chiefly of the prickly *mimosas, cassia auriculata,* &c.

The soil often contains common salt, and on that account is favourable to the growth of cocoa-nut trees, of which there are very large plantations in the valleys.

Having passed the Chittledroog ranges of hills, we descend into an extensive and variegated valley which leads towards the river Tumbudra. Both the eastern and western boundaries of this valley are at a great distance, though they may be observed at times. The low country is variously intersected with flœtz mountains and ridges that seem to be connected with or to bear on one or other of the principal ranges. Some of these are high, and all contain in their rocks much iron and magnesia. The narrow valleys between them have a fine rich soil, which is seldom of the kind called cotton soil, but red and loamy, as it is brought by the rain water from the hills, which are much given to decomposition.

The hills are clad with a fine verdure, and the trees grow on them to a pretty large size, particularly the sandal tree. Grass also seems to be in abundance. North of Mayacondah, a place about half way between Chittledroog and the river, the country becomes long waving. We see here and there single hills or short ranges. The former are mostly sienitic, or granitic, the latter slaty. The nearer we come to the river the more the cotton soil and marl abound. The river is constantly accompanied by ranges of hills. The farthest west of these which I have seen are those of Buswapatam, through which the river winds. They consist of several ranges of mountains. The southernmost is composed of a striped siliceous slate, but those towards the centre consist of clay slate. The soil along the river is mostly black cotton soil, and below it are beds of mica slate.

Hurryhurr is one of the principal places in this part of the country. It lies on the banks of the Tumbudra, is about 1831 feet above the level of Madras, and is probably the lowest point of the whole Mysore. The perpendicular height of the hills here does not exceed four or five hundred feet.

In all these countries the natives distinguish, in their revenue accounts, eight different kinds of soil, for which different productions are particularized. The names of these soils in the Canary language, together with the meaning of the terms, are as follows:

1. Yara, black cotton ground, quite free from stones.
2. Kara, the same, but stony.
3. Kengala, kempu, red soil mixed with loam and vegetable mould.
4. Morallu, molalu, sandy soil.
5. Kallu, murbu, stony and gravelly soil.
6. Bîla, carlu, white stiff loam.
7. Maska, masbu, cabbou, garden soil.
8. Sondu, salt ground.

The productions of these soils will be best seen in the following table. It may be proper to notice that the general division of the country into low and high ground has not been attended to, because the productions of the former are exclusively rice and sugar. Hence wherever such productions are specified they indicate at the same time the situation of the ground on which they are produced. Every other species of grain is the production of high grounds, or of places that cannot be watered. Wheat is chiefly cultivated in the beds of tanks after their water has been expended in irrigating the rice and sugar fields.

Table of the different Soils with their Productions.

NAMES OF SOIL.	PLACES WHERE FOUND.	Grain sown in different Places, on any particular Soil.																						
		Dhaniam.	Chollu.	Ganta.	Korra.	Jonna.	Chama.	Goduma.	Aruga.	Worga.	Kanda.	Wulawa.	Anuma.	Pessara.	Sennaga.	Amda.	Nuwa.	Werrynuwa.	Minuma.	Bobara.	Alsanda.	Pratty.	Cherruku.	Garden Ve-getables.
Black, Yara	Ayamungalum					x																		
	Chittledroog					x		x							x									
	Hurryhurr	o	o	x		xx									x		x					xx		
	Ayrany	o				xx		x			x				x							xx		
	Honelly					xx		x	x		x		x	x	x	x						xx		
	Buswapatam	x				xx					x			x	x				x			x	x	
	Heroor				x	xx		x							x							xx	x	x
	Darmapoory							o							o									
	Sîrah	x	x			x		x							x								x	
Black and *Stones*, Kara	Sawendroog	x	x				x		x		x	x	x	x		x		x	x	x			x	x
	Darmapoory		x																					
	Rutnagherry		o		x						x		x											
Red Soil, Kempu, Kengala	Baetamungalum		xx	o	x	o	o		x		x	xx	x	x					x	x	x		x	
	Colar			o	x	o	o		x		x	xx	x	x					x	x	x		x	x
	Uscotah	x	xx		x			x	x		x	xx	x	x	x	x	x	x	x	x	x			x
	Sewendroog	x	x				x		x		x	x	x	x		x		x	x	x			x	x
	Darmapoory	x	x	x	x		x													x				
	Rutnagherry		x	x	x		x																	
	Sîrah	x	xx			x							x	x									x	
	Bengalore	x	xx		x			x	x		x	xx	x	x	x	x	x	x	x	x	x		x	
	Chittledroog			x							x	x		x			x			x	x			
	Hurryhurr			x		x			o		x	x		x		o								
	Ayrany		o	x	x				x			x	x			o				x	x			
	Annajie			x	x	x	x	x						x		x	x	x	x	x		x	x	
	Honelly		x	x	x	o	x		x		x													
	Buswapatam			x	x						x											x	x	
	Heroor		x	x					x		x	x	x											
	Matod			x	x		x		x			x				x	x	x						

NAMES OF SOIL.	PLACES WHERE FOUND.	Grain sown in different Places, on any particular Soil.																						
		Dhaniam.	Chollu.	Ganta.	Korra.	Jonna.	Chama.	Goduma.	Aruga.	Worga.	Kanda.	Wulawa.	Anuma.	Pessara.	Sennaga.	Amda.	Nuwa.	Werrynuwa.	Minuma.	Bobara.	Alsanda.	Pratty.	Cherruku.	Garden Vegetables.
Garden Soil, Cabbu, Masbu, Maska	Bengalore		x		x			x			x		x	x	x	x	x		x				x	x
	Chittledroog		x																					x
	Buswapatam				x	x	x		x													x		
	Ayrany		x		x				x			x	x			x					x			x
Sand Ground, Molalu, Moralu	Rutnagherry										x	x	x	x		x		x						
	Sirah			x	x		x		x		x	x	x			x		x						
	Talem		x				x					x	x											x
	Hurryhurr															x								
	Honelly		x	o	x	o	x					x					x		x					x
	Buswapatam		x													x								
	Annajie		x	o									x											
	Bengalore		x		x					x	x		x	x	x		x		x					
	Sewendroog		x				x		x		x	x	x	x		x			x					
Stone, Callu, Murbu	Sîrah											x												
	Ayamungalum													x					x					
	Hurryhurr											x				x								
	Honelly		x	o	x	o	x					x					x		x					
	Ayrany		x	o	x				x			x	x			x					x			
	Annajie						x		x			x												
	Heroor								x				x				x	x						
	Darmapoory			x								x												
White Loam, Carlu, Bila	Sîrah	x	x			o																		
	Matod											x												
	Darmapoory				x				x			x												
Salt Ground, Choudu	Chittledroog		x		x	o																x		x

This mark (x) shews that the grain, in the column of which it stands, is cultivated; two (xx), point out the grain as the principal Crop; if the mark (o) appears, it is but in small quantities attended to.

The names of the grain on the table are according to the Telinga language. The following table exhibits the Linnæan names of these vegetable substances respectively:

Dhaniam	Oryza sativa.
Chollu	Eleusine corrocana.
Ganta	Holcus spicatus.
Korra	Panicum italicum, millet.
Jonna	Holcus sorghum.
Chama..........	Panicum meliacium.
Goduma	Triticum aristatum, wheat.
Aruga	Paspalum frumentaceum.
Warga	Panicum pilosum.
Kanda..........	Cytisus cajan, red gram.
Wulawa	Glycine tomentosa, horse gram.
Anuma..........	Dolichos spicatus, cow gram.
Pessara..........	Phaseolus mungo, green gram.
Sennaga	Cicer arietinum, chick pea.
Amda	Ricinus communis, castor oil.
Nuwa	Sesamum orientale, gingelie oil seed.
Werrynuwa	Anthemis? oil seed.
Minuma	Phaseolus minimus, black gram.
Bobara	Dolichos catianus.
Alsanda..........	Dolichos sinensis.
Pratty	Gossypium herbaceum, cotton.
Cherruku	Saccharum officinale, sugar cane.

XII. RIVERS, TANKS, &c.

The largest river in that part of the Mysore of which we have been speaking is the Tumbudra, which may be considered as bounding the country on the north. It comes from the western Ghauts, taking an easterly direction, and to judge from its rapidity and from the depth of the channel which it has cut, it must have a great fall. It receives its waters from rivulets and torrents which, during the rainy season, precipitate themselves in every direction from the hills. It proceeds from the western Ghauts in two distinct streams, called the Tunga and the Budra. These unite not far from Hurryhurr, and then the name of the river is constituted by joining together the two names which distinguished its two branches. From Hurryhurr it runs in a north-easterly direction, and at no great distance disembogues itself into the Kistnah.

As the Tumbudra has cut a deep channel for itself, and is every where surrounded by steep banks, it is quite useless for the purposes of irrigation. During the hottest months very fine musk melons and some other vegetables are raised in its beds.

The wood which grows on the western Ghauts might be readily floated on this river to the coast. It might serve also to convey the products of the Mysore in flat-bottomed boats to the British dominions near the sea.

The only boats at present in use are round baskets covered with buffalo skins. They hold about fifteen men, and, notwithstanding their wretched appearance, have been employed to convey armies and even artillery across the river. The natives often cross the river upon cutchery pots (earthen pots with a narrow mouth), on which they support themselves, and in which they keep their clothes dry.

The smaller rivulets are of more consequence to the farmer, as they convey water into the tanks, without the aid of which the low grounds would yield little or nothing. This water, when it happens to rise from springs, is often brackish in the summer season; yet it answers the purposes of cultivation, and is often drawn laboriously by means of pacotas to water rice and sugar fields. In the rainy season the water of the rivers is usually of a deep red from the quantity of clay, tinged with iron, which it holds in suspension. It is generally sweet, being in fact rain water, and is considered by the natives as peculiarly palatable, and even preferred by them to the waters of the Ganges.

In the southern parts of the Mysore the largest river is the Cavery. It receives several small rivers from the northern parts of the Mysore; two of which, the Arkawatty and Dachanapinnāky, run almost the whole length of the country, rising from the Nundydrug hill, in the north, and flowing into the Cāvery nearly at the southern extremity of the district. These rivers during the rainy season are very rapid and difficult to cross.

There are no lakes in the northern parts of the Mysore; but abundance of tanks or artificial reservoirs in the higher grounds. In the low valleys, where the black cotton soil predominates, there are very few. These tanks receive the water from the neighbouring high grounds, and are employed to water the rice and sugar fields. They are frequently surrounded by stone walls or facings, and are furnished with regular sluices to let out the water.

I conceive that the ground now occupied by tanks might be husbanded much better, by taking advantage of higher and favourable situations, so that many of the spots now covered with water might be cultivated.

The water in these tanks being rain water is always sweet, and though muddy, is preferred by the natives to well water, which is limpid but often brackish. The matter which the water deposites in the bottom of the tank forms a rich soil, upon which fine crops of wheat are sometimes raised after the whole of the water has been employed.

With the natives of India I am much inclined to ascribe to water a number of disorders with which they are afflicted, as intermittent fevers, obstructions in the viscera, and all the multitude of diseases that proceed from this latter cause. I have observed that in those parts of India where the soil is black and calcareous these disorders are general and endemical; I have observed also that those who drink water brought by the rivers in the rainy season are subject at that time to fevers and agues. The precaution used by some officers of my acquaintance of boiling their water, and insisting on those under their command using the same precaution, has kept whole detachments in good health in countries considered as peculiarly injurious to those who are obliged to live in them.

The natives of India have a very simple mode of rendering turbid water drinkable. They rub a little alum or induga (the seed of *strychnos potatorum*) on the sides of a pot, and then pouring the water into it let it remain at rest for a little time. The earthy matter is immediately precipitated, and the water becomes clear and limpid.

XIII. MOUNTAINS AND MINERALS.

Very little can be added to the general description of the country already given. The principal range of mountains is abruptly rising and falling. Distant points appear often as separated from each other by great efforts of nature. The intervening chasm is frequently eight or ten miles long, and very little elevated above the low country.

The western range of hills in the district of Bengalore run so interruptedly that, when among them, we fancy they have no particular direction or arrangement. In the country between the two north and south ranges, which may be called flat or plain, single hills or even whole clusters of them occur of the same nature and appearance as the principal chains. The greatest number of these hills occur near Colar. All these hills abound with underwood and trees, few of which, however, grow to any considerable size. The soil on them is mostly a fine black vegetable mould, very fertile, but not sufficiently deep to afford nourishment for large trees. Springs of excellent water are to be found on most of them. Their surface is usually covered with stones of different sizes, which render the ascent very difficult. They never contain any metallic ores so far as I know, except ores of iron.

Almost all the hills about Bengalore are sienitic; but, to the south-east of Ooscotah, a place between Bengalore and Colar, there occur hills composed of a soft, ferruginous, clay slate. They are low, flat at their tops, and mostly barren. The soil about them is a fine argillaceous red earth. Gold is found in small quantities near these hills, either mixed with the soil, or interspersed in quartzy stones.

Near Sîrah the hills seem to be all of secondary formation. They run in straight lines, in various directions; are quite bare of trees; but, in the wet season, have a green appearance, from the long-hill grass (*anthistiria barbata*), which is almost the only vegetable that grows on them. These hills are almost constantly covered at top with a kind of magnetic ironstone, which withstands the decomposing powers of the air and water much longer than the lower parts of the hills, which seem to be composed of ferruginous slate clay.

The lower ridges, north and west of Chittledroog, consist of a compound in which chlorite, oxide of iron, and sometimes hornblende prevail. They often form basins of considerable size, which have a very fertile soil. Many of them are naked; but some of them are covered with fine grass, and produce trees of a middling size, of which the sandal is the most remarkable.

Having given an idea of the nature of the various mountains which occur in this part of India, I shall now attempt to describe the different minerals which I met with while traversing it in all directions.

1. The great rock, which in fact constitutes the basis of the whole country is a kind of sienite, composed for the most part of four different ingredients; namely, quartz, felspar, hornblende, and mica. The quartz has usually a dull greyish white colour; and veins of it, from four to ten inches thick, often traverse the rock in different directions. The felspar varies in colour, from a silver white to a deep brick red, and is the most copious constituent of the rock. The hornblende is black, very abundant, and very much given to decomposition. The mica is easily distinguished from the

hornblende, even when the stone is nearly in a state of disintegration: the hornblende, in that state, has assumed a brown ochre colour, and has lost all lustre and cohesion; while the mica retains both its colour, lustre, and cohesion to the last, and becomes only more apparent by the progress of disintegration. This is particularly exemplified in the Mysore country, where the waving high ground consists of sienite decomposed into pipe-clay, intermixed with micaceous shining particles, and grains of quartz.

The inland range of the Ghauts is composed of sienite as well as the eastern Ghauts, with this difference, that the felspar is of a beautiful brick red colour, and the predominating ingredient. Mica also abounds in some of the hills. I have seen specimens of mica slate, from mountains situated on the west side of Bengalore; but have never seen any such rock in the eastern range.

The kind of rock just described, which is a very handsome stone, continues to Nidgeul; but, in the range that crosses the country, of which Nundydroog is the principal hill, it becomes intermediate between the sienite of the eastern and inland ranges. The felspar is more red, and the mica more conspicuous than in the eastern Ghauts; but not so beautiful as at Sîwagunga and Sewendroog.

The ranges of hills to which Chittledroog belongs are exactly of the same composition. In some places the felspar is of a fine red, in others of a silvery white colour.

When this rock begins to decompose, it assumes a slaty form, the layers of which are pretty thick; but as the disintegration advances, it scales off in thin laminæ, which are very brittle; and in them the mica is more apparent than in the fresh rock.

This rock is every where given to decomposition, probably on account of the great proportion of iron which it contains; and this decomposition is much farther advanced in the lower than in the higher parts of the mountains. On the summits of the hills the soundest stones are always found, because every thing that has been loosened by decomposition is washed down by the monsoon rains. In the lowest part of the country, usually at some depth below the surface, the same sienitic rock occurs, almost always decomposed, and without cohesion or colour. The felspar is commonly converted into pipe-clay; the hornblende is either entirely gone or changed into ochre; the mica still brilliant, and the quartz entire.

2. Granite (a compound of quartz, felspar, and mica), is chiefly observed

in the low country, where the black soil prevails, almost always in a state of decomposition, and very friable. The felspar is usually large, rhomboidal, silvery, or milk white; often so soft as to verge upon the state of pipe-clay. The mica is in thin plates, little affected by decomposition, of a greyish white colour, and often in large pieces.

In these two rocks, besides the constituents already mentioned, we frequently observe the following minerals:

3. Garnets. In many hills they constitute an integral part of the sienitic compound; but more in the lower than the higher parts of the country. Garnets occur very frequently in the mountains of the Lower Ghauts; but I have not, or very seldom, seen them in the Mysore.

4. Diamond spar. The same observations apply to this mineral as to garnet.

5. Pistazite *, a mineral of a yellowish green colour, sometimes in confused, slender, needle-like crystals; oftener compact, in dots, and overlying the sienite in small stripes. Its hardness is that of quartz, which it resembles much in appearance and fracture. I consider it as merely quartz, coloured with green earth; a substance that occurs in India, as I have seen specimens of it from the Dekan.

6. Granatite of Werner. This mineral I have found in the southern parts of the Mysore.

7. Chlorite slate. This mineral forms the constituent of the hills near Sîrah. It is of a greenish blue colour, with yellowish ochrey spots; lustre silky; longitudinal fracture fibrous; very soft. Cubic crystals of brown iron stone occur in it, from two lines in diameter to one inch. When this mineral is decomposed it becomes quite brittle, red, and ochrey, and stains the fingers. Iron-shot quartz is often found massive in it.

8. Clay iron stone constitutes some ranges of hills near Chittledroog, and the hills north of Hurryhurr.

9. Drawing slate, found in different parts of the country about Chittledroog.

10. Schorl, in quartz, near Hurryhurr.

11. Mica slate, occurs often below the beds of marl in countries where the black cotton soil prevails.

12. Flinty slate, with alternate stripes of a red and grey colour. It forms the cover of most hills here. Magnetic iron stone occurs in it in nests.

* Euclase of Haüy?

13. Bluish black quartz.

14. Pot stone and actinolite occur frequently in nests near Matod. It has a considerable admixture of iron; for when it decomposes it becomes quite red.

15. Asbestoid, found in the pot stone near Talem.

16. Ligniform asbestus, among the Mayacondah hills.

17. Lamellar actinolite, at Hurryhurr.

18. Brown spar. A mineral which I consider as belonging to this species occurs near Talem and Annaji.

19. Captain Warren, formerly an assistant in the Misore survey, has lately discovered that gold was found and extracted from earth and stones by the natives near Betamungalum. By all accounts it was extracted by washing from the alluvial soil; but its quantity was too small to repay the labour of searching for it.

20. Iron-glance is found among the Chittledroog hills, near Talem and other places. It is employed in the glass works at Matod. That mineralogists may have it in their power to determine whether I have named this mineral right, I shall here give a short description of it. Its external colour is brown ochrey, internally it is black. Externally its lustre is dull, internally shining and semi-metallic. Fracture even, inclining to the small granular foliated. Hardness, equal to that of felspar. Specific gravity, 4·95. Streak, red. Its powder is brown. It decomposes into red ochre, which is often found on the fracture when a stone is broken. It occurs in ochrey pieces, coated with an ochrey crust, which feels smooth. It is attracted by the magnet; but not strongly. Large pieces of it show polarity. When heated in a crucible or on charcoal it follows the magnet like iron-filings. To try whether it contained any manganese, I heated a mixture of equal parts of its powder and potash to whiteness. The greatest part of it was scorified black, and a few particles appeared of a dirty green colour. When this mass was put into water scarcely any colour appeared; but when it had stood some time an exceedingly small cloud of an amethystine colour appeared near the slag. On adding a little sulphuric acid the cloud disappeared, and the water remained colourless. This amethystine colour rendering the presence of some manganese in the ore probable, I took ten grains of the powder and digested it twice with five parts of strong nitric acid over a lamp furnace, and exposed the dry powder for some time to the air. I then poured four times the weight of diluted nitric acid on it, adding occasionally a little sugar-

candy. The solution which remained colourless, being decanted off and supersaturated with potash, a very minute quantity of a white powder was precipitated. These experiments, together with some others which I think it needless to recite, showed that only a very minute proportion of manganese was present in this ore.

21. Iron sand, which is, probably, a sub-species of micaceous iron ore, is found in the beds of rivers and nullahs after the rainy season.

22. Clay iron stone is found near Darmaparam, Ruttengherry, and many other places.

From the structure of the country, which is entirely primitive, no coals could be expected. Accordingly none have ever been observed. Indeed if they did occur in India, they would be neglected by the inhabitants, as in consequence of the late perpetual wars, fuel is every where in great abundance.

23. Common salt occurs in this country in considerable abundance. It is usually found in the red soil, upon the surface of which it effloresces in the dry season. It is then swept together in the morning, separated from the earthy particles by percolation, and crystallized again in shallow beds made of mortar. It is manufactured in almost every village on the south side of Chittledroog, and used by those natives who cannot afford sea salt. In consequence of this manufacture, the quantity of sea salt imported into the eastern and southern ports of the Mysore is very small. In the southern districts, about Hurryhurr and Honelly, salt is supplied from the Malabar coast, from which it is brought by the lombardies on the backs of bullocks. The salt obtained from the red soil is conceived, when long used, to occasion eruptions on the skin.

24. Carbonate of soda is likewise found in the Mysore. The greatest quantity of it is manufactured among the hills of the Chittledroog country. It is mixed with a good deal of common salt. The method of procuring it is similar to that just described for obtaining common salt, only that its lixivium is evaporated by boiling. It is sold in all bazars under the name of sobboo. It is manufactured by the washermen, and chiefly used by them. It is employed likewise in bleaching. The glass-makers prepare, by a process of their own, the quantity of soda required for their purposes.

XIV. PRODUCTIONS OF THE COUNTRY.

The shortest and most perspicuous way of conveying an accurate idea of the various productions of this country will be to exhibit them under the form of tables. I have given the Linnæan names of the different plants, the English names when they exist, and I have added the Telinga, Canary, Hindostan, and Tamul names, to put it in the power of every person, who resides in India, to ascertain the nature of the productions which surround him, provided he be acquainted with the name by which it is distinguished by the natives themselves.

TABLE I.

Linnæan Names.	English Names.	Telinga Names.	Canary Names.	Hindostany Names.	Malabar Names.
Oryza sativa	Paddy, rice	Wadlu	Nellu	Dhaun	Nellu
Eleusine corocana	Natcheny	Choda	Raghi	Raghi	Kaewaeru
Paspalum frument.		Aruga	Harka	Kodaru	Wargu
Panicum italicum	Millet spec.	Corra	Nawini	Kogoni	Tennae
——— pilosum	Ditto	Warga	Baruga	Bariki	Kuru warga
——— miliaceum	Ditto	Chama	Sami	Sahmi	Samae
Triticum aristatum	Wheat	Goduma	Godhi	Khaen	Godumae
Holcus sorghum		Jonna	Jola	Jovar	Cholum
——— spicatus		Ganta	Sajja	Bajera.	

Rice being the general food of the country, and cultivated in different soils, seasons, and ways, varieties have been produced, distinguished from each other by their external appearance, size, and colour. In the Mysore I have found twenty-one varieties, the names of which it would be useless to state without giving a particular history of each. The finer varieties are in general less productive than the coarser, and require a much longer time to ripen, often five or six months, when the coarser kinds are ripe in three or four months. It is said that one of the coarsest varieties is ready for cutting down in six weeks after the time of sowing it. The rice most generally cultivated and of a middling kind is chanonghi and kembaddi. It ripens in about four and a half or five months, and two crops are annually expected.

Raghie is the food of all classes of people in most of the provinces in Mysore, and indeed in all the countries on the coast so situated that tanks cannot be constructed for irrigating large tracts of land, or which have not the black soil productive of jonna. There are three or four varieties of raghi, called by the Telingas *choda*, *pedda choda*, and *maddy ruba choda*; besides the *car choda*, which is a new species. On the coast the lowest and poorest classes of people only eat this kind of grain; but in the Mysore it is the food of every person: it is very unpalatable to those not accustomed to it.

The other small kinds of grain, as panicum (*millet*), paspalum, &c. are less esteemed or less productive than raghi, and are therefore sown but in small quantities.

It may be proper to mention, that the names given in the preceding table are in the nominative singular, but in the common language the plural is used when they are spoken of: thus the natives say *ragalu*, *ālu*, &c.

There are nine varieties of *jonna*, which are admitted by all jonnaloo eaters to differ in taste and proportional produce. They are not indifferently cultivated, some being peculiar to particular soils, while others grow in all black and calcareous fields: it grows to the greatest perfection on its own black soil, frequently rising to the height of eight or nine feet, while in the other soils, not so well adapted for its growth, it scarcely exceeds the height of three feet.

Wheat is cultivated but in small quantities in gardens, or in the rich soil of the beds of those tanks which have been left dry after the watering of rice fields. The grains of the Mysore wheat are smaller than those which come from the Mahratta country; on that account it is much cheaper. It is sown in the beginning of the cold season.

TABLE II. *Dry Grains.*

Linnæan Names.	English Names	Telinga Names.	Canary Names.	Hindostany Names.	Malabar Names.
Phaseolus mungo	Green gram	Pessara	Hesaru	Moogo	Patcha pairu
Ditto aconitifolius			Karamanny		
Ditto minimus	Black Ditto	Minuma	Praddu	Manshwurtu	Wulandu
Dolichos spicatus	Cow gram	Annuma	Awira	Ballar	Awarae
Ditto catianus		Bobara			
Ditto Sinensis		Alsanda	Halsanda	Loba	Karamanni
Cytisus cajan	Red Gram	Kanda	Togari	Tuwar	Tovare
Cicer arietinum	Chickpea, Bengal gram	Sennaga	Kadla	Harbirri	Kadle
Glycine tomentosa	Horse gram	Wulawa	Hurully	Kultji	Kollu

These are called *dry grains*, because they are sown on the coast after the rains are over, and on grounds that cannot be watered: but the name does not apply well in the Mysore, where they are usually sown after the first rains along with other kinds of grain.

They are usually boiled into a kind of pulse called *pappu*, and ate along with rice or raghi as a seasoner. The *sennaga pappu*, or dried sennaga, from which the husk has been separated, is eaten as a dainty by young and old at fairs and other public and festival occasions. It requires the best soil, and is often sown in the beds of dry tanks.

The dolichos spicatus, or cow gram, is always sown along with raghi. The raghi is sown by means of a drill plough, which makes ten or twelve furrows, half a foot distant from each other; and between every turn of the plough a single furrow is left for the cow gram.

The phoseolus aconitifolius is only cultivated in the northern parts of the Mysore: it is eaten like green and black gram with jonnalu and rice.

Horse gram is nowhere cheaper or more plentiful than about Bengalore, as it is the only grain that grows on barren elevated situations, which, on account of the crowded population, are here cultivated. Horses not accustomed to feed upon it contract, by using it as food, the disease called the *hot piss*, and camels become itchy.

TABLE III. *Productions not comprehended in the former List.*

Linnæan Names.	English Names.	Telinga Names.	Canary Names.	Hindostany Names	Malabar Names.
Sesamum orientale	Gingelie oil seed	Syuwa	Wallelu	Mitta tēl	Ellu
Anthemis	Oil seed	Werry nuwa	Huckellu	Raw tēl	Pā ellu
Ricinus communis	Large castor oil seed	Per amdah	Dodda harelu	Arandika tēl	Amanak wuttu
Ditto variatio	Small ditto	Chitta amdah	Chitta harelu	Choti arandie	Chittamanak wuttu
Saccharum officinale	Sugar cane	Cherruku	Kabbu	Ganne	Carambu
Gossypium herbaceum	Cotton	Pratti	Katty	Ruvi	Paratti
Crotolaria juncea.	Country hemp	Janapa	Janapa	Sunka jhaud	Janapirri

Sugar is manufactured in many parts of the country about Nundydroog: they understand the process very well; and of manufacturing candy and loaf sugar. In the more northern districts they can make nothing but jaggery and a kind of coarse powdered sugar. The sugar cane cultivated is mostly of the red variety. The farmer does not consider it is a profitable article of culture; it impoverishes the land so much, that three years must be suffered to elapse before sugar can be raised a second time upon the same field.

Cotton requires a good dry situation, as that afforded by the black marly soil, which takes its name from this plant (*cotton soil*). A small shower of rain, if it should fall at the time that it is getting ripe, spoils the whole crop; fortunately this happens but seldom. Cotton is sown by means of the drill plough, the furrows being about a foot distant from each other. It might be cultivated on most of the hills in the country, as the soil on them is very rich.

The werrinuwa * is an oil plant not known on the coast, but found in the higher provinces of Bengal, from whence I received it under the name of verbesina sativa: it grows in all soils, even in the very worst. By the natives it is used for the same purposes as the gingeli oil. All oil used for common purposes is expressed in a mill driven by bullocks. One kolaga of seed yields one mānd and a quarter of oil, and thirty sīrs can be expressed in the course of a day.

The oil from the smaller kind of ricinus communis is used as a medicine, and is chiefly given to children as a laxative. The oil expressed from the larger seed goes in common under the name of lamp oil, and is the cheapest oil in India. The plant grows without the least attention being bestowed on it, and when it has once established itself in any particular place, it is very difficult to root it out completely.

* The following is the botannical description of this plant: syngenesia polygamia superflua. Anthemis proximum genus. An ipsum?

Col. communis hemisphericus, squamis 6, obovato-lanceolatis, acutis.

Cor. composita radiata, corollulæ ☿ tubulosæ in disco. Femineæ ligulatæ in radio ad decem.

Cor. propria ☿ infundibuliformis, 5 dentata.

♀ ligulata, ovata, patens, trifida, lacinulis æqualibus.

Stam. ☿ Filam. 5 tubo longiora, antheræ cylindraceæ.

Pist. ☿ ovarium oblongum. Styl. filiform. stygmata 2, revoluta.

♀ Germ. styl. et stygm. ut in ☿

Per. null.

Sem. ovata, angulata. Pappus nullus.

Recept. palaeceum, paleis linearibus, acutis, striatis.

Caul. herbaceus, scabriusculus. Folia sessilia opposita, lanceolata, serrata. Flores axillares, pedunculati.

TABLE IV. *List of the proportional Produce of one Sēr of Seed of the different Kinds of Grain, and of its Time of Sowing and Reaping.*

Species of Grain.	Place.	Sowing Time.	Reaping Time.	Produce.
Rice	Ooscotah	July	November	10 Seer
	Ayamungalum	January	May	10 Ditto
	Ayrany	August	January	40 Ditto
	Annaji	Ditto	Ditto	20 Ditto
	Bengalore	July	November	20 Ditto
	Sewendrug	May	January	10 Ditto
	Herūr	August	November	20 Ditto
	Harti	Ditto	Ditto	20 Ditto
	Matod	Ditto	Ditto	60 Ditto
	Darmapūry	Ditto	December	13¼ Ditto
	Sīrah	June	November	15 Ditto
	Buswapatam	July	Ditto	10 Ditto
Cholu*	Uscotah	Ditto	Ditto	80 Ditto
	Chittledrūg	November	May	10 Ditto
	Talem	July	November	40 Ditto
	Buswapatam	June	October	50 Ditto
	Ayrany	August	January	40 Ditto
	Annaji	Ditto	Ditto	60 Ditto
	Herūr	September	Ditto	80 Ditto
	Matod	July	Ditto	50 Ditto
	Darmapūry	Ditto	October	270† Ditto
	Rutnagherry	Ditto	November	20 Ditto
	Sīrah	June	Sept. and October	40 Ditto
Gantalu	Ayamungalum	July	October	20 Ditto
	Chittledrūg	June	November	10 Ditto
	Hurryhurr	Ditto	October	100 Ditto
	Honelly	July	November	100 Ditto
	Buswapatam	Ditto	Ditto	80 Ditto
	Ayrany	August	Jan. and February	40 Ditto
	Annaji	July	Ditto and Ditto	40 Ditto
	Herūr	August	November	20 Ditto
	Harti	Ditto	Ditto	80 Ditto
	Matod	Ditto	October	60 Ditto
	Sīrah	April	July	120 Ditto
Corralu	Ayamungalum	October	January	30 Ditto
	Chittledrūg	November	Ditto	20 Ditto
	Honelly	June	October	107 Ditto
	Buswapatam	Ditto	Ditto	20 Ditto
	Ayrany	August	January	40 Ditto
	Annaji	July	Ditto	40 Ditto
	Herūr	August	October	15 Ditto
	Harti	Ditto	Ditto	80 Ditto
	Matod	Ditto	November	30 Ditto

* The produce, on an average, will be about fifty-fold.

† The raghie is here transplanted and watered like paddy at other places, hence the great difference in produce.

Species of Grain.	Place.	Sowing Time.	Reaping Time.	Produce.
Corralu	Sīrah	June	August	60 Seer
	Ayamungalum	October	January	20 Ditto
	Chittledrug	November	February	10 Ditto
	Ditto	Ditto	May	10 Ditto
	Hurryhurr	June	October	48 Ditto
	Honelly	July	November	213 Ditto
Jonnalu	Buswapatam	Ditto	Ditto	40 Ditto
	Ayrany	August	Dec. and January	80 Ditto
	Annaji	June	Ditto and Ditto	80 Ditto
	Herur	September	Ditto and Ditto	20 Ditto
	Harti	Ditto	Ditto and Ditto	80 Ditto
	Sīrah	June	November	120 Ditto
	Talem	July	February	24 Ditto
	Honelly	Ditto	October and Nov.	27 Ditto
	Buswapatam	Ditto	Ditto and Ditto	20 Ditto
Chamalu	Annajie	Ditto	January	40 Ditto
	Sewendrug	May	December	20 Ditto
	Matod	September	November	30 Ditto
	Sīrah	June	August	40 Ditto
	Ayamungalum	October	January	6 Ditto
	Chittledrug	November	February	10 Ditto
	Honelly	February	April	32 Ditto
Godumulu ..	Ayrany	Ditto	Ditto	40 Ditto
	Annaji	Ditto	Ditto	20 Ditto
	Herur	July	October	10 Ditto
	Sīrah	January	May	6¾ Ditto
	Hurryhurr	June	October	10 Ditto
	Honelly	Ditto	October and Nov.	160 Ditto
	Buswapatam	Ditto	October	40 Ditto
	Ayrany	August	January	40 Ditto
	Annaji	July	Ditto	40 Ditto
Arugalu	Bengalore	September	Ditto	20 Ditto
	Sewendrug	May	December	20 Ditto
	Herur	July	November	20 Ditto
	Matod	June	December	20 Ditto
	Sīrah	Ditto	November	60 Ditto
	Ayamungalum	August	Ditto	4 Ditto
	Chittledrug	June	Ditto	7 Ditto
	Honelly	July	Ditto	11 Ditto
Candulu	Ayrany	August	January	40 Ditto
	Annaji	July	Ditto	20 Ditto
	Buswapatam	Ditto	October	10 Ditto
	Ayamungalum	October	January	8 Ditto
Wulawalu ..	Chittledrug	June	November	10 Ditto
	Talem	August	January	12 Ditto

Species of Grain.	Place.	Sowing Time.	Reaping Time.	Produce.
Wulawalu	Hurryhurr	September	November	4 Seer
	Honelly	July	Ditto	27 Ditto
	Buswapatam	June and July	October	20 Ditto
	Ayrany	August	January	40 Ditto
	Annaji	July	Ditto	60 Ditto
	Bengalore	September	Ditto	20 Ditto
	Sewendrug	Ditto	March	10 Ditto
	Herur	Ditto	November	20 Ditto
	Harti	Ditto	March	80 Ditto
	Sīrah	Ditto	November	16½ Ditto
	Matod	August	October	20 Ditto
Anumulu	Uscotah	July	November	40 Ditto
	Talem	Ditto	February	11 Ditto
	Honelly	June	November	11 Ditto
	Ayrany	August	January	40 Ditto
	Annaji	July	November	40 Ditto
	Herur	September	January	2 Ditto
Pessarlu	Aymungalum	August	November	30 Ditto
	Chittledrug	June	Ditto	10 Ditto
	Honelly	June and July	Ditto	27 Ditto
	Annaji	Ditto and Ditto	January	20 Ditto
	Bengalore	September	Ditto	40 Ditto
	Sewendrug	Ditto	March	6 Ditto
	Herur	August	October	10 Ditto
	Sīrah	September	November	8 Ditto
Sennagalu	Ayamungalum	August	Ditto	8 Ditto
	Hurryhurr	October	January	5 Ditto
	Honelly	February	April	11 Ditto
	Buswapatam	Ditto	Ditto	10 Ditto
	Ayrany	Ditto	Ditto	40 Ditto
	Harti	Ditto	Ditto	80 Ditto
	Sīrah	January	May	20 Ditto
Amdalu	Ayamungalum	June	August	5 Ditto
	Honelly	Ditto	October	21 Ditto
	Buswapatam	Ditto	Ditto	10 Ditto
	Sewendrug	September	Ditto	10 Ditto
	Herur	July	November	15 Ditto
	Harti	Ditto	Ditto	80 Ditto
	Matod	June	March	20 Ditto
	Sīrah	Ditto	November	40 Ditto
	Hurryhurr	Ditto	February	5 Ditto
	Ayrany	August	January	40 Ditto
Nuwulu	Ayamungalum	June	August	5 Ditto
	Chittledrug	Ditto	November	4 Ditto
	Hurryhurr	Ditto	September	80 Ditto
	Honelly	Ditto	November	11 Ditto

Species of Grain.	Place.	Sowing Time.	Reaping Time.	Produce.
Nuwulu	Buswapatam	June	November	20 Seer
	Herur	July	Ditto	20 Ditto
	Harti	Ditto	Ditto	80 Ditto
	Matod	June	August and Sept.	20 Ditto
Verrynuwulu	Talem	September	December	10 Ditto
	Hurryhurr	Ditto	Ditto	20 Ditto
	Bengalore	Ditto	January	20 Ditto
	Sewendrug	Ditto	March	6 Ditto
	Herur	November	February	10 Ditto
	Harti	Ditto	Ditto	80 Ditto
	Matod	September	November	20 Ditto
	Sīrah	Ditto	Ditto	40 Ditto
Minumulu ..	Ayamungalum	August	Ditto	3 Ditto
	Honelly	June	October	27 Ditto
	Annaji	July	January	20 Ditto
	Bengalore	September	Ditto	20 Ditto
	Sewendrug	Ditto	March	6 Ditto
	Sīrah	August	November	8 Ditto
Bobarlu	Chittledrug	June	Ditto	3 Ditto
Alsandalu	Ditto	Ditto	Ditto	6 Ditto
	Ayrany	August	January	40 Ditto
	Bengalore	September	Ditto	40 Ditto
	Sewendrug	Ditto	March	6 Ditto
Pratty	Ayamungalum	October	February	5 Ditto
	Chittledrug	November	Ditto	12 Ditto
	Hurryhurr	October	Ditto	3 Ditto
	Honelly	June and July	Ditto	4 Ditto
	Buswapatam	Ditto and Ditto	Ditto	6 Ditto
	Ayrany	August	January	6 Ditto
	Annaji	Ditto	April	3 Ditto
	Herur	June	November	4 Ditto
Cossumba	Hurryhurr	November	February	5 Ditto
Wainta	Ditto	June	October	3 Ditto
	Ayrany	August	January	40 Ditto
	Annaji	Ditto	Ditto	40 Ditto
	Bengalore	September	Ditto	20 Ditto
Cherruku ..	Venketgherry	April	April	40 Ditto
	Colar	Ditto	Ditto	100 Ditto
	Buswapatam	March	March	160 Ditto
	Annaji	April	April	80 Ditto
	Sewendrug	March	February	200 Ditto
	Sīrah	February	Ditto	50 Ditto
Pogaku	Sewendrug	September	March	7¼ Ditto

The difference in the proportional produce of grain in different places, as exhibited by this table, is really astonishing; it may be ascribed to the soil, to the time of sowing, and to the mode of cultivation; but in many cases I have little doubt it is rather apparent than real, originating in the false statements of the farmers: I suspect the accounts of Chittledrug, in the preceding table, fall under this predicament. When grain is transplanted after it has been sown, the produce is greatly augmented. Rice, below the Ghauts, is mostly sown by the hand, and not afterwards transplanted; hence the reason why its produce in that province is so small.

TABLE V. *List of Vegetables, the Leaves of which are used by the Natives in their Curries or Stews.*

Linnæan Names.	English Names.	Telinga Names.	Canary Names.
Amaranthus oleraceus	Country Greens ..	Tota kura	Soppoo
——— doglakura R.		Doggali kura	Doggalie soppu
——— chilakatota kura		Chilakatota kura ..	Chilkivy soppu
——— oleraceus		Perugu kura	Dandoo soppu
——— oleraceus candidus		Rajighirry tella-totakura	Bila soppu
——— quoitotakura		Koitota kura	Harewa soppu
——— cherikura		Cheri kura	Chicka soppu
Achyranthes muricata		Chentsali kura ..	Hakivy gorijie
		Pulla chentsali	
Achyranthes triandra		Pomaganty	Pommaganta soppu
——— lanata		Pendi konda kura	Guddahattoo soppu
Arum esculentum		Chamakura	Kasewadoo soppu
Aeschynomene grandiflora, var. 2.		Awisi	Awisah soppu
Basella rubra & alba & var.		Pedda mattu . Yerra batsali ..	Dodda batsali
Boerhavia diffusa		Adika mamady ..	Belawaraga
Cassia tora		Tantipa kura	
Canthium parviflorum		Balsu kura	
Chenopodium virid.		Chackrawarta	Chackrawartikura
Coriandrum sativum	Coriander	Cottimerry	Cottimbiry
Cleome pentaphylla		Wahinta	Narobeda
Convolvulus esculentus		Tuti kura	
Corchorus olitorius		Parinta	Kotnagoreja
Hyperanthera morunga	Morunga	Munaga kura	Malgina soppu
Hibiscus cannabinus		Gong kura	
——— sabdariffa		Nelly kura	
Marselia minuta		Chitlinta	Panlie bajili

Linnæan Names.	English Names.	Telinga Names.	Canary Names.
Mollugo diffusa		Chandarasi kura..	Kaindas ala
Portulacca meridina		Pulla batsali	Hulybatsali
——— crystalliana		Banka pavali	Doddagona
Sinapis alba..............	Mustard........	Awa kura	Sasoo soppu
Trianthema decandra		Galjeru	Gaija soppu
Phlomis esculenta		Dumpa kura	
Trianthema monogyn		Budu pavali kura	Nutsoogona
Trigonella fœnu græcum ..	Fenugreek	Menty kura	Menta soppu

Some of these vegetables are cultivated in the gardens of the natives, while others grow wild; the leaves of them only are used in their curries, or boiled with chillies to be eaten along with rice. There may be many other plants in India, the leaves of which are employed for similar purposes; but the preceding list contains all that I am acquainted with.

TABLE VI. *Fruits and Seeds of Trees and Plants used in Curries.*

Linnæan Names.	English Names.	Telinga Names.	Canary Names.
Aeschynomene grandiflora ..		Awasi kay	
Artocarpus integrifolia	Jack fruit	Panasa	Haliscna
Bryonia umbellata		Tia donda	Tondakay
Capparis zeylanica		Adonda	Totlikay
Cucurbita alba............	Pumpkin......	Burdave Pdæva gummudu	Dodda kembady buda
Cucurbita lagenaria........		Tappana kura	Dodda sora
Cucumis acutangulus		Garybīra kura ..	Hīrakay
Cucumis pentandra........		Nedy nunabhīra ..	Toppa bīra
Cucumis species		Nakka dossakay ..	Huly souta
Cucumis utillatissimus	Country cucumbers	Pandali dossa ..	Soutakay
Dolichos lablab		Yerra chickudu ..	Manavary
Dolichos lablab, var.		Tella chickudu ..	Billa manavary
Dolichos minimus		Chickudu......	Ghattawary, ackimanavary
Dolichos spicatus	Cowgram	Anapa	Doddamanavary
Dolichos suratu		Suratikay	
Hyperanthera moronga	Morongal fruit ..	Chettumunakay	Nuggakay
Hibiscus esculentus........		Bendakay	Bendakay
Momordica dioica		Potti kakara	Giddagalu
Momordica operculata		Metta kakara....	Chickakura
Momordica species........		Kakara kay	Hagalkay
Musea paradisiaca, 3 var. ..	Plantain........	Amartapanny .. Chackrakaly .. Bonta kay	Bala sara bala Puttabala Kattenabala

Linnæan Names.	English Names.	Telinga Names.	Canary Names.
Solanum longum	Brinjal	Niru wankay	Niru bajany sanna
——— melongena		Metta wankay ..	Dodda bajany, subajany
——— varietas		Conda wankay ..	Molalu bajany gudda
——— trilobatum		Wustakay	Wuchinta
Trichosanthus nervifolia		Potlakay	Podamakay
——— cucumerina ..		Lingapotlakay ..	Pichi kapotlakay
——— kakydonda ..		Kakydonda	Karadonda
Trigonella tetrapetala		Goru chickudu ..	Gorikay

When fruits are introduced into curries, they are usually employed before they are ripe; when ripe they are unfit for this purpose.

Many species of cucumber seem to be quite unknown in the Mysore.

Of pumpkins or cucurbita, the natives reckon no fewer than three species; but these in the present state of our knowledge must be considered as mere varieties.

TABLE VII. *Roots used in Curries.*

Linnæan Names.	English Names.	Telinga Names.	Canary Names.
Arum manchy canda	Good arum	Kanda	Churnagada
Arum esculentum	....	Tohama	Kaswagada
Convolvulus batatos	Country potatoa ..	Mohana dumpalu	Ghenusagedda
Daucus carota	Carrots	Gazerragedda	
Dioscorea sativa	Yams	Pendalum	
Raphanus sativus	Raddishes	Mulanghi	Mulamgadda

Among these roots the carrot is unknown in the gardens of the natives on the coast. The yam is so little cultivated in Mysore, that for a long time I thought it an exotic. The country potatoe is here in its greatest perfection.

6

TABLE VIII. *Garden Fruit Trees.*

Linnæan Names.	English Names.	Telinga Names.	Canary Names.
Annona reticulata	Bullock's heart ..	Rama palam	
——— squamata	Custard apple....	Sīta palam	Beranji hannu
Anacardium occidentale....	Cashew	Jīdymamady	Jirika
Artocarpus integrifolia	Jack	Panasa	Halisana hannu
Averhoa carambola	Carambola		Kamarak
Bromelia ananas	Pine apples	Anasa	Nalalesana hannu
Carica papaia	Papay..........	Madhuranakam	Parenky hannu
Citrus aurantium	Orange	Nareja	Kittali
—— spec.	Sweet orange	Kamalapalam ..	Sikittali
—— variatro	Musk orange	Idapalam	Kirikittali
—— decumana	Pumplemoss	Pomparamossu ..	Chacoti
—— medicus, var.........	Lime	Nimma	Nimba
—— dubba	....	Pulla dubba	Haralli
—— spec.	....	Madalapalam ..	Madalahannu
Cocos nucifera	Cocoa nut	Narika, kobari	Tenghenakay
Eugenia jambos	Rose apple......	Pannīrupalam ..	Pannīru hannu
Ficus carica	Fig............	Anjuru	
Mangifera indica	Mango	Mamedy........	Mavidy
Musa paradisica	Plantain........	Ariti	Bala
Phyllanthus cherimella		Rasah wuserikay	Kirinelly
———— emblica		Wuserikay	
Psidium pyriferum	Guava	Jama	Tshep-panlu
Punica granatum	Sweet pomegranate	Tiadanemma	Sedalimba
——— variatio acid. & dulcis	Sour ditto	Pulla danimma ..	Huledalimba
Pyrus malus, var.	Apple..........	Sewu palam	Sēwu hannu
Vitis vinifera	Vine	Kissimissy	Dracha

The vine is cultivated in many gardens of the natives, particularly by moormen: in the higher provinces of Hindostan it is said to be very common; several species of it are growing wild on the hills of this country.

The cocoa-nut palm is of great importance in some of the northern provinces south of Chittledrūg: topes of them are seen every where, and some valleys appear like forests of them. The nuts are transported on bullocks to the more northern countries. The fibres of the cocoa-nut are made into cables called kayr, but I have no where observed any manufactory of it, nor have I seen any oil expressed from this nut in Mysore. The success with which this tree is cultivated in the centre, as one may say, of the peninsula, refutes the old opinion that it will thrive only on the coast; but it requires a soil impregnated with common salt, similar to that which occurs in the neighbourhood of Sīra.

The palmyra is almost an exotic in the Mysore, though I am confident that it would grow as well as it does on the coast, and would be of service both to improve the aspect of the country, and to furnish the inhabitants with wood for building: it would grow on all the barren high grounds at present unproductive.

The mango tree is a great favourite of the natives of India: it grows on any soil to a considerable size. About Bengalore it is cultivated in great abundance, and the kind planted is very good. On the north of Nidgcul these trees are rather scarce, and to the north of Chittledrug they are extremely so.

Of plantains the variety is not great, nor were any of the better kinds cultivated till very lately: the delhi, rajah, red, and other plantains are now introduced.

There are two varieties of jack fruit distinguished by the natives; one bearing its fruit on the branches of the tree, and the other on the stem and roots under ground. The former only is found in the Mysore.

There are two varieties of the averhoa; one quite sweet and pleasant, and the other sour and only fit for pickling.

Some plants might be introduced into the Mysore with every chance of success and profit. Among others I conceive the following of most importance.

1. The Mauritius and Nankeen cotton. Cotton thrives very well about Bangalore, and might be cultivated on the inland range of hills, where it would grow with luxuriance.

2. The tea plant from China is, in my opinion, a plant that deserves notice among those which might be advantageously introduced: if the best kind could be procured from China, I have little doubt that the climate would be favourable for its cultivation.

3. All kinds of European and Chinese fruit trees; as the apple, pear, chesnut, bread fruit, lichi, wampi, loquat, &c.

4. Coffee, some of which indeed is already cultivated, and sold in the bazars of Bengalore and Seringapatam.

TABLE IX. *Jungle Fruit Trees and Plants.*

Linnæan Names.	English Names.	Telinga Names.	Canary Names.
Aegle marmelos	Wood apple	Weleka	Beldannu
Amyris, spec. nov.			
Bassia longifolia		Ippa pu	Ippa pu
Carissa carandas		Wankay	Kaliwy
Canthium parviflorum		Balsu	
Clausena (Amyris)		Kariwēpu	Kariwa hannu
Eugenia caryophyllata		Nēredu	Kara hannu
Grewia arborea		Pushinika	
Alangium decapetatum		Adeka	
Limonia pentaphylla		Golluga	
Memecylon capitellatum ..		Alli	Kalliwa hannu
Phœnix dactylifera		Ita	
Phlonus jujuba, & var.		Rhegu	Bora hannu, or Elcha hannu
Rubus mysorensis			
Semicarpus anacardium		Nallajidy	Karrajirika
Ximenia americana		Ura neekra	Nackri

This list is more defective than any of the preceding, because it often happened that I saw the fruit without the flower, or the flower without the fruit; but the jungle or wild fruits are but few in number. The best of them is the clausena of Jussieu, a species of amyris which tastes much like the grape, and grows to a fine shrub only on the highest parts of the country, as about Nundydrug, Siwaganga, &c. The Ximenia Americana is also a very pleasant fruit, the juicy part having a sweet and agreeable taste, while the kernel tastes like that of the cherry: it ripens in May and June. I have found it only on the Chittledrug hills. The rubus is a new species, a kind of raspberry; I have only found it wild on the Nundydroog hills: it bears a very pleasant fruit, of the taste and appearance of the blackberry. There is another species which has been brought from the Cŭrg country.

Bichy, probably a species of gardenia, is a very good fruit; I have never seen it but in the bazar at Hurryhurr and Honelly.

TABLE X. *Garden Vegetables not comprehended in the preceding Lists.*

Linnæan Names.	English Names.	Telinga Names.	Canary Names.
Allium cepa	Onions	Wully, nirully	Kembally
——— sativum	Garlick	Welluly	Belluly
Ammomum zinziber	Ginger	Allum	Hassa sonty
Arachis hypogæa	Ground nut	Weru sennaga	Bĕrukadla
Capsicum annuum	Chilly	Miriapukay	Maenisanakay
Carthamus tinctorius	Safflor	Cusumba	Cusumy
Coriandrum sativum	Coriander	Cottimiry	Cottimbiry
Cuminum cyminum	Cummin seed	Jilakarra	Jiry
Curcuma longa	Turmerick	Passupu	
Nicotiana tabacum	Tobacco	Pogăku	Hogasoppu
Papaver somniferum	Opium	Gassagassalu	Garagamalu
Sinapis alba	Mustard	Awalu	Sasu
Trigonella fœnugrœcum	Fenugreek	Mentulu	Mentealu
Bixa orellana	Annotto		

Among the trees or shrubs introduced by Tippoo is the anotto; I found many plants of it in the Bengalore gardens, and on Sewendroog hill. At the former place I collected the seed, with a view to send it to England by the first opportunity, as I recollect that some years ago a considerable premium was offered for the first ten pounds of this valuable dye from the East Indies. My object was, that it might be ascertained whether the anotto raised in India be as good as that from South America. It might be cultivated on all the hills in this country; indeed it grows on Sewendroog with great luxuriance and almost spontaneously.

Carthamus tinctorius, or saflor, is chiefly cultivated about Bengalore, and used by the natives to dye their holiday turbans and other cloths of a beautiful red: the moormen are particularly fond of this colour, though it recommends itself rather by its brilliancy than its durability.

Opium was formerly cultivated to a considerable extent about Uscotah: small quantities of it are still produced in that country.

All the other articles in the preceding list are used by the natives as spices and introduced into their curries.

Flax might be cultivated here, as I have found some plants of it growing wild about Hurryhurr. In the Mahratta country this plant is raised on account of its seed, from which oil is prepared and sent to all parts of the coast. The crotolaria juncea yields a similar kind of fibre, and in greater abundance: it is employed for the manufacture of ropes and gunnies*.

* A coarse kind of tape used for gram bags and emballage.

Among the few forest trees that deserve attention, the sandal is the most important: it grows chiefly on the high inland range of hills.

It may be worth while to make a few observations on the mode of manuring practised in this part of the country. The natives, being well aware of the importance of this article, make composts in the villages of all vegetable and animal matter and rubbish that they can preserve, throwing them in a heap near the road, from whence it is carried in carts to their raghie fields.

When they manure leguminous grains, they put a little on each seed at the time of planting; for dry grain the manure is ploughed in. On black cotton soil no manure whatever is laid.

All cattle are driven to the village before sunset, and kept in places surrounded by high walls: the method of folding them on the field, as practised in other parts of the country, is not known. The precaution of securing cattle in a strong place was probably required under a divided and irregular government, and it is still requisite wherever the country swarms with beasts of prey; but in an open country, like the greatest part of the Mysore, the benefit resulting to agriculture from folding cattle on the fields ought not to be neglected.

The shrubs used for hedges round the villages or houses are the agave americana, and the guilandina bonduccella. The former grows very large, and when high forms an excellent fence against all intruders: the latter is astonishingly prickly. Bound hedges, as they are called, are only common south of Nidgcul and about Bengalore; farther north they are not often observed.

XV. QUADRUPEDS, BIRDS, AND FISHES.

Mysore, so far as I know, cannot boast of any peculiar quadrupeds; this is the case at least with that part of the country which I have seen; the following are the most remarkable.

The tiger frequents only the wilder parts of the country, and seldom comes into the open plains; it is a dreadful animal, but too well known to be described here.

The leopard (*felis leopard*, var. Shaw) climbs on trees, whence it is sometimes chased by the tiger: it frequently attacks men, but is often beaten, in consequence of the want of courage, and suffers for its temerity. This animal infests most parts of the Mysore.

The ursine sloth (*bradypus ursinus*, Shaw, probably a real ursus) commonly called the Indian bear, is a very destructive ill-natured animal, and what Ovid says of the real bear is very applicable to this quadruped:

At lupus et turpes instant morientibus ursi.

They acquire, by dint of application and discipline, the same accomplishments which were considered as peculiar to the Polish bears.

Among the hills of this country is a species of wild dog, which attacks larger animals in a body and destroys them; I have never myself had an opportunity of seeing this animal. The Parria dog, a domestic animal, is oftener afflicted with canine madness than the dogs on the coast: at Sirah and at Bengalore many men that had been bit by them were brought to me in the last stages of this horrid disorder. They all expired under much milder symptoms than those that have been observed in Europe. The hydrophobia was by no means well marked, for all to the last could be prevailed upon to swallow fluid medicines, though they preferred dry powders. They all complained of much pain in the throat, just about the palate, and were constantly spitting, though with some difficulty: the delirium was high, and their imaginations chiefly occupied with wild animals, from which however it was frequently possible to divert them merely by speaking to them. The natives are as little acquainted with remedies against this dreadful disease as we are ourselves; they have not even an idea of extirpating the part that has been hurt, which, after the bite of snakes, as well as of mad animals, is in my opinion, the only step which can be depended on for averting the dreadful consequences.

As for the other quadrupeds, such as antelopes, deer, &c., I have been for many years collecting materials for their natural history, as well as for that of the birds and fishes to be found in the country; and I may, perhaps, hereafter lay the result of my researches before the public.

The variety of birds in the Mysore is not so great as on the coast; and I have not observed a single one that was not to be found below the Ghauts.

The buceros, or rhinoceros bird, is rather uncommon upon the coast. It is frequently seen in the Mysore, in those places where trees of the fig kind abound. On the fruit of this kind of tree only I have found them feeding. It is surely a more agreeable food than the nux vomica, with which M. Sonnerat has thought proper to treat them. As far as I recollect, the shrub producing the nux vomica is no where to be found above the Ghauts.

The Bustard Florican (a species of Otis) is equally scarce on the coast. It is found in the Mysore, though not frequently. It is a large bird, above the size of a full grown turkey. Its flesh is esteemed a great delicacy.

Tolerably good fish may be had almost in all seasons, from the larger tanks. The *Silurus asotus* is the most common, and very well tasted. There are several species of fish in the Tumbudra, which never have been described, and which, of course, are unknown to the naturalists of Europe.

Alligators are also found in the Tumbudra. One of them was brought to Col. Mackenzie in my absence. He will probably favour the public with a drawing and description of the animal, which would be highly acceptable, as the specific differences of those found in India are by no means fully understood.

Among the insects, I must notice the Locust *(Gryllus migratorius)*, a flight of which we observed in 1801 at Seerah. They prove at times, when they come in large numbers, very destructive to the country.

That destructive insect the *Carian*, is not so prejudicial to the cocoa-nut trees in the Mysore as it is upon the coast.

In the mountainous parts of the country, many swarms of small bees fix their honey-combs to rocks or trees. In some provinces, the collection of wax and honey forms even a branch of revenue, though not a very productive one. The natural history of those industrious and harmless animals deserves farther inquiry. The same thing may be said of the Lacca insect.

In certain situations, and at the beginning of the rains, a number of snakes infest the country, some of which are dreadfully noxious. The Cobra de capello is, however, less frequently met with in the Mysore than on the coast. I have collected and preserved many species of this animal, which I may describe hereafter.

XVI. PRICES OF PROVISIONS, &c.

The following Table of the bazar prices of grain, at different places, is extracted from my Journals. The measure is every where reduced to one common standard, namely, the sīr, at sixty-four dubs weight, or two pounds.

TABLE XI. *List of the Price of one Sīr of gain at the different Places.*

	Agamungalum		Chittledroog		Hurryhurr		Talem		Buswapatam		Bangalore		Sawendroog		Heroor		Hartee		Matod		Darmapoory		Rutnagherry		Seerah		Honelly	
	F*	C†	F	C	F	C	F	C	F	C	F	C	F	C	F	C	F	C	F	C	F	C	F	C	F	C	F	C
Wadlu or Paddy		53½								37½		13¾		24		25		20		13		71				18		
Chollu				23				9		17¼		8½		13¾		20		25		13¼		71						
Gantalu		64		21½												20		25								13		
Corrallu		64		21½						17¼						20		25		13½								
Jonnalu				21½		32½				21		8				20		25										
Samulu								6				8½		6¾		20												
Godumulu......	2			75								69				40		72									1	40
Kandulu				60		66½						17¼						70		26½		75				20		
Wulawalu......	1								1	6½		8½		20¾		20		25		13¼								
Anumulu								26½				10¼		17¼						13½		48		24				
Pessalu				60		66½						51¾		51¾				64				72						
Sennagalu......	2			60		52				6½		81¾		69		35		40										24
Amdalu........						52						17¼		34½														
Nuwulu........			1	20		43				52		51				50		50		26½								
Verry Nuwulu..												34½		34½				50										
Minumulu......			1	20								43		51¾														
Alsandalu......				60																								
Alu												5¼		6¾		10												

* Fanam $\frac{1}{12}$ of a pagoda = 2d. † Cash $\frac{1}{16}$ of a fanam.

List of the Price of one Sĭr of Bazar Articles at different Places.

	Betamungalum		Colar		Bengalore		Sewendrug		Sirah		Herur		Darmapury		Harti		Chittledrug		Buswapatam		Honelly	
	F	C	F	C	F	C	F	C	F	C	F	C	F	C	F	C	F	C	F	C	F	C
Opium	22	25			69	32					48											
Pepper	2	$15\frac{1}{2}$									2		1	53			1	70			2	
Cardemoms	4	20																			12	
Cummin Seeds					1	36	1	36			1		1	26			1	20				
Mentulu						20		20										$37\frac{1}{2}$				
Turmerick												50										
Cloves																	3 0				39	
Chillies												26						50				
Tamarind		$11\frac{1}{2}$										10		13				15				
Jaggary				$2\frac{3}{4}$				$33\frac{1}{2}$		43		34		33		40		43		20		60
Sugar, first sort																		67				
second ditto												30		20				60				
third ditto			1																			
fourth ditto				67																		
fifth ditto				$53\frac{1}{4}$													1	40				
Sugar Candy			1	20													1	70			·3	

In this table, F signifies a fanam, or $\frac{1}{11}$ of a pagoda; = 2d sterling; C signifies cash, $\frac{1}{16}$ of a fanam.

The great difference in the price of some articles in different places, opium for example, is owing to the duties levied on them. All intoxicating articles, and some others, are yearly assessed and rented out.

XVII. INHABITANTS OF THE COUNTRY.

The Mysoreans are, in general, a healthy, stout race of men, and rather above the size of the Indians on the coast of Coromandel. Their features are more regular than those of the Malabars, and, in the northern parts of the country, their complexion is fairer. Most of them live on raghie, which they prefer to rice. An individual is usually allowed one sīr* of flour at a meal, and they make two meals during each day.

Of the occupations of the Mysoreans little can be said that is not already known; for the Hindoos are every where the same. The same casts, and the same occupations, prevail in every part of the country, whether populous or thinly inhabited. The same similarity reigns among the Moormen all over India. They are all soldiers by profession, and idlers, who would rather starve than support themselves by labour. Some of them, indeed, exercise some easy handicraft, or attempt a little trade; but they carefully avoid every thing which requires much bodily exertion.

The morality of the Mysoreans is perfectly similar to that of all the Indians; and is low to a degree that is almost beyond the conception of every nation in Europe. Lying, cheating, domineering, perfidy, fickleness, dissembling, inconstancy, treachery, adultery, are so common and familiar, that they can scarcely in India be classed among those practices that are considered as vices; at the same time, it would not be fair to conceal the few good qualities which they possess. They are courteous, polite, contented, and possessed of most of the passive virtues.

The population in most districts is very low; owing, without doubt, to former wars and oppressions. And the northern parts are still thinner of inhabitants than the southern districts.

The houses of the natives and their villages are mean and poor; even those in the larger towns, as in Bengalore. Most villages are surrounded with stone walls, or thick hedges; and many have turrets, by way of still farther defence.

* Measured.

Their dress is much more decent than that of the Malabars. The poorer classes have at least a combaly * round them; and all women have *cholies*, which are a kind of jackets that cover their breast, arms, and frequently also the belly. This greater attention to dress is probably owing to the greater coldness of the climate in the Mysore. From the Moorish women they have adopted the custom of covering their faces with a part of their dress, and of blackening their teeth.

There is a difference between the dress of every particular cast; but it would be a difficult task to attempt to make these variations intelligible to the English reader; and even if we were to explain the subject sufficiently, the value of the information would be no compensation for the difficulty of acquiring it.

XVIII. DIFFERENCE BETWEEN THE PRODUCE AND EXPENSES OF CULTIVATION.

A true account of this difference is but seldom to be obtained. It can be procured only by examining both the cultivators and the circar servants, and comparing their statements, as both parties are disposed to warp the truth according to their own notions of utility. My information has been chiefly derived from the cultivators, and this is the reason why the profits appear so small. But my opinion is that they are really small; and not much greater than they are here represented. Hence, no doubt, the reason why the farmers are unwilling to cultivate more ground than they are actually obliged to cultivate; an unwillingness which exists every where along the coast. The circar share, or revenue derived from the lands, is by no means exorbitant. But the vast number of dues to the village and circar servants must prove exceedingly injurious to agriculture. Some of these dues, indeed, are for actual services: as those to the barber and the parria; but it is the village renter and *shanbog*, or accountant, that derive the greater benefit from their services. It is the messages and burdens of these men that they constantly carry, and their houses alone that they constantly attend. The carpenter is best entitled to his share, as he keeps the instruments of tillage in repair; but even his reward might be settled in a more equitable way.

* Coarse woollen cloth.

I am of opinion that all village expenses should be abolished at once, and the village servants paid by those that want them in the best way they can agree among themselves. Should this measure be adopted, the greatest sufferers would be the Bramins; for, even at present, their share is given with great reluctance. The religious beggars, dancing girls, and whatever dues go by the name of religious gifts, would also be greatly curtailed. The circar servants would likewise feel the change. These people, in the Company's dominions at least, are twice paid for their services, namely, by their employers and by the villagers. This double payment is the reason why the Bramins are so eager to be employed in the revenue service.

The following are extracts from my Journals on this head.

CUSBA DARMAPORAM *.

A quantity of high ground for transplanting raghie, as much as two pair of bullocks can plough (the only measure in use here) pays to the Circar

	K.† ps.	fs.
Kist ‡	5	0
Eight pucca sīr of raghi seed	0	0¼
For ploughing it with two pair of bullocks, four times	1	2
Culy§ for taking the plants out of the bed in which they had been sown originally, two men for fifteen days, at the rate of three dubs per day	0	5¼
Culy for planting the raghi plants, four men for fifteen days, each at two dubs per day	0	7½
If transplanted in August it will be ripe in November, hire for cutting	0	4
	7	9¼

The produce will be 1½ candy, the price of it 12 K. P.	K. ps.	fs.
The *low ground* is cultivated for shares—paddy 1¼ tum	0	6
Culy for ploughing it in July with eight bullocks	1	2
Culy for weeding it	0	6
Culy for cutting it, five months after sowing	0	2
	2	6

* Near Sira.

† This account is given in the coins, or, in the way of calculating used by the natives of the country, in Kanteray pagodas and gold fanams. This pagoda, or ten gold fanams, is equal to three rupees.

‡ Rent.

§ Hire.

2

If the produce be one candy*, the shares are

The Circar	7	Tum.
Tallary (peon)	2 †	
Parrias who take care of the crops on the fields	1⅛	
Village servants	0 4/8	
Bramins	0 6/16	
Shanbog	0 6/16	
Shroff (money-broker)	0 3/16	
Massuldar (a Circar peon)	0 2/16	
Goudu, or head ryot	0 2/16	
The head of the jangam matam, or the priest of the people who worship the lingum	0 3/16	
	12	Tums.
Remaining to the ryot	8	
	20 — 1 Candy.	

RUTTENGHERRY ‡.

If on *black* ground, raghie and anuma are sown together, the account will stand nearly

	K. ps.	fs.
The price of one tum of raghi	0	5½
Of anuma ten ballus	0	1¼
For ploughing the ground four times with two ploughs, in July and August	1	2
Weeding it with the weeding plough for four days in the month of September or October	0	1¼
Culy for weeding when it is high	0	5
For cutting it in November	0	4
	2	9¼

Produce 1 candy of raghie and 8¼ tum of anuma,

Of which the Circar receives	10	Tums.
The village parria	1½	
The village servants	1	
The Circar servants	0¾	
The ryot, or cultivator	15	
	28¼	Tums.

* The same as a putty, of which see hereafter.

† One tum of this goes to the Circar.

‡ Near the Sirah hills.

The price of the ryot's share of raghie....... pagodas 3
——————————— anuma............ 2¼

SIRA.

Of a candy of paddy produced on cheruvu sagu (ground watered by tanks) the fixed deductions are

	Tums.	Sīrs.
For the Circar	2	0
The head man in the village	0	24
The shanbog..	0	24
The tallary	0	24
The village parria	0	24
The village barber	0	12
The village carpenter	0	12
The Circar servants	0	24
The village swamy (god)..	0	24
Charitable gifts to Bramins..	0	12
The massuldar	0	6
The man who measures	0	6
	4 Tums.	
Of the 16 remaining tums the Circar gets half (besides the two tums mentioned among the deduction)	8	0
And the other half remains to the ryot..................	8	0

Of a candy of paddy produced on kala sagu, or on ground watered by nullahs, the deductions before-mentioned amount only to half that quantity, the Circar receiving only one tum, and the other claimants in proportion, and of the remaining 18 tooms,

	Tums.	Sīrs.
The ryot received..........	10	75
And the Circar..............	7	21
	18 Tums.	

Of a candy of paddy from kapila * (grounds watered from wells) the deductions are as in the preceding,

The Circar share of the remaining	6 Tums.
And the ryot's	12
	18 Tums.

* This requires the most labour, as the water for it must be drawn either by bullocks or pacotas. In the former it is obtained with less trouble, as it is usually thrown on the fields by baskets. From tanks it is brought on the field by sluices and channels.

Sajja and kanda sown on one toom of high ground,	K. ps.	fs.
To plough the ground five times, two men's wages for one month..	2	6
Sajja 16 sīr seed	0	2
Kanda eight sīr	0	1
Two men's culy for eight days to weed the field with the weeding plough a month after sowing	0	4
Two men's culy for eight days another time, a month after the former	0	4
Weeding it by culies again	0	6
Culy for cutting, forty-two men at the rate of 7 for 1 Sultany fanam........................	0	6
The Circar kist........................	3	0
The village servants........................	0	8
	8	7

	ps.	fs.
The produce, sajja 1 candy	8	0
——— kanda 4 tums	2	4
	10	4

So that there remains to the cultivator 2 ps. 7 fs.

On gadda, or low ground, the expenses and profits of cultivation are, viz.

To two men to plough in 18 days one tum six times	0	7¼
Seed 72 seer	0	6
Weeding it after it has been a month in the ground, by coolies....	0	4
Weeding a second time	0	6
Cutting it	0	3
	2	6¼

The produce is 15 tums, of which three for deductions, remain........................	12 Tums.
Of this deduct for the Circar........................	6
Remain to the ryot	6

which at the rate of ten pagodas is three pagodas after defraying the above expenses, viz. 2 ps. 6¼ fs.—three and a half gold fanams real profit.

If on the same quantity of ground (one tum) sugar is planted, the expenses attending it are,

	K.	ps.	fs.
For ploughing eight or nine times with two ploughs	0	7¼	
For folding sheep on it for some time, at the rate of 5000 for a pagoda for one day	2	0	
To bring manure from the village	2	0	
To 24,000 sugar plants	12	0	
Culy for planting	0	3	
For making a hedge or railing round the garden	1	0	
For hoeing and raising the ground round the plants after they are a month old	0	8	
For digging small water channels, one between three or four rows of sugar cane	1	0	
For tying the sugar canes that sprout out of one plant (the first time) together	1	0	
Two months after again (the second time)	0	9	
———— (the third time)	0	8	
For religious ceremonies after the cane has attained two-thirds of its growth, 60 sīr of rice and ghee for the Bramins	1	0	
For cutting the cane and bringing it to the boiling place, for ten days, at the rate of seven women each, one fanam a day	1	0	
Men at the rate of four for one gold fanam per day, for ten days	3	0	
For building a shed or place to boil jaggary	1	0	
For ceremonies to the swamy of the shed	2	0	
Oil for the lamps	0	6	
For chunam (lime)	0	2¼	
Hire for the sugar mill	0	5	
Hire for the iron boilers	1	0	
Carpenters' pay	1	6	
Sugar boilers' pay	0	5	
Fuel (required besides the expressed stalks of sugar canes)	1	5	
A man's pay for four months, to keep in the night the jackals away	1	2	
Circar's kist	10	0	
	47	7	

The produce in jaggary is in common 100 maund, from which is to be deducted

	Mds.	Seers.
For the man to whom the mill belongs	0	20
For the iron boiler (vat)	0	20

	Mds.	Sīrs.
For the carpenter....................................	0	20
People employed to boil jaggary..........................	1	0
For the mastry*	0	10
Pot-maker....................................	0	10
For the village servants, viz.:		
For the goudu, or head man of the village	¼	0
—— shanbog	¼	0
—— tallary	¼	0
—— parria who takes care of watering the fields..........	¼	0
—— village chuckler (shoe-maker)	¼	0
—— pot-maker....................................	¼	0
—— barber	¼	0
Total maunds	6	0
Produce, remaining 94 the maund at five fanams........pags.	47	0
Pieces of cane for new plantation	12	0
	59	0
Deduct the expenses	47	7
Remain	11	3

As most ryots have their own cattle and their own family to assist them, greater part of the expenses of ploughing may be put to his profit, but that for cutting and weeding, &c. the crops, greatest part goes out of the family.

A ryot thinks himself completely ruined if he loses his horned cattle, and it is the last of his property arrested by his creditors. If he owes any thing to the Circar, they will be seized but never actually taken from him. The taking care of cattle and the doing the harder work of cultivation is most commonly entrusted to a parria, who serves the ryot for a trifle, probably two or three rupees a year, besides his victuals and a small proportion of grain.

The female part of the family prove in common the most advantageous in the household, as no duties or taxes are levied upon the works of their hands, the profit, though small, goes entirely to themselves. It is said besides that the wives of the Hindoos are remarkably saving and economical, and that they do not easily slip an opportunity of improving their fortunes.

* Foreman.

XIX. INSTRUMENTS OF TILLAGE.

These instruments are remarkable only for their rudeness and simplicity. The following descriptions, with the accompanying figures, will give the reader an accurate idea of them:

Plate II. fig. 1, represents the common plough used all over the peninsula: *a* is the ploughshare, a piece of iron 1½ foot long and 1½ inch broad, and the only piece of iron about the whole machine; *b* is the handle by which the ploughman guides the plough; *c c* a piece of wood to which the oxen are fastened; *d d*, the wooden plough about 2½ feet long.

Fig. 2, represents the weeding plough used about Hurryhurr; *e e* is a piece of wood 18 inches long, *m m* pieces of iron; *n* the space between the iron three inches long.

Fig. 3, represents a harrow used about Bengalore to precede the drill plough, *h h* is a piece of wood four feet six inches long, *i* teeth ten inches long; *j*, *j*, the bars of wood to which it is fixed 7¼ feet long, *k* the handle two feet nine inches long.

Fig. 4, is an instrument used about Bengalore to even the ground before sowing. It is made of black wood, and the ploughman usually stands upon it in order to increase the weight. The length from *l* to *l* is four feet nine inches; *m*, *m*, each six feet long.

Fig. 5, is a drill plough used about Bengalore for sowing raghi: *a* is a cup into which the seed is put, four inches deep; *b*, *b*, *b*, hollow bamboos through which the seed runs into the furrows. They perforate the teeth about the middle, and are three feet six inches long. The length from *c* to *c* is four feet nine inches; *d* is the handle, four feet nine inches long. The pieces of wood *e*, *e*, to which the bullocks are fixed, are nine feet long; *f* is a bamboo with a cup to receive annuma seed, guided by a man who follows the large drill which sows the raghi; the bamboo is one foot three inches long, and the cup 1¼ inch deep: *g* is a rope 2½ feet long, by which the bamboo is fastened to the drill plough.

Fig. 6, is a drill plough used about Hurryhurr for sowing jonnalu. The distance between *n* and *n* is three feet; *o*, *o*, *o*, *o*, are hollow bamboos; *p*, *p*, *p*, *p*, are teeth armed with *q q q q*, a share or a piece of iron.

Fig. 7, is a plough used to weed raghi about Bengalore. The distance between *h* and *h* is one foot five inches; *i*, *i*, *i*, *i*, are pieces of iron sticking

$1\frac{2}{3}$ inches out of the wood; *k* is the handle two feet long; *l* the handle to guide, two feet five inches; *m, m,* the pieces of wood to which the cattle are tied, seven feet long.

Fig. 8, is an instrument used about Hurryhurr to even the ploughing ground. The distance between *r* and *r* is three feet; *s, s,* is a piece of iron.

XX. COINS, WEIGHTS, AND MEASURES.

The current coins in this country are in gold, silver, and copper; but the first metal is most abundant. The gold coins are *mohīrs,* which are of Moorish origin; *pagodas,* an original Indian coin, and *fanams.*

Most gold coins are alloyed. Few are of the twelfth colour * or pure gold. The alloy is called *matam,* and consists of three parts silver and one part copper. Pure gold is denoted by the number 12, and whatever is wanting to make up 12 in speaking of gold is to be considered as alloy. Thus gold of the 11th colour means an alloy composed of 11 parts gold and one part of alloy.

The pagoda is used as the standard weight for many of the dearer medicines.

In the determination of the value of the different coins I have used the silver fanam according to the Company's rate of exchange; namely, silver pagoda† at 45 fanams and $46\frac{1}{4}$ cash—and one fanam at 80 cash.

Gold Coins in the Mysore.

	Weight.	Alloy.	Value.	
	Grains.		Fan.	Cash.
Star pagoda	54	$\frac{7}{24}$	45	$46\frac{1}{4}$
Bahadary or Sultany, Heckary, Paroky, Karku (Mettalu), or Madras pagoda	54	$\frac{5}{24}$	49	78
Jamshary or Samagherry		$\frac{6}{24}$		
Harpunpilly, Venketpatty, or Venketrailu		$\frac{7}{24}$		
Porto Novo		$\frac{11}{24}$	42	73
Gold mohīrs, Bahadary or Ammoody			228	40
——— Asheraffy			208	0
——— Mahommeddy			91	0

* The Hindoos distinguish the purity of gold by its colour.

† In mercantile transactions the star pagoda is reckoned at 42 fanams.

	Weight. Grains.	Alloy.	Value. Fan.	Cash.
Putady cash, Venetian		0*	65	5
Sannary		0	65	5
Calcutta cash		0	55	24
Apranjie cash		0	3	26¼

The mode of purifying gold used by the natives is to take equal quantities of brick dust and common salt, a good handful, which is put between two pieces of potter's ware, and into it the gold. These are placed in the midst of a heap of dried cow dung (wratties), lighted at the top in a place where the wind cannot produce a strong fire, and the pagoda or other pieces of gold when taken out appear incrusted with a black crust, which must be removed, and the process as often repeated as the same is reproduced.

Gold Fanams.

	Weight. Drams.	Grains.	Value. Fan.	Cash.
Sultany and Kantiray		6	4	27
Heckary		0	5	40
Silver Coins are				
Company's rupee	2	51	14	51†
Arcot rupee			14	51
Pondicherry rupee			14	51
Rajah rupee			15	0
Sultany			15	0
Silver fanam		15	1	0

The Rajah rupee is the stamp of the present Rajah, and its real value is in no degree greater than the Company's rupee.

The exchange of all these fluctuates very much.

Silver fanams are very scarce in Mysore, and only to be found in the larger places.

Copper Coin.

	Weight. Drams.	Grains.	Value. Cash.
Dutch dub	4	35	26
Arcot duddu	3	30	20

* Pure gold. † In the Company's accounts reckoned as 12 fanams, 60 cash.

	Weight. Drams.	Grains.	Value. Cash.
Elephant or Enne duddu	3	30	20
Double elephant	7	0	40
Sîrah duddu	1	35	14
Masulipatam	4	0	20
Saya duddu			20
Enne casu, or cash		40	7
Madras duddu *	1	44	10

The continual diminution of copper coins is owing to the natives, who get them constantly made into brass or copper vessels, employed by all those who can afford them.

The Kantiray pagoda and the honnu are imaginary coins. The former is used in all revenue accounts, and likewise in settling most of the private accounts of the natives. Probably in former times it was a real coin. Whenever the word pagoda occurs in this work without a particular stamp being marked, a Kantiray pagoda or three rupees is always understood. To the west of Hurryhurr, in some districts formerly belonging to Vizapoor, the word hunn, the Hindostanee term for a pagoda, is used in the revenue accounts, and its value fixed at half a Sultany pagoda, or two rupees.

The weights or dry measures in this country are of two different kinds, both defined very accurately, though gross impositions are practised respecting both. The former is called the bazar weight, and used in the sale of what are called bazar articles, as tamarinds, turmeric, and all different kinds of drugs. The latter is used for grain both in the bazars and in all revenue transactions. The great difficulty lies in the multiplicity of weights used in different districts; for almost every *Cusbah* † of small district has weights and measures differing widely from all those in its neighbourhood. The consequence of this is that the cunning banyans frequently take advantage of this multiplicity to deceive strangers. The inhabitants of the place cannot be so easily taken in, as they are all well acquainted with their own peculiar weights and measures.

The only general and uniform measure and weight is the pucca sīr of sixty-four dubs weight. And the weight of a dub is four drams. This sīr alters according to the weight of the dub. If these be lighter than four

* Of the old stamp.

† A principal town.

drams more dubs will be requisite to make up the sīr, if they be heavier fewer will do. This measure appears in some writings of very old date, as in the Sudra Ganitam; yet it is said to be of Moorish origin. It has made its way into all accounts, and has as it were dislodged all other weights.

Both fluids and dry articles are determined by weight, with the exception of oil, for the sale of which a kind of graduated measure is employed. All kinds of grain by common consent are sold by a measure which is not merely filled, but heaped up as high as possible above the lips. If a person buys only half the measure he loses the heaped part, which generally amounts to $\frac{1}{7}$th or $\frac{1}{6}$th of the whole.

It would be well worth while to ascertain the way that the agents buy grain in times of war. If they purchase by heaped measures and distribute it in a different way, the profits accruing to them and the consequent loss of Government must be considerable. Suppose that each man of an army of 20,000 receive each a sīr a day, the profits of the agent will be 2500 sīrs per day, or 75,000 per month, a quantity which would support the army for $3\frac{1}{3}$ days.

The lowest standard weight seems to be the dub. Smaller quantities are determined by common fractions, with which the lower classes of Hindoos are much better acquainted than the common people in Europe. They ascend regularly by fours. Of decimals, as far as I have had an opportunity of examining their arithmetic, they appear to be entirely ignorant. There is a Sanscrit work of the name of *Līlavaty*, which treats of this subject. In the Telinga there is a work on the same branch of knowledge, called *Sudra Ganitam*, written long ago, or rather translated from the Sanscrit by a man of the name of Mulliah.

The following weights are the standards for the Circars. As they are derived from the Sanscrit, they may be considered as general for Hindostan:

1 Paddy seed........	is one	vīsum	$\frac{1}{2}$ grain.
4 Vīsums	are one	gulivinda * or 1 patika..	2 grains.
2 Gulivindas................		addaga.................	4 grains.
2 Addagas		chinum.................	8 grains.
$2\frac{1}{2}$ Chinums		tsavila	20 grains.
2 Tsavilas................		dharanum...............	40 grains.
2 Dharanums		mada	1 dram 20 grains.
3 Madas		tulam	4 drams.

* Seed of abrus precatorius.

6 Tulams	are one	pavu sīru or ¼ sīr	3 ounces.
4 Pavus		sīru	12 ounces.
5 Sīrs		vīsa or 1 tackeda	3 lb. 12 ounces,
2 Vīsas		yettu	7 lb. 8 ounces.
2 Yettus		arda manugudu	15 lb.
2 Arda manugudu		manugudu	30 lb.
5 Manugudu		yadum or panchakum	150 lb.
2 Yadums		pandum	300 lb.
2 Pandums		Putadu = candy	600 lb.

Dry Measure.

			lb.	oz.
4 Dubs weight	are one	gidda	0	2
2 Giddas		arasola	0	4
2 Arasolas		sola	0	8
2 Solas		tavadu	1	0
2 Tavadus		manika	2	0
2 Manikas		addadu	4	0
2 Addadus		conchum	8	0
2 Conchums		Irasa	16	0
2 Irasas		tum	32	0
5 Tums		yadum	160	0
2 Yadums		pandum	320	0
2 Pandums		puttadu	640	0

List of Candies and Tums reduced to Pucca Sīr, used in different Places of the Mysore, each sīr of 2 lb. English weight.

Bētumungalum	1 Candy is	160 Sīrs and	1 Tum	8 Sīrs
Uscotah	1 ditto	200 ditto	1 ditto	10 ditto
Bengalore	1 ditto	200 ditto	1 ditto	10 ditto
Sewendrug	1 ditto	200 ditto	1 ditto	10 ditto
Kyamungalum	1 ditto	960 ditto	1 ditto	48 ditto
Chittledrug	1 ditto	960 ditto	1 ditto	48 ditto
Matod	1 ditto	960 ditto	1 ditto	48 ditto
Talem	1 ditto	960 ditto	1 ditto	48 ditto

Hurryhurr	1 Candy is	3200 Sīrs and	1 Tum....	160 Sīrs
Ayrany	1 ditto....	1600 ditto....	1 ditto....	80 ditto
Annaji	1 ditto....	1600 ditto....	1 ditto....	80 ditto
Buswapatam	1 ditto....	1600 ditto....	1 ditto....	80 ditto
Rutnagherry	1 ditto....	1600 ditto....	1 ditto....	80 ditto
Honelly	1 ditto....	320 ditto....	1 ditto....	16 ditto
Herur	1 ditto....	1280 ditto....	1 ditto....	64 ditto
Hartie................	1 ditto....	1280 ditto....	1 ditto....	64 ditto
Darmapury............	1 ditto....	1440 ditto....	1 ditto....	72 ditto
Sîrah	1 ditto....	1920 ditto....	1 ditto....	96 ditto

Many different modes might be thought of to reduce this chaos into union. The easiest and most readily understood by the common people, and the least liable to fraud and imposition, would undoubtedly be the best. Stamped measures and weights are very bad modes of preventing deception; because, as they are always made of metal, a very small degree of hammering is sufficient to alter the shape of the one and the weight of the other, and thus render both unfit for the purpose for which they were intended. The surest and best mode of determining measures is certainly by determining the weight which each should amount to. The introduction of English weights would be commodious for Europeans, but on account of the ignorance of the lower classes of Indians, it would expose them to great imposition from the banyans, and on that account would be injurious. The rupee and dub are at present used every where as weights, and might, therefore, be taken as a standard.

A Company's rupee weighs about three drams, or two drams fifty-six grains.

12 Rupees would be $\frac{1}{8}$ Sīr.
24 Ditto. .... $\frac{1}{4}$ Ditto.
48 Ditto. .... $\frac{1}{2}$ Ditto.
96 Ditto. .... 1 Ditto = $2\frac{1}{4}$lb.

The higher weights could be easily settled, for example,

4 Sīr. .... 1 Conchum.
4 Conchum ...... 1 Tum.
20 Tums .... 1 Putty.

The smaller weights might be determined as at present,

¼ Grain	....	1	Paddy seed.
4 Paddy seeds*	...	1	Gulivinda—2 grains.
7 Gulivindas	....	¼	Pagoda's weight.
28 Ditto	....	½	Ditto.
56 Ditto	....	1	Ditto.

The Masulipatam dub, if generally introduced, would be still more commodious. It weighs very nearly half an ounce. Sixty-four of them would make exactly a *sīr* of two pounds.

This is already a received weight in many parts of the Circars. But care should be taken that all *dubs* have exactly the same weight, a circumstance which has not hitherto been attended to.

It is a very common practice to mention, in the settlement of a bargain, the weight to be employed. The common weight fixed upon is the copper coin of the country, and if large quantities of any article have to be weighed, stones, the weight of which has been previously determined, are employed for the purpose.

The common scales are merely flat baskets suspended from a balanced pole, which is tied to a noose. It is the usual practice to weigh the article first in one scale and then in the other, and nobody will buy any article without seeing that this precaution is attended to.

The land measures are still less accurately defined than those of which we have been speaking. In most places the amount of land is determined by the quantity of seed required to sow it. Thus a *sīr* or a *tum* of land means an extent of ground which will take a *sīr* or a *tum* of seed to sow it. This is obviously the vaguest of all the modes of measuring land hitherto devised; as the quantity of seed will vary, not only according to the kind of grain employed, but likewise according to the nature and fertility of the soil. In some places the extent of ground is determined by the quantity of it which a certain number of cattle are able to labour in a day. This mode is likewise inaccurate; though not quite so fallacious as the preceding.

It would be easy and very useful for the revenue officers to establish a general measure of land on the coast. The mode employed in the *Chetri Ganitam*, a work on land measures, might be adopted.

XXI. COMMERCE OF THE COUNTRY.

The commerce of the Mysore was in a very languishing state during the reigns of Hyder and Tippoo, because both of these princes prohibited all intercourse between their dominions and the Company's territories. Indeed the country is not well situated for external trade, nor has it many articles of its own growth or manufacture fit for exportation. The only article of consequence that I recollect at present is sandal wood, which is produced abundantly and of the best quality. All of it that grows wild in the country belongs to the Rajah, and he prohibits his subjects from cutting down a single tree under the penalty of death. Small pieces of it may be purchased in the bazars at a tolerably cheap rate; but the best sandal wood can only be procured from the Rajah or his Diwan.

The core only of the stem of this tree possesses the qualities for which the wood is esteemed, and these qualities are improved in proportion to the age of the tree. It is sent on carts to the coast. Large plantations of it should be established on the hills, otherwise it will very soon become a scarce article.

Lacca is collected in the Mysore, but in such small quantities that it is scarcely entitled to notice when we are speaking of the trade of the country.

Cotton in small quantities is exported from the neighbourhood of Hurryhurr.

Of late years a great deal of grain, as rice, raghi, and horse gram have been exported from the Mysore to the Carnatic; the scarcity in the latter country enabling the merchants to pay the high duties, which amount to about 100 per cent.

The only manufacture in the Mysore is glass or *bangles,* which is carried from Matod all over the country; and steel wires at Chinnapatam; besides those mentioned in other parts of this tract.

All merchandize is carried on the backs of bullocks, and the carriers are called *lambardis* *, a set of people who support themselves by carrying salt from the coast to the interior of the country, and cotton, wheat, &c. from the interior to the coast. They live constantly under tents, and carry their families always with them. When they stop for any considerable time near towns they supply the bazars with wood. This constitutes the occupation of their women, who are generally handsome.

* In some parts of the country they are known under the name of Brinjāris.

The men are stout and well made, fond of smoking their hobble bobble *, and obey a naique of their own choosing, who regulates their marches and settles their bargains. They always travel in large parties. They are all Hindoos, speak Hindostany or Mahratta to each other, and are usually acquainted with Telinga. The men have nothing peculiar in their dress, but the other sex are decorated in a way very different from what is usual among Hindoo women. They have petticoats and cholies, and their arms and legs are all over covered with brass rings.

They are allowed to travel unmolested in times of war, and whatever party falls in with them pays for what is taken, even supposing it known that it was originally intended for the enemy. In some countries they are subjected to a trifling tax; but no imposition is laid upon them in those places where they purchase their salt. They must continue to possess their privileges, as long as the roads remain in their present bad state. They are satisfied with so moderate a profit that it is not likely that the roads will be soon attended to.

A great deal of cloth is manufactured in different parts of the country, particularly about Bengalore; but little of it is exported. In case of a great demand for the European market, it might be obtained from this place in considerable quantity. The cloth at present made is thin, and nearly similar to that manufactured at Salem. Cotton is rather dear, as it must be brought from the ceded districts; but it would soon become cheaper if the demand for cloth were to increase.

The different kinds of cloth made in different places, with their prices, may be seen from the following table:

		Breadth.	Length.	Price of One Piece.	
		Cubits.	Cubits.	Rupees.	
Chittledrug	Coarse white cloth	$1\frac{1}{8}$ to 2	20 to 21		$1\frac{3}{4}$
	Muslins			3 to 15	
	Blue women's cloth	2	15	3	20
	Turbans	2	60	3	16
	Silk women's cloth	$2\frac{1}{8}$	16	6	60
	Silk handkerchiefs			$\frac{1}{4}$	15
Dawanikerra	Combalies			4	50

* A kind of hucka made of a cocoa-nut shell, and a cup of earthenware; the latter for the lighted mixture of tobacco, bang, &c.; the former for water.

		Breadth.		Length.		Price of One Piece.	
		Cubits.		Cubits.		Rupees.	
Hurryhurr....	Combalies...............					1 to 12	
Ayrany	Combalies..............					1	20
	White ditto					1	10
	Coarse cloth............		2		20		1⅛
	Men's dressing cloth .. .					3	15
	Women's cloth.........					3	15
Annaji......	Combalies..............					1	20
	Coarse cloth.............		2		20		1⅛
	Men's dressing cloth					1	10
	Women's ditto ditto......					1	10
Bengalore ..	Women's cloth of different musters and names	2 to 2¼		14 to 18		2	5
	Cholies or women's jackets of different musters	2	2¼	1	1¼	¾	1⅛
		2	2¼	16	18	5	10
	Silk women's cloth of different sorts	2	2½	16	20	7 to 40	
	Silk shawl handkerchief ..	2	2¼	2	2¼	7	21
	Ditto ditto long	1½	3½	3½	7½	7	60
	Silk cholies	2	2¼	1	1¼	¾	3
	Silk cloth, of five sorts.. .	1½	1¾	10	13	3	22
	Men's dressing cloth of eight sorts..........	2¼	2½	18	22	4	16
	Turbans	¾	1½	30	70	4	12
	Broad tapes of cotton....		¼	8	9	¼	¾
	Gunnies of janapa and gong nara *		½	10	22	¾	1½
	Muslins................	1¼	1½	16	32	3	12
	Coarse cotton cloth......	1½	1¾	16	24	1	3⅛
	Flowered cloth, silk and cotton	1½	1¾	22	24	10	42
	Combalies	2	2½	5	6	¾	3
	Tippoo's tiger or spotted cloth	1½	1¾	12	14	2	2⅛
	Coarse chintz	1¼	1¾	22	26	3	4
	Cotton carpets..........	1¾	2½	5	7½	1	4

* Hibiscus Cannabinus. Linn.

		Punjum*	Breadth.	Length.	Price of One Piece.
			Cubits.	Cubits.	Gold Fanams.
Herur......	Coarse cloth..	8	$1\frac{1}{2}$	22	$3\frac{1}{2}$ to $3\frac{3}{4}$
	Ditto ditto	10	$1\frac{3}{4}$	24	$5\frac{3}{4}$ $6\frac{1}{4}$
	Turbans	4	$\frac{3}{4}$	30	$2\frac{1}{4}$ $2\frac{1}{2}$
	Ditto................	5	1	40	4 $4\frac{1}{2}$
	Combalies	22	$2\frac{1}{4}$	6	$5\frac{1}{4}$ $5\frac{1}{2}$
	Ditto	30	$2\frac{1}{2}$	7	$5\frac{1}{4}$ $5\frac{1}{2}$
Hartie......	White combalies	22	$2\frac{1}{4}$	6	$2\frac{5}{8}$
	Black ditto	38	$2\frac{1}{2}$	$7\frac{1}{2}$	

The number of looms about Bengalore amounts, I understand, to about 5000. There is a small manufacture of silk cloth at Bengalore and at Hurry-hurr; but I have observed the same kind of cloth in many parts of the coast. The raw silk comes from Bengal by a very circuitous rout, and is in consequence very dear.

The greatest discouragement to trade in the Mysore is the pointed aversion of the Government of the country to assist a merchant in collecting his outstanding debts. Nothing can be disposed of in any quantity for ready money, and when the arrears are to be paid the Amildar † protects the debtor for a trifling sum.

XXII. SHARE OF THE PRODUCE ALLOWED THE FARMER.

In most places the high grounds are let at a quit rent, while the low or rice ground is let for shares, and these are proportioned to the facility with which every particular spot can be watered.

The cultivator in most parts of the Mysore has nominally one half of the whole produce; but when we deduct the expenses of cultivation, and the dues of the village and Circar servants, this half is reduced to a mere trifle. Hence I am not astonished at the great reluctance which the ryots show to cultivate Circar lands, and at the facility with which they bestow enams ‡ on Bramins. For in the first place they give away what does not belong to

* A punjum is 120 threads lengthways. † The Collector of Revenues. ‡ Gifted lands.

them, and in the second place, by cultivating the enam lands, they get afterwards a real half not liable to any deduction whatever.

But the greatest bane to cultivation on the coast is the *mustacabol*, or advance of money to the Circar before the grain is in the ground, and again at stated periods before it is cut down. As no zemindar, renter, or cultivator has money to advance, he is obliged to have recourse to the *soukars*, or money-lenders, who on a man's known honesty advance money at the rate of two per cent. per month and a present of five per cent. upon the advance. For the second and third kist *, as the crops are then well advanced, a present is not demanded; but when the fourth is to be paid the crops must be mortgaged. Most lenders insist upon an immediate sale, and become themselves the purchasers at the bazar price, which is at that time five or ten per cent. lower than at any other period of the year.

The loss to the cultivator, therefore, upon a thousand pagodas worth of land is as follows:

The first kist 250 at two per cent. per month, for six months......	30
Present of five per cent.	12¼
For the second kist, interest for four and a half months	22¼
For the third kist, interest for two months	10
For the fourth kist, interest for one ditto	5
Loss on immediate sale of grain, ten per cent.	100
	180

The usurers only derive advantage from this sum; it is exceedingly distressing to the losers of it, while Government derives, comparatively speaking, but little advantage from the ready money.

The zemindars manage matters in a strange way; availing themselves of that fondness for distinction which every Indian possesses. They cajole the poor sowkar by fair promises, presents, and familiar condescension, till they drain him of all his money, and then they proceed in the usual method of seizing his effects and turning him adrift: it may be said, that the loss to the revenue would be the amount of the interest of the money at present paid in advance, but the legal interest is trifling when compared with that exacted by usurers. The revenue would run no risk from the abolition of this oppressive practice, if care were taken to secure the payment of the

* Instalment of revenue collection.

whole of the kist before the removal of the crop. I am aware that this oppressive mode of levying money is known to Government, and that, in many instances, steps have been taken to remedy it, by prohibiting mustacaboles to be paid by the cultivators. But this only serves to alleviate the evil a very little, nor is this palliative ever applied where the kist of the general revenue is expected at seasons when cultivation is at a stand.

XXIII. LANGUAGE.

The language spoken by all classes of people, from the eastern Ghauts to the inland range of hills, is chiefly Telinga: Canary and Tamul are understood by most persons; and the former indeed is spoken promiscuously with Telinga. As soon as we cross the inland range of hills at Nidgcul, we hear no other language but Canary; it continues as far as Hurryhurr, where Mahratta begins to be understood, and is used in all writings and accounts.

Telinga prevails in the eastern or Sîrah hills, which separate the Mysore from the ceded districts.

All people of distinction understand Mahratta, and all public orders from the Durbar are written in that language.

Hindostani is also understood, but not so universally as might be imagined.

XXIV. LEARNING.

I have found but few learned men among the Hindoos in the Mysore, as during the reign of Hyder and Tippoo the sciences were by no means encouraged: medicine, or rather quackery, alone was rewarded by moormen; hence pretenders to this science, makers of nostrums and provocatives, and sorcerers, are to be found in abundance wherever the Mahometan religion is established.

All books of science are written either in Sanscrit, in the Dewanagar character, or in Telinga, in the southern, and Mahratta, in the northern provinces; the few Canary works are only translations: as for example, the Ramayana and Bhagavat; and indeed these scarcely deserve the name of translations, as in them the conjunctions only are Canary, and the rest Sanscrit. The songs used by the dancing women are almost all Telinga; the songs of the common people are in that language even in those parts of the country where it is not understood. They have likewise considerable collections of Moorish and Persian songs.

Their dramas are mere travesties of the national epic works, as of the Ramayana and Bhagavat: the promptor, as he might be called, recites the most remarkable passages before every scene, in Sanscrit verse, understood very often by nobody present, not even by himself. It is then acted and spoken over again in the vulgar tongue, and much wit and satire are frequently displayed by the actors: no class of people, not even the ministers of state (*Dewans*) or Bramins, are spared: the former are represented as avaricious, selfish, intriguing; and the latter as hypocritical, dishonest, supercilious, arrogant, dastardly rogues.

In the northern Circars I have seen women of the dancing cast introduced as actresses; but in the Mysore they always employ Bramin boys to act the female parts, and some of them perform the characters with so much skill, that we almost forget they are not women.

A merry Andrew, or buffoon, is a person never to be dispensed with.

Comedies of this kind last for seven or eight nights, beginning at seven in the evening and continuing till day light.

What learning exists is entirely confined to the Bramins; the lower classes are satisfied if they understand common arithmetic, reading, and writing, and few of the cultivators of land possess even this degree of knowledge.

XXV. PAINTING.

The palaces built by Hyder and his son Tippoo Sultan are all upon one plan, but I do not consider myself as adequate to give a description of them: the brilliancy of the colours with which they are painted have attracted the notice of all who have had an opportunity of seeing them. On that account I conceive it will be interesting to give an account of the way in which these colours are prepared and laid on.

The gold colour, so lavishly applied, is one of the best counterfeits that can well be conceived. To make this colour the following articles must be got ready:—linseed oil, two sīrs; chandrasam (yellow resin) one sīr; dickamalie (aloe socotrina), six drams; musambram (a yellowish green gum resin, mixed with small bits of wood: when burnt it smells like benzoin, but when fresh from the bazar like asa fœtida) six drams; kasturi passpu (the bulb either of the curcuma rotunda, or of the amomum zedarea), three drams.

To prepare the *gunna*, as it is called, take a mud pot, coat the bottom of it with red earth, and after it is heated over a fire, put the resin into it and melt it, then mix with it the linseed oil, which must have been previously made boiling hot in another vessel. Now add the remaining articles previously reduced to a fine powder, and boil the mixture over a slow fire for about two hours, or till a drop of it taken out with a stick and put upon a plank may be drawn out when cool into long thin threads. In this state the matter is called gunna.

For gilding take a sīr of tin, and beat it out into very fine leaves, mix it with one quarter of a sīr of liquified glue, and beat them together into a homogeneous mass; wash it with water, and keep it for use.

When a silver colour is wanted, this mixture of tin and glue, moistened with water, is to be laid upon the plank or wall to be painted; it is then rubbed with a serpentine stone till the silver colour appear.

When a gold colour is wanted, the gunna is on three successive days laid thinly over the silver coloured spot with a brush.

To make a white colour, take four parts of white lead and one part of gum arabic, mix them with water, and when the paint is to be used add as much water as is sufficient to bring it to the requisite consistency.

For a green colour take two seers of linseed oil and one seer of chandrasam; mix them in the same manner as described for the gunnah. Lay it with a brush over the white paint, and powder verdigris over it through a fine cloth.

A red colour is made of four parts of cinnabar and one of gum, rubbed together, and mixed wth water when wanted for use.

For a pink colour, white lead, poti (cotton impregnated with a red water colour sold in the Bazars), gum, and water are mixed together.

For yellow, four parts of orpiment and one of gum arabic are mixed up with water.

To make the ground for any colour, take senku sudda (the finest levigated pipe clay), mix it with a little gum and water, and lay it on the walls or plank which is to be coloured, it is afterwards to be rubbed with a stone till it becomes quite smooth. On this ground the various colours above described are to be laid.

XXVI. MANUFACTURE OF LEATHER.

A very pretty kind of red morocco is manufactured at Hurryhurr by a set of people called Muchiker. It is in the first place tanned.

The goat skins (for these only are employed) are dried in the sun for one day; next day they are washed in the river, rolled up and put into a pot, with a mixture (for each skin) of one handful of common salt, as much water, and half of that quantity of the milk of wild cotton (asclepias gigantea). After the skins have been soaked in this mixture for four days the pot is filled up with water, and the leather suffered to remain four days longer in it: the hair now comes easily off the skins when scraped by a piece of broken pot. The leather thus cleaned is laid in the shade, and when dry is rolled up and kept in a house for two or three days, in a place secure from smoke and from insects; it is then soaked for eight hours in pure water, and scraped with a piece of earthen ware till it becomes quite white.

Before the leather is dyed it is soaked for one night in a pucca sīr of water which has been mixed with a handful of jona meal, (holcus sorghum) and warmed on the fire; in the morning it is taken out and dried with a piece of cloth: when well dried it is soaked again for half an hour in water with which one seer of tamarinds has been mixed; it is then spread on a mat and the colour applied.

For the red colour take $\frac{1}{4}$ kutcha seer of lac (18 drams), allie toppalu (leaves of the mimecylon capitellatum) $\frac{1}{8}$ of a dub weight, and the same quantity of the salt extracted from washermans earth (carbonate of soda): pound these ingredients together, boil $\frac{1}{4}$ of a seer of water in a place where there is no wind; put the pounded mass into it, and keep it for a quarter of an hour over a slow fire. To ascertain whether it has acquired the requisite consistence, dip a jonna straw into it; if the liquid does not run down the straw when turned up it is sufficiently done, but if it runs the boiling must be continued for some time longer.

The leather (previously extended on a mat) is, at three different times, rubbed over with this liquid, it is then thrice sprinkled over with tamarind water, and lastly it is steeped for five or six days in a liquid composed of three seers of water and one seer of pounded tanghedu bark* (cassia auriculata): every morning it is taken out, washed a little, and again replaced, till at last it is well washed in clear water and dried: thus prepared it has a fine crimson colour, and is very soft.

* This bark contains a great quantity of tannin.

XXVII. DYING OF COTTON RED.

Not far from Hurryhurr, about six miles north, is a village called Sarti, where red cotton yarn is dyed. This colour is of an inferior quality, owing, I conceive, rather to the imperfect and negligent mode of proceeding, than to any defect of the materials employed. The process is conducted on the same principles as those followed on the coast where cotton is dyed with chay root: instead of this article, considered indispensable on the coast, the roots of the morinda umbellata, called by the Gentoos *togaru*, and by the Canadys *hempu tsira*, are employed; the process is as follows:

Take ten kutcha seer ($3\frac{1}{3}$ lb.) of white cotton yarn, and soak it in five seer ($1\frac{2}{3}$ lb.) of Gingelie oil (sesamum orientale); a strong ley is then made of the ashes of the milk hedge (euphorbia tirucalli) and the yarn steeped in it for four nights, during the day being always dried in the sun. It is then washed in brackish water and dried in the sun. No other mordant is used, but the workman immediately proceeds to the dying process.

Five seers of togaru root, finely powdered, are put into a pot of water together with the yarn, and kept all night over a fire made of cow dung; in the morning it is taken out, and dried during the day in the sun: the same process is repeated for two successive nights and days, after which the yarn is ready for the market.

The colour of the yarn is a dirty crimson, which fades when the cloth is used for any time: in the Harponelly country it is said that yarn is much better dyed with the same materials; indeed I have no doubt, that if the same niceties in animalizing the cotton were followed in the Mysore as are practised on the coast, the root of the morinda would be found to answer just as well as the chay root. The morinda is a shrub which grows plentifully in the jungles of the northern parts of the Mysore. It affords, by a different treatment, a yellow colour, and might perhaps be exported as a useful dying material.

The mode of making combalies in the Mysore, and indeed in all parts of the country, is as follows: the wool of fifty sheep, contracted for at one Kanty pagoda, amounts to one maund. It is cleaned, carded, and spun, and being put into the loom is rubbed over with a thin pultaceous mass, made of kernels of tamarinds, beat into powder and then boiled: after this the combalies are woven in the usual way. A common one is woven in the course of six or eight days.

TRACT III.

ACCOUNT OF THE DIAMOND MINES IN INDIA.

DIAMONDS have hitherto been found only in India and Brazil; and few or no accurate descriptions of the geognostic structure of the countries in which they occur have been laid before the public. Having visited four or five different diamond mines in the peninsula of Hindostan, and examined the nature of the strata in which these precious minerals are found, I propose in the present essay to give a short description of the result of my observations.

The first diamond mine that I visited was at Mallavilly, a village sixteen miles west south-west of Ellore. My visit was paid on the 25th of May, 1795. Mallavilly is one of seven villages in this district near which diamond mines exist. Hence it would appear that the gem is scattered over a considerable extent of country in this part of India. The names of the other six villages in this neighbourhood near which diamonds are found, and where mines formerly existed or still exist, are, Ganipartāla or Partāl, Atkūr, Burthenypādu, Pertalla, Wustapilly, and Codavettykallu. They all belonged formerly to a powerful Zemindar, called Opparow. But for the last eighty years the Nizam has taken them under his own management.

It is said that about a century ago some mountaineers found at the foot of a hill, after a shower of rain, some large stones which proved to be diamonds of inestimable value. Opparow becoming acquainted with this discovery, immediately set people to work upon the hill, who found a prodigious number of very large diamonds. The news of this acquisition soon reached the Nizam, who was the Sovereign. He dispatched his peons and took possession of the villages. Since that time persons authorised by him are alone entitled to search here for diamonds.

Being unacquainted with the nature of the different treaties which have been ratified since that period, I cannot inform my readers how it came to pass that even after the English East India Company got possession of this Circar, these villages were retained by the Nizam, though all the rest of the country on this side of the Kistnah was ceded. Tradition says, "that as soon as Opparow was obliged to give up his mines large stones ceased to be found, and that the size of the diamonds extracted from the earth never exceeded that of a horse gram or chick pea, though before that period they were as large as common flints."

The traditional account of the discovery of the diamond mine at Codavetty Kallu, one of these seven villages, is as follows:—A shepherd one day found near a ravine in the neighbourhood, some stones which appeared to him serviceable flints. He picked up several, and used them accordingly. Sometime after, the poor fellow, while at the residence of Opparow, took in an unlucky moment one of these stones out of his pocket, and employed it to strike a light to kindle his tobacco. The stone was observed by one of the Rajah's lambădies *, who knowing its value, made inquiry how it had come into the possession of the shepherd. The good man heedlessly related all that he knew. He was conducted to the Rajah, who easily prevailed upon him to point out this unknown residence of Stree Latchmie, the goddess of riches. The Rajah was on this occasion so condescending as to go himself to the spot, and was not a little surprised at the riches which the goddess had reserved for him. Penetrated with grateful sentiments to the invisible harbinger of his good fortune, and to the genius of the place, he immediately ordered an offering to be brought, which, for more than one reason, consisted of the head and blood of the poor shepherd. His wife and children being found, upon examination, entirely ignorant of the discovery, were spared, and taken care of by the Rajah as long as the mines belonged to him. Bullock loads of diamonds were found, it is said, near that nullah, until at length the Nizam, being apprized of the discovery, claimed the ground as his own, and deprived the Zemindar of it for ever. But he had been so industrious, during the short time that the mines were in his possession, that all the large gems were removed, and the Nizam was able to obtain only small diamonds of comparatively inconsiderable value.

I have little doubt that the foundation of this account is correct, though it may very well be asked what is become of the bullock loads of diamonds. For at present the family of Opparow is rather poor and dependent, and resident at Ellore.

* Slaves.

Diamond mines are found in different parts of the ceded districts, especially in the eastern and central divisions. In the Chennūr Taluk *, in which Cuddapah is the largest town, there are two places called Condapetta and Ovalumpally, where diamonds occur. In the next taluk, on the west side of this, diamonds are dug at Lamdūr and Pinchetgapādu. Several mines exist near Gooty, and about fifteen gows † from that place a famous diamond mine exists in the Kistna river.

The diamond mines near Cuddapah are about seven miles north-east from the town, on both banks of the Pennar river, which in this place washes the foot of a range of hills. The country in which they occur is bounded on the east by the range of hills just mentioned, which run nearly north and south for about fifteen miles, with a sharp little interrupted ridge. Opposite to Cuddapah they meet another similar ridge, stretching for about eight miles from north-east to south-west. This second range meets a third range running nearly due west, for about twenty miles, and forming the southern boundary of the district. To the westward the country continues plain and open to a great extent: to the northward we see hills and ranges connected with the eastern mountains.

The southern ridges have at their tops a layer of rock between ten and twenty feet thick, which forms a kind of cap, and prevents the mountains from wasting too fast. This cap consists of a kind of jasper or compact felspar, of which indeed the whole hills are composed. I have observed a similar stony cap in other parts of India, particularly about Chittledroog and Hurryhurr; but at these places the hill and the cap consist of different kinds of rock, whereas here they are similar.

Within half a mile of the foot of these hills the country is quite covered with loose stones. This is the case likewise with the hills themselves, which on that account are often very difficult to climb. They are covered with small trees, and yield to the eye, as soon as the rains set in, a fine refreshing appearance. The perpendicular height of the highest range I consider as about 1000 feet above the level of the country.

In the low country the most common stones are a black compact limestone or marble, containing pyrites and a calcareous tuff, both used by the natives in building. The soil near the hills is a red loam, seldom sandy, and in the plain in general a black vegetable mould; the bed situated under the former often a black shell mud, and under the latter always a calcareous tuff.

* The division of a large district. † A gow is eight miles.

The Pennar river comes from the westward. It meets the eastern hills about ten miles north of Cuddapah, and nearly opposite to that place makes its way into the Carnatic through a valley in this range of hills.

The whole of the country is very little elevated above the level of the sea, for the barometer usually stands at 29·7 inches.

The mines at Cuddapah have, it is said, been worked for several hundred years with various success. Not long ago a large diamond was found, which has produced a lawsuit not yet decided. It is said to weigh 1¼ pagoda, or 70 grains, to be full of flaws, and on that account not to be worth more than 1000 pagodas. These mines are within half a mile of the eastern range of hills, and about as far east from the river and Candapetta, and on grounds belonging to a small village called Kanaperty. They are surrounded by cultivated fields, and have the appearance of heaps of stones and pits half filled with rubbish, in the middle of which we find a number of people at work in a new mine.

The labourers were offended at my coming on horseback near the mines, and objected strongly to my approaching the one in which they were at work: saying that Ammawāru (the sanguinary goddess of riches) would not allow such liberties to be taken, at a place under her particular influence. They were, however, soon pacified on being assured that I had come among them by leave of her ladyship.

The mines are pits of unequal extent and small depth, and usually have a four-sided form. The one in which they were at work had been opened only eight or ten days: it was sixteen feet square, and a few days before I saw it they had come to the diamond bed in one corner of it.

All the different places in which the diamond has been hitherto found consist either in alluvial soil or in rocks of the latest formation, and containing such a great proportion of rounded pebbles as to have rather the appearance of a conglomerate than any other species of stone. The diamonds are not scattered through the whole of the beds from the surface in the diamond mines to the greatest depth hitherto dug; but confined to a single bed, always harder than the rest of the accompanying beds, and usually not exceeding a foot or two in thickness. The structure of all the places in which diamonds occur being similar, it will be sufficient to give an account of the beds found in these mines at Cuddapah, which I examined with as much care as possible.

The uppermost, or superficial stratum, consists of sand, or gravel, mixed with a small proportion of loam. Its thickness scarcely exceeds a foot and a half. Immediately under it is a bed of stiff bluish or black mud, similar to what we see in places that have been inundated. It is about four feet thick, and contains no stones. The diamond bed comes next, and is easily distinguished from the incumbent bed, by the great number of large rounded stones which it contains. It is about two feet, or two and a half thick, and is composed of large round stones, pebbles, and gravel, cemented together by clay. It was quite wet at the time that I saw it, owing to the preceding rains; but, in other seasons, it is as dry as the bed which lies immediately above it. In the Ellore district, the diamond stratum is covered by thick strata of calcareous tuff.

The mode of working a diamond mine is this: after all the superincumbent beds, and the large stones in the diamond bed, are removed out of the mine, the small gravel and the other constituents of the bed are carried to a small distance, and put into a cistern about eight feet square and three deep. In this situation water is poured upon it, which separates the lighter loamy particles. The gravel and small stones, which sink to the bottom, are then thrown into a heap close to the cistern, from which they are conveyed to a smooth plain of about twenty feet square, made of hardened clay. Upon this plain the whole is thinly spread. The gravel in this position being slightly moistened, six or seven people go over it several times in succession. The first time, they pick out only the large stones; the second and subsequent times, the smaller gravel is carefully turned over with the flat of the hand, whilst they as carefully watch for the spark from the diamond, which invariably strikes the eye.

These people are not guarded, and do not seem to be under any controul. Every thing is left implicitly to their good faith; which at all times is, perhaps, the best way to ensure fidelity. They do not go in any particular direction over the gravel. At the Candapetty mines they went nearly from east to west, backward and forward; and at Ovalumpally, from north to south. At both places they were working at the same hour of the day, and in cloudy weather.

They would not allow any of my followers to touch the heap of unsearched gravel, though they did not prevent me from doing it. A present of a gold fanam (about sixpence) made the headman very communicative.

He pointed out to me a variety of small stones in the heaps that were thrown away, which he assured me always indicated the presence of diamonds wherever they occur in beds at some depth under ground. These stones were as follows:

1. Tella bendu (in Telinga). Pebbles of a white, earthy, or chalk-like colour, rounded, or with obtuse angles. They are mostly hornstone, the nucleus of which has a bluish brown or grey colour, while the outside is decomposed into a white pipe-clay. Sometimes they consist of jasper, coated in the same way; and sometimes they are species of felspar. The white decomposed crust of pipe-clay seems to be the grand characteristic. It was pointed out to me before, in other diamond mines, though not so forcibly.

2. Binga bendu. Pellucid quartz; pebbles of a lemon yellow colour, and containing distinct, small, shining particles.

3. Patcha bendu. Pebbles with a green covering, or throughout of a green colour. (Pistazite.—Epidote of Haüy). I was long at a loss what name to give to this species of mineral, which occurs abundantly in different parts of the Mysore. Sometimes I have conceived it to be actinolite, at other times to be jade. It is a frequent constituent of sienite in this country, and usually occurs in indistinct acicular crystals, of the hardness of quartz, and nearly of the same specific gravity. Its colour is light green, verging upon yellow. Its lustre is resinous. I have observed it in some places lying over sienite, and then it has all the appearance of jade. It is looked upon as one of the principal characteristics of the diamond bed. But the outside of the stone alone is attended to; for I have found the inside consisting of different species, as hornblende, jasper, felspar, &c. all going indifferently under the name of patcha bendu, provided they had the same external aspect.

4. Gajja bendu. Pebbles with a corroded ochry incrustation. Eruptions on the skin are called gajja in Telinga. Hence probably the name has been borrowed to indicate the appearance of this kind of pebble. The quantity of ochre on the outside of these stones forms the distinguishing mark; for within they differ in their nature. Like the rest of these pebbles, they are indiscriminately hornblende, felspar, quartz, and sometimes of the abovementioned green stone. They are always in a state of decomposition.

5. Baggira. Red, brown, bluish, and black jasper, pebbles, and hornstone, are the minerals distinguished by this name.

6. Karla. Basalt pebbles.

7. Yerra bendu. Sandstone, with an ochry red crust.

8. Kanna. Small globular ironstone, of the size of a hazle-nut. They constitute the most remarkable pebbles in the Ovalumpilly mines. The external colour is brown; the internal, bluish grey. Hardness, that of fluor spar, or rather greater; fracture approaching to even; dull; streak metallic.

9. Corundum. Sometimes found in small fragments, and considered as the most important of all pebbles.

Besides these, there occur a few other stones, which are distinguished by particular names, but which do not deserve a separate description. The greatest number of them consist of sandstones of different kinds.

In the northern diamond mines, particularly those of Partēl, I found in the diamond bed a great number of fine calcedony and carnelian pebbles and garnets.

The larger stones form the greatest part of the diamond bed. They are mostly a coarse hornstone, of a rounded shape, and of the size of a man's head. Their colour is usually grey, and their fracture splintery, often flat conchoidal. Their hardness is not very great. Among them are found jaspers of different kinds, mostly of a coarse texture, and sandstones; all of them in a state of considerable disintegration. They are, in fact, nothing but fragments of the neighbouring mountains. As to the smaller pebbles, and gravel, they have either come from a distance or are the remains of rocks no longer to be found, which have been worn away and destroyed by lapse of time, or by some great catastrophe. The country rises sensibly as we advance westward. Hence it is barely possible that the bed may have come from that quarter, although there are no indications of any such transportation.

The Ovalumpilly mines are on the west side of the river, about six miles from Cuddapah, and three miles from the mines which we have just been describing. They are situated on a gentle ascent, about half a mile from the Pennar, in a well cultivated country, and within a very short distance of three villages. They are chiefly on ground belonging to Ovalumpilly. They are of more recent discovery than the other mines, and it is only forty years since they have been worked. They have rather the appearance of intrenchments than of mines. The soil of the fields surrounding them is sandy, with a small admixture of loam. It forms the surface of the ground where the mines lie, and is not more than a foot in thickness.

Below it is a red clay, not unlike good garden earth, about three feet thick; and immediately below this is the diamond bed. The mine which I examined had been begun only eight days before, and it was only four days since they had reached the diamond bed. This bed resembled, in its nature and constituents, the one which I have already described, excepting that the proportion of large rounded stones was not so great. They were carried out of the mine together with the pebbles, and some women and boys were employed in clearing them from the earth, which stuck to them with some firmness. They are then thrown aside till wanted to fill up the mine, which they do here as they work on.

The diamond bed, both here and in the last described mine, seems to follow the direction of the river, and is, at different parts, of unequal breadth. The diamonds found in it are in the form of small flat or round pebbles, and, as far as I could learn from the miners, never occur crystallized. They are, however, said to be of a superior lustre and hardness, and much better than those found further westward. A few days after I had been here, they found a diamond weighing seven manjalies (fourteen carats), estimated at about 200 pagodas value.

The Hindoos distinguish four kinds of diamond, differing from each other in beauty and value, and called, 1. Bramha—2. Chetra—3. Vysea, and 4. Sudra. These names are derived from the casts into which the whole nation is divided. The bramha diamond is described as of the colour of clear milk; the chetra, of clear honey; the vysea, of cream; and the sudra, of a frog colour, or a smoky greyish white.

The following is a list of the prices of the rough stones at the mines:—

		Madras Pagodas †.
1 Manjaly weight * of	Bramha,	10
	Chetra,	8
	Vysea,	6
	Sudra,	5
2 Ditto ...	Bramha,	24
	Chetra,	20
	Vysea,	18
	Sudra,	16

* One-eighth of a pagoda, or two carats.

† A Madras pagoda is ten per cent. better than a star pagoda, which is equal to eight shillings.

		Madras Pagodas.
3 Manjalies weight of....	Bramha,...........	40
	Chetra,............	37
	Vysea,............	34
	Sudra,............	30
4 Ditto................	Bramha,...........	80
	Chetra,............	76
	Vysea,............	70
	Sudra,............	60
5 Ditto................	Bramha,...........	100
	Chetra,............	90
	Vysea,............	85
	Sudra,............	80
6 Ditto................	Bramha,...........	150
	Chetra,............	140
	Vysea,............	130
	Sudra,............	120
7 Ditto................	Bramha,...........	250
	Chetra,............	240
	Vysea,............	220
	Sudra,............	200
8 Ditto................	Bramha,...........	400
	Chetra,............	380
	Vysea,............	360
	Sudra,............	350
Two diamonds of equal size, weighing both together one manjely, are worth of	Bramha,...........	8
	Chetra,............	6
	Vysea,............	4
	Sudra,............	3
Three diamonds of equal size, weighing altogether one manjaly, are worth, of	Bramha,...........	7
	Chetra,............	6
	Vysea,............	5
	Sudra,............	4

These are prices of stones free from speck, flaw, or crack. The cut stones are valued in a different way. It is often the interest of the dealer to cut large stones into a number of smaller ones.

I was informed that, in this place, the miners are restricted to the spot which they at present work; that it is nearly exhausted; and that, for a long time past, they have not found diamonds of any considerable size. Many places in the neighbourhood they consider as very promising. They pointed out one place at Candapetta, close to the spot in which they were working, and another very extensive one near Currapully. From this last spot they entertain great expectations, as the diamond bed in it is about six feet in thickness, the smaller pebbles in greater abundance, and the soil of a *redder colour* than any where else in the neighbourhood. The land belongs to a Pagoda, or a Bramin; and they say it is not worth more than seventeen rupees a year. The proprietor would give it up for eighty pagodas ready money, but Colonel Munro had refused permission to work it. I mention this circumstance merely to show that the country is by no means exhausted, and that abundance of diamonds might be procured should an increased demand for them arise.

The farmers, or ryots, are also very averse to the extension of the diamond mines, and oppose their encroachments with all their influence. But I think that these men might find plenty of ground to cultivate in the country, much better worth their labour than these particular spots.

The old grounds are rented, I understand, to a headman, who pays the Company the yearly sum of 130 pagodas for ten mines, which he is at liberty to work, at Cundapetta, Osalumpully, and their subordinate villages. He usually works three or four of these mines himself, and lets out the others at the rate of nine rupees a month for each mine. For all diamonds above a pagoda weight, of whatever kind, he is obliged to pay one-third of the value to the Company.

In these districts, the miners, I was informed, are paid by the month. Sixteen persons, men and women, are employed in each mine, and each receives one pagoda of wages per month. Half of them are employed in mining, and the other half in carrying on the subsequent operations. These people are inhabitants of the neighbouring villages, suders, who, from their infancy, are brought up to this work, and with the ideas necessary for the undertaking, they pride themselves on their honesty to their employers.

I tried to persuade these workmen to give me, for a considerable premium, a basket full of the unwashed diamond bed, but was absolutely refused a single handful, till I obtained it from the owner himself. At Ovalumpelly, I took it out of a mine which they had been obliged to abandon, because it had encroached on the cultivated grounds. From the renter I understood that the usual profits on working a mine are reckoned at 5000 pagodas on an expenditure of 2000; and, in my opinion, it cannot be less, the undertaking being considered as a lottery, in which there are blanks as well as prizes; and the real owners seldom or never appear, but entrust the *management* to hirelings, who may be rogues, but who, at all events, must be paid well. The works in the Kistna are, by all accounts, carried on in a different manner.

In the year 1808, I paid a visit to the diamond mines at Banaganpilly, in the Dekan; and, as the bed in which the diamonds occur at that place is a solid, it may be worth while to give an account of it, in order that we may throw all the light in our power upon the nature of the beds in which this precious and rare production of nature has been deposited.

As Banaganpilly is a place of some consequence, its geographical position will easily be found by consulting the map; but I shall here state a few particulars respecting its mineralogy. It is situated at the northern extremity of the plain which commences at the southern range of hills, near Cuddapah, and about sixty miles from that place. It participates in the same climate, the same soil, and the same vegetable productions. The country rises gently from the river Pennar, till within a few miles of Bannaganpilly; and where it is most elevated, at the distance of forty or fifty miles from Cuddapah, some crops are cultivated which are not to be seen at the latter place: as flax, safflour, and wheat.

In India, where art has done little, the general productions of the soil are the best criterions of its composition. The only exception to this rule is rice, which will grow in any soil, provided a sufficient supply of water can be procured. As the soil between Cuddapah and Banaganpilly is mostly vegetable earth, jonna (holcus sorghum) and sajja (holcus spicatus) are chiefly attended to. When it is poorer, and a mixture of red loam, gravel, and vegetable soil, as near the hills, raghie (gleucena corocana) and aruga (paspalum frumentaceum) are the only kinds of grain that will grow.

There are few or no tanks north of the Pennar. Near the villages, the water is raised from wells, for the cultivation of a little rice, and for gardens; while, for food, it is frequently brought from a small river that winds through the country. This river comes from the west, and has frequently very steep and high banks.

About forty miles north of Cuddapa, a range of hills make their appearance to the westward. At first they take a northerly direction, then bend easterly, and at last run nearly due east. This range, together with another to the westward of Cuddapah, that of Ganjecotta, encloses the plain in which the diamond mines are situated on every side. The former consists chiefly of hills, which, in this country, are called table hills. They are quite straight at top, and usually level for some extent, so that even villages are built on them, and some cultivation is carried on at their very summits. Such hills, in the Mysore, consist chiefly of a kind of decomposed green stone, but here, I believe, they are principally slate-clay; for this stone is so abundant in the country through which I passed, that all houses and walls are built of them, which gave the villages an uncommonly regular and comfortable appearance. Calcareous tuff, and black marble, are also found in that part of the country. Hence the water in the wells is often brackish. The black slaty limestone, at Door, is well known, and sent to all parts of the country.

The village of Banaganpilly is situated within four or five miles of the hills, and lies upon their south side. Combum lies about sixty miles east from it, and Goothy about fifty miles south-west. It is the residence of a Jaghirdār * (Assad Ali Khan) of the Nizam's; who, if we can judge from the fine new town (Kottapettah) which he has built, at the distance of about two miles from Banaganpilly, must be a good and a wise manager. He keeps a train of one dummer, one fifer, and about 400 sepoys, foot and cavalry.

As soon as I arrived at the place, I sent a message to acquaint him with my object, and to request his permission to visit the mine; which I knew was the best way of ensuring his good will. One of his officers waited upon me in consequence, with orders to facilitate my pursuits. His attention I easily secured, by a present of a few bottles of wine, of which I deprived myself for some days without the least scruple †.

* A kind of feudal chief.

† Wine and brandy are articles with which every traveller in India should be always supplied, as they almost constantly serve to gain the hearts of the most stubborn Moormen, and even of the Bramin, who sometimes rejects the offer of a bottle in the day-time with apparent indigna-

The country here is sandy and stony, and less fertile than it is a few miles to the south: the stones are chiefly conglomerates, composed of siliceous materials. The village of Banaganpilly is built at the foot of a low ridge of hills, on which the diamond mines are situated; these hills run nearly east and west, and consist of distinct conical elevations from one hundred to two hundred feet perpendicular height. The farthest east of these hills is said to yield the best diamonds, but it has been so completely ransacked on all sides, that most of the mines at present wrought are in the hill immediately on its west side. There is scarcely any vegetation on these hills, a few prickly plants excepted, which grow between the stones and a tree or two near the first ascent.

A very desultory and destructive mode of mining is followed. A man chuses a piece of ground, and if not immediately lucky, which is frequently the case, he speedily leaves it; another person succeeds, and makes an opening at the distance of a few yards: he discovers a favourable spot, and continues to work it for a little way, but finding a diminution in his earnings soon abandons it for another; by this method of proceeding much ground is wasted and much money lost. The undertaking is looked upon as a lottery, in which the enterprizers rather purchase than renew a ticket.

The mines are scarcely any thing else but deep holes, open at top; sometimes indeed the work is carried on for some extent under the rock, which is then supported by stone pillars: I saw none deeper than twenty feet. The gallery under the rock is so low, that the people are obliged to work in it sitting, a mode of working which an Indian prefers to every other. As most of the miners had left this place for the richer mines of the Kishna, I did not see them at work; I know only that they never employ gunpowder to blast the rock, though such an auxiliary would very much facilitate their labours. The solid rock of the hills (which by the bye is not quite destitute of diamonds) is an aggregate consisting chiefly of a coarse grey hornstone, with rounded pebbles of the same species, but of a fine variety of stone, or of jasper of different colours. At some depth this rock becomes a ferruginous sandstone, the grains of which are finely cemented together; and this kind of stone usually forms the roof of the floor of the mines. The floor is generally of a reddish brown colour with shining particles, and strikes fire with steel.

tion, and humbly solicits a glass at night. This happened to me during the present excursion.

Through this solid rock they are obliged to make their way before they arrive at the bed in which the diamonds are usually found. They commence at different places, as their fancy leads them, with a spot about twenty feet square, which, by iron instruments and steel wedges, they break into slabs or fragments of from one hundred to five hundred pounds weight. In this way they sink to the diamond bed, which is fifteen or twenty feet under the surface: this bed extends round the whole hill, and is as regular in its thickness and extent as the other unproductive beds in the same place; it consists of a conglomerate, composed of rounded silicious pebbles, quartz, chalcedony, and jasper of different colours from white to black. The cement appears to be a kind of clay approaching to wacke in its appearance, and is very small in quantity: thus it appears that the diamond bed is of the same nature with the rocks both above and below it, but it is distinguished from them by its superior hardness. The darker colours, as black, leek green, and brown prevail in some pieces; in others the lighter colours, as white, grey, and brick red, are the prevalent ones. Some of the pebbles, when broken, have a pellucid appearance, others exhibit arborizations or dendritical figures. [See plate III.]

This bed is seldom more than a foot in thickness; it is intimately connected with the beds both above and below it, and frequently differs from them in nothing but the greater quantity of pebbles which it contains. The nature of this bed determines the workmen either to uncover the whole, and work in open day, or to drive a gallery for a little way under the rock. This last method is had recourse to when the diamond bed is of trifling thickness, but very productive.

It is obvious that the nature of these hills is quite similar to that of the earthy diamond mine described in a former part of this tract; the constituents are the same in both cases, the whole difference lies in the cohesion. Here the pebbles are cemented together into a stone, while in the mines formerly described they lie loose in the state of gravel.

The diamonds found here are of an inconsiderable size, but usually in crystals; and I dare say they would be all found crystalized if another mode of extracting them were adopted. Those found in the earthy beds are mostly large, and less frequently of a regular form. This difference seems to depend upon the local situation. We may either suppose that the diamonds in the loose beds have been so long water-worn as to have been deprived of their angles, while those in the stony bed have not been subjected to so much attrition: or if such an explanation be inadmissible, we must suppose that in one case the crystalization has taken place so slowly as to constitute regular figures, while in the other case it has been hurried and rapid, and has produced figures destitute of regularity. There is something in the crystalization of the diamond which distinguishes it from all other crystals: the faces are all curvilenear, while in every other species of mineral all curves seem to be constantly excluded: are we to ascribe this difference to any thing peculiar to the diamond itself, or to the slowness with which the crystalization was effected? At present we can have no accurate ideas on the subject, because we are not acquainted with any substance capable of holding carbon in solution, and of course cannot show the particular circumstances under which its crystalization took place. That some solvent of the diamond exists we have every reason to believe, from the way in which that stone occurs, but it would be useless to speculate on the subject till that solvent shall be discovered.

In no place, as far as my information goes, is more than one diamond bed found under the same surface; but this bed frequently varies in its depth within a very limited distance. Near Cuddapah it is within three or six feet of the surface. At Mallavilly and Partēl, in the Masulipatam district, its depth is twenty feet; while at Banaganpilly it varies from ten to twenty feet in a very small extent of ground.

The mass containing the supposed diamonds is carefully cleared from the portions of the roof and floor of the mine that may be adhering to it; it is then carried to another spot of ground, where it is broken in pieces and gradually reduced by means of iron instruments to the size of very small gravel. It is evident that many diamonds must be broken by this mode of proceeding; indeed it is rather surprising that so many are procured in this way in regular crystals: the process followed for separating the diamonds from the rubbish is almost the same as that observed in other places. The portion wanted for immediate use is wetted, spread thinly upon a piece of ground about twenty feet square, over which the workmen go several times on their hands and knees, not losing or neglecting a fragment of diamond worth a penny: the moistening of the gravel is requisite to render the diamond conspicuous. The most common figures which I have seen the diamond assume are the double pyramid, the dodecahedron, and the lens.

The labourers here, owing probably to the small value of the diamonds, are under still less controul than even at Cuddapah; they are of the lowest order of Hindoos, called chucklers*, but from their occupation they are usually called hill people.

Even the better sort of people here, those, I mean, who employed workmen, displayed a very odd turn of mind. They allowed me to take as much as I pleased from any of their heaps of unsearched gravel, or from the diamond bed; but they absolutely refused to give any of it away with their own hands. They did not, however, reject the present of money, which I thought it right to give them.

There are more places in this vicinity where diamonds are found, either in a stony bed or in loose gravel. Some of these are worked, or have been worked in former times. The natives do not scruple to assign periods of thousands of years since the commencement of some of these workings. At present it is customary with these miners to go to the Kishnah, in the hot season, when the waters are lowest, and to spend the rest of the year in these mountain mines.

The diamonds of this place are bought up by merchants, who carry them to Madras, or to other places, where they are chiefly used in cutting those of a larger size. The large crystals would, I conceive, answer the European market, and might be cut into brilliants. For a carat containing five or six diamonds of the finest water, they ask seven rupees.

I have now stated all the facts that have come to my knowledge respecting the situations in which diamonds are found in India. I regret that they furnish so little light respecting the *formation* in which this gem was originally deposited. For all the diamond mines which I have seen can be considered as nothing else than alluvial soil. Nor is it easy to form an accurate notion of the kind of rock from which the pebbles constituting that soil originated. We find among them stones belonging to primitive rocks, and others, which are peculiar to the newest floetz trap. The strong bed at Banaganpilly has some faint resemblance to amygdaloid; but the exact similarity of its constituents to the other loose beds in which diamonds occur, renders it impossible for us to consider it as a true amygdaloid. I have never had an opportunity of seeing the various diamond mines situated beyond the Ganges. An accurate examination of them would enable us to determine whether diamonds are ever found any where else than in alluvial soil; for, in Brazil, it would appear, from the accounts of Mr. Mawe, that they are found in a situation similar to that in the Dekan.

* Tanners, shoemakers, hangmen.

TRACT IV.

OF THE COPPER MINES IN THE CALLASTRY, VENKATYGHERRY, AND NELLORE DISTRICTS, ON THE PENINSULA OF HINDOSTAN.

ABOUT the year 1797, I laid before government a memoir on the copper mines of Agricondalah, near Innacondah, which I had the good fortune to discover. And since that period I have been assiduously engaged in prosecuting the discovery, and in ascertaining the nature and value of the Indian copper ore. I propose, in this essay, to give an account of the facts which have come to my knowledge.

In the year 1799, I observed, in the mineralogical collection of Mr. Petrie *, some specimens of mountain green copper ore, about the size of a pidgeon's egg, or somewhat larger. Mr. Petrie informed me that he got them from a black man, who told him that they came from some northern district. In 1800, when at Madras, I was informed, by Mr. Westcott, of copper ore brought to him about two years before, from a place where it was found in abundance, and which, from his description, appeared to me to be of the same nature with Mr. Petrie's specimens. Hence it was not unlikely that both came from the same place. I was told that the ore occurred in a vein which ran through three different countries. Having obtained the Governor's leave to direct my pursuits to the ascertaining of this object on my way to the Mysore, I went from Vellore northwards, directly towards the principal place of the Callastry country, where I was in full expectation of receiving information on the subject.

At Bomrazepalliam, one of the valleys among those hills through which I passed, the sienite of the more southern parts of the Carnatic changes into hornblende, and a kind of trapose iron ore. After having cleared these hills, we come to other ranges, which have all the appearance of being stratified. They are mostly high, and at their summits naked, but continuous, and not so rugged as the more southern sienitic hills. They are com-

* Now Governor of Prince of Wales's Island.

posed chiefly of compact felspar. In the lower part of the country, and chiefly below the uppermost stratum of loam, there occurs a kind of greenstone, generally so much decomposed as to have assumed the appearance of pipe-clay. I observed this, especially in the bed of a river near Tripetty, where, at a distance, I took the white beds constituting the banks for white marl.

The prevailing rock of the Tripetty hills is a compact felspar. These hills are pretty high, and run south-east and north-west. But, as I had not an opportunity of ascending any of them, I am unable to communicate any accurate information respecting them, though their structure appears to me to merit attention.

At Venkatygherry, about eight miles from Callastry, where I expected to procure information, I staid three days; but notwithstanding the best endeavours of the collector, I could not obtain any intelligence whatever; and, had it not been for Mr. Petrie's kind endeavours at Madras, and a letter from him directing me to Pocūr, in the Condacūr Purgunnah, belonging to the Nellore district, I must have entirely given up the pursuit.

On leaving Venkatygherry, I had the Ghauts on my left. They continued to attend me at some distance, in low connected ranges; and here and there were some insignificant hills and small ranges on the right, or towards the sea. For the first two days the rocks in the low country were mostly foliated hornblende, which at last disappeared, and mica slate assumed its place. At the same time the soil became black, and a kind of marbly tuff appeared under it. This change took place when I was nearly in a line with Nellore. The water became then so brackish that it was scarcely drinkable. I do not know whether to abscribe to it, or to the violence of the heat, the serious illness with which I myself, and the greater part of my followers were attacked: an unfortunate circumstance, which not only retarded our progress, but almost frustrated our designs.

When I passed Chennūr, a village about twenty miles north from Nellore, I was informed that diamond mines existed in its vicinity, and that not many years ago diamonds had been found there of the first water, or, as the Hindoos express it, male diamonds. The black soil, and the capacious layers of calcareous tuff below it, may be considered as indirect proofs of the veracity of this assertion.

At Bramhanakaka, a place about ten miles farther north, I obtained the first positive account of the existence of copper mines in that vicinity;

though none of the inhabitants could tell exactly where. Some persons, however, were pointed out, who, about two years before, had carried the ore to Madras. They resided at Cavelly, six miles from the place where I was. Cavelly is within eight miles of Ramapatam, a place well known to all travellers, between Ongole and Nellore.

We were informed that the districts in which the copper mines existed were those of the Callastry and Venkatigherry country, which lie between the Nellore and Guntoor circars; and several places were proposed for examination by a man who professed to be perfectly acquainted with them; and Wangapādu was at length selected as the largest, and the one in which the ore was to be found in the greatest abundance.

Our route from Cavelly was at first north-west, for about twelve miles, to Gudlūr. From thence we travelled due west to Linga Samūdram, a village belonging to the Venkatygherry district. Here again the Ghauts appeared in view. They resembled those near Tripetty, but were higher. Several smaller ranges may be observed, running in different directions from the principal chain.

From the latter place the country becomes undulating, jungly, and stony. The stones are chiefly indurated marl and quartz. Where rocks appear they are composed of hornblende and quartz, with a scanty mixture of garnets.

Near Bombartipādu, a village about twenty-four miles from Tripetty, I found on the road pieces of emery, of the size of a hen's egg, or larger; which I discovered to have been detached from rocks which appeared at no great distance, and which were composed of hornblende, a good deal disintegrated, and emery. The hornblende had a foliated fracture, and consisted of irregular bundled columnar crystalizations. It was very soft; the emery was mixed with it, in pieces from the size of a pea to that of a hen's egg, or even larger.

From this place to Kattakindapalle, I found garnets, interspersed in mica slate and in sienite. I observed marl likewise, both in beds and in veins. Rich diamond mines had been formerly wrought in this place. Round the village several pits were to be seen, that looked not unlike old diamond mines. They were filled with water. The principal bed here was of marl.

Hills now make their appearance on all sides, and at a very small distance. Some few of them stand single, but the greater number are in ranges, which usually run eastward. The most extensive ranges are on the north side of the village, which is about forty miles west of Ongole. The Ghauts, visible to the west, in large connected chains stretching north and south, send some ranges eastwards, which, with very little interruption or variation in the nature of their constituents, approach the eastern ocean not far from Ongole. To these ranges belong several remarkable hills, as the Chicota, celebrated for the frequent earthquakes originating at it, and spreading over the country; and the Ongole hill, which seems to influence the compass in an uncommon degree. To them also belong the hills of Wangapādu, which contain the copper mines, the object of my search.

Wangapādu lies rather lower than the country from which we came. The soil round it is black; whereas at the former places it had been chiefly gravelly and stony. This village is very small. It lies at the foot of a rising ground, and opposite to a range of hills, which run nearly east and west, and which abruptly terminate their eastern extremity at this place.

On my arrival, I was astonished to find that my conductor had never been there before, but had proceeded with me upon the bare report that this was the place where the greatest quantity of copper had been found. He was, however, by no means discouraged, but led me to the high ground on the east side of the village, which had been pointed out to him by the villagers. The appearance of this place was not very favourable. We saw merely a few white quartz rocks rising here and there above the surface, and which exhibited no trace of any cupreous efflorescence upon their surface. The soil was red and stony, and covered with small jungle. At last an inhabitant of the village, with much hesitation, shewed us some rocks that had the appearance of having been broken and excavated, as far as they appeared above ground. He told us at the same time, that this place went under the name of the *brass mines*, and that those of copper were on yonder hills, pointing out a range at no great distance.

Suspecting that my conductor, who was a goldsmith, knew but little of those places, I sent for another person, who was said to be perfectly acquainted with all the copper mines in this neighbourhood. Every one, till this moment, seemed anxious to keep us ignorant of these mines; and, indeed, if we had asked about the most common stone, they would have denied its very existence, though, perhaps, sitting upon it at the very time the question was put to them. This to some may appear an exaggeration, but it is a literal fact which happened to myself. Being lately at Bomrāzepalliam, in a village called Allatū Satrum, where I was visited by the Aumildar and one of the Rajah's Sirdars, I asked, during the course of conversation, whether any limestone could be got there. They hesitated for some time, but, at last, unanimously assured me that not a thing of the kind could be found in the Rajah's country. Yet, not fifty yards from the choultry, people were picking up limestones out of the black ground; three or four limekilns were smoaking in our view, and the very choultry itself was a storehouse for chunam*. I was told the very same story respecting iron, which they said came from Madras; though, not two miles from the place, there were a number of iron furnaces, where the metal was smelted in considerable quantities. This strange conduct originated in both places from the same cause: the mandate of the Rajah to conceal every thing, as far as possible, from the prying eyes of an European.

The man who had been sent for, made his appearance about ten o'clock. He was, at that time, an inhabitant of one of the Commum villages, and therefore under no restraint in this district. He acknowledged that, according to the tradition of his ancestors, (and he was himself an old man), the adjacent country abounded in copper mines, which he was very ready to point out, though he declared himself utterly ignorant of the ore, and of every thing else respecting it. Being anxious to ascertain a fact of so much importance, I immediately proceeded, in company with him, to the farthest east hill of the above-mentioned range, which was situated on the north side of the village. It was about two miles distant. The nearer we approached, the more stony and jungly did the road become. A foot-path, paved with stones, led up the hill, to the place which was shown me as one of the mines. It was situated two-thirds up the hill, and might be about 400 feet above the level of the village. An open gallery cut into the rock, demonstrated that it had been formerly wrought. And as the stones, which lay in abundance near it, were all tinged or overlaid with mountain green, there could be no doubt that the ore extracted had been copper.

Many other places containing copper ore were pointed out; but to acknowledge that I did not go to see them, will, I hope, appear to my readers excusable, when I state, as a reason, the very bad state of my health, and the excessive heat of the sun in the beginning of May. Indeed, when I returned to Wangapādu, I was more dead than alive, and was strongly impressed with the idea of approaching dissolution.

* Quick lime.

Before I went away, some of my trusty servants were dispatched, with the goldsmith, to the place from which he had got the specimens of copper ore that had been brought to Madras. This place, according to his information, was about sixteen miles off, and not far from Linga Samudram, which we had passed on our way thither. Not being very sanguine in my expectations, I did not go myself; and, indeed, I could hardly have ventured upon such an excursion without the utmost hazard of my life. I went straight on to Ongole, where, the day after my arrival, I was agreeably surprised by the return of the small party I had sent with a great quantity of the richest mountain green, both in solid lumps and in powder. They had been at a village called Yerrapally, in the Pannūr Purgannah, where they obtained the ore by employing a few men, for six fanams, to dig a hole in the ground, about nine feet deep. The quantity which they brought was sufficient to make about twenty-five pounds of copper. The only stone mixed with it was quartz, which either enclosed it or was aggregated with it. They informed me that they had found various places round the village which were said to have been worked in former times. They brought, likewise, a piece of heavy slag, shown them as the remains of former smelting of the ore.

I shall now endeavour to give an oryctognostic description of the minerals which prevail in this country, especially of those which exhibit traces of copper ore. I shall attempt, likewise, a short geognostic account of the country, and mention such other particulars as may enable us to form a competent judgment of what reasonably may be expected should the mines be again opened, or new ones searched for.

The range of hills which I visited seemed, at first view, to be composed of a kind of hornstone, or compact felspar, which, in many places, assumes a slaty appearance, and might be called siliceous schistus; but, when carefully examined, we find it an aggregate, in which quartz is the prevailing ingredient. This quartz, when it occurs in small grains, is often crystallized and very pellucid; but when in large masses, it is most commonly iron shot, and opake. Schistose hornblende is the ingredient which exists in the greatest proportion after the quartz. It occurs either in minute particles, interspersed through the quartz, or in masses of a considerable size. In the latter case, it has a fine black shining colour, and is composed of thin plates, which in the cross fracture have a hackly appearance, but in the opposite direction are obscurely fibrous. Its streak grey; it is very soft, and its specific gravity is between 2·93 and 3. It has more the appearance of mica than of hornblende; but the specific gravity induces me to consider it as belonging to the latter species rather than the former: from this description there can be little doubt that the rock is a variety of mica slate. Mountain green enters into the composition of this rock here and there in particles, sometimes scarcely visible, sometimes of the size of a pea, sometimes in large masses constituting nests in the rock.

Quartz makes its appearance in the rocks on the rising ground south of the village; it was of a milk white colour and opaque, but in every other respect resembled common quartz; it probably constituted a bed in the mica slate.

Mica slate appears in the low country wherever the ground is laid open to a certain depth; as where wells have been dug in the villages, &c. Its colour is bluish grey and silvery, with black round dots: lustre, shining and semimetallic; opaque; texture undulating, large foliated, somewhat uneven, it is not easily split into lamellæ, though this may be done. It is almost every where intersected with marlaceous tuff, or what might be called semi-indurated earthy limestone. This mineral in the low country indeed seems to form a regular and general bed immediately under the soil: it has the appearance of marl, is greyish white, porous, knobby, breaks with an earthy fracture, effervesces strongly in acids, and does not stick to the tongue. This bed is always covered by one of black mould, and where the mould is supported by gravel or stones, local causes may be easily assigned, as the vicinity of a decomposing rock, or the elevation of the ground from which the rain has carried away all the fine vegetable and decomposed particles. This marl never contains any petrifactions or remains of marine products. When it happens to be mixed with any quantity of gravel or iron ochre, it disposes the whole to harden to a considerable degree: this is the case at the red hills near Madras, at Nellore, and at various places in this neighbourhood, especially near Cāvelly. When this marl has a considerable thickness, which is seldom the case, and is mixed with large pebbles, incrusted with ochre, diamonds are very often found under this stratum.

It renders the water which runs through it brackish: hence it happens that in all parts of India which have a black soil, we find the water of the wells and rivulets nauseous, and on examination it is found impregnated with common salt or muriate of lime: in many parts of the Nellore district, it seems to hold pure lime in solution, for it has the taste and smell of lime water.

Fortunately for the inhabitants these depositions of lime are generally found in the lowest parts of the country, through which the larger rivers take their course; from these rivers the inhabitants are enabled to procure water for culinary purposes. The well water in these districts is unhealthy, and all disorders which may be traced to that source are more common in such countries than in any others.

There is always a bed of black mould lying over the calcareous bed; the formation of this mould, I conceive, is owing to the energy with which the lime attacks all vegetable substances, and reduces them to soil: the plants which spring up in the rainy season are destroyed by the lime during the warm dry weather that follows: even the strong stubble of the jonna is incapable of withstanding this powerful action, but is soon reduced along with the other vegetable bodies to a fine soft mould. This mould, while it continues moist, is remarkably favourable for the growth of plants. The mimosa arabica, jatropha glauca, cassia auriculata, and cassia senna, var. are the only plants that flourish in it during the hot season: many, however, spring up in it during the rainy season. They must all arise from seeds, for no traces of the roots of any of them can be discovered before the rains begin: thus it appears that the seeds of plants are capable of withstanding the decomposing energy of lime much better than the roots, a curious fact not easily accounted for.

From the preceding statement it appears, that the mountains in this country are primitive, and consist chiefly of mica slate; the other rocks which occur in them are probably subordinate, and seem in some measure connected with primitive trap. The lime and marl in the low country is, no doubt, of very late formation, and probably originated from depositions of stagnant water with which the country at one time was probably covered. Several of the copper mines seem to be situated immediately under the bed of marl.

All accounts agree that the working of these mines have not been given up for want of ore, but from the jealousy of the Rajahs, who wished to hide such a treasure as long as possible from their superiors. It was, therefore, with the greatest reluctance that I could prevail upon any of the inhabitants of these places even to speak of it. The copper mines at Agricondah are not far off, and probably are connected with those which I have just been describing; they are situated in a fine clay slate, which I conceive a more favourable rock for containing rich copper ores than those we meet with here. The extent of country through which this ore is distributed is a good symptom, as it shows us that the quantity of ore must be very considerable.

The general use of copper or brass utensils among the natives of Hindostan, and the preference given to them before all other descriptions of vessels, together with the tenacity with which they adhere in every point to the customs of their forefathers, seems to me a very strong proof that copper has been formerly obtained in India in considerable quantity. The constant wars in which the native princes have been engaged, and the consequent depopulation of this part of the country, are probably the true causes why these mines have been so long neglected.

It appears probable, from the information I obtained, that the copper ore occurs in veins, and that quartz is at least frequently the vein stone; but I had not the means of ascertaining either the size or direction of these veins. I have no doubt myself that the size is considerable, and that the copper ore might be obtained in great abundance; but it would be requisite to determine this point by an actual survey before the East India Company make any attempt to work the mines.

As to the nature and richness of the ore, these have been determined. Specimens of it were sent to London. It was analysed by Dr. Thomson, who found it a new species of copper ore, which he called *anhydrous carbonate of copper*. It differs from the two carbonates of copper at present known, in the absence of water. Both of the former specimens are hydrates: the one containing carbonate of copper combined with one atom of water, the other with two atoms. The following are the constituents of this ore, according to the analysis of Dr. Thomson:

Carbonate acid........	16·70
Black oxide of copper..	60·75
Red oxide of iron	19·50
Silica................	2·10
Loss	0·95
	100·00

Thus it contains half its weight of metallic copper, a very unusual proportion for the ores of this metal, which are generally poor. If we were to suppose the oxide of iron to be accidentally present, and not to pervade the whole vein, in that case the proportion of copper would be increased about a fifth, or would amount to about sixty per cent. The carbonic acid gas is driven off by roasting the ore, so that when the roasted ore is smelted, and specimens are chosen quite free from quartz crystals, the metallic copper amounts to at least sixty per cent. of the whole.

This ore possesses another advantage over copper pyrites, the usual copper ore in Great Britain, and indeed in every part of Europe where copper mines occur,—it is more easily smelted and reduced to the metallic state; so that the expense of smelting it would not be so great as usually incurred in similar cases.

All these considerations render these copper mines of sufficient importance to draw the attention of the British government in India: if they were wrought with skill and success they would not only be the source of a considerable revenue, but would greatly benefit the country; and from the total absence of lead, antimony, and arsenic, they would probably produce a copper of sufficient purity to be used as an alloy of gold.

Malachite and mountain green probably constitute the great mass of the ore in the copper veins, but an immense nest of the anhydrous carbonate of copper was found at Ganypittah, a village belonging to a Jaghierdor in the Venkatygherry district, about 40 miles west of Ongole. It exists there in a rock of the nature of gneiss, but considerably disintegrated, and the quantity of it must be immense, as forty coolie's loads were procured by a little digging, and sent to Mr. Travers, the collector for the district, and almost as much remained which had been dug out, but was not carried away.

TRACT V.

ON THE PROPAGATION OF THE CHRISTIAN RELIGION IN INDIA; AND ON THE MORAL CHARACTER OF THE HINDOOS.

I AM of opinion that every body is interested in this subject; the prince as well as the people, the deist as well as the Christian: no consideration is of more importance than the propagation, among a depraved race of men, of principles capable of rendering them good subjects, peaceable and happy. The question at issue is this; is it, or is it not, of political consequence to encourage the religion of Christ in opposition to that of Bramah?

Now if it be true that the followers of the one are good subjects on religious principles, and that the others are dangerous and faithless on the same principles, can there be any hesitation about the nature of the answer? If it be true that the religious opinions of the one lead them to support your government, while the religion of the other induces them to undermine, and if possible to subvert it, what will be the conclusion drawn by every native of Great Britain?

It is unnecessary to dwell for a moment on the principles of the Christian religion, or to inquire whether its ministers and professors have ever done any harm to any government in the world. I lament only that it is too little known how much real good the ministers of the Christian religion have done in India, and how much more they might do, and would have done, if encouragement had been held out to them; but it is necessary to show that the followers of Bramah are such as I have stated them to be,—the enemies of the British Government, and miserable wretches in their private life.

The religion of the Hindoos is commonly represented as inspiring its professors with meekness and charity, and with every virtue that can diffuse happiness around themselves and others. If this representation were correct, I should be sorry to see any change introduced into their religion.

I would allow them a little idolatry, (from which few of us are entirely free) and would recommend them to the mercy of an all-benign Father.

But our opinion will be materially altered when we inquire into the nature of this boasted meekness and charity, and find that their meekness terminates in assassination and rebellion; their charity in extravagance, rapine, and plunder. It is but natural for one wretch to pity another in the same situation with himself, and for the ignominious and weak to bear injuries from their superiors with apparent resignation; but can inference be drawn from this that from disposition and principle he is naturally mild, peaceable, and kind? No. Give him power to revenge himself, and see what he will do: then you will be able to judge whether his former placidity and humble resignation proceeded from good nature and sentiment, or from want of spirit and conscious weakness. A slight observation may convince us that the latter is the case with the Hindoo, and that treachery lurks concealed under his meekness. In disaster and dependance he is always humble and resigned, but when fortune smiles upon him be becomes arrogant, implacable, revengeful; and nothing can atone for the injuries he has suffered but the life of his enemy.

The history of India (a history of assassinations) exhibits numberless examples of horrible designs, long disguised, and harboured in bosoms the least suspected; which broke out at last upon enemies, upon relations, and upon those who had been for years the steady benefactors of the culprits. Yet no consideration of this kind could save the unhappy victims, as soon as an opportunity offered to commit the horrid deed with impunity. Instances of similar occurrences in modern times would, I am afraid, not be wanting, were the perpetrators of such crimes sufficiently conspicuous to warrant their being held out as examples of imitation by the poets of India, and of detestation by the historians of Europe. Of other eastern nations it has been said, that it would be in vain to attempt reconciliation, to make the most abject concessions, or to throw one's self on the mercy of any deeply offended individual among them; that the powerful villain would exult in his situation, glory in the humiliation of his enemy, and quench his vengeance in his blood. I should be sorry to avow this to be the character of the Hindoo; yet should I dread the worst, were my fate in the power of a real enemy of that tribe, for unrelenting vengeance is justifiable by the example of their gods and heroes.

Let us descend into common life, and observe a good natured officious bramin, or any other Hindoo, invested with some power, as an amildar *, sannadar †, dubash ‡, &c. All of a sudden he becomes arrogant and tyrannical; he punishes without mercy, squeezes juice out of a stone, and extracts life from a dead coal: you see him look at the object of his avidity or revenge with a placid smiling countenance, and order the lock at a poor man's ears to be screwed a little tighter §: in short, you see him become all at once a remorseless tyrant in miniature.

It is a fact, for the truth of which *I appeal* to many gentlemen now alive in several parts of Great Britain, that mussulmen treated the officers in Hyder's prison with more humanity than Hindoos, and that among the latter the bramins were the most hard-hearted tyrants of all their keepers.

This disposition must finally end in rebellion. As treachery is not reckoned a crime, as the most sacred promises and oaths may be made, and, when life and property are at stake, lawfully broken and disregarded, who can deny that rebellion against government is lawful? The history of India is nothing but a series of cowardly revolts against legitimate power: most of the present great families have not many years back risen from the dust by treachery and assassination.

It is generally known that, in private life, any man who possesses influence or money, may procure as many witnesses as he pleases to vouch for the truth of any thing whatever. Woe to the man who stands before a court of justice, and whose life depends upon an implacable Hindoo, who considers perjury as no crime: in my opinion it is really astonishing that the evidence of a Hindoo upon oath can be lawfully taken, as his religious principles are known to acquit him of all guilt, provided he can get wages for his iniquity ||.

* A collector of revenues. † An overseer.

‡ An interpreter, head servant of a great man.

§ A mode of enforcing payment of revenues practised by the natives of India.

|| I was once accused of having destroyed the embankment of a watercourse, and publicly called upon by the collector as responsible for all damages, rated at six thousand pagodas. He had discovered my guilt in consequence of a very strict inquiry from upwards of one hundred witnesses, who swore that I and my attendants had been personally guilty of this and other outrages. I received this tremendous letter on my arrival from a place three hundred miles from the spot where the misfortune had happened, and where I had been on official business for

To a Hindoo, all means whatever of attaining riches, power, or any other desirable thing, are equally justifiable. His constant prayer to his idol is for riches; and his sacred writings inform him that assiduity in this respect has been frequently rewarded, by furnishing the suppliant with opportunities to rob another of his property. Many of their popular tales end in this; and these, with an ignorant people, may be said to have become articles of their creed.

From a meek disposition we should expect tolerance; and I know that the Bramins have been cried up as paragons of this virtue; but their pretensions to it are not better founded than to other good qualities. I have only to say that, unless the wise policy of the British government prevented it, we should soon see persecutions raised against all the Mahometans in the Mysore. Even as it is, they are tormented in such a way as often literally to run their heads against the walls. Is it not known that, in former times, whole nations and sects have been extirpated on account of their religious opinions (the worshippers of Bhud and Bhūd, for example); that, at present, the worshippers of Siwen and Vishnu are mortal enemies, and that the whole inhabitants of Hindostan are unanimous in wishing every native of Europe any where but in India? The Bramins, and the populace, instructed and guided by them, are at present in anxious expectation of an emperor of their own nation and religion, called Vīrabhogavasanta Rail, who is born already, will suddenly make his appearance, for whom all hidden treasures are reserved, and who will raise the Hindoo name and religion to their former lustre. Who does not see what facility such a notion would give to a cunning enterprising man, who might even impose upon himself, and set all India in an uproar?

He would be mightily supported, I doubt not, by our own good Dubashes, the greatest villains that the earth ever produced. Much has been said about these monsters: but it is impossible to say too much until the whole race of them, both with an English jargon and without it, are entirely eradicated. They will correspond with your enemies; they will plunder you of your property; and, after they have enriched themselves at your expense, they will throw you into jail. Such examples are too common, and too well known to require specification. All currency is in their hands, hoarded up and lost to

upwards of six weeks, during which time the crime was proved to have been committed. The good collector was not a little astonished at my laconic reply, and I never heard any thing more about it.

the state. They lay out, at usurious interest, just as much as will support their families; the rest never sees the light. When have they come forward with loans in critical times? They will and have trusted their money to rich individuals, whom they conceived to be secure; but when have they tendered it to Government?—Never.

Who will be bold enough to say that Government is secure among a race of men possessed of such principles? It is secure only as long as it is formidable. Instances may be brought against me of real attachment to the British Government. I acknowledge that a few such examples may be produced; but they are so rare as to be entitled to a place only among the exceptions, or *lusus naturæ*. In such a light I would view a Hindoo faithful to an European government. If a native remains steady in perilous times, you may be sure he has his reasons for his conduct. He has an implacable enemy on the opposite side; or his family and his property are in your power; or he hopes to acquire wealth by your destruction; or, what is most probable of all, he is employed upon you as a spy.

I shall now say a few words on their private morals. These indirectly affect the government of a country, like all other vices that have a strong tendency to destroy good order and regularity.

Charity claims the first place; and, from the frequent exclamations of darmam (charity), one would really conceive it to be a national virtue. It would be more proper, in the present case, to call it a national failing. It is only on particular occasions that the rich Hindoo opens his purse; and never to the poor; but to the Bramins, to his own wealthy relations, who must be drowned in ghee and crammed with dainties. They must be filled till they are ready to burst; they must be clothed in sumptuous garments, and feasted with sumptuous entertainments. The poor dependents may look on at a distance, and contribute to the banquet with the sweat of their brows; they must not expect even the crumbs that fall under the table: for, with the Bramins, it is a mortal sin to leave even a grain of rice that has once been placed before them. At the nuptial feasts of the Zemindars, Amildars, Renters, and other great men, every dependent must contribute either labour, or food, or money. Even the lowest pariar is rated; and, while thousands of Bramins are wallowing in luxury, the poorer classes are actually deprived of the means of subsistence. This is called charity!

When calamity oppresses the land, and scarcity and hunger reign paramount, what is the conduct of the rich Hindoo? Thousands of miserable

2

wretches may be seen perishing before his well-filled godowns (warehouses), without even drawing a tear of cold pity from his eyes. The famines are mostly all artificial, and brought on by the charitable Hindoo.

In all village accounts we find a head marked "Charitable Expenses." But we should err very much were we to suppose that this money is laid out upon widows and orphans. No, it is bestowed upon religious beggars, Bramins, dancing girls, comedians, rope dancers, and people of this description. A poor old man, or a helpless child, may starve for want of food in the richest village*. Water, whey, and butter-milk, are the only things that a Hindoo will vouchsafe to bestow upon a poor man under such circumstances. Charity is only for Bramins. This is the doctrine of all their writings: a Bramin is born to receive, not to give: hence we find among them the most flinty-hearted misers.

It must be acknowledged, however, that they are charitable without bounds when they act for the relief of the handsome wife of their brother, their neighbour, or any other man. In such a case they stop at nothing. To carry diseases into another man's house and family, is the greatest of all enjoyments to a Bramin and pious Hindoo. I will not repeat their own sentiments of each other on such occasions, they are too shocking for any but an Indian ear. What M. Sonnerat says of them in this respect is almost literally true, notwithstanding the fine pathetic speech in one of the Madras newspapers some years since. The depravity of the Hindoos in this latter respect is almost beyond conception.

Lying and stealing are esteemed great accomplishments. To give a man the lie direct is not considered as the smallest offence; to be found out in a lie is no disgrace: indeed one expects nothing but a lie in reply to any common question.

As to gratitude, no Hindoo has hitherto made any pretensions to it. There is even no word in the language to express a sentiment of the kind.

Can happiness dwell with men of this description? The thing is impossible. The best among them are only negatively virtuous. The greatest of their virtues turn on privation or negation, as their abstinence, resignation, and acts of devotion. Indeed I may safely say that *indolence* is, in every respect, the greatest of their virtues, and that it can be overcome only by a thirst for gain, by revenge, and by absolute starvation.

* A friend of mine saved a child from dying of hunger in the rich village of Goodcatum, near Vellore, in a plentiful season.

Such being the character of the Hindoos, can any man be bold enough to say that the substitution of the mild doctrines of the Christian religion for the wretched superstition of Bramah; that the introduction of benevolence, charity, sobriety, justice, and truth, in place of the opposite vices which taint all the inhabitants of Hindostan, is not a consummation devoutly to be wished? But it will be said, and it has been often and exultingly affirmed, by the self-constituted philosophers of the new school, that the attachment of the Hindoos to the national religion is inviolable, and not to be overcome. I do not believe the assertion. How great the number of Siks is in the northern parts of India, is now pretty well known to every person who has visited that peninsula; and every body acquainted with the history of that country knows in how short a space of time that great number was converted from the worship of Bramah to the doctrines of their prophet. Are the arguments in support of the Christian religion less forcible than those in favour of the tenets of Nana? Are its attractions smaller, or the rewards which it holds out less powerful and animating?

Hitherto the conversion of the Hindoos to the Christian religion has not been fairly nor properly attempted. Some of the missionaries have been well-meaning enthusiasts, rather than enlightened Christians. The English government, instead of supporting them and facilitating their progress, have rather viewed them as intruders, and have discouraged rather than encouraged conversion. The missionaries themselves, in many instances, have fallen into a mistake of a very injurious nature to their rapid or even ultimate success. In converting a Hindoo to Christianity, they oblige him to adopt a line of conduct by which he loses his cast; this, in India, is considered such a disgrace, that it must present a powerful obstacle to conversion. But the political division of the Hindoos is no part of their religious tenets, though it has been so mistaken by the most enlightened. The Bramins naturally endeavour to perpetuate this erroneous opinion, in order to preserve their supremacy. Learning at first enobled them, and the same badge confirmed the pre-eminence to their families and descendants; who now, indeed, are the only nobility in the country, and, as such, entitled to exclusive prerogatives. In giving to the Hindoos the Christian religion, allow them to retain their casts, and they would be found to embrace it without reluctance, and in considerable numbers.

TRACT VI.

TRANSLATION OF SOME INDIAN BOOKS.

I. KALPASTANUM.

In order to enable the European reader to form some judgment of the merits of the native Indian physicians, I have ventured upon this translation, which, though not a sastrum, is a book of great note, and is in fact a compilation of every thing that the sasters have written on the subject.

It is common in India to hear the native physicians represented by some Europeans as a set of ignorant cheats, and extolled by others as miracles of knowledge and wisdom. The fact however is, that the great body of medical men in India consists of illiterate pretenders to knowledge, few being entitled to be considered as possessed of real knowledge. Most of them are quacks, possessors and venders of nostrums. The medical works of the Hindoos are neither to be regarded as miraculous productions of wisdom, nor as repositories of nonsense. Their practical principles, as far as I can judge, are very similar to our own; and even their theories may be reconciled with ours, if we make allowance for their ignorance of anatomy, and the imperfection of their physiological speculations.

Most Hindoo works of any note have been originally written in Sanscrit, from which they have been translated into the modern dialects, as Tamul, Telinga, &c. But the translators are not always equal to their task; and many errors may have crept into the Telinga translation, from which in all probability the original was free. I attempted at first a literal translation of this work, but after many trials I was obliged to give up the task as beyond my power. My next plan was to make an extract; but this the aphoretical style of my author rendered very difficult. What I here present to the reader is a kind of medium between the two plans. In some places I have adhered to my author very closely, while in others I have abridged, and have omitted many quotations which appeared to me quite useless to an European reader. I conceive it impossible to make a literal translation of any Oriental work into the English language, on account of the complete difference in the genius of writing in the two languages. They are all written in a kind of poetical style, and abound in similes, metaphors, and all kind of figures; and they are of course also replete with allusions to their own customs, propensities, and religious ceremonies, unintelligible to an European.

The author of the Kalpastānum intended it, I conceive, as a kind of compendium for beginners, to make them acquainted with the general rules of pharmacy, and the opinions of different learned men on the subject. It is full of quotations, which till I discovered them to be such, puzzled me exceedingly. The author's name is seldom mentioned, and one quotation often differs so little from another in meaning, that I thought the book merely a collection of needless repetitions. I have been at pains to exhibit the meaning of the author correctly, and to give the botanical names of the plants which he mentions as far as I was able to understand them.

The unsteadiness of orthography which exists in the Telinga language, and the fashionable absurdity of displaying the learning of the author by abstruse, obsolete, and strange words, contributed very much to the difficulty of the translation. In answer to a question put by some learned men in Europe concerning the difference and uncertainty that prevails in spelling Indian names, I beg leave to observe that, though the Indian languages are all related to one another, yet each has its peculiarities in pronunciation and orthography. On that account gentlemen who write in India will spell differently according to the place of their residence, whether in Bengal or among the Telingas or Malabars. In Bengal, for example, a man learned in the Sacred Writings, is called *saster;* among the Telingas he is called *sastru,* and by the Malabars *sastry.* In like manner we have in these different languages *Sanscrit, Sanscritu, Sanscritam; Siwen, Siwa,* and *Si-mudu.*

I have translated only the first section of this work, which treats of vegetable medicines. The second section, which treats of mineral medicines, is less abstrusely written; but I was unable to make them all out for want of the third, which gives an account of the different stones and minerals mentioned in the second. This third section was wanting in my copy, and I have not had an opportunity of perusing it.

THE KALPASTANUM.

Section I. Treats of the climate, weather, and nature of the different soils; the proper method of collecting medicines, as prescribed in the sastrums, and the manner of making nectar-like medicines of the same.

All countries are respectively situated either high or low; or they hold a middle place between the two. The first, called *jangala dehsam*, is a high mountainous country, in which most of the shrubs are thorny and the trees very large. Salt water may be found by digging very deep in the ground *. The air is commonly clear and serene, and the horizon appears at an immense distance from us. The natives of such countries are usually thin and fond of their home †. Adversity affects them much; and the few disorders they are subject to are chiefly of the nervous kind (*wadum*).

The second is called *anopa dehsam*, or low country. A rich luxuriant appearance proceeding from the general verdure and the abundance of tanks, which are covered with nāsu (*utricularia stellaris*), and reservoirs for numberless fish are the characteristics of such a country. The whole of it is encompassed by high mountains; the trees grow on it to a large size, and all parts of the plain appear intersected and surrounded with palmeyras and date trees. The inhabitants are subject to catarrhal and hæmorrhoidal disorders, to obstructions in the abdomen, and to swelled legs. They are in general indolent, large, and have a soft flesh. The slime disorders (*chestum*) are the prevailing ones. The plants growing in such countries yield plentiful juices, but mostly of the sweet kind.

The third kind of country, called *sâdāranam*, approaches, according to its position, either the one or the other of the two kinds of country already mentioned; and on that account is called, according to circumstances, either *jangala sâdaranam* or *anopa sâdaranam*. The best medicines may be procured in these kinds of country, provided we pay attention to the weather and the season of the year.

The rules to be observed respecting the soil from which medical plants may be collected are the following:

All plants that grow on sandy, stony, or salt ground, in pools or white

* This is true in the inland and hilly countries on the coast of Coramandel.

† The mountaineers in Switzerlaud, and even in Germany, are particularly fond of their home; and when in foreign countries subject to a particular sickness, called by them the *heim-wehe*, or longing after home, to be cured only by returning to their own country.

ant heaps, in places that are frequented by men, and places where corpses have been burnt, in church yards, flower gardens, shady places, and places impregnated with the juice of rotten leaves, should never be collected for medical use. Neither ought those plants to be chosen which are for a considerable part of the year under water, and on which the darba grows *. Airy and open places alone are those upon which salutary plants are to be expected.

We have likewise to attend to five different kinds of soil. 1. Soil in which the earthy principle prevails. This soil is very fertile, of a shining brown, yellowish, or black colour, and very stiff or consistent. All trees grow on it to a large size; and grass and every kind of crop come to perfection in it. 2. Soil in which the water has the greatest share. Its nature is cold, and it has a whitish colour; but its surface has a delightful fertile appearance, and is covered with luxuriant plants and trees. Its tanks are constantly filled with water. 3. The fire soil. It is light and has a greyish colour. The trees that grow on it have a sterile grey appearance. It produces climbing plants in abundance. 4. Soil in which the air is the prevailing constituent. It has an ash colour. The trees that grow on it are usually rotten in the inside. Its crops are thin, and it produces only such as grow in cold weather. 5. Ether ground. Its colour is blackish; it is stony, and produces trees that yield resins and oil †.

Plants that grow upon the two first of these kinds of soil may be usefully given as medicines. The three last kinds yield only good emetics and drastic purges.

Every season produces plants peculiar to itself. There are even peculiar parts of plants that belong to each season. The sasters give the following general rules.

Woods, branches, and sprigs must be collected in the rainy season, or warasha rutuwu; leaves in the wasanta; old leaves, petiols, peduncles, and roots in the sisa and greeshna rutuwu; in the former those that are of a cooling, in the latter those that are of a heating, nature. In the hemanta, collect the roots of trees, and the different kinds of yams; in the siradra, bulbous roots, barks, and the milk of different plants. Flowers and fruits must be collected when they can be found.

* Several species of reedy grasses.

† The reader will perceive that the names and divisions of soils here are derived from the five elements of the Indian philosophy; namely, earth, water, fire, air, and ether.

One of these authors says that young sprouts, flowers, and young leaves, roots that descend from the branches to the ground, gums, resins, and oils may be had from most trees in the wasanta rutuwu.

Another rule, mentioned by some authors as a general one, is to collect medicines of a cooling nature, and of a bitter or sweet taste in the warasha, sīradra, and hemanta; in the other three seasons medicines of a heating nature, and of an acid or saltish taste, are to be collected.

Some desire to gather leaves in the warasha, roots in the siradra, gums in the hemanta, milk of plants in the wasanta, and expressed juices in the greeshna rutuwu.

Here follows a list of plants most in use as medicines.

Tuberous and Bulbous Roots.

Sanscrit Names.	Telinga Names.	Linnæan Names.
Manjishta	Manjishta	Nymphæa lotus var. flore rubro
Kushta	Changalà koshtam	Costus arabicus
Chora	Kachōra	Kaempferia rotunda
Bidārika	Nēla gummadi	Vitis tomentosa
Hiridra	Passupu *	Curcuma longa
Māmsi	Jatamāmsa	Cyperus stoloniferus
Musta	Tungamusta	Cyperus rotundus
Wari	Challa	Asparagus racemosus
Rāsdra	Dumparāsdra	
Gunapria	Attewaja	
Shariba	Sugandhiepālē †	Periploca indica
Adraka	Allum	Amomum zingiber
Warahi	Nēla tāti	Curculigo orchioides
Wacha	Waja	Acorus Calamus

* There are two kinds of turmerick, one that grows in the low country and the other on the hills: the latter is esteemed the best, and is a great medicine among the natives; it is used also in their curries, and as a cosmetic by the Indian ladies.

† Is not a tuberous root, but much in use as a good substitute for sarsaparilla. I found, not long ago, a kaempferia of that name, the roots of which are tuberous.

Sanscrit Names.	Telinga Names.	Linnæan Names.
Abdi tunga	Samudra tunga mustalu	Cyperus spec.
Wanasurana	Adivi kanda	Tacca pinnatifida
Nikumba	Nēla ameda	Jatropha glauca
Amlika	Pulla chinta	Oxalis corniculata
Wajie ganaha	Pennēru	Physalis flexuosa
Shukasana	Chilakamuka	Crotolaria ?

Roots.

Sanscrit Names.	Telinga Names.	Linnæan Names.
Brahety	Tella Mulaka	Solanum indicum
	Nēla mulaka	Solanum jacquini
Amshumatydivandiva	Nēla ponna	Cassia sennæ
	Kola ponna	Cassia fistula
Balapanchacum	Chittamutti	Hibiscus micranthus
	Perahmutti	Hibiscus zeilan.
	Chetumutti	Nepeta malabarica
	Moga bīra	Cucumis acutangulus
	Adi bīra	Ditto, with many female flowers
Barbhara	Wāwinti	Cleome pentaphylla
Tandulioka	Chirrikura	Amaranthus prostratus
Gokanta	Pallēru	Tribulus terrestris
Kundali	Wuppi	Capparis sepium
Punki	Wempali	Galega cœrulea
Wāluka	Kuruwēhlu	Lavendula carnosa *
Lamaja	Wattiewēhlu	Andropogon muricatum
Yosha	Ponna	Callophyllum inophyllum
Ahinsra	Totla	Capparis grandiflora
Himsa	Jalāri	Shorea laccifera.
Yosha	Tietekasandi	Tragia involucrata

* I have not yet well examined it.

Sanscrit Names	Telinga Names.	Linnæan Names.
Dwapanarnawa	Tellagaljēru	Trianthema decandra
	Nallagaljēru	Trianthema monogyn.
Sawarchalah	Poddu tirrugada	Helianthus annuus
Päta	Agulu sunti	Cissampelos pata
Kurantakha	Gorinta	Lawsonia inermis
Shiāma	Mogali	Pandamus odoratissimus

Bark of Roots.

Sanscrit Names.	Telinga Names.	Linnæan Names.
Shiāma *	Tegada	Convolvulus turpethum
Ashwagna	Gannēru	Nerium
Agni	Chittramūlam	Plumbago zeilan.
Nilia dua	Nīla	Indigofera tinctoria

Bark of large Trees.

Sanscrit Names.	Telinga Names.	Linnæan Names.
Lodra	Maddi	Morinda citrifolia
Arimada	Tumma	Mimosa arabica
Katwanga	Peddamānu	Tamarindus indica
Därwie	Māni passpu	A yellow wood sold in the bazar
Jambu	Naradi	Myrtus cumini
Lawangaka	Lawanga	Caryophyllus aromaticus
Karamji	Kānuga	Galeduppa pungam
Kamshuka dwandwa	Moduga	Butea frondosa
	Mullu Moduga	Erythrina corollodendron
Shambiaka	Rēla	Cassia fistula

* Seems to be a name given to different vegetables.

Sanscrit Names.	Telinga Names.	Linnæan Names.
Chiravrutchali	Juwie	Ficus benjamina
	Rāwi	—— religiosa
	Marri	—— indica
	Mēdi	—— oppositifolia
	Bramha medy	—— glomerata
Shalmalie	Buruga	Bombax pentandra
Kutaja	Kolamucka	Echites antidysenterica aut tomentosa

Trees possessing a Peculiar Smell.

Sanscrit Names.	Telinga Names.	Linnæan Names.
Madhūka	Ippi	Bassia longifolia
Chandana dwandua	Strī gandham	Santalum album
	Rakta ganham	Pterocarpus santalinus
Amara buruhi	Dēwadāri	Erythroxylon areolatum
Badirah	Chandra	Mimosa sandra
Rohinie	Kāmanchi	Stapelia quadrangularis
Asana	Nemma	Melia azedarach
Nimba	Wēmu	Melia azedarach

Leaves.

Sanscrit Names.	Telinga Names.	Linnæan Names.
Brunga	Guntagaljēru	Eclipta erecta
Alarka	Tigamullamusta	Solanum trilobatum
Arjata	Nēla wuserikay	Phyllanthus neruri
Chilly	Korikūra	Amaranthes tristis Rgh.
Hari	Dūlagovilah	Aristolochia indica
Manjirika	Gakaraku	Ocymum basilicum
Amlika	Pulla chinta	Oxalis corniculata
Wapanadamghri	Hamsapadi	Adiantum spec.
Manshinka	Kuppy	Acalypha indica

Sanscrit Names.	Telinga Names.	Linnæan Names.
Duttura	Wumetta	Datura metel
Karawehla	Kakara	Momordica charantia
Patolika	Chedu polla	Momordica sp.
Machadruku	Ponnaganty	Illecebrum sessile
Nirgundy	Wāvely	Vitex negundo
Banjy	Wēravary	Convolvulus gemella
Kundali	Tellavuppi	Monetia barlerioides
Kasamarda	Nallavuppi	Copparis sepiaria
Mandukaparni	Mandūkabramhi	Phlomis leonurus
Lavanika	Kangundy	Ceanothus racemosus
Talapota	Tanghedu	Cassia auriculata
Arkah	Jillēdu	Asclepias gigantea
Kimshuka	Mōduga	Butea frondosa
Jaia	Adivi malle	Jasminum mucronatum
Agni manta	Wusilika	Phyllanthus emblica
Sharinyari	Batsali	Basella alba et rubra
Sharinishta	Guriginja	Tragia chamelea
Dwepunarnawa	Tellagaljēru	Trianthema decandra
	Nallagaljēnu	———— monogyn.
Bramhie	Vandalaga	Hydrocotile indica
Kurutaka	Juttupāku	Asclepias vomitoria
Anunta	Sahadēvi	Amaranthus spec.
Harie pria	Vishtu Krānta	Evolvulus alsinoides
Latchmie dwetaya	Kupanti	Physalis minima
Jivanti	Pālakura	Asclepias esculenta Rgh.
Durwa	Garika kassuwa	Panicum lineare
Wastuka	Chackrawarikūra	Chenopodium viride
Waluka	Chantarasa	Pharnaceum mollugo
Pushia	Dossa	Cucumis utilatissimus Rgh.
	Donda	Bignonia teadonda
Agukami	Yalakachevi	Evolvulus emarginatus
Kalinga	Puchakay	Momordica elaterium
Tumbadia	Tumma	Philomis indica

Flowers.

Sanscrit Names.	Telinga Names.	Linnæan Names.
Champaya	Sampinga	Mitchelia chambacu
Katali	Mogali	Pandanus odoratissimus
Ashoka	Ashōka	Guilandina spec.
Patilie	Kalagotti	Bignonia spathacea
Punnaga	Ponna	Callophyllum inophyllum
Bhurja	Bhuja patrī	Nepeta spec.
Wakula	Pōgâda	Mimusops elengi
Mādāwi	Bandiguraginja	
Jāji	Jāji	Myristica officinalis
Mallika	Malla	Jasminum sambac
Nepāla	Nepāla	Jatropha curcas
Yudika	Malla	Jasminum auriculatum
Sigru	Munaga	Hyperanthera morunga
Satapatra	Tamara	Nymphæa nelumbo
Nrupadruma	Rēla	Cassia fistula
Warāla	Lawanga	Caryophyllus aromaticus
Dhātika	Ara	Bauhinia spicata
Nandawartam	Nandawardha	Taberna montana grandiflora
Wadpala	Kāluwapu	Nymphæa rubra et lotus
Japādayaha	Dasalampu	Hibiscus sinensis

Fruits.

Sanscrit Names.	Telinga Names.	Linnæan Names.
Drācha	Dwēpadrācha	Vitis vinifera
Dādimma	Dadimbha	Punica granatum
Karchōra	Karjūra	Phœnix dactylifera
Rumbā	Ariti	Musa paradisiaca
Panasa	Panasa	Artocarpus integrifolia
Chūtika	Māmedy	Mangifera indica
Tāla	Tāti	Borassus flabelliformis
Bilwaka	Māredu	Feronia elephantum

Sanscrit Names.	Telinga Names.	Linnæan Names.
Tangadru	Tenkay	Cocos nucifera
Slaeshtmantaka	Weregi	Cordia sebestina
Kapata	Valaga	Aegle marmelos (cratæra religiosa)
Naranga	Narada	Citrus aurantium var.
Lunga	Madala	Citrus, Clove orange
Likucha	Gaja nimma	Citrus medica var. largest kind
Parawata	Royabora*	Zizyphus jujuba
Sura	Dēwadāru	Erythroxylon aseolatum
Souvera	Rēgu	Zizyphus jujuba
Badara	Chinna rēgu	Ditto, var.
Gunja	Guruginja	Abrus precatorius
Karkendu	Sanna rēgu	Zizyphus jujuba var.
Torana	Wallepala	

Seeds.

Sanscrit Names.	Telinga Names.	Linnæan Names.
Ructadwa	Yerra rajanālu	Oryza sativa, best rice
Mudgah ‡	Pessara	Phaseolus mungo
Yerandah	Ameda	Ricinus communis
	Chittameda	——— var.
Punnaga	Ponna	Callophyllum inophyllum
Nagmarjin	Pally	Gossypium herbaceum
Chackramarta	Giriza, tagesy	Cassia occidentalis
Prialu	Marali	Celtis orientalis
Nimbha	Wēpa	Melia azedarachta
Wackulu	Pōgada	Mimusops elengi
Muni	Agesi	Aeschynomene sesba

* The name of the fruit in the Mysore.

† This cannot be, as the tree is leguminous, and bears small red seed.

‡ Means all leguminous grains.

Sanscrit Names.	Telinga Names.	Linnæan Names.
Sackeva	Munaga	Hyperanthera morunga
Karanga	Kānuga	Galeduppa pungam
Joutishmati	Kangundy	Ceanothus racemosus*
Kubaeratcha	Ghetsakay	Guilandina bonducella
Sambimugmam	Catla	
	Karuwēpa	Bergera koenigū
Chūtaka	Māmedy	Mangifera indica
Jutapāla	Jājekay	Myristica officinalis
Yala	Yalakā	Amomum cardamomum
Tackola	Tackola	Clerodendrum inerme
Bramhamdwa	Mōduga	Butea frondosa
Maywraka	Wūtarēnu	Achyranthes aspera
Shunakabarbara	Kuekawawinty	Cleome viscosa
Pepata	Pippalu	Piper longum
Merecha	Mirialu	—— nigrum
Ajajie	Jīlakarra	Cuminum cyminum
Yaevani	Wāmum	Sison ammi
Dhanwa	Cotumbêri	Coriandrum sativum
Sarshapa	Awa	Sinapis nigra
Kataka	Chilla	Strychnos potatorum
Arūshgara	Jīdi	Semicarpus anacardium
Chennaka	Jennaga	Cicer arictinum
Pativa	Kara (kay)	Terminalia chebula
Dhatri	Wuseri (kay)	Phyllanthus emblica
Wībrītaka	Tandra (kay)	Terminalia spec.
Wakuchy	Bawanji	
Amkola	Wuduga	Alangium decapetalum vahl.
Badara	Rēgu	Zizyphus jujuba
Waella	Wayuvilangālu	

* Cannot be, as it is a small seed unlike that of ceanothus.

Acrid and Astringent Vegetables.

Sanscrit Names.	Telinga Names.	Linnæan Names.
Trevety	Tegâda	Convolvulus turpethum
Chitraka	Chittramūlam	Plumbago zeilanica
Gandira	Yēruvanga	Solanum spec.
Bramhie	Jemmadi	Euphorbia antiquorum
Pūty	Tappashi	
Duepoonarnawa	Tellagaljēroo	Trianthema decandra
	Nallagaljēroo	Trianthema monogyn.
Chavia	Chāviam	
Attaroosha	Adhasaram	Justicia adhatoda
Shionaka	Dondila	Aeschynomene aquatica
Pataty	Kalugoty	Bignonia spathacea
Parībadraka	Wēpa	Melia azedarachta
Wara { Datri	Wuselikay } Tripalalu	Phyllanthus emblica
Wara { Sheva	Karakay } Tripalalu	Terminalia chebula
Wara { Karshapalah	Tandrakay } Tripalalu	Ditto spec.
Kannia	Juttupāku	Asclepias vomitoria
Arka	Jillēdu	——— gigantea
Wartaka	Wankay	Solanum melongena
Pallasha	Mōduga	Butea frondosa
Kimshukah	Mullu mōduga	Erythrina corallodendron
Gavachi	Pāpata	Gardenia pavetta
Mallika	Mallatiga	Jasminum scandens
Sankani	Ghilliginta	Crotolaria cærulea
Hiaghri	Wākudu	Solanum diffusum
Chudra	Nēla mulaka	Solanum jacquini
Nirgundy	Wāweli	Vitex negundo
Kundali	Tella vuppi	Monetia barlerioides
Nisha	Passupu	Curcuma longa
Nili	Nili	Indigofera tinctoria
Kettaki	Mogali	Pandanus odoratissimus

Sanscrit Names.	Telinga Names.	Linnæan Names.
Mundy	Budatramu	Spilanthus acmella
Prattiakipūshpi	Wuttarēnu	Achyranthes aspera
Ajagandika	Kuckapāla	Periplora tunicata
Alarka	Mullamusta	Solanum tribulatum
Barbaraduandua	Wāwinty	Cleome pentaphylla
Shunakabarbara	Kuckawāwinty	——— viscosa
Tilla	Nugu	Sesamum orientale
Yeechura	Mulla gorimidy	Barleria longifolia
Wettasa	Prabhala	
Shimshupa	Shamimah	
Dēwampa	Dēwadāroo	Trythroxylon areolatum
Shigru	Munaga	Hyperanthera morunga
Mushkaka	Mockapu	(the male flower)
Bhustranum	Kamanchy	Aesclepias quadrangularis

Milk Plants.

Sanscrit Names.	Telinga Names.	Linnæan Names.
Tilwaka	Nugulu	Sesamum orientale
Arkah	Jillēdu	Asclepias gigantea
Mahavrutcha	Jemmudu	Euphorbia antiquorum
	Aku jemmudu	——— nereifolia
Patrasurkoo	Kalewi	
Warakanya	Jutupāku	Asclepias vomitoria
Aspota	Yērumalla	Jasminum spec.
Bramhi	Bramhadandie	Argemone mexicana

Gums and Resins.

Sanscrit Names.	Telinga Names.	Linnæan Names.
Stounia	Stounia	Sandarac
Sarja	Sarjarassum	Olibanum or frankincense

Sanscrit Names.	Telinga Names.	Linnæan Names.
Strī vasa	Sambranī	Benjanum
Daevadupa	Guggilam	Dammer
Turushkaka	Turushkaradupam	Gum arabic
Palasha	Moduga	Butea frondosa
Shalmalie	Buruga	Bombax pentandra
Guggulu	Mahesache guggilam	
Arishtum	Wēpa	Melia azedarachta
Kanya	Julupaku	Asclepias vomitoria
Patola	Chedupolla	Momordica spec.
Pippaly mula	Modi	Piper longum
Bhynimba	Nēla wēmu	Justicia monanthera
Natta	Grandika tagaram	
Chaira	Chairum	
Attarusha	Adhasaram	Justicia adhatoda
Durwa	Garika	
Prasarani	Lanja Savaram	Convolvulus prostratus
Amlikakya	Chintamān	Tamarindus indicus
Sharinyari	Pulla batsali	Balella rubra
Parpotadayaha	Parpatāku	

The place in which medicines are kept should be clean, dry, and not accessible to rats, white ants, or dust. The drugs ought to be put in nets, or large pots, the mouths of which must be tied over with a piece of cloth, and suspended in a room. Fire, smoke, and water must be kept at a distance.

The house in which medicines are stored should be neither in too high nor too low a situation, and it should not be far distant from places in which medicines may be collected: its front should face either the south or the north, with a convenient viranda before the door of the same side.

The necessary apparatus of mortars, scales, &c. must be kept in a place in the wall that has been consecrated for that purpose by religious ceremonies.

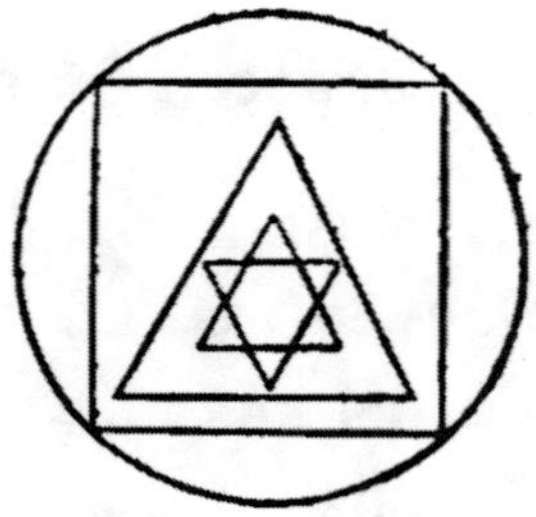

In the middle of the medicine room a place is to be consecrated for the mystical sign.

Proper places are likewise to be adapted for the images of three principal deities, Bramha, Wishnu, and Siwa.

Bramha's pillar must be erected in the eastern side of the apartment. It is the simple trunk of a moduga tree (butea frondosa) with the image of the deity, and the sixteen vowels of the Telinga and Sanscrit alphabets inscribed on as many petals of the nelumbo indica; thus: ă ā, ĭ ī, u ū, ṛu rū, lu lū, e ai, wo, ou, am aha.

After a certain period of time all medicines become unfit for use. Substances abounding in juice cannot be kept longer than one year, if we except sugar, jaggary, and honey, and things preserved in these bodies. Flowers, leaves, and fruits should never be older than one year. All kinds of wood and branches become useless after one year's keeping. Roots should never be used after they have been three years in store. Several seeds and nuts will serve until the fifth year after their collection. Gums and resins may be employed for ten years.

The milk and urine of cows, when wanted, must be taken from young ones; but the horns, bones, and other parts of the body from old and strong animals.

Some medicines, the following for example, may be used when fresh,

Pillapitsera, phaseolus aconitifolius.
Tippatiga, menispermum cordifolium.
Nalla kaliva, nymphæa rubra.
Mula gorinta, barleria spinosa.

The bark or outer covering of some must be removed before they can be applied to any use. This is the case with ginger, garlick, pillapitsera, and menispermum cordifolium. It is not necessary to take off the husks of leguminous grains when used for decoctions, but they must be removed when these grains are baked.

When medical authors, in their writings, mention simply the name of a plant without particularizing the part of it, they always mean the root of that plant.

Physicians are often at a loss what to do when the articles prescribed cannot be procured. The following substitutions may be employed in such cases.

For grapes employ dates or other sweet things.

For long pepper, common pepper.

For dry ginger, green ginger.

For sugar, jaggery.

For honey, oil that has been infused in sweet smelling flowers.

The ghee of cow's milk may be substituted for that of goats; buffaloe's milk for goat's or sheep's milk. If no milk can be procured supply its place with a decoction of green gram (phaseolus mungo). For rajanālu or fine rice take any other kind of rice; for gingelie oil (sesamum orientale) employ lamp oil (oleum ricini), for jungle fowl, peacocks or common fowl. Should the latter not be at hand you may substitute fish. Instead of oysters snails may be given, and if gold cannot be had you may employ silver or even iron.

When ghee and urine are prescribed, without particularizing from what animal, those of the cow are always to be understood.

The word chanuru (moisture) in Hindoo books always signifies gingelie oil. By ashes are understood the residue of burnt rice.

Weights and Measures.

Sun dust cannot be weighed.

8	Paramānum	1	trasa renuwu	
8	Trasa renuwu	1	radha renuwu	
8	Radha renuwu	1	tulagram	
8	Tulagram	1	valagram, as much as a weak wind can carry away	
8	Valagram	1	tilaha	
8	Tilihas	1	kakini	
4	Kakini	1	wrihi (a grain of paddy)	$\frac{1}{2}$ grain
2	Wrihi	1	widalam	1 ditto
2	Widalams	1	guligintsa*	2 ditto
2	Guligintsas	1	manshishda	4 ditto
5	Manshishdas	1	pādam	20 ditto
3	Pādams	1	shanam	60 ditto
160	Wrihi	1	nishkam	80 ditto
1	Wrihy	1	visum weight	$\frac{1}{2}$ ditto

* The seed of abrus precatorius, weighing in common no more than two grains.

16 Wrihys .... 1 fanam's weight * .... 8 grains
10 Fanams .... 1 nishkam .... 80 ditto
8 Nishkams .... 1 palam........ .... 640 ditto
100 Palam .... 1 tūla .... 64000 ditto

Other Weights used by the Shasters.

6 Wamsaha .... 1 marichi
6 Marichis .... 1 sarshapa
8 Sarshapa .... 1 tandulaha
2 Tandolahas .... 1 dannia mashaha
2 Dannia mashias ...... 1 yawaha
2 Yawahas .... 1 mandika, aduga vīsum
4 mandikas .... 1 mashikam, $2\frac{1}{4}$ fan. weight
4 Mashikams .... 1 sānam, 9 fan.
4 Sānams .... 1 panitalam, 36 fan.
4 Panitalams .... 1 mushty, 12 dwt. ℥j ʒij ℈ij viij gr.
4 Mushtys.... .... 1 kudupam...... 4 palams
4 Kudupam .... 1 prastam .... 16 palams
4 Prastam.............. 1 adhakam.... 64 palams
4 Adhakams........... 1 drohnam
4 Drohnam .... 1 waham .... 128 seer

The Weights in common use among the Hindoo Physicians on the Coast are:

1 Paddy grain .... 1 grain
1 Gulighintsa .... 2 grains
1 Sanam ....13 grains
1 Pagoda..............54 grains
1 Pallam ....10 pagodas weight

Long Measure.

1 Ashdakam........8 paddy grains or 1 finger........3 inches
6 Fingers..... ....1 shadankulam or 6 fingers......18 ditto

* A fanam weight is now thirteen grains.

2 Shadankulam, 1 dwada sankulam or witastihy, 12 fingers, 36 inches, 1 yard
12 Witastidwa .. ... 1 aratny, 24 fingers .. ... 72 inches ...... 2 yards
Aratnydwa ...... 1 kishkuhu, 48 ditto..... 4 yards
Kishkuhadwa .... 1 danahū, 96 ditto ...... 8 yards, or 1 p. 2½ yards
1000 Danāhū .. .... 1 danusahasram .... 4 m. 4 fur. 2 poles
2 Danusahasram .... 1 cros (coss)
2 Paruwoo .. . ... 1 cros
2 Coss .... 1 gawutchy
4 Paragu .... 1 Amda
4 Amdas .... 1 yojanum *

Medical authors commonly speak of dried substances, as dry leaves, roots, &c. When these substances are used in their fresh state a double quantity to that prescribed should be employed. This is called dvicūneam. On the contrary, when they avowedly speak of green substances, if these cannot be procured, we may substitute the dried bodies in their stead, but in that case we must employ only one half of the quantity prescribed. But it is only practicable to administer a double quantity of fresh substances in lieu of the prescribed quantity of the dried bodies, when the original quantity prescribed does not exceed an ounce. There is indeed one author, namely, Charakachārlu, who advises to double in such circumstances doses as large as a palam. But he only ventures to recommend this when treating of the leprosis.

According to the country in which the several authors have lived and written, they have made the palam of different weights. According to some it contains eight, according to others twelve pagodas weight. Others, probably from mere whim, altered them according to their own fancy.

A sīr is to be six inches wide and twelve inches deep. This is called a magadaprasdam, and two of them are denominated a loukīka prasdam.

If it be considered better to weigh medicines than to measure them, in that case ten palams weight is to be reckoned equivalent to a seer. A certain author computes magadaprasdam to be equal to thirty-two palams.

Rasaha means the fresh expressed juice of vegetables, obtained either by chewing fresh vegetables, or by pounding them. A little water may be added if they should contain too small a quantity of natural juice to be ex-

* There have been many disputes about a yojanum, the above determination is much larger than that in common use, according to which, a coss is two miles, an āmda four coss, and a yojanum four āmdas, or 32 miles.

pressed. Plants from open places, that have been much exposed to the sun, are the best and most efficacious for these purposes.

Kalkaha is the powder of well dried plants. It may be made into pills or given in substance, or may be mixed with different kinds of medical potions. The common tripala kramam will serve as an example. It is composed of myrobolans, three parts; tādy (terminalu spec.), six parts; and wuscriky (phylanthus emblica), twelve parts. These ingredients being reduced to powder are mixed with water and given.

Sītaha is a cold infusion, composed of one part of a dry ingredient, and twelve parts of a liquid. It must be allowed to stand soaking a whole night. It has but little medicinal efficacy.

Srutaha, kashaiam, and pāndaha are decoctions. Two seers of water are usually required for every handful of dry ingredients. It is to be boiled down to one-fourth of its bulk.

Pāndaha *. The ingredients must be cut into small pieces and put into a clean earthen pot, round the short neck of which an iron wire is to be fastened, in order to move it with ease from the fire. The proper quantity of water being poured over them must be allowed to soak for some hours in the sun or in a warm place. It is then to be boiled over a slow smokeless fire. The whole is then to be strained through a cloth, and the patient must take it without smelling, in the way prescribed by the physician.

The evil spirit that presides over the disorder takes his station on the left side of the patient, and care must be taken that he gets his due portion of the medicine. The cup out of which the medicine has been taken must be placed on the same side; but to prevent the spirit from sipping what might remain, and by that means defiling the cup, it must always be carefully inverted. The patient after taking the medicine may be allowed to chew arrack nut, beetle, or cloves, carraway or the germ of the tamara, a little sugar, honey or green gram, but he must not taste water, or milk, or any thing sour.

Some authors lay it down as a rule that, in disorders from wadum, the decoctions are to be drunk warm; in those from chestum, luke warm; in those from bittum, cold; and in disorders from a mixed origin (dwandarogam), warm or cold, according to the prevailing cause.

As patients are apt to grow worse in the night, double doses of medicine

* No information is given either of the mode of making this medical potion nor any description of what it is; though our author mentions it again, and it seems to be a favourite with him.

should be given them in the evening. These nightly exacerbations are owing to the influence of the moon *, and especially of its beams, which produce injurious effects even on healthy persons. In such cases some physicians order the medicines to be taken at six o'clock precisely, others three hours after the patient has taken his meal; while others, having an eye to the causes of disorders, direct the medicines in wadum to be taken before the meal; in pittum, during it; and in chestum, after the usual supper.

It is a general rule that medicines ought to be given only twice a day, namely, in the morning and in the evening; and at both times the same kind of medicine ought to be administered. Ingredients that have been exhausted by boiling should be thrown away, their contents being nothing but poison.

According to the nature of the disorder the medicine should be taken out of gold, silver, or brass vessels. But if these should not be at hand you may use iron or even earthen vessels.

Ingredients that are added to the decoction after the boiling is over, as syrup, honey, pippaly, salts, &c. are called brativāpam by the sastrums.

It has been observed that to one part of dry ingredients, sixteen, eight, or four parts of water are to be taken. But this is meant only as a general rule; for in particular cases it is the physician's business to judge both of what quantity of water is required to extract the efficacious parts from those ingredients, and how long the boiling ought to be continued.

The bottom of the brazen, copper, or earthen vessel in which the decoction is boiled must be smeared over with cow dung, and for the better managing of it an iron wire is to be fastened to its neck.

The decoctions made with oil are called tailam, the making and application of which constitute a great part of a physician's knowledge. All fluid and solid parts are used to each other in the same proportion as stated before when speaking of kashaiam. The roots are first of all to be put into the boiling oil, then the barks, and lastly the leaves. Along with the oil are often mixed the expressed juices of plants or a kashaiam made with water, &c. In such cases the name is altered to kashaiatailam or swarasatailam.

Should you wish to make a tailam with the ingredients prescribed for a kashaiam, you must in that case double the quantity of oil; and you must

* The Dutch at Batavia entertained, I understand, the same notion of the tendency of this innocent luminary.

proceed in the contrary way if a kashaiam is to be made from the ingredients of a tailam.

According to the nature of the ingredients (whether hard or soft) the quantity of liquid employed may be either increased or diminished. The same observation applies likewise to the time required for boiling. Woods often require fourteen days boiling.

Some authors prescribe decoctions made of meat. Sixteen parts of water are allowed for four of meat, and the water is boiled down to one half. Tailams may be made by mixing oil with such a decoction, or with milk, or with any liquid whatever. Milk and oil in such cases must be mixed in equal proportions.

The physician who has to superintend the boiling of a tailam, must sit down on a plank before the fire, with his face either turned to the south or north, and his eyes fixed upon the boiling mass, gently stirring it with a spatula to prevent it from sticking to the bottom or sides of the pot. The fire must be very slow.

The spot round the fire-place must be besmeared over with cow dung, and painted, according to the Hindoo custom, with chunam and powdered ochre. This part of the business can only be performed by a virgin, or by the mother of sons whose husband is alive. At the same time flowers and rice are to be offered to the immortal gods.

To ascertain when the tailam is sufficiently boiled, a portion must be taken out and formed into a ball. If the tailam is merely to act by applying it to the nostrils, the boiling may be stopped when the ingredients have acquired such consistency as to admit of their being formed into a ball. If the tailam is to be employed for external unctions it ought to acquire such consistency that the ball formed shall feel between the fingers like wax or soap; and when it is to be administered internally it ought to be allowed to acquire still greater consistency.

Some ceremonies are also to be observed when the pot is taken off the fire, and the tailam strained. A spot of ground is to be measured out, four yards square if the tailam be intended for Bramins; three yards square if it be intended for Chetries; and two yards if for Vysias and Soddras. This spot is to be rubbed over with cow dung, and painted with chunam and ochre. Four tums of paddy are to be heaped up in the middle, and the pot with the tailam placed upon them. On its left side must be placed a goblet with water, covered with a clean cloth, and a lamp lighted with ghee; on the north side is to be placed the image of the god Wikneswaradu *. He is to be worshipped, and the sixteen customary offerings of rice, milks, and fruits are to be presented to him in order to insure his interest. Round the whole, heaps of different kinds of grain are to be placed, beginning at the north side with rice. Obeisance being paid to the heavenly bodies, to the Bramins, and cows, music and prayers of the Bramins being muttered in honour of the gods, let the tailam be strained through a new and clean piece of cloth into a new pot. And to hasten the operation it may be gently squeezed with two sticks.

It is to be considered a bad omen for the life of the patient, if by mistake an old piece of cloth has been taken for straining the tailam, or if it has formed a burnt crust at the bottom of the pot.

The dry ingredients, or kalkum, are not to be separated from all kinds of tailams; but they should be removed in all cases when the patient is a child, weak, or old, or when his digestion is impaired.

After the oil is strained give part of it to the fire, or the image of the sun, and part to Wikneswaradu. Then pour it into a gold or silver cup, round the neck of which a clean cloth is fastened by a string of pearls and precious stones, and thus it is to be kept until it is wanted for the patient.

In explanation of these ceremonies we must observe that by the prayers and reading of the Veda by the Bramins, Brahma and Vishnu will be pleased; by the light we conciliate the favour of Bhagavatadu, or the supreme being; by the heaps of the different kinds of grain we please the nine heavenly bodies; by the painted ground in particular we gratify the sun; by the painted goblet, Aswāry, the god of physic; and by the pearls and precious stones we conciliate the favour of Latchmy Davie, the goddess of riches.

The same ceremonies are likewise necessary when the medicine is to be carried to the house of the patient. It is to be placed together with the physician upon an elephant, preceded by music and dancing, and attended by the principal people of the town, and by Bramins invoking the gods by loud prayers, and reading of the vedas. Should any of these ceremonies be neglected from interested motives, the patient will have occasion to repent the omission; for devils of all descriptions will infallibly defile it, as it is no longer guarded by these religious ceremonies.

Before the patient takes the medicine, the god of physic is to be wor-

* Ganisa, the God of Wisdom.

shipped in the person of his deputy, the physician, who (it is seriously recommended for the good of the patient) must be paid well for his services.

The leham, or electuary, is composed of a strong kashaiam of dry powdered ingredients, and some oil, or ghee, and sugar, or honey. As the boiling of it usually lasts very long, iron pots are recommended for its preparation. Besides their durability, they have the advantage of improving the medicinal qualities of the substances boiled in them. If no iron pot can be procured, an earthen pot may be rendered fit for the purpose, by boiling in it 100 palams of lead and iron with water, in the same way as if it was a kashaiam. In boiling a leham, a proper allowance of water is to be made for the quantity which is absorbed by the pot, and likewise for what is spilt during the boiling.

Some lehams must be boiled for twenty days, without ever allowing the fire to go out. The longer one wishes to preserve a leham, the more jaggery must be mixed with it. All decoctions made for the purpose of lehams, must have some Chittramūlum (plantago zeylanica) or Kuddapa roots among the ingredients. The jaggary must undergo a purification before it can be mixed with the leham. It is to be dissolved in water and mixed with the ashes left, with half its weight of tamarind leaves burnt, and boiled down till it acquires the proper degree of consistency.

II. TREATISE OF MEDICINE.

The following translation, or rather abstract, of an Indian Treatise of Medicine, will convey a more complete knowledge of their opinions and prejudices than I could convey by any other method.

Chap. I.—*Advice to Physicians.*

I. The three principal dispositions born with man, namely, wadum *, pittum †, and chestum ‡, occasion his temper and natural constitution. Hence the physician ought to make himself thoroughly acquainted with their nature, so as to be able to ascertain which of the three predominates in any individual; whether they be single or mixed, and what proportion they bear to each other. He ought to know, likewise, the different diseases that may be produced by these three different causes, their nature and symptoms, that he may be able to judge of a disorder by the pulse, and other characteristic signs.

* Literally translated wind. † Bile. ‡ Slime.

II. To form a just diognosis of a disorder, the physician should attend chiefly to the following objects. 1. The heat of the body, which he must ascertain by feeling it with his hands. 2. Its colour: whether pale, yellowish, blackish, &c. 3. The speech: whether weak or loud. 4. The eyes. 5. The colour of the fæces: whether black, green, or yellow. 6. The urine and its colour. 7. The tongue. If all these are attentively examined by an experienced physician, they will soon point out the nature of the disease.

III. Before the physician gives any medicines, he ought to instruct the patient to observe the following rules, without which the medicines cannot have their effect. 1. He is to sleep upon one of his sides, with the hand of the same side put under his head. 2. He must avoid all connection with the other sex. 3. He must rigorously adhere to the diet prescribed. 4. He must not permit himself to lose his temper. 5. He must not let his spirits sink into melancholy. 6. He must not be alarmed about his disease. 7. He must keep his feet always clean.

IV. In the preparation of medicines, the physician ought to be extremely cautious and accurate, especially in taking the different ingredients in the just proportions to one another; in boiling the different portions the exact portion of time requisite, and neither longer nor shorter, &c. The effect of the medicine will be according to the degree of attention that has been bestowed upon these things. For example, the medical oils, in wadum, must be boiled till they admit of being drawn out between the fingers; in pittum, till they gain the consistence of wax; and in chestum, till they may be formed into a ball.

V. In order to give the medicine a proper time to exert its power against the disorder, the physician ought not to disturb the operation of nature by administering it repeatedly on the same day. In disorders of all descriptions, medicines are to be given only twice a-day; once in the morning, after six o'clock, and in the evening at the same hour, or at sun-rise and sun-set. If some extraordinary accidental symptoms should appear, by which the strength of the patient might be much impaired if they were suffered to continue, in such cases alone, medicines either to strengthen the patient or to remove the symptoms may be administered. Still the rule is universal, that we must begin by giving medicines only twice a day. If, after persisting in this course for some time, the disease still continues, then we are at liberty to adopt another.

Chap. II.—*Of the Pulse.*

I. Wadum, pittum, and chestum, the names of the three different morbiferous diatheses in men are likewise the appellations of the three different pulses in the human body. In disorders occasioned by wadum, the pulse of that denomination is perceived; and the same observation applies to the disorders occasioned by pittum and chestum.

II. Four fingers breadth below the navel lies mutadārum, the basis from which proceed in the form of fibres, the arteries that pervade the body; among which, the three called wadum, pittum, and chestum, are alone calculated to enable the physician to judge of disorders. That basis, or root, is four fingers' long, and is the place in which man is conceived. It looks red, like coral; and like it too is full of fringes, which are the roots of so many arteries.

III. Two among these are particularly remarkable, called siwen and danwagy, which are of a yellowish colour.

IV. The pulse siwen is the basis of ten others, the names of which, and their properties and junctions, are as follows:

1. Siwen nariporānen. This presides over the function of respiration, and over the secretion of saliva. It produces also an appetite for eating and drinking. It promotes the faculty of thinking. Its principal seat is under the throat. (Does this allude to the eighth pair of nerves, or to the windpipe? or is it mere absurdity?)

2. Abdomen. The cause of speaking well and lively. Its place is over the navel, and it looks like the lingum. Besides the above-mentioned properties, it promotes the understanding of conceived ideas, and contributes to the extrusion of stools and urine.

3. Wearanen resides in both hips, and reaches up to the sides of the neck and to the eyes. It also extends itself down to the feet.

4. Udānen has its principal seat in the soles of the feet and palms of the hands, but comes up over the neck. It is the cause of sneezing during the act of eating, and prevents the water from entering the stomach, by forcing it upwards again. It directs also the power of opening and shutting the eye-lids.

5. Chaumāṇen* runs from the head throughout the whole body; but it is principally seated in the toes.

* By the termination of most names in *en*, it will be perceived that this translation has been made from Tamul originals.

6. Nāgen in the face and nose, reminds the man of the time in which he is to worship his god.

7. Kurmen counteracts the former, in producing an inclination to put off the time of supplication.

8. Kirugaren produces the power of speaking and laughing.

9. Dewadatten has its residence in the ears, and is the source of hearing; likewise of sneezing and weeping.

10. Dananshien has its source in the sides, upwards and between the shoulders. It remains in action after all the other pulses are dead, and then it causes the swelling of the corpse.

V. To examine the pulse, one of the ten following places may be chosen. 1. The temple. 2. The crown of the head. 3. The neck, under the jaws. 4. The wind-pipe, where it enters the breast. 5. The ancle of the foot. 6. The testicles. 7. The ham. 8. The toes of the foot. 9. The arm-pit. 10. The thumb, down to the wrist. The last is the best, as most conveniently situated, and most distinct in its beats.

VI. The pulse wadum beats exactly at the joint of the hand. Close to it is the pulse pittum, and, a little farther down, chestum. The size of the pulse appears to be that of a rice grain. The pulse, in men, must always be examined on the right side; that in women, on the left *.

VII. In order to examine the pulse, the physician is, with his left hand, to lay hold of the thumb, first and second finger of the patient, and then to lay the first, second, and third finger of his right hand on the pulse. Under the first, he will perceive beating the pulse wadum; under the second, the pulse pittum; and under the third, the pulse chestum. The pulse is in every part of the body.

VIII. If the pulse appears to extend farther than the breadth of three fingers, the patient may be supposed dangerously ill. The fingers ought to be applied to the pulse in the same delicate manner that they are to a wound. The common length of a man is ninety-six times the breadth of his middle finger.

IX. The pulse wadum, when predominant, beats in the same manner that a frog jumps, or as the motion of the creeping rain-worm, the progress of a snake, the motion of a child in a cradle hung in chains, or like the bloodsucker. In pittum, the pulse imitates the fowl when running; she beats the earth with her wings; or it resembles the gait of a peacock, or

* This is carefully observed by the Indian physicians.

the contorted rope, which returns forcibly on itself; or the hopping of a sparrow. In chestum the pulse goes as slow as the fowl walks; as the turtle-dove, or the female crow.

X. The pulse, that goes in the manner that the fowl walks called madakarai, and as the peacock, indicates that wadum and pittum act conjointly. If its motion in the beginning be like the walk of a fowl, and if it change into that of the motion of the bloodsucker (a species of lizzard), and the walk of the bird wichulie, we may conclude that the wadum and chestum are prevailing in equal force. When the pulse beats in the manner that the frog hops, and the goose walks, pittum and chestum are the leading diathesis. Without daily experience in feeling the pulse, none can come to a competent knowledge of it.

XI. The pulse, in sanny, resembles the motion of a large piece of timber balancing upon a man's head; or like the motion of a musk rat, which is at one time extremely quick, and immediately after stops altogether, or becomes extremely slow.

XII. They who smoke much bang *, or tobacco, have a very quick pulse. The same rule applies to a voluptuous man, a fool, and an ideot.

XIII. Hunger, sleep, voluptuous thoughts, always increase the frequency of the pulse. It is irregular in men who are costive, and who labour under obstructions of the bowels.

XIV. The pulse will be found of this latter description immediately after dinner, especially in those who over-eat themselves. Hence at such a time it is difficult to draw any conclusion from the state of the pulse. The same thing happens after washing the head, after sleep, in those who are hungry, who have walked far, or are much fatigued from other causes; who meditate much on religious or abstruse subjects; who are angry; who are possessed with the devil. It happens also after sexual connection, terror, and drunkenness. Likewise to those who are troubled with wind in the bowels, or who have swallowed sulphur, mercury, or poison; who have eaten fowls, hares, frogs, snakes; or who are subject to frequent epileptic paroxisms.

CHAP. III.

I. The diagnosis of the three principal disorders may be farther formed by attending to the following objects. 1. The temperature of the body.

* Cannabis indica.

2. The colour of the face and body. 3. The mode of speaking. 4. The eyes. 5. The stools. 6. The urine. 7. The tongue.

II. In wadum, the abdomen is warm to the touch; in pittum, it is extremely hot, changing from that to a cold temperature. In chestum the body is always a little cold; and the temperature of the valetudinarian varies constantly from warm to cold.

III. The colour of the skin, in wadum, is blackish; in pittum, it is yellowish, or red; in chestum it is pale and whitish; and in the valetudinarian, variegated.

IV. The voice in wadum is natural; neither too weak nor too strong, and of a middle tone. In pittum it is strong, high, and sharp. In chestum it is like that of a man whose throat is compressed. In a man who is constantly sickly, the voice is variable.

V. In wayuvu * the eyes have a blackish tint, which likewise indicate a constant head-ach. The eyes in pittum are reddish and burning, and sometimes of a greenish hue. In chestum, they are pale and whitish; and a matter of that colour is often found to collect in the corner of the eye. The eyes of those who have a weak constitution are red, or sometimes greenish.

VI. If we attend to the alvine evacuations, we shall find them, in wadum, to be small lumps and pieces of a black colour. In pittum, they are like the spittle of those who chew beetle, red and yellowish. In chestum, they are like flame, and of a whitish colour. In those who are constantly sickly, they are of several colours and degrees of consistence.

VII. The urine, in wayuvu, is but little coloured, and is discharged with some difficulty. In pittum, it is red, and often yellow; in chestum, frothy and white.

VIII. The state of the body, with respect to these disorders, may be judged of by dropping gingelie oil upon the urine, while in a state of rest. When the drop extends into a circular form, it indicates wadum; when it divides into many small circles, it points out pittum; and when it produces small air bubbles, chestum. When the drop sinks to the bottom, it indicates sanny wadum, or a state of the utmost debility.

IX. Another mode of discovering the state of the body from the urine, is to expose a portion of it to the sun till it grows quite warm, and then to drop some oil upon it from the extremity of a straw. If the oil extends itself on

* The same as wadum.

all sides, wadum is indicated; if it assumes the appearance of a pearl, it denotes the existence of pittum. If the urine under examination looks like mustard oil, and if the gingelie oil dropped upon it assumes the form of the pearls of the morning dew, then the disorder consists of wadum and pittum united. When the urine appears greenish, and the drop of oil extends itself longitudinally, the disorder consists of wadum and chestum united. When the urine is white, and half the oil sinks to the bottom, it shows that pittum and chestum are united. When the other half of the oil assumes the form of the full moon, or of a square, or of a pearl, a very unfavourable opinion may be drawn respecting the recovery of the patient.

X. The tongue in wayuvu is furrowed, dry, and blackish. In chestum it is white, ash-coloured, and dry. The tongue of a dwantarogam is furrowed, sharp, rough, and destitute of moisture.

Chap. IV.—*Of the principal Diseases which arise from Wadum, Pittum, and Chestum.*

I. From wadum, which, literally translated, signifies *wind*, are derived eighty diseases. The following are the most remarkable of these.

Borowari dandel. Swelling of the legs.

Wirel dale nimittel. Stiffness, inflexibility of the fingers.

Padum dirugle. A sensation of stings in the feet, together with a contraction of the same parts.

Padum polkindy pudle. Spasm in the legs and feet.

Kāl polkindy erudle. Spasms in the calves of the feet.

Narambu poryttel. A protuberance of the veins and sinews.

Narulattel. A weak pulse.

Crudel. Tormenting pains throughout every part of the members, beginning from the extremities upwards, &c.

Trangudle. The same pains, commencing upon the main body towards the extremities.

Muiankāl wīngudle. Swelling of the knees.

Ardamaul wangudel. The intraction of the testicles.

Chiru velaynen shudirukkenachemmudel. Spasmodic contraction of the throat, preventing respiration.

Karundulurudle. A scurviness of the skin, that looks like ashes strewed upon it.

Kāndam bureyttel. Swelling of the sides of the neck.

Orambarāmdirugle. Half-sided head-ache, or megrim.

Dakkaballotudel. Gnashing of the teeth.

Envoborakkannalmunu mudel wanghedel. The intraction of both cheeks.

Kannaduchengle. The distortion of the eye upwards, under the eye-lids.

Kaluden kannatle. Swelling of the foot and legs.

Kureltāney purettel. Griping of the bowels.

Punpolnowudle. A pain of the abdomen, with the sensation of its being covered with wounds.

Wikkum. Swelling of the abdomen.

Udinem kattudle. Swelling in the abdomen.

Uleyboru. Heart-beating.

Trakle. Constant rushing sensation in the ears.

Kunawalittel. Painful contractions of the head-ache downwards.

Dalai danai narukkel. Constant shaking of the head.

Shalailvalittle. Violent head-ache.

II. From pittum (which literally signifies bile) are derived forty diseases, of which the following are the most remarkable.

Engle. Horror and stunning.

Granum. Constant silence, as if meditating on religious subjects.

Parel. Constant singing.

Dungle. Constant sleepiness.

Pattel. Constant chattering of nonsense.

Dondirra cherittel. Constant laughing; indefatigableness in running from one place to another.

Unnadundul. An inclination to put every thing into the mouth.

Karittel. Biting with the teeth, like a dog.

Chinnir iraungudel. Red urine.

Annir wedumbudel. Burning urine.

Arudel parudel. Constant singing and dancing.

Kurudel. Crying out and calling out as if in a great fury.

Nīrdaittel. Constant drinking, without being able to quench the thirst.

Chetikkusteruttel. Giddiness in the head.

Moreadudel wattudel. Meagreness of the whole body.

Urel mogum weluttel. Decoloration of the face and body.

Unu nīrutondudel. An internal sensation of heat.

Oamalnarcittel. In youth the appearance of old age.

Regumarukkudel. Marasm.

Dodawattudel. Nocturnal pollutions.

Ashādy. Drowsiness.

Maidanadel. Pain over the whole body.

Weesimanshanittel. Yellow eyes.

III. From chestum, which signifies liquids and slime, are derived twenty diseases, of which the following are the most remarkable.

Udivium veluttel. Paleness of the blood.

Ullival perudel. Expectoration of much slime.

Adoroniveluttel. Paleness of the lips.

Anninattarittel. Swelling of the tongue, in a manner that prevents speaking.

Dundanshalgerel. A strong catarrh.

Dumbel. Frequent sneezing.

Makkaraittel. Obstruction of the nose.

Areaporamaegam. A white flegm going off together with the urine.

Yrunay. Coughing.

Kainshivasum. An asthmatic respiration.

Kadutta. A sensation of the limbs, as if they were bruised.

Ongievalarumutta durramum. Strong growth of the hair of the head.

Salamalamkarittel. An inclination to make frequent urine, and diarrhœa.

Dalaikarakaraittel. Itching on the head.

Bulaiwaishilandigle. The itch.

CHAP. V.—*Of the Causes of Diseases.*

I. Though these causes are manifold, yet the following are those to which we ought chiefly to direct our attention.

1. Obstructions of the bowels. A man who has not every day three motions, viz. in the morning, at noon, and in the evening.
2. Eating of dishes that have been kept a whole night over.
3. Strong exertions in walking.
4. Negligence in keeping a proper diet and regimen.
5. Great exertions in bodily exercise and working.
6. Long fasting.
7. The swallowing of small stones along with meat.
8. Neglect of washing the head and the whole body.
9. Intemperance in eating.

10. Melancholy.
11. Passion, wrath, and grief.
12. The omission of giving alms.
13. Fear and horror.
14. Licentiousness.
15. Taking medicines that are not purified.
16. Eating of prohibited things.
17. Uncleanliness of the body.
18. Medicines ill applied in disorders.
19. Irregularity in giving medicines, viz. not at the proper time,—twice a-day, in the morning and evening.
20. Excess in sleeping.
21. Unreasonable conduct.
22. A dissolute life.
23. Want of the six daily regular discharges of urine.
24. Neglect in taking monthly a purge.
25. Neglect in taking one hour's sleep after dinner.
26. Sexual connections in the noon time.
27. Eating without hunger.
28. Drinking too much water.
29. Eating too much of roots, as radishes, &c.
30. Retentions of several excretions a longer period than nature claims.
31. Great exertions of the mind.

II. Indigestion is the cause of many disorders, and proceeds itself from the following.

1. Eating before the victuals of a former meal are digested.
2. Throwing down the meat with too great a haste.
3. Sleeping immediately after having taken dinner.
4. Worms in the belly.
5. Obstructions.

Chapter VI. *Of the Diet.*

That the medicines prescribed by the physicians may have their effect, the patient must strictly attend to the prescribed diet; the general rules are as follows. The patient shall not eat any thing sour or bitter; he must neither wade nor bathe in salt water; he must not bathe in cold fresh water, nor drink it, nor touch it; for all these purposes the water must be warm. He must neither snuff, smoke, nor chew tobacco: he must neither eat salt-water fish nor butter that has been salted. He must not expose himself to the wind, and must avoid speaking much.

The diet is called lankanum * when prescribed in fevers. The lankanum requires, that the patient, in fevers occasioned by wadum, shall not eat or drink any thing for the first three days: on the fourth day he begins to take the prescribed physic: other physicians order the patient to abstain from eating and drinking during seven days. In fevers proceeding from pittum, the patient is only condemned to a fast of a single day before he commences his course of medicine, though there are some physicians who prescribe a fast of three days. Fevers from chestum require an abstinence from eating and drinking for seven days, while others more rigid prolong the fast for nine days: the patient may then commence his medicine, and he is to drink some conjie † made of rice one hour after having taken his medicine.

Some physicians go farther in their precautions, and give this conjie in fevers from wadum only at sunset; in those from pittum, at sunrise; and in those from chestum at noon: in the fever dontachūram the fast must continue ten days.

Other physicians prescribe the following lankanum. The day on which the fever begins, the patient shall neither eat nor drink any thing: on the second day some water is to be made warm, and some aratorai leaves, if they can be had, put into it. With this the teeth and tongue are to be cleaned, and the head washed; the head is then tied with a cloth, and the patient ordered to lie on his left side, with the hand of the same side under the head. He must neither attempt to eat or drink the whole day. The third day he may be allowed to drink and eat a tettan kattay (seed of strychnos potatorum). Should the fever return after this, or continue, the lankanum must be persisted in during the 5th, 6th, and 7th days; during

* This word literally signifies, *fast*. It may appear incredible that the Indian physicians prescribe a rigorous fast of eight or ten days to their patients, and still more so that the patients should be able to endure it; but it is literally the fact. This is the common mode of curing the intermittents and hill fevers in this part of the country, and I am a witness that my own servants have fasted from ten to twenty days.

† Water in which rice has been boiled, which is like barley-water.

which time the patient is only to be allowed to drink a little conjie every day. The fever will then disappear entirely, or at least after the administration of medicines for three successive days.

It requires however to determine what persons are equal to a lankanum. It ought never to be prescribed to women that are with child, to lean people; to old men and children; to those that have contracted fever from fatigue in travelling; to those that have sore eyes, consumption, or a diarrhœa: to all such persons it would prove most injurious.

At the end of the lankanum the patient is to drink a conjie, prepared in the following manner. Take one sixteenth part of a medit * of rice and toast it, but not too much; two medits of water are then to be poured on it, and a little piece of ginger is to be added: boil this mixture till one fourth of the water is evaporated. This conjie alone is often sufficient to cure the fever. In fevers from wadum the mixture should be boiled till one third of the whole is evaporated, and the remainder should be administered all at once. In fevers from pittum it must be boiled down to one half, and only one half of the remaining liquid is to be drunk at once. In chestum three fourths of the liquid must be evaporated away, and the remainder is to be drunk at once.

Chapter VII. *Of Fevers.*

I. Fevers are the rajahs, or chiefs of all diseases, and the thirst that accompanies them is like the god of death. They issued from the fiery eye of Ishuren's forehead, when Takka his father-in-law maliciously attempted to dethrone him. In a convention of all the gods he brought a fire offering, with a view to annihilate the great god Ishuren; But Ishuren, informed in his residence Kailāsum of his intention, sent forth from his wrathful eye the burning fever which dispersed itself over all the world.

II. There are seven different classes of fevers, namely,—1. Wadashuram, or the fever that proceeds from wadum.—2. Pittashuram, or the fever that proceeds from pittum. 3. Chestamashuram, or the fever that proceeds from chestum. 4. Būdhashuram, or the fever caused by evil spirits. 5. Ashiranoshuram, the fever from indigestion. 6. Astishuram, the fever of the bones. 7. Dondasūram, the daily fever, or quotidian.

III. In wadashūram the face is blackish; the lips are dry, and blackish; the whole body feels the painful sensation of something running through it;

* A measure of about 2 lb.

there is internal heat and heaviness of the whole body; the breath is drawn with difficulty; the excrements have a yellowish colour.

IV. In pittashuram the patient sleeps much, but jumps up sometimes, and makes efforts to run away; the urine and stools are reddish; he speaks much; the mouth is bitter, and dry, with much thirst; the respiration is often stopped; vomitings and hiccups come on; he becomes melancholy, and seems involved in deep meditation; and this closes the scene.

V. In chestamashuram the face and tongue are pale; a pain, occasioned by coughing and asthmatic symptoms, oppresses the breast; much phlegm is constantly expectorated; the patient complains of flying pains in different parts of the body.

VI. The fever būdhashuram may be known by the following symptoms. Pain all over the body; a deep and difficult respiration; a troublesome cough; a pale tongue; a sweating throat; thirst; rising hair; epileptic fits; unnatural appetite; delirium, exhibiting itself in singing, laughing, bawling, &c. The word budham signifies an evil spirit; and the malignity of this fever is supposed to be caused by such a being.

VII. Ashiranoshuram is the fever in which the body feels very hot, with a sensation of being bruised. The other symptoms are obstinate obstructions, hiccups, eruption of an acid liquor from the stomach into the œsophagus and mouth.

VIII. This last kind of fever is subdivided into four subordinate sets of fever, distinguished by the following names.

1. Reshalhashu chiranum. Produced by eating too many fruits, or drinking milk or conjie water before dinner, which prevents the stomach from properly digesting the meal. The symptoms of this fever are a strong heat of the body, accompanied with head-ache.

2. Witthattamannachiram. In it, the abdomen is extended like a bow, and this is accompanied with a painful heat.

3. Witteracheratchūram. In it, the sensation is felt of a heavy, hard body in the belly, which resists the pressure of the belly; is at the same time very hot, and swells up; sour eructations proceed from the stomach.

4. Tummanachūranam. In it the stomach rises and falls like a pair of bellows, occasioned by the air contained in it. This is accompanied with yawnings, during which the air rushes out of the mouth like smoke. The whole body is hot.

IX. From the bones proceeds the fever astishuram, and it appears after excessive labour. The patient is tormented with much thirst, the whole body feels pain, a profuse sweat overspreads the whole surface, which is followed by great debility. The patient does not speak, lies constantly motionless as if meditating, and desires cool things to eat and drink.

X. Dantashurum is a continued fever, the nature and symptoms of which our author does not relate. In its place he treats of the matselshuram, and says, that it is a fever which regularly returns after an interval of three, four, five, or six days. Those fevers, the paroxysms of which regularly set in at twelve o'clock at night, and which originate either from wadum or from the united influence of wadum, pittum, and chestum, are the most to be dreaded.

XI. There are still several other kinds of fevers, the following will serve as an example of them:

1. Tale portinashūram. It is produced in the head. Its peculiarities are a little heat, much thirst, the pulse as if it were obstructed, head-ache.

2. Elumbai pattinashūram. It has its seat in the bones. The symptoms are, excessive heat, much thirst, copious sweat, pain all over the body. The patient lies without speaking a word, neither does he seem to breathe.

3. Mangashattai pattinashūram. It exists in the flesh. The symptoms are excessive heat and sweat, violent respiration, dryness of the lips, pains of the whole body, rising of the hair, a prickly sensation in the skin, constantly disappearing and returning again, breathing imperceptible.

XII. A fever from pittum and wadum has the following symptoms: the hips and the head are much affected, there is much thirst, internal heat, constant moving and throwing the body about, want of sleep, vomiting. Chestum and wadum produce a fever in which the patient stretches out his arms in a lazy manner, strains frequently, is terrified. A frequent chilliness is perceived, much phlegm fills the mouth and throat, delirium comes on. In the fever from pittum and chestum we find much thirst, excessive heat, bitterness in the mouth, sometimes a violent cold, disquietude, lascivious inclinations. The fever springing from the combined action of pittum, wadum, and chestum exhibits the following symptoms:—The belly is swelled, the patient is afflicted with frequent fits of rigour, and partial sweats in the face at the same time; some times the whole body feels burning hot while the knees alone remain cold. Much phlegm is expectorated. Violent head-aches and obstinate costiveness at once afflict the unhappy sufferer. The taste in the mouth changes from sour to sweet, or *vice versa*. This fever is sometimes called deritūshum, because it owes its existence to the combined action of the three principal disorders.

XIII. The following fevers differ from all those hitherto mentioned:

1. Wishashūrum. A fever from poison. The symptom perceptible the first day is heat, which goes off again. It returns again on the second, third, and fourth days, and disappears on the fifth day. On the twelfth day it sets in again, and continues for some time. It often occupies the upper part of the body only while the lower extremities are cold. The whole body feels heavy and is sometimes covered with froth; during which time the patient despairs of his life.

2. Aimaishūram. Some heat during the day, which is vehement every alternate three hours; in the night it is attended with sleepiness and heart beating. There is a desire to eat, but it is gratified without relish. Weakness is exhibited by the attempts of the patient to speak. A constant trembling of the body.

3. Andirashūram. The symptoms of this fever are much heat, apprehension and fear, vain and constant attempts to vomit, the urine is reddish, the patient lies motionless like a piece of wood. He complains of belly-ache.

4. Churakuram. In this fever the whole body is hot and sweating. The eyes as well as other parts of the whole body are red. The patient is constantly timid; the stools very liquid. The patient sometimes jumps out of bed and tries to run away.

XIV. Shannewadashūram is a fever in which the patient often swoons away. The forehead and breast are covered with sweat, the internal heat is very great. The patient is oppressed with excessive weakness. The eyes have a greenish hue. The breathing is extremely weak. Sometimes the patient lies still without speaking a word, at another he talks incessantly. He is attended with disquietude, pains in the breast, hiccups. The stomach frequently turns up, and the hair bristles.

CHAP. VIII.—*Of the Sanny* *.

I. Sanny is not to be mistaken for kumarak (epilepsy).

* As the word sanny occurs perpetually in the mouths and writings of the Indian physicians, I have been at some pains to ascertain its meaning; but am sorry to say that my efforts have not been successive. I was tempted at first to consider it as apoplexy, but was soon obliged to give up that opinion. At present I am inclined to believe that the three sannys are the names given to the very worst symptoms that occur in any particular disease.

II. Among the thirteen species of sanny—there are six in which life is in no danger; but in the other seven much danger may be apprehended. The names of these thirteen species are as follows:

1. Daham. In it respiration is free; but the members are distorted. The patient finds himself much relieved when his limbs are gently beat every where with the hand.

2. Dalligasanny. The eyes are shut and the whole body burning.

3. Andasanny. Deafness, dumbness, or delirious bawling, internal heat, vomiting, and hiccup unite to characterise this species.

4. Ruttagasanny. Every thing chagrins the patient labouring under this species; he lies down without speaking; the neck feels painful; he throws himself from one place to another, his heat increases, a giddiness comes on, the lips become dry, the forehead and neck are overwhelmed with a partial sweat.

5. Chittapirunay. The symptoms are senselessness, dumbness, head-ache, restlessness, a great degree of heat. The pulse wadum and pittum beat vehemently. Sometimes the patient raves, sings, dances, &c.

6. Shedangusanny. The whole body is cold to the touch and feels much pain: it trembles. The patient labours under a tormenting cough, hiccup, and vomiting. The breathing is interrupted, and the excretions go off involuntarily.

7. Dondirasanny. In this the patient speaks nonsense without interruption; he continually passes his hands over the place on which he lies. His tongue is blackish and rough, the saliva runs out of his mouth, his skin feels dry, his thirst is excessive, his excretions pass off involuntarily. The whole body feels itchy, the eyes are wild and staring, the body is hot.

8. Karedakirubasanny. Sleeplessness, thirst, and drowziness in the head, a protuberance in the sinews of the muscles of the neck, attended with a stiffness of the part, groaning and fear are the symptoms of this species. Sometimes the respiration is interrupted, and the head and body afflicted with much pain. Sometimes there supervene cough, hiccup, and vomiting.

9. Kannikasanny. In this species we find deafness, accompanied with delirious melancholy talking, roughness of the tongue, hiccup, flatulency, and trembling of the whole body.

10. Pakkinasanny. Inability of opening the eyes, from which water is constantly oosing, and when they are forcibly opened by others their ap-

pearing blind; grief, a deep silence, trembling of the body—these symptoms united constitute this sanny.

11. Nalligasanny is present when the tongue and lips are dry and scratched up, the stools bloody or watery, the body both internally and externally hot, the patient is senseless, faints away, is extremely weak, deaf, and subject to hiccup.

12. Iotripadasanny. In it the whole body trembles, the patient utters loud groans, there is much internal heat, thirst, and pain over the whole body, together with coughing and hiccup.

13. Bralabasanny. In it there is much internal and external heat, especially in the soles of the feet; there is thirst, a blackish tongue, beset as it were with thorns and furrowed; the mouth is shut up, and the patient is deaf.

CHAP. IX.—*Of the Prognosis.*

I. To know whether or not the patient will die of his disease, take some of his urine and put it into a place where it may stand undisturbed for a while. Then, from the end of a straw drop some gingelie oil upon it. If it sink, the patient will die; if it swim, he will recover.

II. Life is not in danger when the following favourable symptoms occur:—When the patient takes medicines without aversion; when his voice remains unaltered; when during his well days his pulse is clear and perceptible; when he keeps himself cleanly while asleep; when the hands and feet do not hang inertly from him; when the respiration is free and he does not expectorate too much phlegm; when he prostrates himself and adores his God in the morning, noon, and evening; when his taste is natural, and especially when he can distinguish between sour, bitter, and sweet. Under these favourable circumstances we have no reason to be apprehensive of life, even if the patient should be very weak.

III. Attention to the stars may likewise give us considerable information respecting the fate of our patient.

IV. The symptoms of death are as follows:

1. Want of sleep.
2. A constant murmuring, or unintelligible endeavours to speak.
3. Want of memory.
4. Deep groaning breath.
5. Staring immoveable eyes.
6. Proneness to eat and to drink many improper things.

7. Disquietude.
8. Spasmodic contraction of the hands, feet, and extremities.
9. Failure of the sight.
10. An unsteady pulse, that turns to the right or left when the finger is put upon it.
11. An intermittent pulse.
12. When the body becomes cold and the eyes stare round.
13. Dryness of the breast.
14. The protuberance of the veins, especially of that in the breast.
15. When the sides of the tongue, of the eyes, and of the joints become pale.
16. The swelling of the scrotum.
17. Burned, dry excrements.
18. Swelling of the feet and abdomen, especially of the navel.
19. Total costiveness.
20. Total want of appetite to eat or drink.
21. Constant coughing and yawning.
22. Extraordinary degree of thirst.
23. The sinking in of the eyes.

The absence of these symptoms can give us hopes that the medicines will cure the disorder.

Thus I have finished the translation of this most extraordinary treatise, and I dare say my readers are by this time as fatigued as I am myself. It may be considered as a summary of all the medical knowledge of the Hindoos. We see their absolute ignorance of anatomy, and every thing connected with the functions of the human body; that their system is entirely chimerical and connected with their religious opinions; and the long fasts to which they subject their patients are probably by far the most efficacious of their remedies. I had originally added long notes upon this little treatise, exhibiting the various opinions of other Indian medical writers upon the subjects discussed in the text, but upon farther reflection I have been induced to withdraw them, conceiving that the treatise itself exhibited a banquet of absurdity sufficient to satisfy the most voracious guests; while different views of the same ridiculous opinions could not serve to add to the information of the most inquisitive reader.

I will yet, however, intrude on the patience of my readers, by giving them a few preparations of medicines which among the Hindoo physicians are in great repute. I have chosen such as are taken from the mineral kingdom, as no mention has been made of any of that kind in the Kalpastanum.

Quicksilver in a great variety of forms, particularly as corrosive sublimate (savāram), or as calomel (rassa carpūram), are the ingredients of almost all prescriptions, and are the great nostrums of all Hindoo physicians. These, however, I have avoided to introduce, as they will form the subject of a separate treatise.

Passpom of Tutanag, or Flowers of Zinc.

This medicine is recommended in India, in several diseases that usually prove very refractory when under the care of European medical men.

I once tried it with the best effect mixed with valerian root, in a case of inveterate epilepsy. The patient was a Bramin, who was usually seized with four or five fits a day.

The Hindoos prepare these flowers in the following manner: Zinc is fused in an earthen pot, some green leaves of the euphorbia nereifolia being thrown into the melted mass, which is constantly stirred with an iron spoon. It inflames and burns in the usual manner, and falls to ashes, which are kept in the fire till they acquire a splendid white colour. Only the finest parts of this are kept for medical use. They are separated from the rest by sifting through a piece of fine muslin. This medicine is given in the following diseases, with the greatest confidence. 1. Gonorrhœa virulenta. 2. Nocturnal polutions. 3. Fluor albus. 4. Hæmorrhoids. The mode of administering it in these diseases is as follows:

1. In the meharogam or gonorrhæa it is recommended to take the leaves of ractum mandalappu, to beat them in a mortar to a paste, and to fry them with some ghee, to which is to be added powdered cummin seed and cardamum, of each the weight of one rupee, and sugar to the weight of two rupees. This mass is mixed with four condumanny* of the passpom, and made up into five pills. One at a time, containing two scruples, is the dose to be taken as usual in the morning and evening. As the disorder often continues after the administration of these five pills, the same quantity is to be prepared a second time, and administered as before. The patient must be confined to rice, conjie, and a little boiled mutton, spirits of all kinds, fish and high seasoned meats are to be avoided.

* The seed of abrus precatorius, weighing a little more than one grain each.

2. Nothing can be more distressing to a man than a constant waste of his strength by nocturnal pollutions, and the signs about him of daily increasing impotence in all transactions. It would certainly be a matter of great importance if a man could get rid of so disagreeable an accident by taking for seven successive days, before going to bed, the weight of one condumanny of this passpom, in one ounce of good cow butter, and a glass of good cow's milk after it.

3. In the kusum arogam, or the fluor albus, this medicine is to be given in the following manner:—Take mady kaylu* and pady kaylu,* of each ten, boil them in six ounces of water till half the liquid is evaporated. Then a mixture of two condumanny of passpom, and two rupees of cow's butter is to be taken. After which the liquid just described is to be drunk. The use of this medicine once a day, for a week, will probably complete the cure. But if the disease be very inveterate it will be advisable to administer the medicine twice a day.

4. For the cure of hæmorrhoids, the argerogam of the Hindoos, the following is the prescription: Grind one rupee weight of nēlpusiriga, with ghee, sugar, and cardomum, of each half a rupee weight. Mix the whole with eight condumanny of passpom. Let one half of this be taken in the morning, and the other in the evening. No particular diet is to be observed.

Iron Cenduram.

Both the Tamuls and Hindoos consider the colour of medicines prepared from metals as the greatest criterion of their excellence, and accordingly the colour in their opinion marks the skill and address of the preparer of such medicines. The principal excellence of iron medicines lies in a fine purple colour, which of course they are at great pains to produce. They have a great variety of ways of preparing iron for medical purposes; though in reality their cendurams, as they are called, are nothing else than so many modes of preparing martial ethiops. Vanity, no doubt, and prepossession have occasioned the great increase of these cendurams in India, just as in Europe, they gave birth to such a variety of mercurial and antimonial preparations. And every inventor of course persisted in the superiority of his own peculiar contrivance, and was at pains to spread its reputation and its employment in medicine.

* Terminolia mirabolana, and T. spec. nov.

This accounts I conceive in a great measure for the great number of such prescriptions that are in vogue among the physicians of India, and which are estimated according to the channel through which they have proceeded. Though in other respects they all agree pretty well about the diseases in which these medicines are to be prescribed, as well as the regimen and diet which are to be followed.

When we consider the reputation in which this metal is held by a nation long considered the wisest of the East, we cannot be much surprised to find them possessed not only of our share of knowledge of the valuable qualities of this medicine, but that they even know more of its medical virtues than we do. They have had ample opportunity to obtain this knowledge in consequence of the greater delicacy of their constitutions. I shall, therefore, state a few of their most esteemed prescriptions.

Before sun-rise cut some bark and wood from the samfry chettu (æschynomene sesban) pound it in a mortar and express its juice. Take five pagodas weight of this juice for every rupee weight of iron filings. Put the iron filings upon a plate in the sun, and add the juice at five or six different times. When the whole is completely dried let it be wetted with the expressed juice of the ummatakay (fruits of the datura) and made up into a small cake which is to be laid in the sun to dry between two pieces of cloth. When dry let it be put between two pieces of earthen pot into a heap of dried cow-dung. This dung is to be lighted at the apex, and the cake must be allowed to remain in it for the space of two hours.

Another Iron Cenduram.

Rub for two hours ten drachms of iron filings, with the juice of nago maram (jambolifera pedunculata) obtained from the pounded bark by expression. Form the whole into a little cake, and place it between two pieces of earthen ware into a conical heap of thirty wraties, which is to be lighted at its apex.

After this first ignition mix the powder thus obtained with two and a half pagodas of brimstone, and grind it with the juice of the manatta kally (solanum nigrum) for the space of one hour, and then commit it to a fire of the same kind as before.

This part of the process being finished the iron powder is to be rubbed a third time with the juice of the lahty nardam parham (a species of citrus) and a particular large kind of the sour orange; or, when it is wanting, of the common lemon for an hour. The whole is then to be treated exactly as before, and a fine purple red powder is expected as the result of these complicated processes.

The reader will readily perceive that nothing whatever is obtained by these tedious processes, but the red or peroxide of iron. It is not at all likely that the juices employed in the triturations answer any purpose which might not be equally accomplished by gum and water. For the long continued heat is certainly sufficient to dissipate any peculiar vegetable matter which they might be supposed to contain. Neither can we see any useful purpose which the addition of the sulphur can have. Perhaps indeed a small portion of it may be acidified and remain united with the iron converting it into a salt. I have no doubt that a medicine of equal efficacy might be obtained by giving green vitriol to a gentle heat till the whole of the moisture is dissipated, and then exposing it to a strong heat in a crucible. The colour of such a preparation is quite similar, and I dare say it is in every respect identic with the Indian cendūram.

This cendūram is reputed a very efficacious medicine in the disorder which the Tamuls call ulkachel (the internal fever), the symptoms of which are stated to be a dirty pale colour of the whole body, a particular decoloration of the eye, want of appetite, indigestion, constant thirst, pain in all the limbs, and an extraordinary degree of laziness and indolence which terminates in the last stage of the disorder by a swelling of the belly and a copious diaresis. This fever is produced by an intemperate indulgence of the sexual appetite, by extraordinary exertions and labours, by the constant use of heating things and provocatives. Nothing is more conducive to cure this disease than the cendūram just described. Let from two to ten gold fanams be given daily in a kind of potion made by grinding perincheragam (aniseseeds) and sugar with water. If the fever be very violent the medicine may be continued from eight to twenty days, or rather till the perfect restoration of health, and administered twice a day. The patient must be restrained from the use of pepper, pachapeyr, pomegranates, onions; milk, buttermilk, and rice are recommended.

Is it not improbable that this iron preparation would be useful in those kinds of disorders to which Europeans are frequently subject in India, and which are usually ascribed to obstructions of the liver and intestines. These probably act to a certain extent, but are only secondary causes of the disorder in question.

Tampuru Passpom, or Tambura Bhastmom.

The opinions of European physicians, both ancient and modern, are much divided respecting the use of copper as an internal medicine. Some proscribe it entirely as one of the most destructive poisons, while others extol its virtues when administered in small doses. My own experience induces me to adopt the opinions of this latter class of physicians. About one hundred years ago, it was recommended by many eminent men; as for example Boyle, Boerhaave, Zwelfer, Koenig, and Loesecke.

It must not however be concealed that it has been productive of dreadful consequences when taken internally, though I rather ascribe the deleterious effects to the quantity of the copper administered than to its being inherently injurious to the constitution in how minute a quantity soever it is given. It is well known that the oxides of this metal are violent poisons, and that few metals are more easily corroded and oxydated than copper. But I think there are several cupreous preparations which may be given internally in small quantities with a good effect. The *ens veneris* of the old pharmacopœias, or a solution of copper in volatile alkali, is a medicine of this kind, and I think there are others still less dangerous than it, and which in certain states of health constitute remedies not to be despised. This opinion is founded on the practice of the Indian physicians, who often administer their copper passpoms with much confidence. The Tamuls especially hold the white passpom in the highest estimation. Some may think the proposal of this metal as a medicine, and the Hindoo preparation of it, too frivolous a thing to be proposed to the medical faculty in Great Britain. I shall notwithstanding run the hazard, as the formula is but short. It is as follows:

Take a piece of copper coin, make it red hot, and plunge it into the expressed juice of the tamarind leaves. Repeat this several times. Then melt it in a crucible with an ounce of sulphur thrown into it at two different times. At the first addition the mass will swell up, and after the second fall again. Grind this mass, moistening it with the juice of one hundred lemons, which will render it white.

Such is the Indian process. The chemical reader will at once perceive that the repeated ignitions and sudden coolings of the copper can be of no other use but to diminish its quantity; that the fusion with sulphur forms a sulphuret of copper; that the sulphur is probably greatly in excess; that the juice of one hundred lemons, if allowed to act long enough upon the mass, will take up most of the copper and leave the sulphur. Hence, in all probability, this so much boasted medicine is a hydrate of sulphur, mixed with a portion of sulphuret of copper.

The following is the method of making another cupreous preparation, called Bhastmom.

Melt in a crucible two drachms of copper, adding during the fusion, by small quantities at a time, a powder composed of the following ingredients:

Shells of eggs, two drachms.
Radina nawasagaram *, two drachms.
Borax, six ounces.

It is then alloyed with its own weight of kaylogowankam, and given to the coppersmith, who understands how to purify it. Take then of purified orpiment one ounce, and of borax half an ounce. Rub both together with the juice of lemons, and make pills of it, of the size of small peas.

The orpiment is purified by laying it fifteen times between two strata of fresh burnt lime, which is to be slacked with water.

The copper is then melted a second time, and during the fusion all these pills are to be added one by one.

Of the copper prepared in this manner take one ounce, and the same quantity of sawaram †. When these are rubbed together, they assume at first the appearance of water, then that of wax. We must then add the following ingredients:

Mercury half an ounce.
Camphor an ounce.
White arsenic a drachm.
Wolley aramasy a drachm.

Stir the whole till it acquires the consistence of wax. Balls are then to be made of it, which after being dried in the sun are placed between two pieces of earthenware, and exposed to the heat of two hundred wraties, covered on all sides with earth.

This medicine is to be given in all cases of leprosy, and in several other similar diseases. Milk is always to be drunk after it. In inveterate diseases it may be necessary to give it for forty-one successive days.

* Muriate of ammonia. † Corrosive sublimate.

III. A FREE TRANSLATION OF THE CHETRI GANITAM,

OR FIELD MEASURING OF THE HINDOOS.

Having seen so many contradictory accounts of the land measures of the Hindoos, and the mode used by them for measuring the extent of a piece of ground, I resolved to trace the whole, if possible, to its source, in hopes of meeting with a full account of what is of so much importance in ascertaining the revenue of the country. After many unsuccessful inquiries, I at last fell in with the Ganitam, which, I was told, contained the *ne plus ultra* of all human knowledge in this science, revealed to men by no less a personage than Bramha himself.

This work was originally written in Sanscrit, but was translated into Telinga by Pavaluru Mallaia, a Bramin, who lived, it is said, some centuries ago, at Rajahmundry. It was above a year before I could find a man who was master of it: luckily he possessed at the same time the best practical knowledge of the science, as far as it exists in India.

The other books of the Ganitam are called Păvăluru, Băgărah, Sūvarnah, Mistreta, Benna, Gătă, Chăyah, Sūtra, and Prakīrna. From the inaccuracies that I have observed in many parts of it, from the author's giving his own name to the first book, and from his taking notice only of the Masulipatam circar, in the Chetri Ganitam, I am inclined to think that he has only given a very imperfect extract from the Sanscrit original.

The Chetri Ganitam, or the book treating of land measuring, is the only one of the ten books of the Ganitam that I have seen in Telinga verse. The Sanscrit original is said not to be easily procured, useful as it might have been in correcting the errors and differences with which the Telinga copies abound. I should have been obliged to encounter still greater difficulties in finding a man who could have given me an intelligible explanation of it, as I am myself not well acquainted with this celebrated idiom of Indian languages.

The copy from which I have translated the following pages, appeared to me the most correct of all those that I saw, though it has still many errors, especially in the practical parts of it, which will be easily discovered by any one, though but little conversant in mathematics.

My instructor, a Bramin above eighty years of age, and who could repeat the greatest part of the work by heart, gave me the following account of the other books of the Ganitam.

Păvăluru Ganitam treats of weights and measures, of the fundamentals of arithmetic, as numeration, addition, the five different ways of multiplying, division, practice, rule of three, rule of five, of seven, of nine, and eleven.

Băgărah Ganitam gives an account of the weights used in the valuation of precious stones.

Suvarnah Ganitam. The art of assaying gold and silver by the touch, and of taking their specific gravities.

Mistreta Ganitam. Unknown.

Bennah Ganitam. Practice; treating of weights and prices of things.

Gata Ganitam teaches the manner of measuring the extent of tanks, and the water they contain; the manner of measuring and making channels, fortifications, embankments; explains the different measures in use, and treats especially of the use of the level, in making channels and tanks.

Chaya Ganitam explains the method of finding the height and distance of objects by their shadows.

Sūtra Ganitam contains rules for solving arithmetical, hydraulical, and algebraical questions, and treats of dry measures, of progression, &c.

Prakīrnah Ganitam is the algebra of the Hindoos.

THE CHETRI * GANITAM

Is the sixth book of the work called Ganitam (Mathematics). It treats of superficial measurements, or land measuring; of the terms used in the science of measures, of the mode of measuring, and casting up accounts, and of allowances to be made in measuring, &c.

The fundamental measure is the *inch*, which is determined in three different ways †.

First, by placing three rice corns in a line, lengthways: the space they occupy is called an inch.

Secondly, by measuring the circumference of the second joint of the thumb; half the length of which is an inch.

* Chetri, a Sanscrit word, signifying the ground. Hence the Chetri cast, or Rajahs, are often called husbands of the ground.

† I have tried these three ways, and found that, by all of them, we get a length very nearly corresponding with that of the English inch, provided we take care, in the two latter modes, to have a middle-sized hand to regulate by.

Thirdly, by measuring the second joint of the middle finger: the half of which is also called an inch.

Twelve of these inches are one jana (literally translated a *span*).

Thirty-two janas are one ghada (or bamboo).

Four ghadas (by which is understood one square bamboo) is a kunta.

These measures were used by Kīsary *, and are universally understood.

Land measures used in the middle countries, that is, in the Masulipatam Circar:

12 Inches make	1 Jana = 1 foot.
2 Janas	1 Mura = 1 cubit.
32 Muras.............	1 Bamboo = 64 feet.
4 Bamboos, *i. e.* one square bamboo	1 Kunta = 4096 square feet.
$1\frac{1}{4}$ Kunta............	1 Conchum = 5120 square feet.
2 Conchums	1 Virasa = 10,246 square feet.
2 Virasa............	1 Tum = 20,480 square feet.
5 Tums	1 Yedum = 102,400 square feet.
4 Yedums	1 Putty = 409,600 square feet, or $9\frac{3}{8}$ acres †.

* Kisary was a chuckler (tanner and shoemaker); the very lowest aud most despised cast, whose business it is to do the menial offices in land-measuring. As, according to tradition, the first man was of this cast, and a son or offspring of the earth, the whole ground is considered as their legal inheritance, and still emblematically thus distributed by them. These people are probably the only remains of the aborigines of India. Kisary was ordered, by his Rajah, to measure out a certain quantity of land, which he had reluctantly ceded under the name of Maniams (charity ground) to the Bramins, with positive orders to regulate the length of his ghada by his own span; which, on account of the diminutive stature of the man, was very small, and caused the complaints of the Bramins, who are at all times very clamorous for charity, The good little man, unwilling that charity should be injured through him, and anxious to serve the Bramins at any rate, lengthened his span by an incision through the flesh between the thumb and fore-finger, which enabled him to span twelve inches, or four breadths of a hand. This, in honour of him, has ever since been called a Kisary span, and used in land surveying.

† If to this we add the breadth of a cow's foot between each bamboo, which is enjoined, on pain of losing the favour of heaven, and all worldly good, a putty will be exactly ten acres.

Subdivisions of Kuntas.

1 Kunta, or 4096 square feet, are equal to	2 Ara kuntas.
	4 Pātika.
	8 Paraka kuntas.
	16 Vīssum kuntas.
	32 Aravīssum kuntas.
	64 Kāny vīssum kuntas.
	128 Arakāny kuntas.
	256 Parakāny kuntas*.

To find the number of kuntas in a square, add the number of bamboos of two opposite sides, multiply the amount by that of the two oppo-

* The Indian field-measurers prefer making use of this mode of expressing the smaller parts of kuntas to that of reducing it to yards, feet, and inches, as is our practice.

The kunta used in the Condavier, Innacondah, and Bellumconda districts (in the Guntur Circar), differs widely from the preceding, viz.

80 Cubits are one bamboo, or rope, as they call it there, or 120 feet and a square of

4 Ropes (*a*) one kunta, or 14,337 square feet, and

64 Kuntas, one kuchara, equal to square acres 20, poles 121, and feet $42\frac{2}{3}$, or sq. ft. 904,182.

From the Ellore and Ragahmundry district, I received, from the best authority, the following measurements in use there, viz.

In the Ellore district, 16 Barus are one kunta,

35 Kuntas .. one kutty.

If we take the baru, or fathom, to be six feet, a kutty will contain 322,560 square feet; but as the fathom, as measured in common, will be nearer seven feet and upwards, a kutty of ground, in consequence, may be 439,040 square feet.

About Ragahmundry, the measure agrees nearly with that laid down in the Ganitam, viz.

8 Barus one kunta,

32 Kuntas one kutty; which will be square feet 230,400, if the baru is six feet; and if seven feet, it will be 313,600.

In the Condapilly district, 32 Cubits (Muras) are one bamboo, or 48 feet, and a square of

4 Bamboos (*b*) .... one kunta, or square feet 1,314, and

32 Kuntas.......... one kutty, acres, or square feet, 42,050.

On the Islands of the Godavery,

80 Cubits .... are one bamboo, or 120 feet and a square of

4 Bamboos (*b*) .. one kunta, or square feet 14,337.

60 Kuntas ...... one putty, or square acres, 19; poles, 119; and $20\frac{1}{4}$ yards; or square feet, 860,202.

In fact, every district almost has its own land measure, differing from that of the neighbouring. They all, however, seem to agree in using the common span and cubit, instead of that recommended by law.

(*a*) One square rope. (*b*) Square bamboos.

site sides, likewise add together, and divide the product by four. The quotient will be the number of kuntas which the square contains. Or, take half the amount of two of the opposite sides, and multiply it by half the amount of the two others: the product will be the number of kuntas.

A Table for finding out the Area of a Piece of Ground below the Size of a Kunta.

Length of the field.		Breadth.		Area.		
1/2 bamboo or	32 feet	1/2 bamboo or	32 feet is	1	patika kunta or	1/4 kunta
1/2	32	1/4	16	1	paraka ditto	1/8 ditto
1/2	32	1/8	8	1	vissum	1/16 ditto
1/2	32	3/16	12	1	ditto .... ara ditto ditto or	3/32
1/2	32	1/16	4	1	aravissum	1/32
1/4	16	1/4	16	1	vissum	1/16
1/4	16	1/16	4	1	kany	1/64
1/4	16	1/64	1	1	parakaney	1/256
3/4	48	3/4	48	9	vissum kunta	1/16
3/4	48	3/16	12	2	ditto ditto and 1 kany ditto or	9/64
3/4	48	1/8	8	1	ditto ditto and 2 ditto ditto or	6/64
3/4	48	1/16	4	3	kany ditto or	3/64
3/4	48	3/64	3	2	ditto do. and 1 parakany kunta or	9/256
3/4	48	1/32	2	6	parakany ditto or	6/256
3/4	48	1/64	1	3	ditto ditto or	3/256
3/4	48	1/128	1/2	1 1/2		1/384
3/16	12	3/16	12	9		9/256
1/8	8	1/8	8	1	kany ditto or	1/64
1/16	4	1/16	4	1	parakany ditto or	1/256
1/64	1	1/64	1	1	ghokarakany ditto or	1/1024

The north side of a field is measured by going from the lower end of the field upwards. The left hand side is called *east*, the right hand side is *west*, and when you turn back again and go in the opposite direction you face the south.*

If two sides of a quadrangle are of equal, and two others of different lengths, the figure is called a dursamum.

An equilateral parallelogram is called a samachetaru. An oblong rectangle ayetuchetaru.

* The want of a compass is thus ingeniously enough supplied; but every one must see that the method is by no means adequate to the nicety of land measuring. I have hitherto met with nothing indicating the knowledge of the compass in Indian writings, though in many instances they distinguish the magnet from other iron ores, and ascribe to it peculiar medicinal virtues. The hill people bring many magnets for sale to the low countries.

A trisamum is a square, three sides of which are of equal lengths.

A wishamachetaru is a square, all the sides of which are of different lengths.

In order to find the number of kuntas in an equilateral parallelogram take half the amount of the bamboos of the north and south sides, and multiply it by half the amount of the east and west sides. The product will be the number required. In the same way find the number of kuntas in the wishama, trisama, ayetuchetaru and dursamum*.

Dwisamam.

Rule. Multiply the longest of the four sides by either of the adjoining sides, do the same with the two remaining sides. Add the products. Half this sum is the area required†.

Wishama.

Add the two smallest sides, and multiply half their amount by the longest, the product is the area.

Lokūnis are called those pieces of ground that are in the middle of a field, and for some reason to be deducted from the whole. If they be squares, measure them according to the rules already given, and deduct them from the field in which they are comprised. The same rule applies to the weluchuni, or piece of ground lying on one or more sides, and to be deducted‡.

Mūkōnam, a triangle, of which there are three different kinds.

Rule. Multiply the base by half the perpendicular height, or the perpendicular height by half the base, the product is the area.

Walyacruty (the circle). Multiply the diameter by three, the product will be the circumference. Multiply half the circumference by the radius, the product is the area ‡.

* The reader will perceive that these rules are erroneous.

† The reader will see that the area of a trapezium, which the figure is, cannot be found in this way.

‡ I need not point out that these are not correct. Mathematicians, as the old Bramins are represented to have been, should have known better. It was on this account that I expressed my doubts of the originality of this work.

Or multiply the circumference by the diameter, deduct a fourth part of the product, the remainder is the area.

Maddala acruty chetram and damrugapu.

Double the diameter going through the middle A; add to it the diameter of the two extremities B, C, divide the amount by four, multiply the quotient by the diameter of the length D, the product gives the area.

Madala Acruty Chetram.

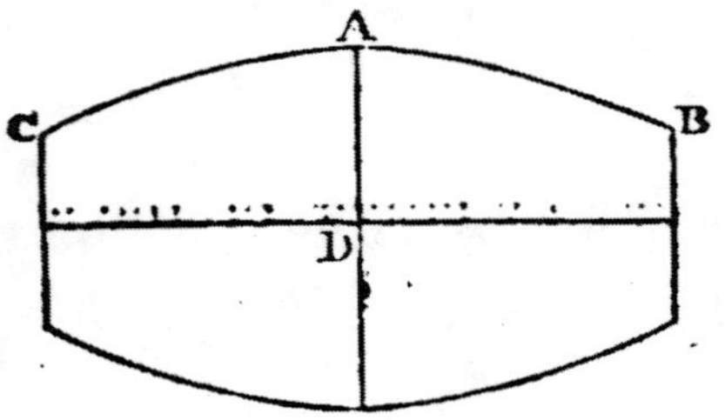

Damrugapu.

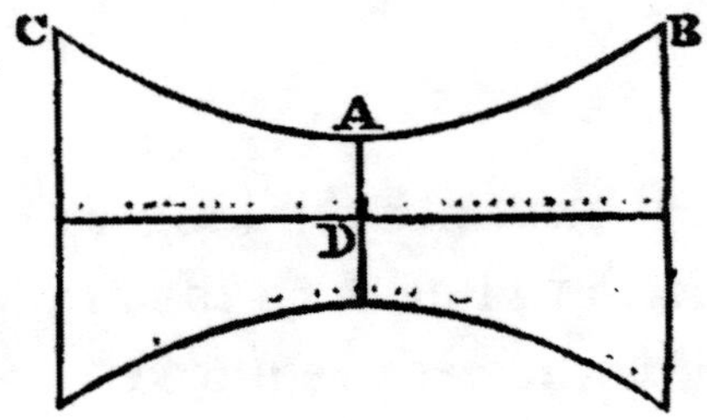

Ardha chendrika. The half moon.

Add the segment A to the distance B, multiply the amount by the same distance B : half the product is the area.

Senka.

Deduct half the amount of the short diameter from the long diameter, square the remainder ; do the same with half of the short diameter, and add the two products together. Multiply the amount by three. Divide this product by four. The quotient is the area.

Ardha Chendrika. The Half Moon.

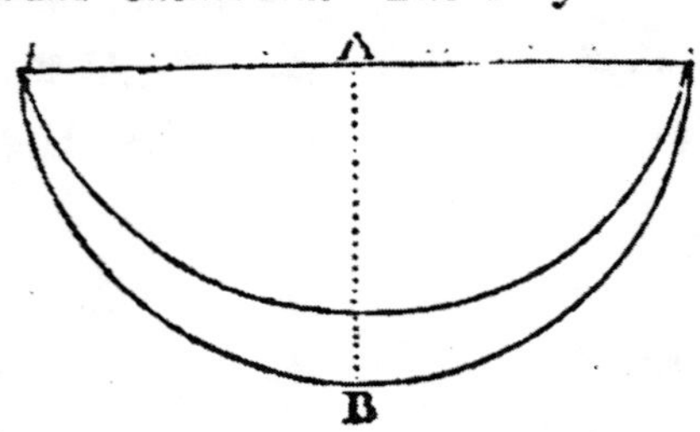

Senka.

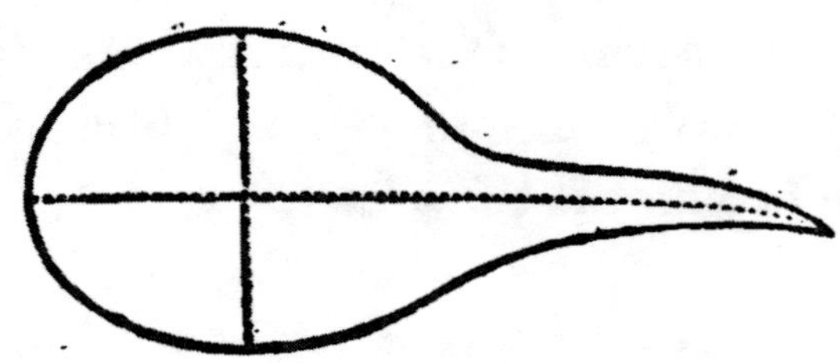

There is a number of other figures, and rules to find their contents ; but I omit them as equally uninteresting and incurious.

*Bijah Prāmānum**. *Kimmuru and Polnad†.*

The Month.	One Puty, or $7\frac{1}{2}$ Acres of Ground planted or sown.	Quantity of Seed.	Produce.
April, Chētram	Sugar garden	Candies‡. 19	Mds. of Sugar§ 1000
July, Ashadam	Chilly garden (capsicum annuum)	Conchums. 4	Candies. 30
	Manchy canda (arum manchy canda)	Candies. 7	70
	Turmerick (curcuma longa)	9	90
	Sweet potatoe (convolvulus batatus)................	9	80
July sown and in August transplanted	Paddy (oryza sativa)	Conchums. 60	30
Sept. Srāvanam	Jonna (holcus sorghum)........	3	25
	Natchinny ‖ (eleusine coracana)..	5	20

* One of the Chapters in the Ganitam treats of the quantity of seed required for one puty of ground, but it is erroneous, or I do not understand the true meaning; in lieu of it I give an account of my own observations, relative to the same subject, which could be easily rendered more complete and extended to all districts.

† The Kimmūr district belongs to the Peddapore Zemindar; and Polnad, another district, to the Pettapore Zemindar: they are watered by the Elysiram river, and except the Delta of the Godavery, are the most productive in the Circars, as they have throughout the year a supply of water.

‡ Ten common basketsful of sugar cane cut into small pieces ($1\frac{1}{2}$ foot long) is called a candy. There are two different candies or putties in use in the Circars.

A Palla putty is a measure used by the Bramins for weighing dry articles, as grain, salt, &c. It has eighty conchums, and each conchum four Pucca sīrs, or fourteen Katcha sīrs (8 lbs.). Seven and a half of these candies are a Coringa garce, or half a Madras garce. It is also to be observed that the size of conchums varies much in different places, that of Samulcotah is one quarter sīr less than that used at Cocanada, though both places are only eight miles distant from each other; but the greatest difference proceeds from the mode of measuring religiously observed at those places, whether at Masulipatam and Cocanada, the measure is filled by a violent throw of it into the heap, or whether it is filled from the grain falling through the hand, as done at Samulcotah, or the heap on the measure increased by keeping the arm round it, as at Rajahmundry.

A Malaca puty is a candy of 200 conchums (as mentioned before), used also in the Circar by the ryots or cultivators.

A mān, or as it is spelled in common, a maund, is 24 lbs.

§ The produce is valued in common at 250 pagodas, out of which is paid to the Zemin[dar] 75, and 80 expended for culy hire, &c.

‖ Price the same as paddy.

The Month.	One Puty, or 7½ Acres of Ground planted or sown.	Quantity of Seed.	Produce.
		Conchums.	Candies.
Sept. Srāvanam	Gingely (sesamum orientale)	5	15
	Brown cotton (gossypium herbac.)	12	30
	Chāma (panicum frumentaceum & miliaceum)	5	15
	Ganta (holcus spicatus)	5	20
	Nella, or black pessara (phaseolus maximus)	12	10
	Minuma (phaseolus minimus)....	10	10
	Pacha, or green pessara (phaseolus mango)	12	6
	Anapa (dolichos spicatus)	10	5
	Lamp oil (ricinus communis)....	10	8
	Sennaga (cicer arietinum)	10	6
	Wulawalu (horse gram, glycine tomentosa)	12	8
	Bobbara (dolichos chinensis)	10	5

In the Yetta-Kotta and Tatipāke Simas.

The Month.	One Puty, or 7½ Acres of Ground planted or sown.	Quantity of Seed.	Produce.
		Conchums.	Candies.
July, Ashadam	Paddy *.....................	63	20
	Red gram (cytisus cajan) *......	1	5
	Cotton (gossypium) *	3	10
	Korra (panicum italicum) *......	5	10
	Natcheny (eleusine corracana) ..	5	15
	Jonna (holcus sorghum)	5	15
	Ganti (holcus spicatus)	5	10
	Allu (paspalum frumentaceum)..	5	15
	Worga (panicum pilosum)......	5	10
	Minupa (phaseolus minimus)....	10	5
	Anapa (dolichos spicatus)......	10	8
	Lamp oil (ricinus communis)....	10	8

Tobacco plants, on one puty, or 7½ acres of ground .. .	1200
Cocoanut trees, on one ditto, or 7½ ditto of ditto	400
Mango ditto, on one ditto, or 7½ ditto of ditto	200

* These seeds are sown together on the same ground, and as they get ripe at different times, easily separated.

TRACT VII.

ON TERRA JAPONICA, OR CATECHU.

THE terra japonica, or catechu, is a dry extract of the fruit of the areca-nut, the areca catechu of Linnæus; and may be had in considerable quantity upon the coast; every where indeed where the areca palm is an object of cultivation. It is called in Portuguese, catch; in Tamul, catakam; in Telinga, kassu. In Mysore, about Sīrah, a great quantity is made, and likewise at some few places in the northern Circars and the southern districts of the coast.

There are two varieties of this extract made on the coast, which possess different qualities; the first, kassu, is very astringent; the second is rather sweet and has very little astringency, and is preferred by the beetle eaters to the former. There is also an inferior kind imported from Bengal.

The mode of preparing both is the following:—Areca-nuts are taken as they come from the tree, and boiled for some hours in an iron vessel. They are then taken out, and the remaining water is inspissated by continued boiling. This process furnishes the kassu or the most astringent terra japonica, which is black, and mixed with paddy husks and other impurities. After the nuts are dried they are put into a fresh quantity of water, boiled again; and this water being inspissated like the former yields the best or dearest kind of catechu, called coury. It is yellowish brown, has an earthy fracture, and free from the admixture of foreign bodies. The nuts are then dried, cut into equal halves, and sold.

This article may be had in considerable quantities, and I conceive that its manufacture might be easily increased, supposing any demand for the article to arise. I do not know at what price it is sold for on the spot; but at Madras a candy (500 lb.) is sold at 36 or 38 pagodas. Now if we take into consideration the numerous hands it has passed through, we may safely deduct 100 per cent. as profit over and above the prime cost. So that where manufactured it is not probably dearer than 18 or 19 pagodas the candy. The Bengal catch is sold at 22 pagodas.

I made some experiments to determine whether the astringent catechu might be employed as a substitute for oak bark in tanning; and as the mode which I followed was the Indian, it will be requisite, in the first place, to give an account of the way in which the process of tanning is conducted by the Hindoos. Tanning of leather is the particular province of the shoemakers' women, as that of manufacturing it for the market belongs to their husbands.

Two goat-skins, as they came from the butcher, were put into a pot that would hold about two gallons of water. They were, in the first place, thoroughly rubbed on the inside with quick-lime, and the pot containing them was filled with water. After continuing soaking in this ley for twenty-four hours, they were taken out, and the hair was easily scraped off, by means of a piece of broken pot, or tile.

Two measured sīrs (or about two pounds) of the coarsely powdered bark of the cassia auriculata, the tanghedu of the Telingas, were then put into a pot, together with the hides, and a gallon of water poured upon them. In this mixture they were allowed to soak for two days. They were then washed and soaked again for twenty-four hours in a similar quantity of bark and water. This process was repeated in water containing two vīs (about six pounds) of Myrobalan nuts broken in pieces, and the kernels thrown away, and tanghedu bark, and continued likewise for twenty-four hours.

The skins were then washed and soaked once more in water containing one sīr of tanghedu bark. They were then washed and dried, and were fit for immediate use. Of skins tanned in this manner, shoes are made in India. The same process is followed in tanning sole leather, which is made of the hides of buffaloes and bullocks. The only difference in the process is, that the sole leather is longer soaked in the infusion of cassia auriculata bark.

At Ellore, and some other inland places, they use the bark of the cassia fistula and mimosa arabica, instead of that of the cassia auriculata.

To see whether the terra japonica would have the same effect, I used it three different times instead of the tanghedu bark, employing about six ounces as a substitute for the two pounds of bark, and mixing, the third time, Myrobalan nuts, in the same proportion as when the bark was used. I found that the skins were at least as well tanned by this process as by the common one.

I tried next an extract which I had made from tanghedu bark, and which weighed twelve ounces. I found it sufficient to tan two skins as well as four pounds of bark. In short, in all my experiments I succeeded just as well by the one method as the other; so that a particular detail of them would only be a tedious repetition.

Besides the Areca nut, I have reason to believe that there are other substances which yield catechu, precisely of the same nature. At Malacca, and other places on the east coast, it is made, I understand, from the leaves of a plant called *camber*, which is a species of nauclea. A description of it has been published in the second volume of the Batavian Transactions; but I have not myself seen that book. The knowledge of this circumstance induced me to make trial of extracts from other substances, in order to determine how far they might be employed for the processes of tanning. The following are the vegetables which yield extracts that, in my opinion, might be most advantageously employed.

1. Cassia auriculata, and the extract made from its bark. In this I place the greatest confidence, as it is known to be the most esteemed in India for tanning and other purposes, and as it can be got in the greatest quantity and at the lowest rate. I think it might be delivered the first year, at the rate of seventeen pagodas per candy; and should the demand for it continue, it might be decreased one pagoda in price every year, till it be reduced to a proper standard. At this rate, however, it could only be delivered to the Company, because the support that their government would give to such an undertaking would be of more value than an additional price offered by individuals. The northern Circars (particularly the district fifteen miles west from Samulcotah), Rajahmundy and Pettapore, appear to me at present the most favourable situations. It may be procured likewise in abundance in the Guntoor and Nellore Circars. I know scarcely any other vegetable in this part of the world of so general a growth and so extensively useful, and which yields so large a portion of extract; no less than one-fourth of its weight. It is one of the articles chiefly employed in the Mysore, in making wütz, or cast steel.

2. Cassia fistula yields a fine extract. Its bark is employed in tanning in some parts of India; but it is neither of so general a growth as the preceding, nor does it yield so large a proportion of extract. It can be got, however, in the Circars, in some quantity. The plant is of a quick growth, and larger than the preceding species.

It is very probable that other species of cassia yield extracts that might be employed for the purposes of tanning. But the two preceding species only, and the cassia orientalis, can be found in such abundance as to render them objects of attention, in a commercial point of view.

3. Mimosa arabica of Roxburgh. The bark of this tree is used likewise in tanning, and it yields a good and pretty abundant extract; but as its wood is very useful in ship-building, particularly for knees of large Donīs*, a demand for its bark would be as injurious to the shipping concerns of India as that of oak bark is in England. At some inland places, however, it might be procured in considerable quantity.

4. Mimosa leucophlæa of Roxburgh. The extract of this tree was tried because the plant bears a considerable resemblance to the preceding species, and because, in Telinga, it is called Tella Tūma, or white Tūma. It is not so frequently met with as the former, but it contains a good deal of extract.

5. Mimosa odorata; so called from the pleasant smell of its flowers. It is a low shrub, and not very common in the low country; but it yields a considerable quantity of extract.

6. Melia azedarachta. From the bark of this tree I obtained an extract which appears very promising and good. The tree itself grows pretty frequently in India, as the backs and hands of the children can bear witness; for it is employed, like the birch in England, in inflicting corporal punishment on children.

I am firmly persuaded that one or other of these substances will answer all the purposes of catechu in tanning; for the catechu itself, imported from other countries, is prepared from almost as many different vegetables. That it is prepared from the beetle nut Dale already knew, as appears from the following passage:

" Palma arecifera; *the Indian or Malabar nut*. In Malabar, aliisque locis Indiæ orientalis succrescit usus. Succus e fructu inspissatus Terra Japonica & Catechu officinis dictus. Est substantia gummosa, indurata, & rufo nigricans, saporis astringentis & austeri, postmodum dulcis & grati, odoris nullius. Duplex est; una purior, degustata leviter in lingua quasi liquescit; altera vero durior & impurior, adeoque fere nullius usus, quæ fortasse decepit Schroderum, ut pro terra habuerit. Vires astringit, ventriculum roborat, nauseam arcet, appetitum excitat, vomitum juvat, fluxum alvi mensium & sanguinis reprimit. De exotico illo medicamento, terra japonica, catechu, seu cattchu dicto, quod nimirum sit non convenit inter eruditos: nonnulli, qui pro vera seu genuina terræ specie, ut nomen sonat,

* Vessels used in the along-shore trade of India.

illud habent inter meralia reperunt. Alii compositum quiddam vitriolicæ naturæ particeps esse existimant. Alli denique, & quidem rectè, vegetabilibus enumerant, pro succo inspissato habentes."

At Malucca it is prepared from a species of nauclea; and in Bengal, from the mimosa catechu. On the Malabar coast it is prepared from the bark of a tree which I have not seen.

At some places on the coast, as at Masulipatam, the tanners use nothing but the myrobalan nuts, the caduka of the Telingas, and the terminalia myrobalana of Linnæus. Should this fruit be found useful, it might be obtained at a very cheap rate from almost every part of India; and should the extract, as obtained in the Indian way, be sufficiently valuable to be substituted for oak bark in the process of tanning, I could point out a plant from which it might be obtained in the greatest abundance, at a very cheap rate, both in England, Ireland, and on the continent.

All these extracts are very soluble in water, and contain, according to my experiments, abundance of tannin. But to enable it to penetrate the pores of the skins, and combine with their fibres, I conceive that a greater degree of heat than is at present employed by the tanners in Europe would be useful, and might probably shorten the process considerably, without diminishing the goodness of the leather. To the temperature of the air in India, and of the water, seldom below 80°, I ascribe the celerity with which the process is finished in Hindostan. It does not last above eight or twelve days. If the leather be longer soaked, its qualities are said to be injured.

The inferiority of Indian leather to English I ascribe to the want of skill on the part of the currier, and to the use of lime-water. The European tanners, both at Tranquebar, and in Bengal and Madras, produce leather scarcely inferior to that made in Europe. At the former place the mimosa nilotica is employed; at the latter, the cassia auriculata.

TRACT VIII.

ON SULPHUR.

SULPHUR is usually found in abundance in the neighbourhood of volcanoes. It occurs likewise combined with iron, copper, lead, and several other metals; but in India it is a very uncommon production. Excepting iron pyrites, I have not observed any other mineral that contains it. Once indeed, as I understand from a very respectable authority, a large lump of very fine brimstone was found at Candapilly, in the trunk of a margosa tree, that had been torn up by lightning, and, as was supposed, shattered to pieces. Being aware of this scarcity of sulphur in India, I was not a little astonished, when in the northern Circars in 1803, a substance in powder, or in small pieces, evidently sulphur, was shown me; and when I was informed that it had been collected on the banks of the Godavery.

The place to which I was directed is not far from Maddepollam and Ammalapore, known for the manufacture of fine long cloth, which is carried on to a very great extent: the circumstance was unknown to all with whom I conversed. My guide, however, convinced me of the truth of his assertion, by conducting me to a small village about twelve miles east from Ammalapore, called Sūra Sāny Yanam, and belonging to Bommadāram muta, one of the Peddassore Rajah's districts: close to it is a lake, at the bottom of which the sulphur is deposited. This lake is narrow, but extends several miles in length from south to north, and seems every where to be very shallow. At its southern extremity it communicates with a branch of the Godavery; it is connected also with a salt water creek, from which it receives its water in the rainy monsoon.

In the warm season it is nearly dry, and the mud then exhales a disagreeable smell which I thought had some faint resemblance to that of sulphureted hydrogen gas.

The first excursion that I made was to a place due west of the village. Here my guides went trampling through the water, and taking up occasionally a handful of mud, which, on examination, had a faint smell of sulphur, but did not at all resemble that substance in appearance which had been shown me some weeks before, and which had induced me to undertake this expensive expedition.

Under the full impression of disappointment I was setting out on my return to the village in my palankīn, scarcely observing that it was surrounded by a number of inquisitive visitors, when on a sudden my attention was caught by the clamorous vociferation of a woman in pursuit of my palankīn bearers, who had robbed her little garden of a pumpkin. She appealed to the renter for protection, but he, like many in his situation, magnanimously made a present of it to the strangers who were carrying it off in triumph: unluckily for them however, I interfered, and ordered my boys to restore the article stolen. This brought on a slight but friendly altercation between me and the renter, which ended in the payment of the pumpkin, and an offer of all the bystanders to conduct me to the place where they collected the sulphur.

In consequence of this offer I followed a man, whom they immediately procured, to the northern extremity of the lake, where we found, without much searching, sulphur in small heaps, and in tolerable abundance. I was told that it may be found still farther northwards, and likewise in small quantities at the southern extremity, where the lake gets soonest dry. It is collected in a loose soft form, or in semi-undurated nodules of a greyish yellow colour, of a very strong sulphuric smell, and never at a greater depth than a foot from the surface of the ground on which the water stands.

This salt lake, I understood, is but of recent formation: fifty years ago it was a cultivated field. The country, for many miles in all directions, is quite plain, not even a hill is to be seen within fifty miles; stones of all kinds are nearly as scarce, except some indurated marl which I found in the bed immediately under the superficial bed. The soil all over this part of the country is either a rich red clay mixed with vegetable mould, which renders it very productive, or it is the black cotton ground, under which is always found a bed of marl. This is the kind of soil which exists on the spot where the lake stands. Earthquakes are entirely unknown here, and volcanic products not to be found.

It may be alleged, perhaps, that the sulphur has been deposited by the Godavery river, with one of the smaller branches of which it is connected; or that it has been thrown up by the sea, with which also it joins. But these explanations are quite unsatisfactory, because sulphur is never found in any of the other numerous branches of the Godavery, nor is it thrown up out of the sea in any of the other creeks or inlets on the spot. We are, therefore under the necessity of supposing that it existed in solution in the lake, and that it is separated and thrown down by some process of nature which has not yet been ascertained.

I tried the effect of a few reagents upon the water of the lake, in order to form some idea of the substances which it held in solution. These trials were the following.

Neither nitric nor sulphuric acid produced any sensible effect.

Soda immediately precipitated a copious white sediment.

Oxalic acid produced a copious precipitate.

Muriate of barytes likewise occasioned a plentiful precipitate.

These experiments are sufficient to show that the waters of the lake contained no sulphureted hydrogen gas, which indeed was sufficiently obvious from its having no smell; they show likewise that it contained a considerable quantity of sulphate of lime. Common salt was obviously present, as the lake communicated with the sea. The only inference that can be drawn from these facts is, that the sulphuric acid of sulphate of lime was decomposed by some unknown agent, and the sulphur deposited. Can decayed vegetable matters produce this effect when in contact with sulphate of lime and water, and assisted by the high temperature of the climate of India? I am much inclined to believe the possibility of such a decomposition: at all events the subject deserves farther inquiry.

TRACT IX.

ON THE METHOD OF SMELTING IRON AT YERAGUTTY, NEAR SATGHUR.

IF the mode followed at this place were the same as that practised in the northern Circars, it would be unnecessary to describe it here, as I have already given an account of that process in the Oriental Repertory; but as it is materially different, is much simpler, less expensive, and more rapid, I conceive that a short description of it will be attended with some utility.

The works or furnaces are under a banyan tree *, near a village called Yeragutty, about four miles south from Satghur. The workmen are only three, from three separate families, who live in constant dread lest they should be pressed for the purpose of carrying burdens for strangers from one village to another, a thing which often happens in the very season when it is in their power to employ their time to most advantage to themselves. As they are exposed to the inclemency of the weather, without any other shelter than the shade of a tree, they can only smelt iron in the driest season of the year, from the beginning of January to the end of March. In the wet season, or immediately after the rains, they are employed in collecting the ore, which is a fine black sand found in small rivulets or nullahs that derive their source from the neighbouring mountains. This ore is covered by a fine silicious sand, and when this sand is removed the ore may be procured in any quantity.

The furnaces are made of red loam mixed with sand, and consist of two parts. The lower and larger is about three spans high, and a foot in diameter, quite cylindrical, and erected over a hole in the ground, about four inches deep; its sides are every where about two inches thick. The upper part is conical, with the higher portion of the cone reversed. It is about

* A species of ficus.

eighteen inches high, and at the opening not quite a foot in diameter. The bellows are of the kind used by the iron smiths, and made of sheep skin: a hole is left near the bottom of the cylindrical part of the furnace to receive their nozzle. A representation of this furnace may be seen in plate IV. figure 1.

In order to smelt iron, they cement the two parts of the furnace with some loam, and fill the bottom part of it with charcoal: this being ignited, they put upon them, with a flat plate made of basket work, one sīr of iron sand, which they cover with four plates of charcoal. After blowing with the bellows for a quarter of an hour, they add another sīr of iron sand, and four plates of charcoal. The third time they add $2\frac{1}{2}$, sīr of ore, and five plates of charcoal; the fourth time one sīr of sand and four plates of charcoal, and the fifth and last time, one sīr of sand and four plates of charcoal. During the interval between each of these additions, which is nearly a quarter of an hour, the bellows are instantly plied. This produces sufficient heat, if not to melt the iron, at least to soften it and conglutinate it with the dross, and at the end of the operation it is found in a solid mass at the bottom of the furnace: water is then thrown upon it, and while yet hot it is cut in pieces, which, however, are not entirely separated from one another. In this state it is sometimes sent to the market, but more commonly it is put a second time into the fire, and subjected to the action of the hammer. By this process it loses two sevenths of its weight, which is usually seven sīr, and in that state a piece of one sīr weight sells at a quarter of a rupee.

As they usually smelt three times a day, they can make about three hundred and sixty pieces, selling at forty rupees. This is all that they get for their labour and skill, and all that they have for the support of three families during the course of a year.

As the quantity of sand used amounts to nine sīr, and produces seven sīr, or when freed from dross five sīr, we must allow this to be one of the richest iron ores, for in the careless manner in which the process is conducted, and the small degree of heat applied, we may safely conclude that part of the iron remains in a state of oxide in the dross, and that another part is lost among the charcoal. The iron thus produced by the first operation is of a very inferior quality, being porous, full of dross and charcoal, and so brittle, that parts of it may be easily knocked off by a few strokes of the hammer: it is in fact what is called cold short iron. This state is doubtless produced, in part at least, by the small degree of cohesion of its integrant particles, though it may likewise be owing in part to the presence of charcoal: by repeated heating and hammering it becomes perfectly malleable and fit for all purposes.

The ore from which it is made is the iron sand of mineralogists, a subspecies of micaceous iron ore. It is attracted powerfully by the magnet like iron filings, except a few particles which occur in small blunt grains, and which are probably iserine, as that species of ore of titanium was found by Dr. Thomson mixed with the iron sand of the river Don in Scotland. The colour of the iron sand is deep iron black; some grains of it are particularly shining with a lustre almost metallic, and these break with a conchoidal fracture: with acids it does not effervesce, and consists in fact of the black oxide of iron probably united to some titanium. The specific gravity lies between 3 and 3·5: the same kind of sand occurs likewise in some places along the shore. From some of these places the specimen, mentioned by Kirwan as coming from the East Indies, was probably taken.

The iron sand mentioned by Lenz is probably of the same kind, or differs only in its cohesion; but he affirms that it yields ninety per cent. of pure iron, which I conceive to be a mistake. If his account were to turn out true, it is obvious that his iron oxide would be the protoxide of iron, for which chemists have been hitherto searching in vain.

I conceived the great fusibility of this ore to be owing to the presence of manganese, though I was not able to determine the point by a few imperfect experiments which I attempted: the want of the proper reagents would have prevented me from undertaking a regular analysis, even if I had possessed the requisite skill; but from the analysis of Dr. Thomson it appears, that this ore contains only oxide of iron.

To account for the place of nativity of this rich ore, as well as for the great quantity in which it is found, we have only to examine the nearest mountains. These mountains, in this part of the Carnatic from Vellore to the Ghauts, consist of a sienite composed of quartz, felspar, and hornblende: the hornblende contains a great proportion of particles, I conceive, of the iron sand. The sienitic hills have a more rugged aspect than the granitic mountains, and it has a kind of appearance of being composed of very thick horizontal strata: this is most perceptible in the highest and most naked rocks; as for example on Kailasghur, the highest hill about Vellore, from which it lies in a south westerly direction; even at a considerable distance its strata are discernible, we find them six feet broad and upwards. They are apt to split into smaller masses, and even to undergo disintegration: they usually crack in a perpendicular direction, and we seldom discover two large masses contiguous to each other, without finding a close resemblance in their surfaces, and that at some preceding period they had been united. Hence the origin of the curious and romantic masses of stones that we often see, with small bases resting upon much smaller stones, or suspended upon the point of a rock, and threatening destruction to every beholder. The great degree of heat to which the naked rocks are exposed, in the sultry climate of India, and the sudden change of temperature produced by a shower of rain, may contribute considerably to the disintegration, and the consequent rugged appearance of these hills. But this cannot be the only cause, otherwise the granite mountains would be equally liable to decomposition, which is not the case. The structure of the stone seems to be the principal cause; it enables the stone cutters to separate large masses by means of a few blunt wedges driven into holes, made in the direction in which they wish to divide the stone.

Plate V. represents a hill in the Tondimans country, remarkable for the great number of detached masses of stones which lie about its summit.

The disintegration takes place chiefly on the surface of the large masses which we find every where scaling off: the smaller stones are frequently affected throughout their whole mass. This property I ascribe to the great quantity of iron, nearly in the metallic state, which exists in the hornblende. When this iron is exposed to the air it attracts oxygen, and loosens, in consequence, the firmness of the whole mass: it is to the complete disintegration of this rock, that the fertile valleys of the Carnatic or Palliam owe their soil. Near the granite mountains the soil is sandy and barren, because that rock is not susceptible of the same rapid and comple disintegration.

These hills, with a very few exceptions indeed, run north and south, and they may be considered as having once been more intimately connected with the Ghauts, which intersect the peninsula of Hindostan: they make their first appearance a few miles on the east side of Arcot. There are indeed some hills near Madras, but I rather consider them as unconnected with those of which we are speaking, as they have a fourth ingredient, garnets, which I have not observed near the Ghauts; they contain likewise hornblende slate.

The usual colour of the most entire sienite is a fine silvery white, mixed with fine black particles. Its specific gravity, tried in water of the temperature of 80° is 2·6. This triple aggregate is very unequal in the proportion of its constituents in different places. Sometimes one and sometimes another of them is most abundant. In some places we find large masses of each of the constituents in a state of purity, without any mixture of any of the other substances of which the rock in general is composed. The quartz is usually white, and reddish yellow in those pieces that are in a state of disintegration. Hence the red gravel at the bottom of the Vellore hill, and at the foot of all the mountains in this district. It is found likewise of other colours, especially various shades of greyish blue; but a dirty white is every where the prevailing colour. Its fragments sometimes affect a rhomboidal form. The fracture is usually splintery and compact; sometimes in the large it is slaty. I have no where observed quartz crystals in any granitic or sienitic mountains, though I have seen them in abundance in rocks of a later date. Along with these crystals occur amethysts, and emery, and fluor spar, and in the same places corundums are found. What is called emery in India seems to me to be nothing but an aggregate of garnets; for its specific gravity, colour, and hardness, exactly correspond with that of the real garnet.

The felspar often traverses the rock in veins. In such cases it disintegrates very readily, and is converted into clay. About Sātghur, and at the foot of the Peddanaigdurgum pass, it is found of a red colour in large masses, mixed more or less with quartz, often in a sound state; but more frequently decaying. But the silver white is the prevailing colour of the felspar in the soundest and most equally mixed sienite. Sometimes it passes into compact felspar.

The third ingredient is a species of hornblende, which I conceive to contain an unusual quantity of iron, and on that account would be disposed to distinguish it by the name of *ferrilite*. It occurs chiefly mixed in small quantities with the other ingredient which forms the sienite. Its fracture is uneven or undulating lamellar, and often resembling mica, from which it is distinguished by its superior hardness, by its streak, and by its fracture. It is very much given to disintegration; and this is probably the reason why the sienite in the Carnatic is so apt to decay. In large masses it traverses the rock in veins, or occurs in it massive, from the size of a hazel-nut to that of a tun or more.

The veins frequently traverse the rock of an uniform breadth for many hundred yards. Their width varies from two to five feet or upwards. These veins occur in many parts of the country, seemingly quite unconnected with the sienite; as for example, near the cavalry cantonments at Arcot.

When this mineral is exposed to the influence of the atmosphere, it is always covered with an ochrey brown crust. Internally it is black, lustre shining, and semi-metallic. Opaque; Longitudinal; Fracture even, and when closely examined fine foliated. The cross fracture frequently exhibits to the naked eye fine columnar crystals, intimately, but irregularly and scantily, mixed with the mass. The specific gravity lies between 3 and 3·09; the temperature of the water in the two trials made being 78° and 82°. When this stone is decomposing its specific gravity is reduced to 2·6. In that state it has a dull colour, a slaty fracture, and a greyish or ochrey appearance, and breaks easily in pieces. When reduced to a fine powder it has a blackish green colour, and is attracted by the magnet.

There is a variety containing white dots, probably of quartz, which is harder than the more common kind, perhaps on account of the quartzy mixture in it. The fracture of this variety is more splintery. When disintegrating it is more gritty and sandy. Its hardness is that of quartz. It differs in some other respects from the common hornblende, especially in containing an unusual proportion of iron.

I do not suppose that our ore is derived from the large masses of the rock, but rather from the disintegrated hornblende, in which, I suppose, these minute grains of iron sand are mixed in abundance. By the heavy falls of rain, we may suppose that many half disintegrated stones of sienite are broken in pieces by being forced along by the torrents and driven with violence against each other. Thus its particles are gradually reduced to sand and deposited according to their specific gravity. The iron sand, being the heaviest, sinks lowest, and the comminuted quartz and felspar cover it. Those portions of the iron, that are mixed with the hornblende in the state of peroxide, are probably washed away with the water in a state of fine mud, and are either carried to the sea or deposited on the fields, to which they communicate the red colour so common in those countries where this kind of sienite prevails.

It probably requires a long time, and a concurrence of many favourable circumstances, to dispose the larger masses of this stone to disintegrate. For we often find some of it in the soundest state, close by others very far advanced in decay; and the *lingums* *, usually made of this stone, are but seldom found encrusted with ochre, though this crust covers all the stones that we find lying at the bottom of the mountains. The purer the stone the less apt it seems to disintegrate.

To see whether the smaller particles of the well-mixed sienite contained iron sand, I reduced a portion of it to powder, and had the satisfaction to find that it was attracted by the magnet, though for obvious reasons not so powerfully, as the iron sand itself.

The only minerals mixed with the sienite, or passing through it in veins, are hornblende slate, garnets, shorlous beryl †, and pyrites. Sometimes the sienite assumes the structure and constitution of granite. The hornblende slate is found in immense masses: large hills of it occur near the mount on the west side of Madras. The principal tracts of these hills are granitic, very much given to decomposition; and indeed large masses seldom occur in a perfectly sound state. The hornblende slate seems to consist of pieces from half an inch to an inch long, united together, probably, by a silicious cement. These pieces have a greenish black colour, their internal lustre is silky, they are translucent on the edges, their longitudinal fracture straight lamellar, their cross fracture striated. They give a greyish green streak. Their specific gravity varies from 3·1 to 3·2. Their hardness does not much exceed that of fluor spar. This hornblende slate seems also to contain abundance of iron; but it is not nearly so apt to undergo disintegration as the common hornblende. It contains many garnets; there are large quarries of it west from Madras, which supply that city with black stone so frequently seen there. I have no doubt that it would take a fine polish.

We frequently find the shorlous beryl, though never in any great masses, mixed with the sienite of the Carnatic, either in place of the hornblende or as a fourth ingredient. I found considerable specimens of it on the Sātghur hills, forming more than one half of the stony aggregate into which it enters. I found it likewise at the Peddanaigdūrgum pass in a nullah, near the encampment of the pioneers, where it is mixed chiefly with red felspar and a little quartz. It occurs in almost all the mountains of the Carnatic in small quantities, forming a kind of incrustation upon the other minerals of which

* A pillar, emblematical of the creative attribute of the Deity.

† Now considered as a sub-species of topaz. Or is it the mineral pistazite?

the mountain is composed. At first sight it bears great resemblance to quartz, having the same dull lustre and hardness, but on a closer inspection we find it in very small columns or prisms, and oblong masses of a white yellowish green colour, its lustre shining, opaque, and though still mixed with quartz and felspar, but constituting the principal ingredient, its specific gravity is from 3 to 3·09. Hence when quite pure it must be a good deal heavier. The pieces least mixed with felspar and quartz affect the form of hexangular columns, truncated at both extremities. The more pure and smaller crystals seem to have the same form. Acids have not the least effect upon it, and in a moderate heat it does not lose its colour.. These characters, I think, are sufficient to warrant my giving it the name of shorlous beryl.

Garnets are found in the greatest abundance in an amorphous state, in the mountains near Madras and Mahavellyporam, mixed with the sienite as well as the hornblende slate. Between Vellore and the Ghauts I have not observed any garnets entering into the composition of the sienite, and as far as I recollect they never occur in pure hornblende. In small pieces of the rock they sometimes, though seldom, form the prevailing ingredient. The mountains in the Guntur Circar, the Condavir hills, and those of Condapilly agree, I believe, in their constituents with those of the Carnatic; but they contain a greater proportion of hornblende, and abound in garnets and what I conceive to be olivins. In these mountains the garnets are frequently found crystallized.

I have found iron pyrites in small cubic crystals on a mountain called Kailasghur. In small particles I have observed it at other places.

The real granite into which the sienite passes, or with which it alternates, I have seen only in large detached pieces. At Mahavellyporam, and afterwards between Conjeveram and Vellore, whole pagodas and choultries are built of it. It is fine grained and not quite regularly compounded; though more so than the sienite. The quartz is white, the felspar silvery white, and the mica in fine black lamellæ. It is not so much given to decomposition as the sienite, and is much harder. It would probably be found by digging between Conjeveram and Vellore: in all probability indeed it forms the basis of all the hills in the Carnatic. I draw this inference from having, in many parts both low and elevated, at a certain depth under the surface, found the remains of a disintegrating or disintegrated granite. Near Conjeveram it occurs near some tanks, in the form of a white clay which adheres strongly to the lips, and near the cavalry cantonments at Arcot in white granular pieces that crumble between the fingers; and here and there some grains present themselves which still retain the fracture of felspar. I found likewise in the same heaps specimens of a beautiful white felspar, in large tabular pieces of a milk white colour, to which some mica and some quartz adhered. This probably exhibited some traces of the appearance of the fresh granite, and the great proportion of felspar accounts for its having been converted by disintegration into clay.

TRACT X.

DESULTORY, BUT WELL MEANING, THOUGHTS ON THE BRITISH GOVERNMENT IN INDIA.

IT is generally acknowledged that no nation in Europe is better acquainted with the art of governing than the British. It has been contended, however, by the French, on mere theoretical principles, that this panegyric does not apply to the management of their colonies. When we take an attentive view of their astonishing success, and of the security with which we find they are established in many parts of the globe, but especially in India, we cannot hesitate to esteem them equally as great legislators in that country as in their own. For my part, I feel myself both unequal and disinclined to enter upon a discussion of such a subject. My object is different. It is an anxious wish that the little knowledge which I have acquired may contribute towards rendering the natives of India as happy under the British Government as I feel myself.

That happiness is ideal, and not real, is a truth with which I am forcibly impressed. Still this ideal phantom, when wanted, renders a man as miserable as the possession of it would produce the contrary effect. Public happiness may be defined the absence of all grievances either real or imaginary, provided they be felt as grievances. The art of governing well consists in an equable distribution of those burdens and benefits which result from a regular government. In order to render the regal power more agreeable to the people the greatest and most shining share of the beneficial branch of government is vested in the King or the Supreme Magistrate. Indeed he is the nominal source of all good. To impose the taxes, and lay on those burdens which constitute the disagreeable part of government, is wisely left in Great Britain to the people at large, through the medium of their delegates. Hence the hatred to which the power that imposes hardships must be exposed is, therefore, only attached to the instruments employed individually in the distribution of them.

2

The only reason why the natives of Hindostan might not think themselves as happy as the nature of things will admit, under the British Government, is, in my opinion, owing to the strange division of the forementioned branches of it. The Company has retained to itself the distribution of evil or the executive power, with the collection of the revenues; but have left the dispensation of the sweets of a good government to native tributary princes, or even to their own native servants, who consequently derive the benefit arising from that situation.

A ryot in the northern Circars, or any other part of the Company's dominions, will candidly acknowledge that the collector takes nothing but the Company's due. This very action, however, is a grievance in the eyes of a Hindoo, who considers possession as real right of property, which by his religious laws and principles he is allowed to retain by the most flagitious and sacrilegious means. The same revenue is exacted by the Zemindar, and probably in greater proportion to the produce; but it is done in a very different way from that of the collectors, and under a combination of happier circumstances.

A Zemindar first tries persuasion; and when he has used compulsion, he endeavours to sooth the poor ryot, or sub-renter, by attention and flattery, by an entertainment, or a trifling present. He tells him that all hardship inflicted is merely at the instance of the Company, who enforce payment of their kists from him with the greatest rigour. The poor plundered man returns home quite proud of the attention, and pleased with the conduct of the Rajah. On his arrival he hears the Rajah praised by the Bramins, who, probably, have returned home with tumbalas * for their enams, or with pattas † for new ones. Or he hears him extolled by the enam peons ‡, who boast of the distinction with which they have been treated, and of the emoluments they derive from the lands which they cultivate. Or the curnum § expatiates with exultation on the allowance made by the Rajah for village expenses. In short, the praises of the darma ‖ Rajah resound from every mouth.

From the collector the ryot returns with far different sensations. When the kist is paid he is dismissed without further ceremony; and comes home brooding over his imaginary losses. The Bramins of the village, who enjoy

* A written order to allow a holder of charity ground to take the yearly produce.

† A grant for charity land. ‡ A kind of militia paid by free lands.

§ Village accountant. ‖ Benevolent Prince.

enams, are silent; those that have none (which constitute the greater part) complain; for not even a chance of acquiring any is left them. The former obtain their tumbalas from the sub-renter, and bless him for it; or, as I know is the case in the northern Circars, they consider their lands as real property, insured to them by means of stipulations between the Nizam and the Company.

From the peons, a very numerous class of the middle and lower ranks of people in India, nothing is heard but complaints. They are not only disregarded but often deprived of their pikes and daggers, which they consider as the very pride of their existence, and sometimes also of their enams or privileges which frequently consist in nothing more than an equal share of the produce of the land which they cultivate; but which are considered by themselves as matters of great importance.

Here I must advert to the position respecting happiness, with which I began this Tract. The Hindoo thinks himself happy, if he as well as the other classes of his nation, especially the Bramins whom he is taught to consider as belonging to a race of beings superior to himself, and to regard as protecting angels, be permitted to remain in the undisturbed exercise and enjoyment of their ancient customs and privileges. The Bramin thinks himself just as much entitled to receive enams and other charitable gifts as the ryot to a share of the produce of the land which he cultivates. Hence when he does not receive them he considers himself as injured. Those who enjoy these donations are never reminded that they are charitable gifts, and of course they are unthankful. Those whose ancestors did not transmit to them these privileges are convinced that they will never obtain them from Government *. Hence their loud complaints, and the readiness with which they would be disposed to support those from whom they might expect a different treatment. They would unite with pleasure in supporting any upstart rebel, whether he were a Hindoo or a Moorman. The lower classes, ever influenced and led by the ministers of their religion, consider the grievances of the Bramins as their own; and as their vanity is never flattered by the Company's Government, which alone could induce them to forget their fellow-subjects, readily join them in lamentations, and would do so likewise in case of a rebellion.

The Bramins in the district of the Zemindar look up to him for charitable

* There have been made some exceptions lately, as those black officers and soldiers who behaved well on some occasions, as at the Vellore mutiny, have been rewarded with lands.

gifts, and are therefore not only ready to support him, but even to prevent a change of administration, because they know that if the country should become amāny * not the least chance of obtaining enams is left them.

It is not uncommon for the lands to be partially resumed by the Zemindar, which enables him to raise his reputation by new gifts, which he fails not to bestow. He takes from one in order to give to another.

I have often heard them declare that the Company's amāny administration was strictly just; but they thought it comparatively not so good as a Moorish Government, and greatly inferior to a Hindoo one. Under the Moorish, say they, a poor man might by chance acquire riches, and experience a turn of good luck, of which in the same Government the richer are often deprived; whereas in the Company's district none are plundered, and consequently none by an extraordinary accumulation of favour rise upon the ruins of others.

If these defects in the British Government in India were generally understood, nothing would be more easy than to remedy them. But I have reason to believe that they are not understood by those who have the supreme direction of affairs in India. Thousands of difficulties indeed start up before my eyes, which I do not venture to mention, because they may, perhaps, be greater in appearance than in reality. Something material, however, might be done, I conceive, without any further investigation, and founded on the strictest principles of justice.

Would it not be advisable that enamdārs of all descriptions and in all districts, whether amāny or under Zemindars, should be publicly announced as under the particular protection and exclusive authority of Government? Even those who have lately acquired, or may hereafter acquire, enams from the Zemindar, should be placed in the same predicament. This would put an effectual stop to the squandering away of lands, and at once detach the greatest interest in the country from the Rajahs. The Curnums would become more independent of the Zemindars, and all accounts would be more open to investigation. Registers might be opened of all enamdārs and enam lands, and those persons who neglect to have them enrolled should be invariably deprived of them, in favour of the informers, or others; for, provided they be given away, it signifies not to whom.

* Under the immediate management of the collector.

To impress the minds of the people with the good intention of Government, printed puttas should be distributed among all registered as enamdārs, in which the Company is represented as confirming their enams, so long as they continue dutiful and faithful subjects. At the same time, it might be made known that all those enamdārs would invariably be deprived of their enams, who, in the event of a rebellion in any district, do not immediately repair with their families to such countries as continue in a state of quietness and attached to the Company. Tumbalas should also be regularly distributed, expressive of the charity which yearly is renewed to the enam holders.

A certain proportion of uncultivated lands might be allotted for new enams, or for such Bramins and Chetris as could prove that they had either themselves cleared and cultivated waste lands, or had encouraged others to do so. By such conduct, I conceive that the Bramins and Nobles of the country would feel at once that they depended solely upon Government, and be encouraged to look forward to favours and emoluments for which there was no opening before.

The consequence of this would be that another and a formidable class of people (I mean the Peons) would be attached to the interests of the Company. They are looked up to, by the rest of the natives, as their natural protectors. They are paid by some trifling enams, or by receiving equal shares of the produce of a certain quantity of their Circar land; and when they are actually employed, they receive daily batta *. They are a proud, haughty, warlike race, who wield the spear with intrepidity in the day of battle. If they can be attached to the Company's interest, nothing is to be feared from foreign or internal enemies. I allude here only to enam Peons, and not to the common rebels, consisting of Moormen and other idlers, whose sole property consists in a sword or a match lock; who readily attach themselves to every upstart, and as readily forsake him. I allude to those Peons who surround the native Princes; whose principle it is to fall in the field of battle with their masters, and who are known rather to sacrifice themselves than survive them. I know it is a favourite maxim to disarm these people; but that can never be effected so long as a bamboo grows in India, or a pointed plough-share is to be met with in the fields. Would it not be a wiser policy to conciliate and secure their friendship? They are all fond of distinction. If they were publicly declared Circar Peons, under the particular

* Daily subsistance, about two-pence each man.

and exclusive authority of the Company, registered as such, and their enams promised to themselves and their families so long as they showed themselves faithful servants; if they were to be assured that they would never be removed from the districts in which they reside, excepting when they were actually employed in war—by these, and similar modes, they might be gained in a very short time. Officers might be appointed in every district, not to drill them, but to become personally acquainted with them, and to lead them into the field when their services were wanted.

Honorary guards might be furnished, out of their number, to the tributary Rajahs, as they are accustomed to this kind of pageantry. They would serve as an effectual guard over them, as soon as they were accustomed to look up to a superior power as their immediate protector.

The great end of all this—the popularity of the present Government with the natives of India—would be secured; and an army, amounting at least to 100,000, would be organized on the coast at little or no expense.

It may be said that consanguinity, or relationship, attaches the Peons to the native Princes. I believe I have heard the observation made; but I do not think it well founded. A slight review of the casts, or tribes, among whom most of this description of men are found, will readily convince any person that no such consanguinity can exist.

To this proposal, it may be objected that all alienations of lands are losses to the revenue, which ought rather to be gradually increased by the resumption of enams to which no ancient title can be produced. I once thought so myself, and was most assiduous in hunting after and pointing out all illegal claims; but, upon more mature reflection, I am of opinion that it would tend more to the advantage of a government so great and powerful as that of the British in India, were they to be indulgent in this respect, and thus evince that attention to the real or ideal happiness of their numerous subjects, which, in other respects, they are so anxious to exhibit. The intention of establishing courts of justice, and of conferring the property of the lands upon the native princes, may be adduced as striking instances. But I am sorry to say that they are not such as will contribute, by their effects, to the happiness of the middle or lower classes of the natives of India.

Samulcotta, 1798.

TRACT XI.

MODE OF DYEING RED COTTON YARN, PRACTISED ON THE COAST OF COROMANDEL.

THOUGH the methods of the Indian dyers are exceedingly tedious and complicated, and though they are utterly unable to explain the rationale of their processes, yet the beauty of their colours cannot fail to be admired, and must inspire us with the opinion that a knowledge of their methods might improve the processes of the European dyers, and might enable them to make some advantageous changes in the art as at present practised; while the application of the light of chemistry to explain the nature of the Indian processes, to enable the enlightened artist to throw out all the useless steps, might contribute more to the improvement of this beautiful art than even the most sanguine is at present aware of.

When I drew up the following essay, some years ago, in India, I was not aware that any of the facts communicated in it were known in Europe. But I find, since my return to England, that this is not exactly the case. The method of dyeing cotton red in the Levant is nearly the same as the Indian method. An account of this process has been published by Chaptal, in the *Annales de Chimie*, and by Berthollet, in the second edition of his *Theorie de la Teincture*; and is well known, I find, to the public in general. It is even possible that the Indian process itself may have made its way into some English book, though I have not yet been able to meet with it. Be that as it may, I shall here venture upon the insertion of my own Essay, which, if I were allowed the liberty of reckoning from the date at which it was drawn up, would be fairly admitted to stand a considerable claim to priority. My knowledge, being all derived from actual inspection of the processes, has the advantage of accuracy, which may be depended on.

I. *Mode of Washing and Arranging the Yarn to be dyed.*

Yarn, before being dyed, requires to be washed and untwisted, that it may not become entangled, and be rendered useless during the numerous processes to which it is to be subjected. It ought also to be in such a state that all its parts may be equally penetrated by the colouring matter, which could not be the case with hard-twisted yarn.

The yarn, after being separated, is divided into little bundles of thirty or forty threads, through each of which, at the middle and extremities, a cotton twine is sewed; but so loosely, that the yarn may be hung on a bamboo, and spread out in such a manner that every single thread is exposed to the powerful rays of the sun. Washing and cleaning are sufficiently accomplished by pouring cold water upon the yarn, and beating and pressing it well with the hands for half an hour, or longer. It is then to be kept in water, in covered vessels, till it acquires a putrid smell, which usually happens after it has stood twenty-four or thirty-six hours, during which time it should be occasionally pressed and worked for a quarter of an hour together. It is now to be washed as clean as possible, beat upon a stone or earthen pot, and then hung up in the sun to dry.

It is obvious that, by these processes, the texture of the yarn must be made as loose as possible; and thus the dyeing ingredients find a facility of penetrating to every part.

The natives of India have a very commodious way of beating their yarn, which requires only to be seen and practised once or twice to enable any other person to perform it as well as themselves. With one hand, they hold the yarn by one of its extremities, giving it a swing at the same time, so as to make it extend quite horizontally, and with the other hand they draw it back into a small compass near their feet: this is repeated ten or twenty times, till the yarn curls, and is as loose as required.

The yarn, after being dried, is not washed again, though it sometimes looks as dirty as ever, but is immediately submitted to that process which may be termed animalization. Every body knows that animal substances receive colours with much greater facility than vegetable. Now the object of the process in question is to communicate to the cotton the same facility of combining with colouring matter that animal bodies possess.

II. *Preparation of the Animalizing Mordant.*

The following ley ought to be prepared during the above described processes to which the yarn was subjected.

Some plantain tree* or other ashes are put into an earthen pot, and cold water poured upon them. This mixture, being well stirred and agitated, is allowed to stand for some hours, to enable the water to extract the alkaline parts of the ashes; for much depends upon the ley being sufficiently strong. This strength the native dyers determine by experiments conducted as follows: they put some of the strained ley into a cocoa-nut shell, add to it about half the quantity of gingelie oil, and give the whole a gentle motion. If this mixture turns immediately white, without any visible globules of oil swimming on the surface, the ley is considered as sufficiently strong. If globules of oil still appear, the ley must be strengthened by an additional quantity of ashes. This experiment is repeated every fourth or sixth hour, till the ley is found of sufficient strength.

The quantity of ley wanted is then carefully poured off, without disturbing the fine black sediment at the bottom, and strained through a cotton cloth. In one half of this ley is dissolved some sheep's dung, in the proportion of two or three ounces of dung to a pint of ley. The solution is again strained through a piece of coarse muslin.

The other half of the ley is mixed with half its bulk of gingelie oil, and with nearly half as much tsicky; and then both liquors are mixed together. We need not be surprised that the Indian dyers are unwilling to allow strangers to be present during their processes. All their actions are mixed with superstition. Now they conceive that, by the propitious cooperation of one of their gods, a milky scum is suddenly produced upon the surface of this mixture; upon which, in their opinion, its efficacy as a mordant greatly depends.

The several substances above-mentioned are employed by them in the following proportions.

To half a pound of yarn they take half a pint of gingelie oil, two pints of ley, a quarter of a pint of tsicky, and about two or three ounces of sheep's dung.

* Musa paradisica.

One fourth part of the mordant thus prepared is poured upon the yarn to be dyed. The yarn is squeezed and wrought in it for a considerable time, adding occasionally small portions of the mordant. This laborious process must be continued till every thread appears thoroughly soaked, which may take place within little more than half an hour, supposing the quantity of yarn not great. A certain dexterity, only to be acquired by practice, contributes much to shorten this part of the operation.

The yarn is now spread upon a bamboo, and exposed to the action of the sun till noon (supposing the dyer to have begun his work in the morning). It is then taken in, and worked up a second time, with an additional portion of the mordant previously diluted with some ley, and hung out to dry as before. At sun-set it is taken in again, and treated with an additional portion of mordant. It is then put into two covered vessels, and allowed to remain till next morning.

If any of the mordant remain, the process is to be repeated again next morning, and the yarn is afterwards to be hung out in the sun to dry: a step, indeed, always taken every day during the whole process.

The strong ley at first prepared is now to be diluted with one third of its bulk of water; the yarn, when taken in at sun-set, is to be moistened in it, and put into two covered vessels during the night, as usual.

Here I cannot avoid making two cursory observations relative to the economical part of the process. 1. No more of the ley is to be added to the yarn than it will readily imbibe. A superfluous quantity would dilute the mordant too much, and would be lost by dropping off while the yarn is hanging on the bamboo, before it had performed the required service. 2. The position of the yarn must be constantly changed, as the containing fluids are always accumulating in the lowest parts, and, if not lost by dropping off, at least become unequally distributed.

Next day, the yarn is to be spread upon a bamboo, and exposed to the sun during the whole day. In the evening it is taken in, and treated with the ley as usual. These alternate exposures to the sun during the day, and soaking in the ley during the night, are to be continued daily without intermission, till it appears that the yarn is saturated with ley; or, to speak more precisely, till the whole of the oil is converted into soap. The time necessary for accomplishing this change is usually five days, supposing the ley sufficiently strong.

This conversion of the oil is ascertained in the following manner. Wash a few inches of one of the bundles of cotton yarn in water, holding some astringent principle in solution. In a short time, a whitish scum will be deposited on the surface. This scum is to be rubbed for some minutes on any part of the skin (usually on the palms of the hands). They readily perceive, by the feel, whether any part of the oil be still free, and also by the shining oily lustre which, in that case, their hands acquire. This separation of the soap would not be produced by common water. The dyers constantly keep the wood and roots of the nalla maram (Phyllanthus umbilica) in those wells from which they take their water for this purpose. The bark of this tree contains the astringent principle, and is often used by the natives to clear turbid water.

After the workman is satisfied that the whole oil is converted into soap, the yarn is subjected to the same treatment for one day more; but it is only wetted with common water, or with much diluted ley, in the morning and evening.

This part of the process being finished, it becomes necessary to dry the yarn in the open air thoroughly. It may then either be washed immediately, or, in order to give the animalizing mordant time to produce its full effect, it may be kept from three to five weeks in a room. The conduct of the dyer is guided by his circumstances. If he can afford to wait, he will keep the yarn, being well aware that the quality of the colour will compensate for the loss of time. I have myself tried both ways several times; and the result of my trials always agreed with the previously conceived opinions of the Indian dyers.

Before the yarn is cleaned properly, it must always be first washed slightly in a small portion of water. This water, which dissolves the soapy particles, is kept by the dyer for future use, and is called by him tsicky. It gradually acquires some consistence, and a disagreeable smell. We have already seen that it enters into the composition of the mordant.

The yarn is then thoroughly washed in a tank, so that nothing of the mordant seemingly remains, except the smell, and a certain softness perceptible to the finger. To ensure the success of the process, the yarn is sometimes subjected a second time to the whole of the preceding treatment; and this repetition appears to me to increase the beauty of the colour. The mordant is prepared quite in the manner already explained, and the quantity of it is only such as will serve for once moistening the yarn. The proportions of ingredients are one part of gingelie oil, three parts of strong ley, half a part of old tsicky, two parts of new tsicky, and a little sheep's dung.

It is unnecessary to describe the way in which this second dose of mordant is made to act upon the yarn; every thing being a mere repetition of what has been already detailed.

III. *Dycing Process.*

The yarn being conceived thoroughly impregnated with this peculiar mordant, the next process is to give it a red colour. For that purpose, a cold infusion in water is made of pounded casah leaves. Some hours afterwards the yarn is put into this infusion, and agitated in such a manner that each of the threads comes completely in contact with the infusion. In this state it is allowed to remain during a whole night. The quantity of leaves employed in forming this infusion is so considerable, that it has a greater resemblance to a paste than a simple infusion of vegetable matter.

Next morning, the water is wrung out of the yarn; the adhering leaves are shaken off; the yarn is beat in an earthen pot, or on a piece of wood. It is then spread out upon a bamboo, and exposed for a whole day to the sun, by which it acquires a fine orange colour.

The old casah leaves being removed, and fresh ones put in their place, together with an equal quantity of chayroot (Oldenlandia umbellata), these are the bodies that contribute essentially to the colour. When the yarn does not exceed half a pound, they may be used to the quantity of a handful each. One or two hours after the formation of this liquor, the yarn is to be laid in it.

The same process is repeated on the third day. By this time the yarn usually changes to a reddish yellow colour, with some red spots here and there appearing. A liquor for soaking the yarn in next night is now made of a handful of chayroot and water.

On the fourth day, the yarn will appear, in the morning, of a light red colour. It is to be treated in the same way as on the preceding days; and a similar liquor to the last is made for soaking it in at night.

On the fifth morning, the yarn is washed in a tank, and afterwards dried in the sun, as usual. In the evening it is laid in a liquor, made in the following manner. Some casah leaves are pounded in a mortar, and mixed with as much gingelie oil as is sufficient to make the whole into a dry paste.

Of this paste, about half an ounce is mixed with the usual portion of water. It is allowed to stand for one or two hours; a handful of chayroot is then added, and the yarn immediately immersed in it for the night.

The mode of proceeding on the sixth day is precisely similar. The liquor for the night is prepared solely of chayroot.

On the seventh day the yarn is washed again, dried, &c. Both on this and the succeeding evening it is soaked in a liquor made of equal parts of casah leaves and chayroot, infused in water; and here finishes the tedious process of infusing, soaking, steeping, &c. which has occupied nearly a month's time.

The liquor of last night is strained in the morning, a handful of chayroot added to it, with as much more water as may seem necessary for giving room to agitate the yarn in it freely.

Though the colouring particles of chayroot strike with much ease, and attach themselves so firmly, and with such facility, to the prepared yarn, that there is no removing them by water, or the other destroyers of colours, yet it is deemed necessary to boil the yarn in the same kind of liquor in which it has been so frequently soaked, in order to make the particles of the colouring matter adhere the stronger. For this purpose a furnace is to be built of some stones, leaving a little room for introducing the fuel. The pot containing the liquor is put upon this furnace, and a brisk fire is kept up till it begins to boil. The fire is then slackened, and kept up just sufficiently to give the water a constant bubbling motion, to be continued till a rose-coloured froth covers the whole surface. This shows that it is time either to remove the vessel altogether from the fire, or, what is more common, to take away the greatest part of the fire from under the vessel, and to suffer the pot to cool gradually without removing it.

The cheapest fuel is the stalks of the chayroot, kept by dyers for the express purpose.

During the boiling, the yarn is often stirred and lifted with wooden sticks, in order to produce an equal degree of heat throughout the whole. But these agitations must be as rapid as possible, to obviate the injury that the yarn would sustain by exposure to the air.

The yarn, when quite cold, is taken out of the pot, washed in a tank, beaten as usual, and dried in the sun.

If its colour, as is frequently the case, should not be of a lively and brilliant tint, the Malabars have ways of improving it. First, by dipping or steeping it once more in a liquor made of casah leaves and chayroot; the former mingled with a little gingelie oil. Secondly, by putting it into a cold infusion of sapan wood (Cæsalpinia sapan). But this method, though it adds greatly to the beauty of the colour, is a mere trick, as the first washing will deprive it of all that the sapan wood has communicated.

IV. *A Process by which only an Inferior Colour was obtained.*

The mode of dyeing usually practised, having been described at great length in the preceding part of this essay, a very short abstract will serve to put the reader in possession of this second method.

First day. The yarn was cleaned, &c. exactly as described before.

Second day. The yarn kept in the water, and occasionally agitated.

Third day. The water smelling very strong was poured off, the yarn hung up to dry, and the ley prepared in the usual way.

Fourth day. The mordant was prepared with gingelie oil, tsicky, &c. Part was immediately applied to the yarn; the rest in the evening.

Fifth day. The yarn, in the evening, was moistened with simple ley.

Sixth day. About noon, and in the evening, treated the yarn with diluted ley. The same was done on the seventh, eighth, ninth, tenth, and eleventh days.

Twelfth day. The yarn having undergone the necessary animalizing part of the process, it was washed at first in a small vessel, to preserve the tsicky, and then in a tank. In the evening of the same day it was once more served with ley, mixed with some part of the new tsicky. The yarn was then suffered to dry some days perfectly in the sun.

Thirteenth day. The yarn being washed and dried again, was plunged into the liquor prepared of pounded casah leaves.

Fourteenth day. The old leaves removed, and fresh ones added to yesterday's liquor.

Fifteenth day. Liquor prepared solely with a handful of pounded chayroot.

Sixteenth day. As yesterday.

Seventeenth day. The yarn being washed in the morning, was dried, and soaked, during the night, in liquor prepared with chayroot.

Eighteenth day. The same as the sixteenth.

Nineteenth day. Some casah leaves were beaten in a mortar, together with a little gingelie oil, and a quantity of this mass, of the size of a walnut, mixed with the usual portion of water, and then chayroot added.

Twentieth day. As yesterday.

Twenty-first. The yarn was washed in the morning, and the infusion prepared as yesterday.

Twenty-second. Chayroot solely used for making the liquor.

Twenty-third. The yarn washed in the morning and evening; laid into a liquor like that of yesterday.

Twenty-fourth. The yarn was boiled in the manner formerly described. Being washed, it appeared destitute of that brightness so much esteemed, and was rather of a darkish shade. This, I believe, was owing chiefly to the negligence of the dyer, in not administering the just quantity of casah leaves, by means of which the former yarn acquired its splendour.

In order to dispose the yarn thus spoiled in dyeing to receive the colouring matter anew, it is necessary to impregnate it again with the animalizing mordant, the same as at first, as there is reason to believe that it has been removed by the repeated washings, and by the boiling. The method which the Malabars pursue is this: they pound some casah leaves with gingelie oil, to a mass of a pultaceous glutinous consistence; part of this is mixed with water, and added afterwards to a handful of chayroot. In this liquor the yarn is soaked during a night; and the process is repeated till the yarn improves in colour. This is the common way of dyeing yarn red on the coast of Coromandel, from Cape Commorin to Palliacotah. But the process, as far as I could learn, is quite unknown on the north side of Kistnah, in the northern Circars, and in Bengal. There are some places in the Guntoor Circar where this method is partly practised; but the colour is of an inferior kind.

V. *Remarks on the Substances employed in this Process.*

Much depends upon the goodness of the yarn to be subjected to this process. The success of the colour, however, is to be chiefly ascribed to a proper regulation of the proportions of the substances employed, and of the time during which the yarn is subjected to each particular process.

The nature of the mordant is peculiar, and could scarcely have been anticipated as one that would answer the purpose. No strong chemical affinity appears to exist between it and the fibres of cotton. Hence one would have suspected that water would have washed the whole of it out. The permanency of the dye, however, and the necessity of the mordant to produce this permanency, are sufficient evidences that this is not the case. The essential constituents of this mordant appear to be the sheep's dung and the gingelie oil. The sheep's dung, no doubt, communicates some animal matter to the yarn, and appears to answer the purpose better than either cow-dung or blood. Instead of gingelie oil, I have used common olive oil, and found it to answer equally well; and I should suppose that tallow would answer still better. The dyers never use the gingelie oil fresh, but always keep it till it becomes rancid. This oil is made to undergo the particular alteration which oil in general undergoes, when converted into soap. The nature of this alteration has not been much examined by chemists, though it is known that, in consequence of it, the oil becomes soluble in alcohol, and that it assumes a much greater degree of consistence than it possessed before.

It is the ashes that produce this change, and the object of the very tedious treatment which the yarn undergoes—the repeated soakings in the alkaline ley, and exposure to the sun,—is merely to bring about this requisite change. It would certainly be worth while to try whether soap, or oil thrown down from soap, might not be used so as to shorten this very tedious part of the process.

As to the ashes employed, I suspect that the plantain is used to produce them, because it can be had at the cheapest rate, and with the greatest facility. But other trees are used when plantain cannot be had. The dry wood and leaves of the plantain are collected into a heap, and burnt briskly in the open air. When they cease to flame, the pieces are extinguished with water, and it is this residuum of charcoal which is employed to furnish the ash. It is well known in India, that the ashes of the plantain yield soda in a state of considerable purity. I have tried both potash and soda, as a substitute for the ashes of the plantain in dyeing, and have succeeded with them both. But I considered the colour as the most beautiful when soda was employed. Soda seems to give greater firmness to oil than potash, as it is known to be essential to the formation of hard soap.

Tsicky appears to be little else than a solution of soap in water; and its use in dying seems rather to favour the supposition that soap might be substituted in a great measure for the mordant.

Casah leaves are the leaves of the memecylon capitellatum, the calamsaly

2

of the Tamuls, and ali of the Gentoos. Dr. Roxburgh gives the following description of this plant.

"It is, in general, a shrub of a middle size; but grows to a pretty large tree, common in most jungles along the coast; is seldom found large except among the mountains, where it is not sought after. It is in general used for fire-wood; flowers during the hot season; the bark is dark, grey, and pretty smooth; the branches, large and small, suberate, rigid; leaves opposite, peteolate, ovate, acuminate, smooth, glaring, solid. Flowers small and purple, very numerous, in little umbels, one, two, or more issuing from where they have stood on the branches. I never saw flowers on the young leaf-bearing shoots, or rarely; always from the branches of twenty-three or more years old. The partial and general peduncles are tetragonal, smooth. Pedicels round and coloured; bracts minute; the calyx bell-shaped; obsolete, four-toothed, purple coloured; corolla four petals, heart-formed, inserted by angles into the divisions of the calyx, coral bluish. Stamina, filaments eight, twice as long as the calyx, in which they are inserted. Antheræ semilunate. Berry of the size of a pea, shining, black, and succulent."

This tree grows over the whole coast. I have found it near Tranquebar, and in the jungles of the northern Circars. But the dyers will never make use of those leaves that grow near their houses, not even when they are obliged to pay dear for those coming, as they say, from a distance, and most probably from the mountains of the coast, and those of Ceylon. And, indeed, the difference is so great, that one would be almost induced to believe that the imported leaves were from quite a different tree, or at least from a different species of memecylon, if we were not aware of the great influence of soil and water, and, above all, of age, to alter the qualities, and even the shape, of vegetable substances. Instances of this kind are so obvious and common, that all farther observations on the subject might be deemed superfluous.

The cold infusion of these leaves imparts a fine yellow colour to cotton, when soaked in it for some time. The leaves have an astringent taste, and all the qualities belonging to that principle. They are, in general, to be had at a very moderate price; for one pound of yarn seldom requires more than a fanam's worth of this article for the purpose of dyeing it. These dried leaves are to be pounded to a coarse powder before being used; but they may be kept a long time in the state of powder without losing any of their virtue. The Tamuls, I am told, sometimes substitute the nunna root (Guilan dina umbellata) for casah leaves, in dyeing cotton red. But as I have not had an opportunity of seeing it tried, I do not know how it answers.

I find that nut-galls will not answer as a substitute for casah leaves. Perhaps some of the trees of Europe, that are known to communicate a yellow colour, might be used in its place. I should be tempted, for that purpose, to try the birch, or the alder.

Chayroot is the principal dyeing ingredient. It is the root of the Oldenlandia umbellata. Dr. Roxburgh's description of it is as follows:

"The Oldenlandia is a small biennial, rarely triennial, plant; grows in a light, dry, sandy ground, near the sea, and is cultivated on the coast of Coromandel. Flowers during the latter part of the season. The seed ripe in January. Root is very long; from one to two feet; with a few lateral fibres. When fresh, the bark is orange coloured. The stem, in the cultivated sort, erect; in the wild, diffuse; in both, round jointed, a little scabrous; below, very ramous. The branches axillary, the under opposite, decussated, spreading, horizontal, and scarcely as long as the stem; above, alternate, or in pairs from the axil. The leaves opposite, tern or quatern pointed, sessile, linear, scabrous, spreading, from three quarters to half an inch long, by 1½ broad. In the axils of the principal leaves are generally fasciculæ of smaller leaves. Stipulas ciliated. Flowers terminal, small, white, very numerous; the whole forming a large umbil. Parts of fructification agree exactly with those of the genus.

"This plant is much cultivated on the coast of Coromandel. It grows but on the purest light sand; there its roots descend to a great depth. The cattle are driven upon the ground for some time to manure it; or some other manure employed, generally the lightest, and the surface of the ground made level and cleared of weeds. The seeds are mixed with much sand, and sown as soon as the rains begin in June or July. The sand is mixed with the seed, to enable the sower to sow it sufficiently thin. It requires to be often watered, if there are not frequent showers. The first watering has a little cow-dung mixed with it, which binds the surface of the soil, and prevents the wind from blowing the seed away. It is then simply watered, till the plants are two or three inches high; after which it requires little or no care. Few weeds grow in such a soil as suits the culture of this plant: of course a very little labour keeps it clean. Much rain injures the quality of the root. Where the wild sort can be had in quantity, it is esteemed one-third or one-fourth stronger than the cultivated; and, what is of more consequence, yields a better colour; and where roots can be had of two years' growth, they are reckoned still better. But the farmer does not find it answer his purpose to let the plant remain longer in the ground than one season."

This root is not less important to the Indian dyers than madder is to the European. Indeed its uses are fully as extensive as those of madder, for it is employed not only in dyeing cotton red, but also in cloth-painting; and very often serves to give other colours a degree of mellowness and beauty which otherwise they could not attain. As the quality of this root varies very materially in different circumstances, it becomes requisite for those that use it to make themselves well acquainted with the different appearances which it assumes that they may avoid the risk of being imposed on by fraudulent people. Particular attention is requisite to be able to discover whether or not the root has been spoiled by accidents, as by rain, or other injuries of the weather; by being kept in a dark room, &c. If a white colour prevail in the inside of the bark, and on the wood, we may be pretty certain that the root is spoiled; whereas a green colour is a sure indication of its goodness.

The Malabars have a method of determining the state of this root, upon which they lay considerable stress. They mix together a little of the pounded root and quicklime. If the mixture in a short time assumes a fine high red colour, the root is considered as good; but if the colour becomes pale or brown, or if no change of colour takes place at all, then the chayroot is considered as of no value.

Water extracts little colouring matter from the chayroot. The infusion has a light reddish tinge, owing to undissolved particles floating in it; for it passes colourless through the filter, but assumes an ale colour on standing. When an alkali is poured into the water the colour becomes a lively red.

Alcohol extracts a yellow colour from chayroot. The addition of a little lime or alkali immediately strikes a fine red.

In India, chayroot is sold in bundles along with the stalks. The dyers do not reduce it to powder till they are going to use it. They then cut off the stalks and the small shoots from the principal roots; then dry the roots in the sun till they become brittle enough to be reduced to powder. The price varies considerably in India according to the season and other circumstances.

In the south of India it is seldom sold for more than a rupee the three pounds' weight, and seldom for less than half that sum.

I have little doubt that madder might be substituted for it in Europe; and that, supposing the Indian method of dyeing introduced, it would furnish almost as fine a colour. Indeed I think it by no means unlikely that, by means of this animalizing mordant, if I be allowed the expression, even cochineal may be applied to cotton cloth, and may communicate to it as splendid a colour as it does to wool.

TRACT XII.

ACCOUNT OF THE METHOD OF SMELTING IRON IN THE NORTHERN CIRCARS.

ABOUT the end of the month of June, 1794, when the thermometer stood at 115°, I set out from Vuppāda for Letchemporam, a small village in the Polaveram district. This village lies about fourteen miles south-west from Rajahmundry. The adjacent country is gently sloping and undulating; and by far the greater part of it covered with jungle. The soil is gravelly, of a red colour, and has the aspect of sterility. There being no tanks, rice cannot be cultivated here. In addition to this disadvantage the country is much infested with tigers, which daily destroy the cattle of the poor inhabitants. I found the people in this village extremely willing to show and explain to me every thing concerning their iron works.

The iron-smelters themselves are a poor set of people, and obliged to plough the land for their subsistence during the wet season, and work as smelters only during the hottest part of the year. The finest and mildest season they employ in cutting wood in the hills, in burning charcoal, and after these occupations are over in recovering their health at home. For besides their repeated experience that every one contracts the fever during his stay among the jungle, we have only to observe their sickly look and their whole appearance, to be convinced that their accounts are correct. To this circumstance, together with the necessity they are under of cultivating the ground for a part of the year, we may ascribe the unproductiveness of their labour as manufacturers of iron. Yet the iron which they produce is considered as the finest in every respect for tools, razors, &c. Hence the demand for it is great, and the number of workmen miserably small; for the miners, smelters, wood-cutters, and labourers, all united together, do not exceed eight or nine men.

Stones containing iron ore in considerable quantity are found every where near the village, from six to eight fathoms under ground, imbedded in a lithomarga, the discovery of which is a sure sign of being near a bed of iron-stone.

These iron-stones lie in beds of a small extent, of irregular thickness, and various in their breadth from side to side; though this is never very great.

They at first mine downwards in a perpendicular direction, till they are obliged by the different directions of the beds to alter their course accordingly. The breadth of their perpendicular shaft amounts to about 2½ cubits, and small steps are cut out in the sides for the conveniency of descending. When they have exhausted a bed of iron-stone, they abandon their mine without any further trial, and dig another in a different direction. This negligent mode of proceeding puts them to many inconveniences, and produces much unnecessary trouble, by obliging them to dig holes almost every six yards, which they fill up again when the iron-stone is exhausted.

The ground in this place, and the ore itself, being of a very soft nature, no other instruments are required for working their mines than a pointed pick-axe. The ore and extraneous stones are drawn up in baskets; the latter (consisting chiefly of clay) is separated, and the former broken by mallets to the size of a hazzle-nut.

This ore has much the appearance of a yellow and brown ochrey clay. It appears also to contain a mixture, or rather coating, of calcareous earth. When reduced to powder it acquires a red colour, and exhibits many sparkling particles.

The miners prepare the charcoal which they require for smelting this ore, by burning the wood of the sandra chettu (Mimosa sandra), which furnishes a solid, good charcoal. But as it is rather scarce in the vicinity of this village, and as a conveyance of twenty-four or thirty miles, the nearest place where it may be had in abundance, is very expensive; this, together with various other obvious circumstances, must render any attempt to establish a large iron-manufactory in this village a very hazardous undertaking. No doubt other kinds of wood might be found which would yield a charcoal that would answer the purpose sufficiently well; but unluckily all the jungle in the neighbourhood of the village consists of very small brushwood.

These smelting-works however, notwithstanding their diminutive scale, attract the attention of every curious observer, on account of the simplicity of every part of the process and the goodness of the iron obtained.

The furnace consists of a small semi-circular mud wall, very much resembling in shape the half of a hen's egg divided longitudinally, with the largest end uppermost. The wall is built of clay or mud. From the apex to the base is usually 4½ feet, while its greatest breadth is three feet nine inches. The external and convex surface has on one of its sides, at the bottom, an excavation serving to receive the scoriæ, which are let out through a hole in the bottom.

The internal surface of this mud wall is plain, except a semi-circular excavation throughout its middle part, commencing at the apex and terminating in a circular hole in the ground, which is 1½ foot deep, and as much in diameter. This part corresponds with the square cavity in European furnaces, in which the iron is collected.

The use of this semi-circular excavation will be understood by considering the temporary part which is destroyed every day after the smelting is finished. It is a thin, convex, semi-circular wall, and is to complete a circular hole with the excavation in the permanent part of the furnace. It is constructed in the following manner:—At five o'clock in the evening, the hole in the ground is cleaned from the ashes and the remainder of the last smelting, and its bottom and sides coated with powdered charcoal moistened with a little water. At the bottom, to the right hand, is a small circular hole for letting off the scoriæ. This hole must also be cleaned, and then stopped up with some moistened clay. Charcoal is then thrown into the hole and placed in such a manner that the apex of the heap touches the margin of the hole opposite to the principal work; and another heap of pounded ore is so placed on the opposite side that the middle of the hole is left an empty space. These two heaps are distant from each other at the apex about a foot, at the bottom about an inch. This is done in order to rest on the charcoal a kind of funnel-formed channel for the admission of the stream of air produced by the constant action of the bellows. The external aperture of the funnel, receiving the nozzle of the bellows, is in breadth five or six inches. Clay is then put upon it, which serves both to fix it and to form the first layer of clay that constitutes the temporary part of the furnace. This part is not to be thicker than two inches, and it decreases in thickness the higher it advances. The funnel itself is made of a mixture of clay and husks of rice; and previous to its application is hardened by fire, and then made firmer in its position by a coat of clay laid over it.

The funnel being fixed in this manner, the wall is raised, becoming gradually thinner, so that when it arrives at the middle part, it does not exceed the thickness of an inch. Then a burnt stone of the same thickness, from ten to twelve inches high and from eight to nine broad, is fixed upon it so that it inclines to the opposite side, the circle becoming narrower the higher it rises. This stone is connected with the principal wall by means of mud. In this manner the circle is completed; some holes of two inches square being left, one or two on each side. On the stone itself is placed a second stone of the same kind and shape, but smaller, and fixed in the same manner. Its apex is on a level with the top of the opposite or principal part of the furnace. The top of the furnace now serves as the basis for a cone, the use of which is sufficiently obvious.

This cone is twelve inches long. Its under aperture rests on the top of the furnace, where its breadth is fourteen inches. At its upper part or apex its diameter is seven inches. To facilitate the introduction of charcoal and ore into the furnace the cone is crowned with a large cutcherie pot, the bottom of which is broken out, and thus serves not only to facilitate the introduction of fuel, &c. but is supposed of much consequence as the representation of a swamy.

It has been already stated that some charcoal and ore had been placed at the bottom of the furnace, and that the funnel for conveying the wind was placed upon this heap. Some lighted charcoal is put before the opening of the funnel, and the whole cavity is then filled with charcoal, and this is continued as the wall advances in height, the charcoal serving as a support to it; for it is so thin that it would not be able to support its own weight. Within the holes left on each side of the stones, which constitute the middle part of the furnace, some lighted charcoal is also placed.

The under part of the cone is also filled with charcoal. Then a small basket of ore is thrown upon it, and upon this likewise some lighted charcoal is placed. Finally the whole cavity is filled up to the top with charcoal.

Matters are allowed to remain in this state till five o'clock next morning, when two pair of bellows are applied to the aperture of the funnel, adapted for the insertion of the nozzles; each pair of bellows is worked by one man. The several vent-holes in the sides of the furnace are stopped up with a mixture of clay and sand. The bellows are then worked without intermission, and an intense degree of heat is soon produced.

The ore is thrown in by small quantities at a time, in small baskets which do not hold above three or four pounds; and for every basketful of ore two basketfuls of charcoal are added. As the charcoal burns the ore gradually sinks downwards, and at last the melted iron and scoriæ make their way to the bottom. The great object of the workmen is to supply the requisite quantity of charcoal and ore, and they continue their additions till within a little of the time when the reduced iron is taken out of the furnace.

A hole was left ready at the bottom to be opened occasionally, in order to permit the scoriæ to run out. This is done regularly every second hour, or six times during the whole operation. They pierce the clay which stops the passage with a pointed iron, suffer the liquid scoriæ to run out, and then secure the hole as before with clay. The cracks produced by the intense heat in the exterior thin wall they take care to stop up occasionally with moistened clay, and now and then they wet the whole with water in which clay is suspended.

At five o'clock in the evening the bellows are removed, and the exterior wall of the furnace knocked down. The iron, which is found in a solid state, is taken out and beaten for about five minutes with wooden sticks, in order to separate as much of the scoriæ as possible. Finally, it is cut with axes into two pieces, in order to show its internal quality.

I do not know the precise quantity of iron-stone which is employed in one smelting process. In general I believe twelve baskets of ore are required, containing each from four to five computed marcals. The whole produce of one process is about 112 lb. of iron, which are usually sold for about a rupee.

The iron, as thus produced, is of a very inferior quality, porous, and its pores filled with scoriæ, and in fact little more than half smelted, if such an expression may be used; for I am persuaded that the whole mass never has been in fusion; as in that case it would naturally have run out with the scoriæ through the hole at the bottom of the fire-place. The metallic particles in the ore are probably at some distance from each other. The fusion of the scoriæ lays them open to the action of the charcoal. They are reduced to the metallic state, tumble down in consequence of their weight, and coming in contact with each other at a welding heat, are cemented or agglutinated together, without having experienced actual fusion.

The iron thus obtained is indeed of such an inferior quality, that none of the names, by which any of the various kinds of cast iron are distinguished, can be applied to it. But if it be exposed to the heat produced by urging a fire by a pair of common bellows, while it is quite covered with charcoal; and, when the scoriæ begins to melt, if it be taken out and hammered, it acquires the properties of steel, and may then be usefully employed in the making of instruments.

The bellows used for this smelting furnace are of the same shape and nature as those used by the ironsmiths on the coast of Coromandel; with this exception only, that they are made of buffaloe hide, and therefore are four or five times stronger than the common bellows which are made of sheep-skin.

Were a manufacture of iron to be established here upon a large scale, the greatest difficulty would probably be the introduction of powerful blowing machines in place of these puny bellows. No doubt the East India Company, if it thought proper, might easily establish such a manufactory in different parts of their extensive dominions; and altogether supersede the necessity of the importation of iron from Europe. But I have strong doubts whether the establishment of extensive iron manufactories, in countries destitute of pitcoal, be a prudent measure. Indeed I think it probable that the iron manufactories of England are in possession of such advantages that no other country is in a capacity to compete with them; and that they must in a great measure supersede and put a stop to the manufacture of iron in all other countries, Swedish iron excepted, which on account of its superior qualities will always find its market and bring its price.

TRACT XIII.

ACCOUNT OF THE IRON WORKS AT RAMANAKAPETTA.

WHILE on my excursion to the diamond mines at Mallavilly, I had an opportunity of seeing the mode of smelting iron, employed at Ramanakapetta, and I think it worth while to give an account of the process in this Essay, in order that the European reader may have as full a view as possible of the various modes employed in India for obtaining this most useful of all metals. The Indian processes are rude and imperfect, and conducted in all cases on a very small scale. Yet they are characterised by a degree of simplicity which throws an air of interest about them. The good quality of their iron obviously depends upon the goodness of their ores, and upon the purity of the charcoal which they employ in their processes. They are too unskillful to produce tolerably good iron from bad ore, and they have never attempted, nor indeed do they possess the means of substituting pitcoal for charcoal as is the practice in England.

Ramanakapetta is a village situated six miles to the northward of Nuzīd. The road to it lies chiefly through a jungle, near which are some fine large tanks, that would supply water in a sufficient quantity to enable the inhabitants to raise large crops of rice, provided there were a sufficient number of hands for the purposes of cultivation. A great number of palmeyra trees, growing in the thickest part of the jungle, sufficiently prove the existence of former villages, and of a greater population.

Ramanakapetta has much better buildings than Nuzīd; the streets are very broad, and the houses, according to the fashion of the natives, good and large. There is an excellent choultrie in the middle of the village; and a fine large tank near it to the south is a great source of comfort to the inhabitants. The nearest hills are eastward, and form a kind of amphitheatre opening to the south. Here lies the village, and here are all the iron mines. Before the late famine, there were forty smelting furnaces in this place, besides a great number of silversmiths and coppersmiths, all in a state of affluence. But the present inhabitants are poor, and indeed in a wretched situation.

The iron mines lie on the north, a mile from the village, and half a mile from the hills. The ore is brought in baskets to the furnaces which are close to the village. The smelters here are a distinct set of people from the miners; neither do they prepare their own charcoal. They purchase both articles: the ore in baskets from the mines; the charcoal from labourers, who bring it from the hills.

The ore constitutes a bed immediately under the soil, and does not exceed a foot and a half in thickness. It consists of small rounded stones lying loose and unconnected with each other. It does not appear to contain any calcareous matter mixed with it. Though it does not exactly agree with any common iron ores in Europe; yet it approaches nearest to *hæmatites.* When moistened it adheres to the lips; it has a fine grain, is easily reduced to a fine powder, which effervesces slightly with acids. I should be disposed to consider it as a *hydrous carbonate of iron,* similar to those which are so frequently employed for smelting in Europe.

The furnaces which, before the famine, amounted to forty, are now reduced to ten. They are exactly similar to the furnace described in the preceding tract, and their mode of smelting is precisely the same as that practised at Letchemporam.

The charcoal which they employ is obtained from the mimosa sandra of Roxburgh, which grows, I am told, in abundance on the nearest hills. But charcoal from any other firm wood is found to answer the purpose sufficiently well. Four gunny bags of charcoal are sold for one rupee. This is the quantity required for every smelting process. The ore is not reduced into small pieces, but thrown into the furnace just as dug out of the ground. The scoriæ are let out only twice during the whole process; the last time is just before they cease to work the bellows.

The process is conducted upon rather more rational principles than that at Letchemporam. For they discontinue to add more ore above an hour before they take out their obtained metal. The whole produce of about one māund is sold for two rupees, after it has been heated and hammered to separate the scoriæ with which it abounds. To be able to dispose of it more easily, they cut it into small pieces, weighing each about two pounds. It is still in a very rude state; but it is soft and malleable, and therefore more easily applied to common purposes. There is a greater demand for this iron than the workmen can possibly supply; though they are constantly smelting during the greatest part of the year.

If the Company were inclined to establish any large iron works, there is no doubt that this place would be eminently worthy of notice. The ore can be obtained in any quantity wanted, probably at a smaller expense than any where else. The neighbouring hills yield plenty of wood; and, what is a material point, there are a great number of people who would be happy to be employed at a business which, under their own management, yields but a scanty subsistence.

Every furnace at present requires nine men, who are chiefly employed in working the bellows. For these, nothing would be more easy than to substitute a simple mechanical contrivance, which, by greatly reducing the number of hands, would contribute materially to the increase of profit.

Besides this village, there are, I am told, six others in the Nuzīd country, in which iron is smelted. Of these, however, I know nothing more than the names; but it is probable that the method of conducting the operation will be similar in them all.

TRACT XIV.

A SHORT DESCRIPTION OF THE BUGGLECONDA HILL, NEAR INNACONDA, IN THE GUNTUR CIRCAR.

THIS hill claims our attention because it is considered by many, both natives and Europeans, as an extinct volcano. It lies about twelve miles to the eastward of Innaconda, and is remarkable for the frequent earthquakes to which it is subject. It runs in a northerly and southerly direction, and has three peaks, of which the middle is the highest. The word Buggleconda signifies in the Telinga language a hill of charcoal; to which appellation the colour and appearance of the stones, of which it is composed, have probably given occasion.

Neither public records, nor tradition, afford any information of any former eruption of lava from this hill; but superstition has given us an explanation of the frequent shocks of earthquakes that originate with this mountain, or are entirely confined to it.*

Though this hill is not high, not exceeding, I should conceive, a quarter of a mile above the level of the plain, yet I ascended it with much difficulty. It is exceedingly steep, and is covered with stones so smooth and large

* The lower classes of natives say, that Madam Buggleconda (for all noisy hills in India are females) quarrels with her husband, the Innaconda hill. The sages among the people give a more intelligent and scientific explanation, by ascribing the noise to the groans of a giant, who in days of yore was imprisoned under the mountain by a valiant dwarf. This must have happened at the time when the warlike gods of Greece and Rome were at war with the giants. This may be inferred from the similarity of the missile weapons in use in both cases. For the combatants often threw huge mountains at each other's heads, as is amply testified by the Ramaiana, (a work celebrating the exploits of Rama) and by many Greek and Latin authors. I have not been able to determine whether it was then that the mountains had wings, and did fly about like a parcel of wild geese. If I am well informed, it was rather at the commencement of that war that one of the Swamy's Dēwandrudu cut off with a diamond sword the wings of all the mountains. These, no longer able to sustain themselves in the air, fell down upon the earth, and by their precipitate fall many a brave giant was buried in oblivion.

that we were obliged to climb from one to another. The heat of the day in the month of April, and my European dress, rendered the undertaking additionally laborious. No more than two out of sixteen natives who attempted the task were able to follow me to the peak, which is the highest except one. Farther than this I myself was unable to proceed.

There grew but few bushes in the narrow intervals between the stones. Most of them are the euphorbia antiquorum, the roots of which seem merely agglutinated to the smooth surface of the rock. Nothing having the smallest analogy to a crater could be seen upon the top of this hill; for from my position I was able to overlook all the peaks with sufficient accuracy. On the east side of the mountain indeed, under the large peak, there is a longitudinal deepening, which a keen volcanist might twist into a crater, though it has every appearance of having existed as long as the mountain itself.

The whole mountain is composed of basalt. At some distance from the hill, I observed some basaltic columns about ten feet high, that had been used by the natives for the erection of little pandals, or small open temples. But whether these columns were natural or artificial, I can not pretend to say. No colums were to be discovered on the mountain itself. In large masses this basalt is as sonorous as iron. Its colour is black, its hardness considerable. When broken it exhibits a great many black shining grains, which I take to be basaltic hornblende, together with some white particles interspersed here and there.

No other stone, except basalt, was to be seen any where upon the hill. We must therefore consider it as composed of a very thick bed of basalt. The stones to be found on the adjacent plain are partly calcareous and partly slaty; so that it does not appear that the basalt penetrates below the surface of the soil. There is a slate quarry at no great distance from the hill, between it and Innaconda. The earthquakes in this hill are often perceived several times in the course of a month, and frequently so strong as to move the furniture of the houses in the adjacent villages, and to roll large stones from the hill into the neighbouring plain. These shocks proceed at times towards all points of the compass, but it has been observed, that they proceed northwards more frequently than in any other direction.

Besides Buggleconda, there are several other hills in India considered by some persons as extinct volcanoes. The Innaconda hill is one of the most remarkable of these. It is a hill with a fort about sixty miles south west from Guntūr. The rock, of which it is composed, is an aggregate of quartz and mica, and is probably connected with mica slate. The quartz is white, and constitutes the basis of the rock; the mica is in large irregular lumps, that are often a quarter of an inch thick and much larger. Its colour is black, and it is so compact that it might be mistaken for schorl. The silicious part of this rock is not uniform; for many quartz crystals of different sizes and shapes appear, as it were, agglutinated together by a quartzy cement. On this hill there are two tanks, which afford a supply of excellent water the whole year round. These tanks may pass for the crater of this supposed volcano.

But neither upon this hill, nor any other of the supposed Indian volcanoes, are the least traces of lava to be observed, nor indeed of any stone, except basalt, which has the smallest resemblance to lava.

TRACT XV.

CURSORY OBSERVATIONS MADE DURING A TOUR FROM BEZWADAH TO TIMMERICOTAH.

I HAVE always considered travellers as so liable to be imposed on by their own imaginations, and by the imperfect information which they obtain from a variety of people, that I must confess I never could bring myself to rely implicitly on the word of my informers, for any observations made during a short stay of my own at the places which I happened to visit. Yet I am still of opinion that much valuable information is often conveyed by travellers. I venture therefore, with the greatest deference, to submit to the reader the following remarks, which I drew up during an excursion from the banks of the Kistna at Bezwadah to Timmericotah, and back again to Innacondah. They were made under too many disadvantages not to require the indulgence of the reader. A connected series of events, or a regular description of the roads and places passed through, will not be expected; but merely such detached and desultory observations as opportunity or objects afforded matter for.

At the village of Bezwadah, I arrived at the latter end of October 1797. Its situation on the northern banks of the river gives it a romantic appearance, which is aided by many venerable buildings of ancient towers and pagodas, most of them now in ruins. From it there is a narrow artificial pass, that leads to Condapilly. This pass, in a military point of view, was formerly deemed of importance. It lies at the south end of a range of hills which run up close to the banks of the Kistna. It constitutes a broad commodious road in form of an arched bridge, cut through a solid rock composed of felspar, mica, garnets, and ochre, aggregated together. Veins of felspar often run through this rock in oblique or horizontal directions. Such veins are much harder than the felspar which enters as a constituent into the rock. The surface of this rock is quite black, owing to the state of the ochre which enters in such abundance into its composition. The felspar is white, foliated, and appears, when in large pieces, transversely striated. It is uncommonly soft, and is entirely disintegrated when long exposed to the air.

Owing to the immense fall of rain, which still in some degree continued, the country was almost inundated, and the only roads lay through jonnalu fields, and were almost impassable.

Roads, in the European sense of the word, scarcely exist in India, at least not in the northern Circars. Hence, travelling in the wet season is exceedingly troublesome: most of the paths passing through rice fields, where the palankeen bearers are up to the middle in water. At all seasons of the year, when we pass through jungles, we must take care not to lose an eye by the branches of thorny bushes which meet each other in the middle of the path, and very soon tear a palankeen to pieces. This is the case even in the roads between the most frequented places, as for example, between Samalcotah and Rajahmundry, and between Rajahmundry, Ellore, Condapilly, and Hydrabad.

Notwithstanding the profusion of water that had fallen from the clouds, the Kistna was scarcely half full: a sufficient proof that the size of this river, as well as that of the Godavery, does not depend upon the rains that fall on this side of the peninsula.

At sunset I arrived at Mundaram, a place situated on the other side of the Kistna, and about four miles distant from that river. It belongs to the country of a powerful Zemindar, called Vassareddy. It is populous and pretty large; and what is very seldom to be seen in India, it had a large pagoda building in it. But what particularly attracted my notice, it seemed to abound with saltpetre earth; and, as far as I could discover, of a much purer taste than in many places where a manufacture of saltpetre had been established. This circumstance deserves attention, because the product, and the price of the article, depend entirely upon the earth from which it is extracted. In appearance there is no difference between the earth which contains common salt or soda, and that which yields saltpetre. All equally attract a little moisture during the night, and appear a black soft dust at the bottom of old walls, or on the streets of populous and old villages. One village, or even one street, frequently produces all the three different salts: and if proper attention is not paid to this circumstance, much loss may be incurred in the manufacture of saltpetre. This I experienced last year at

Ellore and other places, and even this year I have been obliged to throw a great quantity of salt away because it contained too little saltpetre to pay the expense of refining it. The only circumstance which enables one to determine the relative goodness of the saltpetre earth is the taste, when it is not practicable to extract a portion of the salt and determine its nature by crystallizing it.

The country about this place, and indeed the observation applies to the whole Guntūr Circar, appears to be well cultivated, and the jonnalu (holcus sorghum) was much farther advanced than I had observed it on the other side of the river. The soil is black, and would produce any species of grain whatever, provided it could be watered when required. But unluckily the bed of the river lies too deep; and after the periodical rains, which terminate in November, frequently not a drop of rain falls till July, when the rainy season again commences. On this account rice cannot be cultivated here in any considerable quantity. During the months of April, May, and June, the whole animal and vegetable creation suffers so much from want of water, that every thing puts on the appearance of decay, and the face of nature assumes a wintry aspect.

The scene however very speedily changes. The first rain has scarcely fallen when the country assumes a different appearance. The finest verdure springs up every where, the husbandman is every where busily employed in cultivating his fields and his garden, for which in the Guntūr circar he is well paid; for the jonnalu grows here in good years to the height of seven or eight feet, and has ears of a span long, and five or six inches in diameter, and sells at an average for four or five pagodas the candy.

Few trees are to be seen in this neighbourhood, and these few are mostly tamarinds, growing in large topes, which during the hot months afford a refreshing shelter to the weary traveller. Mangoes, cocoanuts, and even palmeyras* seem from their scantiness to be considered as exotics. Indeed

* It is with great satisfaction I observe, that, on my application to the Board of Revenue, Government have been pleased to send this year (1797) 150,000 seed of the black palmeyra. It was not possible to distribute them in the inland countries of this Circar, which, throughout, have a stiff black soil, which, when dry, is so hard that no root can make its way through it. They require no other trouble and expense than that of planting them; and when allowed to grow about twenty-five years in a light soil no tree can be more useful. The black part furnishes a very strong wood for building, the leaves cover houses, and are used as a substitute for paper. Palmeyra wine or toddy is a good beverage, and boiled yields a coarse sugar

none but the latter would thrive without such extraordinary extension as to preclude the possibility of cultivating them with profit.

The natives of this Circar, as is the case in all places where jonnalu is the principal food, are a stout healthy people, and of a larger size than those who live chiefly on rice. This must be owing to the superior nourishing qualities of jonnalu. Even the straw seems to partake of this valuable quality; for the cattle here, during the dry months, have scarcely any thing else to live upon: yet the cows and the sheep grow much larger and fatter than in the Masulipatam and Vizagapatam Circars. The cows, especially, are famous for their size all over the peninsula, though not for their strength; for as soon as they are put to hard work, as carrying baggage, drawing guns, &c. they are found much less able to undergo fatigue than the smaller but hardier bullocks of the Carnatic provinces.

This may be partly owing to a change in their food, to which, in times of war, they are exposed, and which few animals are able to bear. But it is chiefly owing to the size of their limbs and bones, which, in comparison with the bulk of their bodies, are very slender. This last cause was pointed out to me by a Gentleman, high in rank in the civil department, and a set of observations, which I had an opportunity of making during a late tour through this district, have convinced me that it is perfectly just. As this is a circumstance of great importance to Government, it were to be wished that steps were taken to cross the breed with cattle from other countries, especially from the Carnatic. Even the cattle in the Palnād are much better made, and stouter, than those in the Guntūr Circar.

I intended to have taken Chintapilly in my way to Bellumcondah, but the rainy season and the badness of the roads obliged me to alter my plan. Chintapilly was built by the same Zemindar who built Amarēswaram. He was formerly partial to it, and especially to a small fort (as he chose to call it) which he had on the banks of the Kistna, and in which it was thought expedient to keep a guard of sepoys. This having given a stab to his pride, he left the place altogether and built Amarēswaram. This step, however, was not taken without regret, nor before he had done every thing in his power to get the guard removed. For his new place was not so agreeably situated, and wanted those charms which are most attractive to a native of India. It had neither been the residence of his ancestors nor the place of

called jaggary. The roots of the young plant have the taste of a carrot, and are used in the same way by the natives.

his birth. I am glad to hear that he has been again put in full possession of his favourite place.

Bellumcondah, literally translated the *sugar hill*, is a hill fort about twenty-five miles west from Guntūr, and sixteen from the Condavier hills. Here the country begins to assume a hilly aspect. The soil is black, but covered with stones of different kinds. There are some tanks near this place which furnish water for a few rice fields.

The country is but thinly inhabited, and would be more so were it not for the intolerable oppression which the inhabitants of the more fertile districts on the other side of the Kistnah experience from their rulers, the Zemindars*. One would be inclined to consider this as the most barren of all the countries in the east. The soil around is very stony, and the whole country covered with a grey dust. But the stones do not appear to hurt vegetation, as cotton and jonnalu grow pretty well, the former indeed to great perfection.

A good deal of saltpetre is manufactured in the villages near this place. This is the only kind of manufactory which the country seems to be capable of supporting with success. I have observed that this salt is always to be found in greater quantity in villages at the foot of hills, provided they have the other requisites of soil and population.

The country between this place and Timmericotah, furnishes little worth observing. It abounds in different kinds of game, as partridges, hares, wild ducks, and teals.

The Palnād, a district belonging (at that time) to the Nabob of the Carnatic, is for the most part uncultivated, and exhibits scarcely any thing except a continued jungle of underwood. This is partly owing to the natural disadvantages under which it labours, and partly, in all probability, to the present mode of government.

I have scarcely ever seen a tract of land so entirely covered with stones as most of this part of the Carnatic; and from their singularity I think them deserving of a particular description. They are of a calcareous nature, and have a slaty texture; and all the hills with which the country is encircled are composed of the same kind of rock. The district abounds also with many hard stones, some of which are of considerable value.

Many places have diamond mines, which in former ages are said to have been very rich, and might still be profitable if people could be prevailed

* In the Nizam's dominions.

upon to venture their money in such speculations. I am told that when the rains are over, and when the Kistna, which takes its course through the country, has discharged its water, diamonds, cats'-eyes, onyxes, calcedonies and other valuable stones are found in its bed; but nobody is allowed to pick them up without having first obtained an express order from the Nabob. The river is even said to carry particles of gold along with it, and many specimens of that metal have been collected.

All the hills and mountains in the Palnād belong to the floetz class of rocks. The principal ranges run from south to north, and at the south point strike off to the east towards Innacondah. The first of these ranges is but of inconsiderable height; but the latter appear somewhat higher. I conceive the difference to be only apparent, and to arise from the country round the first range being more elevated than that round the second.

One of the most striking objects of curiosity in this district is a cataract six miles west from Timmericotah, on that range of hills that runs from south to north. Some affirm it to be produced by a branch of the Kistna. As this was a circumstance both curious and important in an economical point of view, I could not resist the opportunity of inquiring into the fact; accordingly I went to the place, attended, as it was thought necessary for my personal safety, with a sufficient number of persons armed with matchlocks, and a boy with a tomtom to frighten away the tigers and bears with which the place is infested. Fortunately none of these animals presented themselves to obstruct our passage. The skin, however, of a tiger, which Captain Dess was so obliging as to show me, of an animal about fourteen or fifteen feet long from head to tail, that had scoured the country about Timmericotah for a long time, and had committed great depredations even upon the human species, was enough to have alarmed much bolder adventurers than myself into an observance of the necessary precautions.

The road that leads to this famous spot rises though not suddenly, is exceedingly stony, and so closely lined with very thorny shrubs, that one has a disagreeable feeling in travelling along it. On the plain which forms the top of it, we behold the bed of a small river, which appears as if it were paved in a regular artificial manner. The stones with which it is lined naturally break into regular tables, and thus produce this admirable imitation of art.

The cataract and river under consideration are called by the natives Yedlapādu. According to their accounts it depends upon the accidental fall of rain, as in the dry season the bed of the river is perfectly dry. It runs from south to north, in which direction it precipitates itself over the cataract; then it winds west, and at the distance of about six miles disembogues itself into the Kistna. The Kistna at this place runs in the same direction from south to north, and its bed is situated about sixty feet lower than that of the other small river.

What I have said of the direction in which both Yedlapādu and the Kistna run, as well as the dependence of the former on accidental showers of rain in this part of the country, and the great difference in the height of the beds of the two rivers, cannot I conceive leave any doubt that the former is not a branch of the Kistna, but entirely independent of it; though for political reasons it were to be wished that the contrary were the case.

I despair of giving any description of the place itself, adequate to its natural beauties. A large cataract has always attracted the attention of the curious. It has something majestic in its appearance. The suspended column of water whitened with froth, and encircled with rainbows, the peculiar roaring noise, and the idea of danger with which the spectator is struck, must always render such a spectacle interesting. The peculiar situation of this cascade in a lonely place at the top of a hill, overshadowed with large trees and crowded with places of worship, the simple regularity of the bed of the river above, and of the sides of the basin into which it precipitates itself, render it peculiarly interesting.

The water falls from a height of about sixty feet into a basin more than one hundred and twenty feet in breadth, which, in consequence of the unweildy masses of stone that the torrent has carried along, and which have gradually agglutinated together, is more irregular and uneven than the bed of the water above the fall. The sides of this basin, especially the eastern, are nearly perpendicular, and so regular, that it appears as if it had been constructed by the rules of architecture. This is easily accounted for by the nature of the stones of which it is composed. The front over which the water precipitates itself is also perpendicular, and has clefts that are filled up with roots of banian trees (ficus religiosa), and covered with a species of adiantum, from which the French, who were formerly in this country, are said to have prepared a very good syrup de capillaire.

The roots of the banian, spreading like a net, rendered it easy for me to climb up the perpendicular precipice, and to collect specimens of the calcareous depositions which filled up the fissures between the beds of rock. These soft calcareous stones, a variety of calcareous tuff, often take various forms, which, by the help of a little imagination, are conceived to represent the figures of lingums and other Hindoo deities.

At the time of my visiting this place, there was fortunately a considerable fall of water, but by no means enough to cover the bed from bank to bank. The water was at the eastern side of the fall, and extended in breadth twenty yards. In the middle there was no water; but near the western bank there was an inconsiderable stream, near to which I ascended the precipice.

The places of worship on the western side of the basin consist of Hindoo temples, dedicated to a great variety of deities, among which a small one near the bed of the basin is the most famous. On a certain day all the shepherds of the country round assemble and sacrifice several hundred sheep to the sanguinary Sekty. They do not give over butchering till the blood flows in a stream and mingles with the water in the basin of the cataract.

The other temples or pagodas are somewhat larger, very dark from the large trees that every where surround them; but by no means remarkable for their structure. They are all built of the stone which is found in the immediate vicinity. To the highest of them we must ascend by a flight of steps, and this pagoda, on account of a cavern in it, is the most spoken of. It is said to go under the bed of the Kistna to a port on the opposite bank —an assertion of the Bramins very unlikely to be true. For, besides the hardness of the rock and the great height of the pagoda above the level of the Kistna, the distance, no less than eight miles, makes such a communication utterly improbable. It is, however, firmly believed by the natives of the place. These places are now often the haunts of tigers; and they are defiled in a shocking manner by their numerous inhabitants, the bats, which occasion a smell that is almost suffocating.

A matter of much consequence now offers itself to our attention, namely, whether this cataract can be converted to any useful purpose. The great height from which the water precipitates seems sufficient to enable it to water any part of the Guntūr Circar, were it thought proper to let the water take the same course with the Kistna, though I conceive it would be possible to bring it into the district by a shorter route. But whether the body of water would be sufficient to compensate for the very great expense that it would be necessary to incur, is more than I can pretend to say.

The river being entirely dependent on the periodical rains in this part of the country, is a very unfavourable circumstance, and sufficient to induce the greatest caution in setting about such an undertaking.

The valley through which the Kistna runs in this part of the country is a barren, stony, jungly desert. In the rainy season it is clad with verdure which takes somewhat from its savage appearance; but in the hot season, when all its foliage is withered and the land wind has established its dominion over it, scarcely a vestige of life is to be discovered in it. During that season no country can be more tiresome to the eyes of a traveller than this. A few straggling villages on the other side of the Kistna furnish the only indications of the possibility of meeting with any thing else than beasts of prey. Unfortunately the few human beings that are found there are said to be little else than enemies of the human race. They are robbers who have frequently invaded the neighbouring countries, and some years ago even ventured to attack Tummericotah itself. This place is garrisoned now by a detachment of the Company's troops. There is a small fort, but it is calculated for little more than a defence against straggling parties of native cavalry. The stone wall round it is high, at the upper part thin, and defended by four bastions.

The revenues of the country, of which this is the principal place, (said to be 40,000 pagodas) proceed mostly from duties levied upon the Lombardies, who pass through this country on their way from the inland districts to the sea coast, where they load their bullocks with salt.

There are no manufactures on the Palnād, except those of saltpetre. The product is superior to any that I have seen elsewhere in India. The mode used about Innacondah, of procuring the salt by evaporation, is likewise practised here; and it is doubtless the most profitable in every respect. This article has been hitherto only exported to the inland countries, to Hydrabad, &c.; but from this time it will probably become an article of attention and speculation for the European market *.

* I am astonished that the native Princes pay so little attention to the encouragement of trade. They are the worst politicians in this point of view that ever existed. Taxes are increased and rigorously exacted as soon as an article becomes an object of exportation, whether it be corn or any manufacture. There is not a Zemindar in the Company's dominions who has not been trying to levy customs on saltpetre (since I have commenced making it in a greater quantity than usual), which would exceed the prime cost of the article at least 100 per cent. I could easily show them the impolicy of such a measure; but as nothing that I could say here would

At some places in this country, and on the other side of the Kistna, iron works are established. The only grain cultivated is jonnalu, and the quantity raised is barely sufficient for the consumption of the country. Cotton grows plentifully, and if encouraged might be had to a large amount. It is of the same kind as that cultivated all over the Guntūr Circar. The plant seldom grows higher than a foot and a half, on which account it is called dwarf cotton (gossypium herbaceum). It is sown by the drill plough in lines $1\frac{1}{2}$ foot distant from each other, the plants being scarcely two inches asunder. It yields a brownish cotton, much esteemed by the punjum weavers about Samulcotah.

The cassia sennæ grows abundantly in this country. It is a small branchy plant that spreads itself on the ground, and on that account is called by the natives nēla (ground) tanghedu. It has five or six pair of leaflets, and a petiole without glands and somewhat reddish. The legumen is exactly the same as that found among the senna leaves that are brought from Alexandria. It produces the same effects upon the bowels as the senna of the shops; and

have any chance of ever coming to the ears of these petty grandees, it will be sufficient if I point out in a few words how far the Company may be interested in supporting this manufacture.

1. Saltpetre is made in the hot season when the farmer has nothing to employ him in the fields.

2. The money paid for saltpetre enriches the country at large, as the money obtained for it would be wholly lost if the article were not manufactured. The revenues in consequence are more easily collected.

3. On account of the attention paid to the manufacture, sale, and exportation of this article, it cannot be converted to purposes injurious to the authority of Government. Some years ago all saltpetre manufactured in the Guntūr district was shipped at Kottapam, and carried to different parts of India, especially to the Mauritius; where I am informed a great scarcity of it prevails at present, probably in consequence of the prohibition to export it.

4. The exclusive privilege of selling it belonging to the Company is attended with some advantages. Ill-minded people, of whom there are always a great number, cannot procure it in any quantity to become hurtful to the established Government. The late troubles in the first division of the Masulipatam Circar would certainly not have been quelled so soon, had the insurgents been able to procure saltpetre, for which they applied to me under different pretexts. They had many hundred firelocks, but not a grain of gunpowder.

5. Ballast for the Indiamen is an article much wanted. In time we shall not only procure enough on the coast for the Indiamen, but likewise for the coast army. This will be attended with profit even should our saltpetre continue 25 per cent. dearer than that of Bengal. I have been told that the Captains of Indiamen have declared that a voyage to India could be performed in six months shorter time were the Indiamen not obliged to go for their ballast to Bengal.

in the hands of the French surgeons, who formerly were in India, and acquainted with its properties, it proved a useful medicine.

The jungles in this district are resorted to by the cow-keepers of the neighbouring country, which being mostly cultivated, does not supply them with food enough for their cattle. They pay a sum of money to the Circar, called ballāry, for a certain number of cattle. This forms a considerable branch of revenue; though in fact but a wretched one, considering what might be got if the country were well peopled and well cultivated.

It is now time to begin to turn our thoughts towards returning home; but I shall beg leave to make a few observations on my way to Innacondah.

The road is pretty good till we come to the first pass through the range of hills that turn northward. It then becomes stony, and is so beset with bushes as to incommode the traveller even though lying in his palankeen. There is no want of large trees, though the jungle in the low country is commonly destitute of them. This place a few years ago was very dangerous, being inhabited by a set of people that have committed many murders. Even at present a traveller must be cautious when he finds them in a state of drunkenness, a vice to which they are very much addicted.

At a place on the other side of the pass, called Mallam, I found the water scarcely drinkable, it was so brackish. Several of my people who had waited here for me a day complained of a retention of urine, which they ascribed to the water. This fault in water I have found to be very common in those inland countries. It is remarkable that it contains pure marine salt in considerable quantity. In the neighbourhood of Samulcotah I have observed that the well water is often brackish, but the salt which it contains in solution is muriate of lime.

The second place, called a pass, is not so difficult to travel through. It is about fourteen miles from Innacondah: the country is here well stocked with wood; sufficient, were it in the neighbourhood of mines, to furnish a greater quantity of charcoal than would be required.

The hills through which I came are the same as I formerly described in my account of the copper mines. I happened accidentally to cast my eyes upon a small hill that was situated just in the eastern opening of the pass. It struck me as likely to contain some metallic ores. I ascended it, and found to my satisfaction that it was the same on which I had been before, and on which I had observed the copper mines. I should have known it immediately had I not come from an opposite direction, and ascended the hill on a side quite different from what I had done before.

This hill appears to be composed of clay slate. I found also at its bottom several pieces of writing slate. It seems to contain malachite interspersed through it in very minute particles.

The great quantity of wood at a small distance, and the facility with which it could be procured, is a circumstance worthy attention. It is certainly a great inducement towards re-establishing these mines or even opening new ones.

I observed growing all along the road a great quantity of wild indigo (indigofera pseudotinctoria), and at last came to a spot where a number of people were manufacturing indigo by scalding, according to the process described by Dr. Roxburgh. They told me that the plant grew in abundance among the neighbouring hills, and that they were yearly employed in manufacturing it after the rains. The plant itself grows very luxuriantly, and is wonderfully rich in leaves. This species is known to yield a superior kind of indigo; and manufacturers, who might not wish to settle in this district, where want of hands would render any great enterprize of the kind abortive, would find it a profitable speculation to procure a quantity of the seed.

TRACT XVI.

ON THE MILK OF PLANTS.

EVER since I had an opportunity of observing the surprising properties of the milk of the jatropha cureas, in calcining silver, I have anxiously consulted every chemical and botanical work upon which I could lay my hands, in hopes of obtaining some information respecting the properties or analysis of these vegetable liquids. But I have been completely disappointed. Chemists seem to have overlooked them altogether; and botanists take little or no notice of their peculiar qualities. This silence is the more astonishing, as plants yielding these milky juices may be found every where. Indeed several juices of this kind in an inspissated state are used in medicine, and even in common life; and on account of their usefulness have attracted the attention of the greater part of mankind.

A simple incision made into the bark of some trees and plants causes an effusion of a liquid that soon becomes more consistent, and at last very hard. These substances are distinguished by the names of gum, resin, camphor, manna, &c.

My knowledge is too limited to enable me to assert that azote enters as a constituent into all these bodies; but I do not hesitate to affirm, that it constitutes an ingredient in the milk of all plants that possess any degree of acridity or causticity.

All such juices, while liquid, are either distinctly acid, or at least are apt to become acid under favourable circumstances. Many of these juices contain likewise a very perceptible causticity.

The number of milk-plants in India is considerable. For besides the asclepias, of which we have more than twenty species, there are a great many echilei, neriums, and other contortes, that all abound with a milky juice. The euphorbia is another numerous genus that affords milk. Some convolvuli, one species of jatropha, the cureas (jack sprats nut plant) and all the species of the ficus are in the same predicament.

All parts of the plants, except the wood, yield this milky juice in proportion to their size and to the nature of the plant.

The part below the cut (towards the stem or root) continues for some time to effuse a quantity of this juice until the vessels are closed by the congealed milk itself, which in the open air takes place very soon. The part on the contrary above the cut (farther from the root than the cut) ceases almost immediately to give out any more. Whether this be owing to valves or to what other cause I cannot say.

Adamson (Fam. de Plantes, p. 40, 391) contends that this milky juice is an excrementitious matter. But I cannot see any evidence for this: it never exudes, unless some external violence be inflicted upon the plant, and seems therefore to be entitled to be considered as the true sap, the succus proprius, destined to perform the same purposes in the vegetable economy that blood does in the animal.

This milk, when exposed to the air, soon acquires a degree of consistence and hardness. The milk of the euphorbia tirucalli almost immediately after being exuded is converted into a curdled substance. The milk of the asclepias gigantea keeps somewhat longer liquid. Neither of these acquire much hardness or brittleness. Whereas the milk of the jatropha cureas, though very thin at first, becomes in a few days very hard and exceedingly brittle. At the same time it acquires a purple colour, though the milk, when newly drawn from the plant, is quite colourless. It has likewise the peculiarity of becoming quite soapy and white when rubbed upon the skin. This is the more remarkable as nothing like oilyness can be perceived before the application. By the natives this milk is used externally to remove rheumatic pains. The milk of the asclepias gigantea is rubbed upon the crown of the head, in order to cure the headache. Nothing is more common than to see children blowing air-bubbles in all these milky juices in the same way as is done with soap-water in Europe.

The taste of some of these milks is astringent, of others burning and bitterish; and most of them, when applied to any part of the body deprived of its epidermis, produce a violent inflammation. This is the case especially with several species of euphorbia. I know a case in which a Moorman injected some of the milk of the euphorbia tirucalli into his urethra: the consequence was an inflammation so violent that it almost cost him his life. He had been induced to attempt this foolish injection by the hopes of prolonging or procrastinating the moments of enjoyment.

The leaves of the euphorbia neriifolia, though not sour to the taste, but filled with a milky juice, are put by the natives for a few moments on hot charcoal, and then squeezed between the fingers. The milk is converted into a watery colourless juice, which possesses as much acidity as common vinegar. It is rather pleasant to the taste than otherwise.

The Hindoo medical writers recommend collecting these milky juices for medical purposes in the hottest season of the year; because at that time they may be procured most abundantly, and are possessed of the greatest efficacy.

The gums, or gum resins, that are derived from these juices, differ respectively from each other, like the juices from which they were produced. Some have an astringent acrid taste, others a bitterish and astringent one like that of the jatropha.

A part of some of these milks is soluble in water, while another falls to the bottom in flakes. This is the case with the milk of euphorbia tirucalli, and of asclepias gigantea: the same thing takes place when alcohol is mixed with the milk.

The gum resin of euphorbia tirucalli was found only partially soluble in alcohol: that of the jatropha cureas appeared entirely soluble, and formed with alcohol a strong red tincture.

All the vegetable milky juices that I have tried in India have the property of reddening paper stained with vegetable blue. Hence they all contain an uncombined acid. Once I filled a bottle about half full of the milky juice of the asclepias gigantea diluted with water, and set it aside for a few days loosely corked. It was converted into an acetous liquor, having rather a pleasant smell, and possessing a moderate degree of acidity. I cleared it from the white sediment which occupied the bottom of the bottle in considerable quantity, and added a small portion of solution of potash. It did not effervesce sensibly, but at each addition of the potash gave out a strong smell of ammonia. A good deal of alkali was requisite to saturate the liquid completely, and ammonia was given out during the whole process. Exposed to the air at a temperature between 92° and 108° it evaporated to dryness, but did not crystallize. It had the appearance of acetate of potash, with an excess of base.

I tried some years ago what effect the mineral acids would have upon these milky juices, and observed from the action of the sulphuric and nitric acids some curious effects which I noted down at the time, but have been unlucky enough to lose the paper. Want of a fresh quantity of these acids put it out of my power to repeat the experiments.

The milk of the asclepias gigantea has a strong narcotic smell, which I recollect the addition of a little sulphuric acid immediately changes into a very pleasant one resembling that of sulphuric ether. At the same time a vapour was expelled from the milk, which was only perceptible for an instant or two.

Lime water is not effected by this milk; but the addition of quicklime produces a strong smell of ammonia.

The milk of the asclepias gigantea kept for some time in a damp place separates into two substances, a resinous one, and a watery one. The water becomes gradually sour, and when kept for some time changes its pleasant smell of ether into a strong disagreeable ammoniacal odour, and instead of reddening vegetable blue colours it changes them to green.

The milk of the jatropha cureas, to which I have been always particularly attentive on account of the exclusive property which it seems to possess of oxydating silver, gradually acquires a smell, not strictly speaking ammoniacal, but bordering upon it, and in itself by no means disagreeable.

From these facts I think we may safely conclude, that all the milky juices possessed of any causticity contain not only the constituents of some vegetable acid, or a vegetable acid ready formed, but likewise the constituents of ammonia. Whether the activity which they possess depends upon this acid or upon some other principle, is an inquiry which my imperfect experiments are not calculated to answer in a satisfactory manner.

The singular effect which the milk of the jatropha cureas has upon silver, which is entirely, as far as I know, without a parallel in the vegetable kingdom, makes it very desirable that it were subjected to an accurate chemical investigation, that we might know what its constituents are, and to which of them it is indebted for the great readiness with which it acts upon a metal that resists the action of the alkalies, and of almost all the acids. If a piece of silver be put into this milk, it speedily becomes quite brittle, and may be easily rubbed between the fingers into a greenish powder. The process is this. Heat a piece of silver leaf about a line in thickness between pieces of charcoal, and quench it in the milk of the jatropha. This is repeated twelve or twenty times. I find that the silver must be heated each time, almost to the point at which it melts. The silver is then wrapt up in pounded leaves of any kind of tree, put between two pieces of earthenware in the midst of a small heap of wraties (dry cow-dung), which must be so situated that the wind cannot raise the fire so as to melt the silver. The silver is very little, or not at all changed, when it is taken out after this ignition. But the effect of reiterated heating and quenching in the milk of jatropha moluccana shows the efficacy of the process.

TRACT XVII.

OBSERVATIONS MADE ON A TOUR FROM SAMULCOTAH TO HYDRABAD.

AS soon as my business in the Circars admitted of my absence, I set out from Samulcotah, as well equipped as my circumstances would admit, in July, 1798, with an intention of visiting Hydrabad and the surrounding country, concerning the climate and soil of which, as well as its vegetable and mineral productions, I had heard so much. I was a little surprised at the request of my dubash to accompany me, to which however I acceded after telling him that I would not bear his expenses. My suite consisted of near forty persons: twelve palankeen boys for myself, and one massalji *; six boys and a massalji for my dubash's duly; four coury culies to carry my baggage and provisions, one draughtsman, two plant collectors, two peons, one servant, four invalid sepoys, &c.

In India no person will consider the number of my attendants too great. Not even a single man could have been spared without great inconvenience. But for the information of those who have never been in this part of the world an explanation may be necessary, to account for so great an apparent extravagance. In the first place it was necessary to go in a palankeen, as a shelter against the inclemency of the weather, as the rains were about to set in, in the part of the country to which I was travelling, and I had been informed that the choultries on the road were exceedingly bad. Expedition is another reason for using this mode of travelling in preference to any other, the bearers running daily between twenty-five and thirty miles; but should I ever go that way again I would do it on horseback, as one in that case would see much more of the country, and gain a clearer idea of the whole extent of it; but as a tent would then be necessary nothing would be saved in point of expense.

The four coury culies were thus distributed; one carried provisions, for

* Flambeau bearer.

nothing is to be expected on the road, not even rice; not to mention bread and other necessaries, which in Europe are considered as absolutely indispensable. Another carried my books and paper for preserving the plants; the third my linen, and the fourth my dubash's things.

I intended taking two draughtsmen with me, and should have had business enough for them both; but the best of the two fell sick before I left Samulcotah. I believe, however, his sickness was only pretended, because I would only allow him a little horse to ride on instead of a duly which he expected.

In this country a man who is botanically inclined cannot do without people to collect plants. For botanizing in person for any length of time is quite out of the question. I have some collectors who have made such progress in the Linnæan system as to be able to distinguish male flowers from female in the Dioecious class, in plants which they have never seen before.

A peon or two is always useful to take care of the baggage. A small guard of armed men is likewise necessary as a protection from robbers and tigers. This statement will serve to show the great trouble and expense with which all collections of natural or artificial curiosities are attended. People in England have no conception of the labour and expense which it costs to obtain a box of insects or plants, not to mention the obstacles that the climate often throws in the way.

I staid two days at Condapilly, a noted hill fort, during which time I got a few new plants from the hills, namely, a species of malva, triumfetta, cissus, heliotropium, sida, grewia, vitex, and (as it appeared to me) a new genus of the pentandria monogynia. As plants were daily brought in, I ordered the painter to draw only the outlines with Indian ink; and to colour only one flower, fruit and leaf. By this plan I got a great many more plants drawn than could have been expected during the short time that my excursion lasted.

In the night of the 1st of August I set out with my suite from Condapilly, and arrived in the morning at Gane Parteal *, where I wished to stay in order to make a botanical excursion to the nearest hills. But my palankeen boys objected to it, because it was a Nizam's village, and a Company's village was only four miles farther off, where they could procure pots and rice at a cheaper rate. As they are always absolute, or when they are disappointed make one feel it, I went on with them to Conchumchirla.

* A place where diamond mines are worked.

It was the custom throughout the Circars to furnish the palankeen boys with pots and firewood gratis. This custom still holds in some parts of India. Strangers were provided with the necessaries of life, and their baggage carried from place to place, for the mere payment of batta * to the bearers. In the Circars, in order that none but those who are entitled to such an indulgence (a man for example in the service of Government) may participate of it, it is denied to all such as do not arrive with people of the same description from the neighbouring village. It being supposed that a man of any consequence would have them from the place from which he set out, as well as all the way back again. This rule may at first sight appear a hardship upon the lower classes of people upon whom the drudgery of supplying these articles must fall; but upon inquiry we shall find that the persons who furnish travellers with pots and firewood, or carry their baggage, are actually paid by the Circar (Government). For there is not a potmaker in the country, nor a parria, nor a chuckler, employed in this business, who does not hold enam grounds as a compensation for those very services which he renders to travellers.

The villages only on the most frequented roads through which large detachments of sepoys pass suffer more than their neighbours; but at the same time they make larger profits by selling their things to greater advantage. This is well known to all servants of men in public stations, who in order to enjoy these exclusive privileges, and being acquainted with our mode of judging, represent to their masters hardships that never existed, and make the renters demand remittances on account of expenses which they have never incurred.

Every complaisance of this kind, therefore, is nearly abolished towards European travellers in places that are often frequented by them, or that are under the management of collectors and their dubashes. The latter, however, expect it as far as it concerns themselves, their relations, or any black men in any way connected with their persons: while a gentleman can scarcely get a fowl or a sheep for a curry, although the country abounds with them, and he be ever so willing to pay for it.

I stopped in a fine tamarind tope at the east end of the village, in preference to the choultry at the other side of it, which was occupied by an Armenian. It is under the fourth division, of which Mr. Oakes is collector. The soil about it is black, and it produces a good deal of jonnalu.

* Subsistence, from 1d. to 2d. a day.

About four o'clock in the afternoon we broke up again, crossed a small river about four miles from it, called Kisera or Banjala, which runs from east to west, and was not very deep, though it swells much after a shower of rain. The country between this and the next village, Nandakum, is remarkably pleasant. On the right is a long range of hills, that by degrees strike off to the north-west until they are lost in the distance. The small river winds from village to village, and seems to fertilize the ground. The buildings in the villages are kept in pretty good repair, and the inhabitants seem to be on the whole in comfortable circumstances.

Before sunset we reached Nandikum, a good village with a large pagoda, in which the Hindoo hours were regularly struck. An elephant also belonged to it that had been presented by Vassareddy, the Zemindar, to whom this village belongs. The choultry was occupied by some peons of the Zemindar's, who made room however immediately, and procured me all the comforts that the village afforded, a fowl, milk, rice, &c. Most of these kind of people are Moormen, who are paid by their employers by orders upon villages that owe money to the Circar for their kists, and from which they get from a quarter of a rupee to a rupee a day, until the money is paid. They are usually a set of lazy thieves that would rather starve than work, who cringe in the presence of their masters or any man in authority, and are insufferably insolent to every other person. They have nothing but the dress of sepoys, and often not even that, merely a long sword, or a pike, and a large turban. They seldom use severe measures to make the villages pay, as long as they get their batta, as this would be against their own interest; but they are sometimes obliged to be severe by the positive orders of their employers. The means which they in such cases employ are various. Sometimes they keep the debtor for many of the hottest hours of the day in the sun without allowing him to cover himself; sometimes they refuse him the necessaries of life, especially water; sometimes they fix large padlocks with weights to his ears; sometimes they put heavy stones on his back and feet while he stands in the sun; sometimes they put a pot of boiling oil upon his back, &c. The poor sufferers in such cases frequently put an end to their lives, on which account knives and all offensive weapons are taken from them before their tortures begin. Sometimes they even die under the cruelties inflicted on them. A case of this kind happened about a fortnight before my journey two miles from Samulcotah. A poor ryot, after various other tortures, was kicked violently: his head unfortunately pitched against a tree, and he fell down dead on the spot. His relations complained; but the renter was a rich Bramin, who committed the act, and no steps were taken to bring him to an account.

This was the last * place where I met with a choultry in which one might find shelter in the rainy season, provided the rain does not come from the east, where it is quite open. Most of the choultries in the Circars are nothing but places surrounded by mud walls, twelve feet high, thatched with straw, about sixteen feet long, and from ten to twelve broad. In the walls are holes for putting a small earthen vessel, which is to serve as a lamp in the night. In this the palankeen is placed when the weather is rainy or cold, and around it flock the palankeen boys. An old dirty fakīr, in one of the corners, smokes his chillum. Some of the palankeen boys light their cherutes; others sleep and snore; all combine to make it comfortable to themselves, while their master is almost suffocated by a complication of odours.

Finding the country pleasant, I did not go on early in the morning. This delay enabled me to draw up a description of the plants obtained the day before, and to collect a few more growing near the choultry. On the west side of the village was a tank lately built; the sides of it constituted a regular square, and it was lined with flat stones. In the middle of it was a golamantapam, or a washing place for the swamy (idol), to which he is carried on certain days from the pagoda, and washed, with the accompaniment of a great many ceremonies. The structure of a golamantapam is very simple: it is a square place raised from the middle of the tank, covered by a stone roof and supported by four pillars.

Not far from this tank, under a large tree, I found the Armenian. I invited him to eat a curry and rice with me, and he did not afterwards leave me till I came to Hydrabad. He had with him a great many valuable articles of trade. The small guard I had along with me and my numerous train must have been a great inducement for him to continue in our company. He spoke English pretty well, and imitated the manners and dress of Europeans much more successfully than any others of his countrymen that I have ever seen.

I found near the village some beds in which saltpetre had been lately manufactured; and upon inquiry was informed that, in three other villages besides this, saltpetre had been made by some Moormen about four years before.

* Elegant choultries have been since built from this place to Hydrabad by one of the Nizam's Ministers.

Between this village and Conchumcherla, I found a kind of stone called by the Gentoos, guruwintam *, with which they polish steel. It is an aggregate of small garnets agglutinated by an imperceptible but very strong cement. They are all of an irregular form, a glassy lustre, are very hard; their specific gravity is only 3·1. Probably these stones are detached from the neighbouring hills. Garnets of a regular form, and perfectly pellucid, are found about Condapilly and Bezwadah, and all along the banks of the Kistnah; and formerly, I understand, a profitable trade with them was carried on even to Europe.

About four o'clock we set out from Nandikam, and passed a large village called Nabobpatnam, about eight miles from it: on the west side of which was a very large tank, with immensely high and broad banks. It was furnished also with a sluice to let out the water; a most necessary contrivance both for watering the fields below the tank, and for letting off any superfluity of water that might endanger the banks and the surrounding country by inundation, if they should burst during a monsoon rain, which furnishes in a few hours water enough to fill the largest tank to the brim. This tank cannot be less than three or four miles in circumference. It contains a sheet of water sufficient to irrigate an enormous extent of rice ground. The village seemed to be inhabited by rather opulent people, for the houses were pretty good and large: it belonged to Vassareddy, and is the best I have seen on this side of Condapilly.

From this village we came into a jungle that had lately been in part cleared of its underwood by the Zemindar, to put an end to the many accidents which had happened to travellers from robbers and tigers, with which these jungly plains were infested. On the right hand we passed by a hill called Thieves' Hill, on account of the shelter which it afforded to this description of people, before they were driven away by the Zemindar's sepoys. Nothing is so effectual against the attack of tigers as cutting down all the jungle within twenty yards of the road, so as not to leave the animal any ambush from which he could surprise the traveller. For the tiger never attacks on an open plain; and if he fails in his first leap, he does not attempt another.

The palankeen boys, impressed with the fear of tigers and robbers, made the best of their way, and arrived before ten o'clock at Sĭr Mahomed Pettah, about twenty miles from Nandakum. In the morning another traveller overtook us, a Mr. Harding, a young Irishman, who introduced himself with much

* This is the Telinga name also of the corundum; literally translated, the former means a *heavy* stone.

affability, and we soon became acquainted. He was an adventurer, or a soldier of fortune; had been a Captain in the Rajah of Travancore's service, and conceived high ideas of his future situation at Hydrabad. Judging from the letters of recommendation that he had along with him, and which were almost the first thing he showed me, he had reason to expect that his situation would be at least lucrative *.

Near this village was a large tank, that watered all the rice fields with which the tope, where we had put up, was surrounded. Indeed it might water all the country to Juggampettah, a large trading village about six miles to the south. I thought the country remarkably pretty; the soil was fertile, and nothing was wanting but hands to clear it of its jungle, and to till the ground. The kind of rice cultivated here is that called by the Telinganas kusuma: it is never transplanted, but yields a fine white grain, which has rather a disagreeable smell after being boiled, and is said to produce a flow of bile if it be constantly used.

It is observed by the natives that coarse rice may be eaten in any quantity without producing any indigestion, or flow of bile, or those consequences ascribed to the finer and whiter sorts, which constitute the food of the richer classes of people. I will not decide whether this effect ascribed to the rice may not with greater propriety be assigned to the people by whom it is eaten. It is the food of the rich, who never eat with so much appetite as the poor, nor digest so well.

We went almost round the tank with our guns, and killed some quails and ducks. The Armenian on his side was as happy as possible. He stole unawares upon a couple of doves (not considered as game), and killed them both at once. After our return to our palankeen we took a hearty meal of curry and rice, and opened our last bottle of wine.

We left Sīr Mahomed Pattah about two o'clock, and passed through a great deal of jungle that had the appearance of having been formerly cultivated land: for we saw not only deserted villages and pagodas, but ruined forts and several very large tanks, which, notwithstanding they were out of repair, contained much water, and would be the source of riches in countries supplied with a greater number of hands. Grass was very luxuriant every where, and my fellow-traveller remarked that this country was the best adapted he had ever seen for the breeding of horses. So indeed it ap-

* He was killed in battle a few years ago, commanding a large army of Holcar's, a Mahratta Prince, just as he had gained a victory over Scindia.

peared at present during the rain; but I doubt whether during the dry months it will have to boast of a single blade of grass. Nor will the bushes be covered with any thing else than thorns, with which even at this season they are abundantly furnished, to the great annoyance of travellers.

It appeared to me that I was gradually ascending. Here and there I observed large tracts of rocks, just appearing above the surface of the ground, and which probably in a very few years will be entirely on a level with it, and covered like the rest with earth and herbs. To the right are some hills that give the country around a gay, and in some places even a romantic, appearance.

It was becoming dark when I arrived at Commerabunder, a miserable village, with a more miserable choultry. It had however a fort, if that name can be given to a place of ten or twelve acres of land, inclosed on four sides with high mud walls, and having some ill-constructed bastions in the corners. Mr. H. came in some time after me, and the Armenian long after him. These gentlemen, together with our baggage, had been exposed to a shower of rain on the road. There was another choultry in the village somewhat cleaner than the one that we occupied; but, besides the prohibition laid against our entering it by the cutwall, as it belonged, he said, to a neighbouring Rajah, the entrance was so narrow that it would not admit of our palankeens.

I cannot avoid noticing here a circumstance which I consider as strange, that Europeans still suffer themselves to be excluded by the natives from the best places. It is the more surprising that the natives should attempt this practice, as neither in their customs nor religion does there exist such a rule as denying admittance to any but a parria. It is wrong in Europeans to suffer such a comparison, and much worse to express it even in jest. The Moormen treated the natives very differently; and although now entirely out of power, are still admitted where an European is afraid to show his face. There may be something in our frequently having parrias in our retinue, that makes them dislike our society. But even to this they might be accustomed; and it would prove salutary in the end. Every thing depends upon the first impression which they receive of a European. To prove this I can say that I have been readily admitted into their pagodas, at least as far as any of my servants, both in places where Europeans had lived, who from being well acquainted with their customs had insisted upon it from the beginning; and still more readily in those places where no European had been, before. At other places again I was told "so far such a gentleman went and farther you shall not go." Our servants are often much to blame, who when a suder says, instigated by pride, "Master must not go farther, but I will go and make compliments to swamy;" or when a parria tells his master so, because he dare not venture to go farther himself: the best way is either to go alone or to take an intelligent Bramin or Moorman with you.

There is another insult to which Europeans are subject that presents itself in a still stronger light; and it appears astonishing to me how it could have been overlooked so long. When a European behaves improperly he is liable to be punished by the laws of his country; but a native may commit murder, theft, forgery, &c. without any law in force that can condemn him to capital punishment. It was so at least only a short time ago in the Circar. The Zemindars were forbidden to punish a man with death (they have done it however in private), of course murders and thefts were committed every where, and either no cognisance taken of the perpetrators, or they were kept in confinement for some years until they could make their escape. During the five years I was at Samulcotah, more than ten murders of the most atrocious kind were committed immediately about that place. Very lately a man killed his own wife; another robbed and killed a Bramin; and a third killed a young woman almost under the very ramparts of Samulcotah. All these miscreants are alive and at liberty. Three other murderers have been confined in the main-guard for these three years. The greatest blessing to a European is that the generality of Hindoos are of an indolent and passive disposition; but it is still more fortunate that we have a prospect of soon seeing justice administered, by the measures lately adopted by the legislature of Great Britain.

From this digression, I return to Comadabad, where we slept as well as the musquetoes and the fumigations of our palankeen boys would permit us. It rained a little during the night, but the next morning was fair, and we set off as soon as it dawned, and passed through a great many cultivated rice fields, watered as it afterwards appeared by a large tank near Munagall, which is about twelve miles distant, and the last village in this direction belonging to the Company. It has a mud fort and a small garrison commanded by a native officer. This garrison is necessary to protect the villages from numberless thieves that infest the jungle hereabout like the tigers. They are necessary also to keep the communication open between the Company's territories and Hydrabad; the resident of which place keeps a kind of tappal (post) office here.

I was visited by a petty Zemindar; the terms having been settled previously that we should speak to each other standing, or that he should be allowed to sit down with us. I presented him with a penknife of which they are always in want. When it shuts they consider it as a valuable gift. He offered me a sheep that was carried behind him, and it was delivered to my people according to custom, without being formally presented. He had a great number of peons about him, but seemed otherwise quite poor, and even complained of not having wherewithal to subsist his family. He has a small Zemindary under the fourth division. He belonged to the Reddy family, one of the most renouned in the annals of the Telinga kings. His chief motive for coming to me was that he had heard of my being a physician, a title to which in this country the best passport is of very inferior consideration. He had a complaint to which fat people like him are very much exposed: he had been relieved from it once before by another surgeon; and he requested me now to act that friendly part again. Notwithstanding my best wishes to serve him immediately, I was obliged to tell him that it could only be done if he would send one of his men along with me to Hydrabad: from which place I sent him what I thought would be of service to him.

We had put up at an old but large mosque that stood on a rising ground close to the village. In front we had a fine large tank; and from the top of the building, to which we ascended by a flight of steps, we could see before us a great extent of country, with many scattered hills; the whole covered with an almost impenetrable jungle: while behind us lay the village and a great many rice fields, furnishing a striking contrast between the dominions of the Company and of the Nizam.

We set off about one o'clock in the afternoon, and were carried much against our inclination by the shorter or tappal road, which, on account of the thick jungle through which it goes, is scarcely passable for a palankeen; especially on the other side of Malsāram, a large village about ten miles rom Munagal. A little expense however would make this a very good road. I observed a number of teak trees in the jungle, not very large, but in blossom. I saw also several species of grewia, one of them with ripe berries that had much the taste of cherries.

Rather late in the evening we arrived at Kæsarabad, a village where an officer of the Nizam resides in a mud fort. I sent him my passport, which Captain Kirkpatrick had been kind enough to procure for me from the Nizam. The consequence was, an order to the village curnum to show me a house to live in, and to procure me every thing that the place afforded. The house however had so small an entrance that I was obliged to sleep with my fellow-travellers under a tree, while I gave up the house to my Bramin; and after all the provisions offered, we were obliged to sup upon our own biscuit and some milk.

This being the first Nizam's village in which we halted, my Bramin made every inquiry to satisfy his own curiosity respecting the happiness which he expected to find the Nizam's people in possession of; but he returned early in the morning with a face full of disappointment. He had not been able to procure any thing except a little rice, and that at an enormous price. He had learnt from the Bramins of the village that they were worse off than any other class of people, that their handsome wives and daughters were taken from them by force, that they were deprived of their gold and silver ornaments as soon as they were seen with them; that they had plenty of enam lands; but only nominally so, the product being regularly taken away as a matter of course. They all agreed, and publicly avowed, that nothing more desirable could happen to them than to see the country placed under the Company's protection. He added that depredations upon the property of individuals took place here daily, even in a favoured village, the residence of a great man.

My baggage not coming up till the next morning, I was obliged to stay till ten o'clock. The Armenian stopped with me; but Mr. H. who travelled light, and was impatient to enter as soon as possible on his glorious career, left us to the no small satisfaction of the Armenian. His place was amply supplied, at least in point of numbers, by crowds of all descriptions of people that joined us from all quarters, on our march, conceiving themselves fully protected against thieves in the train of a gentleman.

We passed by a village called Bemāram, situated on a rising ground. We then again passed through a jungle, and arrived about three o'clock at Nāgracall. About Bemāram I observed some palmeyra trees, a sure sign of our being in a country that has a gravelly or sandy soil, in which this tree is more easily propagated than in any other. The reason is that the seeds which are scattered about are soon covered with sand by the wind; they vegetate, take root, and easily make their way through a loose soil. Indeed this kind of soil is so congenial to their growth, that, from the appearance of lofty palmeyras at the greatest distance, we may pronounce without any risk of mistake, that the country is gravelly or sandy. Hence they are found all along the coast, and at the foot of ranges of granite and other silicious hills which by their decomposition constitute a sandy soil. Near hills of a slaty nature, as about Innacondah; or composed of basalt or green stone, as in other parts of the Guntūr Circar, which by their disintegration yield a clayish soil, we may be sure of never finding a single palmeyra. They grow well enough in a stiff black mud; but then they require being planted a foot deep, and in a season when the soil is moist and easily penetrable.

I had looked upon most of the villages on this side of Condapilly as very poor and wretched; but I now saw, for the first time, one that was really entitled to these opprobrious names. There was scarcely a hut that was sufficiently covered to keep out the rain; though the many standing walls of ruined houses convinced us that this formerly had been a good village. We could not get a drop of milk nor a grain of rice. The water was brackish, except what was got from a tank at a little distance from the village. There were several other tanks about the village, most of them out of repair; and the ground, though now overgrown with jungle, still showed marks of having been formerly laid out in rice fields.

Next morning we passed by several villages not much better than Nāgracall. The country continued very pleasant; the ground was undulating and at some distance hilly. At ten o'clock we arrived at Nallagonda, where the choultry being occupied by some of the Nizam's horsemen, we were obliged to put up under a tree. There was a large mud fort in the village, as in fact there are in all the villages belonging to the Nizam. But the villagers had all run away, a few old women excepted. One of them, when asked for a fowl, replied, "And pray, Sir, what kind of an animal is a fowl? The Moors take care we never see any." They complained of the Sirdar, to whose Jaghire this and the adjoining villages belonged. He had by his oppression driven all the people away, and was not likely to persuade them to return. It is, however, no uncommon thing to find the cultivators deserting their villages, just at the time when the renter wishes to settle accounts with them. This step they take in order to oblige him to do them justice. But the practice is often carried too far: the cultivators run off as soon as they are desired to pay their kists, or to settle their accounts, certain of finding protection in the country of the neighbouring Zemindar, probably not more than a mile from their own homes. They are flattered with ample promises from the same quarter if they wish to remain in their new asylum. The renter is then obliged to go in person and settle with them, or to send his curnum (village writer) with full powers, and papers filled with empty promises. On an excursion of this kind, they seldom take their women and cattle along with them. These remain till they see that the renter will not come to terms: then they endeavour to steal them away; but are often prevented from accomplishing their object by the vigilance of the renter. From these disputes a loss of revenue often proceeds: the season for working, which is very short, passes over in sending messages, and drawing up agreements that seldom are meant to be strictly binding. In the Company's dominions such transactions should not be permitted. A Hindoo never wishes to leave the village in which he was born and educated, nor is it his interest to do so, as he is generally much worse treated in any other place where he may choose to take up his habitation. The first year he cultivates the fields in common as a baycastu or stranger, whose share of the produce is half of the whole; but the second and third years he becomes naturalized, and must submit to the same regulations as the old inhabitants, with whom, unless he happens to be related to them, he is never upon a friendly footing.

I was glad to leave this miserable place, where I had been starved a whole day, and thought myself happy to arrive in the evening at Chitteal, one of the best villages I had seen in the Nizam's country. Here I got milk and a fowl, and slept once more under shelter. Not far from the choultry was a small Hindoo temple dedicated to Annamuntu. This swamy has the figure of a long-tailed monkey, and was Rama Sawmy's * generalissimo, when he fought the giants. This I understand is the only Hindoo deity tolerated in the Dekan, probably because it flatters the pride of the Moormen to see the Hindoos degrade themselves by worshipping a monkey.

The village is situated in a semi-circle of hills, and has several streets and good houses. Large flocks of black cattle were driven in towards evening, and the fields round it seemed well cultivated. Among other minerals I found a good deal of asbestos. Its external colour was pearl grey; internally it was darker. Its external lustre was pearly: it was opaque; soft;

* An incarnation of Vishnu.

and its specific gravity was 2·6. The fracture was coarsely foliated and striated; fragments, long and splintery; feels dry, has a grey streak, and does not effervesce with acids.

We set off early in the morning, and arrived about ten o'clock at a beautiful spot, sheltered by large banyan trees, in sight of a long range of hills to the westward. Not far from it we found a large but ruined mosque and other buildings that showed the place to have been in former times the residence of a powerful man. The ground hereabout began to be sandy and the stones silicious, especially on the high ground on which the mosque was erected, and which was covered with a jungle, where we found abundance of partridges, quails, and hares. Not far from it was a well with excellent water. Here I found that my Armenian companion had a quantity of wine and brandy. not indeed of the best kind; but after having been confined for several days to simple water, I was glad to accept of his offer of a glass of brandy and water, as he had freely partaken of my stock so long as it lasted.

The ground for a considerable extent was irrigated by wells from which the water was drawn by bullocks. As this method is very simple, and as far as I know peculiar to India, I shall give a short description of it. Close to the well is a spot of ground considerably elevated towards the edge of the well. It is ten yards long, or more if the well is deep, and just broad enough for a pair of bullocks to walk straight forward upon it. Across the well are placed some pieces of wood in order to support two other perpendicular pieces, on which a wheel moves. Over this wheel goes a leather thong fixed to the upper part of a leathern or iron bucket which ends in a point, to which also a rope is fastened, somewhat shorter than the former. Both of these ropes being fixed to the bullocks, when these animals move in a retrograde direction towards the well, the bucket goes down and is filled with water; and it is drawn up full when the bullocks advance forward. As the small rope fixed to the point is the shorter the point is kept close to the bucket when it goes down and fills, and is extended from it by degrees as it rises up towards a channel into which the water is discharged. (This contrivance will be better understood by inspecting the engraving of the whole in Plate IV. fig. 2.) By this method a great deal of water is raised, probably not less than one-eighth of a ton at a time. I have employed it to fill the cistern for my indigo works, and to water the garden under my care. If the bullocks are broke in, a single man is capable of managing the whole; and even when the bullocks are unaccustomed to the business, a man and a boy are quite sufficient.

During my stay here I received a letter from Captain Mackenzie, which was delivered by a naigue, and a few men of the Bengal regiment stationed at Hydrabad, who had been sent to escort me from Munagall.

My Armenian, overjoyed at finding himself once more protected, opened his trunks and showed me a quantity of fine European silver plate that he intended to present to the Nizam and his Dewan. He told me that his countrymen never disposed of their merchandize to the Nabobs and great Mussulmen in any other way than that of presents, which they found more to their advantage than the usual mode. They all understand Hindostané well, and comply with the customs of the people with whom they have business, even receiving insults with humble resignation. This may be the most profitable way of proceeding; but I doubt whether it will ever be adopted by Europeans, especially now that all the native Princes are as poor as beggars, and not able to be generous.

We set off about three o'clock in the afternoon, went through a pass in a range of hills, near a village called Malkapūr, where the opening was very wide, and at sunset we arrived at Singaveram. On the east side of this place is a river, I believe the Musy, the bed of which is very stony; but it was destitute of water. From this river the ground rises towards the town, which lies on the east side of a semi-circular range of hills.

This town has a wall, and gates that are shut at night. The streets are pretty straight, and lined on both sides with the shops of banians. I was allowed to pass through it without being interrogated by the guard, and put up in a stable that was given me by the Havildar, who commanded a detachment of Bengal sepoys, and who procured us every thing we were in want of that could be obtained. I understood that this detachment was here on account of the Company's elephants attached to the Bengal regiment at Hydrabad. For here they had better and cheaper food than they could have obtained nearer the encampment.

I arrived in the morning about seven o'clock on a high spot of ground, from which I saw Hydrabad to my left in an extensive valley, and the forts of Golcondah and Old Golcondah both upon rising grounds on the other side of it. The air was sharper than I had ever before found it in any part of India, so that I was obliged to shut up the doors of the palankeen. In the cold season, it is so cold here, I understand, that the gentlemen can hardly keep themselves warm; though I am sure the thermometer seldom if ever falls below 50°. It is the suddenness of the change that occasions the disagreeable feeling of cold. A change of 25 or 30 degrees in the course of six hours is common even in covered places. Were we to take the extremes in the open air, they would not fall far short of 100.

The country hereabout has a very barren and rugged appearance; and the range of hills that encircle it on all sides are remarkable for their irregularity. They appear as if they had been thrown upon each other, and you may often meet with an immense block with one of its pointed sides resting on a very small stone of the same nature. So that the visitor is afraid least a blast of wind might roll it from its situation, and bury him under it.

This is probably the most barren spot which the Nizam could have selected in the whole of his dominions for a capital. It is remarkable that the tyrant of the Mysore chose a similar spot for his capital; for the neighbourhood of Seringapatam is, I understand, as barren and stony as the country about Hydrabad. It puts me in mind of some Tartar Princes, who kept a vast desert round their residences to starve their enemies before they could make their approach to them. With a view to effect such a defence for Hydrabad, it is not unlikely that his Highness the Nizam confides the management of the country adjoining the Company's dominions to the most rapacious of his Sirdars. This opinion does not appear so improbable when we hear it affirmed that the interior of his country is much better managed. Gentlemen, who have been there, pronounce the country highly cultivated, especially all over the Table Land, which commences a few miles beyond the western range of hills not far from Hydrabad.

The encampment of the Bengal regiment, at which I arrived about nine o'clock in the morning at my friend Captain Mackenzie's, lies about three miles north from Hydrabad, on the north side of a large tank called the Hussan Sāgar. It stands on a rising ground, and in consequence of the many bungaloes and of the cottages that the Sepoys have erected, has the appearance of a small town. I was received by Captain Mackenzie in the most cordial manner, and introduced by him, as soon as possible, to all his friends and acquaintances, who, I acknowledge very gratefully, have shown me every attention and kindness in their power. Hospitality was exercised in the true Bengal stile. I had general invitations from the gentlemen who dine in mess together, and from Colonel Hyndman their commanding officer.

On the ground and near it are some hares and partridges, which they hunt and shoot; but they dare not pursue them nearer than within two miles of Hydrabad; where nobody is allowed to shoot, lest the deer and antelopes, which the Musselmen delight to see in large flocks near their habitations, should be frightened away.

Two days after my arrival I rode with Captain Mackenzie to the residency, where I was introduced to Captain Kirkpatrick, then acting resident, who received me in the kindest manner, and promised his assistance and influence to enable me to see every thing that was worth seeing.

The resident's house is in a garden on the banks of the Mūsy, which winds round the outer northern walls of Hydrabad. It is built quite in the Moorish stile *, has a lofty hall, the roof of which is supported by large pillars. Round the sides of the wall, where the first story might be, are alcoves, behind the curtains of which the women might be spectators of what is going on at great entertainments below. Every thing was grand, but I think uncomfortable. There were several outhouses for the writers and munshies in the same structure. The garden was formerly a very good one. Cypresses grew here to a great height, and vegetables and grapes to considerable perfection. At present nothing was to be seen of the cypresses but the dried stumps, and the vegetables were not superior to those in the public bazars. Hydrabad and the country round it have been always famous for fine vegetables, especially for carrots, onions, and turnips; and among fruits the grapes are famous. This is rather owing to the climate than the soil, which I am told must be made artificially before any thing will grow on it.

West of the residency, and not a hundred yards from it, are large unwieldy masses of fine sienite. The felspar is of a beautiful flesh colour, and constitutes the greatest portion of the aggregate. The hornblende is black, and rather harder than usual. The quartz, which is the smallest portion of the mineral, is of a light green: it constitutes a beautiful stone which takes a fine polish, and would do extremely well for building palaces.

A resident at the Nizam's court is nothing less than the Ambassador of the King of Great Britain and of the East India Company; and in order to support his character great attention is paid to him. He has an honorary escort from the Bengal establishment, commanded by a captain. He is also allowed a surgeon. Both of these gentlemen reside in their own houses near the resident's; but they live with the resident, as his table is kept by the

* Since that time a noble palace has been built for his accommodation.

Company. All the servants pay him the greatest respect, speak only with the utmost submission, and with up lifted hands. This compliment is paid also to his European visitors. All this is thought to be of great consequence: the Mussulmen themselves being ambitious and ceremonious to a degree. They will measure steps, motions, and words; and glory in nothing more than to get the advantage over one another in the most trifling thing of the kind.

The first Ambassador sent to Hydrabad was, I understand, a Mr. Johnston, who came with all the pomp of an Indian Prince, and insisted upon the Nizam's coming out to receive him; as he had the advantage over him in point of some titles and insignia received from the Mogul Emperor: the Nizam acknowledged his titles to be valid, but pleaded a right to be visited first, as master of the country. It was at last agreed that they should meet each other half way.

Captain Kirkpatrick is fond of natural history, and I understand his brother, a Colonel in the Bengal establishment, for whom he acts here, is a good mineralogist. The Captain was so kind as to show me a collection of minerals which had been purchased from M. Sonnerat. I expected from so celebrated a man to have seen a complete and well-arranged collection of Indian minerals; but I was disappointed when I found only a small number arranged according to the method of Wallerius, and almost the whole of them European; some with German, some with French, and some with English names. The only Indian minerals were a few that Colonel Kirkpatrick himself had added. All the tin ores in the collection were ticketed *galena*. It would appear from this that M. Sonnerat's mineralogical knowledge is not even as extensive as his botanical.

Many stones found hereabout Captain Kirkpatrick was so kind as to give me. Among these the following deserved most attention:

Semi-opal found near Hydrabad inland. The colour of the best is bluish white. Others partake of a reddish and somewhat fiery effulgence, when placed between the eye and the sun. They have a glassy lustre, and are strongly translucent: Fracture conchoidal: hardness equal to that of quartz. Specific gravity between 2·09 and 2·063. They strike fire with steel; which I believe is peculiar to this variety of opal. When exposed to the air it becomes opaque. Along with the opal are found chalcedony, quartz, and sometimes carnelian. Some of these carnelians are drusy on the outside, have impressions of regular forms or different kinds of holes that are filled up with a soft ochrey substance.

Chalcedonies of different colours and shades, at least I consider these minerals as entitled to that name; though their specific gravity is only from 2·06 to 2·100. Among them I observed some very fine mocha stones, onyxes, and sardonyxes. Most of them occur in round pieces, often with a fretted porous surface. The most remarkable of them are the following:—Cachalong, pure white, surface uneven, very easily frangible, strikes fire with steel, fragments sharp-edged; fracture flat conchoidal, sometimes even. Transparent in small pieces, lustre glassy. I was long at a loss what to call this stone until I observed its transitions into onyx and chalcedony.

Chalcedonies in large rounded pieces, hollow in their inside and of a beautiful appearance. The outside is a greyish white, rounded, penetrated every where with small roots of plants, that are not petrified. Were the crystals in the inside formed before, or after, the roots penetrated the stone? If after, how was it possible for them to penetrate the hard mass? If the stone had been in a state of fusion and crystallized in cooling, how came the roots not to be destroyed by the heat, or intimately mixed with the whole stone?

I observed a curious mixture of different crystals in some large masses, consisting chiefly of quartzcrystal, amethyst, prase, pyrites, and calcareous spar. The prase usually in irregular masses formed the basis. It was also crystallized in long slender pyramids in the middle of the substance of the stone. It has a leek green colour, and the colour of the amorphous parts is much duller than that of the crystals. On the surface it seems to be withered, and not unlike green copper rust. When fresh broken it has a glassy lustre; strikes fire with steel.

The amethyst is in large crystals, not of the finest colour, striated. The quartz crystals are of different sizes and transparency. The calcareous spar is usually in very small proportion. The same remark applies to the pyrites.

The soil about Hydrabad is throughout gravelly, excepting where, from cultivation, it has acquired some vegetable admixture. From attending to its appearance we may easily determine the composition of the neighbouring hills. When it is black we may rest assured that mica predominates in the granite of the nearest mountain: where it is reddish, on the contrary, as about the camp, there is a preponderancy of hornblende. In a hole dug in this place, I observed the soil had a reddish appearance, and upon a closer inspection I found that it consisted of felspar with a great admixture of silicious gravel. I went to the nearest hill, about a mile and a half due north, and found it composed of a decomposing sienite, containing much red felspar and white quartz, with some particles of red ochre, that, when exposed to the air, caused the whole to be covered with a reddish coat, and probably contributed much to the easy disintegration of the stone. The beds of which the rocks were composed were in the greatest disorder, some horizontal, others oblique. The surface of all the stones was as if cased by a coat an inch thick: that crumbled away between the fingers. This decayed part the next heavy monsoon will wash down into the plain; and in this manner the whole of the rock will be converted into soil.

The solidity, which the ground near the bungaloes in the camp has acquired, renders it very probable that in time it will consolidate into as hard a mass as the granite hills themselves. On this hill I found a well or reservoir of water that had been cut through the solid rock. In it I observed beds distinguished from each other by horizontal fissures. Not far from the well is a small mosque, near which I observed a vein of hornblende setting through the whole rock, which I traced in both a northerly and southerly direction for a considerable way. It was about six yards broad. About half way between the hill and Captain Mackenzie's house, I observed the same vein again near a tank; and close to it I observed some rhomboidal iron-shot quartz.

On the road from the camp towards the residency, I found granites containing much black mica in a state of decomposition. The ground immediately under these stones consisted entirely of gravel, in which all the parts of the granite were discoverable, and the soil in their vicinity contained them in a more divided state, and was on account of the mica blacker than any other about Hydrabad.

Returning one day from the residency, I took a different road in order to see the Hussan Sagar, which I was told was well worth seeing. In my way to it I took a view of a foundery situated on the right side of the road. A Venetian with whom I was unacquainted was the superintendent of it. They were boring some very large cannon; but were not at that time employed in casting any.

The ground here for many yards deep consists of the gravel of decomposed granites, again conglutinated together. Farther on, near the tank, I found the granites to consist of white felspar, a very small portion of mica, and a little quartz, softer than any other I have as yet seen. The tank, Hussan Sagar, contains in the wet season an immense sheet of water, and is a work worthy of a Nabob. The eastern and only elevated bank is entirely a work of art, and keeps within the bed of the tank the water that collects from all sides during the rains, between the foot of the western hills and itself. It is nearly a mile and a half long, and in some places that require particular strength, 120 feet broad; but its usual breadth is not more than thirty or forty feet. The side of it which faces the water is nearly perpendicular, and constructed of regular square cut stones of stout granite. It has two large sluices, each of which has three stories, in which one can go down by flights of steps to the surface of the water. The whole is very massy, built of the same kind of granite, and cut into large square pieces like the banks.

The whole must have cost an immense sum of money. This tank waters most of the gardens about Hydrabad and a great extent of rice fields. Its water is rented out yearly for about 60,000 rupees to a man who parcels it out again in smaller quantities; by which in good years he is said to gain a considerable sum of money. For the ground itself I understand the proprietors pay nothing, as it is unproductive without much water. But it is not every year that enough of rain falls to fill this tank. The inhabitants of three villages express their gratitude by celebrating the event with festivities. I had the pleasure of seeing it almost filled in the course of a few days' rain; for I was there in the middle of the monsoon which takes place in the month of August.

This circumstance prevented me in a great measure from profiting by the opportunity of seeing what was worth observing, and collecting and preserving the plants that grow in this neighbourhood, which by the bye are very different from those in the low countries. I had planned an inland excursion which the rainy season rendered abortive. I could not even go to Golcondah which Captain Kirkpatrick promised to get me permission to visit, an indulgence seldom granted to any European; and those who have temerity enough to venture without it expose themselves to bad treatment and to insults. The natives say that immense treasures, especially great quantities of diamonds, are heaped up there. This in some measure accounts for their being jealous of European inquirers. But other accounts contradict this.

The diamond mines of Golcondah are not situated near that place. They are the very same that I have described in a former Tract. In the neighbourhood of Golcondah nothing is to be found but sienite; and about forty miles west of it the opals and chalcedony already described. Golcondah is the repository of all large diamonds, to which, though the mines should be in the Company's territories, the Nabob has an exclusive right stipulated by treaty.

The name of the present Nizam is Ali Kān, a man more than eighty years of age, in so feeble a state of health that his death has been expected hourly for this long time past. He got a paralytic stroke by lying in the night (after being heated by a provocative) to cool himself in the open air. After having tried for a long time what medicines from black physicians would do, an English medical gentleman was called in, and the old Nabob seemed to be the better for following his advice. Upon this he returned to his usual indulgencies in spite of the Doctor's opinion. This he still continues to do though only half alive. It is astonishing what a quantity of provocatives the higher classes of Moormen use; and yet they live long and enjoy themselves.

The dominions of the Nizam extend a great way inland. The climate produces abundance of wheat, jonnalu, and other dry grains. The wheat is much better than that which grows in Bengal, and is brought by land down to the coast by the lombardies, who in return take salt. I was too short a time at Hydrabad to ascertain the situation of the different districts or the revenues, which certainly would be immense were they better managed.

It is said the Nizam confides implicitly in his Prime Minister, Munseer Mulk, into whose hands he has entirely given the dominion, and even allowed his daughter to be married to a young Prince, whom in prejudice of his elder brothers he has named successor to the Musnud.

I had not the honour of seeing either of these two personages, owing to the great official business of the resident, now well known to the public. This did not allow him time or opportunity to speak on trifles, though his inclination to oblige me was great.

Of the private characters of these great men we cannot form an idea except by comparing their actions with those of persons of the same class of society, and making allowance for the political situation in which they are placed. Should we judge of them as of other individuals, their names would not be found among the virtuous: they would be justly stigmatized with the epithets of abandoned, unprincipled, treacherous, cowardly. He among them who is most courted and flattered may rest assured that he is on the brink of a precipice, that he is the first victim to be sacrificed to the ambition of another, or to a stroke of policy. Promises and protestations of friendship are then entirely disregarded.

It has been asserted that the Nizam possesses immense riches at Golcondah. But I understand from very good authority that he is as poor as the rest of the Princes on the coast. This must be owing entirely to his own mismanagement, as he is not tributary to any, and possesses a country that is internally rich.

Hydrabad, the capital of the Dekan, is a very large and populous place, bounded on the north side by the Musy, a small river, but rapid during the monsoon, when it is not fordable. There is a large arched bridge over it leading to the northern gate, entirely built of sienite. It is broad enough for two carriages to pass each other, and is on the whole as good a building as I should have expected to see at Hydrabad. The town is surrounded by a low wall said to be nearly square. The ground on which this city is built is uneven. Captain Kirkpatrick was so kind as to give me two of his hircarras, who cleared the way before me, and procured me immediate admittance, which without them I could not have obtained.

I do not know from what motive; but no European is allowed to enter this city, not even an officer of the Company's detachment. Some years ago, I am informed, they were perfectly at liberty to go to any part of it. In order to see every thing as well as possible I traversed the streets on horseback. They are in general narrow, badly paved, and far from straight. The houses are mostly built of wood, few with upstair rooms, and on the whole they have a very wretched appearance. The back houses, wherever I could get a glimpse of them, seemed to be much better and more spacious. But no man, and least of all a European, can get admittance to them: nobody indeed but the master of the house and his eunuchs. They even distrust their sons, who after they have attained a certain age are not allowed to enter the Zenana. Few women are seen in the streets; but they are crowded constantly with men and horses. The small number of females to be seen are either old Moorish hags, or Telinganas, and not the prettiest of them. In one part of the town dancing girls are to be seen in great numbers.

I saw several great Amirs pass in state. They have always according to their rank a number of horsemen before them: their palankeens are very short, and they sit upright in them. Few but themselves are allowed to enter the gates in such a conveyance: this being a privilege that must be granted by the Nizam or his Prime Minister. The Amirs living at the capital are in fact nothing more than state prisoners; none being allowed to go out of the town without particular leave of the Nizam: much less are they allowed to repair to the provinces confided to their care.

As eastern pomp requires a great number of attendants, and large sums to support them, it is easy to see why the capital is so very populous. It makes on the whloe an appearance that may be called splendid in comparison with the other native towns on the coast. I believe we may even call it opulent; for all the money collected in the provinces is spent here; and merchants, though sometimes plundered, soon recover again, on account of the extravagance of the rich and the quick circulation of money. It is one of the maxims of a Moorman never to keep money. They care not for to-morrow: they spend their money among women and merchants as fast as they can squeeze it out of the poor cultivators, or out of the merchants themselves. I did not think much of the bazars that I visited. The china shops here contain a very miserable collection of things, and those of other merchants are not much better. The only place where any thing can be got is the Beghum bazar, of which I shall speak hereafter.

The buildings best worth seeing at Hydrabad are the large mosque and the palace. The former is a grand building, the two domes of which are astonishingly high, engage the attention of the traveller at a great distance, and betray the residence of a mighty and wealthy Prince. The street, before you approach this grand building, is by no means qualified to prepare one for the sight of such an edifice. It leads to a gate where I was obliged to dismount and take off my boots. From this I ascended a flight of steps, and found myself all at once on the esplanade before the Mecca Masjīd. If I am not mistaken it has acquired its name from being built on the same plan as the great mosque at Mecca.

Having no firman I was not allowed to go into the mosque, and am therefore unable to give a description of a place that is so worthy of it. From without I saw that the whole consisted of a number of beautiful and regular porticoes round a spacious centre, where, before a burning taper, I saw the Mahomedan doctors upon their carpets. The pillars were amazingly lofty, and if I am not mistaken composed each of one solid piece of granite, the surface of which was beautifully polished.

Opposite the entrance is a tank or reservoir of water for ablutions. It is a square place with steps descending to the water, which did not appear to me very clean. I even saw some fellows washing their dirty clothes in it.

I observed also here a number of beggars in rags, who made a most disagreeable noise. I do not mean fakīrs, but the same as are met in numbers in all the streets of Hydrabad, who are even impudent enough to seize the bridle of a horse, and not allow the rider to proceed a step until he has satisfied them.

On the same side of the mosque, near the reservoir, is the place where the mother of the present Nizam is buried. It is a small mausoleum erected of coarse marble, very artificially cut, which is said to have cost a great deal of money. It is always covered with flowers of which the Moormen are exceedingly fond.

The Nizam goes to the mosque only once a year on a certain day, though his mahal or palace is quite close to it. I had no opportunity of seeing the palace, for which I am the more concerned as it is said to be one of the few places worth seeing at Hydrabad. It is astonishingly large, being, if we include the Zemana, several miles in circumference. The Zemana, I am told from the best authority, is watched by a guard of women, probably because women are much stricter than eunuchs in watching over the chastity of their own sex. More than 600 beauties are shut up within the walls of the Haram, for the use of an old emaciated cripple. Among them are said to be many Circassians and Georgians, and some Italians.

The beghum, or wife of the Nizam, is said to be of the Vysea cast. He saw her by chance in his younger days when passing through a village, and took her away from her house. Her province now is to watch over the rest of his women, to choose and appoint them regularly, and, as report says, to prepare his curries, which she sends him daily sealed up under a strong guard. Whether it be true that a certain quantity of pulverized gold is mixed with them I had no means of determining; but as all Indians have a very high idea of the strengthening power of this metal, the assertion does not seem to me very improbable.

The Beghum bazar is a kind of suburb inhabited chiefly by Hindoo merchants of the Mahratta nation. It is situated on the northern banks of the Musy, so that you pass through it when you go from the residency to the town. It is so called because the duties levied on all sorts of merchandizè in this bazar belong exclusively to the Beghum or Queen. The streets are very narrow, and the houses mean. I went only to the shops of the druggists who have as great a variety of things as many in Europe. But as they did not understand Telinga, and spoke only Hindostanee and Mahratta, I could not make the inquiries I proposed, in order to get some elucidation of the Kalpastanum or materia medica of the Hindoos. I confined myself therefore to inquiries about mineral articles, of which I shall notice the following, as not every where to be found. I could get no other information respecting the places where they were collected but that they got them from Auanegabad.

Steatite. Colour green of several shades, especially dark ones; no lustre. Opaque. Fracture coarse splintry; takes a polish from the nail; specific gravity 2·606. It is used by the Banians of the country to write with upon wooden tables, which they previously rub over with the juice of green leaves.

Senku sudda. Shistose talc. I was long at a loss what name to give this mineral, as it did not exactly agree with any discription that I had seen. It is used by the natives for giving a gloss to the surface of their finest chunam * work. It is finely ground, put into a piece of cloth, and powdered over the place. It has a greenish white colour internally; lustre pearly—opaque; fracture irregularly slaty—soft; not very easily frangible. Specific gravity 2·74.

Here I may mention that west of Hydrabad are some ancient buildings, the beautiful enamelled surfaces of which have hitherto braved the vicissitude of the weather; the colours are different, blues, yellow, red, &c. All are very bright, and look as fresh as if they had been put on yesterday. The art of doing this is said to be lost.

Chalk of a yellow colour. It has neither lustre nor transparency; but is harder than common chalk. It effervesces strongly with acids, but does not stick to the tongue. It stains the fingers, but is rather too hard for marking. It has an earthy smell, moulders in water and imbibes it, on which account its specific gravity is not easily taken.

Spar. I conceive it to be connected with arragonite. It was white, translucent, in striated prismatic crystals; fragments rhomboidal, sharp edged; specific gravity 3·; effervesces strongly with acids. Used as a medicine.

Spar in rhomboids approaching to cubes. It falls to powder in the fire, sometimes effervesces strongly with acids, sometimes not. I conceive the first of these to have been bitter spar; the second cube spar or anhydrous sulphate of lime.

Calcareous slate. Its colour is a dull greyish black, its surface often

* Mortar.

covered with a calcareous white crust that effervesces strongly with acids. Fracture perfectly slaty, and between the lamellæ are seen a few whitish calcareous particles. Fragments sharp edged; sticks but very slightly or not at all to the tongue; has no lustre nor transparency. Specific gravity 1·765.

Lithomarge. Colour brownish or bluish red, speckled with white dots. The surface is very smooth; it is fine grained, feels soft or greasy. It has no lustre nor transparency; fracture nearly even; very soft; adheres strongly to the tongue; crumbles immediately in water, but does not fall into fine powder. The softest kind soils the fingers and gives a reddish streak.

Besides these minerals I found some fullers' earth, greyish green internally, and a little scaly; but corresponding in all its other properties with the well known appearance of this substance.

The only manufacture I have heard of in this place is a fine kind of combaly, and a very thick cloth for the covering of horses; the former is made of wool, and is 2¼ cubits long and 2 feet broad. Two pieces are always sewed together. The white ones cost about two rupees, and the coloured ones from three to four. This manufacture might, I conceive, be much improved, and being of the texture of the common shawls, might by the middling classes of people, be used in their place. Perhaps they might even do for exportation. I have not heard of any places in the Company's dominions where they are made. The other stuff, called by the Moormen namdha, is also made of wool; but it is not woven. I fancy it must be worked in the same way that the hatters work up their materials; it is very thick, and serves the purpose of keeping horses warm extremely well. The common price of a piece eight feet long and four broad is four rupees.

I went to see the horses that were for sale, and met with a fellow who poured forth a torrent of abusive language against Europeans. Some of the horses were very well looking animals but very dear. In the month of December there is a fair at Malligam, about 40 miles from Hydrabad, where horses, I understand, may be had very cheap. They bring them from all parts of India, being sure of finding a market at a place where the greatest part of the army consists of cavalry. In the vicinity of Hydrabad great numbers of horses are to be seen belonging to the cavalry. They are of all sizes from fifteen hands high to tattoos that are scarcely eleven hands high. This proceeds from the plan which the Nizam follows in paying his troopers. He makes every one provide his own horse, and pays him according to its quality from twenty-five to fifty rupees per month; this sum, were it paid regularly, would be a handsome subsistance. As every Moorman wears a sword when he goes out, and the troopers have no uniform, it is very difficult to distinguish them in the mob.

The Nizam's infantry amounting to about 14,000 men, all clothed and trained, was commanded by M. Piron. Since I left Hydrabad, this body of men has been disbanded and the French interest in the Dekan destroyed. Another small corps of about 4000 men was commanded by Colonel Finglass, who I understand has been likewise dismissed. Both commanders had their jaghire for the payment of the troops, and the former had inherited from his predecessor, M. Raimond, a large arsenal filled with arms of all descriptions. This, together with the profits of collection from the Comam country, had given him an opportunity of amassing a large fortune. His officers, however, were not paid with a very liberal hand, and in consequence have left their families in a distressing situation.

These few imperfect observations were all I had an opportunity of making during my stay. Had the weather been more favourable, my journey might have proved interesting, and better answered my expectations. The greatest acquisition I made was the friendship of Captain Mackenzie, from whose experience and knowledge I have derived great benefit, and from whose correspondence I promise myself a rich harvest. He had always been attentive to mineralogical objects, and had lived a considerable time in that part of the country where the diamond mines are situated. Hence I was not surprised to find among his papers several descriptions of these different mines.

I left Hydrabad on the 24th of August, impressed with lively sensations of gratitude for the kind attention shown me by all the gentlemen to whom I was introduced. I arrived early in the morning at Singawaram, where, after having staid for some time at the Cutwalls Choultry, which is in the middle of the town, I learnt that a gentleman of my acquaintance was encamped near the town with a string of elephants, which he had conducted thus far from Bengal.

Owing to great care and attention he had lost only six out of fifty. Whereas others before him had delivered no more than one half of the original number, and thought themselves lucky when not more than one third died on the way. This circumstance is not a little surprising, as we know that elephants usually live to a very old age, and on that account may be conceived of a constitution capable of undergoing fatigues of all sorts. But the fact is quite different; the least thing affects them. When they are sick they can seldom be prevailed upon to take physic, and die in consequence; gripes is the complaint they suffer by oftener than any other. Sometimes they are seized with a sudden weakness for which nobody can account. Some hours after my arrival a large female elephant, thirty years old, died of the last mentioned disorder. She had been, to appearance, quite well the day before, had eaten fourteen sīr of rice, the usual allowance, and was seized with the fit when going to drink. She laid herself down and was never after able, even with the help of two other elephants, to rise again. One of the signs, which the people that attend the elephants chiefly notice, is the dung: when quite red, it is a sure sign that the animal is in health; but when it assumes any other colour, they are equally certain that the elephant is diseased.

The food of the tame elephant is, besides rice, the leaves of the banian tree (ficus indica) and rice straw; as that of the camel is the margosa leaf (melia azedarachta:) the former is acrid, containing a milk, and the latter very bitter. The price of an elephant varies from 600 to 1000 rupees or more; and that of camels, which on account of their hardiness are the most useful animal, is from 200 to 300 rupees about Hydrabad.

Long teeth in elephants are not admired, they are therefore cut short before the animal is brought to the market, and a copper or brass ring is fixed round them at the extremity. In other parts of India, long teeth semicircularly bent upwards are esteemed a beauty in an elephant.

The ground near Singawaram is very stony and sandy; hence there are abundance of palmeyras on the road towards it. Half a mile west from it I found several layers of iron stones perpendicularly cracked, and not far from these different kinds of trap scattered about.

From this place I set off about five o'clock, and proceeded towards Malkapūr where I arrived late in the evening. The ground is very stony and jungly, and difficult to travel over. With a little brandy I conciliated the Headman's favour, who made room for me and my baggage, together with my small guard of Sepoys, much against the will of a party of the Nizam's cavalry, who had occupied the choultry. This village is at the entrance of a pass through a range of hills running nearly north and south. The hill that terminates the northern range is called Pedda Gudda, and the two hills that commence the southern range are called Pedda and Chinna

Somconda. From what I could observe, these hills must be granite; the ground at the foot of them being sandy, well stocked with palmeyras, and the hills abruptly and variously pointed.

From this place to Narainpore you travel along this range of hills, which are pretty high. The ground is sandy and the road not bad; though the country be but little cultivated. I understand there is another road close by the hills; but it is said to be very stony and disagreeable.

Narainpore, a pretty large place, is the residence of the Rajah Narrain-reddy. It is situated in a pleasant country and in a bason formed by the hills. I put up in a garden on the north side of the village, where a good number of gun-carriages and tumbrils were making, which I was told were for the Nizam's army. They are made here because the tummah wood (mimosa arabica) is cheap. This wood is brought from a place situated on the south side of the village, where the ground is better; for these trees delight in a black stiff mud, such as is common in the Guntūr Circar, and along the banks of the Godavery and Kistnah. East of the village are some barren hills covered with different kinds of silicious stones, though the main hill seems to be composed of solid sienite, as was evident from a well that had been dug at the foot of these hills near the village. It is about sixty feet deep, cut through the solid rock; the sides of it exposed to the air were disintegrated, as was the case likewise with the heap of stones that had been thrown up near it. The sienite was internally of a reddish white colour with a great deal of felspar in large pieces. The disintegrated portions looked whiter, being more detached from the felspar. This disintegrated rock constituted the soil of this place, which contains a good deal of clay on account of the great proportion of felspar contained in the rock.

At the foot of this hill, close to the gardens where I put up, is a small river, in the bed of which I found large pieces of felspar of different colours, but most commonly flesh red or bluish. On the top of the hills, opposite to the fort, are several towers.

I wished to pass through the fort, but was prevented by a surly fellow of a sentry, who refused me admittance until the Zemindar's leave was obtained. I told him I had the Nizam's. He answered that might be; but I must have the Zemindar's also. As I did not wish to stay for that, I went round the place, which was enclosed by a good wall, and proceeded towards Campula. The country here is cultivated and appears fertile; the soil containing more clay than I had before seen.

It rained very much during the night, so that we were obliged to look out for a better shelter than the choultry at Campula afforded; this we found in a Telinga house. After the rain was over I went out with some of the sepoys to kill something for dinner, which after much fatigue was accomplished.

The soil was stiff and black, and stuck to our feet so that we could scarcely disengage them. In a nullah near this place, I observed that this soil covered a thick bed of limestone or rather marl. This if I recollect right was likewise the kind of stone met with in small pieces in the fields mixed with a few fragments of primitive trap and granite.

We set off in the afternoon, but were obliged to halt again at Mungūr, not more than eight miles from the former place. In preference to the Cutwall's choultry, I put up in a banian's shop, as the cleaner place of the two. In the evening after the rain I took a walk round the place. It is surrounded by walls and has a mud fort. At its east end there is a fine pagoda, built entirely of a beautiful and hard granite. The country is waving, and descends perceptibly towards the east. On the west side of the town is a small river, the bed of which is entirely sandy.

Notwithstanding the constant small rain, I set off in the morning and reached Nallagunda, where I went into an old but large pagoda. It was built of a strong granite, regularly cut.

Understanding that an Amir commanded the troops that occupied this place, and knowing how much the natives like being paid attention to, I sent one of my men to him with my compliments, and requested to be kindly treated in a place under his command. He was so much pleased with the compliment, that he immediately sent a chobdār with orders to attend me during my stay, and to turn any man out of his house that I should desire him to clear for my residence. The man brought me to a very good house, inhabited by the Adjutant of Yezami, the Amir's corps, a young man who behaved remarkably civilly to me. I staid in an upstair room with him for many hours, where numbers of his sirdars came probably from mere curiosity to see me. Among the visitors was the son of Yezami, a little stupid boy, of whom however they took great notice. I was always addressed Captain, which seems to be the name they give to all European gentlemen. For though I told them I was a physician, they still continued to call me Captain, and inquired of my servants what rank I held in the army, to which they think every European in this country belongs. From this man I learnt that the horses in the Nizam's cavalry get only three sīr of gram per day,

Their whole allowance is given them at once in the evening, which is thought a much better plan than stuffing them two or three times a day. They expose their horses to all weathers, as I saw them in all parts of the town, and very good ones too. Those in the stables are only kept for show. When I complained that a horse under my care was exposed to the rain, the sirdar ordered his own to be taken out of the stable and mine to be put in its place.

The hill called Nallagunda is close to the town, and has been fortified as well as another opposite to it. The stones appearing at a distance quite black; it is not unlikely that they may be of a basaltic nature; but the constant rain prevented me from being able to ascertain the fact. Both the hill forts are quite deserted and in ruins.

The next day we passed a ridge of hills, the stones composing which appeared to be a species of trap. The surface of the country was in general undulating and covered with jungle: the soil, as usually happens in the vicinity of basaltic mountains, was black, mixed with some sand. Here and there it was entirely sandy, mixed with calcareous tuff in the form of gravel. I observed also palmeyras and mimosas. We stopped a little at Cockrami, near a large tank. The stones I met with were mostly porphyries composed of red felspar, mixed with quartz and hornstone, and incrustated with calcareous tuff. Farther on at Yemmalpilly the ground is quite black with abundance of red felspar and calcareous stones. But it becomes somewhat sandy again at Merialpādū, a pretty good village, at which we halted during the night. Here, as well as in the former places, the inhabitants complained much of Yezami's oppression. Cultivation was not carried on to any extent, and rice in consequence was very dear.

Some saltpetre is made hereabout, a proof that this place must have been populous in former times, and that the soil is good. For saltpetre is never produced without both these requisites.

From this we passed through an even jungly country near a range of hills running south and north. As the tops of these hills were all even it is probable that they were of a slaty or calcareous nature. The soil was loamy.

On the banks of the Kistnah is the village of Wadapilly, a pretty large place, and at this time full of strangers, who had encamped along the banks of the river. They were mostly Mahratta Bramins; were all mounted, and had a martial appearance. They had a number of handsome women with them, and were on a pilgrimage to Tripetty, a large pagoda in the Carnatic.

Wishing to proceed, I wanted to cross the river immediately in a basket boat, the only kind of conveyance which they have here, but I was detained by some Peons who would not let me pass unless I produced a passport from the Nizam. I was therefore obliged to stay till my people came up, when I produced my passport.

The banks of the Kistnah are covered with a black mould some feet deep, under which is a layer of limestone, breaking with a coarse slaty fracture. Of this limestone all the houses in the village and the adjoining part are built. This limestone at a certain depth probably constitutes the bed of the river. Not far from it is found a beautiful white clay which is sent to Masulipatam for cleaning copper and silver. It has no calcareous admixture.

Thus much I have been able to say of the country through which I have hitherto passed. My observations I flatter myself would have been both more interesting and more correct if the constant rain had allowed me to travel more on horseback or to look about me at the places where I was obliged to stop. The situation of the places that I have mentioned may be sufficiently known from the map; but it is to be wished that the nature of the country and its productions could have been more completely described. I shall take a retrospective view and give a summary account of the whole as far as my observations went.

The tracts of mountains on both sides of Hydrabad are the highest that I have seen on this tour. They are in fact the Ghāts or part of the chain of mountains that commence at Cape Comorin and divide the whole peninsula into two parts. They are all sienitic, varying somewhat in the relative proportion of their constituents in different places. As we advance east we find smaller ranges branching out from the principal ones. There are likewise some detached hills composed also of sienite, but containing a greater proportion of felspar. Farther on (at Conrama) we find whole ranges of hills of a mixed nature, containing beds of primitive trap, of limestone, besides the felspar and hornstone, and quartz which belong to the granitic hills. These hills are lower than the granitic ranges, but they almost all run in a southerly and northerly direction. They are more even, but not quite so straight as those we find farther east, which are of a slaty and calcareous nature as well as those near the Kistnah.

If we notice the ground about these ranges of hills, we find it near Hydrabad and the granitic mountains quite corresponding with the hills themselves, abrupt, uneven, and barren. If the quartz predominates we find the soil gravelly; if the felspar, we find it clayey, and tinged red when the granite contains iron. At a certain depth conglutinating again and forming a new kind of rock. This may be seen in deep wells. Palmeyras and a few thorny bushes are the only natural productions of this country. The palmeyras only grow where the soil is sandy and at a distance from the hills. Where the hills consist of trap the soil is more or less black, the surface is waving and covered with a variety of large and small trees, and with mimosas where the soil is very stiff. This is the case about Nallagunda.

Where the mountains are slaty, or of a marly nature, the ground will be even and the soil very rich. In dry weather it will be like dust. The roads and paths appear as if gravelled and of a white colour, proceeding from small pieces of white tuff or conglutinated marl washed down from the nearest hills, and deposited in particular spots. Dry grains are the produce of the latter kind of country and soil; and rice, where it can be watered from small rivulets that stream every where during the wet season from the neighbouring hills. Were these rivulets as well taken care of as the Eliseram, near Samulcotah, they would greatly enrich the country. But at present it is depopulated and poor, and will in a short time be a desert, if it continue under the present management. Here the bed of the Kistna is deep and does not flow very rapidly. The fine black mould which it deposites is a sure sign of its coming from a country having nearly a similar soil. From Captain Mackenzie's account the Table Land on the other side of Hydrabad, from which it comes, is a flat country with a black soil that produces dry grains in abundance.

I would not however argue from this that the soil in the Guntūr Circar, which is black, owes this quality to the river. I am more inclined to ascribe it to the nature of its mountains, which as far as I have observed are mostly of the class of rocks distinguished by the appellation of trap, and by the strata of calcareous tuff that are found all over the low country.

The basket boat in which I crossed the river is quite round, twelve feet in diameter and four feet deep. Some pieces of light wood at the bottom give the traveller a dry footing. These boats have a circular motion in the water and are directed by a man with a bamboo in his hand. Having crossed the river I found myself in the Palnād, which I have already described in a preceding Tract. The ground from the river ascends towards Timmericotah, and every where presents large beds or layers of limestones of different colours, mostly greyish white, white, black, and red. They have all a coarse slaty fracture, absorb moisture, and stick a little to the tongue. The black limestone at first sight looks like plumbago. It burns quite white, a proof that the colouring matter is of vegetable origin. It is used for building; but the red limestone is found not to answer for that purpose, and therefore is not employed. I have observed small veins of quartz running through this limestone for more than fifty yards.

TRACT XVIII.

A BRIEF ACCOUNT OF THE CIRCARS ON THE COAST OF ORISSA.

THE northern Circars are the districts of the peninsula which lie between Ganjam and the river Krishna, on the coast which is commonly called Orissa. Ganjam is the principal place of a district of the same name, situated in the lat. 19°. 24′. The Krishna disembogues itself into the sea south of Masulipatam, and very near that place.

The Ganjam district is the most northern province of those that belong to the Government of Fort St. George, and before the last Mahratta war had the frontier garrisons of the army of that establishment. It is mountainous in general, but it has also large and fertile plains which render it the cheapest to live in of any on the coast. Its climate is reckoned very pleasant and healthy. The land winds, which are so distressing in some of the more southern Circars, are scarcely known there.

Of its mineralogy I can say nothing more than that iron abounds in many places, and is manufactured, in the often-mentioned Indian way, into the necessary tools and instruments. The hills and mountains, to judge of them from a transitory view, appear all to belong to the primitive order.

The next southern district is that of Chicacole and Vizagapatam. These are, generally speaking, mountainous, and intersected by ranges of hills longitudinally north and south, according to the general direction of the peninsula. Those which I have seen were all of the primitive class. At Vizagapatam, the principal settlement of that district, and the seat of a provincial Court of Justice, the hills form a kind of promontory at what is called the Dolphin's Nose, a mountain of about 1500 feet high, which juts out into the sea, and forms, with those a little north of it, a kind of bay.

The valleys which are formed by the intersecting ranges of hills are sometimes of considerable breadth, and are mostly very fertile and highly cultivated. The soil, by being a good mixture of loam, vegetable earth, and gravel, is productive of all kinds of grain cultivated in India, with the exception of Indian corn *, wheat, and cotton. That these articles are cultivated at some places cannot be denied; I mean only that they do not form part of the general crop of the country. The inland parts of Chicacole are jungly and very unhealthy, and the rains continue there beyond their regular periods.

The range of hills which forms a promontory at Vizagapatam (the Dolphin's Nose) continues along, and at a small distance from, the shore, as far as a place called Tūny, where they at once take a south-west direction, and run in high and close ranges toward the place where the Godavery issues out of the hills into the low country near a place called Rajahmunday. The low country which lies between the hills and the sea, and between Tūny and the Godavery is called the Rajahmunday Circar. It is at first very narrow, as the hills commence their course from the sea to the south-west, and the coast runs nearly S. S. E.

The hills as far as I have examined them consist chiefly of a species of stone, called *pindyray* by the Telingas, which is a kind of gneiss, in which adularia and other sub-species of felspar occur. They run very high and in ranges pretty even at top. The valleys among them are very narrow and unhealthy, and are inhabited by a race of men very different in appearance, manners, and language from the Telingas. Those I saw were all of a small stature, had big bellies, broad faces, and lean extremities. They are very warlike, or, what is nearly the same thing, they are fond of plundering. They were formerly, and are probably still, ruled by a woman called the Rampa Rany. In former times they were very troublesome to the inhabitants of the low country, but since the Company's Government has been firmly established they behave very quietly. They make their appearance sometimes in the low country, but when they are stirred up by the Company's Zemindars that live near the hills, as the Palavaram Zemindar, every mischief that is committed is charged to their account.

Among the ranges of the hills of this Circar, there must be some of primitive limestone, as I have found many specimens of it on the banks of the Godavery, and further up among the hills. The beds of the Godavery are generally gravelly with pebbles of the larger kind. They consist of rounded fragments of chalcedony, carnelians, agates, quartz crystals, zeolites, and

* Holcus sorghum.

indigo coloured corundum. The former are brought from the country on the other side of the hills, where I have found the ranges that come along the Godavery to consist of an amygdaloid, in which those pebbles are imbedded. The corundums are found in this part of the country, and indicate sienitic rocks.

The country between the ranges of hills and the sea is, with few exceptions, free from hills, and consists chiefly of a fertile plain, watered by a small river, called the Eliseram, which often inundates the greatest part of it. The only high ground in this Circar runs from Rajahmunday towards Peddapore and Samulcotah, in a direction nearly west and east, and is altogether alluvial, consisting of depositions of sand, and clay stones strongly impregnated with iron.

The soil in the plain is a good vegetable soil, and very productive. Where it is mixed with animal matter, as in large villages, it produces saltpetre in great abundance. In a village not of the largest kind, as Pittapore, 5000 lb. of the best quality is yearly manufactured, and as much more might be collected if more attention were paid to the business. The cultivators of ground use the saltpetre earth here as manure on their gardens and fields.

The high ground which I have mentioned is chiefly covered with jungle, the soil being for the most part sandy and barren. Near the banks of the Godavery there are extensive beds of marl covered by black cotton soil.

The land winds are in this Circar for several months of the year very violent, but the low country is reckoned healthy. The valleys among the hills are notoriously otherwise; the jungle fevers being dreadfully destructive to all strangers that venture among them, particularly after the rains have set in there.

The river Godavery, the largest on the peninsula, is near Rajahmunday about a mile broad, and when full, generally in June and July, it presents one of the finest sights in the world. In the back ground there is an amphitheatre of high towering hills; on both sides of a commanding sheet of water a beautiful and well cultivated and well wooded country; in it are seen floating, rafts of wood, whole trees, herds of cattle, and not seldom tigers; among these are a number of men in pursuit of the wood, which they are endeavouring to drag on shore. These people are ridiculously enough called horse marines, as they sit astride on a log of wood which is turned up before, and gives them at a distance the appearance of sitting or swimming on horseback. This will not sound very marvellous, as it is sufficiently known that some natives of Madras venture out to sea on two pieces of wood slightly lashed together. The beds of the river are very deep, and nearly on a level with the sea, which is at a distance of about thirty miles from Rajahmunday. This explains why in an inundation of the sea, which happened about thirty years ago, ships that had been lying at anchor in the bay or river of Conuga, were found drifted up to Rajahmunday.

The banks on both sides are from twenty to thirty feet high, and consist chiefly of hardened clay marl, and black earth; great portions are therefore often carried away by the torrent, and deposited at distant places, where they form islands. There are some pretty large ones near Rajahmunday, which however every year change their size and appearance, and are often entirely swept away. When new ones are formed they always cause much contention between the villages that lie nearest on the banks of the rivers, as the soil is highly fertile in them, and productive of the most lucrative of all crops, tobacco. Not far below Rajahmunday the river divides itself into several branches, which form larger islands or deltas, known to be the richest and most fertile landscapes in the peninsula.

The next southern district is called the Masulipatam Circar, and comprises the plain between the rivers Godavery and Krishna. To the westward it is bounded by the continuation of the northern ranges, which now however take a more southerly direction; for at Condapilly, a hill fort near the banks of the Krishna, they are only about thirty miles from the sea.

The main ranges and the highest at Condapilly are sienitic, in which garnets from the pyrope to the common garnet occur interspersed and imbedded. The rocks of the smaller ranges in advance of the main, are of the kind called pindyray or gneiss, as before mentioned. The country near the hills is somewhat waving, and the soil sandy: at some depth are beds of lithomarga and bog iron ore; and diamond strata make here their first appearance. The mines at Mallavilly are, to my knowledge, the farthest north. Extensive depositions of marl, often covered with black cotton soil, are very common in this extensive plain, which I believe is not interrupted by a single hill or even a hillock. I need scarcely observe that the tract of the country within a short distance from the sea is sandy, and at some places, as at Masulipatam, it is swampy.

The Krishna river is not near so considerable as the Godavery; it may be compared rather in point of size to some of the larger branches of that river. Its beds are also very deep, and mostly sandy. In some places it is fordable in the dry season, which none of the larger branches of the Godavery are. Its water is remarkably sweet and limpid. Of the diamond mines in its beds I have spoken on former occasions. On both sides of this river are extensive layers or depositions of marl, which generally are covered with the black cotton soil.

South of the river Krishna is the Guntūr district or Circar. It is bounded to the westward, as well as to the northward, by the Krishna river; and to the southward it is terminated by a range of hills which strike off from the main ranges which have the general direction of the coast, and run rather in low and interrupted points eastward, where they approach the sea at Ongole within a few miles.

The western frontier of this district is intersected by ranges of hills which run along the river. Some of these, as that which forms the south-west of Chintapilly, is of a grey transition limestone; some are sienitic, but these are very unconnected, and appear only in high points, as at Bellumconda and Innaconda. Farthest to the west and southward the hills consist of a fine clay slate which contains malachite in nests and beds, as at Agricondala.

Near Innaconda is a basaltic hill, from which, as I have observed in another part of this work, earthquakes are frequently observed to proceed to other parts of the country.

The most eastern range in this district is sienitic, and runs in high and connected points for about ten miles west of Guntūr, in a direction from north to south. The hills which form the southern boundary of this district are chiefly basaltic, and of some other of the later floetz formations. These hills are known for the variation of the magnetic needle, which is observed at sea at some distance from Ongole.

From the ranges which in the Masulipatam Circar consist of the pindyray or gneiss, there is a continuation into the Guntūr district, between the most eastern sienitic and the more western limestone ranges.

The pindyray is here a fine grained mica slate, as the felspar * is not so observable as in that of the more northern countries. One of these hills, opposite Bezoada †, is in some places excavated for temples and caves, in

* The felspar in it passes frequently into adularia, a specimen of which is at the India House.

† A place on the banks of the Krishna, not far from Condapilly.

imitation of Ellora * and Elephanta *. The low country or plains between the different hills and the sea is composed of uninterrupted strata of marl, covered with black cotton soil. In some parts the soil contains a great deal of common salt, as about Innaconda. Saltpetre is also produced in this district, but much contaminated with common salt. In some parts, as in the Palnad †, the black marl rests on a black limestone which yields particularly fine lime for mortar, &c.

The next southern district is that of Nellore, of which I have spoken in the account of the copper mines.

* Ellora and Elephanta, the caves of these places are well known and have been described.

† Palnad, a small district on the banks of the Krishna, noticed in a former Tract.

N. B. Krishna, Krushna, Kishna, Kishtna, names of the river indifferently used by the natives. The second particularly by the Bramins, and the last by Europeans.

TRACT XIX.

JOURNAL OF A TOUR FROM CUDDAPA TO HYDRABAD, IN THE YEAR 1809.

I HAD recovered my health so much during the year and a half that I had lived at Cuddapa, that I began to long for a change of situation, and wished, if possible, to go to a part of the country which I had not yet visited. My application to government, in which I stated the true reasons for making the request, was immediately complied with, and indeed could not be considered as a great boon, since I changed for the worse in almost every point; from a civil to a military, from a quiet to an unsteady and laborious situation, and to one withal which did not hold out the same advantages in point of emolument; but just such a one as shortly after most of the senior surgeons on our establishment were obliged to accept, and to relinquish their old situations to their juniors. I was appointed according to my own request, to the eighth regiment of native cavalry, which was then stationed at Talna, the most northern point at which the Madras army has a detachment. I was blamed for this step by my friends, and I must acknowledge justly; for from this event I must date all the misfortunes and casualties that have happened in my family.

I left Cuddapa in order to join my regiment on the third of January, 1809. The weather ought to have been settled, serene, and cool; but this year it was otherwise. It had rained daily for some time before, and the fields and roads about Cuddapa were all under water. The small torrents, or nullahs, as they are called in India, were full of water to the height of a man, and the Penna, the largest river in the ceded districts, which we had to pass, was reported impassable. Notwithstanding all these discouraging circumstances we ventured out.

Our party consisted of myself, my wife, two children, a relation a boy about five years old, two nurses, a butler, a cook, and some other servants who attended the baggage. I rode generally on horseback. My wife and the youngest child were in a palankeen carried by ten bearers, a nurse and another child in a duly carried by six bearers, and another in a bullock bandy, which is a kind of large box fastened on a two-wheeled carriage. This was particularly designed for an old Malay woman who had been my wife's nurse, on which account she received particular attention, as is the custom in India. The rest of the servants either walked or had a bullock to ride on occasionally. All had their families with them; so that we formed a pretty numerous party. Of baggage or furniture we had no more than two cart loads and eight bullock loads, as I had sent all my collections of plants and library to Madras, to the care of my friend the Rev. Dr. Rottler. The rest of my furniture, as drawers, chairs, &c. I left at Cuddapa, and have never heard any thing of it since.

In this way we moved from ten to sixteen miles in the course of a morning. The tent, which every officer must carry along with him, was in general struck about three o'clock in the morning, long before day-light. About four the baggage left the ground and the family followed. We were generally on the ground again an hour or two before the tent and servants could come up. We either stopped under a tree, or went into a choultry when one could be found. Indeed if the choultry was tolerably clean, we always put up in it in preference.

The road from Cuddapa to Chinnūr we found fully as bad as it had been represented; for the soil is either loamy or black, and becomes deep when once thoroughly wetted. Luckily the Penna was fordable; for otherwise we must have returned to Cuddapa again, as we had sent on the tent sometime before to Cazapet, a place on the other side of the river, where we arrived rather late in the evening.

We set out early in the morning, and passed several villages, as Maidūr and Chintaconda, between which the road was so bad that we were obliged to send the baggage by a round-about way near the hills (where the country is higher, and where of course no rice can be cultivated) which renders this part of the country so impassable. The tanks, of which there are a great number here, were, on account of the late rains, full of water, and in fact the whole country was quite inundated. This to the Indian farmer is the most delightful sight imaginable; for nothing pays his labours so well as rich crops of rice. Every inch of ground here is cultivated: the population being just sufficient for such a cultivation. Every thing is here cheaper than at Cuddapa, to which the greatest part of the produce is sent for sale.

There is no manufactory here, except of coarse cloth chiefly for home consumption. This remark, indeed, applies to almost every part in the inland places of the Peninsula.

I arrived with my family about two o'clock in the afternoon at Dūr. But as the baggage had gone a round of more than four miles, it did not reach us till late in the evening. We halted here the whole of the fifth of January, as our cattle had undergone so much fatigue the day before, and as we had got over so much ground already. Dūr is a large handsome village at the foot of a range of hills, the nearest and lowest of which are only about a mile distant or perhaps not quite so much. Owing to this and to the proximity of the Camūl country, this place has ever been infested by robbers, who found shelter among the hills, or shifted from one country to another as occasion required. On this account we were very grateful to the village people, for sending us a number of peons in the evening to guard our property, especially as we had no Sepoys with us, without whom, I believe, none before us ever undertook a journey of such length in this part of the country. It is the universal custom to take such a night guard, not so much in the Company's territories as in those of the native princes; who indeed without such a precaution would not be safe even in their own villages. The ceded districts had been but a few years in the Company's possession, and the custom, which subjects the villagers to make good whatever is stolen in their village, had not been abolished. In former times large villages, it is said, were often attacked in the middle of the day by bands of robbers; but at present, in consequence of the vigilance of the police and of the courts of justice, they are obliged to confine themselves to nightly depredations, and even these are continually decreasing in number.

I took this day a walk to the nearest hills, and found them covered with fragments of decomposing quartz of different sizes. The hills themselves appeared to be composed of clay-slate.

The weather had now become as fair as could be expected in the season, and the air had some freshness in the morning, which is peculiarly grateful to all Europeans that live in India, though the natives rather dislike it.

January 6. We left Dūr early in the morning, and proceeded through a fine country bearing crops of jonna (Holcus sorghum). The roads in consequence were dry, if they could not be called good. At Chamelmurga, the first village that belonged to the Nabob of Canūl, the axletree of one of our carts broke; but with the assistance of the village people, who were very kind, the damage was soon repaired. The adage, *qualis rex, talis grex*, holds more correctly in India than among the more civilized nations of Europe. The Nabob of Canūl has found it to his advantage to be always a faithful ally of the Company, and has always paid particular attention to officers passing through his country. His subjects or vassal servants, therefore, without any order from him, will be civil to them, and will cheerfully assist them, at least when paid, which is far from being the case at other places. In the Nizam's country the people are obliged to be civil; but they act with a reluctance which plainly shows the temper of the prince, who feels himself under the disagreeable necessity of being a faithful ally. In the old districts belonging to the Company, the natives are saucy; and where the price of labour and of the articles of life is not regulated, they will exact as much from strangers as they possibly can.

At Maddūr, a Company's village, where we staid to-day, the people were at first rather uncourteous, but changed their behaviour in consequence of a friendly expostulation. In general, a gentleman who speaks the language of the country may in this way get almost any thing reasonable from the Hindoos in villages, even their houses for a night, if a decent choultry cannot be found. But in this case it is necessary not to have pariar servants. They will then, as I have frequently experienced, furnish every thing required, and dress all victuals wanted, provided you sit down with them and listen to their stories. I ascribed the uncommon civilities which I every where experienced during the present journey to my having a wife and family with me. For to children Hindoos are always kind, and to a samsāry (wife or honest woman) they pay great deference; particularly as there are but few gentlemen who travel in this way among them. There must have in former times existed a notion among the natives of India that there were no matrimonial connections among the Europeans in their country, as to this very day our ladies go under the name of dora sāny, that is, a gentleman's dancing girl or mistress: and it is but lately that some ladies have opposed this opprobrious denomination, and insisted on those used among the superior classes of the natives; as ayagārū in Telinga, and ammāl in Tamul. In some instances the wives of Rajahs have given the first hints and advised the change, which our servants ought to have done long ago.

To-day the water, which hitherto had been remarkably good, was rather brackish.

There is a good deal of cotton cultivated in this neighbourhood, which, though not so profitable to the ryot as jonna, is usually more saleable, and on that account often cultivated in preference.

January 7. The country through which we passed to-day was still pretty well cultivated; yet many spots of fine ground lay waste, owing to a want of hands, which was very perceptible in the Canūl villages. We saw at times also wheat on the ground about a foot high and not quite ripe; even in the best seasons it never attains a greater height in this part of the country. We passed through a good number of villages, some of which, as Chintagūdam, are large and well built, and have pagodas, mosques, and choultries. The houses are all built of clay-slate, which is every where found here under the black and marly bed that constitutes the surface.

We put up to-day at a choultry in a place called Paducanlu. In general we always availed ourselves of such accommodations, as they saved us a great deal of time and trouble in the morning which was occasioned by striking and packing the tent, &c. There is a small river near the village called Bockilēru, which takes a southerly direction.

January 8. We made to-day but a short stage, though the roads were remarkably good, the weather fine, and every thing as we could have wished it. The waste land increased on all sides, though the soil continued remarkably good, and some large populous villages were in sight. Yerragutty, where we remained to-day, is entitled to that name. It has a small stone fort, with ramparts and a ditch. The streets are broad and all the houses built of stone. It is chiefly inhabited by Lingabaljis, a sect of strict worshippers of Siwa, who always carry his emblem, the lingum, in a large silver box on their breast. They are chiefly traders in grain and cotton, and generally rich. This remark, I believe, applies universally to sectaries, especially if they are enthusiastically inclined.

Forage of all kinds is very abundant in this part of the country; but water is rather scarce and not good.

January 9. The country remains in every respect as yesterday. The weather being cool we travelled on with much satisfaction towards Nundial, the place where the Nabob of Canūl at that time resided. We arrived about ten o'clock, and put up in a tamarind tope, about a mile north of the town, as it is in general not very safe to come too near a place of the kind, there being always a great number of thieves and rogues about the court of a great man in India.

We had scarcely arrived when we received a present of milk and grass, which was delivered as coming from the Nabob, and with his compliments. Such a present is always very acceptable, as it is difficult to procure such things in a large place after the day is somewhat advanced.

Nundiāl is a large populous place in which the Nabob occasionally resides. The small river which runs on the north side of it supplies water both for the accommodation of the inhabitants and for the cultivation of rice. The town is surrounded by a mud wall, and for its farther defence has a mud fort near it.

We were visited in the afternoon by the Company's vakīl, a Bramin under the immediate authority of one of the collectors in the ceded districts. He is a very necessary personage, were it only to observe the conduct of travellers, as well as that of the natives to them: he left with us a person belonging to the Nabob, who was ordered to procure every thing we wanted, and to settle our accounts with the inhabitants of the place. This, on all occasions except the present, a traveller never should omit to do himself. For if it be left to the dubash or head servant, he either forgets it altogether, or he charges one half more than he actually pays. He never fails at the same time to impress the natives that it is "master's order that he shall pay no more." In districts belonging to native princes, the inhabitants have no other way of getting their due than by refusing to furnish the people necessary for carrying part of the baggage or for showing the road. For were they to complain to their own superior, it is ten to one he would take the part of the traveller and punish them for their presumption. In the Company's districts the villagers complain in the first instance to the gentleman whom they consider as highest in rank, and who too often does not understand them; or he relies on the asseverations of honest ramasay who "*sures master they are too much great thieves*," and when they become loud and troublesome he takes his advice and threatens and kicks them out of his presence. The next step taken by the villagers is to proceed in a body to the judge or collector of the district with a clamorous and exaggerated complaint, who never, or seldom, fails of geting them the utmost of their demands: or when biassed, as it may happen to the best, he forwards the complaint to government; when the poor unfortunate subaltern suffers severely for his ignorance and misplaced confidence. That the ill treatment, as it is called by the natives, is less owing to the imperious and oppressive character of gentlemen travelling in India than has been imagined, is evident from this circumstance, that officers are never better pleased with the treatment they receive on the road than in Mysore, where the Rajah's government has fixed rates for every thing required; a list of which in English is handed to him by a peon, who produces every thing that is ordered, and receives payment for it. In other countries it is advisable for travellers to take a receipt for what they pay from the accountant of the village. By doing this he will keep both the villagers and his own servants in check, and prevent them from imposing upon him.

It must be acknowledged likewise that the natives of India are much given to take every possible advantage of travellers, and cheat them and plague them whenever they can do it with impunity. That the native princes are very sensible of the difficulties under which Europeans labour, particularly those caused by their own servants, is plain from the steps which they have taken in many places with a view to obviate them. Here the Nabob generally sends a peon to attend the travellers to the frontiers of his country, who is to provide them with every thing they want at a moderate price, and with a pint of milk and some straw gratis.

In the evening we were surprised with a procession moving slowly towards our tents. When it came nearer we perceived that it was loaded with provisions. It was a dinner sent us from the Nabob's kitchen, and consisted of a profusion of pilõws, curries, pickles, &c. They came unluckily after our dinner was over, otherwise I should have feasted upon the Nabob's present with much pleasure. The curries of the Moors are all made of meat, and are highly seasoned with spices, and swimming in ghee; whereas those of the Hindoos are made chiefly of vegetables, and contain more turmeric and tamarinds than the former.

As nothing can be done without presents in India, I gave the people who brought the curries two rupees; but I was told in plain terms that they expected a great deal more. As, however, I knew that Indians are not satisfied however much they receive, their murmuring was of no avail.

I cannot avoid observing here that the rewards or presents given to servants in India, though trifling in themselves, are in reality greater in proportion than those given in England or any other country in Europe. I mean greater, when compared with the price of necessaries, or of living in general. Two rupees was probably as much as the monthly pay of any one of the men who brought the present; yet it was thought too small a reward for five or six of them: while a gratuity of three or four pounds, to which the monthly pay of a servant in England may amount, would be thought very handsome for an equal number for a trifling piece of service. I have known some gentlemen in high situations, who never gave moret han one rupee on any occasion whatever. A set of palankeen boys who had carried them miles, or a set of dancing girls who had exerted themselves for hours, all were alike rewarded with a rupee.

The government of the Nabob of Canũl does not appear very oppressive, and seems to have more system and regularity than that of the Nizam. The country therefore is comparatively populous and well cultivated.

Banaganpilly, a place which I mentioned in a former tract on account of its diamond mines, is about twelve miles west of this place.

The black cotton soil, which is the prevailing soil in this part of the country, I found at a village not far south from Nundial, lying immediately above clay-slate rocks without any intervention of calcareous marl. This is a circumstance which I have no where else observed. In every other place I have uniformly found marl the substratum of this kind of soil.

January 10. Soon after we left Nundial, the country became rather jungly. The bushes and shrubs on black cotton soil consist chiefly of some mimosas (particularly the Mimosa Arabica) and the Cassia auriculata, both of which trees yield a bark that serves remarkably well for tanning. But a jungle composed of them is usually very thin. The country had still a pleasing aspect; but most of the villages through which we passed were in ruins.

The ranges of hills, which had accompanied us all along on the right, became now much loftier, and retired to a greater distance to the east. A small range, that comes from Banaganpilly west of us, loses itself in a swelling ground on which the village of Gadamalla, where we rested to-day, is situated. The soil still continues black, but stony; the surface here is thickly strewed with fragments of clay-slate and of quartz.

Palmeyra trees make their appearance again here: in the ceded districts, and in those parts of Canūl, through which we had come, they are very scarce: they are a sure sign of a poor and barren soil.

January 11. The jungle increases as we advance, and of course cultivation diminishes in the same ratio. The soil however continues the same as before, only rather more stony. I observed repeatedly small tracts of country with long grass on it. This on black cotton soil I had never seen before; it may be owing to the undisturbed operations of nature. In the Company's territories good soil like this is constantly interrupted by the plough. I do not mean here to praise the Company's government; I speak merely in allusion to the properties of that soil which produces an abundant crop only once a year; when it has sufficient moisture to enliven the grain thrown into it, and to revive the roots of those vegetables that are natural to the soil, and which have withstood the action of the calcareous admixture. When the process of vegetation is over, the fields become bare in cultivated grounds; and on waste plains, as here, they are covered with dry grass, constituting a kind of natural hay.

We came to Paramansala, a decent looking village, in which however little was to be got for ourselves and cattle, and being rather unwell, I determined to halt the whole of the twelfth of January. Of the apparent scantiness of all articles of life, and the causes of it, I cannot speak with any degree of precision, as I was not able to walk about, and make the necessary inquiries; but I think it is in all probability owing to the great proportion of Mussulmen who are settled in this village, for these people are seldom or never disposed to be industrious.

Water being scarce, the Hindoos and Mussulmen take it from one well; and to prevent the Parriars from defiling it, they have agreed to fill the pots placed at the top of the flight of steps leading down to the well; every Hindoo or Moorman, when he finds an empty pot at the top of the stairs, fills it, and then returns for another load for himself.

January 13. We had to-day a long and fatiguing march through an uncultivated country, which became worse and more stony and rocky the nearer we approached to the river Kishna. Close to the river and all along its banks there are hills connected by lower ridges, many of which are naked and barren. The higher hills are in general fortified, and were in former times considered as places of great strength. Mūrconda, at which we arrived to-day, lies on the banks of the Kishna. It is now but a poor place, but must formerly have been of great importance: it is inhabited by Hindoos, who chiefly live by the strangers whom they carry over the river. The fort is quite deserted; it is not large, but is situated on a very elevated spot which commands the river; it is built in a most singular style, quite different from any I have yet seen in India; I conceive it to be the pure Hindoo style unadulterated by that of their Mussulman conquerors. It is full of small temples dedicated to Swamys, which would never have been suffered to remain undisturbed had the Mussulmen ever thought proper to occupy it.

I omitted making a memorandum of the nature of the stones and rocks that are found hereabouts, but if my memory does not much deceive me, they are all granite or primitive trap.

January 14. We were employed the greatest part of this day in getting our baggage across the river, which proved a troublesome affair, as the only basket boat at that place was small, and not in the best condition. My wife seemed at first rather alarmed to entrust herself and our children to a vessel which, on the slightest accident, as a cut through the leather covering, would infallibly sink and destroy them. But seeing that the first boat arrived in safety, she ventured to embark, and reached the opposite bank without any accident, except a good deal of fatigue, as a great part of the sandy bed of the river was to be walked over. The Kistna is here about half a mile broad and mostly very shallow; a few miles further down, it is rocky, and the water dashing against the rocks give it the appearance of the surf of the sea in miniature. I have never observed these basket boats used any where except upon this river and the Tumbudra, not even in those parts of Hindostan where simplicity in every thing else is carried furthest.

About six miles west from this place is the junction of the Kistna with the Tumbudra, which of course is reckoned a place of great sanctity by the pious Hindoo, who considers all rivers as Gods, or emanations from the Deity. We saw the junction very distinctly, and it had certainly something inspiring solemnity. The Tumbudra appeared the broadest and the clearest. The Hindoos were most fervent in their wishes to be allowed to discharge their sins by ablution in that holy spot, but they were obliged to be satisfied this time with a distant adoration, which they performed by repeatedly lifting their folded hands above their heads, and saying, dhannam, dhannam, samy! The water of the Kistna is here particularly sweet and clear, and my family declared it the finest they had ever tasted. This excellence is ascribed to the Tumbudra, which is proverbially in this part of the country preferred to that of the Ganges.

The bed of the river is a fine white sand, and in many places it is intersected by rocks, among which nothing but a pliable basket boat could survive in bad weather. This river, like the Godavery, has very steep, indeed almost perpendicular banks during its whole course, which renders it altogether useless for agricultural purposes, such as watering the countries through which it flows: both the banks are higher than the adjoining country as I ascertained by barometrical observations.

The Kistna, as far as I know, is the only river in India in which diamonds are found. There is a place not far from this, where the Banaganpilly diamond miners yearly employ themselves during this season in diving for them: there are others situated in the Palnād, a district mentioned in a former tract, which the government of Madras offered lately to the public, but no person was found adventurous enough to engage in them.

The man whom the Nabob of Canūl had sent with us left us here, as we now entered into the dominions of the Nizam, where he would have been of less use than he was in the dominions of his own master. My servants I found were in general very happy to avail themselves of his services; but I thought always that I could myself with a good word, and a little money, procure things more easily than the peon, armed as he was with the rod of power, and disposed as he was to use it very frequently if I had permitted him. The difference is indeed very striking between the Company's districts and those of the native powers. In the former a collector's letter or note to the village people will ensure a cheerful reception and compliance with every thing reasonable; whereas here the mandate with a person to enforce it met with sullen indignation, and often with a flat refusal when they found themselves strong enough to resist. The Hindoos seemed by no means satisfied with their master, though the Mussulmen extolled him as a perfect saint. To me this at once explained his character, for *pious*, when applied to a Mussulman, means a man who lavishes his money upon fakīrs and women, and has no mercy on caffres or unbelievers.

"Oh, when will the Dharma Company take care of us also?" is the general exclamation of the ryots on the frontiers of the districts belonging to Mussulmen sovereigns. We learned here that the Nizam's government had lately applied to that of Madras to forbid the receiving of their cultivators in the Company's districts, as they had emigrated in such numbers that they were afraid of a diminution in the revenue. A rumour of this kind may have been spread merely to deter the people from making further attempts to leave the country. It is a common practice for ryots to leave their villages and take refuge in other districts, whenever they feel themselves aggrieved by the renters and zemindars; terms are then generally offered and accepted, and guaranteed by the zemindar in whose district they have taken refuge.

Masulgutta, the place on the banks of the river where we staid all night, has a large stone-built pagoda, in the verandas of which we put up and found ourselves well accommodated. The Mussulmen had defiled this place, as they have all places of religious worship within their dominions: the figures of the idols, as well as those with which the temple is decorated, were mutilated; and as the cutting off a man's nose is looked upon as one of the most humiliating punishments for crimes, they have directed their pious zeal against this feature of the Hindoo gods.

We obtained here every thing we wanted without the least difficulty, and, for the first time, horse gram (Glycine tomentosa), which however was not much relished by our cattle, who had been always fed on Bengal gram (Cicer arietinum); it was as little relished by our servants, who were obliged to boil this gram, whereas the other required only soaking, and might be given to horses even without any preparation. This change in the bazar articles showed us at once that we had entered into a country where the soil and its products were different from those of that which we had just left. The horse gram is only cultivated on a red gravelly or loamy soil: on rich soils Bengal gram and other valuable crops are raised.

My servants were surprised at the colour of the horse gram, which here was perfectly black, whereas usually it is brownish yellow; what grows here, however, is not specifically different, but a variety which is considered as superior to the common.

January 15. Close to the last place is Jettabol, a fine large village in which many Moormen have established themselves. The country immediately about it is rich and well cultivated. The curse of Moslaism however soon becomes perceptible, for at the distance of a few miles all becomes dreary and jungly. Further on the soil becomes barren and stony, and the roads almost impassable. Palmeyras are now very abundant.

We arrived early at Tūmgūnta where we were obliged to remain all day, there being no other place within a reasonable distance where we could have found a safe night's quarters. This place belongs to a polygar, who is a vassal of his highness the Nizam: the village is large and has a small fort for its defence. The water is very brackish here, and as we had lately feasted on that of the Kistna, we thought it undrinkable. The stones lying about are granite, in which a red coloured felspar prevails.

January 16. We travelled to-day towards the Pāngull hills, a small ridge that runs nearly east and west. The soil is red, but not so poor as it was yesterday; here and there it is stony, and the loose stones are all fragments of granite.

We passed some tanks, under which rice is cultivated. The country had upon the whole a very barren aspect, at least at this season, when most of the trees had lost their leaves, and the grass, which during another part of the year adorns the country, was completely burned up. We arrived about noon at Pāngul, a village at the foot of a hill fort of the same name. I applied to the killedār or commanding officer of the fort for leave to botanize on it, but was civilly refused. The hills are not high, they are pointed and appear to be granite. There are plenty of fine cattle here, and provisions are very cheap.

January 17. The jungle, through which we passed, during the whole of this day's journey, was as unproductive as yesterday for my collection. I regretted that I had not been detained a month longer, as then every thing about us would have been in blossom! The weather, indeed, in that case would have been very hot, but the trees would have recompensed me for all my sufferings a thousand fold. The greatest harvests for a botanist in India are the hottest season of the year and the period just after the rains. In the first of these seasons he has to look for trees, in the other for annuals of all kinds. The road was tolerably good for our cattle and baggage; the *pass*, as it was called, was imperceptible both in its ascent and descent. The country was gently undulating with insulated hills at some distance. Wanamparty, where we staid to-day, is the residence of a polygar, from whom we received a very civil reception, but for a long time we could scarcely get any thing else. The civilities consisted in the deputation of a bramin and some of his servants, to congratulate us on our arrival, and to tender us his services; they expressed at the same time a hope that I would visit the Rajah after I had recovered from the fatigue of the day's journey, and in the mean time brought me a watch and a telescope for my amusement. The watch had never gone since it had been in the Rajah's possession, and the spying glass had been quite dark. Some gentleman who had passed this place, had given it as a present to the Rajah; "In his hands it had brought things many miles off close within their reach, but now it represented nothing but darkness."

The watch had never been wound up, nor did they know how to do it, and the shutter over the eye glass of the telescope never had been opened. They were delighted at finding that the spell was so easily removed. But it required no small degree of trouble to instruct them how to prevent similar accidents from happening in future. The management of the telescope was particularly difficult for their comprehension.

In the evening I went to see the polygar who had expressed a strong wish for farther acquaintance; and to please him, as I was told it would, I drove in my chaise to his cutchery in the fort. He was a good looking young man, a Hindoo, very polite, and I believe thought himself very condescending. He spoke Telinga fluently, but seemed to prefer Hindostany, though I believe the former was his mother tongue. Our conversation at first turned chiefly upon the watch, and as he had heard that I had even a much better than his, he requested that he might see it, but was not a little surprised to hear that it had cost 100 pagodas. I am sure that he did not believe me, and equally sure that no zemindar, polygar, or any other Hindoo, who styles himself a Rajah, in the country would give half the price for the best watch England can produce. They are always much pleased and ready to take a gun, a watch, looking-glass, &c. as a present, but they would never think of paying more for it than the value of the gold or silver about it. The Moormen are somewhat though not very different in this respect. The thermometer, which at the request of my morning visitors I had brought along with me, was matter of great astonishment to the Rajah, particularly when he plainly saw that heat could be measured by it; which at the beginning he seemed to consider as fabulous, or as a trick similar to those of his jugglers. He introduced a brother of his whose foot was in a leprous state, a disease to which these people are as much exposed as those of meaner classes; as neither the cause nor remedy of such a nauseous disorder is known.

His house I had not an opportunity of seeing, as it lay in what was called the inner fort. The cutchery in which he received me was rather mean; it was situated in the outer fort, which, like the inner, consisted merely of a high mud wall.

A detachment of the Nizam's horse was quartered in the village to collect the revenue; this is the custom, for without compulsatory measures none of the petty vassals of his Highness would ever think of paying their tribute.

January 18. The country was mostly jungly during the whole of this long day's journey, and it was scarcely possible to discover any vestige of a road. There were, however, but few stones, and these few were granitic. At a distance to the eastward appeared a high range of hills running in a north and south direction. Small clusters of hills were visible in different points, and we halted to-day under a hill that was fortified, a place called Gunpūr. This place must in former times have been of some consequence, probably the seat of a grandee of the Nizam's court, as the mosque in which we put up was one of the finest buildings I have seen of the kind. It was built entirely of quarry stones, had a great number of arches, and was the largest mosque I have ever seen, except the one at Hydrabad. The fakīr who had the charge of it told us it was built 300 years ago; consequently, at a time when the power of the Moguls was in its highest lustre, when the country was so far flourishing, that it had not been ravaged by petty contending factions, which in later times have so utterly destroyed and impoverished the territories which were subject to the Mussulman powers. At present I think even the Nizam would find it difficult to construct a building of this kind in this part of the country; for, supposing him to have money enough for the purpose, he could scarcely find hands to execute his orders, unless he were to send them from Hydrabad.

That this country has been more populous at a former period, and that it has been highly cultivated, appears evident from numerous proofs. Traces of ruined towers and villages are to be found all over the jungle, and marks of the old divisions of the land and of former cultivation may be distinctly seen. It is a sad reflection, but a true one, that as long as this country continues under the dominion of a Mussulman, it will invariably proceed on in desolation, and will in a short time be a desert, in which no human being will be found except some straggling lombardies with their herds. Destruction is the delight of a pious Mussulman—He is the destroying angel!

Every thing was dear here; the fakīr however obtained for us what we wanted, and seemed to be very grateful for the rupee which he received as a gratuity. Mosques are generally used in India as places of repose for travellers; and where a fakīr has the superintendance of them, they are much cleaner than other choultries.

January 19. We passed through a country exactly similar to that of yesterday, and on our arrival at Allūr, we put up in a pagoda which was small but clean. The buildings in which this Swamy, a long-tailed monkey, the generalissimo of Ramaswamy's forces, presides, are every where open for the accommodation of travellers, and are in fact the only Hindoo places of worship to be found at present in his Highness the Nizam's dominions. I cannot divine why Hannamuntū should be the god or protector of travellers, unless it be that the *wind*, which the word in Sanscrit implies, is thought particularly necessary in order to enable a traveller to proceed comfortably on his journey. In some places I understand this god is invoked as the emblem of life: *spirit*, analogous to *wind*.

The sanctuaries of the other Hindoo deities are all defiled by the vile bigots the Moormen, and these are tolerated, probably because they are looked upon as more like choultries than places of worship. There was some rice cultivated near this village.

January 20. We met to-day with a detachment of the Nizam's horse, who so far behaved well as not to meddle with us nor abuse us, as ten years ago would have been the case. Fear, however, is at present the only motive that keeps them quiet, for in their hearts they are full of rancour; I say this of that part of the Nizam's army only which is not officered by Europeans; and his peaceable subjects, particularly the Hindoos, have different interests and different wishes.

The country here still remains a wilderness, but the jungle is very productive of fine grass, which yields food to numerous herds of cattle belonging to the lombardies. Here these people seem to be at home, if the place to which they retire with their cattle, after an expedition to the coast or to distant inland countries, may be called their home; here they reside when they are not upon such expeditions, or when not employed by a campaigning army, to which in India they are an indispensable appendage.

We passed a few small villages in which rice was chiefly cultivated.

January 21. The country and its productions were just as yesterday.

We staid at Funucknagur, a large village with a fort, where provisions were pretty cheap.

January 22. From this last place the country takes a different appearance; it becomes waving like the Mysore, and there are no hills in sight; the soil is red, it is a good mixture of gravel, loam, and vegetable earth, and produces excellent crops of rice. It changed however for the worse again before we came to the end of our day's journey. Jungle covered the whole country round, and the unfruitful soil was strewed with stones. Had we been asleep in our palankeens during the whole of our journey, the appearance of the village Shāpore, in which we halted, would have sufficiently indicated the poverty of the country, for we had not seen a more miserable one during the whole of our journey, at least we had never been obliged to put up in one so bad during the night; we could not even get a drop of milk for our breakfast. The water during the last three days was good and sweet.

On some stony ground near the road we passed by some lime kilns; the lime stone which they burn is a calcareous tuff, which is found in most parts of India, as a deposition from tanks.

January 23. We had but a short march to Shumsabad, which is a large town, built on a rising ground, and the seat of a grandee of the Nizam's court. The cyprus gardens, which make their appearance here, gave the place a solemn aspect, and reminded us of Bengalore, a town so dear to my family. The walls round the city are built of stone, the streets are generally broad, but the houses are mean. We encamped close to the town in a place enlcosed with a hedge, and were not disturbed, which, near such a place, is seldom the case in India.

As the country resembles Bengalore so closely, we expected to treat ourselves with the same kinds of fruit which abound in that country, and which this place, if in proper hands, would equally produce; but we could get nothing except a few small guavas, and for them we paid handsomely.

I have already observed that the country here resembles the Mysore, and as it is nearly on the same elevation with Veniatigherry, at the commencement of the Mysore Table Land, the climate contributes to the similarity; for in the mornings we found it rather cold, and during the day never too hot: the high grounds are long, waving, and the valleys between them rather shallow. The soil is red and fertile in the valleys and gravelly on the high grounds. To the northward many pointed mountains and ranges of hills make their appearance. The well water is very good.

January 24. We came soon in sight of Hydrabad, the capital of the Dekan, and the residence of the Nizam. It had a pretty appearance with its high minorets and large buildings rising above the thickly crowded mansions of the vulgar. On all sides of it are hills; those to the west, among which Golcondah is the most remarkable, approach nearest; all have a northerly direction, and none are very high except those at a great distance east of the place.

We passed through the suburbs, and, what astonished me, without being once abused by a pious Mussulman. What a difference from the treatment which I saw and experienced ten years previous! At that time it was with the utmost difficulty that I could get admission into the city, and, when unprotected, I seldom passed a Moorman without receiving an opprobrious appellation: now the gates were wide open, English sepoys were seen parading every where in the streets, and many a Moorman as he passed would salute us with a salam.

We came about noon to Secunderabad, the English cantonment about three miles north of the city. It had become quite a large and handsome place, and was very different from what I had seen it in 1798. Dr. Kennedy, the superintending surgeon, had been good enough to procure a house for me and my family; and the commanding officer, Colonel Montresor, permitted me to remain until I should see my family comfortably settled, as in those troublesome times it did not appear advisable to take them with me to Jālna.

To give the reader a more accurate idea of the height and the temperature of the country which we passed, I have thought it worth while to insert the following table of the heights of the barometer and thermometer.

Date.	Place.	Distance.	Barometer.			Thermometer.		
Jan. 1809.			Morn.	Noon.	Even.	Morn.	Noon.	Even.
	Cazapetta............	..	..	..	..	..	..	..
4	Dūr	..	..	..	..	..	..	..
5	......	..	29·59	..	..	..	76	..
6	Maddūr	..	29·6	..	..	..	78	..
7	Padacanlu	..	..	29·71	..	..	74	..
8	Yerragutty	..	..	29·60	..	..	80	..
9	Nundial	..	..	29·60	..	..	78	..
10	Gadamala............	..	..	29·40	..	..	74	..
11	Paramansah	..	..	29·30	..	..	75	..
12	......	..	29·28	29·22	29·19	55	88	74
13	......	..	29·30	..	..	59	..	..
	Mūrconda	..	..	29·30	..	..	78	..
14	Ditto	..	29·42	..	..	64	..	..
15	Jettabol..............	..	..	29·17	..	..	76	..
16	......	..	..	..	28·90	..	..	82
17	Wanamparty	..	..	28·80	28·90	..	82	71
18	Gunpūr...............	..	..	..	28·80	..	..	73
19	Allūr	..	..	..	28·50	..	..	70
20	Rajampore...........	..	..	..	28·40	..	..	74
21	Furrucknagur	..	..	..	28·29	..	..	71
22	Shapūr	..	..	..	28·20	..	..	70
23	Shamsabad	..	..	..	28·23	..	80	71

The incidents in a journey in India, particularly through a country depopulated and desolate, as was the case with the greatest part of that through which we came on our way to Hydrabad, can be but few and uninteresting: hence a journal of it can only be worth the attention of the reader, as far as it records facts relating to natural history, antiquities, and the general character of the inhabitants, and the causes physical or moral of its devastation and desolation.

For botanical observations the season in which I travelled was most unfavourable, as the trees were mostly leafless, and the tapestry of the ground faded and burnt up. In my mineralogical pursuits I hoped to be very successful, as the accounts of the country, which I had previously received, led me to expect much novelty. But in these expectations I was considerably disappointed, as I did not find a single mineral different from what I had seen in other parts of the country.

I have ascertained however to what natural divisions of the country the different districts through which we passed belong; their aspect, climate, elevation, productions, and general character: and of these I shall give a summary account, in the way which I have followed in some of the preceding Tracts.

The ceded districts, and of these I can speak with some confidence, as I resided nearly two years in them, when taken in a political point of view, are those countries of the dominions of the Sultan of Mysore, which had fallen to his Highness the Nizam's share in the late partition, and which were shortly after transferred by him to the Company, for the payment of the troops in his territories, which are called the subsidiary force of Hydrabad. I believe the revenue was estimated at seventeen lacs of pagodas, which is equal to about 680,000*l.* But it is said that by proper management they will yield ten lacs more.

The southern parts of this country consist of valleys lying between the Ghauts, which stretch from near Colar, in Mysore, as far north as Gurumconda, and from thence west towards the Nidgcull and Sira inland mountains.

North of these are the districts of Cuddapa, Gooty, and Bellary. These are bounded on the south by the hilly districts above mentioned; the rocks in which are almost all granite or sienite. In point of elevation they are considerably lower than the lowest valley among those mountains, as is very evident when we descend from the hills near Cuddapa into the district. The western frontiers are the hills from Nidgcull to Sira, among which the hill forts of Paghur and Bellary are best known. The Tumbudra and Kistna rivers form the boundary on the north side. Low ranges of hills, consisting of silicious schistus and hornstone, of clay slate, slate clay, and wacke, run along the eastern frontiers of the Cuddapa district. Among these hills there are many fine valleys which belong to the Zillah of Cuddapa. These hills recline on the most eastern branch of the Ghauts, which are highest at the points called the Pulicat Mountains, and run from thence in an interrupted chain through the Nellore district towards Guntūr, Innaconda, and Condapilly, where they allow the Kistna to slip through the Guntūr district into the sea.

This large plain is intersected in different directions by low ranges of hills, which branch off and lose themselves among the southern granite ranges. The most western branch is that on which Pennaconda is situated. At the bottom I found the rocks mostly hornblende, and, at the top, consisting of a sandstone mixed with mica, which frequently runs through it in perpendicular bands, and forms, when the sand is disintegrated or detached, a kind of honey-combed edge. These hills are very naked of trees, and have altogether a very barren appearance. They are pretty straight at top. I have only crossed them near a place called Nimadola on the east side, and at Pennaconda, at their western side. They have a parallel direction to the high sienitic ranges which run through the Mysore from north to south.

On the east side of this range there are several groupes of hills and small ridges, mostly composed of sienite, abounding in felspar, and containing a good deal of hornblende. The next interesting range of hills is that in which the Gooty mountain is the most prominent. This mountain stands by itself between two branches which divide south of Gooty and run north, the one on the west and the other on the east side of this mountain. This mountain, as well as the range on the west side of it, is composed of sienite in which red felspar prevails. There often occurs in it, massive or in plates, a green stone which does not look unlike jade, of a grass green colour, resinous lustre, and soapy feel. The barometer on the top of the hill near the flag-staff stood at 27·93 inches, and near the gate of the petta (town) below at 28·89. The thermometer was 82°. This gives the height of the hill 988·5 feet above the pitta, and 2245·5 feet above the level of the sea.

The hills on the east side of Gooty I passed in the night. They are very rugged and interrupted, and the stones which I found on the road were mostly sienite. They are covered on the east by a range of floetz trap rocks consisting of conglomerate, containing jasper, flint, hornstone, &c. united by a silicious cement. At the bottom of these hills I found in detached pieces, heliotrope, porcelain jasper, red, black, and striped jasper, and lydianstone in six sided prisms.

The late Tippoo Sultan, who seems to have been attentive to every thing that promised to be useful to himself and his empire, conceived that the jaspers and flints in this conglomerate would make good gun flints, and ordered a quarry to be opened from which many cart loads of the best were sent to Seringapatam. There still continue, as I was told, some storehouses full of them at Raylcheru, a place at the foot of these hills. It would seem that they did not answer the purpose, as the work was soon ordered to be discontinued.

Farther east are other ranges of hills which are rather low, and run even at top. Among these, especially towards the north, appear table hills, or conical hills truncated at top and presenting a flat summit. These summits, in some parts of the Carnatic and the Mysore, are often very extensive, and are cultivated and inhabited. In the low country west of them, as near Tarpatry, there occurs a silicious schistus with vegetable impressions, and not far from it hornblende in large decomposing masses, in concentric, inch thick layers. These hills are known by the name of the Ganjicotta Hills. There is a gap in them at this place through which the Penna river has forced its way into the plain of Cuddapa. This gap would seem to have been formed by a violent operation of nature, as it is very narrow, and its opposite sides almost perpendicular. On the southern precipice is the hill fort of Ganjicotta, which has given its name to the whole range of hills. The rocks at the summit of this hill are a stratified iron-shot sandstone, which rests on a stratified flinty slate. This range has a barren appearance, and is almost naked of trees. It runs for some distance to the north north-east, and then turns directly east and connects itself with those of Banaganpilly, which contain crystallized diamonds in a conglomerate belonging to the newest floetz trap, if not to an alluvial formation.

In the country at the foot of these hills, and especially on the banks of the Penna, appears a limestone rock of a black colour, which from its granular texture obviously belongs to the primitive class of rocks.

The country lying between these ranges of hills is, generally speaking, plain and even, and connected with the low country on the coast. Near the sienitic ranges indeed it is more waving and higher, as west of Gooty and west of Pannacunda. The soil in the large plains is universally the black cotton soil, having a sub-soil of calcareous marl resting either on compact limestone or on clay slate.

A red loamy, gravelly, sandy, and all other varieties of soil, occur frequently at the foot of or near the different ranges of hills which either encompass or intersect this part of the country; yet even in the valleys among the hills the black cotton soil very frequently appears. The other varieties of soil seem to be only superficial, and to be washed down from the hills by the rains.

The natural productions of the black cotton soil are the mimosa arabica, (gum arabic tree); the cassia auriculata, used for tanning; the jatropha glauca, aristolochia bracteata, some species of euphorbia, and a few other annuals. Few trees will thrive in it: the tamarind and jamblang are the only fruit trees that I remember to have seen growing on it in topes. The margosa and ficus bengalensis I have observed near villages. There is indeed a great scarcity of all kinds of trees in the ceded districts, and gentlemen who have camels find it a difficult thing to procure food for them. I have observed the same scarcity of trees in all countries where this soil prevails.

It would be endless or impossible to enumerate the natural productions of the loamy and other soils, as they comprise, according to their peculiarities, all the botanical productions of the country. The mountainous ranges, which form the eastern boundary, may be remarked as peculiarly rich. Trees grow on many parts of them to a very great height; among which the red sandal wood tree *, which is used about Cuddapa for building, is particularly distinguished.

The climate and temperature are such as might be expected in a low flat country in this latitude, not only at a considerable distance from the sea but separated from it by thick ranges of hills and mountains. The mean heat according to my meteorological journal which I kept at Cuddapa is 86°. The highest point to which the thermometer rose was 105′, the lowest to which it sank 71°. In Gooty and Bellary the heat is said to be much greater, at which I am rather surprised as Gooty is much more elevated above the sea than Cuddapa. All over India the months of April and May are the hottest in the year. At that season the hills here are all on fire, and present a spectacle, the magnificence of which is easier conceived than described. Yet there are here no real land winds; not such at least as those which I have described on the coast. Short puffs of them indeed sometimes precede rain from the eastern hills. They have by no means any regularity in the times at which they set in, and during which they last; nor are they accompanied by the same phenomena as on the coast.

The rains here set in generally much sooner than they do in the Mysore, and during the months of May and June they are heavier than in that country. It happens however not unfrequently that this district is visited with a long drought. This was the case in 1807, the year before I went to the country. The calamity produced was so great that from ten to twenty thousand head of cattle died for want of food in a few months. The great monsoon rains are here in common with the rains on the coast. While they con-

* Pterocarpus Santolinus.

tinue the country is almost impassable, as the water does not run off so fast as it would do in a waving country; and it penetrates the soil which is here naturally soft, much more than it would do if it were of a harder, loamy, or gravelly nature.

In the months of April and May there are frequent heavy thunder storms. The corruscations are very vivid and the explosions loud. They come universally from the eastern ranges towards Cuddapa. I never saw any hail here, nor heard any thing particular about it.

From the barometrical journal, it will be seen that the country from Cuddapa towards the river Kistna is nearly on a level, or rather ascends a little towards the river. This is a remarkable circumstance, as rivers usually occupy the lowest part of the country through which they run.

The principal river in this country is the Penna. It rises in the hills of Nundydroog in the Mysore, receives the greatest part of the water from the Pennaconda hills, winds with a very shallow bed towards the hills of Ganjicotta, passes through a gap in them, then winds to the eastern ranges, which it enters about five miles above Cuddapa, and glides through them to the Nellore district, where it finds its way into the sea. Its beds are in general sandy, and in many places, as on the east and west side of Ganjicotta, rocky. These rocks consist usually of a black compact limestone. The water in the hot season, when the river is almost dry, is very brackish, and has a taste somewhat like that of lime water.

About Ganjicotta I found that the water of this river was used for fertilizing the country, channels being cut in different directions to the fields. In other parts, as about Sidhout, the beds are cultivated in the hottest season of the year for melons, which it produces of a superior flavour. They are famous as the best on the coast. Those of the size of a large apple with rough skins are reckoned the best.

Some small rivers come from the districts on the south side of the Kistna, and mix their waters with the Penna; but they are of no consequence as to size. The Penna is never broader in these districts than the Thames about Blackfriar's bridge; and as it is very shallow I do not believe that any boats are employed to cross it. There are only a few days of the year on which it is unfordable. It is not quite destitute of fish, and these are well-flavoured.

The river of Cuddapa, which takes its rise on the hills south-east of the place, is remarkable for its independence on rain, as it has springs of fine water all along its course.

Some of the rivulets or torrents that come from the hills supply the tanks, constructed in favourable situations, with water. This is the case at Cuddapa, along the eastern range of hills, at Chintagunta, &c. The smaller tanks are chiefly filled by rain water, on which account they are only to be found in a waving country or at the foot of hills.

The water generally speaking is in this part of the country brackish in the hot season, and good and sweet during the rains. There are however places where it is at all times remarkably fine, as that from the springs all along the Cuddapa country. The well water in the low country, where black cotton soil exists, is always hard on account of its passing through calcareous strata. Few countries in the world produce so many varieties of salt, and in such various ways, as India. In the northern parts there is borax: rock salt occurs also in Hindostan; but every where are to be found soda, common salt, and saltpetre. The soda is found most frequently, if not exclusively, on a red ferruginous soil, as in those districts among the Pennaconda hills and those of the eastern ranges which encompass this country. These spots for a considerable part of the year are swampy and moist. They may be immediately discovered by their barren aspect and by the black colour which the mould that covers them assumes in the morning. This is occasioned by the salt having imbibed moisture from the air, and by its retaining it till the heat of the sun forces it to part with it again. When purest, it is collected by the washermen and used by them instead of soap; hence it is known by the name of washerman's earth. It is not uncommon also on black cotton soil; but there it is mixed with a great proportion of common salt, which forms the principal object of a manufactory carried on by the people, called *tank diggers* by Europeans, and *salt people* by the natives. Salt works of this kind are found in all parts of this country, which renders the importation of salt from the coast very trifling. The mode of manufacturing it is exactly similar to that practised for obtaining saltpetre.

Of the manufacture of saltpetre I can speak with much confidence, as I have introduced it on a large scale into the northern Circars, and had the superintendance of that establishment for several years.

It is found in India, and, I believe, in all hot countries, in places and soils which have a due proportion of animal and vegetable matter. As in old populous villages built on black cotton soil, or in rich garden earth, as we find it in many parts of the northern Circars. In such places we find that the streets, and particularly the lower parts of mud walls with which their houses are built, or their yard surrounded, from the beginning of the dry season in February till the rains begin again in May and June, appear wet and black in the morning, and crumble down into a fine soft earth which collects in a heap under the walls. This when collected by sweeping, as is done every other day, contains about one-fifth of its weight of crude saltpetre. It is observed by the natives that such years are most productive of this article in which the preceding monsoon rains have been strongest, and accompanied by a great deal of thunder and lightning. A heavy thunder storm in April or May is likewise reckoned very favourable for the manufacture. After the saltpetre is extracted from this earth, it is thrown on a heap and spread out when the monsoon is over. After lying a year or two it is found to yield, by sweeping it every other day, saltpetre earth fit to be manufactured again. These are the only saltpetre grounds with which I am acquainted. Whether those in Bengal and Spain have been formed in the same way I will not pretend positively to affirm; but from the nature of the salt, and its component principles, it appears to me very probable.

It is found in the manner just described in very considerable quantity: about two gallons of saltpetre earth at the foot of each yard of wall. And in a large village, as that of Pettapore, in the Circars, which contains about two or three thousand inhabitants, from two to three hundred candies may be manufactured in the course of a season, which yield about five or six thousand pounds of the best refined saltpetre. I have observed that the saltpetre, gained from grounds that have a black cotton soil for their basis, yields a product that contains more common salt than that which is obtained from garden earth; this is the case in the Guntūr district, and in that of Cuddapa, where the common salt is of as much consequence to the manufacturer as the saltpetre.

The mode of obtaining the saltpetre here and at Guntūr is by evaporation, and formerly it was obtained in the northern Circars by boiling the lixivium. The process of elixiviation, or of extracting the salt from the earth, is performed by putting the earth in inverted conical pits, which are made on a rising ground from two to three feet deep, and as wide at the mouth. A little straw is put into the bottom of this pit before the earth is put in. The water is strained through this straw, and by means of a bamboo is conveyed through a common channel into a reservoir. Water is added till every thing soluble is extracted from the earth. The same water is then poured through a fresh quantity of saltpetre earth. It is then generally strong enough to be evaporated or boiled for its contents.

The boiling is performed in earthen pots that hold about three gallons; but is so expensive that I soon relinquished it. A candy or 500 lbs. of crude saltpetre cannot be made under six or seven rupees, which are about fifteen shillings sterling. And a candy of refined saltpetre, which requires $2\frac{1}{2}$ of crude, could not be delivered in a warehouse on the coast under eight pagodas or three pounds four shillings sterling.

The cheapest way is to evaporate the liquid in shallow beds made of mud, and lined with a covering of mortar. They are filled with water to the depth of about four inches, which from the heat of the climate is half evaporated in four or five days, and then the saltpetre begins to crystallize. The first product is always the purest, and consists of prismatic crystals of different degrees of thickness, often not larger than a needle. The second day's product contains nearly half its weight of common salt. In the third day's product there is scarcely one-fourth of saltpetre. The remaining liquid, which is thrown on the elixiviated earth, has a caustic burning taste, and contains scarcely any thing else than nitrate and muriate of lime.

The refining of saltpetre is always done by boiling. For clarifying it different substances are used, as soap, milk, eggs, the twigs of the milk hedge (euphorbia tirucalli), &c. Five hundred pounds weight of this single refined saltpetre, which still contains about twenty-five per cent. of common salt, is delivered by the manufacturer at three pagodas or twenty-four shillings sterling. It would be easy to divest it entirely of its foreign salts even at the first boiling, though this is never done, not even in Bengal. But the Bengal saltpetre does not contain so much common salt as other impurities which might be still more easily separated. Hence it has a browner look than the saltpetre of the coast.

Common salt is prepared by evaporation, exactly in the same way as saltpetre. But soda is boiled down to dryness after it has been extracted from the earth that contains it. It is very common in India to hear gentlemen speak of the saltpetre grounds which they have observed in their travels, and of the great quantity of ground which lies neglected in this way—nay, even of saltpetre works they have seen. These grounds, however, I have found universally to be nothing else than grounds impregnated with common salt or soda. They are often found in the middle of a cultivated field, and the ploughman takes great care not to touch them that he may not contaminate the rest of the ground. I suspect that the supposed saltpetre grounds in Bengal, and at the Cape of Good Hope, are similar impregnations of the soil with common salt or soda, and that saltpetre is always originally the product of animal and vegetable matter.

That the saltpetre earth, after being once elixiviated, should again produce new saltpetre after a certain time is not surprising. It is similar to other laws of nature by which the productive process gradually proceeds after it has received the first impulse, until the basis is exhausted. After copper has become once tainted with verdigris, the corrosion goes on till the whole metal is destroyed. If saltpetre has been kept or prepared in an apartment, it will be difficult to prevent the destruction of the walls by the continual production of that salt. This I have found to be the case at least in India.

The saltpetre which is made near Cuddapa, chiefly at a place called Podatūr, is partly used in the country for fire works at feasts and marriages. The rest is exported to Madras, and to the Nizam's country.

I have already given a general idea of the position and direction of the hills in this country. But it will be requisite to give a more particular view of their nature and structure before I notice the mineral productions of this part of India. The principal hills in the country are primitive, and either consist of granite or sienite. They seldom contain any other metal except iron, with which our globe appears as it were cemented. The quantity of it which exists in hornblende is known to be so great (amounting frequently to thirty per cent.) that this mineral may, and sometimes actually is in India employed as an ore of iron. Among these ranges of primitive mountains there occur others of later formation, and which seem all to belong to the class of floetz rocks. They consist about Cuddapa, as far as Tripety, in the Carnatic, of flinty slate, or hornstone mixed with more or less of mica without any petrifactions or vegetable impressions. It passes into slate clay soon after the ranges have proceeded beyond Cuddapa. At this place the primitive rocks become clay slate, and these rocks in this place are rich in ores. Here the rich copper mines of the Nellore and Calastry districts occur. Ores of lead are likewise found, and a galena rich in silver. This ore has been lately discovered in some parts of the Nellore district, and I found it myself in some mines about eight miles north of Cuddapa, which had been formerly wrought by order of Tippoo Sultan. They were abandoned because they were not sufficiently rich. I found pieces of galena both massive and disseminated in the deserted mines, which consisted of open galleries cut in various directions in the sides and on the tops of several hills. I received larger pieces from the natives, who had kept them from the time that the mines had been worked. This ore was analysed in Bengal by the Company's assay master, and "found to contain eleven per cent. of silver *." In the present scarcity of this metal in Europe it would be worth while to make farther search and inquiry into this mine, so uncommonly productive of silver, particularly as it might be done at a very small expense. Copper is found in many places in great abundance; but I have already entered into sufficient details on this subject in a preceding Tract.

The central ranges of hills here consist of clay slate, sometimes with a wavey or undulating fracture, and a silky lustre. I have never found petrifactions or vegetable impressions in it. Hence, as well as from its other characters, I have no doubt that it is primitive clay slate. At the bottom this rock is covered by beds of limestone, which appear of a posterior formation. They have generally a black colour, and white veins of calcareous spar frequently run through the rock. The fracture is compact and splintery, the splintery fragments appearing greyish while on the black ground. This limestone is generally covered with a bed of marl more or less thick. This bed is on many accounts very remarkable. It occurs, as I have just observed, among the clay slate hills, and likewise in the low country, in the ceded districts, and in all parts of the coast where a black cotton soil is found. The upper parts of the bed are usually free from stones of any size. But about the middle of the bed they make their appearance in the state of large rounded masses of silicious stones of the size of a man's head and upwards. These stones have a smooth surface. Below these there appears a collection of smaller pebbles of jasper, hornstone, quartz, &c. in different states of decomposition and colour, and among these, not unfrequently, diamonds are found. Where rocks of limestone cover the clay slate at the foot of the hills, we find them accompanied by calcsinter, peastone, ludus helmontii, &c. In some parts of the coast, as at Nellore, at the red hill near Madras, and among the clay slate hills, we find the beds of marl mixed with rounded pebbles, and of a reddish and yellowish colour. So long as it is somewhat moist it is soft, but when exposed to the air it contracts a de-

* Dr. Roxburgh in a letter to the author.

gree of hardness, and is used like bricks or stones for building. The marl is mixed with ferruginous particles, which strongly unite and form a natural cement.

It is remarkable that I never could find any remains of animals or vegetables in this marl. The calcareous part of it is no doubt derived from the compact limestone over which it lies. The large masses of silicious stones are certainly fragments from the neighbouring ranges of hills. But it is not easy to conceive where the jasper and chalcedony pebbles come from. I have mentioned a range of hills near Ramcheru, some miles east from Gutty, the rocks of which consist of a conglomerate, and the Banaganpilly hills are composed of a similar rock. But how comes this floetz or alluvial mixture to lie here, under the masses belonging to primitive rocks, and whence do the jaspers and chalcedonics originally come?

I was formerly of opinion that limestone, or a compound in which lime forms the predominating constituent, would be found the matrix of the diamond. Nor was this opinion unreasonable as in general the bed in which diamonds are found is covered or mixed with calcareous marl. But since my acquaintance with the Banaganpilly mines, and with those of Buwapatam, I have been obliged to change my opinion. In the former place we find them in a conglomerate in which no calcareous admixture is discoverable, and in which an argillaceous matter, probably wacke, forms the cement; and in the latter place the mines are absolutely in mountains composed of wacke, in which I have not discovered any jasper or other pebbles. The latter mines are particularly remarkable. They are said about eighty years ago to have furnished the largest gems to the Nizam's collection. At all events they deserve future and particular investigation. I made an excursion to them in 1808; but, when there, was so ill and so weak that I was barely able to walk to the hills where the diamond mines had been worked. They are very extensive, on a kind of table land, which is intersected with ranges of hills on which those mines wind from one to another. In them occur beds of hematites, which are worked for iron.

All the diamond mines in this part of India, with very few exceptions, lie between the river Kistna and the Penna; such at least is the situation of the mines of Golconda; for in the province so called no diamond mines whatever occur. The mines of Mallavilly and Parteal are the only ones with which I am acquainted on the north side of the Kistna, and these may be said to lie upon its banks. I would not be understood to infer that diamonds never occur in India except between these two rivers, but merely that the diamond mines known under the name of those of Golconda, which occur particularly to every person's mind when the diamond mines in India are mentioned, are exclusively to be found in the districts that lie between these two rivers.

I have stated that limestone is the general substratum of the black soil and marl: in the northern parts however of the Cuddapa district, particularly in Canūl, I have seen the black soil covering clayslate rocks without the intervention of any marl. Whether this clayslate constitutes merely a local deposit I will not venture to affirm, though I rather suspect that this is the case. Its layers have an oblique and sometimes nearly vertical position. If this be the case, it is not impossible but limestone may lie immediately below this clay slate bed.

The objects of agriculture in the ceded districts are perfectly similar to those in other parts of India; where there is a command of water the principal crop is always rice, and in favourable years they raise two crops. The first and principal crop in this district is sown in June during the first rains, and is reaped before the heavy rains in October commence; the second is sown during the October rains, and is ripe in January and February. Rice being a grain which depends entirely upon a sufficient supply of water, the cultivation of it is entirely regulated by the rains, or by those sources which are capable of supplying the husbandman with a complete command of this element. In years when the rains are late, I have seen them commence sowing it in the latter end of August or the beginning of September. In consequence of the structure of the country, the cultivation of rice is chiefly confined to those parts which lie along the different ranges of hills which surround and intersect these districts.

The principal crop in the ceded districts, and in Canūl which has the same local situation, is jonna (Holcus sorghum), a grain which requires a good soil as the cotton ground is known to be: it produces yearly but one crop. Wheat is cultivated on the same kind of soil in the northern parts of these districts, but only in small quantities. It seems to be raised merely for the consumption of the higher classes of Mussulmen, many of whom have come from the northern provinces of Hindostan, where this grain is generally cultivated. It is sown here in the the coldest season of the year after the rains. Flax is also cultivated in small quantities for lamp oil.

Cotton is cultivated in many parts of this district on the same black soil, and constitutes an article of much importance to the farmer. Government some years ago sent a commercial servant to ascertain how much could be procured, and it was then generally believed that a factory would be established for the purpose of collecting and exporting that article; at present it is sent on bullocks to Bengalore, Salem, Wallajanagar, and other places in the Carnatic.

The high grounds near and among the hills are cultivated with small grain, as aruga (Paspalum frumentaceum), samy (Panicum miliaceum), korra (Panicum Italicum), &c.; and in many places indigo engages the attention of the husbandman. The way of manufacturing it here is that described by Dr. Roxburgh, by boiling or scalding it. Among the hills, where the Nerium tinctorium of Roxburgh grows plentifully, the natives mix the leaves of that plant with real indigo, a practice which I have not observed any where else. It is known that the leaves of that plant alone produce a very tolerable indigo. This article, as brought for sale here, is not made up into cakes, but left to dry after it is strained, and of course is either in powder or lumps of a small size; it is also very spongy and light, and contains far less colouring matter than that which has been prepared by fermentation, and which has undergone the different processes instituted for refining and compressing it for the European market. The mānd of about 25lbs. is sold at Padālu by the merchants, in common years, for eighteen or twenty rupees; they themselves purchase it from the ryots for about ten or twelve rupees.

It may be worth while here to notice a mode of manufacturing indigo which of late years has been much practised on the coast, though not with that success which was anticipated, since the indigo produced does not sell so well in the English market as that from Bengal. The process is as follows:

The indigo plant, when cut, is exposed to the sun till the leaves are dry and can be easily separated from the stalk: they may then either be kept or manufactured immediately. When they are to be kept they must be deposited in a very dry place. The indigo is manufactured by steeping the leaves about six hours, then straining the water, beating it in the common way, and indeed conducting the whole exactly as usual. The only difference is using the dry leaf instead of the green. If this process had been equally successful, it would have been attended with great advantage to the manufacturer; much time and labour is saved, and there is less risk of injury, for the green leaves are often spoiled on their way to the works. In fact there is a saving of fifty per cent. upon the mode of manufacturing with the green leaf.

This process has been long in use on the coast, and practised by the natives about Tranquebar, Cuddalore, Puorto Novo, places formerly and even at present famous for the finest blue dye upon cotton. The natives are, or at least some years ago were, so partial to this indigo that they pretended their fine blues could not be produced from any other. I think it produces at least as fine a colour as that from Bengal, and that if any difference really exists, it must be in the colouring matter not being so much compressed. It is not unlikely that both the boiling process and the dry leaf, yield a colouring matter which does not admit of the same compression as that from the green leaf by fermentation.

The vegetables cultivated in gardens are all over India nearly the same. I may therefore refer for a list of them to the second tract in this volume, which gives a statistical view of the Mysore. At Cuddapa these vegetables are reckoned larger and better than in most other places, particularly the brinjals (Solanum melongena) and bendacays (Hibiscus esculentus). At some places on the banks of the Penna, particularly at Sidhout, the melons are reckoned the best in India. They have a great number of varieties, distinguished by particular names, and to each of which they ascribe particular properties. They raise them in the bed of the river during the hottest season of the year.

About Cuddapa, and in all places along the hills, where the soil is not altogether black cotton soil, there are many orchards (called topes) as of mangoes, guavas, and plantains. Where the black cotton soil prevails, I have seen only tamarinds and sometimes jamblang, and I have already observed that trees of all kinds are very scarce on this soil. In general it may be said, that orchards are found in India only in the neighbourhood of large cities, and that a guava, mangoe, or plantain near common villages is an unusual sight. Along the coast indeed, and in the Carnatic, orchards are found in smaller villages.

The former Mussulman governors have introduced in places the cultivation of the grape, but only in such a way as to show that it will grow and produce fruit with little trouble. The same may be said of the fig.

The cocoa palm is not cultivated in this part of the country, nor is the palmeyra often to be seen, and only near the hills in high and dry situations, as south of Cuddapa. The black cotton soil does not seem to suit either of these trees.

On the mode of collecting the revenues, on the share assigned to the cultivator of the soil, and on whatever belongs to the internal economy of the country, I can say even less than I was able to do of the Mysore. There I had an opportunity of making some inquiries; but here, by my situation as surgeon to the Court of Justice, I was debarred from all means of information.

Every judiciary division of the country, of which there are two in the ceded districts, has a collector of the revenues, who lets the lands belonging to every village to a renter, or to the inhabitants of the village, generally at a quit rent to be paid by several instalments. The renter again parcels it out to the ryots for shares which in most parts of the coast are pretty much alike.

Hitherto no great landholder or zemindar has been established in these districts, and it is to be hoped there never will; for in my humble opinion they are equally injurious to the cultivator and the Company.

The people who inhabit these districts are mostly Hindoos. In the larger places, as at Cuddapa, Bellary, Canūl, &c. there is a small proportion of Mussulmen. The former are a healthy industrious race, who live, upon the whole, in a very comfortable manner; while the latter have scarcely any thing to support them but their pride. The Hindoos speak Telinga, and in some parts of Canūl, Canary. This latter language was particularly spoken, as I observed in this tour, by the Bramins. At Cuddapa there are a great number of old Patan families, who speak Hindostany in its greatest purity. They might be suspected of being at heart inimical to the British Government, yet I have seen them all turn out in support of the Judge, when a mutiny had broken out in the prison, which threatened destruction to all about the Court.

Not long ago Cuddapa was the residence of a Nabob similar to that at present at Canūl, a vassal or feudary of the Nizam; and near it is a place where a battle was fought in which the Nabob was slain. The palace where the Nabob resided still remains in a mud fort close to the Pettah, on the banks of the Cuddapa river. It is now converted into a court of justice for the Zillah. Near it is a garden with a pretty summer-house, small, but very neat and airy, quite in the Indian style. The prison, likewise situated in the fort, consists of a number of choultries (open buildings) separated from each other, and surrounded by high mud walls, which have been erected by the convicts that inhabit it at present. It contained when I was there between six or seven hundred prisoners, the greatest part of whom (upwards of 500) where convicts condemned to work in irons from one to fourteen years, according to the nature of their crimes, which mostly consisted of theft, housebreaking, and highway robbery. The remainder are persons not yet tried, or debtors; of the latter description indeed there are but few, and they are kept separate from the rest, as likewise are the women. Among the prisoners there are persons of all casts, from the Bramin down to the Chuckler, all huddled together without distinction in the same prison; yet even here they rigidly follow the precepts of their cast respecting eating and drinking, and notwithstanding express orders to the contrary, the Bramins are always treated with more leniency than the others. A Bramin, however depraved or however loaded with crimes, is always looked upon as belonging to a higher class of beings. The prisoners are guarded by peons, and when they are at work out of prison there is usually one peon for every two convicts. Their work consists chiefly in repairing the roads, clearing the ground in the vicinity of the prison, and in assisting to erect and repair the public buildings; but as they cannot be employed at any great distance from their prison, they will soon be in want of employment. I had chalked out some useful and constant work for them in the neighbouring districts; but the discontinuance of my appointment, which by Sir George Barlow was thought useless, prevented me from laying it before Government.

The convicts and untried felons are allowed daily one sīr of the cheapest kind of grain, as the alū corralū, or natcheny; and one dubb, a copper coin, equal to about a halfpenny. On this they are not only able to live, but some of them save both grain and money, or contribute to the subsistence of their families. The debtors are allowed two-pence per day: the felons are not allowed meat even when they are willing to pay for it, unless at the recommendation of the surgeon, who is obliged to attend them when sick. The articles for their food, which are exposed for sale in the prison at stated hours, consist of salt, chillies, onions, and tamarinds. While at work, they collect wood for firing, and herbs which they boil into curries; in fact they live better than most of the common people of Hindostan do even in their own houses.

"The Company's donkalūs (thieves) look like bridegrooms" is a common

6

saying among the people of Cuddapa; they mean that they look sleek, fat, and comfortable like people in good circumstances; many of these men have themselves declared to me that they never lived better in their lives, and others, that they would not leave such an asylum as long as they could help it. Yet a smaller allowance certainly could not be given, it is what Tippo and all Indian princes have been in the habit of allowing to their prisoners, both prisoners of war and felons. It is really astonishing on how little an Indian can subsist apparently with comfort; yet their mode of living is such, that an European would be loath to see his enemy reduced to it. The Sunday, on which no work is done, is to them a great satisfaction; but no attention is paid to their own festivals.

Murderers, after their condemnation, are kept separate from the rest; they are doubly ironed and handcuffed until the time of their execution, which is often delayed for months after their trial and conviction, as the sentence of death must be confirmed by the Suddar Adaulat (Highest Court of Justice) at the Presidency, and the warrant signed by the Governor. A delay of this kind is not only expedient but highly commendable, as the Mussulman code, the criminal law of India, is in some instances improperly severe, condemning a man to death who killed another even in self-defence. In such cases it requires to be mitigated and corrected by a superior power. The Cazy is in fact the judge at the quarterly sessions; and the circuit judge, a servant of the Company, only a commissioner.

Punishments that do not affect the life of a culprit are executed immediately after the sessions are over, by the Zillah judge. They consist in condemnation to work for a certain number of years, and a number of stripes on the bare back, not exceeding forty, with a rattan, similar to what is called a *wellcome* in some houses of correction in Germany. This part of the punishment is severer than most people are aware of; but it is the mode or the instrument with which it is inflicted, not the pain that is caused or the ignominy entailed on the sufferer, against which an exception could be made. Many of the culprits become victims to this punishment, dying soon after of a locked jaw. This is ascribed, and I believe with reason, to the rattan. When it is used, as generally happens, quite new, its outer covering, which is very thin and sharp, is apt to splinter and to insinuate itself into the skin, where it occasions that irritation, which is apt, without much external inflammation, to produce a locked jaw. I have several times lost three or four persons after an execution of this kind, nor did I advert to the cause of it till too late, otherwise a proper representation would have obviated the misfortune. That such deaths are not owing to the severity of the punishment, or to the constitutional inability of the Indians to bear it, is pretty clear from what is known of military punishment, in which many have suffered 800 or 1000 lashes at a time, without dying in consequence.

Sentence of death is commonly received with perfect unconcern: the culprit returns to his cell, after having asked to be indulged with some tobacco and a good meal, which he enjoys with the greatest satisfaction, just before he sets out on his fatal journey. He converses with his friends and relations, or with those about him, on indifferent subjects; and when reminded of his misfortunes, says *karmam!* (ill fate!) This word, in all stages and vicissitudes of life, is the Hindoo's comfort; it was karmam that made him commit the crime. By *bākiam* (good luck) he would have escaped, by karmam he suffers. The strumpet, the thief, the murderer, alike plead in their defence *karmam.*

Bramins commonly behave with most obstinacy when condemned to die; probably because they conceive themselves to be inviolable, which would be the case under all Hindoo governments. I knew of one at Rajahmundry, who absolutely abused the judge and every body about him, when going to the place of execution. Nothing mortifies them so much as to be hanged by a Chuckler, the lowest of all outcasts, or when it happens that one of the latter description is to suffer with them upon the same gibbet.

Let us now take a glimpse of the private life of the common Hindoos. That of the cultivator, the labourer of the class of suders, may be called a happy one, and it is so in fact, as he seems to be content with his lot: none but a Hindoo however would be happy in such a situation. A sufficiency of food is the sole object of the wishes of a Hindoo: whether it be rice, which he seldom tastes, or the coarest of all grain, aruga, makes no difference to him; this is boiled and seasoned with salt, with chilly and onions, which his garden affords, and a few leaves of the tamarind tree are added to give the whole a relish. The conchi or water in which his food has been boiled constitutes his beverage at meals, and water, coloured with a little sour milk or butter-milk, supplies him with a refreshing draught during the day. In villages in the country, the husbandman scarcely tastes animal food oftener than once a year, probably at the sacrifice of a goat. Sometimes, indeed, his flock may happen to be visited by sickness and death; in such câses even the best of sûders does not hesitate to feed on the carcases of his sheep and goats. Our servants and dubashes, well aware of the abomination in which they would be held by their masters, will deny this fact; and they act herein wiser than we, who disregard their peculiarities in every respect.

The common Hindoos are very fond of spirituous liquors: even the women will take a glass of brandy when offered by an European. Of their morals and propensities I have already spoken in a preceding Tract.

The ceded districts are reckoned very healthy, as is the case with most countries in India that are open, and on which jonna is cultivated. I know of no endemic diseases here, such as the jungle and hill fever in other parts of India, nor have heard of any epidemic disorders that have visited these districts for some time past, except the small-pox, which even during my residence committed great havock. Vaccination had been practised by a surgeon about two years before, and the escape of all the children that had been vaccinated from the small-pox made such an impression on the inhabitants, that they petitioned Government for practitioners, who had been allowed to all other Zillahs except this. There is one disorder however which occurs here oftener than in other parts of the country in which I have been; it attacks only women shortly after they have been delivered, and consists in a profuse cold perspiration, accompanied by low spirits and apprehensions of death; the pulse is natural, and all other functions go on regularly. The patient however soon becomes exhausted and dies imperceptibly. This disorder makes its appearance in the hottest season. The remedy which the natives use, and have found most efficacious, is theriac in large doses.

The domestic animals in this district do not differ from those in the Carnatic or Mysore, excepting that the cows are not so hardy as in the latter, nor so large as in the neighbouring Nellore districts. There are but few goats, and no woolly sheep here. There are fewer wild animals in the northern parts of this district and in the plain country than in any other part of India in which I have lived. There are no tigers nor chittas here, though these animals infest the northern hills about Buswapatam and Commum. The cobra de capello is very frequently seen in the fields, but other snakes are not so numerous as on the coast.

Trade is on the whole in a very languishing state, and unless it be carried on with ready money it cannot be attended with profit. It is entirely in the hands of a few individuals, and only nominally in those of the *shroffs* (native bankers); for these persons can hardly be considered in any other point of view than as the brokers of men in power: artificial wants are thus created as circumstances may require. If revenues are to be paid in silver, it disappears; when pay is issued in gold, it falls in value, and so on. Even copper coin is a rich source of gain by its fluctuating exchange. Large fortunes have lately been made in this way, quite openly, and it would appear without apparent disadvantage to Government. Who the sufferers must be I need not point out. Some years ago there was a good deal of trade carried on at Podatūr, a village not far from Cuddapa, with a kind of cloth called Percallas: it is of a thin texture, and more similar to the Bengal cloth than that of the coast; it is about ten yards long and one broad, and costs from one and a half to ten rupees and upwards the piece. It is manufactured in this part of the country, and sent to Madras and to the southward for sale. It is well fitted for the Indian market, as it is a very light wear. Muslins of every quality are made among the hills from Gurrumcunda to Cumbum, and formerly they were in request for Pegu. Along the banks of the Penna, chiefly west from Gutty, much chintz is manufactured, particularly of the coarser kind.

TRACT XX.

ACCOUNT OF AN EXPEDITION FROM JALNA TO SERONGE, IN NORTH LATITUDE 25°.

SOON after the disturbances in the Madras army in 1808 and 1809 were settled, Colonel Close came to Jālna, and formed a considerable army, with which he crossed the Nurbudda and penetrated Hindostan as far north as Seronge, which lies between the twenty-fourth and twenty-fifth degree of north latitude. Respecting the causes and effects of this expedition it is not my business to expatiate. We never saw an enemy, though we often suffered privations, and were even plundered of our goods and cattle by a set of robbers called Pindāries, who infest the country.

Our first marches were in the Nizam's part of Berar, which is, without exception, the most depopulated and desolate part of India that I have seen. The soil is rich and produces abundance of fine grass, and it strikes a traveller coming from the Nizam's territories, that it might easily by rendered the garden of India. The climate is excellent; it is sometimes hot in April and May, but the heat does not last long. The nights are always cool and refreshing. In the cold seasons the thermometer sinks below 40°, I have frequently seen it early in the morning at 39°.

The soil is generally black cotton soil, which might perhaps be denominated the Indian soil; for nearly four-fifths of all the surface of the country that I have seen is composed of it. The kinds of grain principally cultivated in Berar are wheat, Bengal gram (chick pea), peas, vetches, and flax. These are all sown after the rains are over in September and October, and are ripe in January. The Nagpore wheat is celebrated as the most nutritive and productive in India. It requires only three months to come to perfection; it grows from two to three feet high, and its ears are loaded with seeds. It yields a very fine spirit; I made some which, under the name of whisky, acquired much celebrity in the camp. The peas are of an inferior kind, small and black, I believe, a new species: when young they were sweet, and were generally used on our tables, which did not abound in vegetables. Flax is cultivated merely for its seeds, from which they express an oil.

The second crop in the year is jonna (Holcus sorghum); it is sown after the violent rains of June and July, and is ripe in October; it grows here to the height of eight or ten feet or upwards. I have seen from a rising ground several regiments of cavalry as if drowned in it, when they marched through an extensive field of it. This grain, together with wheat, is the common food of the natives of the country. They make a kind of bread or flat cake, which they eat either alone or with some curried vegetables and chillies. Near the villages some barley is cultivated, and it seems to require a better soil and more care than the wheat. I could not ascertain to what particular uses this grain was applied. Carrots, onions, melons, &c. are cultivated in all gardens; but fruits, as plantains, oranges, grapes, are only found in large places. We were chiefly supplied from Nagpore, and though at the distance of eighty miles, we were generally furnished with oranges and grapes at a very moderate price, for under such circumstances I call twelve oranges for a rupee cheap.

Berar is a large tract of country on the northern bank of the Godavery, which there is called Gunga. It is intersected by low ranges of hills running in naked even ridges, and consisting of an amygdaloid, in which the Hydrabad opal, chalcedony, zeolite, and heliotrope, are found. In the lowest beds, particularly near the Gunga, I have found beautiful specimens of agate and calcareous spar in it.

Aurungabad and Omrasatty are the largest places in the western provinces belonging to the Nizam. The latter place is, I understand, the emporium of all inland trade, and has lately been fortified by high stone walls, which are sufficient to secure it against the inroads of Pindāries, and the cavalry of native Princes. The houses here, and particularly at Aurungabad, are mostly built of stone, and are often two or three stories high, and in every respect different from those in the southern countries. The pagodas resemble in their external appearance the common dwelling houses of the natives; but mosques are to be observed every where, and some of them in former times must have been superb buildings.

Mahratta is the language spoken by the Hindoos, who constitute the bulk of the nation, and in the large towns Moorish is generally understood. The lowest classes of people are much fairer than the Bramins in the Carnatic. Here the Bramins are sometimes as fair as Europeans. The women are not afraid of being seen, and are, I think, generally handsome.

After leaving the Bunslows Berar, we came into a wild uncultivated country. We crossed the Tapti or rather stepped over its source at Molty. From thence the country becomes mountainous, and continues rising to the mountains of Nurbudda, which belong, I believe, to the Vindyan, famous in Indian mythology. We passed through them not without great difficulty. It took us more than eight days, encamping in narrow valleys, inhabited by hordes of bears and tigers. Had we been attacked by ever so small a force we must have perished, if from nothing else, from want of water and provisions. These mountains, some of which are about 3000 feet in height, are composed of granite, though it is neither so hard nor so beautiful as that which forms the constituent of the mountains that run north and south through the peninsula.

The mountains here run east and west on both sides of the Narbudda, which is one of the finest rivers I have seen in India. We encamped on its southern bank, near a small fort called Hussingabad, and crossed it about a mile east from that place. The river here is about half a mile broad, the stream runs gently along, and the water is remarkably sweet. It abounds in good fish and tortoises, which are as large as any in the sea. The stones in the bed of this river are red and black jasper, and other hard argillaceous minerals. On its banks, which are very steep, and in its bed, I found several plants belonging to genera common in colder climates; as ranunculus, veronica; and in nullahs, or small rivulets, near it there occurs abundance of the sweet smelling grass roots, the Andropogon muricatum. The valley through which the Narbudda runs is but scantily cultivated, and only in the neighbourhood of villages, which here lie at a considerable distance from each other. The jungle, when we passed it in December, was mostly bare of leaves, but in January the beautiful Grislea tomentosa, which was every where in blossom, enlivened the dreary scene; and in February the whole country appeared for a short time as if covered with the brightest scarlet, from the flowers of the Butea frondosa; at the same time the Bassia latifolia perfumed the air in its peculiar way, for its scent is not equally agreeable to all.

The flowers of this tree are gathered by the natives, and when dry have the appearance of a berry. They are as sweet as raisins, and are chiefly used by the natives to obtain a good vinous spirit by distillation. The flower has in its dried state a smoky flavour, and might be used in small quantities to impart this peculiar taste to gin and whiskey, as the amateurs of these liquors are, I am told, particularly fond of such a flavour in them.

After we had crossed the Nurbudda, we had to march through mountains, wilder and more unfriendly if possible than those on the south side of that river. Luckily they were not so steep. After a forced night's march we came to Racīn, a strong hill fort where we expected to find enemies, but they were fled, and we were told that the Bassal Nabob had come to terms, and that we were no longer in an enemy's country. From thence we went on to Bilsa, famous for the best tobacco in India. It is a very large town, and the country all around it is well cultivated and rich. A few miles north of it we passed the Bedowa, a river which falls into the Jumna. At this season of the year it was every where fordable. Seronge was the last and best place that we came to in Hindostan. It lies in a charming situation at the foot of a small range of hills, and at the end of a most extensive and well cultivated plain, which furnishes wheat, sugar, &c. in the greatest abundance. Mīr Cān had left the place before our arrival. Not one of the inhabitants had abandoned their habitations, they even threatened those who annoyed them that they would complain to Colonel Close; and I am sure they have in no one instance been disappointed by him. About this time the Colonel was so much liked by the army, (a few great commanders excepted,) that he might have done with it any thing he thought proper, which was by no means the case in the beginning of the campaign. We were at times, even in this rich country, very badly off for provisions, particularly for our cattle, gram selling in our bazars at five or six sīr for a rupee: while at the distance of ten miles 50 or 100 sīr could have been purchased at the same price.

Cloth of the coarser kind was manufactured here, and was very cheap. I bought a piece ten yards long and a yard wide for one rupee. It was a kind of cloth that would make excellent tents; many tents were made up for the Company here, and I think they must have got a private tent for about 7 or 8 pagodas, which is 100 per cent. cheaper than the price in the northern circars. Coarse cloth was always to be had very reasonable from the time that we left Omravatty.

In this part of the country we were obliged to substitute the spirits made from the flowers of the Bassia latifolia for arrac and brandy. The Com-

6

pany, I dare say, would purchase it for a rupee a gallon, as I made it for about half that sum, and much better than what was served out to the Europeans. I cannot believe that the Company paid six rupees per gallon as was said, or that they paid fifty pagodas for a private tent made up in the camp!

Near Seronge, where we encamped for a fortnight, I felt the greatest cold I ever experienced in India. The thermometer was generally 38° in the morning, and twice it fell to 32°, and we had ice. Our southern people, notwithstanding this, liked the country, to which the general healthiness of the army must be ascribed. The Europeans on the contrary suffered considerably, especially the 34th Regiment of British Infantry. This might be owing to the new manufactured spirit which they were obliged to drink.

The regiment to which I belonged and another of cavalry were sent towards Bundlecund to bring a supply of gram; and I must say, that I never saw so fine a country in my life as that between Ruttunghur and the Nurbudda. It was entirely covered with wheat, gram, and flax, all ripe for being cut down; but what was curious, in the whole immense plain not a house or village was to be seen. We were told that the cultivators lived at a great distance, and came here only in the sowing and reaping time; they sell their crops to the Brinjaries as they stand upon the field. About this time of the year the Pindaries, a lawless set of rebels, make their appearance likewise, to share the fruits of industry with the buyers and sellers. I consider this as the finest country and the finest climate in the world. What a pity it were not inhabited by industrious well protected Europeans.

In February we recrossed the Nurbudda, and the force to which my regiment belonged, remained in that place about a month, in expectation of being stationed in Hindostan, as a subsidiary force to the Bunslow. But ultimately in the beginning of April we returned through Candeish to Jālna, where we arrived in May. The rest of the army had gone by another rout under Colonels Conran and Hare to Jālna and to the Carnatic.

Candeish is a mountainous country, and in the valleys a very hot one. The Tapti which runs through it is already a large river, with very deep and steep banks, consisting throughout of a black firm earth. Near it the country is curiously intersected with ravines from thirty to forty feet deep, that often wind along for several miles; as the road lies frequently through them, a whole regiment frequently disappears for an hour, and re-appears again not a quarter of a mile in a straight line from where it first entered the ravine, all covered with dust and almost suffocated.

Berrampore is the capital of Candeish, which belongs to Scindiah. We passed close under its walls, but no European officer was allowed to enter it. By all accounts it is the best built city in India, and to judge from its outside it must contain may fine large buildings. It lies in a beautiful valley on the banks of the Tapti. The country about it is well cultivated, and the villages are the neatest that I have seen in India. About fifteen miles south from it is the range of hills that separates Candeish from Berar. These we ascended by the Adjunta Pass, where we encamped near a fort of the same name. Not far from this place I found monuments to the memory of some of my dearest friends, who had been wounded in the battle of Assaye, and had died here. The field of battle we also saw and encamped close by it. No mark or vestige of that famous action remained, except a single button marked 74, that was picked up by some of us.

Soon after our arrival at Jālna, I found myself unexpectedly in orders for the factories of Ingram and Maddepollam, an appointment the more agreeable, as it was the place where my two poor remaining children had found an asylum in the house of Mr. George Yates, without whose kind care I must have lost them altogether.

TRACT XXI.

REMARKS ON MAHAVELLYPORAM.*

As I have nothing left me by preceding travellers either to admire or to describe about Mahavellyporam, and yet do not wish to be considered as an inattentive or idle spectator, I must endeavour to represent things in a different point of view from my ingenious predecessors. Should the doubts or observations which I am about to bring forward deserve refutation, the good cause will gain by my opposition in acquiring clearness. My propositions are the following:

First. That there never existed, and consequently never was swallowed up by the sea, such a town as Mahavellyporam is represented to have been.

Secondly. That new Mahavellyporam, or the town said to have been built on the destruction of the former, never has been better or larger than at present, or at least never has been a place of any consequence.

Thirdly. That the sculptures on the rock and the pagodas are very little, if at all, superior to many others in the country.

The grounds for believing the former existence of such a town have been rested on the alleged danger to vessels if they approached the coast within many miles of it, lest they should founder on the remains or ruins of the buildings still remaining, though buried for some thousand years in the bottom of the sea. Secondly, On a stanza in the Bhagavat, expressive of the existence of a large town on the south east point of Ceylon. And thirdly, On the tales of the Bramins. This simple statement seems to me to go far to establish my position; but as the two latter allegations have

* This paper was addressed to Mr. W. Petrie, now Governor of Prince of Wales's Island, after an excursion with him to Mahavellyporam: a gentleman to whose support and politeness I feel particularly obliged.

been in a particular manner connected with the first, and as they must all stand or fall together, I shall pursue the subject a little further.

It is certainly true that vessels cannot approach the coast, because for many miles both north and south it is very rocky; and here in particular we can observe two miles out in the sea, opposite to the pagoda near the surf, a ridge of rocks on which the sea breaks very violently. These, in my opinion, are the buildings so much spoken of, which have braved the monsoons and currents for these several thousand years.

Respecting the two verses, I must refer to Mr. Chambers's account, as also for the truth of my observation. The only book that would lead to a certainty in determining points of this kind is the Stalapūrānam*, for though poetical, its avowed scope is to perpetuate the memory of remarkable places. Any other poetical work, as the Bhagavat, Ramayana, &c. cannot be admitted as evidence either for the description or situation of a place, any more than the Iliad, Æneid, or Lusiad on the same subject.

The tales of the Bramins, whether proceeding from ignorance, superstition, or indigence, are all alike unworthy of confidence. They found it answer their purpose to persuade people that the rocks out in the sea were roofs of pagodas; that in a dream they had information from a mighty Swamy of his intention to move out of the briny element into a more dry and comfortable place. This explanation is not only perfectly consonant to the mode of thinking and acting of the people in India, but it is the very story of the Bramins of this place.

A more direct proof of the mere imaginary existence of this place is the account of the founder of it, Mahabali, who is said to have reigned in the saly yūgam (the golden or first age), that is, about Noah's time, if we compute according to Mr. Bentley's tables. This is part of the story of the Bramins, which would not become more likely, even if we were to suppose that Mahabali were the same with Balin, who lived in the dwepa yūgam (the brazen age), about the 3098th year of the world.

In order to prove my second position, I shall state the traditions, the only intelligible documents that we have remaining; and I trust, by comparing them, not only to make good my assertion, but also to throw some light on the real history of the place.

* Since writing the above I found the Stalapūrānam at Conjeveram. It contains a dystich, which, literally translated, is as follows: "The town of Conjie is 300 yojanam from Benares and five from the Eastern Sea." Now if the yojanam, as in common, be taken at four coss (eight miles), this agrees pretty exactly with the respective situation of the place.

First. The inhabitants that escaped the general calamity are said to have been the first founders of the present village, once a large town.

Secondly. About 500 years ago a Poligar of the name of Balicota Simcomnaidū lived here, and began to build a little fort on the top of the rock, some ruins of which still remain, as bricks, &c.

Thirdly. It is said also that Krishnarailu, who lived about 250 years ago, employed some workmen, who had been driven from the north into the Carnatic in search of bread, in erecting a gopāram or a choultry, the walls of which being the solid rock, represented Krishna, his brother, and a number of shepherds and milkmaids, cows, &c. in the plains of Madūra. The same people were probably also employed in the execution of the sculptures in the rock close by, and the pagodas and rhadams most worthy of attention: for much older than 200 years they cannot be, if we judge from their appearance, and compare it with the nature of the rock, which, as shall be observed hereafter, under certain conditions is liable to decomposition, and in many places is actually far advanced in disintegration.

By comparing these different accounts, we may with a great degree of probability conclude that, before the reign of Krīshmaraylū, this place was the seat of a Polygar or manager of a small district, who, at the persuasion of the Bramins first built the two brick pagodas for the reception of the half drowned god. In consequence of this and other circumstances, the place became known to Krīshmaraylū, who in order to employ a set of half-starved labourers set them to work in carving the rock. But as there are no remains or ruins of palaces, walls, large tanks or wells, to be found near the place, and as the space between the rocks and the sea (half a mile) would not allow of a large establishment, we may safely conclude that this has never been a place of any consideration.

It remains for me to make good my third assertion; and by examining the objects thought most worthy of attention, this will be easily accomplished.

The pagoda on the sea shore is the most talked of, though I do not see why, for it is neither remarkably large, nor uncommonly beautiful, nor in any way singular. It is built of stone upon a rock which supplied the materials. In respect of size it does not even rank with the middling in the Carnatic. It seems to have been once inclosed by a brick wall, and the number of stones lying in the surf and near the pagoda on which the marks of the tool are to be traced, shows that some smaller buildings or temples, which are very common near large pagodas, have formerly existed here.

A pillar of about fourteen feet high, opposite to the door facing the sea, is washed by the surf. We see the like Garuta Stambham before all pagodas, but they are usually much larger than this; it does not appear ever to have been higher, no marks of violence being discoverable.

This pagoda viewed from a small distance has a pretty appearance, on account of its pyramidal form; but this is a form by no means uncommon in India. There is one, for example, of the same kind on the west side of Conjevaram. When closer examined we find that the stones of which it is built are by no means uniform either in size, species, or shape. The sculptures of Sīva and Pārvatty in the inner rooms, and those of the Dii Minorum gentium, are neither beautiful nor singular, nor do those on the outside of the walls represent any thing else than figures and historical incidents, which are very common in other places, and explanatory of mythological events.

The uncouth figure in a lying posture, cut in the rock in a gallery behind the pagoda, cannot well be Wishnū, as some have imagined, it having none of the insignia that characterise that deity, as the chacram, sankam, &c.; and because this pagoda is consecrated to Sīva, whose worshippers certainly would not suffer Wishnū to occupy a corner in the temple of their favourite deity.

Let others admire the sculptures on the rock, for my part I consider them as hideous caricatures. The cats resemble hyenas; the angels or devatas look like rickety children with big heads and swollen bellies; the heroes have thighs like spindles, while the nymphs and milk maids have waists as thin as their arms. The only tolerable figure is the old man Arjūnas fencing master. The cows and elephants I have seen equally well executed in other places. Lions represented in their proper form with a mane are to be seen in many other parts of India; for example, at Besoadah, at Samulcotah, at Ellore. The goddess Mahirhārura Maidānī (with a buffaloe's head) is always seen upon the back of a proper lion. It is not necessary to trace the sphynxes to Egypt, we find them ready made to our hand all over the country under the name of Gūnti Simha in almost all pagodas. In the Conjeveram pagoda there are pillars resting upon sphynxes. Neither is there any occasion to have recourse to Arcadia for the origin of the flutes. The Telinga shepherds call them pillam gravi, the Sanscrit scholars wēnū: hence Krishna is called Wēnū Gopāl, the flute playing cowherd. The instruments applied to the mouth, as the flute and flageolet, go under the same name.

The temples on the rock and about it, of which we found a good number, and which are mostly cut out of one stone, are very insignificant and more like models than real Hindoo temples; many of them are left unfinished, and appear as if but lately come out of the hands of the stone-cutter. The Rhadams, to the south of the main rock are also cut out of single stones. Whether they are models of Hindoo palaces (mahal) as has been suggested, or places of worship, as the lingums and sculptures on them seem to indicate, I cannot pretend to decide; but the architect who planned the largest of them must not have understood his business well, for by excavations and galleries he weakened his building so much that, when about sixty years ago it was struck by lightning, it burst asunder from top to bottom. On the outer walls of this building are many figures, some of which appear to be decorated with large wigs. This may furnish hints whence the custom of wearing them in our western world was derived, and may prove that the credit of the invention is by no means due to Louis the Barber!

I shall now make a few observations on the mineralogy of the rocks and buildings, which may perhaps throw some additional light on the antiquity of the place.

The rocks are all granite, composed of quartz, felspar, a small quantity of mica, and some garnets; though I have some suspicion, from the superior hardness of what I call mica, that it is in reality hornblende, and that the rock in fact is not granite but sienite. The felspar seems to be sometimes compact, sometimes common, and it readily disintegrates, as we find to be the case in the buildings of Mahavellyporam, and even in the quarries at which they are at present at work; for we see that the pieces broken off and lying about are much tarnished and different from the appearance of the recent stone.

On examining the surface of the rock we find it scaling off in large flakes, half an inch thick, and this the more the nearer it is to the sea. The pagoda near the surf, for example, is coming off not by piecemeal, but very rapidly indeed. When I saw it last, two months had scarcely elapsed since the preceding monsoon, yet handfuls of sand and silicious gravel could be collected from the neighbourhood of the stones. That this speedy disintegration is peculiar to the rock we are speaking of is evident from this circumstance. Some blocks of another kind of granite are met with here and there in the pagoda, but they are quite fresh, having undergone no disintegration whatever. There is likewise a black stone, of which all the lingums are made, probably hornblende, which does not readily undergo decomposition.

The granite of this place, as indeed is the case with granite in general, splits very readily, as is evident from large masses of it found lying close together, the nearest opposite sides of which demonstrate by their form that they were once united. The stone-cutters cut out pieces of it with great ease, and supply Madras and other places with quarry stones of all sizes. To split an immense large mass into two pieces they have nothing to do but to make square holes of about an inch in every direction and about the same distance from each other, throughout the whole length of the stone, and to drive blunt wedges of the form of the holes into them, striking upon them in succession, and in a few minutes the business is done. The making of the hole seems the most difficult part of the business. They do it with a kind of chisel and iron hammer. These, together with a pair of common bellows, constitute their whole apparatus.

These people are probably the descendants of the workmen from the north country mentioned above. And, if we are to judge from the many unfinished single stone pagodas on which recent marks of the tool appear, they still amuse themselves with creating objects for the admiration of posterity.

I had almost forgotten to mention that this rock does not seem to suffer so much from the action of the sea, as from the atmosphere; for the stones washed by the sea are by no means so much disintegrated as those upon dry land. They are smooth indeed like all stones washed regularly by the tide, but quite hard and solid. The same observation applies to the figures sculptured on the walls of the Gopāram, even those on the inner room of the pagoda near the sea, which are usually moist. They appear not nearly so much injured by time as those at a greater distance from the shore. The air near the sea seems to possess more corroding power than that at some distance from it, owing probably to the particles of common salt which it contains.

It has been observed by others, that the bottom part of the lowest range of figures on the rock near the Gopāram is considerably sunk in the ground, not less than a foot or more. This can be ascribed to nothing else than to the gravel or sand accumulated from the decomposing rock above, and an eye the least accustomed to mineralogical objects will easily distinguish in this gravel all the constituent parts of the rock.

In consequence of the uncommon facility with which this granite flakes off, we may judge pretty well of the time that has elapsed since the construction of the temples and rhadams in this place. Suppose the formation of a flake a quarter of an inch thick required 100 years, to form which I conceive to be a very full allowance; on such a supposition 200 or 250 years is the most distant period that can be assigned for the cutting of the figures and the formation of the pagodas, for hitherto that surface has not lost an inch.

It may be worth while to notice some blocks of a beautiful granite that are to be found in the pagoda near the sea. It is composed of white felspar, quartz, and mica; the mica is usually in the smallest proportion. It is quite fresh. I do not know from whence it came, but I have seen blocks of the same kind of granite in a deserted pagoda near Conjeveram.

TRACT XXII.

JOURNAL OF A TOUR FROM BENGALORE TO TRICHINOPOLY, IN 1802.

DURING my stay in the country near Sira, in the latter months of last year, I had been attacked by the jungle fever, an intermittent which seldom is subdued without a change of climate. In milder cases this change need only be from one part of the country to another, particularly from an inland province to the coast; but in the more violent and inveterate, a voyage to China or Europe is often required. I received, on my application to Government, permission to proceed to the coast; and being at liberty as to the particular place, I chose for several reasons a tour through the Baramāl to Trichinopoly. I had never been in that part of the country, which is so celebrated by the wars in the last century between the English, French, and some Native Powers; as well as for its general surface and its natural productions. The accounts varied so much, that I was happy to have an opportunity of satisfying my curiosity.

I left Bengalore on the 13th of January, a time of the year above all the most agreeable for travelling in India. The weather is then cool, the sky serene, the country still clad in colours of a lively hue, which in little more than a month give place to others of a darker complexion, and to an atmosphere heated by a vertical sun, obscured often by sultry clouds. I travelled to-day under a somewhat cloudy sky, towards Ryacotta in an E. S. E. direction, the ryots were still employed in reaping their harvest of horse gram, which is the last on the fields in this part of Mysore.

The general aspect of the country is the same as about Bengalore. Gentle elevations alternate with fertile valleys; the higher grounds are generally uncultivated and covered with a low jungle, which serves as a cover for hares, partridges, and rock pidgeons (a species of grouse), and which in this season afford food for sheep, goats, and cattle of all descriptions. The first ascent is laid out, in general, in fields for raghy, gardens, and topes of fruit-trees, and the vallies are cultivated with rice, or, according to circumstances, with sugar. The want of trees however, and palms on the higher grounds, which form, if not the most extensive, certainly the most striking part of this country, give on the whole a barren and often a bleak appearance. I arrived in the afternoon at Attapilly, a village eighteen miles from Bengalore. I was in hopes of receiving accounts here of the gold mines which were reported to be at no great distance from this place; but, as happens too often in India, the persons to whom I applied either did not choose to impart their knowledge from prudential motives, or they were actually ignorant of what existed at such an immense distance as twenty or thirty miles from their homes. I heard enough however to determine me to proceed to Kellamungulum, as a place likely to get better information.

January 14. After travelling for some time in a country similar to that of yesterday, we came in sight of the Eastern Ghauts. The soil of the country changed for the worse, and its aspect became blacker and wilder. Cultivation seems to be confined to the valleys and to the grounds immediately round the villages, which on the whole, however, had a tolerably good appearance. Near Kellamungulum, a village not far from some hills, the ground became very jungly and barren, and the soil gravelly and stony. It belongs to the district of Ruttungerry, one under the Company's Ammāny, of which Mr. D. Cockburn is the collector. The regulated prices of such necessaries as are required by travellers in India, appeared to me remarkably reasonable. This object of a good police is, I believe, more attended to in those provinces that have been added to the Company's dominions since the fall of Tippoo, and in Mysore, than in their ancient possessions; and is indeed far more necessary here to prevent altercations and misunderstandings between the European traveller and the natives, particularly as the latter would not know how to obtain redress should they conceive themselves aggrieved, and might probably take the law into their own hands and cause extensive troubles. The tariff, or price of articles, in English and in the country languages, which the village can furnish, is handed to every traveller as he arrives, by a peon stationed in it for the purpose, who himself is to produce the required articles, and to receive payment for them. It happens certainly sometimes, that a fellow of that description, elated with the dignity and power with which he feels himself invested, becomes insolent; but this is an abuse not chargeable on the system: in general all parties separate contented, the present of a fanam (two pence), or two at most, settles all differences that might have arisen.

The farther we advanced to the eastward, the more jungly and stony became the country, and the poorer the appearance of the villages which we passed. This is the case in all mountainous tracts in India, and in such we found ourselves to-day. About noon we arrived at Hurrydrūg, a hill fort, at the foot of which is a poor and almost deserted village. I ascended the rock in the afternoon accompanied by a few peons that were stationed here in charge of the fortifications, which in times of yore were esteemed very strong. Just when I was at the summit, my attention was arrested by the warlike sound of the collary horn and the tomtom, and on looking about I saw several bodies of armed men pass the village without however in the least molesting it or my baggage. On inquiry I was told they were rebels against Government, or rather against the collector of the revenues. I understood further, to my great disappointment, that their place of rendezvous was Pungampilly, a village within a few miles of the gold mines of Suttergul, and which I had to pass on my way to them. Under these circumstances it would have been extremely hazardous to pursue my design, for though it is in general by no means dangerous for a stranger unconnected with the object of their revenge, particularly for a military officer, to pass through the midst of such people, it has happened that insults of an unpleasant nature have been offered. The attempt would have proved fruitless at all events, as most villagers in the vicinity of those places had left their houses and joined the rebels, or had removed to other more peaceful situations. I am not able to give an account of the nature of the present discontent: the rebels blamed the collector; and others ascribed it to the intrigues of a Polygar who had stirred up the credulous multitude, which in those cases is in general the true cause. For reasons already stated, I was not afraid to remain during the night in this village, and I had a guard of Sepoys with me, with whom, if the worst had happened, I could have defended myself in the fort; but I thought it prudent to break up earlier than usual in the morning, and to push on for Ryacotta, a place of security, and where a military force was stationed.

January 16. I passed in my way through thick jungle, and between a number of unconnected hills, to the range or assemblage of which that of Ryacotta belongs.

To my no small surprise I found on my arrival that in the earlier part of this day's journey I had passed through the very heart of the present troubles, which had become so alarming that Mr. Cockburn the collector had been obliged to fly for security to this place, as the malcontents had manifested a particular animosity against his person.

It is remarkable that this place is very healthy though on all sides surrounded by jungle, and among a number of hills, and at no great distance from contiguous ranges. It lies near the entrance into the Table Land of Mysore, and commands one of its principal passes. It was, before the last war that terminated the Mussulman Dynasty in Mysore, a frontier station of that power, and deemed a place of great strength. It is still a place of some consequence, commanded by a colonel, and garrisoned by a detachment of troops.

A petta, or town of considerable importance for an Indian one, lies close to the lower fort, which defends the only place from which the upper or the hill fort is accessible. In it reside the European officers, the garrison, and a number of private families of the natives of the country.

The day after my arrival here I ascended the hill, which is not above 800 feet in perpendicular height, and not steep except at the gates of the hill fort, from whence it rises very suddenly and terminates in an almost naked rock.

The climate of this part of the country resembles that of Bengalore though it is not quite so high above the level of the sea by from 5 to 600 feet; it is on the whole very pleasant.

The rocks hereabout are, as far as I have seen them, all sienitic, similar to those described in some former tracts. The hills are very interrupted in single points, which however both south and north of this become more contiguous and form ranges. At no great distance east of this are the higher ranges of the lower Baramāl, and south west appear those of the higher.

The jungle with which the greatest part of this country is covered, and which comes up to the very fort of Ryacotta, consists of the very same kind of shrubs as are common in the eastern parts of Mysore, so that I made no acquisition for my botanical collections. It is much infested by tigers, which made it dangerous even to go to any distance from the fort; indeed these furious animals very often carry men and cattle off from the very environs of the place. The monkies domineer on the hill and are remarkable for their impertinent intrusion to the houses near their regions.

The death of the Rev. Mr. Gericke may, as I am told, be ascribed to the fright which they occasioned him when he slept in a bungalore belonging to the commanding officer of that station which is near the brow of the hill.

The soil immediately about Rayacotta in the lower grounds appears to be very good, as it produces not only the vegetables and fruits of this country, but such as have been introduced from others, in great perfection. Peas, sallad, cabbages, carrots, asparagus, &c. are found here in all months and seasons of the year. Potatoes do not grow quite so well here as at Bengalore and Nundydrug, where they are now almost generally cultivated. It is not however quite clear to me whether they would not thrive here as well if the culture was carefully attended to: at the former places they were first introduced in the gardens, particularly of the Nundydrug hill, by Colonel Cuppage, and since 1800 by me among the natives, whom I was enabled by Government to supply with seed potatoes of the best kind from the St. Helena stock, and to offer them a sale of their produce, which, however, they soon found for themselves in all parts of the country where Europeans reside. Since that time they have even supplied Madras, where they are preferred to those of Bengal, at which place they seem to have degenerated. The Mussulmen and Hindoos, with the exception perhaps of the Bramins, eat them with great eagerness, and seem to give them the preference to their yams and sweet potatoes. It is not surprising that the Bramins should not eat them, as there are other vegetables, particularly bulbs, from which they abstain, as onions, turnips, and raddishes. Apples, peaches, and grapes come to great perfection in the gardens of this place: the first are of the kind cultivated in the Bengalore gardens, and were originally sent from Persia; they much resemble the nonpareil in taste and appearance. The regular season of produce is February and the beginning of March, but with a little management they may be had in all other seasons. They often grow as bushes, but if properly pruned, grow pretty trees of the smaller size. The peaches are about a month later than the apples, they are also very well flavoured, and grow as large as any produced in England. They have been introduced from the Isle of France, whence they were sent to the late Sultan, who, like most Mussulmen, was fond of gardening: at present they are chiefly propagated by cuttings, but grow equally well from the stones, which usually require less than eighteen months from the time in which they are put into the ground to that of yielding a large crop on a tree which in so short a time is grown upwards of twelve feet high. The grapes produced here are not inferior in size and flavour to any raised in the hot-houses in England. It is a pity indeed that no attempt has been made to cultivate the vine on a more extensive scale, as it grows so well in all parts of the country where it has been attended to. At Pondicherry it comes to great perfection, and grapes in the season are abundant; in Aurangabad in the higher parts of the Dekan, they are sold as other fruits of the country in the public bazar; at Seringapatam and here they are by no means scarce.

The common wood strawberry, which was introduced by the Right Hon. Lady Powis when Governess at Madras, grows in great luxuriance and of delightful flavour. Many other fruit-trees of Europe, as the cherry, pear, plum, chesnut, walnut, olive, would, I am persuaded, thrive with equal luxuriance in Mysore; and ere long I am in hopes the noble personages interested in the welfare of India will succeed in their generous endeavours of securing these comforts to their countrymen, than which scarcely any thing awakens a more lively sense of the *amor patriæ,* and the enthusiastic desire of returning to it and to the friends of their youth.

January 18. I left Ryacotta again, proceeding southward through a wild jungly country between ranges of high mountains; it became however as we advanced soon open again, and we found ourselves in a well cultivated district, that abounded with tanks, rice fields, and villages. The rice was about a span high; the soil had also changed for the better, was often black; it was nowhere so stony and gravelly as near Ryacotta and the earlier part of our day's journey. The stones which lay about were mostly sienitic, but contained more felspar, hornblende, and pistazite than quartz. Hereabout and more north of Ryacotta, I found in the road pebbles of staurolite, which I could not discover in the solid rock near those places from which however they must of necessity have been derived. We put up for the rest of the day at Palicol, a fine large village built in the style of those in the Carnatic. We saw here the first palmeyras again, which in Mysore are not to be found. Cocoanut gardens made also their appearance near the villages.

January 19. The ranges of hills as we proceed retreat on both sides, and leave a broad well-cultivated valley, in which we often fell in with black cotton ground and marly stones. We passed through a number of good villages, and staid at Darmapore, the largest, in which Captain Read, formerly the Collector of the district, has a bungalore: his memory is still respected, as he did ample justice not only to his employers, but also to the natives of the country. There was a number of native servants of the revenue department here, to whom I applied for milk and sheep for myself and servants; but, as happens frequently, those gentlemen wished to impress me with a due sense of their authority and dignity, and suffered me to go without it.

January 20. We travelled to-day along a range of hills for the first ten miles in a well cultivated country, in which dry grain were chiefly attended to; but all at once it became jungly and barren. I found here a detachment of the 1st Battalion of the 18th Regiment of Native Infantry, with the officers of which, Captain Muirhead and Lieutenant Hay, I was well acquainted, and now spent a few hours with them. In the evening I left them again and descended through the Tapore Pass into the Lower Baramāl; this pass is rather long, but no where so abruptly steep as that of Peddanaigdurgam; it is the one through which the English armies in former times have entered Mysore, and from which the Mysore forces have often invaded the Carnatic. During the night I staid in the choultry, at the foot of the pass, which is by no means good or commodious.

January 21. The road from the choultry, though it leads through a wild stony country, is broad and good, and has avenues of trees which by Colonel Munro have been planted throughout the Baramal leading to the principal places. I need not observe that they will prove a great comfort to the weary traveller, but cannot help expressing the wish that his example may be followed in other parts of the country. In the Tanjore country are many avenues that have been planted by the ancient sovereigns of that country, which to this time make travelling in it so pleasant. I passed to-day a river with running water, and staid during the night at Vommelūr, a fine large village.

January 22. Rose rather early and came at day-break to a high ground which ran from east to west towards the high range of hills from which we had descended. I have lost the specimen of the rock that constituted the forementioned low ridge: in my memorandums I find it was intersected by calcareous tuff, and contained in small nests a semipellucid greenstone, which, in its decomposed state in which it principally occurred, crumbled into a powder which is carbonated magnesia. The sound stone is about the hardness of serpentine, striated, and looks not unlike the famous *image* stone in China, which however is said not to contain magnesia as a constituent. The soil hereabout is chiefly a black cotton ground. Foliated hornblende appears often in rocks above it. The country is charmingly cultivated.

Salem, to which we now came, is a large, populous, and beautiful village, in which there are many handsome choultries. The Company have here a factory for the purchase of coarse cotton goods of the same kind as their northern punjums, which are so much esteemed and in great demand in the European market. The cloth is not so dear here as in the northern Circars, but it is not so strong. I presume it is pretty well known that a punjum is a certain number of threads that run lengthways through a piece of cloth; that of course a piece of twelve punjums must have twelve times the number of threads which constitute one, and that twenty-four punjums in the same breadth must have twice the number of threads as those of twelve punjums. Here two punjums are designated by *first call*, so that twelve punjums of cloth is called *six call*, and so on.

Mr. Carpenter, the Resident of this factory, received me in the politest manner, and his hospitality detained me a day longer than I at first intended to remain. I wished much to go to a high mountain which lies S. W. of the place, and is reckoned the highest in the Baramāl, but found that it would cost me several days, though it appeared so near, and not above 2000 feet high; but so much time I could not spare. There are several villages on it I understand, and a kind of table land.

Saltpetre is very cheap here, being sold at the rate of nine rupees for 225 lbs. in the bazar.

The country is chiefly cultivated with jonna and rice: of the former they get two crops in the year from the same field, which shows that the little monsoon in April, when the first crop is sown, must be sufficiently strong to prepare the strong cotton soil for the nurture of the grain, which in the more northern country I have no where found to be the case. The second crop is sown, as in most other places on the coast, in September, before the setting in of the great monsoon. The first seems to be the principal one, and the species of jonna is the *white* variety which is expected to produce thirty-two fold; the second is called *red*, and yields only twenty-four fold. After the two crops are reaped, sennaga (Cicer arietinum) is sown on the same ground, so that a field in this part of the country actually produces three times in the course of a year. A great deal of cotton is grown in this and the adjoining districts, particularly on Coimbatore. There are also two species, the white and the brown; the former is an annual plant, the latter biennial and even triennial. The water is very often brackish in this district.

January 24. I proceeded on my tour towards Malūr, a village eight miles from Salem, to which the roads were exceedingly good, and as all in the Baramūl, broad and commodious; the country between the hills is well-cultivated.

January 25. On leaving Malūr early this morning before sun-rise we heard on all sides the creaking tones of the sugar mills, which sounded much like the singing of a devout congregation at some distance, and awakened ideas which a machine of that kind would appear very unlikely to call forth. The stones which I found to-day were granite in which the felspar was red and in great proportion to the other ingredients. Calcareous tuff accompanied as usual the black cotton ground, and salt works of the kind as noticed in my former Tracts were not uncommon. The country during the latter part of this day's journey fell off in point of cultivation from what it was in the earlier. I staid during the night in a choultry near Chittūr.

January 26. We travelled on our way to Namcull chiefly on elevated ground, and had on our left ranges of high hills. Namcull, like most fortified hills, is detached from the rest of the range to which it probably belongs. A pretty large town is at the foot of it. The hill of itself is steep but not high; its rock is sienitic, in which white quartz and felspar prevail: in some places it contains garnets in hornblende and a greenstone which possesses the characters of felspar and is composed of the same constituents; the latter compound seemed to prevail, particularly in the lower country, in which the rocks that appeared near and in the road to-day consisted chiefly of it. The sand in the nullas and in some part of the road was mostly an aggregate of small garnets and hornblende. We staid but a short time during the hottest part of the day at Namcull, and proceeded afterwards to Malleapetta, where we crossed some small rivulets which had running water, and reached in the evening Vadagapetta, where we staid during the night. At the former place the cultivation of rice begins again, for which they draw the water from the channels with pacotes, and at the latter place we found a great number of plantain gardens.

January 27. Our journey to Totteam was to-day again on high uncultivated and stony ground; and near this place the avenues which had all along

6

lined the roads discontinued, which we took as a sure sign (as was really the case) that we had left the Baramāl and entered the Carnatic. The soil about this place is mostly black, and saltpetre is produced in the village in great abundance. The cultivation about this place is chiefly confined to that of rice, as the country can be watered from the channels of the Cavery, on the banks of which river we travelled for the rest of the day. We passed here often through very high grass, which came up and sometimes overtopped the horse's back and the rider, and after a very long march we arrived in the evening at Musery. The villages on the banks of the Cavery are very thickly strewed with plantations of cocoanut, plantains, and other fruit-trees. The country in general is one of the best cultivated on this coast. The soil we had passed to-day was mostly of the black kind, and the stones that lay scantily about were fragments of quartz and granite. I have observed that black soil, with its accompanying calcareous strata of marl and tuff, rest in common on granite, indicated by rocks of this nature appearing above its surface; that on the other hand a red soil prevails where sienite forms the apparent groundwork. I conclude from this that granite is at the bottom of all, and sienite is only superimposed; for the latter appears only in the elevated or higher parts of the country, and the former in the lowest, which is generally covered with alluvial strata.

January 28. The channels or canals, which water the adjacent country on both sides of the Cavery, have been constructed often with great expense, the sluices belonging to them being built with solid masonry. The villages are often mean and poor in appearance, a sign that the inhabitants work more for their masters than their own benefit. There are often three crops of rice produced on the same field, a fertility of which scarcely any other country in India can boast: this however can only be done when the cultivator confines himself to the coarsest kind, which from the time it is planted to that in which it can be reaped requires only seven weeks; the middling sort takes about four months, and the finest nearly six months before it can be reaped.

January 29. I crossed the Cavery to-day very early in the morning before sun-rise, when I could observe nothing but that the water was very low. It is the most useful river in the peninsula; for in Mysore near Seringapatam, it fertilizes the country, and the Carnatic owes the former importance and splendor of its princes to the waters which this river yearly distributes in its provinces. Its beds as long as it is above the

Ghāts are stony, and its banks no where deep. Not far W. from Ryacotta it precipitates itself abruptly, and forms a number of beautiful cataracts. After it has entered the Carnatic it slides quietly along, and distributes its blessings as it proceeds towards the sea. It depends for the first and principal supply of water in the month of May on the rains that fall in the western Ghāts, or on the Malabar mountains on which it takes its rise. Its tributary streams collect the water of the eastern and southern parts of the Mysore in June and July, and in the latter part of the year it is again filled by the monsoon rains of this eastern coast of the peninsula. The coming of the "fresh water from the country," as it is called, is every where hailed and celebrated with festivities by the natives of the Carnatic, who worship it as one of the greatest of the most benignant deities.

I arrived early this day at Trichinopoly, and put up with my friend the Captain, now Colonel G. Lang, who commanded a Battalion of Native Infantry, with the determination of staying some time with him, which however I was prevented from doing; I had however time enough to see what was remarkable in and near the place.

To speak of its history and former importance would be presumptuous in me, but a few words of what it is at present will not be uninteresting. It is still one of the principal military stations under the Government of Fort St. George, and the head-quarters of the officer commanding the southern division of the army. The cantonment of troops consists of a Regiment of His Majesty's Infantry, at that time the 12th Regiment; a Regiment of the Hon. Company's Native Cavalry, and one or two of their Battalions of Infantry, with detachments of European and Native Artillery. The fortification is now quite neglected, and it appears surprising that it could have been ever of any importance. The hill, which probably attracted the first founders of the settlement, is an elevated rock of no great height: I think not much above 600 feet from the foot of it to its greatest summit. On its northern and eastern side is the pagoda which makes so eminent a figure in the view, which as the best of any I have seen, I thought my readers would be pleased to find in this work;* I have been favoured with it by Dr. Wilkins, the Superintendant of the Hon. Company's Museum and Library at the India House, where the original is deposited. The rock is of the common sienite of the Carnatic, and of no beauty whatever in its composi-

* See Frontispiece.

tion. The flat country in which it raises its head is altogether alluvial, and to a great extent on all sides low and even.

I visited during my stay here the famous pagoda of Striringam, which during the seige of Trichinopoly was the principal station of the French army. It has seven high walls, within the range of which live a great number of Bramin families who exist on the revenues of the temple, or on the misplaced charity of its pious visitors. Pillars of immense size support the gateways and the building erected on it. They are all of sienite composed of quartz, felspar, garnets, hornblende, and mica, singly, often aggregated in spots and stripes. It is astonishing indeed how people with so few mechanical means as the natives of India possess, should have erected such buildings, and transported such immense masses; for on the spot where they are now, and its vicinity, there is no vestige to show that they have been found. The present race is so degenerated as firmly to believe that none but supernatural beings could have effected such prodigies.

When they at present attempt to set up a pillar of any height, as there is always one before every pagoda (garuta stampam), they raise a mound of earth of the height of the pillar, and fill up the space behind, on which they roll it by main force, so that at last it stands upright and firm in the middle of an artificial hill which they carefully afterwards have to remove, supporting the pillar, and particularly strengthening it by a pedestal as occasion requires.

Trichinopoly is also a principal establishment of the Civil Power of Government, as it is the station of the Southern Judicial Courts of Circuit, in which three of the Circuit Judges reside when they are not on the quarterly visitation of the subordinate Zillahs. During their presence they form a Court of Appeal, in the first instance, from the Zillahs in all cases of civil law, while in their circuit, cases only of a criminal kind come before them. This establishment is of all others of the greatest importance to the country and its inhabitants, whatever may be thought or said of the Zillahs; as these latter only relate to property, which often can be guarded or acquired only by possessors of great means, which may lead often to very bad consequences; while the former guards the personal safety of the peaceable subject of Government and its own stability. In former times robberies and murders were committed often with impunity, and hence increased to an alarming degree; which now are followed by immediate and legal punishment, and become scarcer every day.

The Tamuls, or Malabars as they are often called, are, like all other Hindoos, an industrious gentle set of people, who are not given to any flagrant excesses of any kind, who are in general strenuous idolaters, and mostly worshippers of Siwen. They have the failings of the other Indians; and of those we have spoken enough in another place. To judge from their features and appearance, they seem to be a distinct race from the Telingas who inhabit the valleys of the Baramul and the Palliams farther north, as also the whole country beyond the Penna to Ganjam, and the whole of Golconda and Telingana inland. Their faces are flatter, the forehead shorter and more depressed than that of the Telingas, they are shorter also and much darker in complexion. Their extremities are not so well formed; their feet particularly are broader, and the hollow part is often filled up with muscle or fat, which gives them an unseemly appearance. Their women also are not so elegantly formed as those of the Telingas, nor are they so decently dressed, as they are often seen in the country quite naked to the loins. The young ones among them stain their faces, arms, and feet with turmeric oftener than the other, and extend their ear-laps with rolls of paper so that they often hang down to the very shoulders.

In this part of the country the Christian religion has made some progress, particularly about Tanjore, where the late Rev. Mr. Swartz and other Divines of the Mission of the Established Church of England, have in former times spared no exertions which zeal could prompt and prudence devise, and where at present their successors the Rev. Messrs. Pole and Kohlhoff do not labour in vain. Want of assistants and fellow-labourers confines their attention now chiefly to the flocks which have been collected, and to the schools to which all classes of natives have admittance. The Christians of this mission are not deprived of their cast: they on the contrary sometimes marry from among those Gentiles who yet profess the religion of their fathers, and who on this occurrence adopt that of Christ with the perfect consent of their relatives. I am myself witness of a connivance of the kind that happened about twenty years ago at Tranquebar, where a Christian of this mission, Gniāna Pragāsam, the interpreter of the Danish Government, a man of a respectable cast, married the daughter of a Hindoo at Madras, who with his family came and lived with the new couple for some time, and remained bigotted idolaters. I have since understood that marriages of this kind are by no means uncommon.

Much has been said of the *rice* Christains, as those were called who received a small allowance of food when they were instructed in the tenets of the Christian religion during a famine, some of whom recanted or returned to their families and their gods after it was over. In my opinion this is proof positive that the adoption of the Christian religion in itself is not followed by the privation of their cast or their situation in political society; it shows, on the contrary, the laxness of Hindooism, which readmits apostates either quite unnoticed or after a trifling penance. Loss of cast incurred by some crimes is on the contrary irrecoverable.

The climate in this part of the Carnatic is wholesome, and not so burning hot as its situation might give reason to expect. The extensive sheets of water which at all times of the year cover the country where rice is cultivated produce such evaporation as keeps the ambient air to a great degree cool and agreeable, whilst the temperature is yet so high as to dissipate and render them innoxious, which in climes less ardent, as in Spain where rice is cultivated, would prove the source of unhealthiness to its inhabitants.

TRACT XXIII.

DESCRIPTION OF THE GLASS WORKS AT MATOD.

THE glass works that I have seen in India are at Matod, among the hills south-west of Chittledroog, and in the ceded districts; but this last is smaller. I confine my observations to the first of these.

The materials used in this manufacture are, 1. Soda. 2. Quartz or compact ironstone. 3. Compact specular iron ore. 4. Copper.

1. The soda is mixed with a notable proportion of common salt. It is obtained from a sandy earth found in many places along the coast on the surface of the ground, and from its use is commonly called washerman's earth. At some places hereabout the salt is extracted from that earth by elixiviation, and the lixivium evaporated by fire, and sold in the bazars under the name of *sobbu*. For the purpose of making glass it is gained in the following manner:—*

Some pits about a foot and a half deep are filled with salt earth, and water is poured upon it. The same portion of water is poured successively upon different portions of salt earth till it is conceived to be sufficiently impregnated with saline matter, which is judged of by its brown colour. This water is then worked into a pultaceous mass with cow dung, and spread upon a straw mat about an inch thick, and dried in the sun. Another layer prepared in the same way is applied the next day, and for twelve successive days it is kept moist by the addition of fresh portions of lixivium of soda. The large cake is then divided into smaller pieces, which, when quite dry, are piled up into a heap and burnt. The fine ashes which are found along with the more solid pieces are kept separate. The latter are reduced to

* I have reason to think that borax exists in some quantity in it; a substance of which the soda of other places on the coast which I have noticed is quite destitute.

powder, stored up, and called *soudu sāram* (essence of soda); because they contain the largest quantity of soda.

2. Quartz (in the language of Canara, bellakallu). What is used here is a little ironshot.

3. Gorykallu. This is an iron ore that comes nearest to the compact brown ironstone of Kirwan (hydrate of iron).

4. Kimmidu kallu (iron glance). Specular iron ore of Kirwan; red oxide of iron, as appears from the experiments of Bucholz; though as the ore in question was attracted by the magnet, I consider it as rather a mixture of black and red oxides of iron than a pure specular iron ore. It is found in sufficient quantities after heavy rains in a nullah near a village called Kadavigada, in the Budela district. The nullah comes from the north side of a hill which probably contains the ore in rocks. This ore is reckoned best when firm and sound. If red ochre appear in the fracture, the specimen is esteemed inferior to the best kind, in the proportion of two to three. And accordingly a greater quantity of it is considered as necessary in the manufacture of glass.

From these few materials the four following kinds of glass are made:— 1. Bīza or mother glass. It is a soft, imperfect, porous glass; and is used only as a substratum or basis to the other kinds of glass made here. 2. Red glass. 3. Green glass. 4. Black glass.

Bīza is made of the following ingredients:—

1. The ashes, which remain when the soda is made, and which, as was mentioned before, are kept apart. If these ashes do not contain many grains of salt, five parts of them are taken; but if they are mixed with much salt, three parts are deemed sufficient.

2. Pounded quartz, or bellakallu, one part. These two ingredients are separately pounded and then mixed together, put into clay pots and kept in the heated furnace for eight days. To see whether glass be formed, an iron hook fastened to a long bamboo is dipped into a pot containing the glass materials. If the mass adhering to it be of the consistence of wax, the operation is finished. If not another day's heat is given.

Red Glass.

It is of a hyacinthine colour, penetrated with large round white spots. It is composed of

Bīza	7 parts.
Soda, or soudu sāram	21
Kimmidu kallu	10
	38

All the ingredients are first separately reduced to an impalpable powder, and then mixed. It requires first three days of slow heat, and then seven days of the strongest fire that can be given.

If more than the stated quantity of kimmidu be taken, the glass acquires a black colour; if less, it assumes a lighter shade of red.

Green Glass.

This glass is composed of the following ingredients:—

Soda, or soudu sāram	21 parts.
Bīza	7
Kimmidu kallu	$0\frac{6}{7}$
Copper filings	$0\frac{6}{7}$
	$29\frac{5}{7}$

This glass has a dark emerald green colour with opaque spots.

Black Glass.

This glass is made of the following ingredients:—

Soudu sāram	3 parts.
Bīza	1
	4

Four days moderate heat is enough for obtaining it. The charcoal of the soudu sāram probably gives it the black colour; as it will lose it if the fire be too long continued or too strong. This glass is the least esteemed of all. It is quite opaque and has a close resemblance to enamel.

The common salt contained in the soda separates itself from the other ingredients, and is found covering the glass or bīza in a firm crust of one inch or more in thickness. It is very fine and white, and used like sea salt.

The only use to which these different kinds of glass are applied is the manufacture of bracelets, with which the poorest as well as the richest of the Hindoo women (the widows alone excepted) ornament their arms.

TRACT XXIV.

ACCOUNT OF THE METHOD OF MAKING STEEL IN THE MYSORE COUNTRY.

THE place where I first saw steel manufactured in this country is a small village among the hills, south-west of Chittledroog, in the Talem purgunna. The iron from which it is made comes from Malsinganhally, a village at a small distance from the former. The preference given to the product of that work seems, however, owing only to its vicinity, as iron is made from the same kind of ore at fifteen other places in this district, and exactly in the same manner. The place where the ore is found is a hill near Kalwarangapamapetta farm, whence it is conveyed on asses to the different iron furnaces in this district.

Near the furnaces I found it in small tabular pieces of a brown ochrey colour, with shining particles scantily interspersed, nearly friable, and of an earthy fracture. It is not magnetic, and appears to me either decomposed hornblende, or iron glance, which is very common in this country. It yields about 0·269 of metal.

The process of making iron commences with filling the furnace with charcoal. After it is heated, which requires an hour, a basket of ore, containing about 33 lb. reduced to pieces of the size of a pea, is put into the funnel and covered with charcoal; an hour afterwards a similar basketful of ore is put in, and this addition repeated three times, at the stated intervals: care being taken that it is always covered with charcoal, and the furnace supplied with a sufficient quantity of this article. About an hour after the last replenishment the process is finished, which lasts altogether from five to six hours.

It must be mentioned also that after the third addition of ore, a small hole is made at the lowest extremity of the temporary furnace, to let out the dross.

After the charcoal has been consumed, the temporary part of the furnace is pulled down, and the iron collected at the bottom of it is taken out with a long forceps, carried to a small distance, and beaten with large wooden clubs. During this operation a great quantity of scoriæ are seen running from the porous mass of iron.

When the red heat is nearly over, it is cut into three pieces. In this state it is very porous, and worse in appearance than any crude iron of European manufacture.

To prepare it for the market, it is several times heated to whiteness, cut into thirteen pieces of about 2 lb. each, and hammered into cylindrical pieces of eight inches in length. It is in this state a good soft iron, answering all purposes for which it is wanted in cultivation and building. The mānd of this iron (27 lb.) is sold for about two rupees.

The people engaged in this work are of an emaciated sickly appearance, forming a striking contrast with the other inhabitants of this part of the country. This I have observed at all other iron works on the coast, but am not able to account for the circumstance.

In order to convert the iron into steel each piece is cut into three parts, making fifty-two in the whole, each of which is put into a crucible, together with a handful of the dried branches of tangedu (cassia auriculata), and another of fresh leaves of vonangady (convolvulus laurifolia). The mouth of the crucible is then closely shut with a handful of red mud, and the whole arranged in circular order, with their bottoms turned toward the centre in a hole made on the ground for the purpose. The whole is then filled up with charcoal, and large bellows are kept blowing for six hours, by which time the operation is finished. The crucibles are then removed from the furnace, ranged in rows on moistened mud, and water is thrown on them whilst yet hot. The steel is found in conical pieces at the bottom of the crucibles, the form of which it has taken. The upper or broader surfaces often striated from the centre to the circumference.

In some crucibles half of the iron only is converted into steel, and others are found empty, the smelted metal having run through a crack in the crucible, and is deemed useless.

I could not discover any slag at the top of the metal, although it had lost about one-fifth of its original weight.

These conical pieces are sold at the price of fifteen gold fanams the mānd, about ten shillings and eight-pence for 27 lb. Sometimes they are heated again and hammered into small bars of four or five inches long.

It is probably not quite indifferent what crucibles are used in this operation: at all events they must be able to stand a strong fire. The loam employed for these crucibles is of a brown red colour, of an earthy appearance and crumbles between the fingers; mixed with white sand and some shining particles: it has no earthy smell when breathed upon, nor effervesces with acids.

From this the finer particles used for crucibles are separated by water, which keeps them suspended for some time, during which it is drawn off and left to deposite them.

The dried sediment of many of these washings is compact, has a liver brown colour, with some shining particles; of the consistence of chalk; a conchoidal fracture, feels soft and soapy, and takes a polish from the nail. It makes a pretty good brown paint. Of this the crucibles are made, by moistening it and mixing it with the husks of rice. It is then dried in the open air.

The stone used in the construction of the fire-places of the iron and steel furnaces is called ballapam by the natives; a name applied to all stones of the magnesian order, which have a soapy and greasy feel, and little hardness. Here it is a potstone of a leek green colour, easily scraped with the nail into a greenish white powder, longitudinal fracture inclining to the even, with abrupt irregular rugosities, faintly striated, cross fracture, irregularly slaty, foliated, lustre silky, verging to the semi-metallic; specific gravity 2·782 to 2·802, the thermometer being 81°; opake; exposed to the air its surface is corroded, the colour changes into red, it easily crumbles to pieces, and its appearance becomes more slaty.

Along with it is found asbestinite of a light green colour. The fracture of the mass undulating; it is composed of needle and arrow-formed crystals, confusedly aggregated; the former are often scopiform. It has a harsh feel, cannot be scraped with the nail, but easily with the knife into a white powder; lustre glassy, translucent; specific gravity 2·894.

The rock of the mountains on which these stones are found consists chiefly of the following kind of stone:—In its sound state it is in the gross slaty, longitudinal fracture, undulating or even, cross fracture hackly. External colour a silvery green, and where decomposing red; internal greyish green, with many silvery shining particles. External lustre (where not red) silky verging to the semi-metallic; hard; gives fire with steel; specific gravity 2·64; thermometer 81°. It is much given to decomposition, becomes then softer, but does not lose its shining greenish colour, though it is evidently mixed with a great quantity of red; sticks a little to the tongue, cross fracture earthy, slaty. From the total decomposition of this stone is derived, I think, the red loam of which the crucibles are made, which in the wet season is washed down on the plain.

Another place where iron and steel is manufactured, and where I attended the process, is Kākerahally, a small village on the road from Bengalore to Seringapatam. The iron ore used there is the magnetic iron sand common all over the coast, and even found on the sea beach near Madras. The furnace used here, and the process of smelting iron, is similar to that described on former occasions.

Before the iron is made into steel it is heated, hammered, and reduced into pieces of eight inches length, and two inches breadth, and half an inch in thickness. It is then still so brittle that it breaks under the hammer. Its grain is coarse and white. Twenty-eight rupees' weight of it is put into a crucible, and upon it a handful of the dried branches of cassia auriculata. This is covered with the green leaves of the convolvulus laurifolius (tallāku), and the opening of the crucible is closed with a handful of loam.

The furnace consists of a hole in the ground about 1¼ foot deep; it is one foot broad where widest, and ¾ foot at the opening. This hole is filled with charcoal, and in and about the opening of it seventeen crucibles are placed; these are covered with a heap of charcoal, and bellows are kept playing on it until the contents of the crucibles are liquified, which is known by its perceptible fluctuation when taken out for the purpose of trying it.

The operation seldom lasts longer than three hours; and is usually made four times in the course of the day, and three times in the night.

The loss in twenty-four rupees is only one or 1¼ rupee weight and less. The steel is found in conical pieces striated at the broader surface. When it has run accidentally through a crack in the crucible, it is smelted again, and sold to the goldsmiths, who use it in making fireworks.

One hundred pieces, each weighing about twenty-eight or twenty-nine rupees, are sold for four Cantaray pagodas, *i. e.* fifteen pounds; cost about seven shillings.

As it seems indifferent what kind of iron is used for making this steel, a manufacture of it, if deemed expedient, might be established near Madras, or any other shipping place.

The principal point of making steel by fusion seems to consist in the exclusion of atmospheric air from the crucible, and the use of fresh vegetables instead of charcoal, by which means, it is probable, a higher temperature is obtained than could easily be procured by the use of common charcoal. Hence the iron is more certainly fused, and at a smaller expense. The crucibles are made here of a stiff loam mixed with the burnt husks of rice.

The grain of the steel is much finer than that of the ore; but there still appears spots which are not well fused.

I fancied that the iron manufactured here was a kind of natural steel; but a drop of diluted nitric acid left a whitish green spot, a sign, according to Kinman, that it is iron. On the steel of this place a brownish black was produced.

The specific gravity of the finest steel is 7·852; but I found the product here only 7·664.

Cassia auriculata (tanghedu of the Telinga) is one of the most common shrubs on the coast; but grows most luxuriantly on black soil. It is used in medicine, but more for tanning.

The extract, which it yields in great abundance and most readily, and which I recommended as a tanning material in lieu of terra Japonica, was rejected at first as useless by persons engaged practically in this manufacture at Calcutta; but since used by the very same persons in the Madras tanning, which has been established. It is rather scarce about Bengalore, and by no means luxuriant. It agrees with the Linnean description in all but the leaves, which are here from five to seven feathered.

The Convolvulus laurifolia, is a new species that contains some milk; it grows in most parts of Mysore and many other inland countries. I do not think it is very material for the manufacture of steel, except that it furnishes uncharred vegetable substance.

Since my arrival in England I have endeavoured to obtain information of what is known here of Indian steel, and of the result of experiments which have been made with it; and I am happy in being permitted to lay before my readers a letter from Mr. Stodart, an eminent instrument-maker, to whom I was recommended for the purpose by Dr. Wilkins, which equally proves the importance of the article, and the candour and ingenuity of the writer. The Letter is as follows:—

" Agreeable to your request, I herewith transmit to you a few remarks on the wootz, or Indian steel. I give them as the results of my own practice and experience.

"Wootz, in the state in which it is brought from India, is, in my opinion, not perfectly adapted for the purpose of fine cutlery. The mass of metal is unequal, and the cause of inequality is evidently imperfect fusion: hence the necessity of repeating this operation by a second and very complete fusion. I have succeeded in equalising wootz, and I now have it in a very pure and perfect state, and in the shape of bars like our English cast steel. If one of these is broke by a blow of a hammer it will exhibit a fracture that indicates steel of a superior quality and high value, and is excellently adapted for the purpose of fine cutlery, and particularly for all edge instruments used for surgical purposes.

"A very considerable degree of care and attention is required on the part of the workmen employed on wootz; the metal must on no account be over heated, either in forging or hardening; the fire ought to be charcoal or good coke.

"The art of hardening and tempering steel is admitted, by all who have attended to the subject, to be of vast importance; the excellence of the instrument depending in a great measure on the judgment and care with which this is performed. I find the wootz to be extremely well hardened when heated to a cherry-red colour in a bed of charcoal-dust, and quenched in water cooled down to about the freezing point. In the process of tempering, a bath of the well known fusible mixture of lead, tin, and bismuth, may be used with advantage; linseed-oil will also answer the purpose, or, indeed, any fluid whose boiling point is not below 600 degrees. The temper is to be ascertained by a thermometer, without any regard to the colours produced by oxidation.

"It is worthy of notice, that an instrument of wootz will require to be tempered from 40 to 50 degrees above that of cast steel. For example, if a knife of cast steel is tempered when the mercury in the thermometer has risen to 450, one of wootz will require it to be 490; the latter will then prove to be the best of the two, provided always that both have been treated by the workman with equal judgment and care.

"Upon the whole, the wootz of India promises to be of importance to the manufactures of this country. It is admitted, by the almost universal consent of intelligent workmen, that our English steel is worse in quality than it was some thirty or forty years ago. This is certainly not what one would expect in the present improved state of chemical science; but so it actually is. The trouble and expense of submitting wootz to a second fusion will, I fear, militate against its more general introduction. If the steel makers of India were made acquainted with a more perfect method of fusing the metal, and taught to form it into bars by the tilt hammers, it might then be delivered here at a price not much exceeding that of cast steel. Whether this is worth the consideration of the Honourable Directors of the Company is not for me to judge. I am of opinion it would prove a source of considerable revenue to the country. I have at this time a liberal supply of wootz, and I intend to use it for many purposes. If a better steel is offered me, I will gladly attend to it; but the steel of India is decidedly the best I have yet met with.

"It is eighteen years since I was favoured with the first cake of wootz (for so it is called) by the Right Honourable Sir Joseph Banks, to whom, I think, we are indebted for its introduction, and to whom, as to the friend of science and the arts, I shall always be happy to acknowledge my obligation. From this cake I at that time formed some few very valuable little instruments, but not without considerable difficulty; some parts of the cake being scarcely malleable, and the whole of the mass very unequal, owing, I have no doubt, to imperfect fusion."

LETTERS

ON

SUMATRA.

LETTER I.

On board the Harleston, 10th March, 1812.

DURING a residence of near twenty years in India my health had been so much impaired, that it could not reasonably be expected to hold out much longer without renovation in a more congenial clime; my children also, though still very young, could not be kept with any propriety much longer in this country, where hitherto they had enjoyed parental care from Mr. G. Yeats and his lady, at Ingeram, for whose friendship and kindness I shall never be able to find terms to express my feelings of gratitude. I availed myself therefore of the indulgence of a furlough of three years, which is granted to the Honourable Company's military servants after ten year's service.

I had lately been stationed on the northern Circars, at a place from which the distance to Calcutta was not considerably greater than that to Madras, from whence I should have embarked; I obtained leave therefore to proceed to that place, where I could have the pleasure of paying Dr. Roxburgh, one of my oldest patrons and friends, a visit, and of seeing the botanical garden, now the only establishment of the kind in India. There was besides a prospect of my getting a free passage for attending a ship's company in my medical capacity: but in this I was disappointed.

I took a passage in the Harleston, an extra ship, which, with another of the same kind and size, of about five hundred tons burthen, the Minerva, was destined to take in a cargo of pepper at Bencoolen, and left Saugur (where we embarked) on the 5th of January, 1812. Our Captain was a young gentleman of pleasing manners and much humanity, of the name of Thomas Walker. The reason that I preferred so circuitous a route, when I could have got a passage at least cheaper, if not better, in a regular Indiaman, many of whom were then lying ready to sail for England directly, you will discover in my natural disposition of rambling about in the world, and of admiring the works of God and nature in whatever corner they can be found.

The incitement to visit Bencoolen was particularly great, as so little of it is yet known; but enough to raise the curiosity of an amateur to much greater exertion. We hear frequently in India of the gold brought from Sumatra, of benjamin, camphire, pepper, all articles of great importance, of which the natural history is almost unknown; and as frequently of its murderous and dastardly inhabitants, who had lately assassinated their Governor, and are in the constant custom of plundering such ships as they can master, or are not on their guard against insidious attacks. There was certainly little reason to expect that I should make any discoveries in so short a space of time as that to which our stay was limited; yet something might be done; so much at least might be seen as to incite future inquirers and travellers to the objects worthy of particular attention.

Our passage from Sagur to Bencoolen was short but boisterous: we were even in some danger of going to the bottom, on account, as it was thought, of the ship being overladen, badly stowed, and withal sadly incumbered. The cabin, which, *pro tempore*, had been allotted to me, was so small, and so full of baggage that had been thrown in without arrangement, that I became really sorry for having undertaken this voyage in such a ship. The younger of my two children was also taken ill with a bowel complaint, the most alarming of all disorders in that clime, and under such circumstances, that I could not ascribe the disease to any thing else but his getting frequently wet in the bed in which he slept, the ship taking in much water at all times. In short, I was as unhappy and depressed as possible; when, after a fortnight's misery, the fog dispelled, and we found ourselves in sight of land, and came shortly after near a country, which in beauty and grandeur of appearance surpasses any I have yet seen.

To the children, of which we had thirteen on board, the sight of the cocoanut-trees seemed to be particularly interesting, and the prospect of going on shore, and of enjoying the luxuries to which they had been accustomed, made them forget all the hardships they had suffered.

We anchored in the roads of Bencoolen within a few miles of Fort Marlborough, the principal settlement in the Island of Sumatra, and at a distance of about four miles from Rat Island, where the Company's ships are brought as soon as pilots can be obtained, both on account of the greater security in the basin of that place, and for the convenience of more easily freighting them.

The day after our arrival I went on shore with my two children, and after

2

a few days' stay had the pleasure to see the younger recover very rapidly. But I felt now the want of a servant more than even on board the ship, for it prevented me from going about as I should have wished, and from becoming acquainted with the objects of research that were within my reach.

The people in a public house, though very kind and friendly indeed, could not be expected to pay much attention to such unprofitable customers, and I had no invitation from any of the surgeons, which in other parts of India would not have been wanting. As living in a public house is rather expensive here, four dollars a day for myself, and as much for my children, I was soon obliged to return to the ship, and from thence with the other passengers to Rat-island, where we spent our time as comfortably as circumstances would allow, and not altogether unprofitably.

I visited from thence several times the main land, and at other times the coral rocks, which on all sides surround the island, and which during low water afford a deal of amusement to those inclined to fish, or to collect shells and insects.

The passengers to and from India are generally of much consequence to the Captain, as they pay him very liberally for their entertainment. The price for a passage for officers from India is regulated according to the rank which they hold in the service, and by the same rule are their accommodations regulated, which on the whole are liberal to a high degree. I paid for myself and two boys three hundred pounds sterling, and had one-third of the great cabin. My next door neighbour was a lady, Miss S., who had been but six short weeks in India, and returned in the same ship in which she had arrived, without having seen a brother to whom she intended to have paid a visit. She had under her care two little boys, her nephews. Next came Mr. Stansbury and family, which consisted of his wife and two grown up girls and five other children, of which the youngest was but a few months old. Mr. S. had been in the earlier part of his life in the army, but latterly a partner of a very respectable trading house at Calcutta; a man of good understanding and integrity. We had besides two Dutch officers, who lately had been sent as prisoners of war from Batavia: they were both gentlemen in their conduct, and were treated with much humanity and generosity by Captain Walker, at whose table they dined. One of these, a native of Holland, had been forced by General Daendels into the military service, though he always had belonged to the civil. He was a very intelligent clever merchant.

From Bencoolen we got another passenger, Mr. B. formerly in the civil service, from whom and his writings I received much intelligence relative to the establishment.

Among the ship's officers, which consisted of four mates, a surgeon, and purser, I can complain but of one, the rest were genteel beings, with some of whom none but the Captain had reason to be dissatisfied. Among the ship's crew there were men of all nations of Europe, Russians, Greeks, Italians, Germans, Swedes, Spaniards, Portuguese, &c. besides Americans and Lascars from India. We had but few English sailors, and only such as had been discharged from his Majesty's ships as unable for service. They behaved on the whole very orderly, and were treated with great leniency. From among these I have a young German to wait occasionally on my children and myself, as the boy whom I intended to take with me from India for the purpose had not arrived in time to embark with me, a loss which, on many accounts, I shall feel very severely.

The mode of living in the Company's ships is very comfortable, and almost splendid. We have for breakfast, between eight and nine o'clock, tea and coffee, plenty of milk, as there is a cow on board which gives nearly four gallons a day. Fresh rolls are served up every day, and rice for such as chose to eat it with fried meat or salt fish. For dinner we have daily fresh meat, there being an immense stock of fowls, sheep, and hogs, which in Bengal can be procured at a very low rate indeed. There are two kinds of soup daily, pea and gravy; and a pudding and tart. Of Madeira, port, and claret, as much as every body chooses to drink; but we are all very moderate. In the evening, about six o'clock, there is tea again; and about nine o'clock, supper for such as choose to eat any.

It is not likely we shall have any dancing, as there frequently is on board the outward-bound ships, where there are often gay young ladies, and at all times young gentlemen, who have much time on hand. Want of the latter will prevent such amusements on the Harleston.

After a stay of near five weeks on Rat-island, where during the latter part we had been much annoyed by a number of unruly drunken soldiers among the European detachment that was quartered in the same house on the ground-floor, we were happy on being summoned on the 8th of March to the ship, which had completed its cargo of pepper, and where the Captain had built himself a round house (as it is called) on the deck for his own accommodation, as he had given up his share of the great cabin to me and my children.

The day after, it being Sunday, esteemed a lucky day by sailors to commence a voyage, we were piloted out of the bason, and set sail in the afternoon with a very faint and not quite unfavourable breeze.

LETTER II.

On board the Harleston, 12th March, 1812.

We continued in sight of Sumatra for many days after we had left Bencoolen, as the wind was neither fair nor strong when we sailed, nor has it changed in the least until the present moment. The currents alone seem to be in our favour.—Tedious as our progress has been however, we have enjoyed by our detention the finest prospect imaginable, for the coast of Sumatra is certainly the richest I ever saw in my life. The knowledge also which I have been able to obtain, defective as it is, of its productions, inspires me with an ardent wish to revisit it for a longer period, and under more favourable circumstances. It is in my opinion highly deserving the attention of the natural philosopher, as well as of the general observer.

Bencoolen is the principal settlement of the Honourable East India Company on the Island of Sumatra. Not long since, it was the seat of a distinct government, but it is now incorporated with that of Bengal. The civil servants of the Sumatra establishment were understood in India to have been all transferred to Fort St. George; but some I found had been allowed to remain, and, very properly, all those of colour; while others were permitted to retire on pensions of from 90*l.* to 260*l.* a year. A number of the former are now in situations of profit and responsibility on the new-modelled establishment.

The Representative of Government, at present, is a Mr. Parker, of the Bengal civil service, who is styled Resident in all public addresses, Governor by his more immediate dependants, and Commodore by the native Malays. He enjoys all the honours, if not more, than were granted to former regular governors. He has a body-guard of cavalry; holds levees, where he expects homage from his inferiors, and such strangers as wish to partake of his public dinners, which are provided at the Company's expense; and he has occasionally salutes fired for himself, when he thinks proper to awe the natives with a display of his power and splendour.

The next in rank to him are the senior assistants, of whom the first is also a Bengal civil servant, who as such is chief secretary and treasurer. He may hold other situations besides; but this depends entirely on the Resident, who has also the sole and exclusive patronage, like the Honourable Company's Governors on their other Indian establishments. The rest of those assistants are mostly men of colour, but they are covenanted servants of the late Bencoolen establishment. These preside at the different offices at Marlborough, or they are residents of the factories in different parts of the country. They have trifling or no salaries, but they thrive very well notwithstanding: the former on the commissions to which they are entitled; and the latter, on the pepper contracts which they make with Government, and the trade of their districts, which they monopolize, there being no competitors.

The junior assistants, otherwise called monthly servants, are a motley crew of all colours. They are employed in the offices as sub-secretaries, clerks, chaplains, &c.—Some of them are Jews, as the chief chaplain at Bencoolen; others are Christians of some description or other;—but all consider themselves very great men, particularly when admitted to the Resident's table, which exhibits as party-coloured a groupe as can well be imagined.

The nature of the civil government at Bencoolen, and in the districts subject to it on the west coast of Sumatra, is I believe as undefined, if not more so, than that of any municipality in the world. The native chiefs are recognized as proprietors of the soil, and as independent princes; yet such is the perplexing constitution of their own statutes, that it becomes necessary for the Resident to take the law often into his own hands, and to judge and punish even the greatest in the land as the exigencies of the times require.

Seven chiefs not many years ago were hung in chains after they had suffered death in various ways for the murder of Mr. Parr: one of them suffered after he had, on the promise of pardon, betrayed the others; or, in other terms, after he had turned King's evidence. His death, it is thought, had become absolutely necessary as a warning to some instigators and accomplices of that horrid deed who could not be brought forward, at least not to condign punishment.

Some of the culprits on this occasion were blown off from the mouth of a cannon, and their remains gibbetted *in terrorem*. Summary proceedings of this kind should only be resorted to when they become necessary for the preservation of a settlement and its peaceable inhabitants. That the occasion called for vigorous measures is beyond doubt, yet there are some at Marlborough who assert strange things which it is not for a traveller to repeat, who cannot possibly form a correct judgment of intricate affairs which may have been hushed up to avoid farther well deserved severity.

It is necessary here to observe that there is not even a justice of the peace, far less any other legal magistrate at the principal settlement of Bencoolen, which is Marlborough; yet there is a jail in which even Englishmen have been occasionally confined. On the other hand, many heinous crimes have escaped punishment, though the offenders were sent for trial to Calcutta, as it was impossible to take legal depositions here, and as much so to send witnesses a distance of 2000 miles.

Many applications have been made by the local authorities to the supreme Government in Bengal on this account as it has caused all along many difficulties and apparent irregularities. Yet nothing could be done legally to remedy this defect, as this settlement had not been included in the acts of parliament which authorise the appointment of justices of peace, and the execution of the British laws.

According to the original compact between the Honourable East India Company and the native princes in this part of the country, the former are constituted the Supreme Arbiters or Protectors of the Constitution of what may be termed the Confederation of the Princes on the West Coast of Sumatra, and as such their Representative presides at the Supreme Council of Malay Princes called the Pangaran's Courts, and has a right to affix a negative to any of their decisions, on the plea of its being against the fundamental laws and constitution of the realm. As such he also confers and confirms titles to estates and principalities, and in fact he has the same or greater authority and influence than formerly Emperors of Germany had in their Diets. By the charter, however, he is not allowed to do any thing without the consent of the Pangaran's Court, much less to exercise any jurisdiction.

The Residents in out-stations preside at the provincial courts of justice, which of course gives them vast influence among the natives, and secures to them the monopoly of every thing valuable there; but they derive no direct advantage or any share of the fines in which all punishments consist.

The system of government among the natives seems still less settled. It appears partially patriarchal and despotic. They have Rajahs or Chiefs of much apparent authority, yet every Malay thinks himself perfectly independent; he avenges his own wrongs, and is absolute in his family. The chief indeed cannot interfere in their private quarrels, nor in any of their transactions, though he does it occasionally when supported by the Resident.

Of the character, peculiarities, and customs of the natives of Bencoolen, as far as I have become acquainted with them, I shall speak in another letter. I have only to observe here that the allegiance or duty they owe to the Honourable Company consists chiefly or solely in keeping up their pepper plantations according to the original agreement, and in delivering the produce at a certain rate to their factors.

The agreement is, that each person of age is to cultivate 500 pepper vines, and to deliver the produce at the rate of three dollars per cwt. (formerly two) to the Company's agent. In default, the provincial Resident is authorised to punish them by confinement or otherwise, and when the case is atrocious he is to send them to Fort Marlborough for punishment. The Pangarans agree to these latter measures, as they receive a certain allowance of from $1\frac{1}{2}$ to 2 dollars for each bar (500 cwt.) of pepper produced in their districts; which makes them even solicitous to find out and produce all such persons as are of age to cultivate this article.

As is the case in most uncivilized countries, the natives have frequently petty warfares among themselves: to prevent these and the losses that might accrue to the plantations and to the quiet inhabitants of the country, the Government has been often obliged to interfere with a military force, and, as in all other parts of India, have always with little difficulty succeeded in re-establishing quietness.

* * * * * * * * * * *

To oppose the refractory, or to secure submission, the Company's factors in out-stations are to keep up a guard of Peons, or native soldiers, for which they have a handsome allowance; and a regular force of natives of the country officered by persons of rank among them, besides these a detachment of some companies of Bengal marines; a company of European and native artillery is also stationed at Marlborough. The latter is, I think, chiefly intended for the defence of the fort, which has been much strengthened lately, and may be yet a place of importance. Much money has been thrown away without obtaining any adequate advantage.

In times of alarm all Europeans and other settlers are summoned to the fort by the firing of three successive guns; and from that moment they become subject to military law and discipline. This was the case after the murder of Mr. Parr, and continued some time after the execution of the assassins. This alarm is a circumstance at all times much dreaded, as the Malays have then a full opportunity of indulging in one of their favourite amusements, that of plundering the unprotected houses of the settlement when the owners are absent in the fort.

The Company's districts, as those provinces are called which acknowledge the superiority of the English Government, comprise the whole extent of coast from Tappanouly (a district which borders on the country subject to the King of Achem) to the Straits of Sunda, and stretch as far inland as the second of the three ranges of hills which divide the island.

From these extensive districts the Company receive no revenue, and in fact derive no other advantage than what arises from their exclusive trade in pepper, which under existing regulations is far more beneficial to their servants than to themselves.

The resources which the Company have to assist them to pay the heavy expenses of the Government here, and the defence of their settlement and factories, consist chiefly in their farms and the land and sea customs levied at Marlborough.

The farms are those branches of revenue which arise from the retail sale of spirituous liquors, of palm wine, and opium, and the licenses for cock-fighting and other gambling houses, amusements to which the Malays are much addicted. It is needless to particularise the several sums, but it is understood that more has come to the Company's treasury for those farms since Mr. Ewer's administration; as they were, before his time, only nominally let out, but really proved a source of wealth to the members of Government, who were the actual renters. The yearly income on all those several branches cannot amount to much more than 60,000 dollars.

In the time when Mr. E. Cole was Governor, (in about 1788—9) the expenses of Bencoolen exceeded the profits or income, it is asserted, by

77686 dollars. Then also the Company paid ten dollars per bar (500 cwt.) of pepper at Croy, one of the factories, and lost 500 dollars on that establishment.

I should not forget here to mention the profits arising from the sale of articles sent from England, consisting chiefly of woollen and cotton cloths, marine stores, &c. but these cannot amount to much, and the sales in all probability are scarcely sufficient to pay the costs and charges on the articles.

It would lead me too far were I to relate what opinions I have heard or formed myself on the present system or management of affairs at Bencoolen, but it will strike you, from what has been said already, that it admits of, nay calls for, improvement. The expenses are too great, personal and general security too small, and the advantages that might be derived from a country intrinsically rich are neglected, or given up to private individuals.

The principal objects will be: In the first place to increase the income so as to meet the necessary expenses of the local Government. The East India Company should also get their pepper at least on the same terms with the Dutch in former times, and with the Americans at present. The next great objects will be to provide for the safety of their European settlers, the gradual improvement of their native subjects, and of the country, which is so capable of it—requisites which are so intimately connected with each other, that one can scarcely be attempted without the others being influenced or accomplished.

After a little further acquaintance with the subject I shall probably venture to give my humble opinion on the best method of attaining the objects just mentioned. At present I beg leave to close this letter, and to subscribe myself, &c.

LETTER III.

Harleston, at Sea, 13th March, 1812.

We were alarmed this morning upon finding the ship at day-break within a mile of Triest, and standing right in for that island. Luckily, the current which had carried us into this perilous situation was not strong, and the wind was just sufficient to favour our clearing the land and the rocks which were at no very great distance from the ship. Happier should we have been had that small breeze continued longer, or only so much of it as would have caused a circulation in the air to allay the disagreeable sensations and uneasiness produced by the sultry heat of an Indian sun.

Our prospects indeed are by no means flattering, for by some accident a number of casks of water belonging to our stock had been lost at Bencoolen, and a want of this necessary of life, even in apprehension, is certainly of all the most dreadful. Captain Walker, our good commander, is therefore very right in imposing restrictions; and the share of water to which I and my children are reduced is only three pints a day, independent of what is used at table. Such a quantity would do very well in a cold climate, but here it is barely sufficient to allay the thirst of my children, and for washing ourselves we must use salt water. A melancholy subject will therefore best accord with my present state of mind. I shall at least commence with one, by giving an account of the murder of Mr. P. or rather of the causes which led to that catastrophe, as they have been related to me.

Before I begin this disquisition I must state that the sentiments that occur in dispraise of any person connected with it are to be understood as not my own, but of those persons with whom I have become acquainted at Marlborough or whose writings I have perused since on that subject. I must add likewise, that I have been so unfortunate as to become acquainted only with persons who had espoused a different interest from that of Mr. P. and who of course interpreted all his actions solely according to their own prejudiced notions.

To give a history of that assassination would be unnecessary, as it happened not many years ago, and has been made known through different channels. It would be scarcely excusable to dwell on the causes which led to so atrocious an act; if such an inquiry were not intimately connected with the tendency of my letters, namely, that of giving, as far as lies in my power, a general account of that settlement.

Mr. P. was one of the first Residents at Bencoolen after the abolition of the Government there; for Mr. E. before him, was styled Commissioner, and was sent on purpose to that settlement to inquire into affairs, and to effect a reformation, which their previous mismanagement demanded.

From all I could collect when at Bencoolen, and subsequently from manuscripts, I firmly believe that Mr. P. was a generous and hospitable man, kind and humane to those about him, indeed much like the generality of the Honourable Company's civil servants in India; but unfortunately for himself he was, as is asserted, haughty, inconsiderate, and even despotic in his conduct.

His deportment to inferiors seems to have given almost general disgust, and the ideas which he entertained of the cowardice of the Malays made him sadly improvident and inattentive to the advice of his best friends.

It is certain, that he received a letter from Bengal three months before his assassination, informing him of what would befal him shortly, if he did not alter his behaviour towards the natives, and relinquish all rigorous measures. It is also well known, that all settlers at Marlborough felt conscious of what would happen, and that many of his friends endeavoured to set him on his guard, but to no purpose; as he would not use the most common precautions against an attack of robbers, having even put away the weapons of defence which he commonly had about him. A pair of pistols and a gun were removed from his sleeping room, where he usually had kept them, on the very day of his assassination.

Captain C. a particular friend of his, not many hours before the perpetration of the murder, refused the invitation to spend the evening with him, (in a country house,) apprehensive, as he intimated, that he should not return alive to his family, were he to stay much longer.

All this may appear singular, but considering that the whole country was in a state of open rebellion, brought on, as is pretended, by his obstinancy, and the knowledge which all of the inhabitants, himself excepted, had of the character of the natives, it is not very astonishing that they should have timed the fatal event so accurately.

The principal or rather ostensible cause for the general disaffection of the natives was the attempt which he made by strenuous measures to introduce the culture of coffee in Sumatra. It had been found by experience that this article might be produced in great perfection on that island, and one of the Pangarans expressed himself willing to give the scheme of raising it every support in his district, and undertook also to persuade the other chiefs to accede to the measure whenever it should be proposed. On this, without regularly consulting the Pangarans' Court, as is customary, Mr. P. is said immediately to have issued positive orders, that all persons in the province of Bencoolen should establish plantations of coffee, to a certain specified extent, under pain of severe punishment, if the order were not found to have been obeyed at the termination of a specified period.

The chiefs, not accustomed to any arbitrary proceedings, objected to the scheme from the first as impracticable, or at least as utterly unprofitable; they were however at length persuaded by the Pangaran mentioned before to accede and even to promise their exertions in favour of the ordinances, as Mr. P. had condescended to confer with them on the subject.

It is the nature, or rather the custom, of all Indians, not to give a positive denial to any requisition made on them, though they should be ever so much disinclined to the granting of the request; they promise therefore readily enough, particularly if pressed by a superior, preparing themselves, however, for nothing but evasion and plausible excuses. This was exactly the case at Bencoolen; at first they gave the fairest hopes and flattering reports, whilst they really were intent only on counteracting the plan and defeating Mr. P.'s measures.

Mortified at the miscarriage of his favourite scheme, and incensed at the instigators of the opposition and their adherents, he issued new mandates, which contained severe threats against all non-performers of his former orders respecting coffee plantations, and announcing at the same time, that, at the stated period a Company's servant should be sent to inspect the plantations, with power to punish the disobedient.

From this moment, the natives prepared for resistance, and resolved rather to exterminate all Europeans in Sumatra, than to submit any longer to the humiliating treatment which in this instance and many others they had received from the Commodore.

It is suspected that on this occasion some European settlers, apprehensive of what inevitably must take place, should Mr. P.'s plans be vigorously pursued, industriously intimated to the natives, that the Resident alone was to be blamed, and that they themselves had great reasons to complain. In this way, to put the mildest construction upon it, they made common cause with the malcontents, and thus directed their vengeance against the Resident alone, but saved themselves and the settlement, which otherwise would have been destroyed.

Within a short time of the period fixed for the inspection of those imaginary plantations, Mr. P. actually ordered, as is averred, a military detachment, and appointed an officer to command it, to accompany the inspector. Fortunately for them all, (for none of them would have returned alive,) the military officer refused to proceed, on the plea of the insufficient strength of his party against the numerous armed hordes, which were known to hover about and concentrate themselves in the vicinity of Marlborough.

The rebels now commenced hostilities in their usual way, by setting fire to the houses in the plantations that were at the greatest distance, proceeding gradually toward the settlement. So serious a pledge of their intentions affected Mr. P. so far, that he withdrew his injunctions with respect to the establishment of coffee plantations, and requested the malcontents to disperse, holding out to them several promises of indulgence, &c. These measures in all probability would have had the desired good effect, but most unfortunately his letters were either inadvertently or maliciously detained a whole day, and as he could not be persuaded to leave Mount Felix and retire to the settlement, a party of Malays rushed, in the middle of the night, into the room where he was asleep, cut off his head, and wounded his wife, who most heroically defended him.

Some of the assassins were killed by a small party of soldiers stationed there as an honorary guard, and by the manly exertions of a young gentleman, Mr. P.'s assistant, Mr. M. who a few days after died of a fever, which he had contracted on that dreadful occasion. The rest of the conspirators retired completely satisfied that the Commodore's head was off, and dispersed without committing any further mischief.

Thus is the story told at Marlborough, and thus did I find it confirmed in its leading particulars, in a paper which I had an opportunity of perusing, written by a gentleman who lived there when that deplorable event occurred. But as it is totally improbable that a single act of Mr. P. should have produced such inveteracy against him, I will select a few others, which, if they actually happened as it is stated, in my opinion would make a much deeper impression on the minds of rational beings, than a mandate, however strict, the good tendency of which could not possibly be mistaken.

The Pangarans and other chiefs, though by no means independent of the

English Government, still think themselves very great men; and former Governors were at some pains to cultivate their friendship, as they have much influence among the lower orders. To destroy this preponderance, particularly as he often found them somewhat difficult to manage, Mr. P. treated the chiefs (in order to lower them in the eyes of the other natives) with open disrespect, degraded them, and even laid violent hands on their persons, when their behaviour towards him did not appear so respectful, as he conceived was due to his exalted rank. The deportment of the Malays is certainly widely different from that of the same class of men in Hindoostan, where the conquering sword has left a deeper impression of superiority, than a simple contract, such as that at Bencoolen, could produce.

With a view of obtaining the phantoms which his ideas of propriety had suggested, he insisted that all natives without distinction should dismount from their horses or carriages, and pay their respects standing, whenever they should meet him on the road.

This, I understand, was the etiquette at Batavia, which was observed even by Europeans of the first distinction towards the Governor; and at present this mark of respect is shown in many parts of Hindoostan to the judges and magistrates by the natives of their respective districts.

It unfortunately happened once that a son of the Dyan, one of the greatest chiefs in Bencoolen, and particularly in the Company's interest, omitted the compliment of dismounting from his chaise when passing the Resident in the streets of Marlborough. Incensed at this insult, he ordered his body guard to drag the youngster out of his vehicle; but finding them hesitate in performing his command literally, (as they were wont to look with reverential awe on all the members of that family,) he himself applied the horsewhip on the head and shoulders of the young man, to bring him to a proper sense of his misdemeanour.

A few days after that exploit, he confined in the common prison a near relation of the same chief, for a similar offence.

Mr. P.'s friends indeed assert that there were circumstances, nor do I feel disposed to doubt their existence, which would not only excuse Mr. P.'s proceedings, but place them in such a light as to prove that he had acted with strict propriety. I can only say that I should feel rejoiced were it in my power to adduce them.

Another instance of violence, dictated by his notions of the respect due to him, was that of ordering one of the Pangarans, who appeared in European habiliments before him, to be stripped of them in public court, and afterwards to be confined in the public jail for his arrogance and misbehaviour.

It must be observed, that the man in question took at all times a delight in dressing after the English fashion, as there are some at this time who get their jackets made in Bengal, to be certain of their being fashionable. The latter are particularly such as have been in the Company's military service. It is a propensity which, in my opinion, should be particularly encouraged, for similarity in appearance is no inconsiderable step to assimilation in character.

The last act of Mr. P. of which I shall take notice, is one which would have given deeper umbrage to a more enlightened nation, but was likewise felt and severely reprobated by the Malays; it was the controul he took in the administration of justice. The Pangarans' Court, which is chiefly a judiciary one, he held, it is asserted, entirely subservient to his direction, consulted them only when he pleased, and altered their sentences according to his own discretion. This would have been in some manner excusable, had his decisions been always the wisest. But it is stated, among other charges, that he executed* a man who had only been condemned to suffer *eventually*, and who, by a delay of a few days, might have escaped; that besides, an hour after his execution, a large portion of the charges against him was found entirely false. And once, rumour says, that he burned a village and imprisoned the inhabitants, on the mere suspicion of their having been concerned in a robbery, of which they afterwards could not be satisfactorily convicted. All the reparation of the injuries they received consisted in the liberty of rebuilding their houses, and the consolatory assurance, that they should be severely punished if they ever were found guilty of such crimes as now had not been clearly proved against them.

It would be absurd to think that such a mass of folly proceeded from a mind intrinsically bad or malevolent—I have said already that he was humane and generous, nor was he destitute of understanding; and I repeat it again: but if part only be true, he certainly was not fit to be a Governor,

* He probably did it to prevent the chance of escape from punishment for a horrid deed, by paying that, in Sumatra, customary fine for murder.

though he might have made an excellent secretary to a government. All his errors may have proceeded from a scanty knowledge of mankind, and of the means required to mould them even to the best purposes. His primary objects, I think, were to establish the interests of his employers on a firmer basis; to increase the revenues and the resources of the country; and to reform the abuses and absurdities which had crept into the system of the Malay constitution and the management of the Company's own affairs. All this might readily have been attained by steady but mild perseverance, by personal example of economy on the one hand, and useful enterprise on the other, by strict justice tempered by mercy and forbearance.

But his measures seem to have been, in the very outset of an undertaking arduous even to the wise and experienced, decidedly precipitate and injudicious.

Allow me now to state a few instances of villany that have been perpetrated in that settlement. They are horrid, but I am afraid they are not unique in the annals of that country in remoter times.

During Mr. E.'s administration, it was ordered by the Supreme Council in Bengal to destroy Government papers to a considerable amount. The ceremony of burning them was also observed; but, wonderfully phœnix-like, those very papers were soon discovered in their pristine vigour and in full circulation, after having done all the mischief against the Company, and all the good in their power to their preserver.

A more complicated story of iniquity is the following. It is known that the French Admiral L. came during a war with a fleet to Bencoolen roads, landed a party in Pulo Bay, and burnt the Company's pepper warehouses of that place, which is about twelve miles south from Marlborough. The loss of pepper on that occasion amounted only to 315 tons, as Mr. T. B. the Resident reported; but Mr. E. desired, that 405 tons should be brought to account as burnt, to cover the quantities due by himself and some friends, which they ought previously to have delivered, and which in that case must have been destroyed with the rest!

A ship but lately arrived from Bengal was next captured, but not before the commander of it had landed twenty-four chests of opium in a creek where it was thought they would be secure. Against the enemy they were indeed safe; but on examination some chests were missing, and most of the remaining plundered of part of their contents.

On the amount of loss being ascertained, payment was decreed; and as the owners or commanders of the small craft had not suffered much by the enemy's fleet, and as some of them might have been concerned in the robbery, it was thought but fair that they should pay half of the whole loss, which they were soon compelled to do, to save their vessels from confiscation; I understand their share amounted to 5000 dollars. It was also very likely that the inhabitants of the nearest village to that creek had pilfered a great deal, for these rogues are very fond of opium. To make them pay was rather difficult, as they would have secreted themselves, had the demand been made openly. It was thought safest therefore to surprise them; they were surrounded by a party of soldiers, conducted by one of the civil servants, Mr. B., in the night when at one of their rejoicings, and fifty of them led to Marlborough, to be taken to account, or rather to pay for the lost opium. On examination, they were however found unable or unwilling to pay, but they were ordered to be kept to hard labour in Mr. E.'s plantation, where many are said to have died during the confinement.

It is farther said, that the underwriters in Bengal were obliged to pay for the supposed loss of opium; and that the Honourable Company's account was ultimately charged with it again.

A relation of this kind, for I have forborne all comments, appears so improbable, that I deem it necessary so far to substantiate it, as to say, that I have it from a manuscript now on board, in possession of a gentleman who has himself been involved in the transaction, and can vouch for its veracity.

In honour and justice to our Indian Government it should however be publicly known, that Mr. E. was instantly removed from his situation as soon as his iniquitous practices became known, that he was punished as far as the law would allow, and that he actually died shortly after in jail at Calcutta, to which, on the suit of Government, he had been committed.

LETTER IV.

Harleston, at Sea. March 20, 1812.

ALLOW me now to introduce you to the society at large in and about Marlborough—a group of odd characters, whose peculiarities form probably the only claim they have on our attention, as in their mode of acting and living there will appear more to reprehend than to approve, and I am afraid little or nothing to applaud.

It is said of the people there in general, that they are disunited amongst themselves, and agreed only in one point, that of making the most of strangers who may happen to come among them: how far this may be true I am unable to say.

I have felt that the people in general are not so hospitable as they are in other parts of India, which may be owing to the greater expense with which the exercise of that virtue is attended here. It is, however, remarked by all strangers that have lately visited this settlement.

There are but few Europeans in the settlement besides those in the Honourable Company's civil and military service: and those are adventurers, who, for any thing that is known, may have dropped from the clouds; or they are runaways from ships, mostly from menial situations; all of whom by various means (some by industry, or even by holding situations under Government, others by successful blundering in trade) have amassed wealth, and consequently acquired consideration. They are all in their own estimation gentlemen of consequence, and live in hopes (as money in their opinion is the only qualification in England requisite for a great man) "to spend some jolly days with the Prince Regent, the Duke of York, and such other good company!" Their occupations chiefly consist in trading to the interior of Sumatra, and to the eastern islands, which they hitherto have supplied with opium, and with English and India goods, which were of late much wanted by the Dutch. It is to be wished that there were a greater number of the latter description of men on this island, as by nobody sooner than by them, would the resources of the country be discovered, provided a reasonable latitude and support were given them in trading, manufacturing, and labouring, as also proper restraint laid on their behaviour towards the natives.

There were formerly a great number of Germans here, mostly artificers, of whom but one is alive, a pensioner on the charity of Government. I have not been able to ascertain in what way they were employed.

Next to them come the gentlemen of colour, from yellow to jet black—the descendants of Jews and Christians of all nations, by Malay or Bengal women: some of them, as has been observed before, are covenanted servants of the Honourable Company; others are monthly writers in the offices at Marlborough and the outstations. All are gentlemen of vast consideration, particularly when basking in the sunshine of residential favour. By speaking so slightly of the men of colour here, I beg you will not suspect me of an antipathy against the whole race. By no means, I know some that bear an excellent character, and I believe even that those who have enjoyed a liberal education are in general greater ornaments of society than the generality of men of similar advantages.

All are traders here, even the greatest among them will indulge himself so far as to buy a plantation, when it can be knocked down to him at a little less than half its value. Many of them would not assist a stranger with the least advice, nor would they put him on his guard against the wiles of the traders; nay, they would see him imposed upon under their eyes, and cheated in their houses! They beg leave "to decline all interference" when their opinion is requested—and they experience the same good turn from their neighbours on similar occasions.

The Chinese inhabit a part of the settlement separated from the rest of the inhabitants, which is called the China Bazar. They have a magistrate of their own, who is styled the China Captain, in general the wealthiest and most respectable of the tribe, as much consequence is attached to the situation. The Chinese, as a nation, are much like the Jews, always and every where the same: it is needless, therefore, to take any further notice of them here, than to say that ten or twenty thousand more would soon give another face to the country.

Their number at present does not amount to one thousand, I believe.

There are a great number of Bengalese settled here, as handicraftsmen and servants. All tailors and washermen at Marlborough are of this description. They are very extravagant in their charges, and the servants of this class are exceedingly knavish. To make a common jacket the tailor charges four dollars; and for 100 pieces of linen, a washerman demands six dollars. The liberal minded inhabitants at Marlborough support them even in these extravagant demands; and appear astonished, when strangers by exciting competition (as we do) reduce the price to half of the original demand. The Bengalese here are mostly, if not all, Mussulmen, and intermarry with the Malays; and soon lose themselves so far, that their progeny look, act, and speak like other Malays; their numbers, therefore, remain inconsiderable, as they always depend upon new supplies from Bengal.

The slaves claim our attention in the next instance. The Company have about 800 of them, and a greater number live dispersed among the settlers. Those of the latter are mostly of Malay extraction; and the former in the same proportion Negroes. They all look stout and hardy, are well clothed, and seemingly well fed. They are always frolicksome, singing at work, as well as after it is over; when they often amuse themselves with a dance to the strains of an unharmonious fiddle, or to that of their better-toned throats. The younger women show themselves in this exercise amazingly nimble, and trip a reel like the best taught Miss at a country boarding school.

It is said their numbers are always decreasing; a circumstance which must be owing entirely to their profligate way of living, for their treatment is very mild, so much so that most of them, particularly the elder, have refused their freedom when it was offered them for a very trifling consideration; and it is thought it would not be accepted by them on any condition.

Some of the younger are emancipated at times by their parents and relations, at the fixed rate of forty dollars for a child under ten years of age, and sixty dollars for a female, and eighty for a male slave above that age.

The few puny looking children among a number of stout wenches, I have observed, belong in common to the ugliest and oldest of these women.

The good treatment received by the slaves in private families makes them much attached to their masters and to their children. I know some that have followed them all over the world, and proved themselves most attentive and useful servants.

I cannot but mention here an observation which I have often heard made, that half-cast Europeans and the Indians themselves are much better masters to their slaves and servants than Europeans: they are more attentive to their wants and comforts, which indeed are much the same as their own; they treat them, if not with familiarity, at least with greater placidity and indulgence; and in return are better served, and get servants who will adhere to them in all vicissitudes of life; whereas Europeans always complain of the rascality and ingratitude of all their Indian servants and followers, and are forsaken by them and robbed as soon as it suits their convenience.

The slaves of the Honourable Company are employed in all public works, about their warehouses, in public buildings; and the women particularly in carrying pepper and other heavy loads; they are also very handy to all individuals in any way connected with the service of Government.

A class of men yet to be mentioned are the convicts. Great numbers of them were formerly sent from Madras and Bengal; and most of them were expatriated for life. At present the greater number under such sentence at both Presidencies are transported to the Prince of Wales's Island. Here they have proved themselves very useful and faithful subjects. They have even been employed in times of emergency as soldiers, and have acquitted themselves manfully! It was one of the complaints or grievances urged against Mr. Parr, that he disbanded a corps of convicts, after they had for a length of time served as Sepoys, and crushed in a distant province a rebellion among the Malays, not without much bloodshed and hard service on their part; and, in fact, after they had conciliated the good will and confidence of all, by their services and attachment: yet were they sent back to their work as other convicts!

A description of men I believe quite peculiar to Sumatra are the bondsmen or debtors. They consist of all such natives as are indebted to the richer classes, and have no other means of satisfying their creditors than personal servitude. Upon these the European and other settlers depend as workmen in their plantations, as the price of labour is extravagantly high in Bencoolen, at all events dearer than the planters can afford or choose to pay for it. I cannot say how the agreement is made in such a case, or how the labour is rated, but should imagine the proceedings are occasionally arbitrary, and sometimes unjust: I approve in some measure of the plan; it is at least a thousand times, and for a thousand reasons, better than that of shutting a man up for years in a horrid jail. The greatest objection I have against it, is the abuse that can be made of it, particularly when entirely left to the discretion of an individual; but to the same objection all other plans are in some way liable, and it matters very little if a man is ill used by the laws of his country or by individuals.

The debtors thus working receive three fanams (six pence) per diem for their subsistence.

The natives of Sumatra may be divided into the aborigines, or the prior inhabitants of the island, and the Malays. The former occupy the centre parts of the isle among its high ridges of mountains, and are Gentiles. In the northern parts they are called Batties, and in the southern Lampoons, besides a number of smaller tribes. The Batties are described as very untractable; but the Lampoons are mentioned with more complacency, particularly their women, who are said to be very handsome and well behaved.

The Batties are said to be on many accounts the most remarkable of all the natives of Sumatra, and of which they seem to be the aborigines. They worship three gods and four devils, and have a heaven for the good and a frying pan or a hell for the bad. Their language is different from all the rest.

They eat the flesh of all animals, the human not excepted. The plea that they only feast on that of their enemies or of culprits is too trivial to be admitted in excuse or palliation.

Double adultery is punished with death, but murder *at most* only with slavery; for if the murderer can be at the expense of feasting with the friends or relations of the slain, no further notice is taken of the crime.

Unnatural crimes are punished in the severest way by drowning the culprits.

They use match-locks in their wars, which are made in their own country.

All their agriculture consists in the propagation of the benjamin tree; and where this will not grow, in the cultivation of their low and high lands with rice and some fruit-trees.

In a manuscript which I have seen, the Lampoons are represented as savages, even without the least notion of a Supreme Being, but at the same time very much afraid of evil spirits, whom they consequently and exclusively adore. They are said to be very superstitious, and to believe in an existence after death, or rather in a kind of metempsychosis; whence they worship such animals as frequent their houses, or are seen after the burial of their relations near their graves, as they suppose the souls of their friends have animated those animals, and have become tutelary saints to their families.

The greatest reward for a well spent life is to be allowed to return in the human form. They give, occasionally, feasts to the souls of their departed.

relations and friends, and of course feast afterwards themselves on the provisions remaining. They abstain from eating certain vegetables, or other food, not as the Hindoos, from any religious motive, but in consequence of vows they have made individually on certain occasions, or that have been made by any one of their forefathers for the whole family collectively: they religiously abide by them under the idea, that such a substance has been cursed.

They are very courteous and hospitable to strangers, and on such occasions bring all their young women to dance and sing before them in their public houses; but woe to him who should take any improper liberties with them.

They are jealous of their wives, whom they buy from their parents. Should the whole price be paid down by the husband, all relationship between the wife and her parents and other relatives is totally dissolved: she does indeed no longer belong to the family; and should her husband die, she becomes the property of his brother, who at all events must take care of her. It is therefore very often the case, by mutual consent, that a small sum is left unpaid, in order that the *tie* of relationship may not *be cut*, as the expression signifies.

They take great care, in every respect, of their young daughters; but should it happen that a *faux pas* notwithstanding has been committed, she has only to mention the gallant, and she is sent to his house at a reduced price. Strange it is, that she could not be returned, should she have fathered the child on, and be sent to, a man who never had the least connexion with her!

They are very fond of dancing and singing, and their music is said to be very harmonious.

Murder can be expiated by a sum of money, which is the law in all parts of Sumatra. If the culprit cannot pay, nor the chief of his village or clan for him, he suffers death inevitably. The usual mode of execution is by throwing spears at him until he expires.

There are certain days and occasions when a man cannot be dunned for debts, except for some of a particular nature (for example that for the price of a wife); as days of public festivals and rejoicings, after the return from a journey before he has washed himself and taken victuals, in his sleeping room, or when walking on the high road, &c.

The Malays, properly so called, are the natives that inhabit the coast to a certain extent inland. These are Mahometans, or a sect of that religion, for among the Mussulmen in India they would hardly be acknowledged as truly faithful.

The character they bear among Europeans is very bad. They are described as a dastardly, treacherous, piratical horde of savages, in the best of whom, no faith nor confidence can be placed. A long intercourse however with them on Sumatra, as well as at other places, should have modified or rather rectified this general opinion of their manners and natural propensities, and more attention to the "*audietur altera pars*" should also have been paid. A merchant or a captain of a ship, who meets with cruel treatment at a place, vociforates his complaints and sufferings wherever he goes, but carefully avoids mentioning the causes which subjected him to that ill treatment. He forgets to mention that he seduced the wife of the man who attempted to creese (stab) him; or that he fired at and killed some half-starved wretches, whom he observed pilfering some handfuls of rice, and in consequence he cannot appear in public without danger; or that he insulted or beat a man of respectability among the so called savages; or that he defrauded the customs and was found out, which subjected him to a whipping, which in any other, even of the same nation, would probably have been punished with death. These are all things that have actually happened, and to some of my acquaintance.

In their appearance they resemble the Chinese so much, that I have often taken one for another, particularly their women and children.

They are remarkably well limbed, and have the appearance of strength and sturdiness. Many of the women are exceedingly fair, and notwithstanding the flatness of their faces and the smallness of their eyes, have something very soft and pleasing in their countenances.

Their hair is lank and black, which the women allow to fly loose for a moment, when they mean to give an amorous invitation.

Their dress is very different from that of any other Indian nation. Round the head the men tie in common nothing but a handkerchief, or a fine piece of blue striped cloth, wrapped up somewhat like a turban; on the body they wear a loose kind of shirt of a blue colour; and the richer sort, over this, a garment much like a dressing gown, of white cotton cloth. In their houses they wrap a large piece of cloth round them, in which they are imitated by such settlers as live in the out stations.

The favourite colour of the Malays is blue; and blue and white, and red striped Indian cotton cloths and chintzes are also much admired. The Rajahs and Chiefs are said to be very splendid in their dresses; those I saw were accoutred quite in the European style, and were such as had been or still continued in the Honourable Company's military service. They seem on the whole not to have such an aversion to the European manners and dress as the natives of Western India. It was even thought necessary by Mr. Parr to restrain them from it by very severe means. In Hindoostan I have seen but one young man of rank who dressed in an European uniform and cocked hat: it was the son Salabad Khān, one of the greatest generals of the Nizam, who often paraded in this way to the scandal of all the *faithful* at General Close's, in the last Mahratta campaign.

By the bye, it always struck me as very curious, that the Indians should not have so great an aversion to a cocked hat as they undeniably have to one of the common round kind.

The richer classes among the lower orders, as merchants, affect a plainness in dress which borders too much on meanness.

The Malays are very fond both of smoking and chewing tobacco: the latter they do in the most disgusting way; as they have always a quid of half an inch sticking out of their dirty muzzles. Their manner of smoking is also peculiar. They roll a little tobacco in a small piece of plantain leaf, or in that of any reed, and after it is lighted, take only a few whifs, and throw the rest away.

Their teeth are black and altogether very disgusting to behold. Some, by way of ornament, get holes bored through them, which they fill up with gold. Others, but not at Marlborough, file their fore teeth into sharp points.

Their principal and favourite diversions consist in cock-fighting, games of hazard, and in exhilarating themselves with opium, which however often amounts to intoxication. These vices lead to each other, and both to the commission of the greatest crimes. It is therefore not very politic to encourage these propensities by license, which, though probably the most productive branch of revenue for the time being, must be the most cancrous and self-destructive in its effects.

The Malays are the most determinate gamblers in the world: they will hazard every thing in their possession on a battle in which a favourite cock is engaged, and as a last stake even their families and themselves. In the choice of their heroes they are very whimsical, as they depend mostly on the lucky marks of a cock, and on the number and colour of the scales on his legs, the colour of his plumage, &c. Hence it often happens that Europeans, who frequently indulge themselves with the same amusement, win their money, as they judge by more substantial diagnostics. The bets are from one to 100 dollars, which to prevent disputes are paid, before the commencement of the battle, to the renter of the farm who superintends all matches, and sees that every thing is conducted fairly and honourably. The Chinese seem to be equally fond of this cruel diversion; and indeed the regular established cockpit is in their Bazar, where, as on an exchange, every evening about four o'clock all cock-fighters and amateurs assemble.

The spurs used here are, like those in vogue in Western India, lancets or knives of different shapes, all as sharp as art and the greatest attention can make them; a battle therefore is often as soon over as it is begun.

Another vice of which the Malays are accused is their *indolence;* but this in my opinion is much overrated.

In our colder climes it is as much as a labouring man can do to procure a livelihood by his work for himself and family. Far otherwise is it in that happy country where the requisites for the support and even the enjoyment of life are fewer, and most of them freely offered by bounteous nature.

The wife of a Malay, the drudge of the family, can alone, by fishing or other little work, procure rice for them all. Vegetables and spices of the most exquisite kind grow wild about their habitations; the poultry yard furnishes them with fowls for a treat, and the wilderness with game; and of course the lord of the house may lull and enjoy himself in indolent supineness, and hazard even the produce of his pepper plantation at the gambling house, without material injury (should he lose all) to his family concerns.

If one wife should not be able to manage the affairs of his household, a second and a third may easily be had, who can work and bring forth sons and daughters; the latter of which are an excellent article of speculation, and are on this account in every respect well treated.

Persons who have long sojourned among the Malays grant that they can form attachments to strangers, and that they are capable of friendship, which is more than can be allowed to the Western Indians.

The Malays are polite to strangers, but very independent in principle, and impatient of haughty controul; and withal very superstitious.

Though revengeful to the last degree when the least open attempt on their brows is made, they are said (at least many of them) to wink at profitable intercourses of their wives, provided always, that every thing is conducted with secrecy and apparent decency! The creese, or oftener poison under the cloak of friendship, is otherwise administered without hesitation or the least remorse.

Private injuries are never forgiven, and the revenging of them is bequeathed by the father to the son as a dying request.

I have observed that the inhabitants of all ranks at Bencoolen, the Resident perhaps excepted, live in apparent ease and confidence. I know many live in the country among the Malays without the least apprehension, nor is there an instance on record, I believe, of an assassination of any, but such as have amply provoked it.

The Malays are thought by some warlike, by others cowardly. To judge from their propensity to assassinate and poison, and from the excitements they require before an engagement, which consists in their taking opium to intoxication, they certainly cannot possess much natural courage, though for acts of bravery they have been much esteemed by the Dutch in their former Eastern establishments.

There is indeed much contradiction in the character of the Malays, but much more in the opinions that have been formed of it by strangers.

I should not be afraid to spend a few years among them, and flatter myself even with the prospect of advantages which would be derived by all parties.

LETTER V.

Harleston, at Sea, March 30, 1812.

WHAT would I not give for another view of Sumatra, were it only to aid my recollection of those things of which I wish to give you an account, and of the variegated scenes with which it abounds, and the singular productions of nature.

As it is, I can scarcely pretend to any thing else than an enumeration, which however may be of use, as the local knowledge of the existence of a gold mine, though the ore, or its matrix, should remain doubtful.

On this principle, I shall attempt to touch on such subjects of natural history as have forced themselves on my observation, and leave a minuter account of them to others better informed than myself.

Sumatra is called *Andelo* by the inhabitants of the island. It is on the whole populous and fertile, though swamps and wildernesses are not wanting.

The chain of hills which runs through the island divides it nearly into two equal parts, of which neither is more than sixty miles broad.

The natives divide the island into three parts. The first, or southern, commences from the Straits of Sunda, and comprises the districts of Palambang, Lampong, and Bencoolen. The principal product of this division is pepper. It is called by the natives Ballumang, or Kampang.

The second division commences on the east coast of this island at the frontiers of the Palambang empire, and extends to the river Seak, on the west coast from Majatta to the river Sinkol, and comprises the kingdoms Jambe, Andraghiri, Manningeobo, and Indrapūra. This division is rich in pepper, rice, gold, benjamin, camphire, cocoanuts, and cotton. There are also some silver mines.

The third and most northern part of this island is called Balla, and contains the kingdoms of Achīm and its subordinate states, Peder, Pacem, and Dely.

The coast of Sumatra, viewed from the sea, has an aspect rich and beautiful beyond description. Ranges of high mountains, at a distance behind each other, whose summits appearing involved in clouds and smoke, and their sides invested with the densest verdure, give the whole a most majestic appearance. A waving country rising at the bottom of the mountains, interspersed with hillocks, and clad with a continued forest of palm trees, until close to the sea beach, adds to the magnificence of the scene. To compare the whole to a rich Persian carpet, to a fanciful landscape drawing, pictured in even the liveliest colours, would be detraction from what it is in reality.

The ranges of mountains begin in this part of the country at the distance of about twenty miles from the sea, when they rise rather abruptly to a considerable height: on other parts of the coast they draw nearer the ocean.

Some raise their cloud-capt heads singly above the rest, as the famous Sugar-loaf, which overtops most of its neighbours in the nearest range. Three ridges of these mountains may be distinctly observed, of which the farthest off is of course the highest. They do not run in straight lines at the top, neither are they much broken or interrupted by pointed or rugged prominences, and hence they are plainly neither of the primary granitic order of mountains, nor of the later formations.

The Sugar-loaf, which is one of the highest hills in Bencoolen, and advances in front of the rest, is, in my opinion, about 4000 feet above the level of the sea; it is of great use to the mariner in steering his course into the Bay of Bencoolen. It is about twenty miles in a northerly direction from Marlborough; I mean in a straight line, for as the roads wind it is above twenty-eight, according to Dr. Lumsdaine's accounts.

I understand that a few years ago a friend of mine, Captain Daldorf, in the Danish service, ascended it in spite of all the reports of dangers the settlers could invent: I only hope that his premature death has not deprived the world of an account of the excursion which few would be better able to give, and none with more accuracy. He had a general knowledge of all the departments of natural history, and a profound one of the living creation.

About sixteen miles, in a more easterly direction from Marlborough, is a volcano, which frequently emits flame, and is almost constantly smoking. During the short time of our stay we witnessed an eruption, though by no means a dreadful one. The weather, before and after it, was very unsteady and turbulent: thunder, rain, and storms appeared at a time when but little expected; even a few smart shocks of an earthquake were felt, which however alarmed none but our female passengers, who evinced much timidity on the occasion.

The inhabitants of Bencoolen are not afraid of them, as they never have experienced any harm from those their frequent visitors. Lightning they look upon as the most terrible of the two phenomena.

Besides this volcano, which is but of minor consideration, there are three others in this island, which throw out much sulphur and lava. The highest lies a day's journey east from Priamang, and the other two near Postamang and Tegabla Cottas.

The low country in this part of the island is undulating and gradually rising from the sea-shore towards the mountains. On closer examination, we find the swelling high grounds intersected by narrow vallies, formed by torrents that poured down from the mountains during their long and heavy monsoon rains, which in those climates have not only the appearance, but are really powerful rivers, that sweep every thing before them which opposes their career.

On the coast of Orissa I have seen tigers and whole herds of black cattle carried along by what are called freshes, and trees of immense size.

There is in most, if not in all these vallies, abundance of water, either in pools or small rivulets, even in the driest season: all which might be rendered useful, were the country better cultivated. Their dependance at present is on the rains, which seldom fail to irrigate the country in nightly showers in all seasons.

There are no rivers of any consequence on this, the western coast of Sumatra. In the provinces north of Bencoolen, from Tappanouly to Padang, are a good number of such as require ferries or boats to cross, and which even admit small craft; but to the southward of Marlborough they are, with the exception of some trifling ones, almost entirely wanting. It is not unlikely that here the waters from the mountains take an easterly direction, and form the large river that disembogues itself near Palambang.

Swampy and marshy grounds abound in this country so as to render it unhealthy both to natives and strangers. There is a very extensive one about twelve miles south of Marlborough, at a place where the Company have pepper warehouses and an establishment of servants, who at all times suffer much from sickness. The place is called S———, and is near the landing-place of Pulo Bay. North of Marlborough, is old Bencoolen, similarly situated, from which the whole country has derived the character of its great unhealthiness.

The climate in general seems to be very mild and salubrious, and the changes in its temperature are not so great and sudden as in other parts of India. The heat of the day is allayed by a breeze from the sea, which regularly sets in about nine o'clock in the morning and continues until five in the evening, when it slackens, but is soon succeeded by the land wind, which, contrary to what is experienced on the other side of India, is also very cool and pleasant. To account for this difference we must observe, that here this wind comes from high ranges of mountains which are constantly moistened by ever dripping clouds; whereas in western India this wind is only the forerunner of rain, and carries along with it the caloric which has been disengaged in the formation or condensation of the gaseous substances into liquids, as I have hinted in an Essay on the Land Winds of the Coast of Coromandel. *

The heat in the day-time is, however, here very great in the sun, and after nine o'clock nobody can with impunity expose himself by walking about in the place. An umbrella is then but a poor defence against the power of his serene majesty! It is only in well covered houses where men can exist; but there it can be done even with comfort, particularly in such parts as are exposed to the sea breeze.

We were at Bencoolen from the lattĕr end of January to the beginning of March, during which period the thermometer seldom exceeded 84° in the day, and never fell at any time below 78°; and as it is known that the temperature of the air is nearly the same throughout the year, the medium is probably nearly the same as at Madras, between 81° and 82°, but more equally divided.

The weather in January was rainy and boisterous, which I ascribe to the convulsive efforts of nature before mentioned. The inhabitants called it the procrastinated breaking up of the monsoon rains. The morning and the early part of the day were in common clear and serene; but about noon cloulds began to gather all over the eastern horizon, with distant murmuring thunder, which towards evening increased, and in the night broke out into violent torrents of rain accompanied by the loudest and alarming claps of thunder and vivid lightning.

There are in Bencoolen, as in other tropical regions, two seasons for periodical rain. The first in the year sets in with the change of the wind to

* Published without my knowledge in the Transactions of the Medical Society of London, Vol. I. Part I. p. 189. Dr. Roxburgh's name is prefixed to the paper instead of mine by mistake.

the southward, about the month of March, and lasts till August. The first months of this reign are turbulent and rainy until May, in which the weather becomes settled again. This is what we should call, on the coast of Coromandel, the little monsoon. In September the principal monsoon rains begin, and last with little intermission to the beginning of January. During this time the north-west wind prevails, which is always more stormy and boisterous than the former.

The soil about Bencoolen is generally a fine red vegetable mould, and such it is said to be all over this country, only richer and more productive in the more inland parts of the island. The sample I brought with me was indifferently taken in a plantation about three miles from Marlborough, and from a garden in that place, and will be admitted to be of the best kind, in which, with a due proportion of moisture, any thing will grow in the greatest luxuriance. Indeed, it cannot be otherwise where abundance of rain produces a constant succession of vegetation; which by the excessive heat of the sun is almost as quickly destroyed and decomposed, and thus formed into an increasing stratum of the richest mould. I must say that I have not beheld the like in India, and few have seen more of that country than myself. The richest soil on the coast and in Bengal is that which is called black cotton soil, which is also a vegetable earth, but with too great an admixture of calc tuff, which indeed at no great depth forms the principal sub-stratum.

Some tracts indeed in Bengal and the coast, particularly such as for the greatest part of the year are under water, and are cultivated with rice (paddy) have a fine black vegetable mould, but it is so situated that it could not produce any thing else than a crop of the above mentioned grain; whereas in Bencoolen even that of the higher parts of their swelling grounds is much of the same discription, and grain and plants, and trees of all kinds would grow in it with luxuriance. At present it produces nothing but a coarse lank grass of little or no value.

There are few stones lying dispersed about the country; those I have seen were fragments of basalt of a black colour, which in their decomposition become red, and probably give that tinge to the soil.

The water, as in most other mountainous countries, is sweet and good in wells and rivulets, and in abundance. In pools it is plain that it must be far from salubrious, as it is absolutely pernicious after it is decomposed and mixed with atmospheric air. The quickness of vegetation, which improves the soil, renders the standing water in the same degree pernicious. All extractive particles of plants that have either perished in it, or are carried thence by the rain water, must impart qualities destructive to animal life, either by their very substance, or their decomposition.

The air in general is light and wholesome at a certain height *above* the *surface* of the ground, and where its circulation is not obstructed by underwood or the numerous thick forests of trees, which the inhabitants of these regions delight in having round their habitations. This strikes me as one of the principal causes that Marlborough is not so healthy as it might be considering its elevated situation, exposed to a fine never failing sea breeze. Of late years, I understand, a very great deal of wood has been cut down in and about the town; but there is yet so much left as to give it more the appearance of a large plantation, in which the proprietors have built themselves comfortable garden houses, than that of a fort and town.

There are a great number of garden houses within a few miles of the settlement, which are mostly erected on high commanding spots, and they are consequently very airy and healthy. Some of them, I believe three, and the best and largest, have been built by former Governors, at the expense of course of the Honourable Company. Mount Felix is one of them, the principal country seat of the Residents here, and that in which Mr. Parr was murdered. It is a very commodious large building, from which there is a beautiful prospect over all the country round, and the bays of Bencoolen and Pulo. It is at present quite abandoned. Mount Edgecombe is another chateau of the same kind, and said to be more elegant than the former.

Near the country seats of individuals large spice plantations have been established, which are now a source of amusement as well as of speculation to their sanguine proprietors.

Every house almost in the settlement has an orchard and a garden; in the former they however solely attend to the fruit-trees of the country; and in the latter to their spice plants more than to the raising of flowers and vegetables, for which they say the climate is too hot and labour too dear. The Chinese, who must be well paid for their trouble, are their gardeners. It may become matter of speculation, should the settlement ever become larger, or should others near it spring up, to establish gardens at the foot of the inland mountains, or at some considerable ascent among them, for the production of European vegetables, as potatoes, cabbage, &c. which certainly would grow as well there as they do in similar situations on the Island of Java.

The conveyances which the inhabitants use to carry themselves to their plantations and about the place are single horse chaises (buggies) and palankeens on a low wheel carriage, drawn by a single horse, for the Malays have not yet condescended to carry them on their shoulders, as is the custom in India.

The disorders which prevail here, and are reckoned most pernicious, are fevers contracted by exposure to the sun, and by residence in marshy places.

The former are of the remittent bilious kind, which soon terminate in typhus; and the latter are intermittents owing to obstructions in the abdominal viscera, of which an indurated or greatly enlarged spleen is frequently the consequence.

A more than liberal use of calomel is the remedy chiefly, if not entirely, depended upon by the surgeons in both cases; and that they frequently succeed is pretty plain from the great partiality shown to it, and from the extravagant praises bestowed upon it by the inhabitants of Bencoolen.

In the case of the (indurated) spleen, the native Malay physicians are more expert, were one to believe the assertions of the inhabitants of Marlborough, who are by no means averse from taking their advice in preference to their own medical men. Simples and charms are the remedies on which the Malays depend.

The medical establishment at Fort Marlborough consists of three assistant surgeons, of which the senior has the superintendance. The gentleman who is at present in this situation has amassed in fifteen years a very ample fortune, on which he will retire as soon as he is promoted. Thus the service loses men, owing to the regulations by which only juniors can hold situations of emolument (I might add of *trust* also), who if employed in active, unprofitable military service whilst young, would have proved the ornaments of their profession, and of the greatest moment to the public by their acquired skill in situations of greater importance, when called by public emergency into action.

This will be also the case on our (the Madras) establishment. Young men of parts or interest will get civil or other lucrative or easy situations, in which, if prudent, they will endeavour to get a competency to retire from the service, to avoid the drudgery of a military life, which they must enter after they are promoted.

Those only will remain whose want of providence or skill has left them but negative acquisitions.

LETTER VI.

Harleston, at Sea, April 7, 1812.

The only inducement the Honourable East India Company could have to accept the supreme rule over the Princes of Sumatra, clogged as it was with stipulations, must have been the exclusive trade in pepper on the lowest terms at which it could be procured, which was offered them as a recompence for the trouble and expense of a Government.

In those times (upwards of 100 years ago*) it was well worth accepting, when India and its productions were so little known, and so highly esteemed in Europe, and when particularly pepper was an article of the first importance.

At present, perhaps, a country would not be occupied which held out no advantage except one article of trade, and which had no revenues or resources adequate to support great establishments; unless it should happen that, by doing so, another power could be kept out of its possession. Pepper in particular must be of little consideration to the Honourable Company now, as it might be obtained in any quantity from their Malabar provinces.

It is well known to you that pepper is the berry of a large vine, which in appearance and in every respect resembles that which produces the betel leaf, so much used by the inhabitants of Madras. It is indeed of the same genus; this the piper betel, and the former the piper nigrum of Linneus.

The Malays in Sumatra cultivate the pepper vine in plantations regularly laid out, in which it is planted at the distance of five cubits in every direction. To support the feeble vine, a large faggot, or green stick of mutchy wood (erythrina corallodendron), is put in the ground along with it, which

* In the year 1680, deputations from Atcheem and Bencoolen arrived at Madras, with an invitation from the Princes of Sumatra to protect and govern them.

soon takes root and strikes out branches before the vine comes to any size. Other reasons, besides its quick growth, for preferring this tree as a supporter, are, its spongy and prickly bark, and its thin foliage, when it has any at all; for during a long time in the course of a year it is quite naked of leaves; the former aids the creeper in its ascent, and the latter admits the parasite to bask in the sun and to expand.

The pepper grows most luxuriantly in places where it has much moisture; and hence the valleys with which Sumatra abounds are found to be the most favourable situations for their pepper gardens. Like most other vegetable productions in hot climes, it requires after the first planting but little trouble or attention: in fact, the cultivator has almost nothing else to do than to collect the produce in the proper season.

When the natives make a pepper plantation, they first cut down the wood that grows on the spot, then plough the ground and sow rice in it; among which they afterwards plant the layers.

On the Malabar coast the pepper vine is often raised from seed, and I know a gentleman possessing extensive plantations who gives the preference decidedly to this mode of propagation. In Sumatra, on the contrary, it is uniformly raised from layers and cuttings, though the other method is equally understood. Their reason for preferring this plan is seemingly very substantial, and would do credit to people less blamed for indolence than the Malays. The vine raised from the seed, they say, although it produces fourteen years (which is double the time reckoned upon that propagated in the other way), yet it yields smaller crops, and berries of less size and inferior quality: the latter circumstance alone should be of sufficient weight to urge the adoption of the other method.

The usual time of putting the layers and cuttings into the ground is in the beginning of the greater monsoon, in September. The plant is afterwards left to its fate for twelve or eighteen months, when it is buried with all its branches in such a way, that only a small arch of the stem remains above ground. From this arch new shoots soon sprout out, three or four of which are allowed to climb up the tree, and expected to produce flowers and fruit in a year after this operation.

It is reasonable to suppose that, by the practice just mentioned, the strength and vigour of the plant by the multiplication of its organs of nourishment, the roots, are so much increased that it can not only produce large crops of flowers, but bring the fruit also to its greatest perfection. To me it proves farther that the omission of this manipulation in the Company's plantations at Samulcotta, in the northern Circars, which were established by Dr. Roxburgh, was the cause of our failure. The plants that were raised from cuttings seemed indeed to thrive well, and soon produced blossoms; but such as had male flowers only. To account for this circumstance we supposed that the hermaphrodite plant had been withheld by the people who sent us cuttings from their hills, where pepper is cultivated to a small extent, when, in fact, we had starved our plants into celibacy. It seemed, at first, matter of astonishment to the Malays, when I mentioned pepper plantations that had produced no other than male flowers; but as they very quickly and shrewdly guessed the cause, I believe the same must have occurred to them occasionally.

There are two seasons in the year in which this vine produces fruit, as is the case with most others in India. The flowers of the principal crop appear in September at the time of the first monsoon rains. They consist in a cylindrical string of a little more than a line in thickness, densely covered with small flowers, which can only with difficulty be analized by the naked eye of ordinary acuteness. In the latter end of December the berries begin to ripen, and are gathered during January, as they get to maturity. It is said that a plantation of pepper in these months presents a most beautiful sight, rich beyond comparison with any in the vegetable world. The whole part which covers all parts of the tree, is decked with bunches of green, white, and red berries, resting on the shining deep green of its foliage, must, I can imagine, produce a pleasing, if not a grand, effect on the eye.

The finest berries in the second state towards maturity are selected for the purpose of making white pepper, which not long ago was supposed to be the fruit of a different plant. The process is very simple, and consists in steeping those berries for three or four days in running water, and then drying them well in the sun.

A gentleman of my acquaintance, who has long resided in Bencoolen, chiefly engaged in the pepper trade, maintains that even black pepper may be converted into white by sufficient steeping in running fresh water.—*Relata refero.*

The flowers of the second crop appear in March and April, with the rains of the little monsoon; and the fruit ripens and is gathered about July and August; and it is probably owing to the want of moisture that this is so much inferior to the former, and more scanty.

One thousand vines are reckoned to produce about 10$\frac{1}{7}$ cwt. of pepper in the course of a year, and consequently each vine yields about 1$\frac{1}{8}$ lb. value 4d. to the cultivator, at the rate of three dollars for each cwt. for which they must sell it to the Company.

The ryots in Bengal and in most other parts of India would think themselves most amply rewarded were they able to earn with their helpmates thirty-two dollars a year; but such is the difference in the price of labour, that here it is looked upon so inadequate a sum for the article delivered, that an increase of 100 per cwt. cannot prevail upon the Malays to increase their exertions in the least.

To lessen the weight of an expensive establishment by the increase of the quantity of pepper, it was proposed to offer an advance on the price of all pepper produced in plantations, to the establishment of which the people could not be obliged, and which were distinguished by the name of Free Gardens, and their produce rated at six dollars per cwt.; a sufficient encouragement it was thought to double in a short time the yearly quantity. The accounts of the state and number of the free gardens were also very promising on paper; but, as usual, experience has not satisfied the sanguine expectations of the projectors, as the real produce of the whole establishment still remains about 700 tons yearly, whilst the nominal is 1000 as before.

The free gardens were chiefly to have been established in the province of Bencoolen, by the vicinity of which to Marlborough the expenses of carriage to the warehouses would have been considerably less than from any of the out-stations.

It is difficult to say with certainty where the fault lies, whether in the indolence of the natives, or in the mismanagement of the whole affair: this much is true however, that not many years ago the Americans might have got as much pepper as they wanted in Sumatra at the rate of six dollars per hundred weight.

It would be very difficult to estimate the real price at which the East India Company get the pepper at the period of its being shipped for Europe; but it appears they pay much dearer for it than the Americans, who have no establishment of their own on Sumatra; and the Dutch, who had a factory on the east coast—Palambang; and another on this—Padang.

In former times the pepper Residents advanced money, on account of the

Company, for pepper to the natives, and collected the produce, debiting all the expenses as they occurred: all of which we may suppose was done in the most economical way; for besides a liberal pay and allowances, they were in situations most favourable for private trade. Mr. Ewer, however, found out a way which reduced the expenses, and consequently the price of pepper, still lower, by making contracts with the Residents themselves, leaving them to settle in the best manner they could with the natives *, and for the contingent expenses. Accordingly they deliver the pepper from eight to fourteen dollars per cwt. as their contracts may be, which is inclusive of all charges, salary not excepted. The only allowance they have is for keeping up a guard of native soldiers for the defence of the warehouses, &c. It has been observed in another place that they were allowed to trade in all other articles on their own account, and as they are the representatives of Government, and have the same influence and power in the provinces in which they preside as the political Chief has at Marlborough, it is possible they are not very backward in exercising or enforcing what they think their exclusive right, the monopoly of every thing valuable which the country produces.

It is but fair that men should be well rewarded who devote the whole or the best part of their lives to the service of the Honourable Company, far from their native country, and in a region where they are deprived of the greatest comforts of life: but if it should happen that the business in which they are employed could be done twice as much better without them, which I conceive to be the case here, it then becomes matter of imperious necessity that means should be used by which the loss incurred on their account should be reduced and ultimately abolished. Government was probably prompted by a generous motive to reward deserving old servants, to ratify those favourable contracts with the gentlemen now employed as Residents,

* It is said that the Resident's gain is chiefly derived from the price of articles which they alone are allowed to sell: these are—

Salt at the rate of	1 Dollar for 32 lb.
Tobacco	15 ditto for 1 kranjang.
Java cloth	2 ditto for 1 piece.

The Dutch are said to deliver these articles to the subjects of the King of Palambang much cheaper; indeed at the following rates:—for 1 dollar salt 320 lb.—5 dollars for 1 kranjang of tobacco—and ½ dollar for a piece of cloth.

who all belong to the old Bencoolen establishment; but since they are become affluent, it is but just that measures should be taken to bring the pepper at a proper price to the Company's warehouses.

There are at present four Residents who transact the Company's business in the out-stations of this establishment. The most northern is Tappanouly, which to the Resident is the most lucrative, as the country thereabout abounds with the richest articles of trade that Sumatra produces, such as camphire, benjamin, cassia, wood for ship-building, &c. The Company have but few pepper gardens here, for which the Resident draws a salary of 300 dollars monthly, though the produce of them does not amount to more (it is said) than a boat load. This, though reckoned one of the finest parts of the country, is thinly inhabited, on which account but little pepper is cultivated. It may be had in great quantity from Sisu, a neighbouring province, where the Americans bought their pepper lately from six to ten dollars per cwt. and from whence also the Company's Resident draws the quantity which he sends on his private account for sale to England.

The country from Atchīm to Tappanouly is reckoned to produce yearly 4000 tons of pepper.

This part of the country (Tappanouly) abounds with rivers, and the hills approach very near the coast. There is here also one of the finest and safest bays of which India can boast, in which it is said 500 of the largest ships could lie in the greatest safety. The Resident lives on an Island at a small distance from the main land.

The country belonging to this Residency extends from the river Sorum, north, to the river Baddang Ferro, south, about sixty miles in length. The valleys are mostly cultivated with grain. A numerous tribe of savage batties inhabit the wildernesses of the interior, with whom there exists but little intercourse, and over whom the Resident has no authority, except when they apply to him, as they sometimes do, to settle their differences, after they are tired of warfare.

The country about Battang Ferro abounds with wood for ship-building—and much trade was carried on at this place some time ago in benjamin.

Nattāl is a place about thirty miles south of Tappanouly, where formerly also a Resident lived; but which is now subordinate to the former. A savage tribe of cannibals live at no great distance inland from this factory. The Company has no trade here.

Mr. Prince has 4000 dollars a year to keep up a kind of military establishment for the defence of the two factories. He is allowed to appropriate also the duties which formerly were levied for the Company. The batties purchase here a great deal of iron, steel, piece goods, salt, brass wire; and carry it inland: they pay in camphor, gold sand, and ivory.

Padang, a place nearly under the line, was formerly a Dutch settlement, and is governed now by a Resident, who, as a political officer, has little or nothing to do with the Company's pepper trade: he is at liberty, however, to trade in it on his private account.

There are still a number of Dutch inhabitants or people of that extraction at that place, who supply Bencoolen with almost every article that is required for the support of their tables, as poultry, sheep, dried fish, vegetables, &c. They are sent there on prows, whose principal cargo is pepper. Without those supplies it would be absolutely impossible to get ships' provisions at Bencoolen, and the inhabitants themselves would be starved, or obliged to rear those articles of food themselves. The people at Marlborough very composedly ascribe the abundance of those articles at Padang to the cruel oppression of the Dutch Government, who obliged the poor Malays to work and procure a livelihood by such drudgery!—All articles in consequence of that oppression, however, are now 400 per cent. cheaper than they are at Marlborough, though there cannot be produced a single good physical reason for such a difference.

For the district of Bencoolen there is a pepper Resident at Marlborough, who manages both the Company's and the free gardens, should there be any of the latter discription.

Saluma and Manna, farther south and inland, were formerly separate Residencies; but latterly they have been put under the management of one factor. The greatest quantity of white pepper comes from thence, I understand.

Croy is the most southern Residency, and from thence the greatest quantity of pepper is obtained. The country there is said to be extremely fertile, and as the Lampoons are beings of a more tractable nature than the rest of the natives of Sumatra, much might be done to extend the cultivation of pepper and other valuable productions.

The smaller islands along the coast of Sumatra would produce pepper in large quantities, as they abound with valleys and situations most eligible for such plantations; and trials have been made by former Governors of Bencoolen which promised great success.

I have not heard that the pepper vine grows wild in any part of Sumatra, nor do I know of any on the continent of India. Some species of an herbaceous kind I have collected in Mysore.

The Island of Sumatra produces some other plants yielding substances of great utility and in universal demand; and which might have formed lucrative branches of trade to the Honourable Company, to Europe, and China, if they had not been given up to the private traders, or rather to their servants residing in Sumatra.

In the first instance I mention camphor, which is produced by a tree as yet not well known. It was formerly thought to be a species of laurus, as a tree of this genus on Java and other eastern islands, really yields a similar article. Doctor Roxburgh, who has examined dried specimens of the former, supposes it to belong to a new genus, which he denominates *Shoreă*, (sāl of the Bengales), but which I, with equal right, called *Clivia*, as Lady Powis was the first who discovered a species of the same, a large tree near Vencatygherry in Mysore, and recognized it as a non-descript. This however is destitute of any aromatic quality as is the sāl in Bengal; and it is only remarkable that the lacca insect builds on it, on the hills about Nundidrŭg, in preference to any other tree.

The camphor tree of Sumatra flourishes in the northern parts of this island, particularly about Tappanouly, and the camphor is from thence sent to Bencoolen, China, and India.

The camphor tree propagates itself among the mountains without any trouble or labour to the natives. Each tree yields about 3lb. which is found in grains or scales, whereas in Japan it must be distilled from the wood of the tree; the former is less volatile than the latter. The places where camphor trees grow are reckoned particularly unhealthy, owing probably alone to the nature of the soil, or the situation required for the flourishing state of that tree.

There are two sorts of it; one lamellar which is the best, and the other of a grainy fracture. The latter, as the worst, is for the India market, where it is sold in all bazars, and chiefly used by the Hindoo physicians. It is not very pure, but always appeared to me much stronger in smell and taste than any refined which comes from China and Europe.

The prime sort is reserved for China, where it sells about 3000 dollars per pecul, which costs 1500 in Sumatra. It is probable that the Chinese buy it for home consumption, as the camphor refined is sold by them for 1500 dollars, or it may be used by them to give to inferior kinds when refined, a superior appearance.

I am sorry it was out of my power to procure a quantity, as it certainly would be very desirable to become better acquainted with a drug so very valuable, particularly if it should be really superior to what is generally used in England.

Another product of this island is benjamin or benzöe, and one, if I recollect right, to be found exclusively here. It is obtained from a tree which is also a native of the northern parts of this island, Styrax Benzöe.

The natives distinguish three sorts; the first of them, called Europe Head, contains the white talc-like shining substance in large lumps, and in great proportions; the second is called Indian Head, and should have about one-third of its weight of white substance; the worst, called Caffre's Head, is of a grainy, greyish, brittle mass, with only here and there a particle of the abovementioned white ingredient. The best sold at Bencoolen at 80 dollars per pecul, is by no means the best sort. Of the second and third, great quantities are sent to India, where both Hindoos and Mussulmen are very profuse of it in perfuming themselves, their houses, and temples at festival times. The physicians of those nations, both male and female, smoke their patients, to drive out pains and the devil.

Cassia is a bark well known as a substitute for cinnamon. In former times great quantities of it were sent to Europe; but now it is only exported to China, and that in small quantities. It is principally found in the northern districts of this coast about Tappanouly.

A drug called by the Portuguese in India catacamber, and here gambier, is a vegetable product of the inland parts of this island. They called it at Bencoolen a kind of gum, but it is assuredly nothing else than the inspissated juice of the leaves of a tree, and probably of a nauclea, for the plant I saw had quite the habit of this genus. It tastes like the cutch of India or the terra Japonica of our shops. This particular kind is chewed by the Indians along with the betel and areca nut, and is considered as giving it an additional flavour.

As cutch contains a great deal of tannin, it would be well worth inquiry, whether this drug does so in the same proportion; and, in this case, whether the tree grows in such abundance as to ensure a large and constant supply for the purposes of tanning.

LETTER VII.

Harleston, at Sea, April 12, 1812.

After the capture of Amboyna and other eastern islands from the Dutch, in the year 1798—9, the British Government in India showed themselves very solicitous, and expended considerable sums, to indigenate the nutmeg, clove, and other spice and fruit trees, for which those islands are famed, in their own colonies on the continent of Asia.

The greatest proportion of plants that were received at Madras was sent to a place near Pallamcotta, one of the most southern situations on the coast of Coromandel, as its climate and soil approached nearest to that from which they had been transplanted: another considerable share was entrusted to my care, and planted in the Sultan's garden at Bengalore; and a small but choice collection was retained for the Government's garden at Madras.

Of the latter, I am sorry to say, there were none but the caiput tree remaining alive, when I saw the garden about four years ago, not even the mangustans, which you will recollect seemed to thrive and take to the soil amazingly. That garden, indeed, is now totally neglected and barren, which under Lord Clive's auspices flourished so much. The soil which then was so much improved that it appeared a fine rich mould, has regained its natural preponderance of sandy sterility; and the water of the large wells, then perfectly sweet, from neglect of cleansing has become quite brackish, and hence destructive to many vegetables.

I cannot make a better report of the plants sent to Bengalore. The climate seemed to be too cold for the spice trees, all of which died during the first cold season, whilst I was employed on the survey of Mysore under Captain (now Colonel) M'Kenzie. Some of the fruit-trees however prospered, as the mangustan, rhambudan, and dorian, and of the Iju palm a great number flourished when I left that place. Whether any of them are in existence now I do not know: in the garden there are certainly none, as a negro to whom the garden was given as a reward for faithful services, disposed of all the trees; those that could be transported he sold to the gentlemen in the cantonment, and the rest he cut down for fuel. The garden in which you so much delighted is now, I understand, mostly converted into paddy and rhaggy plantations.

A number of spice trees are yet remaining in the plantations near Pallamcotta, as I hear; but none of them have yet produced, which they would have done had any attention been paid to their culture.

Bencoolen received about that time also a large stock of spice plants from Amboyna, and on account of the vicinity to this place, and the similarity of climate, it might reasonably be expected that the chance of success was greater here than at any other place. Mr. Cole, a civil servant of that establishment, was the first who in the year 1798 took measures to cultivate the nutmeg and clove plants, on a scale that merited attention. His plantation however was the only one of its kind until 1803, when it began to produce, and convinced the sneerers that the spice did not only grow well, but produced in the greatest perfection. From that period, plantations sprung up on every side, a great deal of money has been realized by the first speculator, chiefly on the sale of young plants, at the rate of one dollar for each; and much money has been sunk by others in buildings and purchases, and the settlement has been thereby wonderfully improved.

The number of plantations amounts to about thirty-three, most of which have trees bearing, the produce of which in the market is equal to that from the Eastern Islands, particularly the mace and cloves: the nutmegs are not quite so large as those from Banda.

The Company's plantation, established by the late Dr. Campbell on Mount Carmel, about sixteen miles south of Marlborough, might as well, in my humble opinion, be sold now, as it is too small to answer any other object than that which has been obtained, and as there is no person at that place in the plantation possessed of knowledge to make the establishment otherwise useful to the country and its inhabitants.

The expense at which those plantations are established and kept up is very great, as labour of all kind is extravagantly dear in Bencoolen, but the profits, as they are calculated by the planters, are also immense. I have been promised an estimate of both by a gentleman, who possesses one of the largest and best plantations, of which I shall endeavour to procure a copy.

Whether those plantations ever shall become of national importance, and thus prove the ruin or fortune of the planters, will entirely depend on the peace that in time must be made. Should then the Spice Islands be retained by England, the plantation at Bencoolen must fall, as they never will be able to cope with those of natural and ancient establishment; but if they are given up, Bencoolen will become of the greatest importance to England, and prove the source of wealth to its inhabitants, while it causes an increasing loss to the former monopolizers of the spice trade.

One of the prisoners of war on board the Harleston, a Dutch officer, who had been but lately in possession of a large nutmeg plantation at Banda, very ingenuously gave his advice to the planters of Bencoolen as to the best mode of cultivating the tree, and of preserving and garbling the nutmeg, which latter operation seemed here but imperfectly understood.

The nutmeg is liable to be attacked by worms, which in a short time multiply at such a rate, that all in a warehouse or a ship in which they are stored are soon entirely destroyed. To separate such as have worms from the rest, becomes therefore highly necessary, and of this particular consists the art of garbling. It is easy enough to find out those from which the worm has escaped, by the hole which it has made; but to discover those in which it is yet at its destructive work, requires some knowledge and an experienced eye. The basis of the nutmeg where it has been attached to its shell must be examined; should this be found more than usually depressed, the opposite point will be raised or swelled a little, and the outer pellicle will easily come off by scratching with the nail, and discover the lurking-place of the enemy.

The small and shrivelled nutmegs that gentleman advised to be separated from the better sorts, and to be used for the distillation of oil, and making of nutmeg soap.

The nutmegs which are smoothest on their outside are reckoned the best, as containing the greatest quantity of oil.

There are some cinnamon trees in the plantations of Bencoolen, which flourish in every respect, except that of producing ripe seeds; a circumstance rather astonishing, as they yield them in great abundance in Bengal and on the coast of Coromandel, in situations far less similar than this to the island in which they are indigenous.

An intelligent enumeration of the fruit and principal forest trees of Bencoolen would be, I am sure, acceptable; but here also my information is so scanty and limited, that I have nothing to offer but desultory and partial remarks, which I hope, however, will not be altogether void of interest.

On fruit trees in general, it may be said, that Sumatra resembles a frontier station of the Eastern and Western world of those latitudes, where individuals of both live and thrive together as valuable citizens of the respective commonwealth.

There are mangoes in Bencoolen, (to commence with the finest fruit,) but in no great abundance, nor any way to be compared to the best in India in point of flavour.

The guava grows also there, and is mostly planted in their burying ground, whence these go in general under the name of Guava Gardens.

Of plantains there is great abundance and variety on this island, and it is said the Malays distinguish about 100 different kinds by appropriate names. The finer kinds, as the rajah and the red plantain, are, I believe, unknown here.

Oranges seem to be in tolerable abundance: the best have large knobs or protuberances on the rind. Pompelmusses and jack fruit are very common.

The cocoanut appears to be more at home here than on the continent of India, as the tree attains a greater size than at any other place where I have observed it; and as it produces more abundantly, and fruit in every respect of greater perfection. Forests of it are seen to extend to the very water's edge, and the trees, as already observed, are of great height and size; farther inland they however become scarce, and in the middle of the island there are none to be found. This palm indeed thrives only in places where the soil is impregnated with salt; and where it is not naturally so, it must be supplied artificially; it is necessary there to put a quantity of salt under the roots of the young plant when it is transplanted the third and last time.

The Malays seem to be particularly fond of the water of the young fruit, which is certainly very delicious and cooling in this burning clime, but the enjoyment of this luxury deprives them of the more substantial part of the fruit, the kernel, which affords real nourishment. It is indeed entirely to be ascribed to the epicurism of the natives, that it is necessary to import ripe cocoanuts from Padang and other places; for besides the water of the nut, they are also fond of the palm wine, in which they indulge very freely, which, as is well known, is drawn from incisions into the flower stalks, which prevents its bearing fruit.

In the bazar of Bencoolen, 100 cocoanuts are usually sold for one dollar.

To fetch cocoanuts from the tree as they are wanted, the Malays have trained monkeys, which are more expert at the business than any toddy-man on the coast of Coromandel.

I was at first astonished that cayr, or the fibres which surround the cocoanut, was not an article of trade in such extensive cocoa forests, which on account of the great size of the fruit would be of a superior quality; but recollecting the daintiness of the Malays in regaling on the young fruit, my wonder soon ceased, as that article can be only procured from the fruit in its greatest maturity.

Among the fruits of the eastern parts of India, the mangustan stands foremost. It is of a particularly delicate flavour, and the favourite of both natives and strangers. By the former it is always carefully noticed that any quantity may be eaten with impunity, which is not the case with most other fruits of this country. From the inside of the mangustan, which is very astringent, exudes often a kind of gamboge which stains the otherwise snow-white pulp with its own colour, and imbues it with its disagreeable bitterness.

I once tasted a dorian, a fruit of the size of a melon; but its smell is so offensive, and the clamminess which it produces on the palate so disagreeable, that I should not be easily persuaded to taste it a second time. The natives and some Europeans, as our Dutch prisoners, seemed to be very fond of it. They ascribe to it a *heating* quality: an expression so vaguely used in India, that it is difficult to define its meaning. All acid fruits, as lemons and tamarinds, are heating, and so are cucumbers, melons, and plantains; but when it is applied to the dorian, it must mean some other fanciful or real property, as it has more aromatic or pungent qualities, which as in chilly, pepper, ginger, &c. are called *cooling*.

The jambo is an insipid fruit, of which there are some species and varieties at Bencoolen. Rhambustan, lansu rayer, juba, and some others, I have also tasted; they have all but little substance, but they are pleasant enough, and, on account of their acidity, cooling; but they are not reckoned very wholesome.

There are two species of bread-fruit, which I am told are indigenous. Both resemble that of the South Sea islands, in habit, fruit, and leaf.

The coast of Sumatra abounds with palms of different descriptions; of which some, as the sago palms, are peculiarly useful. Like the cocoanut tree, they are only found on the coast, and some of them actually grow in sea water. Palms appear to me to be mostly insular productions; for beside the date palms (Phœnix dactylifera et Elate), and the palmeyra (Borassus flabellifernus), I scarcely recollect any other that grows on the continent of India at any distance from the sea; and these thrive even better on the coast in barren sand.

There are four species of palms from the pith of which sago is made here; and of these the Iju is the most remarkable, as every part of it is useful and valuable. Each leaf on its evolution is enveloped with black hair-like fibres, which are worth at least one dollar, as they are in great request, on account of their tenacity and strength for cordage. The tree begins to bear blossom after it is ten years old, and these, on account of the great quantity of palm wine which they yield, are very valuable to the owner. This wine is boiled into sugar, and that of one bunch is sold for forty dollars; which is as much as twenty-five palmeyra or cocoanut trees would produce. The fruit of this tree is of the least consequence among all its other parts, as it is merely used, preserved in sugar, as a dainty. When the tree is old and exhausted, it is cut down, and its pith prepared into sago. The leaves are used for thatching houses. There are as yet but few trees of this kind about Bencoolen; they were, I understand, brought from the Eastern Islands.

The other three species of sago palms are found in great abundance on the Poggy and other islands along Sumatra, but, as has been observed, they are also indigenous here.

Rattans: several species of it are found in great abundance along the coast, and are exported to China. Bamboos grow to a large size, and are very common in the wildernesses of the interior. They use them in various ways about their houses, particularly for fetching water from the wells, for measures, &c.

The Java poison-tree is also an inhabitant of this island, and by Dr.

Lumsdaine's* account, is a species of ficus. It is scarcely necessary to mention, that it is by no means so deleterious in its effects as has been represented: on the contrary, it is known that many officers have pitched their tents and lived under it with impunity.

The iron-wood tree of Sumatra is well known, as also many species of oak and of pine that grow there; and on diligent inquiry, I am persuaded, different kinds of valuable wood would be found, both for ship-building and cabinet-work.

There is no want of culinary vegetables on this coast, of which many bulbous and tuberose roots are particularly nutritive. Of the latter, I shall only mention yams, the Indian and China, red and white, of which the latter are most esteemed; also dacca pinnatifida, arum, which grow both wild and cultivated in the country. They have all varieties of melons, cucumbers, and pumkins, which India produces, and mostly of a larger size.

Beans are found in great variety in their bazars; some, of which they seem particularly fond, have an abominable smell. I brought some seeds of it on board with me, which however were soon found out, and thrown overboard.

Agriculture is quite in its infancy, and according to the accounts of the inhabitants of Marlborough, discouraged in favour of the culture of pepper. This, however, I cannot believe. An enlightened Government, like that of the Honourable Company, is too well aware that abundance of food is the most effectual means of increasing productions of all other descriptions. The Bencoolen Government probably insists that the natives shall cultivate the stipulated number of vines, but neither would they, I am sure, nor could they prevent them from cultivating rice besides, or any thing else which they conceived to be useful: for which they have abundance of leisure.

From others I heard that the Malays cultivate as much rice as they want for their own consumption, and that the quantity yearly imported from Bengal is scarcely sufficient for the inhabitants of the European settlements. I have seen several kinds of Bencoolen rice in the bazars, all in the husk, of a black colour, and of rather a small grain. The rice I have

* Senior Assistant Surgeon at Marlborough.

also tasted and found it very palatable. The Malays give it the preference to that brought from Bengal.

The way of ploughing the ground in the southern provinces is unique and deserves mention.

After the trees and underwood are cut down and burnt, on new ground, or after the crops of cultivated grounds have been taken away, a number of buffaloes are penned upon it, not with a view of manuring it, (as is done in India,) but absolutely of turning it up by ambulating, for the reception of the seeds, which are thrown or scattered about on the field; nature is, after this, left to herself until the crops are ripe to be cut down.

Besides rice, there are some kinds of grain cultivated, which appeared to me to differ specifically from those of India.

Sugar is cultivated, but only in small quantities in their gardens, as a delicacy for the women and children who enjoy the juice of the cane. The colour of it is a deep purple, and the joints are very short, but thick and juicy.

I could mention many other subjects belonging to the vegetable kingdom, both of curiosity and utility, that have come to my knowledge; as plants yielding hemp, medicinal herbs, and beautiful or curious flowers; but as it is not possible I could have sufficient information of the former, and as the latter are mere objects of scientific research, I pass them over in silence.

LETTER VIII.

Harleston at Sea, 5th April, 1812.

RAT-ISLAND is, I believe, one of the smallest islands that are inhabited; but it is one of more importance than many others of a hundred times its size. To the settlement of Bencoolen, and to the Honourable Company's shipping, it is of much consequence, as it forms, with some coral rocks, a basin in which three large ships can lie with the greatest security in almost all seasons of the year, which in the open bay would be exposed to great danger.

This Island is about nine miles in a westerly direction from the settlement, and is inaccessible on all sides but one, from the basin, and here only by those acquainted with the channel that leads from it to the landing place near the northern wharf. I have seen a boat from the Cornelia frigate upwards of an hour attempting in vain to find out that passage, and it required several weeks' experience before our ship's boats could find their way, without getting aground on the coral rocks.

For want of other means to ascertain its dimensions, I have paced the island several times in all directions, and found it took 650 of my steps to circumscribe it near the highest water mark, which I ascertained to be 1620 feet. Its greatest length from north to south is by the same measure one furlong and a quarter, and its greatest breadth between the warehouse and dwelling-house one-eighth of a furlong. It is not long since it was twice as large, and in several respects of more than double its present importance to the settlement at Marlborough. There was then among other buildings an hospital for the European sick and convalescents, as the air is so much purer and cooler here, and consequently more wholesome than on the main land.

The reduction of the island to its present size was very sudden, and embittered by the loss of many lives. The cause of it was the injudicious choice of a place for a wharf, on a spot where at all times a strong current was setting on the land. It happened that soon after the building was finished, a violent swell of the sea from the south-west arose without the least alteration of wind either in strength or direction, probably occasioned by an earthquake, a circumstance said to be not uncommon on this coast, which in the course of a night swept away both the building and that part of the island with which it was connected.

My opinion is that, ere long, the whole island will experience the same fate; nor do I see how it well can be prevented. My apprehension is founded on the knowledge I have of a current, which (I believe but lately) has found its way through the southern coral rocks, rushing along the western shore of the island, on which it daily encroaches, and which, from any strong commotion from that quarter of the sea, must absolutely wash the superficial part of the island into the deeps of the ocean.

That current may be best observed at low water, where it is seen to run like a rivulet along the shore into the channel which leads into the basin. At the southern extremity an attempt has been made to set bounds to its encroachments by a stone wall, which runs about 150 paces to the northern wharf, and hitherto it has proved sufficient; but no flimsy contrivance of this kind can be expected to save this island long from destruction.

As yet this little spot affords a pleasant retreat from the noisy uncomfortable dungeons of a ship, to such as can obtain the Resident's permission to reside in the house which originally was built for the use of the Governors.

This building and the pepper warehouses are in the centre of the island, at the distance of about fifteen yards from each other. The pepper-house is built in the European style, with virandas round it, which serve for the accommodation of the detachment of Bengal Sepoys, and the slaves employed in the weighing and carriage of pepper from it, to the northern wharf and the ships' boats.

The dwelling-house is erected in the style peculiar to Sumatra, of which in the sequel I shall take particular notice.

It is occupied when ships are here by the European soldiers, who are sent here for the protection of the ships and warehouses, and by one of the Government's servants, who superintends the weighing and delivery of pepper, a situation given in common to a monthly servant, a dependant in favour with the Resident, as an allowance is admitted of three dollars a day to defray his extraordinary expenses. The person who was sent this time, and whom we were obliged to admit among us, turned out to be, what is too common among his tribe, disagreeable in many respects.

The plan of building houses in Sumatra consists in erecting the habitable part of them on pillars of from five to twelve feet above the surface of the ground. The space that would constitute the ground floor, is used by the natives generally, as a poultry yard, and by the Europeans it is laid out in godowns, which means store-rooms and warehouses.

The parlour and sleeping rooms are thus elevated from five to twelve feet over-ground at Marlborough, and in the inland parts of the country sixteen feet and upwards. In front there is generally a broad viranda, extending all along the house, which is entered by a staircase, or in meaner houses by a ladder; and in the country by the trunk of a palm tree, which is notched for the easier ascent in the day-time, and drawn up in the night.

The Malays imagine that their forefathers adopted this mode of building as a protection against tigers or other ferocious animals: in my opinion they had wiser motives; they did it to defend themselves against much more formidable enemies—the effluvia of the ground, which in a climate and soil like that of Sumatra, we know to be extremely noxious. They consist probably of carbonated or hydrocarbonated gases; the former abundantly secreted from a luxuriant vegetation, and the latter from decaying substances, which, particularly the former, are best avoided by residing some distance above ground, near which they remain on account of their great specific gravity.

I have heard from a friend, (the Rev. Mr. Haensel, who has resided for a considerable number of years in the Nicobar Islands,) that the natives there construct their dwellings in a similar manner on pillars or posts considerably elevated; and I am convinced, that if the Moravian Brethren and the Danish Settlers had imitated the natives in this point as they did in others, they would not have experienced that dreadful mortality which obliged them to relinquish that settlement. The people of Nicobar could not, at all events, have intended to guard themselves by this way of building against any ferocious animals, as they have scarcely any other quadrupeds but hogs on those islands.

I sincerely hope this plan may get a fair trial in countries of reputed unhealthiness, as in Surinam, and many other places of America and the West Indies. I have suggested it to some of my friends in India to try it among the hills of Orissa (the Northern Circars), in those parts particularly which to our knowledge abound with the finest teak wood, which both Europeans and the lowland natives are deterred from visiting, by the destructive fever which never fails to assail them after the first setting in of the rains, as soon as vegetation becomes luxuriant. The natives ascribe that deleterious fever to the effluvia of the marking nut tree (Semicarpus anacardium), and with which those forests abound, but unjustly, I believe.

Rat-Island is completely covered with vegetation, though the soil is not much above a foot deep. There are about 150 cocoanut trees on it, some trees of a species of ficus, hedysarum umbellatum, phyllanthus emblica, tamarindus indica, butea frondosa, viola baccata, &c. Among the smaller vegetables the most conspicuous are, verbena, dolichos, convolvulus pes Capræ. The whole flora amounts to about seventy species, of which I have lost the catalogue which I had carefully prepared.

The superficial soil consists of black mould mixed with shells, pieces of coral, and sand. The latter ingredient prevails near the beach, where it is thrown up from the sea; the foundation of the whole is a coral rock.

There are two wells on the island which yield but little and brackish water, so that it is necessary to supply the detachment of Sepoys stationed here, and the slaves, with it from the main land. It is said that the water in these wells was both in greater abundance and sweeter before the reduction of the island to its present size. To me it is matter of astonishment that there should be any drinkable water at all on a coral rock, which is scarcely elevated above the level of the surrounding sea. There must be a simple process which nature uses to separate salts from sea water, besides heat, and which I am not quite without hopes will yet be discovered.

I was formerly of opinion that all sweet water in wells, situated as just mentioned and on the sea coast, was entirely derived from veins proceeding from the nearest high lands, but never from the sea: but my opinion has changed considerably, since I have observed that wells within a distance of more than 100 yards from large reservoirs of water are regularly affected by the changes that occasionally take place in the latter. On the island of Coringa, where the well water is in common so brackish that the Europeans residing there get supplies from distant places, or store up rain water, it becomes perfectly sweet in those wells as soon as the freshes in the Godavery make their appearance; and it continues so till the sea water has regained its ascendancy in the creeks with which that part of the country is intersected. I must observe that it often happens, particularly in the earlier part of the seasons, in June and July, that the freshes come down the Godavery in the fairest weather, preceded and accompanied only by strong westerly winds, so that the sweetness of the well water cannot be ascribed to atmospherical supplies. It is farther true that the water in the wells of that island is at all times on a level with that in the creeks.

I will, however, by no means maintain that all well water in the vicinity of the sea, or of any other large reservoir, is derived from that source; on the contrary, I still think that most comes from the higher parts of the adjacent country.

There is, I understand, a person of the name of Beaumont at Calcutta, who for a premium of 25,000*l.* has offered to Government to disclose the secret of converting salt water in large quantities at a time, without the agency of heat, and with very little trouble and expense, into sweet and drinkable water. He pretends that the process is so simple, that he scarcely can speak of it without betraying his secret. I wish him success with all my heart, and will gladly subscribe to the statue which he deserves, should his expectations be realized. He is a man, I understand, who has made himself useful to many manufacturers in Bengal, particularly to those of indigo and tanning, by his suggestions of improvements; and he deserves, on that account, some attention.

There are no stones on the island, but such as evidently have been brought hither for the purpose of building, or that have been discharged from the ships as superfluous ballast. The former are a kind of basalt from the main land, and the latter flints. It is in compliment only to my informers, that I said these latter had been cast on shore from the ships at anchor in the basin, as, in my opinion, it is more likely they have been thrown up by the sea, as they are small both in number and size, mostly rounded pebbles coated with chalk.

The rats are not so conspicuous here as might be expected from the name of the island; they are however the only quadrupeds on it, if you except lizards, and of the latter there are some varieties.

There are no snakes here, but thousands of scorpions and numberless other insects, many of which I have never seen before; though in the earlier part of my residence in India, I have by no means been inattentive to this branch of natural history.

I mentioned before that this island was surrounded on all sides by coral rocks, and I wish it was in my power to give you a full account of them; for they are so rich in different productions, richer than I can give any idea of, or than can be well imagined. They absolutely swarm with animals, appearing, in short, as if alive.

The most conspicuous of the coral rocks run out for more than two miles in a north-west direction from the island; and at high water, indeed at all times, present a tremendous surf. At low water they appear as part of the island. From thence they extend round the western shores of the isle, half a mile and upwards in breadth. They become lower, after having doubled the southern extremity; and those to the eastward are, though extensive, mostly covered with water at ebb-tide, and of course the surf is here not very perceptible.

The animals inhabiting those rocks are fish, shell-fish of all descriptions, polypi and other insects, which at low water live in the pools formed by the coral rocks, or adhere to the branching corals, corallines, and sea-weed, from which, those that are useful for the various purposes of man are easily taken by the natives.

The shells of this part of the world have been long known as particularly beautiful; and as they are easily preserved, and strike the eyes of even uncultivated persons, they have long since found their way into the collections of the curious. The fish which they contain are mostly eaten by the Malays in preference even to those of the real oyster, of which several species are found here and along the coast.

Polypi are found in the greatest abundance and variety, of which those in the form of leeches and snakes are the most remarkable. The former were absolutely taken by us at first for leeches, and, I believe, most of our shipmates are still of opinion that they are a harmless species of that kind. I was soon undeceived by the fringes which they occasionally spread about their mouths: they are mostly black, about a foot long, and three inches in circumference. From a species of these the tripa is made, which is an article of food or luxury much in request in China. An extensive commerce is carried on from some islands of the Eastern Archipelago with this article to China.

The polypi in the form of snakes are of different length, colour, and consistence. Some of them are six feet long, beautifully variegated, and of as firm a substance as the former; others seem to contain nothing but water which extends the extremities of the animal, when it is suspended from the middle. They appear then like a part of the thin intestines of one of the larger animals, which is slightly filled with water.

The corals are remarkably fine, and of a thousand different forms. Some, particularly the solid flat ones, are often found of the brightest colours, red, blue, and yellow; those of shrub and tree-like form are commonly white, and their ends tipped with a yellow, red, or blue colour. Some appear full of warts, others are decorated with a beautiful net of the finest fillagré.

Those rocks abound also with real vegetables of the Neptunian empire, of which the *fuci* are very numerous and remarkable. Some are in the form of hair, and are called Caffre hair or Malay hair, as they are lank or curled; some are in the shape of capsicums; others in that of the winged fruit of the combretum, a species of terminalia and the ventilago. Some of these contain a kind of seed which the Malays find very palatable.

These open like a capsule from the apex, and I have never seen them adhering to the rocks, but always as if torn from the parent plant. Some are in the form of bunches of currants, and are eaten by the natives with pepper and vinegar. But the objects of this kind are here so many and so remarkable, that it would require years to describe them scientifically, and in any other way than that they are not worth your attention.

I must, however, still mention a kind of sponge, which is found on the most northern coral rocks in some abundance. It is full of a yellow or orange coloured matter, which must be expressed, and what remains extracted with boiling water before it can be used.

The native inhabitants of Rat-island live in the style peculiar to the country in some huts built in its southern extremity. The principal personage among them is called Rajah, and said to be the hereditary proprietor of the island. Like the rest of his subjects he is a fisherman, and supplies the ships in the basin and the strangers on the island with fish, and sometimes with fruits and vegetables, which he himself purchases on the main land; for the little gardens which are about their houses never would supply enough of corn for their consumption. The poultry yard under their houses I found tolerably well stocked, but the price they ask for their poultry is very extravagant. The same may be said of the fish which they have for sale.

The mode of fishing here differs as to the place in which it is proposed, and as to the object. If the Malays mean to catch large fish, they choose a place where the water remains at some depth during the ebb; they inclose there an extensive spot with a fence of bamboos, through which the fish cannot escape after they once have entered during high water, and where of course they are easily caught when it becomes shallow. In deeper water they cast the net, in which they are said to be very expert.

On the coral rocks, which at a distance appear quite dry during low water, there are still extensive pools full of smaller fish, eels, and shell-fish. These are persecuted by the Malays, and driven out of their skulking holes by poison with which they impregnate the water. The material they use on these occasions is the root of a creeping shrub, in appearance a smilax, and which, in a dried state, is sold in all bazars in Sumatra. It is said that the Malays often use it for the iniquitous purpose of ridding themselves of their friends. The name of it is aguer tuba. I had one of the plants of it in a box in my cabin, where it withstood the attacks of the rats longer than any other, but at last it was also destroyed, though apparently not without its revenge.

The way of using it to catch fish, is to take a small handful, and to beat and bruise it slightly with a stone, and then to dip it into the water, agitating it slightly, until the fish make their appearance. Every thing living is soon seen in the greatest distress, the two-valved shells open, the crabs and prawns crawl about in great confusion, the fish gape, and try to throw themselves out of the water; but all soon becomes quiet again, languidity precedes apathy and death, and they are without a struggle taken from the surface.

This seems to be the favourite way of fishing of the Malays, as they even at night are seen to traverse the rocks at low water, with a flambeau in one hand and the tuba in the other.

The fish caught on the rocks about this island are deemed by the inhabitants of Marlborough inferior to those got on the deeper banks in the bay of Bencoolen. The difference however lies more in the kind of fish than the place; for the former are, as on the coast of Coromandel, mullets, pomfrets, soles, searfish, skates, &c. whereas on the rocks I have seen few others but those called parrot-fish, which have little else than their colours to recommend themselves to our attention. These are certainly exquisitely beautiful, yellow, green, blue, and black, mostly remarkably bright in spots and zones.

Fish, generally speaking, are in great abundance all along the coast of Sumatra, and comparatively cheap.

The only way of preserving the fish, here in use, is to dry them in the air; in which state a great quantity is brought from Padang, where the "*cruelty*" of the former Dutch Government taught the natives to seek food and employment even in the ocean!

A much better way of preserving fish is that in use on the coasts of India, where they are first salted, and then dried in the sun or smoked.

There are many sharks about Rat-island and along the coast of Sumatra, of which some species are relished as food by the Malays, as indeed is the case also in Western India.

LETTER IX.

Harleston at Sea, 12th April, 1812.

VERY formidable enemies to the natives of Sumatra are the elephants, of which large droves issue from the wildernesses, and lay waste all plantations of grain, sugar, and trees that come in their way.

The natives destroy them on those occasions by arsenic, which they introduce into sugar cane, of which these animals are known to be particularly fond. They do this not only to rid themselves of very troublesome visitors; but also with a view to get their tusks, which sell well at Bencoolen, for exportation to Europe and China. I have observed that a great number of the tusks brought there were as large as any I have seen in India, and must have belonged to animals of very large size. As elephants are not used here as they are in India, it would be very desirable that they should be extirpated, as independent of the mischief they do to plantations, they often destroy men, women, and children, when they unluckily fall in with their haunts.

The most destructive, however, of all wild beasts is the tiger in all its species.

The large royal beast attacks and preys upon all larger animals, there being none which he cannot master, the elephant generally excepted: and the smaller sorts prove as destructive to the timid and small species. This country is so infested with them that some ascribe the manifest depopulation of it in some parts to the ravages which those animals commit on the human race; an opinion to which, however, I would not implicitly subscribe, there existing other causes productive of greater destruction to the human species, as constant public and private warfare, unhealthiness of the climate, &c.

They certainly must exist in great numbers, as they very frequently come close to the settlement of Bencoolen, and carry off men and animals out of the very plantations. Pecuniary rewards for destroying them are here held out by this Government as in other parts of India: but it is very seldom indeed that any is claimed; the Bencoolese being too superstitious and too indolent for such enterprises. The heathenish part of them look upon those ferocious animals with reverential awe, perhaps with a kind of pride, as beings animated by the souls of their forefathers and relations, which they feed and worship (to be sure at a distance) until they happen to make away with one of the family—then certainly all connexion is cut, and the spirit of revenge shows itself more powerfully than that of religion. The Mussulmen either silently cherish the same opinions with the former, for all in India are idolaters in some degree, or their predestinarian ideas are so predominant that they despise all precautions.

The most useful animal in Bencoolen is certainly the buffalo, as it not only supplies the inhabitants with milk, butter, and meat, but is also employed in their agricultural and mercantile pursuits. Those which I have seen are of a reddish grey colour, and generally larger than they are on the continent of India. They are much more docile than could be expected from an animal apparently so stupid and sluggish.

Those broke in for carriages, when driven to a heap of bags of grain, will put their horns, it is said, under one of them, throw it upon their backs, and walk off with it to the place where it is to be delivered. The Company's pepper is carried by these animals to the rafts on which it is floated down the rivers, or to the warehouses from which it is exported.

There are but few cows in Bencoolen, and those are wretchedly degenerated, which is owing, probably, to the coarse rank grass on which they must feed. Cows' milk therefore and butter are a luxury of which few can boast but the Resident, and such as have plantations where the soil is so far meliorated as to produce a better kind of grass.

Sheep are very scarce here, as nobody takes the trouble of breeding them, which might be surely as well done here as at Padang, from whence I saw a flock of very good looking animals.

The Achem horses are so well known in India as excellent draught horses, and so generally used in single horse chaises, that I need not describe them to you.

Those here are certainly of the same origin, but they look more like those brought from Pegu; they have stronger necks, but do not possess equal breadth of chest. They are in other respects equally well made, well limbed and knit, and high-spirited without being vicious. They are in common from 11 to 12½ hands high, and as they are very strong, hardy, and indefatigable, would, in my opinion, answer very well for a few regiments of native cavalry in the Honourable East India Company's establishment. I know that a charge of a body of this kind of horse would not be so powerful as that of the larger sized animals from the Cutch and the Mahratta country; but I am persuaded it would be quite powerful enough against any infantry which the native powers of Hindostan could bring into the field. They would be very useful also for escorting and bringing in forage, for which lately the Mysore horse have been chiefly employed; a wretched and despicable sort of beasts in every respect!

It would be advisable even to introduce that breed of horses into India to supplant the wretched Pariar race; and that could be done easily enough.

There are a number of wild animals in the forests and mountains of Sumatra, which I pass over altogether, as I could give no other than vague accounts of their names as well as of their peculiarities.

In the gardens of Marlborough, and even in Rat-island, I have seen a great number of birds which appear to be strangers in Western India. Some of them are fine warblers, others are extremely beautiful. Of the latter I will only mention the loories, of which some species are always offered for sale for a few dollars apiece in the bazars: and on Rat-island I was often delighted with the songs of a small wagtail that had taken up its abode in a banian tree before the house.

Sparrows, crows, and ravens, which I always thought were inhabitants of all countries of our globe, are not to be found in Bencoolen. The inhabitants of Marlborough say that there are some ravens in the interior of this island, and sparrows; but the latter are not of that species which is common about the houses in Europe and Asia. The former, I am astonished, should be found in places where they have nothing to feed upon but sour berries and pepper, and not in populous places as Marlborough (comparatively so at least), where they might find something more congenial to their tastes and pleasanter to their palates. I suspect almost that the ravens of Bencoolen will be found on better acquaintance a different kind of bird from the common.

From this circumstance, however, I am inclined to suppose that Sumatra has never been part of the Asiatic Continent, though the distance in some parts of the straits of Malacca is very small indeed; so much so that it is astonishing that those birds should never have ventured over in pursuit or being pursued. That they are common in Siam, &c. on the islands near that peninsula I know from an anecdote which I heard from the Rev. Mr. Haensel, with whom I was very intimate about twenty years ago in India.

A native of Bencoolen had followed him to Jangzeilan, an island near Siam, who, in the greatest fear imaginable, came to him crying out, "there is the devil," pointing at a crow that was sitting on one of the trees cawing, whilst the vessel was passing up the river.

On the coast of Coromandel and in Bengal crows and sparrows are in greater abundance than they are in any part of Europe.

Poultry of a very superior kind is common all over this island. I have already spoken of their game cocks, which are reckoned to be of the first blood; and in taste they are certainly not inferior to any other; besides having the advantage of being very dear in Bencoolen.

The minerals with which this island must abound, to judge from its aspect, are but little known. Of metals, we only know gold to exist in some abundance. It has been said that copper is found also; and I have seen at Madras a sulphuret of it, which was said to have been brought from Achem. It was quite compact, black and heavy, and effloresced with blue and green carbonate of copper. The latter in beautiful concentric needle-form cristallisations, and but for this efflorescence I should have taken it for an artificial production. Tin, I believe, is not found in Sumatra, at least not in any considerable plenty. The great quantity of this metal which was yearly sold by the Sultan of Palambang to the Dutch Company, was procured by him from the Island of Banca, as I have learnt from our Dutch officers, who in civil and military capacities had been formerly employed in that part of the world.

The quantity of gold which is obtained on this island is mostly exported to India, in exchange for opium, calicoes, and other articles. Whether the ophyr of the ancients is in this country I leave to others to prove, better versed in hypothetical lore than myself. It is chiefly found in the northern parts of the island and in districts which do not belong to the Company, though these also are not quite destitute of such mines. The Dutch, it is said, went to much expense to work some mines near Padang, and an enterprise of this kind was set on foot a long time ago near Bencoolen; but both attempts failed from want of hands, such chiefly as could do the laborious part of the business.

The gold occurs in small particles among river sand, and is then called gold-dust, sometimes it is found in pieces weighing an ounce and upwards, and in mines which by the description are open galleries of small extent, probably much like the diamond mines on the coast: which I have noticed in my former reports. In those mines the metal is found in grains dispersed in quartz. The largest piece of the kind, which I saw some years ago, is in the possession of Mr. Petrie, at Madras; it contains large lumps of this metal of the greatest lustre and perfection. I understood at Marlborough that this specimen had been sent to him as the largest that had of late years been obtained. I forget what he paid for it, or the value of the gold it contained, but it is a very considerable sum.

In the mountains of Sikilany and Passaman, the latter of which is almost under the equinoctial line, much gold is found, which is reckoned the finest of any on the west coast of Sumatra, holding generally from twenty-one to twenty-two carats.

Three days' journey to the eastward of Padang are the rich mines of Songipago, Songhiabo, and Sohanjong, of the strata of which I have received the following accounts:—the first or superficial is a clay of one fathom thickness, covered and mixed with quartz stones of a white colour. Next comes a white clay of two fathoms, lying on a black sand of one fathom depth. This is probably decomposed from rocks of a bluish colour on which it rests, and which is also but one fathom thick. Immediately under the latter is found, as a sure sign if it does occur of a rich vein of gold, a rock of a yellow hard stone kind of the thickness of five fathoms. The tigablas cottas yield about 3000 tail of gold in a year, of which five are about a mark.

Coals have been discovered near Bencoolen, and a Captain Cox of that place has taken great pains and expended great sums of money to make them useful to the settlement. The want of success is to be ascribed to the difficulty of water carriage, or indeed to its total deficiency.

I received a quantity of coals as a specimen of those found here, but discovered that coals lately brought from Port Jackson had been substituted. For my own part, I see no great reason to lament, except on his own account, that the enterprise of Captain Cox has failed, as Bencoolen and all other parts of Sumatra abound with wood for fuel, which in my opinion is always preferable to sea-coal, and the cutting of which will materially assist in rendering the country healthier.

I mentioned in my last Letter that the stones of Rat-island were chiefly basaltes; and such only I have found on the main land.

From Captain Cox I received a large lump of aggregated quartz crystals, which he said had been taken out of a rock in the surf, in a state almost quite soft, and that they had acquired the state of hardness, in which I received them, after a few months' exposure to the air. They are still extremely brittle, but very pellucid and beautiful.

I could say a great deal more on this and the other subjects which I have mentioned, but I am afraid of my information.

Of those which I have noticed, I have been very careful in selecting such information as I could procure from good documents, in the possession of Mr. T. Blair, a gentleman formerly in the service of Bencoolen, and a fellow passenger in the Harleston; or from other creditable authority. That which rests on my own observation I submit to your knowledge of my humble pretensions.

Some subjects of statistical import yet remain, of which I will offer some fragments of my own gathering.

Trade is, generally speaking, in a very languishing state on the coasts of Sumatra, notwithstanding that nature has been very kind, and blessed it with its richest productions. But they are not articles that require many hands and many vessels, which alone enliven trade, and render it useful to the country at large. The natives, on the other hand, require but few commodities from other countries, for the possession of which they would make any unusual exertion; and the nature of the inhabitants is such that they will not submit to labour for others in consideration of a scanty pittance; or to please a great man of their own community. The father of a family may persuade its inmates to collect gold, camphor, benjamin, and other things for him: but a Pangaran, or a chief of a village, would find himself in an awkward predicament should he use means to force his nominal subjects to similar labours for the common good, or for his own private ends. Whoever will gather gold in Sumatra must, therefore, bring labourers from other countries.

Pepper is one of the few articles on this island which is bulky and requires hands to cultivate and to collect it, and vessels of all descriptions to carry it away. Notwithstanding the monopoly of the East India Government, it is not so much engrossed as to exclude individuals altogether. They on the contrary are allowed to buy from such as have no specific contracts with the Company, and to send it for sale in the Company's ships to England.

Camphor and benjamin, so much esteemed in Europe, India, and China, belong chiefly to the provinces not under the Company's authority; and the Resident of Tappanouly is the only English subject at present who can deal in them to any considerable amount. Dammer is an article I have not mentioned before. It is the product of a species of pine, a rosin much used in India for their ships; the soft as well as the hard drug. From this island it is obtained as yet in small quantities: in Pegu it is a considerable article of trade.

The principal article imported is Bengal opium, of which the Company, I am told, send about 100 chests, and half as much more may be reckoned to be brought by individuals. From that country is also imported calico, muslins, rice, wheat, sugar, tobacco, and rum. From the coast of Coromandel, long cloth, chintzes, brown, blue, and red striped goods, and Pulicat handkerchiefs, &c. From Europe is wanted, broad cloth, chintz, marine stores, &c. all articles of necessity and luxury for the use of the small society of Europeans. These are brought yearly by a ship that touches here in its way to China, and which is emphatically called the Store-ship.

The pepper and other articles sent to Europe is commonly taken away by a ship sent for that purpose from Bengal, of which there are two this year, the Minerva and the Harleston, as none had been here last year.

The coasting trade is carried on in Malay prows, which are vessels that carry from twenty-five to fifty tons. These bring pepper and provisions from the provinces to Marlborough; and carry opium, European and India goods to the out-stations, and to the Eastern Archipelago. Among these, it is said, that some men of war and privateers have made sad destruction of late years; taking indiscriminately all property they found, burning the vessels, and ill using the owners and sailors, &c.

I feel it repugnant to my feelings to give much credit to all this, and mention it merely as a matter of conversation, and of complaint among a certain class of people in Bencoolen. All have lost of late years in India; and more than the rest, the army and such individuals as were obliged to give their hard-earned property to agents and merchants, many of whom, as they only could lose the money of others, boldly speculated, lost their ships, and became bankrupts, and continue to live in splendour. I speak freely on the subject, for I have also lost, with most of my friends, all the scanty savings of a military pay, and must now leave my children, whom I have brought to England for education, without any resources, should I die after my return to India, except the limited allowance of the medical fund!

The boats used on the coasts of Sumatra are called sampans. They look much like the Norwegian boats, are like them very narrow and sharp at both ends. To prevent their upsetting, to which by the formation they are very liable, a four-sided parallelogram of single bamboos is fastened on them nearly the length of the whole boat, and projecting on both sides four or five feet, which has the desired effect. Even with this apparent incumbrance they sail very fast, faster than most of our ships' boats.

The upsetting of the boats in itself is not much regarded by the natives, as long as they have nothing of value to care for, and on that account they use those boats, and the smallest kind of them very often without that apparatus, for they are very expert swimmers, and soon know how to set matters to right again. When out at sea they wear shallow broad brimmed baskets on their heads, which gives them the appearance of Chinese at a distance, but which defends them much better against the heat of the sun than the conical straw caps or palmeyra leaf used by the boat people about Madras.

The Malays are reckoned good sailors, better at least by far than the Lascars of Bengal and Bombay, who have adopted a great number of sea phrases (or cries) from the former, which in itself implies, I think, an acknowledgment of superiority.

The only articles of ingenuity and curious workmanship I have observed at Marlborough, are thimbles and small boxes made of gold fillagree, which are offered for sale on very moderate terms. They are not equal, however, to what I have seen in some parts of India, of which I possess some specimens.

In many parts of the island the natives make their own clothes from the fibrous part of the bark of some trees; also of silk which they raise about their houses.

It is curious that, in a country where gold is found in some abundance, there should not be a coin of that metal. It should be, I think, the interest of the East India Company to stamp as much as they possibly could with their arms, adding some imaginary value to the product, as this would in some measure prevent its being sent to any other than their own dominions.

The currency at Marlborough is entirely silver, and a little copper. The dollar goes for two sicca rupees; and this for twelve Madras fanams, which of course are rated at about thirteen per cent. more than they are worth.

LETTER X.

London, September 28, 1812.

I HAVE rather precipitately in my first letter engaged to come forward with proposals for ameliorating the state of things in Sumatra.

A reformation is certainly much wanted, and that country, even more than any other in India with which I am acquainted, merits the particular attention of the East India Company; but I am afraid that this is neither the time, nor am I the person likely to make an impression with respect to subjects of such importance.

Allow me to advert for a moment to the times, as they form a particular obstacle to changes in existing regulations.

Independently of their being awfully momentous in general, they are particularly so to India, and to every subject connected with it. That vast flourishing continent may be most materially affected by a single vote on the question, which soon must come for decision before that august Assembly: whether India shall be any longer governed by its present rulers, who acquired it, and under whose auspices it has flourished; or in other words, which in my humble opinion are nearly equivalent, whether it shall any longer form part of the English empire! Before this grand point is decided, no scheme can be attended to, at least nothing ought to be expected or determined upon, that in any way could change the present routine of things.

I would pass this subject over in reverential silence; but, as I feel deeply for the good of the best of masters, and very interested in the welfare of a country in which I have spent the best part of my life, in which I have enjoyed and suffered so much, and of which I have seen a greater proportion than comes to the lot of most who have been like myself twenty years in India; and as it has been my particular business during the greatest part of my residence there to render myself acquainted with the nature of the country, and its inhabitants, revenues, &c. I hope you will not think me impertinent if I proffer my humble opinion on the subject under discussion, so far, however, only as I may be supposed to be able to judge of these matters. There are some points, however, of political expediency and economy, of which I have but confused ideas, and which I neither ought nor will attempt to canvass.

Justice in home or family concerns ought to be balanced as nicely as possible; a family will never be so happy as when strict attention is paid to this particular. It creates mutual confidence which is the stimulus for joint exertion! England would not stand on that proud eminence which she enjoys among the nations of the world, were it not for her impartial, I might almost say, unrelenting justice to her children.

The primary and principal object of the East India Company was certainly trade. They gained considerably when they attended to nothing else. Circumstances, however, and particularly wars in which the mother country was engaged, made it necessary for their own existence, as well as for the interest of England, to take arms in those distant regions: had they not done so, the enemies of Great Britain, (viz. the Dutch and French who were nationally engaged in the traffic and transactions of that country,) would have destroyed the gem in its crystallization, which now shines the brightest in her diadem.

Thousands have bled in expelling the enemy from the formidable situations which they occupied; and millions have been expended to encourage the brave and adventurous; many things have been accomplished, which at the outset it would have been thought madness to expect. The history of India is too well known to require any elucidation of my assertions.

From that time, however, the *profits* and the *prosperity* of the Company decreased, almost in proportion as that of their sovereignty increased. They were obliged to keep up large armies of their own, they paid all the King's troops, and ships that were lent them; they supported their Allies, lest they should be driven out with them; they repelled their enemies and aggressors; incorporated their possessions with their own; they conquered countries for his Majesty, and added to his dominions the richest empires in the East, which for centuries had enriched a rivalling nation—but with a rich, plentiful prospect, they became in some degree impoverished themselves.

Had the Honourable East India Company, like ancient and modern bar-

barians, plundered their subdued subjects; or had they subsisted their armies on the countries which they in the course of wars invaded; or exacted forced loans—they might have filled their coffers, and might now look with indifference at the result of parliamentary resolutions. India would not be worth contending for had they not shown clemency and justice to its natives; but this they now expect themselves on this occasion from their mother country.

The security of the Indian possessions is but of a very recent date: the exact periods are the conquest and victories obtained under the auspices of the Marquis Wellesley. Before that time, Madras and its dependencies were under constant apprehensions from the Mysore and Hydrabad tyrants, and the Southern Mahratta states; for had these ever heartily united, the event of a long war could not have been doubtful.

Bengal was at all times threatened by the then mighty Mahratta Empire, the Seiks and the Vizier of Oude, of which, had they ever cordially and systematically combined, not all the resources of Bengal and its subordinate provinces could have withstood the shock. All lie prostrate now by the force of genius and money: for comparatively but few lives have been lost in that immense struggle. Millions were spent, but judiciously—not squandered away, as it may have happened in former times, but expended in procuring the means of resistance and aggression. The troops, both white and black, were in those campaigns regularly paid and well supplied in every respect; success in all their undertakings was hence secured.

The results of such gigantic efforts were immense: they were superior to every expectation that could have been formed by any other than the genius that planned them. The dominions under Fort St. George are now so secure from foreign enemies, that since the last Mahratta war, notwithstanding the vast territorial extension, not a corps of any description has been raised; nay, the number of men in many instances has absolutely been diminished. The income on the other hand has been raised by the revenues of conquered and ceded countries. This presidency is no longer dependent on Bengal for the payment of her establishments, and the other can remit the surplus of her finances for the payment of her debts and dividends.

The time indeed has commenced when the Honourable Company are to reap the fruit of all that which genius, from Lord Clive down to the Marquis Wellesley, combined with the perseverance, courage, and bravery of their troops, and all that liberal encouragement and immense sums, have accomplished.

The time is come, when the mother country will derive the assistance to which she, for her cherishing care and protection, is so eminently entitled; but which, in my humble opinion, she will by no other means receive so effectually, as through the East India Company as at present constituted.

This in justice cannot certainly be the time that the East India Company should be deprived of the sole management and the profits which they are to derive from the countries which so lately and with so much expense have been added to their stock; when scarcely one-tenth of the purchase money can have been realized! This certainly cannot be the time when any part of their estates should be taken from them; for by disuniting the military from the civil, the latter would become ineffective and would lose its respectability. A contrary interest would soon appear, where closest union is required for ensuring existence!

My knowledge of politics is too limited to say, or even to guess with any degree of precision, what changes will be proposed, or what alterations are intended; but I am much inclined to think, that any material ones will be attended with the worst effects.

The great bulk of the ancient subjects of the East India Company's possessions feel themselves perfectly happy and contented under their government; they call it emphatically *Dharma* Company, as they formerly applied the same epithet to one of their greatest kings, who still is remembered and worshipped under the name of *Dharma* Rajah, meaning the good, the charitable. Indeed, the lower and working classes are superlatively happy in India: they are at least more so than any set of mortals with whom I am acquainted.

Another class of those men, particularly the subjects of the newly conquered provinces, and those attached by long habit to the families and institutions of former days, begin just to be reconciled and to feel themselves comfortable; but they are by no means so much so, that they would not on a change of fortune, or any material one in the state of affairs, begin to waver, or to cherish and encourage hopes for greater alterations in their favour. If the natives should see that the army was no longer under the entire controul of the Local Government; or if the judicial department should be alienated from the present establishment; they will be struck with amazement, they will probably begin to think it not impossible to bring about another, yet greater revolution.

If the Dharma Company can be so easily dissolved, the Maha Rajah (of whom they have seen so many got rid of,) could, in their opinion, be also dispossessed!

Any change at present might be attended with the worst consequences.

The Company's servants both civil and military, before they get any material controul, must render themselves acquainted, in subordinate situations, both with the nature of the Company's affairs, with that of the natives, their language and manners; indeed they must become in some degree naturalized. It is more than probable, that the greater part, if not the whole of them would be retained in his Majesty's service. But it is as certain also, that gentlemen would be sent to India, and in situations of the greatest consequence, who are destitute of all those qualifications which now are reckoned absolutely necessary for the management of those affairs. These, with the best intentions, might propose reformations, and introduce practices which may be attended with the same or worse effects than the *caps* and *stocks* of Sepoys are believed to have brought about on a recent occasion. Should it happen that an old spendthrift arrives among them, with a determination of recruiting his broken fortune in as short a time as possible; then woe to the poor Hindoos in the first instance, and mercy on his countrymen in the sequel! A dozen of these characters, with half a dozen of the former, would be the loss of India.

This creates in my mind the most gloomy apprehensions for the safety of India, if it should be taken from the hands of the Honourable Company, without gradual preparation.

The only thing, which in my humble opinion could be attempted with safety now, is to teach and to accustom the natives of India to look up to Majesty as the source of mercy, honour, rank, and justice.

Commissioners appointed by the King should alone have the power, in the name and behalf of his Majesty, of signing death-warrants, granting reprieves and pardons: the same should be authorized to sign, on the recommendation of the Local Government, the commissions of the native officers of the army: confer titles, as Rajah, Subadar, Zemindar, &c. the most powerful of all means to attach an Hindoo, and one most successfully practised by former Emperors and Kings of Hindoostan; for there is certainly not a child prouder of a father than a Hindoo is of a bauble of that kind. The Dutch granted and sold the privilege of using an umbrella or a walking stick; and, limited as their possessions were on the continent of India, I have myself known persons who have paid many thousands of pagodas for that pledge of honour. This Court might be also one of ultimate appeal in causes of peculiar magnitude.

It is scarcely necessary to say, that to avoid great extraordinary expenses, the Governor and Royal Judges in the different Presidencies might be constituted into this Royal Court of Commissioners.

APPENDIX.

APPENDIX A.

Annalysis of a New Species of Copper Ore. By Thomas Thomson, M. D. F. R. S. and E. From the Philosophical Transactions. Read before the Royal Society, November 18, 1813.

THE mineral which constitutes the subject of this paper was discovered, by Dr. Benjamin Heyne, about the year 1800, in the peninsula of Indostan, near the eastern border of the Mysore.* From Dr. Heyne's description, it is probable that it occurs in nests in primitive rocks, which seem to be green stone, or at least connected with primitive trap. These rocks appear to be subordinate to mica slate. But I purposely omit all particular details, because I understand Dr. Heyne has himself a work in the press, in which the mineralogy of this country will be particularly described.

Copper mines had been wrought in these mountains some centuries ago; but they had been abandoned probably on account of the various revolutions to which this part of India has been subjected. The most common ore which occurs in these mountains is malachite, and it seems to occupy very extensive veins; but the species which I propose to describe here occurs also in considerable quantity. It had been already made the subject of various experiments, with a view to determine how much copper it contained, but I am not aware that any person had subjected it to a regular chemical analysis, or recognised it as a new species.

All the specimens of this ore which I have seen are amorphous; so that, as far as is known at present, it never occurs crystallized. Quartz crystals indeed are imbedded in it abundantly and very irregularly. Sometimes they

* In the Vincatygherry and Calastry country, below the Ghauts, vide Tract on Copper Ore.

are single, sometimes they constitute the lining of small cavities to be found in it. These crystals are all translucent. In some rare cases they are colourless; but by far the greater number of them are tinged of a yellowish red, and some few of them are green. The mineral is likewise interspersed with small specks of malachite; and with dark, brownish red, soft, particles, which I found to consist of red oxide of iron.

The colour varies in consequence of the irregular distribution of these extraneous substances. One specimen, which was the most free from the malachite and the red particles, was of a dark blackish brown colour. But in general the colour is a mixture of green, red, and brown; sometimes one, and sometimes another prevailing. Small green veins of malachite likewise traverse it in different directions.

The fracture is small conchoidal, and in some parts of the mineral there is a tendency to a foliated fracture. The lustre is glimmering, owing, I conceive, to the minute quartz crystals scattered through it. The kind of lustre is resinous; and on that account and the variety of colours, this ore has a good deal of the aspect of serpentine.

It is soft, being easily scratched by the knife. It is sectile. The streak reddish brown. The specific gravity 2·620.

It effervesces in acids and dissolves, letting fall a red powder. The solution is green, or blue, according to the acid, indicating that it consists chiefly of copper.

After a few preliminary trials to ascertain the nature of the constituents of this ore, I adopted the following mode of analysis.

1. 100 grains in the state of a coarse powder were put into a phial containing diluted sulphuric acid, and the mouth of the phial was stopped with cotton wool. The loss of weight, when the effervescence was at an end, amounted to 16·7 grains. This loss was owing to the escape of carbonic acid gas.

2. 100 grains of the ore were treated in the same way with muriatic acid. The green solution was decanted off, and evaporated nearly to dryness, to get rid of the excess of acid. A plate of zinc was then put into the liquid previously diluted with water. The copper precipitated weighed 48·5 grains.

On repeating the analysis, I found that the muriatic acid had likewise taken up a portion of iron. I therefore supersaturated the solution with ammonia, and threw the whole upon a filter. By this means the red oxide

6

of iron was separated. The ammonical solution was then neutralized by muriatic acid, and the copper thrown down by a plate of zinc. But during my first analysis, none of the iron was taken up by the cold muriatic acid, owing, no doubt, to the state of its aggregation.

3. The red powder, which remained undissolved after the muriatic solution was drawn off, was boiled for several hours in nitromuriatic acid. The matter gradually diminished in bulk and became white, while the acid acquired a golden yellow colour. The acid was now separated from the undissolved powder, evaporated nearly to dryness to get rid of the excess of acid, diluted with water, and mixed with an excess of ammonia. A brown powder fell, which was separated by the filter, and which, after being exposed to a red heat, weighed 19·5 grains. A little of this powder being dissolved in muriatic acid was precipitated dark blue by prussiate of potash. The remainder being mixed with tallow, and suddenly heated in a covered crucible, became black, and was attracted by the magnet. These properties leave no doubt that the powder was peroxide of iron.

4. The ammonical solution had a light blue colour, I therefore neutralized it by muriatic acid, and put into it a polished plate of zinc. I obtained a sensible deposit of copper; but so small, that I was unable to collect and weigh it. I estimate it at about 0·1 grain.

5. The white undissolved matter being heated to redness weighed 2·1 grains. On examining this matter attentively, I found it entirely composed of fragments of quartz crystals which had been interspersed through the ore, and had from their minuteness escaped my observation.

6. From the facility with which the copper dissolved in muriatic and sulphuric acids, there could be no doubt that it existed in the ore in the state of an oxide. But the red colour of the ore made me uncertain whether the oxide was the red or the black. I therefore put 100 grains of the ore into a tall narrow phial, filled the phial full of water, and then by means of a funnel poured a quantity of muriatic acid into the bottom of the vessel. The ore was immediately attacked, and the solution from the very commencement apeared green. This I consider as a demonstration that the copper in the ore was in the state of black oxide. Now, black oxide of copper is a compound of 100 metal + 25 oxygen. So that the 48·6 grains of copper, extracted from the ore when in the state of black oxide, must have weighed 60·75 grains.

From the preceding analysis, it appears that the ore is composed as follows:—

Carbonic acid	16·70
Peroxide of copper..........	60·75
Peroxide of iron	19·50
Silica.....................	2·10
Loss	0·95
	100·00

The silica was obviously accidental, and derived from the quartz crystals; so that the ore, in fact, consists of carbonic acid, peroxide of copper, and red oxide of iron. In the different analyses, I have found the copper to vary a little. The least quantity I obtained was 48·6, the greatest 51 grains. The red oxide of iron and siliceous matter varied also somewhat. The least quantity obtained was 19 grains, the greatest 25 grains. These variations are owing chiefly to the admixture of quartz crystals, and partly to the specks of malachite and red oxide of iron with which the ore is interspersed.

The carbonic acid is obviously combined with the black oxide of copper, so as to constitute carbonate of copper. Now carbonate of copper, as I ascertained by a direct analysis, is composed of an integrant particle of carbonic acid, and an integrant particle of black oxide of copper. An integrant particle of carbonic acid, as I have shewn elsewhere, weighs 2·751, and an integrant particle of peroxide of copper weighs 10. Now 2·751 is to 10 as 16·7 is to 60·75, so that there can be no doubt that the carbonic acid and oxide of copper are united in the ore. As to the oxide of iron, I am disposed to consider it as only mechanically mixed; because in one experiment I dissolved almost all the copper without touching the iron. Yet it deserves attention, that 77·4 and 19·5, the weight of carbonate of copper and oxide of iron found by the preceding analysis, correspond with three integrant particles of carbonate of copper, and one integrant particle of peroxide of iron.

We were previously acquainted with two other native species of this salt, namely, *malachite* and *blue carbonate* or *copper azure.* But both of these are hydrous carbonates containing water as a constituent, and if any confidence be put in the analyses of Klaproth, whose precision is sufficiently known, malachite contains twice as much water as the blue carbonate. Blue carbonate is a compound of one integrant particle of water, and one integrant particle of carbonate of copper, while malachite contains two particles of water. Our ore is an *anhydrous carbonate of copper*. When heated to redness, it loses its carbonic acid, but undergoes no further change. Some specimens lost about half a grain more than their carbonic acid. This I ascribed to the water in the malachite, with which the ore was occasionally mixed.

APPENDIX B.

TABLES OF THE THERMOMETER AND BAROMETER,

AS OBSERVED IN DIFFERENT PARTS OF

THE PENINSULA OF HINDOSTAN.

MARCH. 1800.

Names of Places.	Day of the Week	Day of the Month	Thermometer.			Barometer.
			M.	N.	E.	N.
Madras	Mon.	10				30·169
	Tues.	11				30·2
	Wed.	12				30·03
	Thurs.	13				30·03
	Fri.	14				30·05
	Sat.	15		93		30·
	Sun.	16				29·966
	Mon.	17				29·85
	Tues.	18				29·666
to	Wed.	19				29·525
	Thurs.	20				29·525
	Fri.	21				29·525
	Sat.	22				29·533
	Sun.	23		98		29·5
	Mon.	24				29·16
	Tues.	25				29·
	Wed.	26		93	81	29·
	Thurs.	27	69	95	82	29·
	Fri.	28	66	95	81	29·09
	Sat.	29	69			29·266
	Sun.	30	71	86	81	29·266
Peddanaigdurgam	Mon.	31	72	94	87	28·92

Mean height of the thermometer $77\frac{1}{3}$.

APRIL. 1800.

Names of Places.	Day of the Week	Day of the Month	M.	N.	E.	N.
Vincatygherry in Mysore	Tues.	1	72	93	86	27·7
	Wed.	2	74	92	83	27·6
	Thurs.	3	73	94	84	27·4
	Fri.	4	69	91	84	27·4

APRIL (continued.)

Names of Places.	Day of the Week	Day of the Month	Thermometer.			Barometer.
			M.	N.	E.	N.
	Sat.	5	75	94	87	27·4
	Sun.	6	76	97	90	27·4
	Mon.	7	75	94	86	27·28
	Tues.	8	74	93	86	27·28
	Wed.	9	74	93	84	27·3
to	Thurs.	10	74	93	80	27·39
	Fri.	11	73	92	80	27·28
	Sat.	12	70	89	80	27·21
	Sun.	13	70	93	84	27·23
	Mon.	14	$72\frac{1}{2}$	93	86	27·25
	Tues.	15	$72\frac{1}{2}$	93	87	27·37
Bengalore	Wed.	16	$72\frac{1}{2}$	93	88	27·25
	Thurs.	17	$72\frac{1}{2}$	93	88	27·25
	Fri.	18	66	90	83	27·2
	Sat.	19	64	91	86	27·23
	Sun.	20	70	92	86	27·25
	Mon.	21	71	95	84	27·25
	Tues.	22	72	$93\frac{1}{2}$	86	27·25
	Wed.	23	74	94	86	27·25
	Thurs.	24	72	94	86	27 25
	Fri.	25	72	96	82	27·25
	Sat.	26	74	95	86	27·25
	Sun.	27	74	84	83	27·2
	Mon.	28	74	89	82	27·2
	Tues.	29	74	91	82	27·2
	Wed.	30	72	92	86	27·2

Mean height of the thermometer $83\frac{1}{4}$.

Greatest variation of ditto in the course of one day .... 27°.

Ditto ditto in the course of one month 33°.

MAY. 1800.

Names of Places.	Day of the Week.	Day of the Month.	Thermometer.			Barometer.
			M.	N.	E.	N.
Bengalore	Thurs.	1	72	93	86	27·2
	Fri.	2	74	92	86	27·2
	Sat.	3	74	95	84	27·3
	Sun.	4	74	94	82	27·3
	Mon.	5	73	89	84	27·3
	Tues.	6	71	92	82	27·25
	Wed.	7	71	94	86	27·25
	Thurs.	8	71	99	90	27·3
	Fri.	9	73	96	90	27·35
	Sat.	10	73	96	89	27·15
Left Bengalore travelling towards Sira	Sun.	11	73	96	86	27·15
	Mon.	12	70	98	90	27·5
	Tues.	13	74	97	90	27·65
	Wed.	14	76	99	92	27·82
	Thurs.	15	76	99	92	28·7
	Fri.	16	78	98	92	28·1
	Sat.	17	78	96	90	28·1
	Sun.	18	74	95	90	28·06
	Mon.	19	74	100	90	
	Tues.	20	75	98	90	27·96
	Wed.	21	75	94	90	27·78
	Thurs.	22	74	94	86	27·75
	Fri.	23	74	94	85	27·75
	Sat.	24	74	92	84	27·80
	Sun.	25	74	94	85	27·80
	Mon.	26	74	93	81	27·65
	Tues.	27	74	85	76	27·65
	Wed.	28	74	88	76	27·73
Chittledrūg	Thurs.	29	74	85	74	27·73
	Fri.	30	74	90	84	27·7
	Sat.	31	74	91	84	27·7

Mean height of the thermometer 82·03.
Greatest variation of one day 28°.
Ditto ditto in one month 30°.

JUNE. 1800.

Names of Places.	Day of the Week.	Day of the Month.	Thermometer.			Barometer.
			M.	N.	E.	N.
Chittledrūg	Sun.	1	74	94	84	27·7
	Mon.	2	74	90	74	27·7
	Tues.	3	74	88	74	27·7
	Wed.	4	72	86	74	27·7
	Thurs.	5	72	88	74	27·7
	Fri.	6	72	86	73	27·65
	Sat.	7	72	82	73	27·65
	Sun.	8	71	80	71	27·65
	Mon.	9	72	78	69	27·65
	Tues.	10	72	80	73	27·65
	Wed.	11	73	80	73	27·65
	Thurs.	12	70	82	72	27·65
	Fri.	13	70	82	74	27·65
	Sat.	14	70	82	74	27·65
	Sun.	15	70	80	76	27·65
	Mon.	16	74	82	79	27·66

JUNE (continued.)

Names of Places.	Day of the Week.	Day of the Month.	Thermometer.			Barometer.
			M.	N.	E.	N.
Chittledrūg	Tues.	17	74	86	78	27·65
	Wed.	18	74	83	78	27·65
	Thurs.	19	74	90	79	27·65
	Fri.	20	72	86	79	27·7
	Sat.	21	71	89	74	27·7
	Sun.	22	74	86	79	27·7
	Mon.	23	74	88	76	27·7
	Tues.	24	70	76	74	27·7
	Wed.	25	72	89	76	27·7
	Thurs.	26	72	86	75	27·7
	Fri.	27	72	86	74	27·6
Mayconda	Sat.	28	74	84	74	27·8
	Sun.	29	74	81	76	28·1
	Mon.	30	76	89	82	28·13

Mean height of the thermometer 75·5.
Greatest variation of one day 20°.
Ditto ditto in one month 24°.

JULY. 1800.

Names of Places.	Day of the Week.	Day of the Month.	Thermometer.			Barometer.
Hurryhurr	Tues.	1	76	89	81	28·15
	Wed.	2	75	91	80	28·17
	Thurs.	3	75	82	76	28·17
	Fri.	4	74	82	75	28·17
	Sat.	5	75	87	75	28·27
	Sun.	6	76	91	75	28·26
	Mon.	7	75	90	75	28·27
	Tues.	8	75	86	78	28·26
	Wed.	9	76	82	75	28·27
	Thurs.	10	76	82	76	28·27
	Fri.	11	76	82	76	28·17
	Sat.	12	76	86	75	28·16
	Sun.	13	76	83	75	28·27
	Mon.	14	75	82	75	28·26
	Tues.	15	75	88	75	28·26
	Wed.	16	75	86	75	28·27
Yalahelly	Thurs.	17	75	86	79	28·27
Conuntalla	Fri.	18	75	86	78	28·27
Honelly	Sat.	19	75	83	76	28·28
	Sun.	20	75	78	71	28·18
	Mon.	21	73	76	72	28·15
	Tues.	22	73	81	74	28·15
	Wed.	23	74	79	74	28·15
	Thurs.	24	74	81	74	28·15
	Fri.	25	74	81	74	28·15
Arakere	Sat.	26	74	78	73	28·2
Buswapatam	Sun.	27	72	80	73	27·9
	Mon.	28	73	80	73	27·9
	Tues.	29	73	80	74	27·9
Conavarahully	Wed.	30	74	85	76	28·1
Hurryhurr	Thurs.	31	76	84	78	28·3

Mean height of the thermometer 77½.
Greatest variation in the course of one day 15°.
Ditto in one month 20°.

AUGUST. 1800.

Names of Places.	Day of the Week	Day of the Month	Thermometer. M.	N.	E.	Barometer. N.
Hurryhurr	Fri.	1	75	86	78	28·3
	Sat.	2	75	86	78	28·3
	Sun.	3	75	70	82	28·3
	Mon.	4	75	88	80	28·33
	Tues.	5	75	87	78	28·33
	Wed.	6	74	88	80	28·33
	Thurs.	7	75	87	80	28·33
	Fri.	8	75	87½	79	28·37
	Sat.	9	75	86	79	28·37
	Sun.	10	75	84	78	28·35
	Mon.	11	75	84	78	28·33
	Tues.	12	75	84	78	28·27
	Wed.	13	75	84	76	28·27
	Thurs.	14	75	84	78	28 27
	Fri.	15	75	84	78	28·27
	Sat.	16	75	87	78	28·37
	Sun.	17	75	85	79	28·37
	Mon.	18	75	89	79	28·37
	Tues.	19	75	87	79	28·37
	Wed.	20	75	84	78½	28·37
	Thurs.	21	74	83	74	28·37
	Fri.	22	74	84	76	28·27
	Sat.	23	73	80	77	28·27
	Sun.	24	74	80	77	28·27
	Mon.	25	75	82	76	28·27
	Tues.	26	75	82	76	28·27
Chicka Bedery ...	Wed.	27	75	84	76	28·27
	Thurs.	28	75	82	76	28·2
	Fri.	29	75	85	78	28·33
	Sat.	30	74	85	78	28·33
	Sun.	31	74	88	80	28·2

Mean height 79¼.
Greatest variation in one day 14°.
Ditto in one month 17°.

SEPTEMBER. 1800.

Names of Places.	Day of the Week	Day of the Month	Thermometer. M.	N.	E.	Barometer. N.
Hurryhurr	Mon.	1	74	91	80	28·27
	Tues.	2	74	87	78	28·27
	Wed.	3	74	85	78	28·27
	Thurs.	4	74	83	77	28 27
	Fri.	5	74	81½	77	28·27
	Sat.	6	74	86	77	28·27
	Sun.	7	74	88	77	28·27
	Mon.	8	74	86	76	23·23
	Tues.	9	74	86	76	28·27
	Wed.	10	74	85½	76	28·27
	Thurs.	11	74	85	78	28·27
	Fri.	12	73½	86	78	28·27
	Sat.	13	73	90	81	28·27
	Sun.	14	74	91	81	28·27
	Mon.	15	74	89	81	28·27
	Tues.	16	74	86	78	28·27
	Wed	17	74	87	78	28·45
	Thurs.	18	73	87	79	28·4

SEPTEMBER (continued.)

Names of Places.	Day of the Week	Day of the Month	Thermometer. M.	N.	E.	Barometer. N.
Hurryhurr	Fri.	19	74	89	80	28·4
	Sat.	20	74	92	80	28·2
	Sun.	21	73	89	75	28·2
	Mon.	22	74	92	81	28·3
	Tues.	23	76	94	82	28·3
	Wed.	24	76	87	81	28·23
	Thurs.	25	70	78	75	28·23
	Fri.	26	76	90	78	28·23
	Sat.	27	76	88	82	28·33
	Sun.	28	71	88	82	28·37
	Mon.	29	72	83	75	28·36
	Tues.	30	74	86	75	28·35

The remarks of the thermometer are taken usually at 2½ P. M.—20th at 12½ 94.

Mean height 79½.
Greatest variation of one day 17°.
Ditto in one month 23°.

OCTOBER. 1800.

Names of Places.	Day of the Week	Day of the Month	Thermometer. M.	N.	E.	Barometer. N.
Hurryhurr.......	Wed.	1	73	87	80	28·3
	Thurs.	2	74	94	86	28·2
	Fri.	3	75	92	80	28·2
	Sat.	4	74	92	81	28·2
	Sun.	5	75	88	83	28·2
	Mon.	6	75	90	82	28·2
	Tues.	7	76	87	79	28·2
	Wed.	8	76	87	79	28·13
Mallagandenhully	Thurs.	9	72	90	70	28·65
Annaji	Fri.	10	74	82	71	27·87
	Sat.	11	70	88	71	27·8
Ballahull	Sun.	12	71	84	70	27·8
Chittledrūg	Mon.	13	70	82	71	27·8
	Tues.	14	70	84	78	27·8
	Wed.	15	69	86	78	27·8
Aiamungalum	Thurs.	16	70	90	80	28·
Erūr............	Fri.	17	72	80	73	28·
Jangunhully	Sat.	18	71	88	71	28·
Sirah	Sun.	19	71	92	77	27·95
	Mon.	20	71	90	76	27·95
Sesuppanhully....	Tues.	21	70	90	76	27·6
Bidery	Wed.	22	70	90	76	27·45
Tūmkūr.........	Thurs.	23	70	80	74	27·33
Nidgicul	Fri.	24	70	80	74	27·25
Nellāmungalum ..	Sat.	25	70	76	74	27·05
Madavaram	Sun.	26	64	78	75	27·2
Bengalore	Mon.	27	70	90	75	27·1
	Tues.	28	70	75	74	27 05
	Wed.	29	71	78	75	27·05
	Thurs.	30	71	78	75	27·05
	Fri.	31	71	78	74½	27·05

Mean height 76½.
Greatest variation of one day 20°.
Ditto of one month 30°.

NOVEMBER. 1800.

Names of Places.	Day of the Week	Day of the Month	Thermometer.			Barometer.
			M.	N.	E.	N.
Bengalore	Sat.	1	71	78	77	27·15
	Sun.	2	73	77	76	27·07
	Mon.	3	76	77	77	27 07
	Tues.	4	76	78	77	27·07
	Wed.	5	74	77	76	27·07
	Thurs.	6	74	77	76	27·07
	Fri.	7	74	76	75	27·07
	Sat.	8	72	74	73	27·07
	Sun.	9	73	74	72	27·07
	Mon.	10	70	73	73	27 07
	Tues.	11	70	72	76	27·07
	Wed.	12	76	86	84	27·07
	Thurs.	13	68	$71\frac{2}{3}$	72	27·07
	Fri.	14	69	72	72	27·07
	Sat.	15	69	74	74	27·07
	Sun.	16	69	76	74	27·07
	Mon.	17	70	75	75	27·13
	Tues.	18	72	$75\frac{1}{2}$	75	27·13
	Wed.	19	73	$76\frac{1}{2}$	76	27·2
	Thurs.	20	72	76	76	27·15
	Fri.	21	72	76	75	27·15
	Sat.	22	70	74	73	27·15
	Sun.	23	70	75	74	27·15
	Mon.	24	70	74	74	27·15
	Tues.	25	70	74	74	27·07
	Wed.	26	68	$73\frac{1}{2}$	78	27·07
	Thurs.	27	68	76	75	27·13
	Fri.	28	66	74	$71\frac{1}{2}$	27·13
	Sat.	29	67	76	73	27·13
	Sun.	30	65	76	73	27·13

Mean height $73\frac{1}{2}$.
Greatest variation in one day 11°.
Ditto in one month 21°.

DECEMBER. 1800.

Names of Places.	Day of the Week	Day of the Month	Thermometer.			Barometer.
			M.	N.	E.	N.
Bengalore	Mon.	1	65	74	73	27·13
	Tues.	2	64	73	71	27·13
	Wed.	3	65	73	71	27·2
	Thurs.	4	64	73	71	27 2
	Fri.	5	64	73	71	27·2
	Sat.	6	65	75	73	27·1
	Sun.	7	66	75	73	27·1
	Mon.	8	64	75	73	27·1
	Tues.	9	66	75	73	27·1
	Wed.	10	66	75	73	27·1
	Thurs.	11	70	77	75	27·1
	Fri.	12	66	77	75	27·1
	Sat.	13	66	77	75	27·1
	Sun.	14	68	77	75	27·1
	Mon.	15	67	75	73	27·1
	Tues.	16	65	71	69	27·1
	Wed.	17	64	73	71	27·1

DECEMBER (continued.)

Names of Places.	Day of the Week	Day of the Month	Thermometer.			Barometer.
			M.	N.	E.	N.
Bengalore	Thurs.	18	65	75	73	27·1
	Fri.	19	65	73	70	27·1
	Sat.	20	63	71	70	27·1
	Sun.	21	65	71	69	27·1
	Mon.	22	64	73	71	27·1
	Tues.	23	66	73	71	27·1
	Wed.	24	67	71	69	27·1
	Thurs.	25	64	71	69	27·1
	Fri.	26	63	71	69	27·1
	Sat.	27	65	71	69	27·1
Bengalore	Sun.	28	67	72	70	27·1
Kistnarajapore ...	Mon.	29	68	72	70	27·2
Ooscotah	Tues.	30	68	76	73	27·2
Taverikera	Wed.	31	66	80	72	27·15

Mean height $70\frac{1}{2}$.
Greatest variation in one day 14°.
Ditto in one month 17°.

JANUARY. 1801.

Names of Places.	Day of the Week	Day of the Month	M.	N.	E.	N.
Colar	Thurs.	1	66	78	73	27·35
Bētamungal......	Fri.	2	64	80	73	27·55
Venketigherry....	Sat.	3	64	80	71	27·75
Peddanaïg Pass ..	Sun.	4	64	80	71	28·83
Sātghur	Mon.	5	64	86	75	28·83
Gudiatum	Tues.	6	68	76	71	29·1
Erinjiporam......	Wed.	7	66	77	75	29·4
Vellore..........	Thurs.	8	68	78	74	29·43
Tengary	Fri.	9	70	80	76	29·5
Jemmadhengy....	Sat.	10	74	86	76	29·73
Balachitty Suttrum	Sun.	11	74	86	77	29·83
Virapermāl Ditto..	Mon.	12	76	86	81	30·
Ammāramattū....	Tues.	13	75	88	78	30·1
Pogākū Mettū ...	Wed.	14	73	88	78	30·23
Madras	Thurs.	15	73	88	76	30·25
	Fri.	16	71	35	76	30·25
	Sat.	17	71	$85\frac{1}{2}$	76	30·3
	Sun.	18	70	85	76	30·23
	Mon.	19	70	86	77	30·23
	Tues.	20	70	87	77	30·23
	Wed.	21	70	87	76	30·23
	Thurs.	22	70	87	77	30·23
	Fri.	23	70	87	77	30·23
	Sat.	24	70	86	77	30·23
	Sun.	25	70	87	77	30·23
	Mon.	26	70	86	77	30·23
	Tues.	27	72	87	76	30·23
	Wed.	28	70	87	76	30·27
	Thurs.	29	70	86	75	30·23
	Fri.	30	70	86	76	30·23
	Sat.	31	70	85	76	30·23

Mean height $76\frac{2}{3}$.
Greatest variation in one day 22°.
Ditto in one month 24°.

FEBRUARY. 1801.

Names of Places.	Day of the Week	Day of the Month	Thermometer. M.	Thermometer. N.	Thermometer. E.	Barometer. N.
Madras	Sun.	1	69	86	78	30·23
	Mon.	2	69	84	78	30·23
	Tues.	3	69	82	78	30·23
	Wed.	4	70	82	78	30·23
	Thurs.	5	70	82	78	30·23
	Fri.	6	70	85	77	30·25
	Sat.	7	70	86	77	30·25
	Sun.	8	70	86	78	30·25
	Mon.	9	70	84	77	30·25
	Tues.	10	70	84	77	30·25
	Wed.	11	70	84	77	
	Thurs.	12	70	85	77	
	Fri.	13	70	82	77	
	Sat.	14	70	83	77	
	Sun.	15	70	83	77	30·2
	Mon.	16	70	83	77	30·2
	Tues.	17	70	84	77	30·2
	Wed.	18	70	86	77	
	Thurs.	19	70	86	77	
	Fri.	20	70	87	78	30·2
	Sat.	21	71	85	77	30·2
	Sun.	22	70	85	77	29·9
	Mon.	23	70	83	77	30·
	Tues.	24	70	85	79	30·
	Wed.	25	71	85	79	30·1
	Thurs.	26	71	84	79	30·1
	Fri.	27	71	85	79	30·1
	Sat.	28	71	87	70	30·1

Mean height 77½.
Greatest variation in the course of one day 17°.
Ditto in one month 18°.

MARCH. 1801.

Names of Places.	Day of the Week	Day of the Month	Thermometer. M.	Thermometer. N.	Thermometer. E.	Barometer. N.
Madras	Sun.	1	70	86	79	30·2
	Mon.	2	71	88*	79	30·22
	Tues.	3	72	87	80	30·25
	Wed.	4	72	89	80	30·22
	Thurs.	5	73	87	80	30·22
	Fri.	6	73	85	80	30·1
	Sat.	7	71	87	80	30·1
	Sun.	8	71	86	80	30·2
	Mon.	9	71	88	80	30·2
	Tues.	10	71	88	80	30·2
	Wed.	11	71	90	82	30·25
	Thurs.	12	73	90	82	30·25
	Fri.	13	73	89	82	30·25
	Sat.	14	73	89	83	30·2
	Sun.	15	71	90	84	30·2
	Mon.	16	72	89	85	30·2

* At twelve o'clock 93°.

MARCH (continued.)

Names of Places.	Day of the Week	Day of the Month	Thermometer. M.	Thermometer. N.	Thermometer. E.	Barometer. N.
Madras†	Tues.	17	72	89	84	30·2
Sadras	Wed.	18	71	89	84	30·1
Pondicherry	Thurs.	19	72	90	85	30·25
	Fri.	20	72	89	85	30·23
Cuddalore	Sat.	21	72	90	84	30·25
Tranquebar	Sun.	22	72	90	84	30·15
	Mon.	23	72	90	84	30·15
	Tues.	24	72	90	84	30 15
	Wed.	25	72	89	84	30·15
	Thurs.	26	72	90	84	30·15
	Fri.	27	71	90	85	30·1
	Sat.	28	70	91	86	30·1
Korungū Suttrum	Sun.	29	70	90	86	30·$\frac{2}{3}$
Shially	Mon.	30	75	93	83	30·07
Chillembrum	Tues.	31	74	90	84	30·

Mean height 81$\frac{1}{6}$.
Greatest variation of one day 21°.
Ditto in one month 21°.

APRIL. 1801.

Names of Places.	Day of the Week	Day of the Month	Thermometer. M.	Thermometer. N.	Thermometer. E.	Barometer. N.
Ucūr	Wed.	1	76	91	83	30·
Mattadūr	Thurs.	2	78	101	86	29 9
Gingi	Fri.	3	78	96	84	29·9
	Sat.	4	82	92	86	29·9
Vermamungalum .	Sun.	5	82	96	88	29·93
Arnie	Mon.	6	84	96	89	29·9
Chiltra Choultry .	Tues.	7	84	96	89	29·4
Vellore	Wed.	8	84	102	89	29·4
	Thurs.	9	84	100	90	29·4
	Fri.	10	84	99	89	29·4
	Sat.	11	84	100	89	29·4
	Sun.	12	84	99	90	29·4
Lalapettah	Mon.	13	84	99	89	29·4
Ramkistnaraze Petta ..	Tues.	14	86	98	90	29·5
Allatur Suttrum ..	Wed.	15	86	98	90	29·53
Bomrās Palliam ..	Thurs.	16	86	94	88	29·5
	Fri.	17	86	96	89	29·23
Bahader Petta....	Sat.	18	74	101	89	29·6
Tripetty	Sun.	19	78	97	94	29·6
Yērped	Mon.	20	86	101	94	29·7
Yellaganaru	Tues.	21	86	101	95	29·75
Venketigherry	Wed.	22	87	96	92	
	Thurs.	23	86	95	90	29·8
	Fri.	24	86	102	96	29·8
Sidaporam	Sat.	25	87	102	94	29·8
Podlacuru	Sun.	26	88	105	96	29·8
BuchyreddyPolliam	Mon.	27	84	99	94	29·87
Chennūr	Tues.	28	86	102	96	29·85
Bramhanacūka . ..	Wed.	29	86	96	87	30·05
Cāvilly	Thurs.	30	84	97	88	30·

Mean height 90$\frac{2}{3}$.
Greatest variation of one day 27°.
Ditto of one month 31°.

† On a tour from Madras to Tranquebar, Gingi, Vellore to the Copper Mines, Ongole, Commum, ceded districts to Bengalore.

MAY. 1801.

Names of Places.	Day of the Week	Day of the Month	Thermometer. M.	Thermometer. N.	Thermometer. E.	Barometer. N.
Gūdlūr	Fri.	1	86	91	84	30·
Irrincotah, in the night at Linga Sundrum	Sat.	2	84	96	87	29·8
Bombartipādu	Sun.	3	80	98	87	29·8
Kuttakindapallet	Mon.	4	80	98	87	29·6
Vangapādu (copper mines)	Tues.	5	82	102	90	29·63
	Wed.	6	82	107	98	29·8
Kunlagunta	Thurs.	7	80	95	87	29·83
Ongole	Fri.	8	82	95	89	29·8
	Sat.	9	84	94	89	29·8
	Sun.	10	86	98	91	29·8
	Mon.	11	86	99	96	29·8
Nutialapādu	Tues.	12	86	$107\frac{1}{2}$	96	29·75
Yellamunla	Wed.	13	86	107	95	29·6
Kunlametta	Thurs.	14	87	106	94	29·4
Caljavalpādu	Fri.	15	86	96	92	29·33
Commum	Sat.	16	86	95	91	29·33
	Sun.	17	85	95	89	29·33
Pussalapādu	Mon.	18	86	99	90	29·33
Pottypulle	Tues.	19	87	95	90	29·2
Hullinagur	Wed.	20	84	98	90	29·15
Porimamalu	Thurs.	21	84	102	92	29·35
Ambaram	Fri.	22	84	102	97	29·3
Unupenta	Sat.	23	85	107	99	29·5
Podatūr	Sun.	24	87	101	97	29·5
Jonalamurga	Mon.	25	88	102	96	29·5
Talia Podatūr	Tues.	26	89	102	96	29·4
Turpattry	Wed.	27	89	101	96	29·27
Royelchervu	Thurs.	28	88	101	96	29·05
Gutty	Fri.	29	84	101	96	28·8
	Sat.	30	84	101	96	28·85
	Sun.	31	84	106	96	28·8

Mean height $92\frac{1}{2}$.
Greatest variation in one day 25°.
Ditto in one month 27°.

JUNE. 1801.

Names of Places.	Day of the Week	Day of the Month	Thermometer. M.	Thermometer. N.	Thermometer. E.	Barometer. N.
Pāmdy	Mon.	1	84	106	94	28·8
Anantapore	Tues.	2	76	98	90	28·8
Darmārum	Wed.	3	75	101	90	28·8
Cottapulle	Thurs.	4	76	90	88	28·8
Hussainpore	Fri.	5	76	89	84	28·1
Pāghur	Sat.	6	72	89	84	28·$\frac{2}{3}$
	Sun.	7	76	89	86	28·$\frac{2}{3}$
Pareghi	Mon.	8	76	90	87	28.$\frac{1}{2}$
Sowluru	Tues.	9	78	91	88	27·9
Tondabary	Wed.	10	74	94	88	27·5

JUNE (continued)

Names of Places.	Day of the Week	Day of the Month	Thermometer. M.	Thermometer. N.	Thermometer. E.	Barometer. N.
Ballapore	Thurs.	11	70	91	89	27·1
Bengalore	Fri.	12	70	90	86	27·1
	Sat.	13	70	84	76	27·1
	Sun.	14	70	80	78	27·1
	Mon.	15	70	79	78	27·1
	Tues.	16	70	79	78	27·1
	Wed.	17	70	80	78	27·15
	Thurs.	18	70	80	76	27·1
	Fri.	19	70	80	76	27·$\frac{1}{2}$
	Sat.	20	70	80	76	27·15
	Sun.	21	70	80	76	27·15
	Mon.	22	70	79	76	27·15
	Tues.	23	70	79	76	27·1
	Wed.	24	70	80	76	27·
	Thurs.	25	70	80	76	27·
	Fri.	26	70	84	76	27·1
	Sat.	27	71	86	75	27·1
	Sun.	28	72	88	75	27·1
	Mon.	29	71	86	77	27·1
	Tues.	30	70	86	75	27·1

Mean height $79\frac{7}{9}$.
Greatest variation of one day 26°.
Ditto of one month 36°.

JULY. 1801.

Names of Places.	Day of the Week	Day of the Month	Thermometer. M.	Thermometer. N.	Thermometer. E.	Barometer. N.
Bengalore	Wed.	1	72	89	76	27·1
	Thurs.	2	73	88	75	27·1
	Fri.	3	72	87	76	27·1
	Sat.	4	71	86	75	27·1
	Sun.	5	70	84	79	27·1
	Mon.	6	72	86	76	27·1
	Tues.	7	72	87	78	27·1
	Wed.	8	72	86	76	27·05
	Thurs.	9	72	87	76	27·05
	Fri.	10	72	87	75	27·05
	Sat.	11	72	86	74	27·1
	Sun.	12	72	85	75	27·
	Mon.	13	72	86	75	27·1
	Tues.	14	72	86	75	27·1
	Wed.	15	72	86	75	27·1
	Thurs.	16	72	87	77	27·1
	Fri.	17	72	86	77	27·1
	Sat.	18	72	80	75	27·1
	Sun.	19	72	79	76	27·
	Mon.	20	72	79	78	27·
	Tues.	21	72	81	75	27·05
	Wed.	22	71	82	79	27·05
Madavāram *	Thurs.	23	70		82	27·19
Bagūr †	Fri.	24	76		81	27·19

* On a tour from Bengalore to Sīra.
† From Bagūr through Savagunga, Tumkūr, Bedery, Columbella, to Sīra, made no observations.

OCTOBER. 1801.

Names of Places.	Day of the Week	Day of the Month	Thermometer. M.	N.	E.	Barometer. N.
Sira	Fri.	9	74	82	78	27·97
	Sat.	10	74	82	77½	27·95
	Sun.	11	74	82	78	27·9
	Mon.	12	73	82	78	27·93
	Tues.	13	72	82	80	27·9
	Wed.	14	70	82	80	27·93
	Thurs.	15	74	83	80	27·93
	Fri.	16	74	83	80	27·93
	Sat.	17	72	83	80	27·8
	Sun.	18	70	82	80	27·8
	Mon.	19	74	83	79	27·8
	Tues.	20	72	83	79	27·8
	Wed.	21	72	82	79	27·87
	Thurs.	22	74	84	79	27·9
	Fri.	23	74	84	79	27·9
	Sat.	24	74	83	77	27·9*
	Sun.	25	74	78	76	27·9
	Mon.	26	73	76	74	27·95
	Tues.	27	73	81	79	27·9
	Wed.	28	74	82	79	27·9
	Thurs.	29	74	81	77	27·95
	Fri.	30	72	77	75	27·9
	Sat.	31	72	76	73	27·75

Mean height 77½.
Greatest variation in the course of one day 12°.
Ditto in one month 14°.

* At the time it rained, which was about 3½ P. M. the barometer fell to 27·85, and thermometer to 78.

NOVEMBER. 1801.

Names of Places.	Day of the Week	Day of the Month	Thermometer. M.	N.	E.	Barometer. N.
Sira	Sun.	1	74	79	77	27·8
Sira glacis, near the	Mon.	2	74	80	78	27·8
fort gate	Tues.	3	75	81	78	27·85
	Wed.	4	75	81	78	27·9
	Thurs.	5	74	82	78	27·9
Sira	Fri.	6	75	84	77	27·85
	Sat.	7	73	83	77	27·85
	Sun.	8	67	83	77	27·85
	Mon.	9	70	83	76	27.85
	Tues.	10	72	80	73	27·85
	Wed.	11	68	78	72	27·85
	Thurs.	12	68	78	74	27·87
	Fri.	13	72	79	74	27·87
	Sat.	14	74	82	75	27·87
	Sun.	15	73	83*	79	27·85
	Mon.	16	72	83	77	27·85
	Tues.	17	69	83	78	27·83
Sira Petta	Wed.	18	62	83	71	27·97

* At nine o'clock A. M. the thermometer 85°.

NOVEMBER (continued.)

Names of Places.	Day of the Week	Day of the Month	Thermometer. M.	N.	E.	Barometer. N.
Sira Petta	Thurs.	19	56	83	72	27·97
	Fri.	20	57	82	72	27·97
	Sat.	21	58	82	72	27·97
	Sun.	22	58	83	72	27·97
	Mon.	23	62	85	72	27·97
	Tues.	24	62	85	70	27·97
	Wed.	25	62	85	70	27·97
	Thurs.	26	60	84	70	27·97
	Fri.	27	62	84	71	27·97
	Sat.	28	67	82	73	27·97
	Sun.	29	65	84	74	27·97
	Mon.	30	60	85	74	28·

Mean height 74⅔.
Greatest variation of one day 27°.
Ditto one month 29°.

DECEMBER. 1801.

Names of Places.	Day of the Week	Day of the Month	Thermometer. M.	N.	E.	Barometer. N.
Sira	Tues.	1	60	85	74	28·
	Wed.	2	58	85	74	28·
Balker †	Thurs.	3	59	85	75	28·
Demunwelly	Fri.	4	59	86	74	27·75
Toinkere	Sat.	5	58	77	70	27·3
Corretekera......	Sun.	6	67	83	70	27·3
Bunwatty.........	Mon.	7	67	82	70	27·6
Gundumgherry‡..	Tues.	8	67	86	74	27·7
Ballapore........	Wed.	9	72	80	73	27·2
	Thurs.	10	69	77	74	27·1
Yellavenkum	Fri.	11	69	78	74	27·3
Bengalore.......	Sat.	12	68	78	72	27·2
	Sun.	13	66	72	68	27·2
	Mon.	14	64	70	68	27·2
	Tues.	15	64	70	68	27·1
	Wed.	16	64	70	68	27·1
	Thurs.	17	64	70	68	27·1
	Fri.	18	64	70	69	27·1
	Sat.	19	66	70	68	27·1
	Sun.	20	68	70	68	27·1
	Mon.	21	66	72	70	27·1
	Tues.	22	69	72	70	27·1
	Wed.	23	71	74	72	27·15
	Thurs.	24	70	74	72	27·15
	Fri.	25	70	74	72	27·15
	Sat.	26	70	74	72	27·15
	Sun.	27	70	71	68	27·15
	Mon.	28	68	71	70	27·15
	Tues.	29	68	74	70	27·15
	Wed.	30	66	74	76	27·15
	Thurs.	31	68	74	70	27·15

Mean height 71.
Greatest variation of one day 27°.
Ditto of one month 27°.

‡ Near Maukallydroog.

† On a Tour from Sira through the hills to Bengalore.

JANUARY. 1802.

Names of Places.	Day of the Week	Day of the Month	Thermometer. M.	N.	E.	Barometer. N.
Bengalore	Fri.	1	60	74	74	27·15
	Sat.	2	70	74	73	27·15
	Sun.	3	70	72	71	27·15
	Mon.	4	70	74	73	27·15
	Tues.	5	68	72	72	27·15
	Wed.	6	70	72	72	27·15
	Thurs.	7	68	74	72	27·15
	Fri.	8	70	72	71	27·15
	Sat.	9	70	72	71	27·15
	Sun.	10	70	70	71	27·15
	Mon.	11	70	70	71	27·15
	Tues.	12	70	70	71	27·15
Attepally *	Wed.	13	68	72	70	27·15
Tellamungalum...	Thurs.	14	68	82	78	27·45
Huridurgum	Fri.	15	70	76	74	27·5
Rayacotah	Sat.	16	70	82	78	27·6
	Sun.	17	70	80	78	27·6
Palicole	Mon.	18	74	80	78	28·5
Darampury	Tues.	19	74	82	79	28·7
Tapur Suttrum ...	Wed.	20	74	86	82	29·
Vomillore	Thurs.	21	76	92	80	29·3
Salem	Fri.	22	76	89	86	29·2
	Sat.	23	66	85	83	29·1
Mallūr	Sun.	24	66	88	86	29·2
Chiltra Choultry..	Mon.	25	70	88	84	29·3
Vadavavatty	Tues.	26	70	85	83	29·65
Musiri	Wed.	27	70	87	85	29·65
——— Choultry ..	Thurs.	28	70	83	80	30·
Trichinopoly	Fri.	29	70	87	81	29·8
	Sat.	30	68	87	82	29·8
	Sun.	31	67	87	82	29·8

Mean height 75.
Greatest variation of one day 22°.
Ditto of one month 26°.

FEBRUARY. 1802.

Names of Places.	Day of the Week	Day of the Month	Thermometer. M.	N.	E.	Barometer. N.
Trichinoply......	Mon.	1	66	87	82	29·8
	Tues.	2	68	87	84	29·8
	Wed.	3	69	87	84	29·8
	Thurs.	4	66	87	84	29·8
	Fri.	5	70	90	86	29·9
	Sat.	6	68	90	84	29·9
	Sun.	7	66	89	82	29·9
	Mon.	8	70	89	85	29·9
Coilluddie	Tues.	9	70	90	84	29·9
Tirware	Wed.	10	70	88	80	29·8
Sawmymalle	Thurs.	11	74	90	86	29·85
Mayāvaram	Fri.	12	75	90	85	29·85
Tricalore	Sat.	13	74	90	87	30·
Tranquebar......	Sun.	14	73	90	82	30·1
	Mon.	15	72	86	80	30·13
	Tues.	16	73	87	79	30·15
	Wed.	17	72	88	80	30·15

FEBRUARY (continued.)

Names of Places.	Day of the Week	Day of the Month	Thermometer. M.	N.	E.	Barometer. N.
Tranquebar	Thurs.	18	68	86	70	30·15
	Fri.	19	69	86	70	30·15
	Sat.	20	70	88	80	30·15
	Sun.	21	70	86	70	30·15
Shially	Mon.	22	68	90	76	30·15
Chellumbram	Tues.	23	69	87	75	30·13
Tawden Sultrum..	Wed.	24	69	86	72	30·15
Majecopom	Thurs.	25	70	89	72	30·15
Cundapa Mudellir Suttrum ..	Fri.	26	74	89	85	30·2
Umma Suttrum ..	Sat.	27	74	89	83	30·2
Pāl Suttrum	Sun.	28	74	89	85	30·2

Mean height 79⅔.
Greatest variation in the course of one day 23°.
Ditto in one month 24°.

MARCH. 1802.

Names of Places.	Day of the Week	Day of the Month	Thermometer. M.	N.	E.	Barometer. N.
Pallagāren Suttrum	Mon.	1	72	86	80	30·2
Motakaron Ditto..	Tues.	2	73	89	80	30·2
Madras	Wed.	3	73	89	80	30·2
	Thurs.	4	73	86	73	30·1
	Fri.	5	73	86	73	30·1
	Sat.	6	74	86	70	30·2
	Sun.	7	74	86	79	30·2
	Mon.	8	75	86	79	30·2
	Tues.	9	75	88	79	30·2
	Wed.	10	75	88	79	30·2
	Thurs.	11	75	88	79	30·2
	Fri.	12	75	87	83	30·2
	Sat.	13	75	87	83	30·1
	Sun.	14	75	87	83	30·25
	Mon.	15	75	87	83	30·25
	Tues.	16	75	88	83	30·2
	Wed.	17	76	88	84	30·2
	Thurs.	18	76	88	83	30·2
	Fri.	19	75	88	82	30·2
	Sat.	20	75	87	82	30·2
	Sun.	21	75	88	83	30·2
	Mon.	22	75	87	82	30·25
	Tues.	23	76	87	85	30·15
	Wed.	24	77	87	85	30·15
	Thurs.	25	77	87	85	30·2
	Fri.	26	76	87	85	30·2
	Sat.	27	75	88	86	30·05
	Sun.	28	75	87	85	30·05
	Mon.	29	75	87	85	30·05
	Tues.	30	76	87	85	30·2
	Wed.	31	76	87	85	30·15

Mean height 81·04.
Greatest variation of one day 23°.
Ditto of one month 24°.

* On a tour from Bengalore to Ryacotta, to Trichinopoly, &c.

APRIL. 1802.

Names of Places.	Day of the Week	Day of the Month	Thermometer. M.	N.	E.	Barometer. N.
Madras	Thurs.	1	76	88	86	30·15
	Fri.	2	76	90	87	30·15
	Sat.	3	76	90	87	30·15
	Sun.	4	76	90	87	30·15
	Mon.	5	76	90	87	30·1
	Tues.	6	76	89	86	30·15
	Wed.	7	75	89	87	30·1
	Thurs.	8	76	89	87	29·95
	Fri.	9	76	89	86	29·95
	Sat.	10	79	89	86	29·95
	Sun.	11	78	84	80	30·
	Mon.	12	78	84	82	29·9
	Tues.	13	82	86½	85	29·95
	Wed.	14	83	87	85	29·9
	Thurs.	15	83	87½	85	29·9
	Fri.	16	83	87	85	29·9
	Sat.	17	84	91	88	29·8
	Sun.	18	84	91	88	29·85
	Mon.	19	84	91	88	29·85
	Tues.	20	84	90½	88½	29·95
	Wed.	21	84	90	88½	30·
	Thurs.	22	84	91	89	29·95
	Fri.	23	84	89	88½	29·95
	Sat.	24	84	88½	86	29·95
	Sun.	25	84	91	88	29·95
	Mon.	26	83	88½	86	30·05
	Tues.	27	83	88	87	30·
	Wed.	28	83	89	87	30·
	Thurs.	29	83	89	87	30·
	Fri.	30	83	89	87	30·

Mean height 81⅓.

MAY. 1802.

Names of Places.	Day of the Week	Day of the Month	Thermometer. M.	N.	E.	Barometer. N.
Madras	Sat.	1	83	88½	87	29·9
	Sun.	2	83	89	87	29·9
	Mon.	3	83	88½	87	29·9½
	Tues.	4	84	89	87	30·⅓
	Wed.	5	84	89	87	30·
	Thurs.	6	84	89	87	30·
	Fri.	7	84	89½	87	30·
	Sat.	8	84	89½	87	30·⅓
	Sun.	9	84	89½	87	30·
	Mon.	10	84	89½	87	30·
	Tues.	11	86	90	88	30·
	Wed.	12	86	90	88	29·8½
	Thurs.	13	86	90	88	29·9
	Fri.	14	86	89	88	29·9
	Sat.	15	86	89	88	29·9
	Sun.	16	86	89	88	29·9
	Mon.	17	76	90	89	29·9

MAY (continued.)

Names of Places.	Day of the Week	Day of the Month	Thermometer. M.	N.	E.	Barometer. N.
Madras	Tues.	18	76	90	89	29·9
	Wed.	19	78	91	89	29·9
	Thurs.	20	78	93½	90	28·8½
	Fri.	21	79	92	90	29·9½
	Sat.	22	80	92	90	29·9
	Sun.	23	76	88	87	29·9
	Mon.	24	78	92	89	29·9
	Tues.	25	80	93	90	29·9
	Wed.	26	78	94½	89½	28·8½
	Thurs.	27	78	94	89	28·8½
	Fri.	28	78	94	90	29·8½
	Sat.	29	80	93	90	29·8½
	Sun.	30	80	93	90	29·8½
	Mon.	31	80	99	90	29·8½

Mean height 85⅓.

JUNE. 1802.

Names of Places.	Day of the Week	Day of the Month	Thermometer. M.	N.	E.	Barometer. N.
Madras	Tues.	1	80	94	90	
	Wed.	2	79	93	90	
	Thurs.	3	80	94	90	29·9
	Fri.	4	82	93	90	28·8½
	Sat.	5	82	92	90	29·9
	Sun.	6	82	94	90	29·9
	Mon.	7	82	96	91	30·
	Tues.	8	82	94	90	29·9
	Wed.	9	82	92	90	29·9
	Thurs.	10	78	92	89	29·9
	Fri.	11	80	92	89	29·9
	Sat.	12	80	92	89	29·9½
	Sun.	13	82	93	89	29·9½
	Mon.	14	84	95	90	29·9
	Tues.	15	84	93	90	29·9
	Wed.	16	84	93	90	29·9
	Thurs.	17	84	92	90	29·9
	Fri.	18	84	92	90	29·9½
	Sat.	19	84	90	90	29·9½
	Sun.	20	85	90	90	29·9
	Mon.	21	85	90	89	29·9¼
	Tues.	22	64	89	88½	29·9½
	Wed.	23	85	90	89½	29·9½
	Thurs.	24	85	90	89	29·9½
	Fri.	25	85	90	89	29·9½
	Sat.	26	85	90	89	29·9½
	Sun.	27	85	89	88½	29·9½
	Mon.	28	85	89	88½	29·9½
	Tues.	29	85	90	89	29·9
	Wed.	30	85	91	90	29·8½

AUGUST. 1805.

Names of Places.	Day of the Week	Day of the Month	Thermometer. M.	N.	E.	Barometer. N.
Bengalore	Thurs.	1	72	76½	75	27·
	Fri.	2	73	77½	76	27·
	Sat.	3	73	73½	73	27·
	Sun.	4	71		72	
	Mon.	5	70	72		26·99
	Tues.	6	70	73		26·98
	Wed.	7	70½	74		26·95
	Thurs.	8	71	75	72½	27·05
	Fri.	9	71	75		
	Sat.	10	70	75		27·
	Sun.	11	70	75	73½	27·
	Mon.	12	71	75		27·03
	Tues.	13	71	75		27·03
	Wed.	14	70	75		27·03
	Thurs.	15	71	76		27·04
	Fri.	16	72	77	76	27·10
	Sat.	17	73	75½		27·08
	Sun.	18	71		72	
	Mon.	19	70½	75	72	27·
	Tues.	20	70½	74	73	27·03
	Wed	21	71	74	72	27·03
	Thurs.	22	70	75		27·02
	Fri.	23	70	75	75	27·05
	Sat.	24	73	76½	77	27·08
	Sun.	25	73	75	74	27·06
	Mon.	26	73	76	76	27·08
	Tues.	27	72	76	74	27·05
	Wed.	28	73	75	75	27·05
	Thurs.	29	73	76	74	27·12
	Fri.	30	72	74½	73	27·12
	Sat.	31	71	75	73	27·10

SEPTEMBER. 1805.

Names of Places.	Day of the Week	Day of the Month	Thermometer. M.	N.	E.	Barometer. N.
Bengalore	Sun.	1				
	Mon.	2	71	75		27·06
	Tues.	3	72	74		27·07
	Wed.	4	72	75		27·02
	Thurs.	5	72	75		27·05
	Fri.	6	71½	75½		27·08
	Sat.	7	71	75		27·06
	Sun.	8				
	Mon.	9	71	74		27·05
	Tues.	10	72	75		27·10
	Wed.	11	72½	76	76	27·09
	Thurs.	12	72	77		27·10
	Fri.	13	73	78		27·10
	Sat.	14	72	77		27·10
	Sun.	15				

SEPTEMBER (continued).

Names of Places.	Day of the Week	Day of the Month	Thermometer. M.	N.	E.	Barometer. N.
Bengalore	Mon.	16	72	77		27·03
	Tues.	17	74	78	77	27·03
	Wed.	18	73	76		27·05
	Thurs.	19	73	75		27·10
	Fri.	20	72½	77		27·05
	Sat.	21	73½	77½		27·03
	Sun.	22				
	Mon.	23	72	73½		27·05
	Tues.	24	72½	75		27·05
	Wed.	25	74	75		27·05
	Thurs.	26	74	77		27·05
	Fri.	27	73½	76		27·05
	Sat.	28	74	76		27·05
	Sun.	29				
	Mon.	30	73	67		27·05

OCTOBER. 1805.

Names of Places.	Day of the Week	Day of the Month	Thermometer. M.	N.	E.	Barometer. N.
Bengalore	Tues.	1	73	76½		27·
	Wed.	2	74	76		27·04
	Thurs.	3	73	74½		27·10
	Fri.	4	73	74½		27·03
	Sat.	5	72½	73½		27·04
	Sun.	6				
	Mon.	7	72	74		27·10
	Tues.	8	72	74		27·08
	Wed.	9	72	73		27·09
	Thurs.	10	71	71½		27·08
	Fri.	11	71	72		27·09
	Sat.	12	71	73		27·04
	Sun.	13				
	Mon.	14	71	73		27·
	Tues.	15	71½	73½		27·
	Wed.	16	71	73½		27·
	Thurs.	17	72	74½		27·05
	Fri.	18	72	74		27·05
	Sat.	19	72	72		27·04
	Sun.	20				
	Mon.	21	71	73		27·10
	Tues.	22	71	72½		27·10
	Wed.	23	71	73		27·08
	Thurs.	24	72	74		27·09
	Fri.	25	72	74		27·10
	Sat.	26	72½	74		27·15
	Sun.	27				
	Mon.	28	73	75		27·05
	Tues.	29	73	74½		27·13
	Wed.	30	73	75		27·15
	Thurs.	31	72	74		27·18

NOVEMBER. 1805.

Names of Places.	Day of the Week	Day of the Month	Thermometer. M.	N.	E.	Barometer. N.
Bengalore	Fri.	1	72	74		27·16
	Sat.	2	72	72½		27·13
	Sun.	3				
	Mon.	4	72	75		27·13
	Tues.	5	72	75		27·13
	Wed.	6	72	75		27·13
	Thurs.	7	71	73		27·
	Fri.	8	71	73		27·
	Sat.	9	71	73		27·
	Sun.	10				
	Mon.	11	70	73		27·
	Tues.	12	69	73		27·
	Wed.	13	70	73		27·08
	Thurs.	14	69	73		27·08
	Fri.	15	69	73		27·12
	Sat.	16	69	73		27·12
	Sun.	17	69	72½		27·12
	Mon.	18	69	72½		27·12
	Tues.	19	66	72		27·12
	Wed.	20	66	72		27·12
	Thurs.	21	66	73		27·12
	Fri.	22		74		27·17
	Sat.	23		74½		27·17
	Sun.	24				
	Mon.	25		74½		27·17
	Tues.	26		75		27·17
	Wed.	27		75		27·17
	Thurs.	28		74		27·18
	Fri.	29		73½		27·20
	Sat.	30		72		27·20

DECEMBER. 1805.

Names of Places.	Day of the Week	Day of the Month	Thermometer. M.	N.	E.	Barometer. N.
Bengalore	Sun.	1				
	Mon.	2		73		27·20
	Tues.	3		73½		27·20
	Wed.	4		73½		27·20
	Thurs.	5		73		27·20
	Fri.	6		73		27·20
	Sat.	7		73½		27·20
	Sun.	8				
	Mon.	9		70½		27·15
	Tues.	10	64	70		27·16
	Wed.	11		71		27·16
	Thurs.	12		69		27·16
	Fri.	13		69¾		27·05
	Sat.	14		70		27·10
	Sun.	15				
	Mon.	16		69		27·15
	Tues.	17		68		27·10
	Wed.	18		68		27·10

DECEMBER (continued.)

Names of Places.	Day of the Week	Day of the Month	Thermometer. M.	N.	E.	Barometer. N.
Bengalore	Thurs.	19		67		27·10
	Fri.	20		69		27·13
	Sat.	21		68½		27·15
	Sun.	22				
	Mon.	23		69		27·15
	Tues.	24		69		27·15
	Wed.	25				
	Thurs.	26		70		27·16
	Fri.	27		70		27·16
	Sat.	28		70		27·16
	Sun.	29				
	Mon.	30		68		27·16
	Tues.	31		68		27·16

JANUARY. 1806.

Names of Places.	Day of the Week	Day of the Month	Thermometer. M.	N.	E.	Barometer. N.
Bengalore	Wed.	1		69		27·16
	Thurs.	2		72		27·16
	Fri.	3		72		27·15
	Sat.	4		72		27·15
	Sun.	5				
	Mon.	6		72		
	Tues.	7		72		
	Wed.	8		70		
	Thurs.	9		71		
	Fri.	10		72		
	Sat.	11		73		
	Sun.	12				
	Mon.	13		72½		
	Tues.	14		72		
	Wed.	15		72		
	Thurs.	16		69		
	Fri.	17		71		
	Sat.	18		72		
	Sun.	19				
	Mon.	20		72½		
	Tues.	21		71½		
	Wed.	22		71		
	Thurs.	23		73		
	Fri.	24		73		
	Sat.	25		73		
	Sun.	26				
	Mon.	27		73		
	Tues.	28		73½		
	Wed.	29		73		
	Thurs.	30		73		
	Fri.	31		73		

FEBRUARY. 1806.

Names of Places.	Day of the Week	Day of the Month	Thermometer.			Barometer.
			M.	N.	E.	N.
Bengalore	Sat.	1		74		
	Sun.	2				
	Mon.	3		74½		
	Tues.	4		76		
	Wed.	5		76½		
	Thurs.	6		77		
	Fri.	7		76		
	Sat.	8		76½		
	Sun.	9				
	Mon.	10		76½		
	Tues.	11		76½		
	Wed.	12		77		
	Thurs.	13		77		
	Fri.	14		77		
	Sat.	15		75½		
	Sun.	16				
	Mon.	17		75½		
	Tues.	18		76		
	Wed.	19		77½		
	Thurs.	20		77½		
	Fri.	21		77½		
	Sat.	22		79		
	Sun.	23				
	Mon.	24		78		
	Tues.	25		78		
	Wed.	26		77		
	Thurs.	27		78		
	Fri.	28		79		

MARCH. 1806.

Names of Places.	Day of the Week	Day of the Month	M.	N.	E.	N.
Bengalore	Sat.	1	71	79	79	
	Sun.	2	71		79	
	Mon.	3	71	81	79	27·20
	Tues.	4	72	82	79½	27·20
	Wed.	5	72	81½	81	27·20
	Thurs.	6	73½	81	81	27·20
	Fri.	7	74	81½	81	27·25
	Sat.	8	74	80	79	27·25
	Sun.	9	69		79	
	Mon.	10	67	80	81	27·23
	Tues.	11	68	81	80½	27·25
	Wed.	12	68	82	81	27·28
	Thurs.	13	69	81	80	27·28
	Fri.	14	71	81	80	27·20
	Sat.	15	70	81	81	27·20
	Sun.	16	72		82	
	Mon.	17	72	81½	81	27·20

MARCH (continued.)

Names of Places.	Day of the Week	Day of the Month	Thermometer.			Barometer.
			M.	N.	E.	N.
Bengalore	Tues.	18	72	81½	81	27·19
	Wed.	19	71½		82	
	Thurs.	20	72		83	
	Fri.	21	72		83	
	Sat.	22	72		82	
	Sun.	23	72		82	
	Mon.	24	72		81½	
	Tues.	25	72		82½	
	Wed.	26	73		83	
	Thurs.	27	73		82	
	Fri.	28	72		81	
	Sat.	29	73		81½	
	Sun.	30	73		82	
	Mon.	31	73½		81	

APRIL. 1806.

Names of Places.	Day of the Week	Day of the Month	M.	N.	E.	N.
Bengalore	Tues.	1	74½	84	82	27·22
	Wed.	2	74½	85	83½	27·22
	Thurs.	3	75½	84½	83½	27·20
	Fri.	4	76	85	85	27·20
	Sat.	5	74	83½	83	27·22
	Sun.	6	75		83	
	Mon.	7	75	85	82½	27·22
	Tues.	8	75	86	84	27·23
	Wed.	9	76	86	86	27·23
	Thurs.	10	76	85½	83	27·20
	Fri.	11	76	85	84	27·20
	Sat.	12	76	85½	84	27·20
	Sun.	13	76	85½	84	27·20
	Mon.	14	76½	85½	84	27·15
	Tues.	15	77	87	81½	27·15
	Wed.	16	77	85	85	27·18
	Thurs.	17	75	83½	84	27·18
	Fri.	18	75½	85	85	27·15
	Sat.	19	76½	85	84	27·12
	Sun.	20	75		84	27·12
	Mon.	21	75½	85	84	27·18
	Tues.	22	76½	85	85	27·18
	Wed.	23	77½	85¾	86	27·18
	Thurs.	24	78	87	87	27·20
	Fri.	25	77	86	86	27·20
	Sat.	26	78	86	87	27·20
	Sun.	27	78	87	87	20·20
	Mon.	28	78½	87	86	27·20
	Tues.	29	74	85	77	27·20
	Wed.	30	74	86	86	27.15

MAY. 1806.

Names of Places.	Day of the Week	Day of the Month	Thermometer.			Barometer.
			M.	N.	E.	N.
Bengalore	Thurs.	1	77	86½	85	27·15
	Fri.	2	76	89	89	27·15
	Sat.	3	76½	87½	86	27·16
	Sun.	4	76½		86	
	Mon.	5	76½	88	87	27·16
	Tues.	6	77	87	87	27·19
	Wed.	7	77	86½	86	27·20
	Thurs.	8	78	86	81	27·17
	Fri.	9	74	86	80	27·17
	Sat.	10	74	85	81	27·17
	Sun.	11	76		81	
	Mon.	12	76	86	85	27·20
	Tues.	13	76	86	83	27·20
	Wed.	14	73	83	81	27·20
	Thurs.	15	73	82½	79	27·15
	Fri.	16	74	83	81	27·15
	Sat.	17	74½	84	81	27·15
	Sun.	18	74½		78	
	Mon.	19	74	81	78	27·15
	Tues.	20	74	82	77	27·10
	Wed.	21	73	81	81	27·10
	Thurs.	22	74	81	79	27·10
	Fri.	23	74	80½	80	27·10
	Sat.	24	71	80	79	27·10
	Sun.	25	70		76	
	Mon.	26	74	81	79	27·05
	Tues.	27	74	81	81	27·09
	Wed.	28	74	81	82	27·09
	Thurs.	29	75	82	82	27·10
	Fri.	30	76	82	80	27·10
	Sat.	31	75	81½	79	27·10

JUNE. 1806.

Names of Places.	Day of the Week	Day of the Month	M.	N.	E.	N.
Bengalore	Sun.	1	74		75	
	Mon.	2	72	79	76½	27·10
	Tues.	3	72	78	72	27·10
	Wed.	4	70	77½	75	27·10
	Thurs.	5	70½	77½	72	27·10
	Fri.	6	70½	78	74	27·10
	Sat.	7	71½	77	75	27·12
	Sun.	8	72½		75	
	Mon.	9	72½	75	72	27·05
	Tues.	10	69	73	70	27·06
	Wed.	11	68	75	73	27·10
	Thurs.	12	70	76½	75	27·10
	Fri.	13	70	75	75	27·10
	Sat.	14	70	76½	76	27·10
	Sun.	15	71		75	
	Mon.	16	71	78	76	27·10

JUNE (continued.)

Names of Places.	Day of the Week	Day of the Month	Thermometer.			Barometer.
			M.	N.	E.	N.
Bengalore	Tues.	17	71½	78½	76	27·10
	Wed.	18	72	78	77	27·10
	Thurs.	19	72	79	79	27·07
	Fri.	20	73	79	74	27·07
	Sat.	21	72	79	79	27·00
	Sun.	22	73		76	
	Mon.	23	73	78½	79	27·10
	Tues.	24	72½	79	78	27·10
	Wed.	25	73	78½	79	27·10
	Thurs.	26	73	79	79	27·12
	Fri.	27	73	79	79	27·09
	Sat.	28	72½	76½	75	27·09
	Sun.	29	72½		75	
	Mon.	30	71½	77	74	27·09

JULY. 1806.

Names of Places.	Day of the Week	Day of the Month	M.	N.	E.	N.
Bengalore	Tues.	1	71½	77	77	27·12
	Wed.	2	71½	77½	77	27·13
	Thurs.	3	71½	77	75	27·12
	Fri.	4	71	76	75	27·10
	Sat.	5	70½	76½	75	27·10
	Sun.	6	70½		75	
	Mon.	7	70	76½	75	27·05
	Tues.	8	71½	78½	76	27·
	Wed.	9	70	78	75	27·05
	Thurs.	10	70	77	75	27·05
	Fri.	11	70	78	74	27·03
	Sat.	12	71	78	75	27·03
	Sun.	13	71½		75	
	Mon.	14	72	76½	75	27·03
	Tues.	15	72	75	74	27·03
	Wed.	16	70½	76½	72	27·03
	Thurs.	17	70	76	71½	27·03
	Fri.	18	70	75½	72	27·05
	Sat.	19	70½	76½	72	27·05
	Sun.	20	70½		73½	
	Mon.	21	71	77½	75	27·05
	Tues.	22	71½	77	76	27·05
	Wed.	23	71½	76½	74	27·13
	Thurs.	24	70	76	74	27·13
	Fri.	25	70	76	76	27·13
	Sat.	26	72	77	72	27·13
	Sun.	27	72		74	
	Mon.	28	70	77	74	27·13
	Tues.	29	71½	78	78	27·13
	Wed.	30	72	78½	79	27·13
	Thurs.	31	74	79	77	27·13

AUGUST. 1806.

Names of Places.	Day of the Week	Day of the Month	Thermometer. M.	Thermometer. N.	Thermometer. E.	Barometer. N.
Bengalore	Fri.	1	73½	79½	78	27·13
	Sat.	2	73½	79	76	27·13
	Sun.	3	73½		77	
	Mon.	4	71	77	77	27·13
	Tues.	5	71	77½	74	27·10
	Wed.	6	70½	76	74	27·10
	Thurs.	7	71	77	76	27·10
	Fri.	8	71½	77	76	27·10
	Sat.	9	72	77		27·10

NOVEMBER. 1806.

Names of Places.	Day of the Week	Day of the Month	Thermometer. M.	Thermometer. N.	Thermometer. E.	Barometer. N.
Bengalore	Thurs.	20	65	71	69	27·20
	Fri.	21	65	72	71	27·20
	Sat.	22	67½	73½	71	27·22
	Sun.	23	67		72	
	Mon.	24	67	71	68	27·20
	Tues.	25	63½	72½	72	27·10
	Wed.	26	66½	74½	78*	27·12
	Thurs.	27	68	75	70	27·15
	Fri.	28	69	76	70	27·20
	Sat.	29	69	76	72	27·20
	Sun.	30	68		72	

DECEMBER. 1806.

Names of Places.	Day of the Week	Day of the Month	Thermometer. M.	Thermometer. N.	Thermometer. E.	Barometer. N.
Bengalore	Mon.	1	69	74	72	27·20
	Tues.	2	64	73	72	27·20
	Wed.	3	63	73	71	27·20
	Thurs.	4	63	72	70	27·20
	Fri.	5	62½	72	70	27·20
	Sat.	6	62	72	70	27·20
	Sun.	7	58		68	
	Mon.	8	58	71	68	27·20
	Tues.	9	58	70	69	27·20
	Wed.	10	58	70	68	27·20
	Thurs.	11	58	69	69	27·20
	Fri.	12	58	70	70	27·20
	Sat.	13	59	70	70	27·20
	Sun.	14	60		70	
	Mon.	15	60	74	74	27·20
	Tues.	16	60	74	72	27·20
	Wed.	17	66	74	72	27·20
	Thurs.	18	62	72	68	27·20
	Fri.	19	62	70	69	27·20

DECEMBER (continued.)

Names of Places.	Day of the Week	Day of the Month	Thermometer. M.	Thermometer. N.	Thermometer. E	Barometer. N.
Bengalore	Sat.	20	64	70	68	27·20
	Sun.	21	62		68	
	Mon.	22	68	70	69	27·20
	Tues.	23	64	70	68	27·20
	Wed.	24	62	70	68	27·20
	Thurs.	25	61			
	Fri.	26	64	70	68	27·20
	Sat.	27	62	70	68	27·20
	Sun.	28	61½			
	Mon.	29	61½	71	71	27·20
	Tues.	30	62	72	72	27·20
	Wed.	31	62	71	71	27·20

JANUARY. 1807.

Names of Places.	Day of the Week	Day of the Month	Thermometer. M.	Thermometer. N.	Thermometer. E	Barometer. N.
Bengalore	Thurs.	1	62	70	70	27·20
	Fri.	2	62	70	70	27·20
	Sat.	3	62	70	70	27·20
	Sun.	4	62		71	
	Mon.	5	62	71	71	27·28
	Tues.	6	62	71	70	27·28
	Wed.	7	62	71	70	27·28
	Thurs.	8	61	71½	70	27·28
	Fri.	9	60	71	70	27·28
	Sat.	10	60	70½	71	27·28
	Sun.	11	60		71	
	Mon.	12	60	71½	71	27·28
	Tues.	13	60	71	71	27·28
	Wed.	14	59	71	71	27·28
	Thurs.	15	59	70½	70	27·28
	Fri.	16	58	70	70	27·25
	Sat.	17	59	71	71	27·25
	Sun.	18	61		71	
	Mon.	19	62	71	71	27·25
	Tues.	20	62	71½	71½	27·25
	Wed.	21	64	72½	72	27·25
	Thurs.	22	64½	73	72	27·25
	Fri.	23	66	73	72	27·25
	Sat.	24	67	73	73	27·25
	Sun.	25	67		73	
	Mon.	26	67	73	73	27·25
	Tues.	27	67	73½	73	27·25
	Wed.	28	69	74	74	27·25
	Thurs.	29	69½	74	74	27·25
	Fri.	30	69	75	75	27·25
	Sat.	31	65	74		27·25

FEBRUARY. 1807.

Names of Places.	Day of the Week	Day of the Month	Thermometer.			Barometer.
			M.	N.	E.	N.
Bengalore	Sun.	1	65		74	
	Mon.	2	65	72		27·25
	Tues.	3	62½	71	71	27·25
	Wed.	4	62	71	71	27·25
	Thurs.	5	62	72	72	27·25
	Fri.	6	63½	74	74	27·25
	Sat.	7	66	74	74	27·25
	Sun.	8	66			
	Mon.	9	66	74	74	27·25
	Tues.	10	66	74	76	27·25

FEBRUARY (continued.)

Names of Places.	Day of the Week	Day of the Month	Thermometer.			Barometer.
			M.	N.	E.	N.
Bengalore	Wed.	11	65	76	76	27·25
	Thurs.	12	67	77	77	27·25
	Fri.	13	68	76	76	27·25
	Sat.	14	68	76	76	27·25
	Sun.	15	68			
	Mon.	16	68	78	78	27·25
	Tues.	17	69	78	78	27·25
	Wed.	18	69	77	77	27·25
	Thurs.	19	69	77		27·25

APPENDIX C.

Route from Cuddapa to Hydrabad, with Distances in English Miles.

Cuddapa to	M.	F.
Chinnūr	6	0
Puttūr	6	2
Cazapetta	0	3
Mydacūr	6	2
Chintagunta	4	4
Gudipādu	3	0
Dhūr	2	6
Cānagundūr	4	7
Chugulmitty	4	4
Muddūr	3	8
Bhojanam	3	2
Condacūr	3	6
Pāla Samūdram	2	4
Gubuguntlam	4	0
Nellagutla	2	4
Battalūra	2	1
Yērgutla	2	4
Govindapilly	5	1
Sāmbram	4	6
Nandiāl	5	2
Pūlmurry	4	4
Panagūru	3	6
Chintacūr	3	0
Gadimala	3	4
Comalūra	1	6
Pārmansala	7	2
Mandalam	6	2
Codiāl	5	4
Mūrconda, on the banks of the Kistna	6	6
Munselgutta	1	6
Gopalpūram	4	0
Tūmgūnnta	4	5
Wullavaram	3	7
Hytapully	2	2
Pangul Hill Fort	4	7
Dājipilly	3	1
Top of the pass	2	7
Wanampurty at the bottom of the pass	3	2
Chintiāl	2	3
Chinna Mandry	5	1
Solapūr	3	0
Manandyjetta	2	6
Petta of Gunpūr Hill Fort	3	1
Cūla Mulghira	5	1
Cotūr	3	7
Enūr	3	3
Junchila Fort	3	5
Mudrapīlly	4	6
Rajapetta	1	6
Pūlmāmdy	2	6
Nagampilly	3	3
Rycul	4	0
Furrucknagur	4	5
Nundigām	5	0
Palamcull	5	7
Shāpūr	3	2
Shamsabad	5	1
Bridge over the river Musery close to the west gate of Hydrabad	9	2

APPENDIX D.

Route from Bengalore to Trichinopoly by Ryacotta.

Ryacotta to	M.	F.
Kirrianūr	3	2
Chinnadubba	2	4
Wodapilly	2	4
Ampimattam	1	6
Palicōl	3	2
Cadamada	2	0
Somampilly	3	0
Sangumputty	3	0
Chellamputty	1	1
Darmapūry road	1	0
Adamancotta	4	7
Appanaipālliam	3	4
Beginning of the Tappūr pass	2	2
Top of ditto	1	0
Bottom of Tappūr pass and Choultry	4	4
A Tank on the road	3	0
Mucanūr	4	0
Tattiambetty	4	6
Unealūr, or Wombinellīr	4	4
Shettapettaguta	3	4
Munguppam	2	6
Shoramangalam	2	1
Salem	4	0
Pudūr	4	3
Attampetty	2	0
Mallūr	1	6
Canampalliam	4	2
Andatūr	3	0
Munuchoudy	2	4
Velattampatty	2	7
Calangūny	2	5
Madalapetty	5	6
Namcul	2	2
Tusūr, on the right bank of the Kurravatūvēr, which is here crossed, estimated	5	4
Pāvittrum ditto	12	4
Viramshampetta, ditto	12	0
Munsurpet, ditto	19	0
Trichinopoly	6	1